D0262924

STREET ATLAS
Tyne & Wear
Northumberland

First published in 1996 as
'Tyne & Wear' by

George Philip Ltd, a division of
Octopus Publishing Group Ltd
2–4 Heron Quays, London E14 4JP

First colour edition 2001
First impression 2001

ISBN 0-540-07808-5

© George Philip Ltd 2001

O𝕊 Ordnance
Survey®

This product includes mapping data licensed
from Ordnance Survey®, with the permission
of the Controller of Her Majesty's Stationery
Office. © Crown copyright 2001. All rights
reserved. Licence number 100011710

No part of this publication may be
reproduced, stored in a retrieval system or
transmitted in any form or by any means,
electronic, mechanical, photocopying,
recording or otherwise, without the
permission of the Publishers and the
copyright owner.

To the best of the Publishers' knowledge, the
information in this atlas was correct at the
time of going to press. No responsibility can
be accepted for any errors or their
consequences.

The representation in this atlas of a road,
track or path is no evidence of the existence
of a right of way.

Ordnance Survey and the OS Symbol are
registered trademarks of Ordnance Survey,
the national mapping agency of Great Britain

Printed and bound in Spain
by Cayfosa-Quebecor

Contents

II **Key to map symbols**

III **Key to Navigator® map symbols**

IV **Key to map pages**

VI **Route planning**

X **Administrative and Postcode boundaries**

1 **Street maps** at 2½ inches to 1 mile

98 **Street maps of Newcastle upon Tyne and Sunderland city centres** at 5 inches to 1 mile

104 **Navigator® mapping of Northumberland** at ⅝ inches to 1 mile

136 **Town maps** of Alnwick, Amble, Berwick-upon-Tweed and Rothbury

138 **Index** of towns and villages

140 **Index** of streets, hospitals, industrial estates, railway stations, schools, shopping centres and universities and places of interest

Digital Data

The exceptionally high-quality mapping found in this atlas is available as digital data in TIFF format, which is easily convertible to other bit mapped (raster) image formats.

The index is also available in digital form as a standard database table. It contains all the details found in the printed index together with the National Grid reference for the map square in which each entry is named and feature codes for places of interest in eight categories such as education and health.

For further information and to discuss your requirements, please contact Philip's on 020 7531 8440 or george.philip@philips-maps.co.uk

II **Key to map symbols** on pages 1–103

(22a)	**Motorway** with junction number	Walsall	**Railway station**
	Primary route – dual/single carriageway	M	**Tyne and Wear Metro station**
	A road – dual/single carriageway		**Private railway station**
	B road – dual/single carriageway		**Bus, coach station**
	Minor road – dual/single carriageway	◆	**Ambulance station**
	Other minor road – dual/single carriageway	◆	**Coastguard station**
– – –	**Road under construction**	◆	**Fire station**
	Pedestrianised area	◆	**Police station**
DY7	**Postcode boundaries**	✚	**Accident and Emergency entrance to hospital**
·—·—·—	**County and unitary authority boundaries**	H	**Hospital**
	Railway	+	**Place of worship**
– – – – –	**Railway under construction**	i	**Information Centre** (open all year)
	Tramway, miniature railway	P	**Parking**
	Rural track, private road or narrow road in urban area	P&R	**Park and Ride**
	Gate or obstruction to traffic (restrictions may not apply at all times or to all vehicles)	PO	**Post Office**
– – – – –	**Path, bridleway, byway open to all traffic, road used as a public path**	Ⅹ	**Camping site**
	The representation in this atlas of a road, track or is no evidence of the existence of a of a right of way		**Caravan site**
98 / **84**	**Adjoining page indicators** (The colour of the arrow indicates the scale of the adjoining page - see scales below)	▶	**Golf course**
		✕	**Picnic site**
102	The map area within the pink band is shown at a larger scale on the page indicated by the red block and arrow	Prim Sch	**Important buildings, schools, colleges, universities and hospitals**
		River Medway	**Water name**

Acad	**Academy**	Mkt	**Market**
Allot Gdns	**Allotments**	Meml	**Memorial**
Cemy	**Cemetery**	Mon	**Monument**
C Ctr	**Civic Centre**	Mus	**Museum**
CH	**Club House**	Obsy	**Observatory**
Coll	**College**	Pal	**Royal Palace**
Crem	**Crematorium**	PH	**Public House**
Ent	**Enterprise**	Recn Gd	**Recreation Ground**
Ex H	**Exhibition Hall**	Resr	**Reservoir**
Ind Est	**Industrial Estate**	Ret Pk	**Retail Park**
IRB Sta	**Inshore Rescue Boat Station**	Sch	**School**
		Sh Ctr	**Shopping Centre**
Inst	**Institute**	TH	**Town Hall/House**
Ct	**Law Court**	Trad Est	**Trading Estate**
L Ctr	**Leisure Centre**	Univ	**University**
LC	**Level Crossing**	Wks	**Works**
Liby	**Library**	YH	**Youth Hostel**

River, stream

Lock, weir

Water

Tidal water

Woods

Houses

Church **Non-Roman antiquity**

ROMAN FORT **Roman antiquity**

■ The small numbers around the edges of the maps identify the 1 kilometre National Grid lines ■ The dark grey border on the inside edge of some pages indicates that the mapping does not continue onto the adjacent page

The scale of the maps is 3.92 cm to 1 km
2½ inches to 1 mile • 1: 25344

0	¼	½	¾	1 mile
0	250 m 500 m	750 m 1 kilometre		

The scale of the maps on pages numbered in red is 7.84 cm to 1 km • 5 inches to 1 mile • 1: 12672

0	220 yards	440 yards	660 yards	½ mile
0	125 m	250 m	375 m ½ kilometre	

III

Key to Navigator® map symbols on pages 104–135

Motorways		
M6	Junction	Service area — Corley Services

❷ Restricted junction

Under construction

A20 **Primary route** – dual, single carriageway
Primary route under construction
Narrow primary route
LINCOLN **Primary destination**
A1031 **A road** – dual, single carriageway
A road under construction
Narrow A road
B1200 **B road** – dual, single carriageway
B road under construction
Narrow B road
Minor road
Drive or track
Ring road
5 ✱ 5 **Distance in miles**
Tunnel
Toll **Toll, steep gradient** – points downhill
National trail – England and Wales
Long distance footpath – Scotland
NEWINGTON **Railway with station**
Level crossing, tunnel
ROLVENDON **Preserved railway with station**
National boundary
County / unitary authority boundary
Car ferry, catamaran
Passenger ferry, catamaran
Hovercraft
Internal ferry – car, passenger
Principal airport, other airport / airfield

National park, area of outstanding natural beauty, forest park
Woodland
Beach – sand, shingle
Linear antiquity
R. SEVERN **Navigable river or canal**
Lock, flight of locks
☀ ▲ 965 **Viewpoint, spot height** – in feet
✕ 1066 **Site and date of battle**
🆃 **RAC / AA telephone box**
Caravan site, camping site

✛ **Abbey / Priory**
Aquarium/Dolphinarium
☐ **Art collection**
Art collection / Museum
Bird sanctuary / Aviary
Castle
▲ **Cathedral**
✝ **Church**
Country park – England and Wales
Country park – Scotland
County show ground
Farm park
○ **Garden**
Golf course
Historic ship
■ **House**
◉ **House and garden**
Local museum
⚓ **Marina**

◈ **Maritime museum Military museum**
Motor racing circuit
Museum
Ⓐ **Picnic area**
Racecourse
Roman antiquity
Safari park
Steam railway Miniature railway
Tourist Information Centre – open all year
Tourist Information Centre – open seasonally
Transport collection
★ **Viewpoint**
△ **Youth hostel**
Zoo
∴ **Ancient monument Earthwork Windmill Watermill Other place of interest**

The scale of the maps on pages numbered in green is
0.98cm to 1km
⅝ inches to 1 mile
1: 101 987
0 ½ 1 1½ 2 miles
0 1 2 3 kilometres

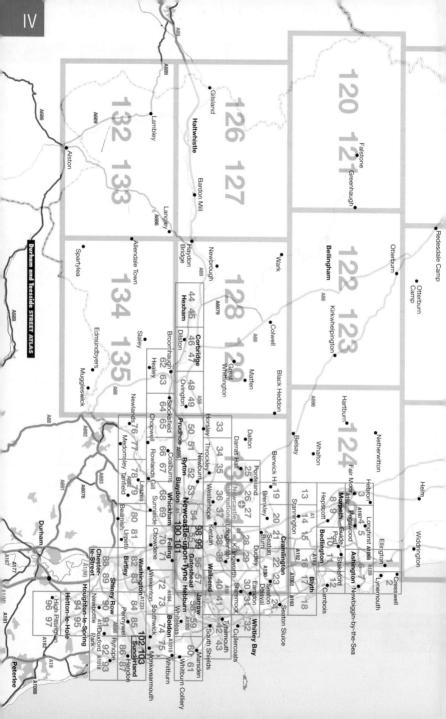

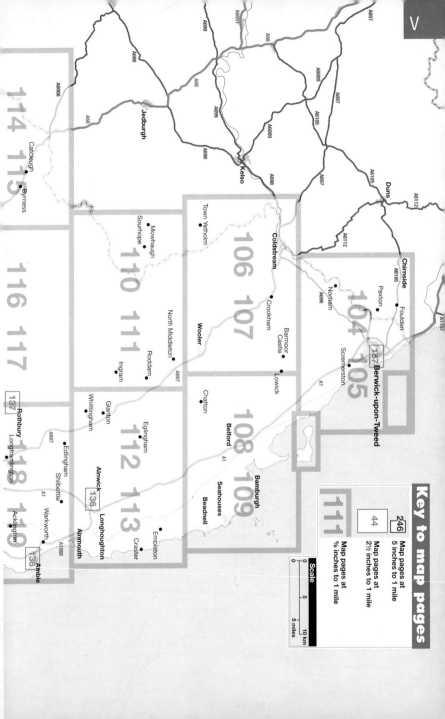

V

Key to map pages

246	Map pages at 5 inches to 1 mile
44	Map pages at 2½ inches to 1 mile
111	Map pages at ⅝ inches to 1 mile

Scale

0   5   10 km
0   5 miles

A897

A699

A68

A698

A68

A699

A6089

A6105

A697

A6112

Jedburgh

A6088

A68

Catcleugh

Byrness

Kelso

A698

A697

A6089

A698

Duns

A6112

Chirnside
A6105

Paxton

Foulden

A6112

A698

Coldstream

Town Yetholm

Norham

Mowhaugh

Sourhope

106 **107**

Crookham

Barmoor Castle

Paxton

104 **105**

Scremerston

187 **Berwick-upon-Tweed**

A1

110 **111**

North Middleton

Roddam

Ingram

A697

Lowick

Wooler

Chatton

108 **109**

Belford

Bamburgh

Seahouses

Beadnell

114

113

116 **117**

Whittingham

Glanton

Eglingham

A697

Edlingham

Shilbottle

A1

112 **113**

Alnwick

136

Longhoughton

Embleton

Craster

Alnmouth

137 **Rothbury**

Longframlington

Warkworth

A1068

136 **Amble**

Acklington

118 **119**

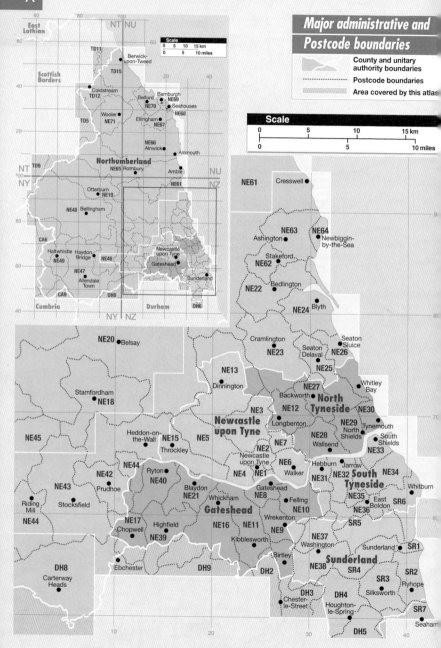

Major administrative and Postcode boundaries

County and unitary authority boundaries

Postcode boundaries

Area covered by this atlas

Scale

| 0 | 5 | 10 | 15 km |
| 0 | | 5 | 10 miles |

East Lothian

Scottish Borders

TD11
Berwick-upon-Tweed
TD15
Coldstream
TD12
TD5
Wooler
NE71
Belford
Bamburgh
NE69
Seahouses
NE70
NE68
Ellingham
NE67
NE66
Alnwick
Alnmouth
NE65 Rothbury
Northumberland
Amble
NE61
Otterburn
NE19
NE48 Bellingham
CA6
Haltwhistle
NE49
Haydon Bridge
NE46
NE47
Allendale Town
CA9
DH8
Cumbria
Durham
TD9
NT
NY
NU
NZ

Newcastle upon Tyne
Gateshead
Sunderland

DH6

NY | NZ

Scale

| 0 | 5 | 10 | 15 km |
| 0 | | 5 | 10 miles |

NE61
Cresswell

NE63
Ashington
NE64
Newbiggin-by-the-Sea

Stakeford
NE62
NE22
Bedlington
NE24
Blyth

NE20 Belsay

Cramlington
Seaton Delaval
NE23
Seaton Sluice
NE26
NE25
Whitley Bay

NE13
Dinnington
NE27
Backworth
North Tyneside
NE30

NE3
NE12
Longbenton
NE29
North Shields
Tynemouth

Newcastle upon Tyne
NE28
Wallsend
South Shields
NE33

Stamfordham
NE18
Heddon-on-the-Wall
NE15
Throckley
NE5
NE2
Newcastle upon Tyne
NE7
NE6
Walker
Hebburn
Jarrow
NE32 **South Tyneside**
NE34

NE45
NE44
NE42
Prudhoe
NE40
Ryton
NE4
NE1
NE31
Whitburn

NE43
Blaydon
NE21
Whickham
Gateshead
NE8
NE35
East Boldon
SR6

Riding Mill
Stocksfield
NE17
Chopwell
Highfield
NE39
NE16
NE11
Gateshead
Felling
NE10
Wrekenton
NE9
NE36
SR5

NE44
Kibblesworth
NE37
Washington
Sunderland
SR1

DH8
Carterway Heads
Ebchester
DH9
Birtley
NE38
Sunderland
SR4
SR2
Ryhope

DH2
DH3
Chester-le-Street
DH4
Houghton-le-Spring
SR3
Silksworth
SR7
Seaham

DH5

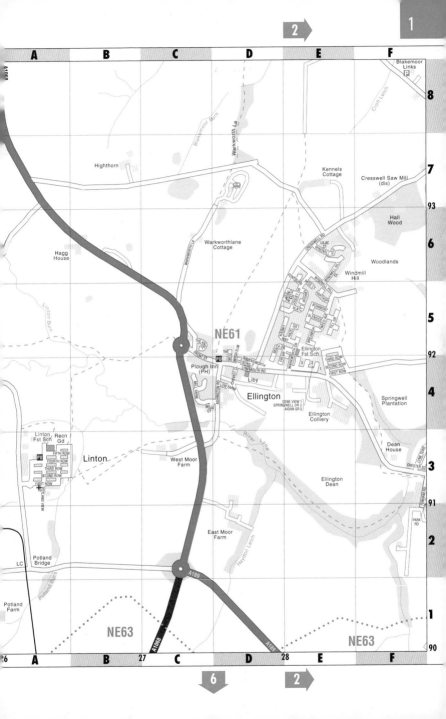

A B C D E F

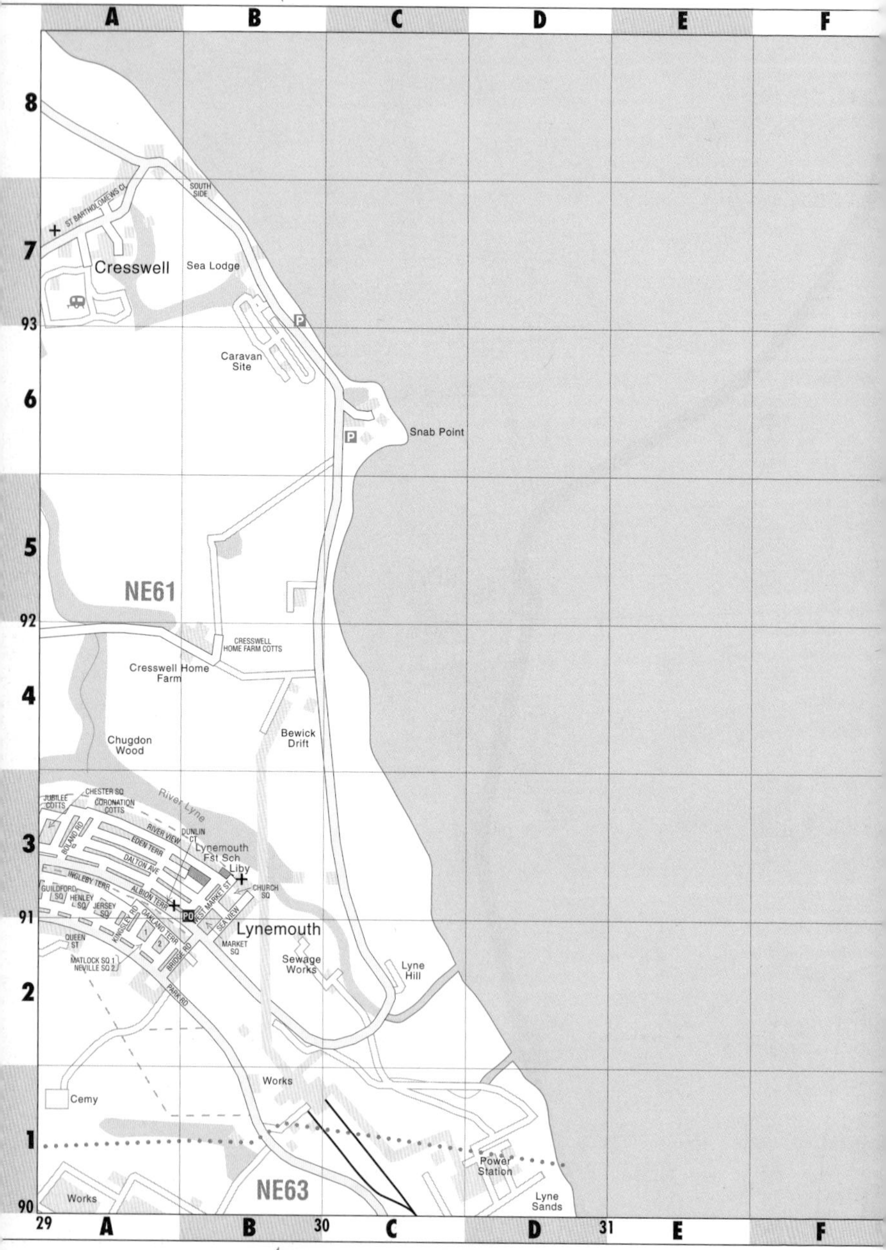

8

SOUTH SIDE

ST BARTHOLOMEWS CL

7 Cresswell   Sea Lodge

93

Caravan Site

P

6

P   Snab Point

5

NE61

92

CRESSWELL HOME FARM COTTS

4 Cresswell Home Farm

Chugdon Wood   Bewick Drift

River Lyne

JUBILEE COTTS   CHESTER SQ
CORONATION COTTS
RIVER VIEW   DUNLIN CT
3   EDER TERR   Lynemouth Fst Sch   Liby
DALTON AVE
INGLEBY TERR   ALBION TERR   CHURCH SQ
GUILDFORD   HENLEY   ARCADE ST
SQ   C SQ   JERSEY   Lynemouth
C SQ   PO
91   ORCHARD TERR
QUEEN ST   MARKET SQ
MATLOCK SQ 1
NEVILLE SQ 2   Sewage Works   Lyne Hill

2   Pear Rd

Works
Cemy

1   Power Station
   Lyne Sands

90   Works   NE63

29   A   B   30   C   D   31   E   F

7

	A	B	C	D	E	F

Alder Wood

Hare Wood

WHISSY LA

Heighley Gate Farm Nurseries

High Highlaws

Strafford House

Hebron West Farm

Hebron East Farm

Hebron

8

Shieldhill Burn

Flake Hill

Quarry Hill

7

89

Low Heighley

Low Heighley Rigg

Warreners House

West Shield Hill

Shieldhill Burn

Silver Hill

6

Heighley Wood

NE61

Wr Twr

WEST VIEW

East Shield Hill

5

88

H

Southernwood

Fair Moor

A192

Northgate & Prudhoe NHS Trust

Fulbeck Grange

Cottingwood Common

4

East Benridge

Benridge Bridge

A192

East Lane End

St George's

H

3

87

Benridge Burn

West Lane End

Morpeth Wansbeck St Aidan's CE Fst Sch

Peacock Gap

POTTERY BANK

NORTHLANDS RD 1
UPPER FENWICK GR 2
OLYMPIA HILL 3
NORTHBOURNE AVE 4

The King Edward VI Sch

2

MORPETH

PINEWOOD DR

LESLIES VIEW

POTTERY BANK CT

Morpeth Chantry Mid Sch

COTTINGWOOD GDNS

SOUTH TERR

Dean ouse

Spital Hill Farm

Morpeth Newminster Mid Sch

BULLER TERR

DOGGER BANK

B6343

NEWGATE ST

1

Spital Hill

PH

B6343

A197

B6343

MITFORD RD

River Wansbeck

CHALLONER'S GDNS

CORPORATION Sch YD

A192

86

	A		B	18	C		D	19	E		F

F1
1 HOWARD TERR
2 HOWARD RD
3 MARITIME PL
4 ST JAMES TERR
5 MORRISON RD
6 OLYMPIA GDNS
7 ABBEY VIEW
8 ABBEY TERR
9 BACK RIGGS
10 GREYSTOKE GDNS
11 WELLWAY CT

A **B** **C** **D** **E** **F**

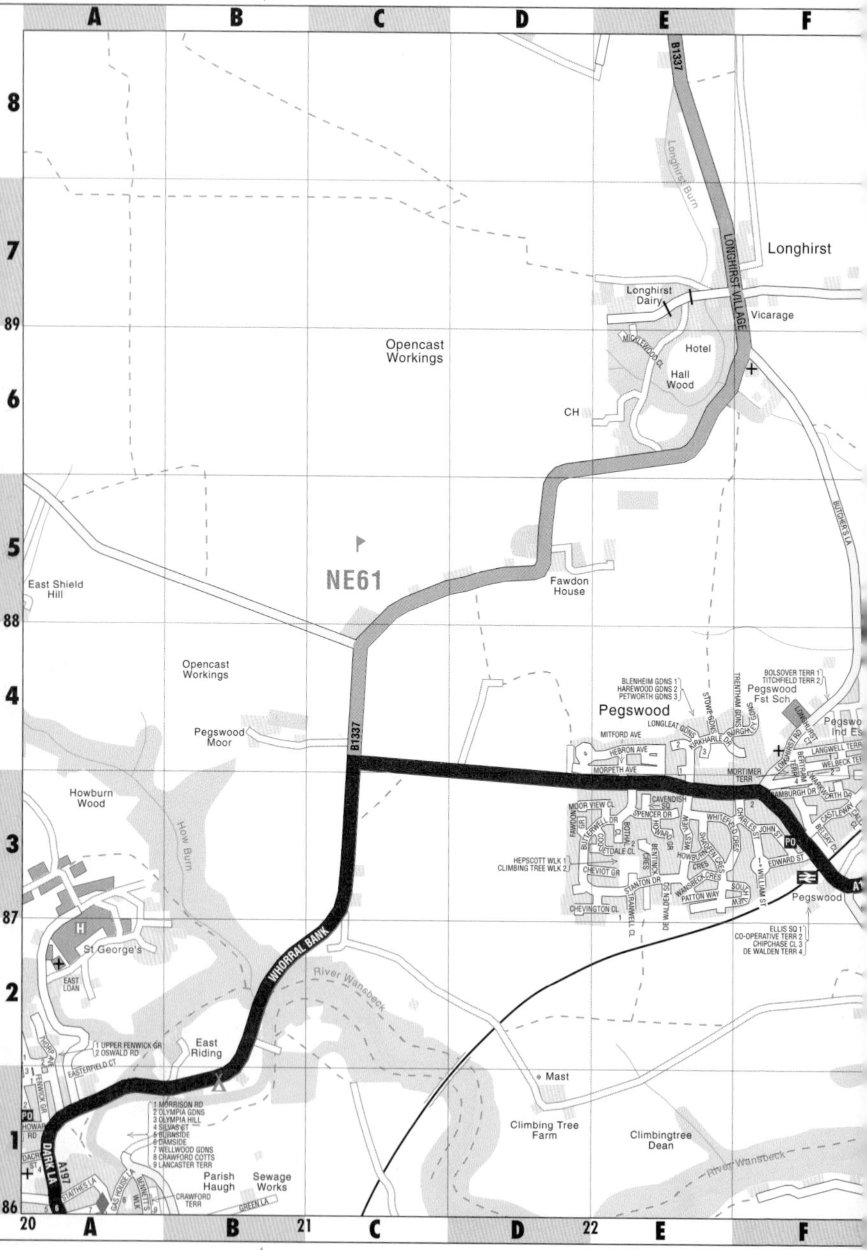

8

7

89

6

5 NE61

88

4

3

87

2

1

86

20 **A** **B** 21 **C** **D** 22 **E** **F**

Longhirst

B1337

Longhirst Burn

LONGHIRST VILLAGE

Longhirst Dairy

Vicarage

MICKLEWOOD

Hotel

Hall Wood

CH

Opencast Workings

Fawdon House

East Shield Hill

Opencast Workings

Pegswood Moor

Howburn Wood

How Burn

St George's

EAST LOAN

1 UPPER FENWICK GR
2 OSWALD RD

East Riding

EASTERFIELD CT

PO

HOWARD RD

DARK LA

A197

STAITHES LA

1 MORRISON RD
2 OLYMPIA GDNS
3 OLYMPIA HILL
4 SQUARE ST
5 BURNSIDE
6 DAMSIDE
7 WELLWOOD GDNS
8 CRAWFORD COTTS
9 LANCASTER TERR

WHORRAL BANK

River Wansbeck

Parish Haugh

Sewage Works

Crawford Terr

GREEN LA

Mast

Climbing Tree Farm

Climbingtree Dean

River Wansbeck

B1337

BLENHEIM GDNS 1
HAREWOOD GDNS 2
PETWORTH GDNS 3

BOLSOVER TERR 1
TITCHFIELD TERR 2

Pegswood Fst Sch

Pegswood

LONGLEAT

MITFORD AVE

HEBRON AVE

MORPETH AVE

Pegswo Ind Es

MORTIMER TERR

HEPSCOTT WLK 1
CLIMBING TREE WLK 2

CHEVINGTON CL

Pegswood

A197

ELLIS SQ 1
CO-OPERATIVE TERR 2
CHIPCHASE CL 3
DE WALDEN TERR 4

EDWARD ST

PO

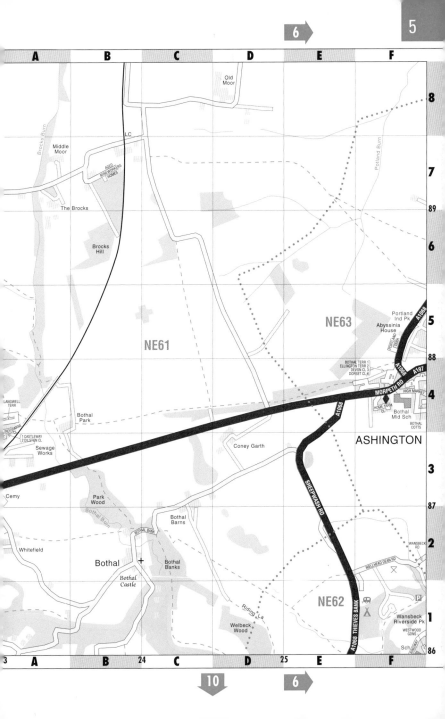

8

7

89

6

5

88

4

3

87

2

1

86

Old
Moor

Brocks Burn

Middle
Moor

LC

AGED MINEWORKERS
HOMES

The Brocks

Brocks
Hill

Portland Burn

NE61

NE63

Portland
Ind Pk

Abyssinia
House

PORTLAND
TERR

A1068

BOTHAL TERR 1
ELLINGTON TERR 2
DEVON CL 3
DORSET CL 4

A197

A1068

MORPETH RD

HIGH MARKET

LANGWELL
TERR

Bothal
Park

HONEY FARM
CL

Bothal
Mid Sch

BOTHAL
COTTS

LINDISFARNE

1 CASTLEWAY
2 DILSTON CL

Sewage
Works

A1068

ASHINGTON

Coney Garth

Cemy

Park
Wood

Bothal Burn

Bothal
Barns

SHEPWASH RD

87

Whitefield

BOTHAL BANK

Bothal
Banks

WANSBECK
RD

Bothal

Bothal
Castle

NE62

WELLHEAD DEAN RD

Wansbeck
Riverside Pk

P

WESTWOOD
GDNS

Riding La

A1068 THIEVES BANK

Welbeck
Wood

Sch

NE61

NE61

A1068

A189

New Moor Cottages

LC

Whinny Plantation

Hotel

P

Haydan Letch

89

Third House Farm

Queen Elizabeth II Ctry Pk

6

Hawthorn Cottage

A1068

Woodhorn Colliery Mus

NE63

Works

Wansbeck Bsns Pk

WOODHORN COTTS 1
AGED MINER'S HOMES 2
ST BATHOLOMEWS CL 3
ST CHRISTOPHERS CL 4
ST DAVIDS CL 5

5

A197

1 DUKE ST
2 CHARLTON ST
3 COUNCIL RD
4 CRESSWELL TERR
5 WANSBECK SQ
6 GREENSIDE
7 HILLSIDE

LC

BLUNTONVILLE PARKWAY

A197

88

A197 MORPETH RD

ELEVENTH ROW

ROTARY PARKWAY

NINTH ROW
EIGHTH ROW
SEVENTH ROW
STATION RD

HALBOURNE ST

NORTH VIEW

VIEWLANDS

P

Alexandra Mid Sch

Wansbeck General

1 ESILGTON MEWS
2 KIDLAND CL

High Market

WELLHEAD TERR

FIRST ROW 1
NORFOLK CL 2
SUFFOLK CL 3
SURREY CL 4

HENDON

Ashington Wansbeck Fst Sch

PARK VIEW

PARK VILLAS

LANGWELL CRES

SOUTH VIEW

Lib'y

4

AGED MINERS HOMES

Ctr

1 MORVEN TERR
2 MOREN PL

ASHBOURNE CRES

ARUNDEL
DARNLEY PL
RISDALE CL

1 HOLLY ST
2 BOLSOVER TERR
3 CAVENDISH GDNS
4 BERTRAM TERR
5 ACACIA TERR

1 MOORHOUSE EST
2 FONTBURN CRES
3 HEBRON PL

Ashington Alexandra Fst Sch

St Benedict's RC Mid Sch

ASHINGTON

Ashington Comm High Sch

KIELDER RD

COUPLAND RD

GREEN LA

Sch

Hirst

CAVENDISH AVE

GARDEN CITY VILLAS

87

3

LC

SENET ENTERPRISE WORKSHOP

FAIRNE AVE

Hirst High Sch

Ashington Farm

The Steadings

WEST PASTURES

5 OATFIELD CL
6 RYEDALE CL
7 LINNET CT

ELDERWOOD

EAST PASTURES
FALLOWFIELD WAY

TITCHFIELD TERR 1
FELTON TERR 3

CHELTENHAM

GOODWOOD

WETHERBY

NORTH SEATON RD

LONGHIRST AVE

2

HENSHAW CT 1
BELLSBURN CT 2
SHOTLEY CL 3
HOUNDSLOW CL 4

BARRASFORD

MAUREEN

ORCHARD

1 ORRINE CT
2 SHALLON CT

EPSOM

Coll

WALLINGTON RD

NELSON CL 1
COLLEGE PL 2
NYE BAVEN HO 3
BEECH TERR 4
CEDAR TERR 5

MONKSEATON TERR 1

FOXCOVER
ANCROFT

B1334

P

P

Wansbeck Riverside Pk

Wellhead Dean

River Wansbeck

CELANDINE CT 1
BURNETT CT 2
PRIMROSE CT 3
CRANEMARSH CL 4

Jubilee Ind Est

Schs

NEWBIGGIN RD

P

PO

North Seaton Ind Es

1

NE62

RUNGWAY

ALLENDALE CRES

WESTRAY

5 JASMINE CT
6 LILAC CT
7 LARCHWOOD DR

1 PERCY GDNS
2 FARNDALE AVE
3 WESTWOOD GDNS

A196

B1334

BLACKCLOSE BANK

LC
BLACKCLOSE EST

1 SWALLOW CL
2 SANDPIPER WAY
3 WATERFORD CL

86

26

A

B

27

C

D

28

E

F

F2
1 LINSHIELS GDNS
2 LINDISFARNE HO
3 SIMONBURN LA
4 SALLY DAVISON CT
5 CALLERTON CL
6 HESLEYSIDE
7 ALWINTON SQ
8 WINCHESTER SQ
9 SALISBURY CL

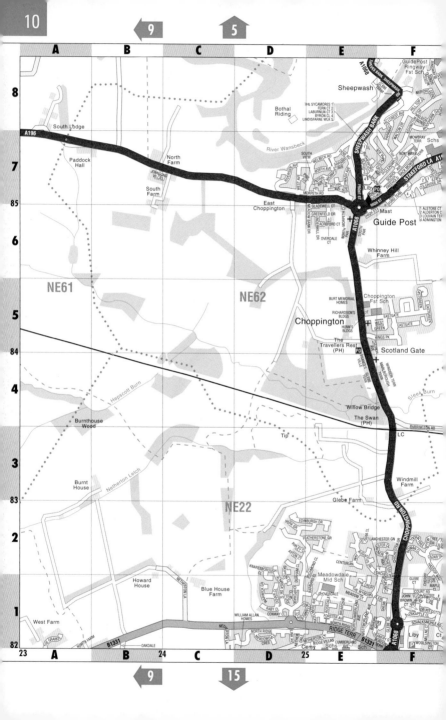

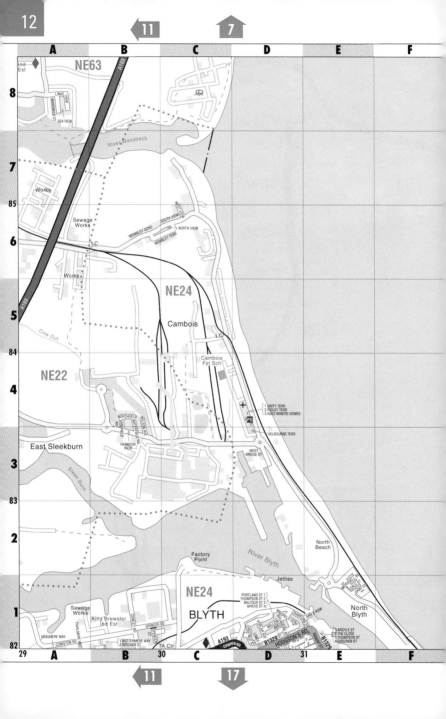

NE63

NE24

NE22

Cambois

East Sleekburn

NE24

BLYTH

North Beach

North Blyth

River Wansbeck

River Blyth

Sewage Works

Works

Works

Cow Gut

Steek Burn

Sewage Works

Kitty Brewster Ind Est

Factory Point

Jetties

Cambois Fst Sch

WEST BRIDGE ST

SELBOURNE TERR

1 UNITY TERR
2 RIDLEY TERR
3 AGED MINERS HOMES

PORTLAND ST 1
THOMPSON ST 2
BALFOUR ST 3
GREIVE ST 4

1 ARGYLE ST
2 B THE CLOSE
3 THOMPSON ST
4 GOSCHEN ST

GRASMERE WAY

CONISTON RD

THIRLMERE WAY

1 BUTTERMERE WAY
2 BEECHER ST

SPENCER RD

TA Ctr

A193

COWPEN RD

B1329

HODGSON'S RD

B1329

LINKS VIEW

WANSBECK ST

SEA VIEW

WEMBLEY GDNS

WEMBLEY TERR

SOUTH VIEW

NORTH VIEW

WEST ST

NORTHFIELD RD

SANDFIELD

WILSON RD

WATERFIELD RD

HARBOUR VIEW

LC

LC

LC

PO

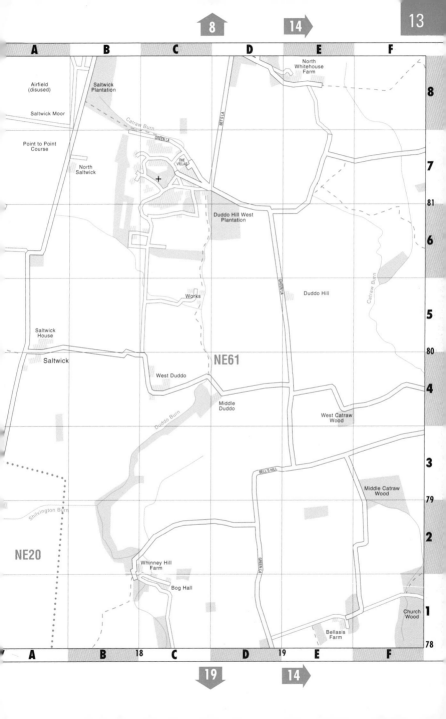

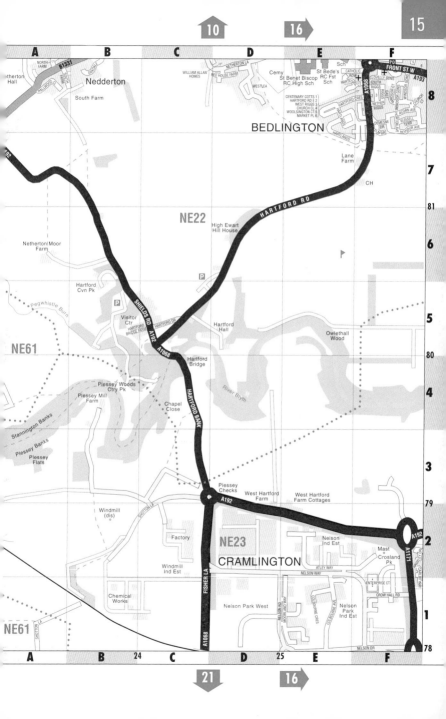

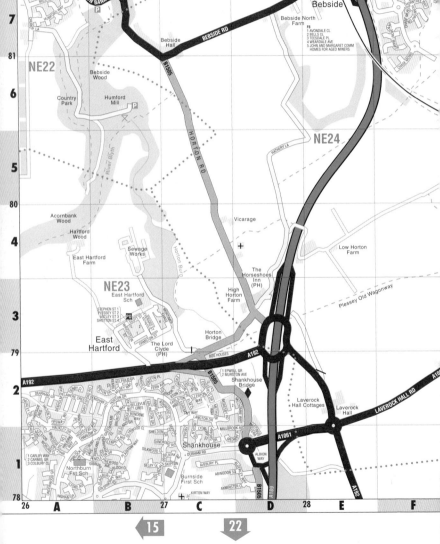

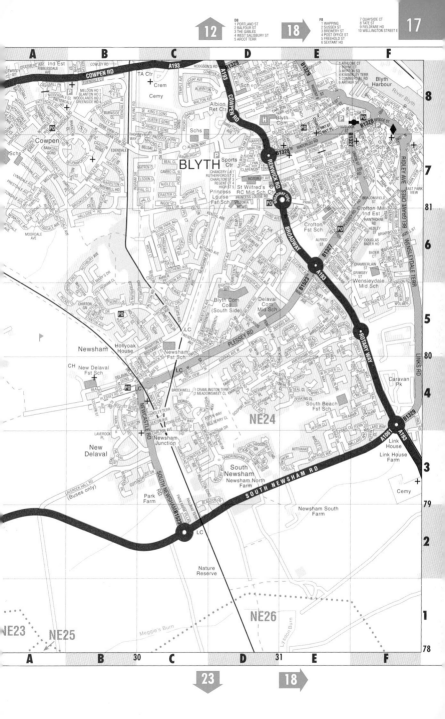

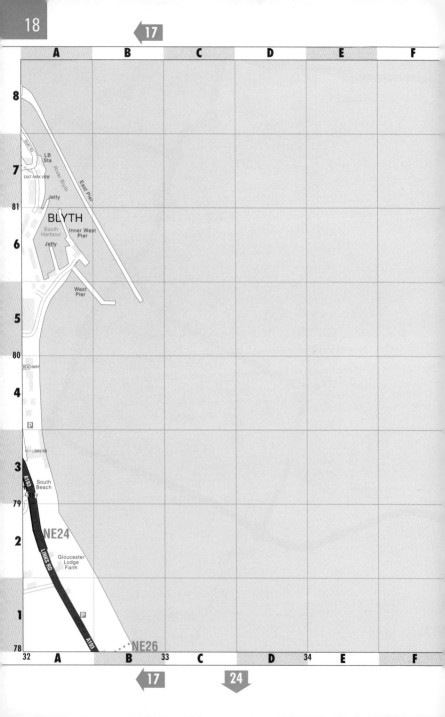

8

BOAT RD

LB
Sta

7

EAST PARK VIEW

East Park View

River Blyth

East Pier

Jetty

81

BLYTH

South
Harbour

Inner West
Pier

6

Jetty

West
Pier

5

80

BEACHWAY

4

P

LINKS RD

3

A193

South
Beach

Quay

79

NE24

2

LINKS RD

Gloucester
Lodge
Farm

1

P

A193

78

NE26

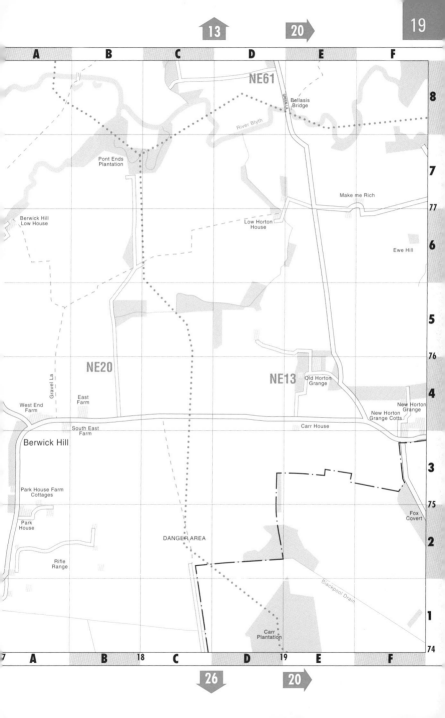

A B C D E F

NE61

Bellasis
Bridge

8

River Blyth

Make me Rich

7

77

Berwick Hill
Low House

Pont Ends
Plantation

Low Horton
House

Ewe Hill

6

5

76

NE20

Gravel La

East
Farm

NE13

Old Horton
Grange

New Horton
Grange

4

West End
Farm

South East
Farm

New Horton
Grange Cotts

Carr House

Berwick Hill

3

Park House Farm
Cottages

Fox
Covert

75

Park
House

DANGER AREA

2

Rifle
Range

Blackpool Drain

1

74

Carr
Plantation

19
14

A   B   C   D   E   F

8

Ewe Hill
Blagdon Lake
Lake Plantation
Election Plantation
Home Farm
New Kennels
New Cottages
Shotton
Shotton South Farm
NE61

7

Lake Wiseman
Old Kennels
Cascade Dene
Twist Plantation
Bog House
Blagdon Hall
North Wood
Coal Wood

77

6

Grove Pond
Deer Park Wood
Blagdon Park
Shotton Edge
North Wood
Snitter Burn
Fusilier Plantation

5

Thornhill Cottage
Park House
Shotton Grange
LEDGES DR
SOUTH DR

76

Milkhope Ctr
Milkhope Plantation
NE13

4

Hoys Wood
Shotton Edge South

3

Brenkley
North Farm
South Brenkley
East Brenkley Farm
Crow Wood
Seven Mile House

75

2

Trinidad Plantation

1

Gardener's Houses Farm

74

Carr Grange Farm

19
27

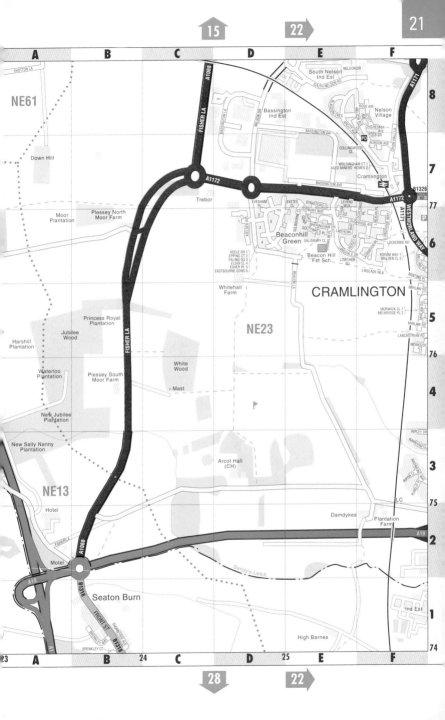

23
18

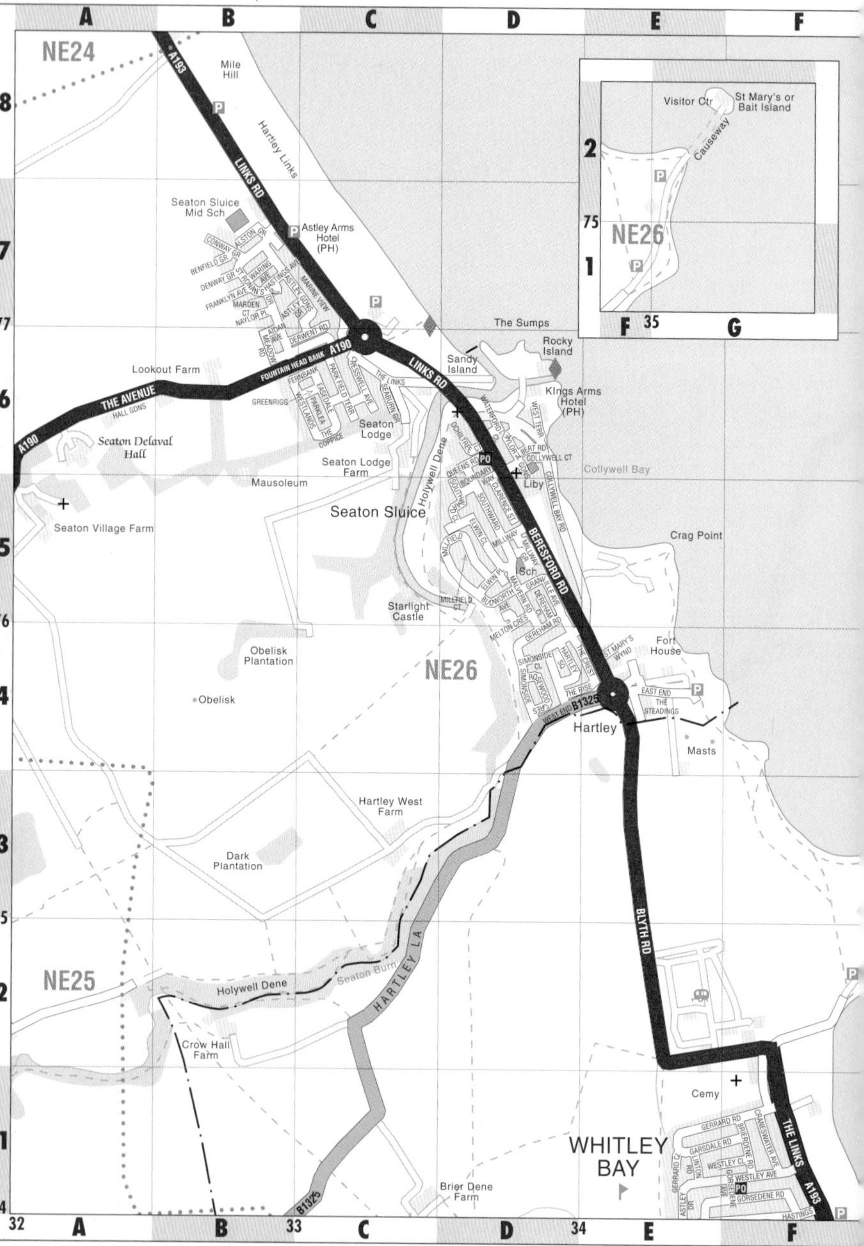
A
B
C
D
E
F
NE24
A193
Mile Hill
Hartley Links
LINKS RD
Seaton Sluice Mid Sch
Astley Arms Hotel (PH)
CONWAY GR
ALSTON GR
BENFIELD GR
DENWAY GR
ST RONAN'S
WARING AVE
HASTINGS AVE
ASTLEY GDNS
MARINE VIEW
FRANKLYN AVE
MARDEN CT
NAYLOR PL
AIDAN AVE
MEADOW RD
DERWENT RD
The Sumps
Rocky Island
Sandy Island
A190
FOUNTAIN HEAD BANK
Lookout Farm
THE AVENUE
HALL GDNS
FERNBANK
EASEDALE
PARK FIELD TERR
CRESSWELL AVE
THE LINKS
SEABURN GR
GREENRIGG
WESTLANDS
PARKLEA
THE COPPICE
Seaton Lodge
Seaton Lodge Farm
Kings Arms Hotel (PH)
WATERFORD CL
WEST TERR
OCHILTREE CT
TAYLOR GDNS
BERT RD
COLLYWELL CT
Collywell Bay
Seaton Delaval Hall
Holywell Dene
QUEENS RD
BOUNDARY WAY
CLARENCE ST
SOUTHWARD
ELWIN CL
Liby
COLLYWELL BAY RD
Mausoleum
Seaton Sluice
Seaton Village Farm
WILLFIELD
MILLWAY
Sch
BERESFORD RD
Crag Point
ELWIN PL
BUDWORTH AVE
MALVERN RD
GRANVILLE AVE
DEREHAM CT
DEREHAM RD
MILLFIELD CT
Starlight Castle
MELTON CRES
Obelisk Plantation
NE26
SIMONSIDE CL
HARTLEY SQ
THE CREST
ST MARY'S WYND
Fort House
Obelisk
ROSEWOOD CRES
THE RISE
B1325
WEST END
EAST END
THE STEADINGS
Hartley
Masts
Hartley West Farm
Dark Plantation
BLYTH RD
HARTLEY LA
NE25
Seaton Burn
Holywell Dene
Crow Hall Farm
Cemy
GERRARD RD
BRIERDENE RD
CRANESWATER AVE
THE LINKS
WHITLEY BAY
GARSDALE RD
WESTLEY CL
WESTLEY AVE
LINTON RD
GERRARD CL
GORSEDENE AVE
GORSEDENE RD
ASTLEY DR
Brier Dene Farm
B1325
HASTINGS
A193
PO
P
8
77
7
6
5
76
4
3
75
2
1
74
32
33
34
Visitor Ctr
St Mary's or Bait Island
Causeway
NE26
2
75
1
F
35
G

23
31

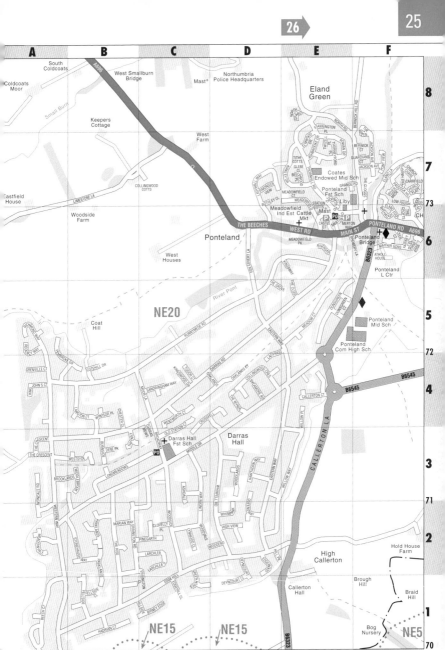

A   B   C   D   E   F

8
7
73
6
5
72
4
3
71
2
1
70

South
Coldcoats

Coldcoats
Moor

West Smallburn
Bridge

Mast

Northumbria
Police Headquarters

Eland
Green

Keepers
Cottage

West
Farm

Castfield
House

COLLINGWOOD
COTTS

LIMESTONE LA

Woodside
Farm

Coates
Endowed Mid Sch

Ponteland
Fst Sch

Lib'y

Meadowfield
Ind Est Cattle
Mkt

THE BEECHES
WEST RD
MAIN ST
PONTELAND RD   A696

Ponteland

Ponteland
Bridge

West
Houses

River Pont

Ponteland
L Ctr

Athol
House

NE20

Coat
Hill

Ponteland
Mid Sch

Ponteland
Com High Sch

B6545
B6545

Darras Hall
Fst Sch

Darras
Hall

CALLERTON LA

High
Callerton

Hold House
Farm

Brough
Hill

Braid
Hill

Callerton
Hall

Bog
Nursery

NE5

NE15
NE15

B6323

15
16

A **B** **C** **D** **E** **F**

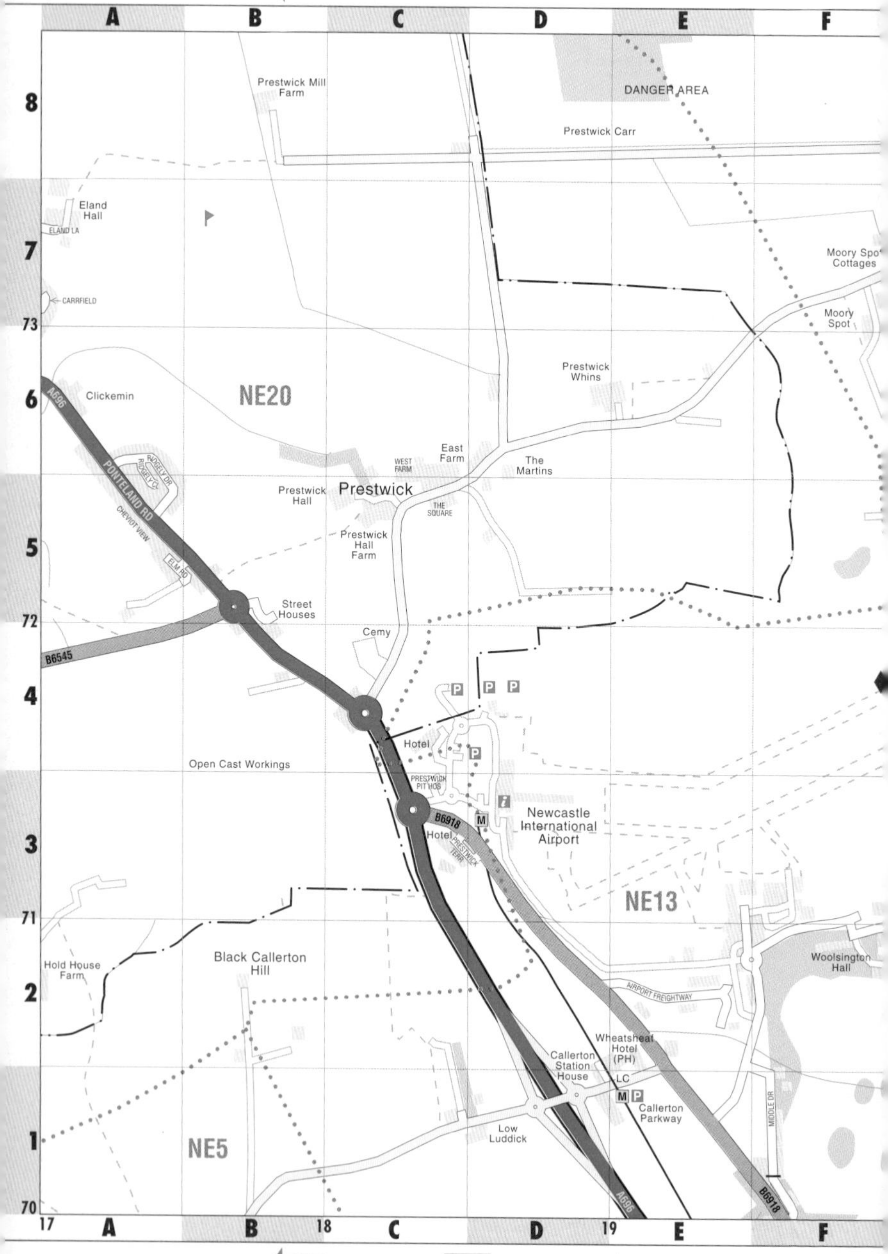

Prestwick Mill Farm

DANGER AREA

8

Prestwick Carr

Eland Hall

ELAND LA

7

Moory Spo Cottages

CARRFIELD

73

Moory Spot

NE20

Clickemin

6

A696

Prestwick Whins

PONTELAND RD

WEST FARM

East Farm

CHURCH VIEW

Prestwick

The Martins

Prestwick Hall

THE SQUARE

T.L.M. RD

Prestwick Hall Farm

5

Street Houses

72

Cemy

B6545

Open Cast Workings

4

P P P

Hotel

P

PRESTWICK PIT HOB

B6918

M

i

Newcastle International Airport

Hotel

PRESTWICK DRIVE

3

NE13

71

Hold House Farm

Black Callerton Hill

Woolsington Hall

2

AIRPORT FREIGHTWAY

MIDDLE

Wheatsheaf Hotel (PH)

Callerton Station House

LC

M P

Callerton Parkway

1

NE5

Low Luddick

A696

B6918

70

17 **A** **B** 18 **C** **D** 19 **E** **F**

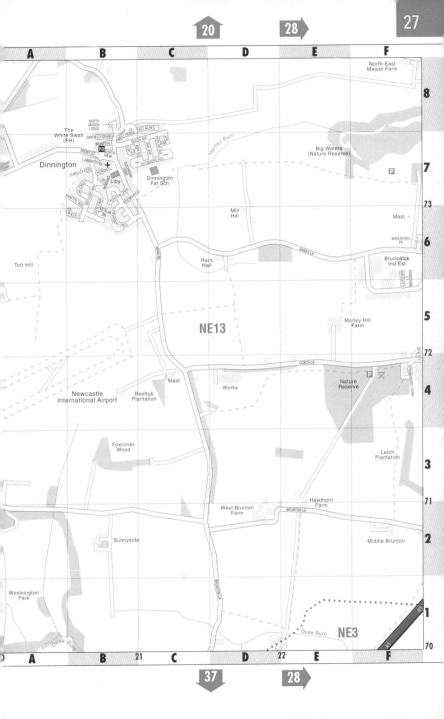

A   B   C   D   E   F

8

North-East
Mason Farm

NORTH
MASON
LODGE

The
White Swan
(PH)

OAKFIELD GRANGE

WEST ACRES   EAST ACRES

BRIARDALE

PO

FRONT ST

NORTH
VIEW

Dinnington

DUNSLEY GDNS

FARNDON

CHURCH CL

SYCAMORE AVE

BEECH AVE

OAK AVE

PINE

Hartley Burn

Big Waters
(Nature Reserve)

P   7

SHAFTOE WAY

MITFORD DRV

CHURCH CL

Liby

HERON CL

MORTON CRES

BELSAY

PORTIA

BEDELI AV

HEDGELEY CRES

Dinnington
Fst Sch

73

Mill
Hill

Mast

WATERFORD
PK

6

BICKEN CL

MAIN RD

Toft Hill

Hack
Hall

SANDY LA

Brunswick
Ind Est

SANDYSON

HARTLEY CT

NE13

5

Morley Hill
Farm

72

COACH LA

Mast

Works

Nature
Reserve

P

STRAWBERRY TERR

25 FT ST

4

Newcastle
International Airport

Beetbub
Plantation

Foxcover
Wood

Letch
Plantation

3

71

Hawthorn
Farm

West Brunton
Farm

BRUNTON LA

Sunnyside

Middle Brunton

2

Woolsington
Park

BALDON LA

Ouse Burn

NE3

A1   1

70

Ouse Burn

A   B   21   C   D   22   E   F

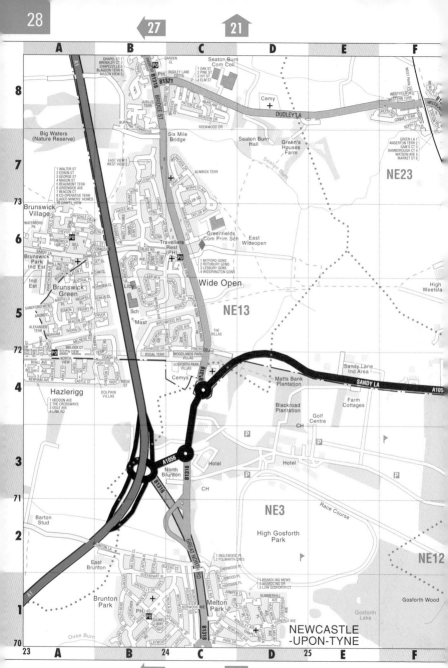

A · B · C · D · E · F

8

NE23

West Field

7

Holywell Grange Farm

East Holywell

Fenwick's Close Farm

73

6

West Holywell

NE25

Burdene Burn

Cem

B1322 West Farm

Middle Farm

BACKWORTH LA

Church Mews

ECCLES CT

LC

Wks

5

THOMAS TAYLOR COTTS

ST AIDAN'S LS

MELROSE AVE

CHURCH RD

STRETTON WAY

Backworth Park Prim Sch

Recn Gd

CLARA AVE 1
LOWER CRONE ST 2
UPPER CRONE ST 3
CO-OPERATIVE TERR 4
EARSDON VIEW 5

72

NEALSBURY

KILLINGWORTH LA

CASTLE SQ

RUSHBURY CT

NE27

Shiremoor Mid Sch

PH

Recn Gd

RYWE GR

KILLINGWORTH AVE

CH

ECCLES RD

Moor Edge Farm

MORLEY PL 6
HUGH AVE 7
CHARLES AVE 8
JAMES AVE 9

Shiremoor

4

A19

Backworth

Moor View

Holystone Farm

MOOR EDGE RD

MATSON GR

ANN ST 1
HARROW ST 2

PO

M

1 GARFIELD CL
2 HARWOOD DR

ST MARKS CT 1
CO-OPERATIVE TERR 2

EARSDON RD

3

B1317

East House Farm

HAYDON GDNS 1
HAVELOCK RD 2

STATION RD

NEW YORK ROAD A19

BOYNE GDNS

Shiremoor Prim Sch

Hypermark

71

NE12

A186

BRENKLEY AVE

2

Killingworth Moor

Holystone Farm

A191

NEW YORK RD

PH

BRUNSWICK RD

Brunswick SQ

Holystone Prim Sch

PH

THE SILVERLINK

Algernon Ind Est

A19

1 PALMERSVILLE
2 CO-OPERATIVE TERR
3 CLARABAD TERR
4 BANNISTER DR
5 THORNTON TERR
6 ELIZABETH CT
7 ELIZABETH CT
8 KELVIN PL
9 ROSEBERRY GRANGE

Holystone

ST CUTHBERT'S RD

HOLYSTONE WAY

PO

The Allotment

Silverlink Park

Mon

1

Palmersville

LAUREL AVE

End of Palmersville

Benton Square Ind Est

ST CUTHBERT'S

ST AIDAN'S SQ

BACKWORTH TERR 1
HOLYWELL TERR 2
RYTON TERR 3

CARLISLE CL

West Allotment

B1505

GREAT LIME RD

FEETHAM

Benton Square

B1505

70

E1
1 NORTH TERR
2 ECCLES TERR
3 CARLISLE TERR
4 BUDDLE TERR
5 MAUD TERR
6 LAMB TERR
7 GRIFFITH TERR
8 TAYLOR TERR
9 EARSDON TERR
10 CRAMLINGTON TERR
11 CO-OPERATIVE TERR
12 PRESTON TERR

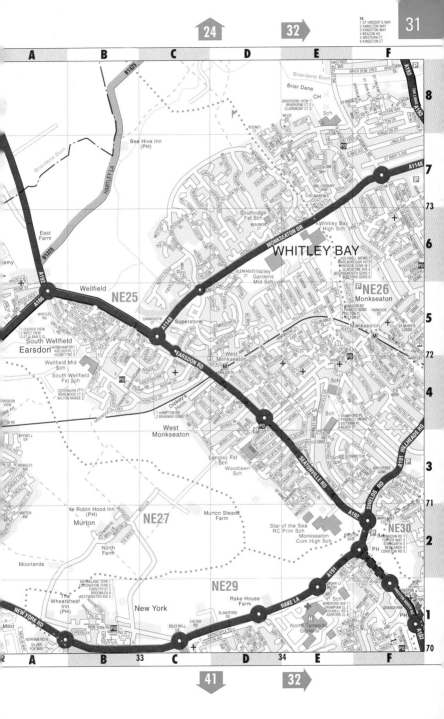

WHITLEY BAY

NE26

NE25

NE30

Marden

Monkhouse Prim Sch

Marden High Sch

Cullercoats Prim Sch

Cullercoats

Tynemouth North Point

Tynemouth Sealife Ctr

Brown's Bay

Brown's Point

Whitley Bay

1 ESPLANADE AVE
2 LINDEN TERR
3 TREWIT RD
4 VICTORIA MEWS
5 SMEEKING ST

B4
1 ALBANY GDNS
2 CLARENCE CRES
3 ALEXANDRA TERR
4 ALBERT TERR
5 WATERFORD CRES
6 DEVONSHIRE TERR
7 GLADSTONE TERR
8 STANLEY CRES

1 GORDON TERR
2 ROCKCLIFFE

1 ROCKCLIFFE GDNS
2 GUARDIAN CT
3 COLLINGWOOD TERR
4 ROMNEY CL
5 WESTMINSTER CL

1 EGLINGHAM AVE
2 RENNINGTON AVE
3 AYDON CL
4 SEACREST APARTMENTS

1 EDENGARTH
2 NEWLANDS
3 CONISTON RD
4 BLENCATHRA

1 THE DRIVE
2 PARKSIDE CRES

1 BRAESIDE CL
2 SHADEN PARK RD

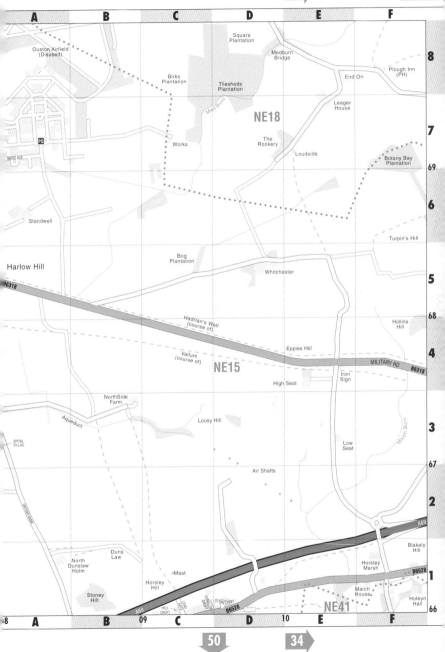

A   B   C   D   E   F

Ouston Airfield (Disused)

Square Plantation

Medburn Bridge

End On

Plough Inn (PH)

8

Birks Plantation

Tilesheds Plantation

Leager House

NE18

7

69

PO

Works

The Rookery

Loudside

Botany Bay Plantation

WADE AVE

6

Standwell

Turpin's Hill

Harlow Hill

Bog Plantation

Whitchester

5

68

B6318

Hadrian's Wall (course of)

Hollins Hill

Vallum (course of)

Eppies Hill

MILITARY RD   B6318

4

NE15

High Seat

Iron Sign

NorthSide Farm

Low Seat

3

Aqueduct

Lousy Hill

SPITAL VILLAS

Air Shafts

Marsh Burn

67

2

A69

DEVILS BURN

Blakely Hill

Duns Law

Mast

Horsley Marsh

North Dunslaw Holm

Horsley Hill

March House

Stoney Hill

HILL CROFT

LEAD ROAD

STONECROFT

DUNSLAW CROFT

B6528

B6528

NE41

Holeyn Hall

A69   09   C   D   10   E   F   66

8   A   B

1

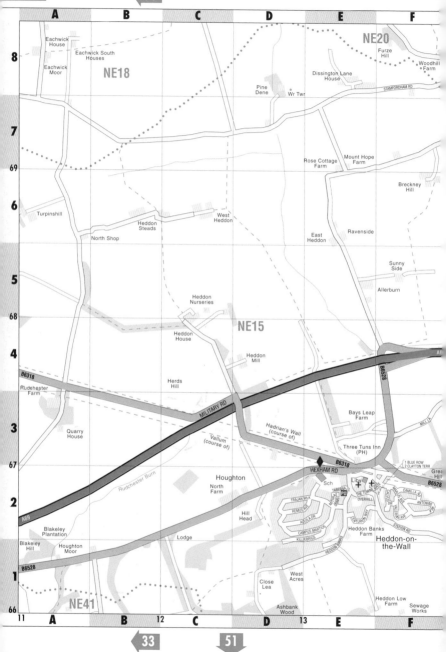

A   **B**   **C**   **D**   **E**   **F**

8

7

69

6

5

68

4

67

3

2

1

66

11   **A**   **B**   12   **C**   **D**   13   **E**   **F**

Eachwick House
Eachwick South Houses
Eachwick Moor
NE18
NE20
Furze Hill
Woodhill Farm
Dissington Lane House
STAMFORDHAM RD
Pine Dene
Wr Twr
Rose Cottage Farm
Mount Hope Farm
Breckney Hill
Turpinshill
Heddon Steads
West Heddon
East Heddon
Ravenside
North Shop
Sunny Side
Allerburn
Heddon Nurseries
NE15
Heddon House
Heddon Mill
Herds Hill
B6318
Rudchester Farm
MILITARY RD
Hadrian's Wall (course of)
Bays Leap Farm
B6528
A6
Quarry House
Vallum (course of)
Three Tuns Inn (PH)
1 BLUE ROW
2 CLAYTON TERR
Gre Hill
B6318
Rudchester Burn
HEXHAM RD
Houghton
North Farm
Sch
Lib
THE TOWNE GATE
OVERHILL
MILL LA
B6528
A69
Hill Head
TRAJAN WLK
REMUS GR
AQUILA DR
CAMPUS MARTIUS
KILLIEBRIGS
THE TOWNE GATE
CAPITURIS
TABERNA CL
VITINA GR
CAMILLA CL
CLAUDIO
VALERIAN AVE
ANTONINE
Heddon Banks Farm
Heddon-on-the-Wall
Blakeley Plantation
Lodge
HEDDON BANKS
STATION RD
Blakeley Hill
Houghton Moor
B6528
Close Lea
West Acres
Heddon Low Farm
Sewage Works
NE41
Ashbank Wood

35
26

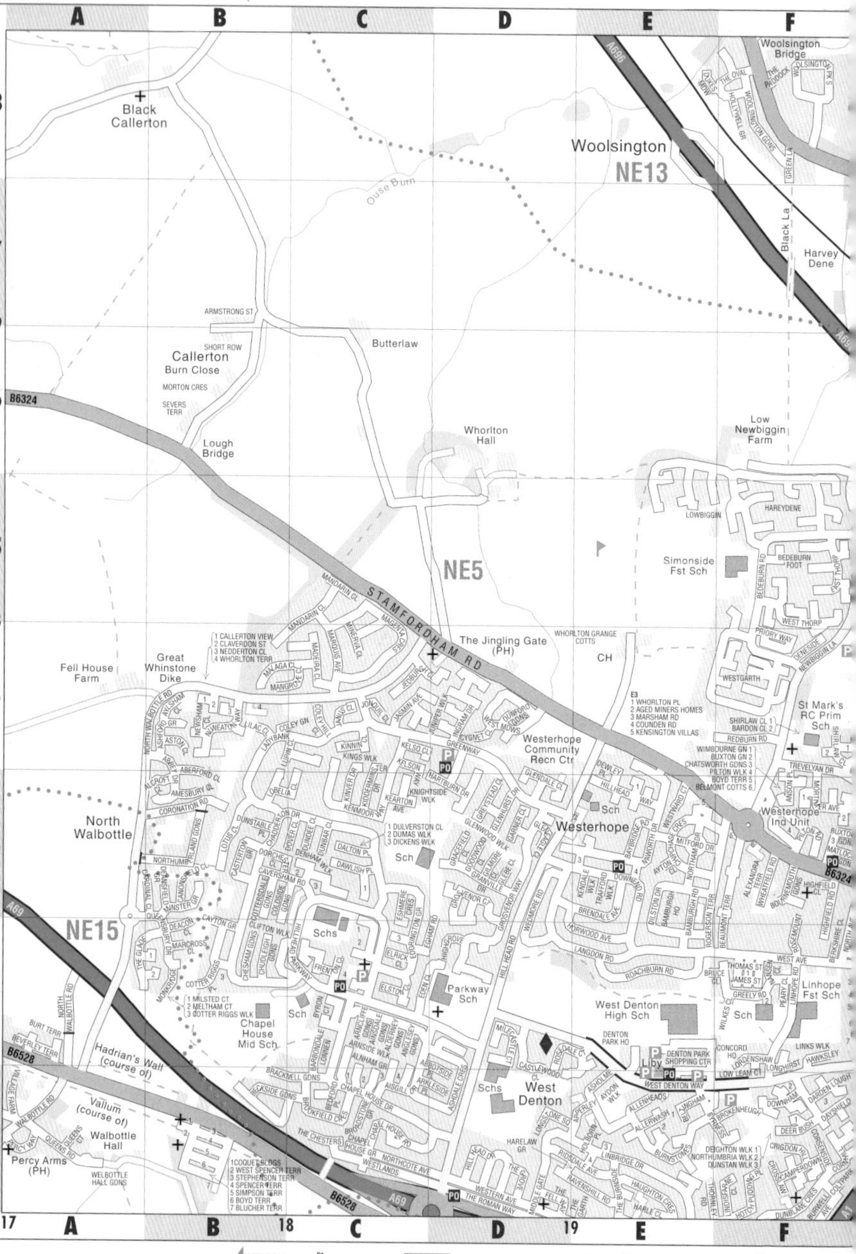
A
B
C
D
E
F
8
7
69
6
5
68
4
3
67
2
1
66
17
18
19
Black Callerton
Woolsington Bridge
Woolsington
NE13
A696
THE OVAL
DUKES MDW
HOLLYWELL GR
WOOLSINGTON GDNS
THE PADDOCK
WOOLSINGTON PK S
GREEN LA
Ouse Burn
Black La
Harvey Dene
ARMSTRONG ST
SHORT ROW
Callerton
Burn Close
MORTON CRES
SEVERS TERR
Butterlaw
B6324
Lough Bridge
Whorlton Hall
Low Newbiggin Farm
LOWBIGGIN
HAREYDENE
NE5
Simonside Fst Sch
BEDEBURN FOOT
BEDEBURN RD
EAST THORP
WEST THORP
PRIORY WAY
DENESIDE
NEWBIGGIN LA
STAMFORDHAM RD
MANDARIN CL
MAGNOLIA CRES
MINERVA CL
MARQUIS AVE
MADEIRA CL
MALAGA CL
MANGROVE CL
1 CALLERTON VIEW
2 CLAVERDON ST
3 NEDDERTON CL
4 WHORLTON TERR
Fell House Farm
Great Whinstone Dike
The Jingling Gate (PH)
WHORLTON GRANGE COTTS
CH
WESTGARTH
E3
1 WHORLTON PL
2 AGED MINERS HOMES
3 MARSHAM RD
4 COUNDEN RD
5 KENSINGTON VILLAS
St Mark's RC Prim Sch
SHIRLAW CL 1
BARDON CL 2
REDBURN RD
WIMBOURNE GN 1
BUXTON GN 2
CHATSWORTH GDNS 3
PILTON WLK 4
BOYD TERR 5
BELMONT COTTS 6
TREVELYAN DR
Westerhope Community Recn Ctr
Westerhope Ind Unit
Westerhope
Sch
North Walbottle
NORTH WALBOTTLE RD
AYLSHAM CL
ASHFORD GR
ASTON CL
NEWSHAM CL
NUNEATON WAY
LILAC CL
COLEY GN
COLEY HILL
LADYBANK
LUPIN CL
JANUS CL
JONQUIL CL
JASMIN AVE
JEDBURGH CL
JUNIPER WLK
INGRAM DR
CYGNET CL
WEST MDWS
DUNFORD GDNS
KINNIN
KINGS WLK
KELSO CL
KELSON WAY
GREENWAY
MARTBURN DR
KNIGHTSIDE WLK
KEARTON AVE
KENMOOR WAY
KINVER DR
KIDDERMINSTER DR
LOBELIA CL
ABERFORD CL
ALCROFT CL
AMESBURY CL
CORONATION RD
LOTUS CL
DUNSTABLE PL
CHADDERTON DR
DOVER CL
DUNDEE CL
DUNBAR CL
1 DULVERSTON CL
2 DUMAS WLK
3 DICKENS WLK
DALTON PL
DENHAM WLK
DAWLISH PL
CASTERTON GR
CAVERSHAM RD
DORCHESTER CL
NORTHUMB
CARDINAL CL
DANSFIELD CL
CANONSFIELD CL
MINSTER GR
OUSEBURN RD
CAYTON GR
DEACON CL
MARCROSS CL
THE GLADE
COTTER RIGGS PL
MONKRIDGE
1 MILSTED CT
2 MELTHAM CT
3 COTTER RIGGS WLK
CHESHAM GDNS
CHUDLEIGH GDNS
CLIFTON WLK
COTTERSDALE GDNS
COLDSIDE GDNS
HILLHEAD PARKWAY
FRENTON CL
ELRICK CL
ELSTON CL
ESHMERE CRES
EDDRINGTON GR
EGHAM RD
EDEN CL
HIGHGROVE
GRACEFIELD CL
GOODWOOD CL
GILMORE CL
GLEBE CL
GRANVILLE DR
GROSVENOR CL
GROSVENOR WAY
GLENWOOD WLK
GREYSTEAD CL
GLENHURST DR
GARNER CL
GLENDALE CL
HILL HEAD RD
DEWLEY PL
HILLHEAD WAY
BAYBRIDGE RD
HAWORTH DR
WESTWARD CT
CHIPCHASE CRES
MITFORD DR
AYTON CL
NORTHAM CL
DOWNEND RD
KENDALE WLK
TRAFFORD WLK
BRENDALE AVE
HORWOOD AVE
LANGDON RD
WEDMORE RD
DILSTON DR
BAMBURGH HO
BAMBURGH RD
ROGERSON TERR
BEAUMONT TERR
ROACHBURN RD
ALEXANDRA TERR
WHEATFIELD RD
BOURNEMOUTH GDNS
HIGHFIELD CL
HIGHFIELD RD
ROSEMOUNT
BERKSHIRE CL
WEST AVE
BRUCE CL
THOMAS ST
JAMES ST
GREELY RD
LINHOPE RD
PEARY CL
WILKES CL
Linhope Fst Sch
NE15
Schs
Sch
Chapel House Mid Sch
Parkway Sch
West Denton High Sch
DENTON PARK HO
DENTON PARK SHOPPING CTR
Liby
WEST DENTON WAY
LOW LEAM CL
CONCORD HO
LORDENSHAW
LONGHIRST
LINKS WLK
HAWKSLEY
West Denton
Schs
MILECASTLE CT
ROSEDALE CT
CASTLEWOOD CL
ASHOLME
AYDON WLK
ALLENHEADS
ALLERWASH
BRIGHAM
BYRNESS
BROKENHEUGH
DOWNHAM
DARDEN LOUGH
DAYSHIELD
DEER BUSH
CRIGDON HILL
CAMPERDOWN
CORBRIDGE
DUNBLANE CRES
BURWELL AVE
COLTPARK
DEIGHTON WLK 1
NORTHUMBRIA WLK 2
DUNSTAN WLK 3
THORNLEY RD
LINDISFARNE CL
HOTSPUR WAY
CROSSWAY
BURNSTONES
LINBRIDGE DR
HAUGHTON CRES
HARLE CL
THE BURNSIDE
RAVENSHILL RD
RIDSDALE AVE
APPERLEY
HOLBORN PL
LONGSTONE SQ
HARELAW GR
MIDDLE GATE
THE GARTH
FELL WAY
HILL HEAD DR
THE GROVE
WESTERN AVE
THE ROMAN WAY
NORTHCOTE AVE
WESTLANDS
THE CHESTERS
CHAPEL HOUSE GR
CHAPEL HOUSE DR
CHAPEL HOUSE RD
BROADSTONE GR
BROOKFIELD CRES
BEDFORD PL
BECKSIDE GDNS
BRACKNELL GDNS
BARBONDALE LONNEN
BYRON CT
ARNCLIFFE GDNS
AINSDALE GDNS
ALDERNEY GDNS
ANGLESEY GDNS
ARNSIDE WLK
ALNHAM GR
AISGILL CL
ABBOTSIDE PL
ARKLESIDE PL
ASHDALE CRES
BURT TERR
NORTH WALBOTTLE RD
BEVERLEY TERR
B6528
Hadrian's Wall (course of)
Vallum (course of)
VILLAGE FARM
WALBOTTLE RD
PERCY WAY
QUEENS RD
QUEENS CT
Walbottle Hall
Percy Arms (PH)
WELBOTTLE HALL GDNS
1 COQUET BLDGS
2 WEST SPENCER TERR
3 STEPHENSON TERR
4 SPENCER TERR
5 SIMPSON TERR
6 BOYD TERR
7 BLUCHER TERR
A69
A1

35
53

C1
1 ANGRAM WLK
2 ASKRIGG WLK
3 AUDLAND WLK
4 AUSTWICK WLK
C2
1 HANOVER WLK
2 HANOVER CL
3 ELGAR AVE
4 THE SHOPPING CTR

E1
1 BIRKSHAW WLK
2 BICKERTON WLK
3 KNARSDALE PL
4 HIGHWELL LA

F2
1 FRANKHAM ST
2 BARENTS CL
3 FAIRSPRING
4 FENTON WLK
5 FORESTBORN CT
6 FOURSTONES
7 FORDMOSS WLK

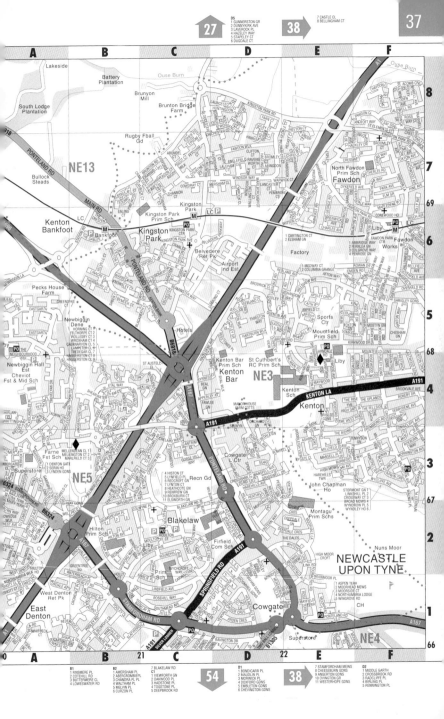

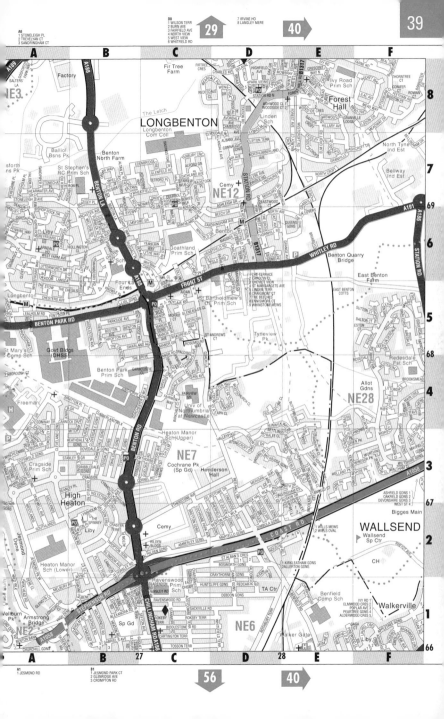

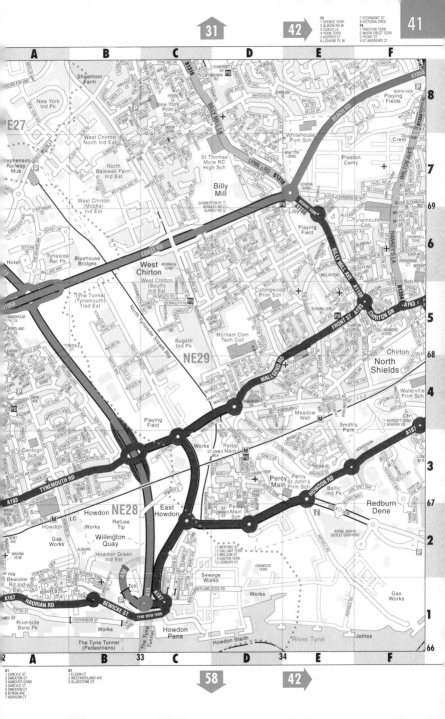

F5
1 SPENCE TERR
2 ALBION RD W
3 COACH LA
4 YORK TERR
5 HOPPER ST
6 LOVAINE PL W

7 STORMONT ST
8 VICTORIA CRES
F6
1 PRESTON TERR
2 MOOR CREST TERR
3 FRONT ST
4 ST ANDREWS CT

	A	B	C	D	E	F

Shiremoor Farm
New York Ind Pk
White Fox Way
SOMERSET ST
STIRLING DR
AIRBIL
NORTH VIEW

E27
West Chirton North Ind Est
New York Prim Sch
BILLY MILL LA

North Balkwell Farm Ind Est
St Thomas More RC High Sch

West Chirton (Middle) Ind Est

Stephenson Railway Mus

West Chirton North Ind Est
WESTMORLAND RD

Billy Mill
GUNNERTON PL 1
BERKLEY RD 2
SURREY RD 3

Whitehouse Prim Sch
Preston Cemy
Crem

8

7

69

Tyneside Ret Pk
Bluehouse Bridges
Hotel

West Chirton
COAST RD
NUNWICK GDNS

Tyne Tunnel (Tynemouth) Trad Est

West Chirton (South) Ind Est

BILLY MILL AVE A1108

Tynemouth Coll

Collingwood Prim Sch

NE29

Bugatti Ind Pk

Norham Com Tech Coll

North Tyneside Steam Rly

WALLSEND RD

FRONT ST
CHIRTON GN A793

Chirton
North Shields

Collingwood House

6

5

68

Waterville Prim Sch

Meadow Well

Smith's Park

L Ctr
1 MORCOTT GDNS
2 NEWARK SQ

A161

4

Denbigh Sch

Playing Field

Works
Percy St John's Main
St John's Main

Percy Main
Percy Main Prim Sch

Baltic Ind Pk

Redburn Dene

HOWDON RD

67

3

TYNEMOUTH RD
A193

Howdon NE28
LC
Works
Willington Quay
Gas Works
Refuse Tip
Howdon Green Ind Est

East Howdon

St Mark's Main Sch

ROYAL QUAYS OUTLET SHOPPING

Gas Works

2

Bewicke Rd Ind Est
A187 HADRIAN RD
BEWICKE ST
Riverside Bsns Pk

Toll
TYNE VIEW TERR
A161

Sewage Works

1 MITFORD ST
2 GALLANT TERR
3 MELDON ST
4 EASTEN TERR
5 LESBURY ST

OAKWOOD TERR

Works

Jetties

1

66

The Tyne Tunnel (Pedestrians)
The Tyne Tunnel
STEPHENSON ST
Works

Howdon Pans

Howdon Staith

River Tyne

	A	33	B	C	D	34	E	F

A1
1 CARLYLE ST
2 SMEATON ST
3 HANOVER GDNS
4 CARLYLE CT
5 SMEATON CT
6 BYRON AVE
7 ADDISON CT

B1
1 ELDON CT
2 WESTMORLAND AVE
3 GLADSTONE ST

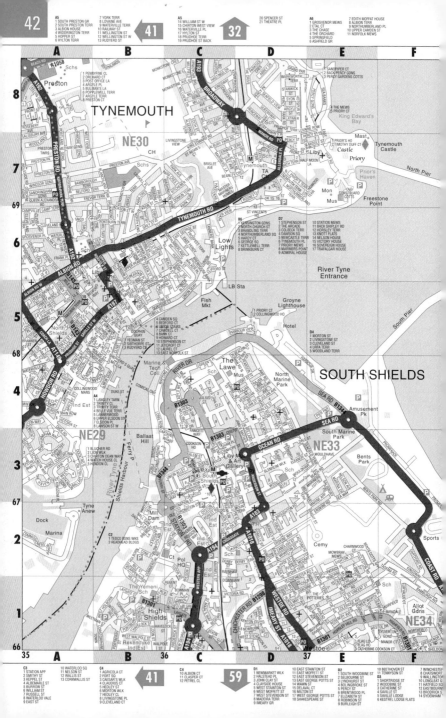

	A	B	C	D	E	F	

North Pier

South Pier

Trow Point

P
PH
NE33

Trow Lea

1 BIDEFORD GDNS
2 CHEVIOT RD
3 NORHAM AVE N
4 SHELDON RD
5 SOUTHFIELD RD

Frenchman's
Bay

NE34

Frenchman's
Lea

COAST RD
A183

8

7

69

6

5

68

4

3

67

2

66

1

48   A   B   39   C   D   40   E   F

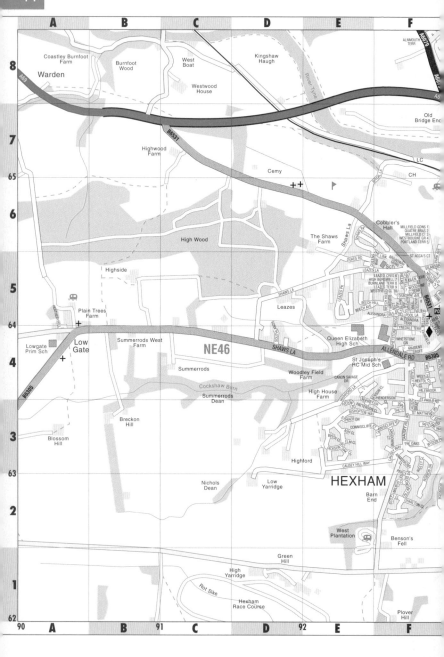

A4
1 PRIESTLANDS AVE
2 CROFT TERR
3 ST OSWALD'S RD
4 HENCOTES CT
5 GIBSON HO
6 ST WILFRID'S CT
7 ETHEL TERR
8 HENCOTES MEWS
9 SELE CT

10 HIGH ST CUTHBERT'S AVE

B4
1 NEWMAN'S WAY
2 JUBILEE BLDGS
3 DIAMOND SQ

46 ►

45

A   B   C   D   E   F

8

Beaufront Castle

The Park

Knoll Hill

Hampstead House

CORCHESTER LA

Cor Burn

7

Beaufront Red House

Red House Plantation

A69

A69

A69

CORCHESTER TWRS

B6529

Corbridge Mid Sch

THE DEAN

65

Prior Thorns

Redhouse Burn

Redhouse Haughs

CORSTOPITVM ROMAN FORT

CORCHESTER TERR 1
CORCHESTER AVE 2

STAGSHAW RD

ROMAN

LEAZES TERR

PRIOR TERR

ST HELEN'S LA

AVENUE

6

NE46

River Tyne

TRINITY TERR

COCKSHOTT

MANOR COTTS

WEST TERR

PRINCE

ST HELEN'S ST

ORCHARD TERR

WATLING ST

Widehaugh Nursery

WELL BANK

HILL ST

B6529

MIDDLE ST

MARKET PL

FRONT ST

5

Wide Haugh

Dilston Haughs

Corbridge Bridge

Sam's Island
LC

B6321

STATION RD

64

A695

Cemy

Corbridge Bridge

B6529

TINKLER'S BANK

4

Dilston Plains

DILSTON HAUGH COTTS

B6321

LC

NE45

Corbridge

Dilston Park

The Scrogs

Dilston Haugh Farm

B6307

A695

3

Dilston South Park

Bowlingally Hill

Dilston Mill

Dilston

Scurl Hill

LADYCUTTERS LA

Roecliff Lodge

63

Dilston Park

Dilston Hall

East Haugh

Devil's Water

High Town

West Fell

2

Park Wood

Birchside Wood

Snokoehill Plantation

Snokoe Hill

1

West Haugh

Birchy Sike

Quarry Cottage Belt

Swallowship Wood

B6307

Birchy Wood

Temperley Grange Farm

62

Swallowship Hill

96   A   **97**   B   C   **98**   D   E   F

A   B   C   D   E   F

B6321

8

Gallow
Hill
Gallowhill

Thornbrough
High Barns

7

Thornbrough
Kiln House

AYDON RD
CRAGSIDE
JACKSON LA
DESCHENE LA
BEECH AVE
WOODSIDE AVE
BIRCH DR

Aydon
Grange

65

Piperclose
House

Quarry
Wood

Linn Burn
Wood

6

Corbridge
CE Fst
Sch
SYNCLEN TH
TERR
ST HELEN'S LA

1 CHANTRY EST
2 AYDON RD EST
3 ST HELEN'S ST
4 WINDSOR CT
5 AYDON GR

Crooks
Hill

NE45

RINCES ST
WINDSOR COMMERCIAL
AYDON GDNS
ELANDS RD
ORCHARD
CRES
APPLETREE RISE
CARIL
CARL
CATTELLA

Corbridge

Howden Dene
Farm

Thornbrough

UN ST   B6530

Cricket
Plantation

Thornbrough
Buildings

5

Howden
Dene

Sidle Hill

Brocks
Bushes

64

Gallow
Hill

Thornbrough
Haugh

East
Lodge

A69

B6530

4

Eales

Thornbrough
Wood

Styford
Toll Bar

Styford
Lodge

Tynedale
Park

Gravel
Pit

River Tyne

3

A69

Farnley
Haughs

NE43

High
Barns

Farnley
Grange

Gravel
Pit

63

YOUTITERS LA

Whinney
Corner

LC

Styford
Cottages

Farnley
Gate

2

Grey
Court

Abbeybank
Wood

Prospect
Hill

NE44

Riding
Hills

A695

1

Mast

Styford
Park

Styford
Hall

62

A   B   00   C   D   01   E   F

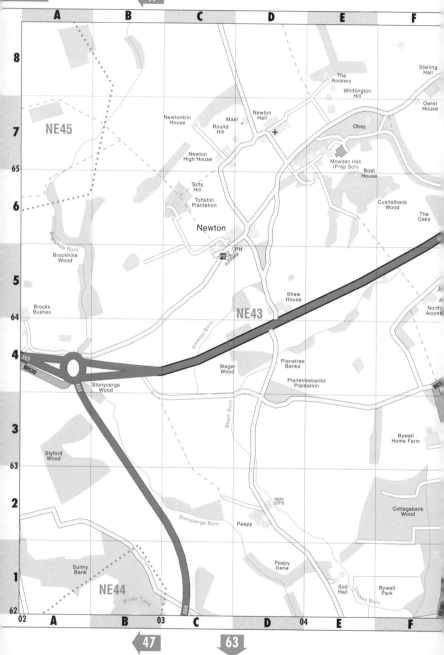

47

8

7

NE45

65

6

5

64

4

A69
B6530
A68

3

63

2

1

62

A   B   C   D   E   F

02   03   04

The Rookery
Whittington Hill
Stelling Hall
Owlet House

Newtonkiln House
Mast
Round Hill
Newton Hall
Obsy

Newton High House
Mowden Hall (Prep Sch)
Boat House

Tofts Hill
Toftshill Plantation
Cushatbank Wood
The Oaks

Newton

Brockhole Burn
Brockhole Wood

PO
PH

NE43
Shaw House

Brocks Bushes
North Acomb

Newton Burn

Stonyverge Wood
Wager Wood
Planetree Banks
Planetreebanks Plantation

B63

Styford Wood
Beam Burn
Bywell Home Farm

PEEPY COTTS

Stonyverge Burn
Peepy
Cottagebank Wood

Peepy Dene

Sunny Bank
NE44
River Tyne
Sod Hall
Bywell Park
Clockey Burn

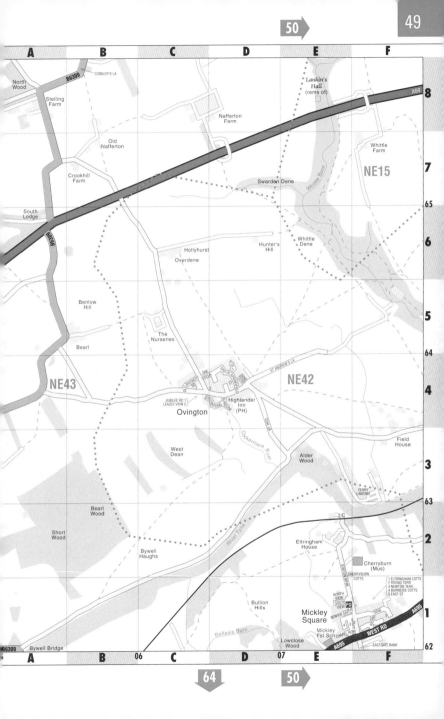

49　33

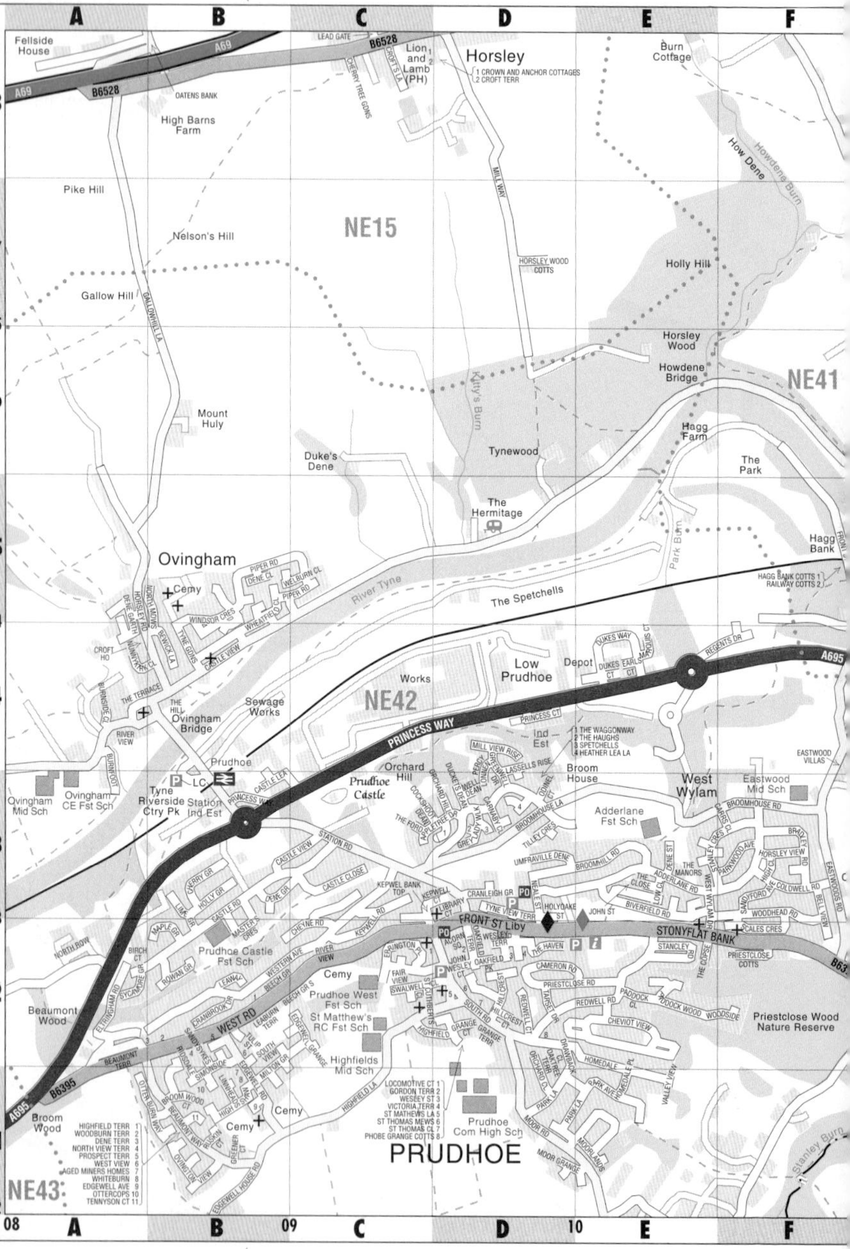

A　B　C　D　E　F

Fellside House

A69

LEAD GATE

B6528

Lion and Lamb (PH)

Horsley

1 CROWN AND ANCHOR COTTAGES
2 CROFT TERR

Burn Cottage

B6528

OATENS BANK

How Dene

Howdene Burn

8

High Barns Farm

CHERRY TREE GDNS

MILL WAY

Pike Hill

NE15

Nelson's Hill

HORSLEY WOOD COTTS

Holly Hill

7

Gallow Hill

65

Horsley Wood

BALLOWFIELD LA

Howdene Bridge

NE41

6

Mount Huly

Duke's Dene

King's Burn

Tynewood

Hagg Farm

The Park

Park Burn

The Hermitage

Hagg Bank

HAGG BANK COTTS 1
RAILWAY COTTS 2

5

Ovingham

PIPER RD

DENE LA
MELBURN CL
PIPER RD

River Tyne

The Spetchells

WINDSOR GDNS

WHEATLANDS

Cemy

Works

Low Prudhoe

Depot

DUKES WAY
DUKES EARLS

A695

REGENTS DR

4

CROFT HO

THE TERRACE

NE42

NE42

PRINCESS WAY

PRINCESS CT

Ind Est

1 THE WAGGONWAY
2 THE HAUGHS
3 SPETCHELLS
4 HEATHER LEA LA

EASTWOOD VILLAS

THE HILL
Ovingham Bridge

Sewage Works

MILL VIEW TOP

LASSELLS RISE

Broom House

West Wylam

Eastwood Mid Sch

BROOMHOUSE RD

RIVER VIEW

Prudhoe

Orchard Hill

Adderlane Fst Sch

HORSLEY VIEW

Ovingham CE Fst Sch

P LC

Tyne Riverside Station Ctry Pk Ind Est

Prudhoe Castle

PRINCESS RD

TILLEY CRES

UMFRAVILLE DENE

ADDERLANE RD

THE MANORS

SADDLER ST

COLDWELL RD

WOODHEAD RD

3

Ovingham Mid Sch

STATION RD

CASTLE VIEW

CASTLE RD

CHYNE RD

KEPWEL BANK

CRANLEIGH GR

BROOMHILL RD

RIVERFIELD RD

THE CLOSE

BIRKDALE

PRIESTCLOSE COTTS

CALES CRES

STONYFLAT BANK

63

MAPLE CL

BIRCH CL

JUNGTON

CRANBROOK

FRONT ST Liby

JOHN ST

STANCLEY

THE DURSLEY

B6395

Beaumont Wood

Prudhoe Castle Fst Sch

RIVER VIEW

Cemy

OAKFIELD

PRIESTCLOSE RD

PADDOCK WOOD

2

WEST RD

WEST RD

Prudhoe West Fst Sch
St Matthew's RC Fst Sch

FAIR VIEW

EWBANK

GRANGE TERR

CAMERON RD

REDWELL RD

CHEVIOT VIEW

WOODSIDE

Priestclose Wood Nature Reserve

BEAUMONT

Highfields Mid Sch

HIGHFIELD LA

LOCOMOTIVE CT 1
GORDON TERR 2
WESBY ST 3
VICTORIA TERR 4
ST MATHEWS LA 5
ST THOMAS MEWS 6
ST THOMAS CL 7
PHOBE GRANGE COTTS 8

HOMEDALE

VALLEY VIEW

1

Broom Wood

Cemy

Cemy

HIGHFIELD TERR 1
WOODSBURN TERR 2
DENE TERR 3
NORTH VIEW TERR 4
PROSPECT TERR 5
WEST VIEW 6
AGED MINERS HOMES 7
WHITEBURN 8
EDGEWELL AVE 9
OTTERCOPS 10
TENNYSON CT 11

Prudhoe Com High Sch

MOOR GRANGE

PRUDHOE

Stanley Burn

A695

NE43

62

08　A　B　09　C　D　10　E　F

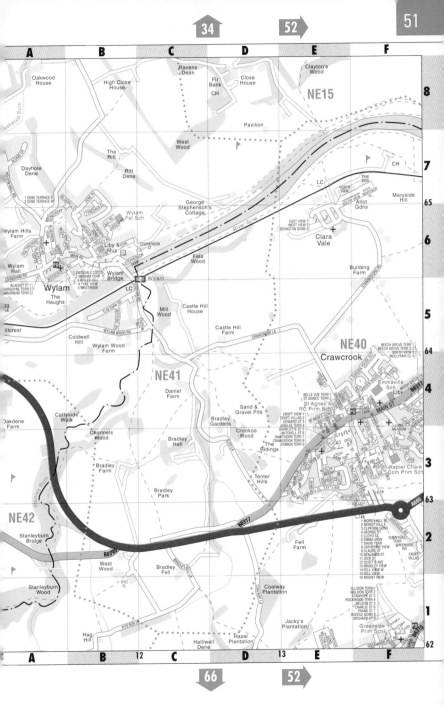

A   B   C   D   E   F

8
7
65
6
5
64
4
3
63
2
1
62

Oakwood House

High Close House

Ravens Dean

Fir Bank
CH

Close House

Clayton's Wood

NE15

Pavilion

West Wood

The Rift

Rift Dene

Dayhole Dene

George Stephenson's Cottage

River Tyne

LC

NORTH VIEW
TYNE VIEW
MARYSIDE
SOUTH VIEW

Maryside Hill

Allot Gdns

CH

Wylam Hills Farm

EAST VIEW 1
WEST VIEW 2
EDINGTON GDNS 3

Clara Vale

Liby & Terr
Wylam Fst Sch

Wylam Mus

1 DENE TERRACE E
2 DENE TERRACE W

STEPHENSON CT

STEPHENSON

Eels Wood

Building Farm

Wylam Hall

1 SWINDALE COTTS
2 INGHAM TERR
3 WYLES HILL
4 TYNE VIEW
5 WEST VIEW

Wylam Bridge

Wylam

BLACKET CT 1
BURGOYNE TERR 2
LABURNUM TERR 3

Wylam

The Haughs

LC

ELM BANK RD

Castle Hill House

Mill Wood

Castle Hill Farm

CRAWCROOK LA

NE40

Crawcrook

BEECH GROVE TERR 1
BEECH GROVE TERR S 2
SOUTH VIEW 3
MOLLYFAIR CL 4

llcrest

Coldwell Hill

Wylam Wood Farm

WYLAM WOOD RD

NE41

Daniel Farm

Sand & Gravel Pits

Bradley Gardens

Crookoe Wood

BELLE VUE TERR 1
ST AGNES TERR 2

St Agnes RC Prim Sch

CROFT VIEW 1
CROFT VILLAS 2
EDWARD ST 3
JUBILEE TERR 4
CHARLOTTE ST 5
MITCHELL ST 6
HAWTHORN TERR 7
CRAWCROOK TERR 8
DONKIN TERR 9

The Ridings

Emmaville Sch Liby

MAIN ST

LONG MEADOW

Kepier Chare Com Prim Sch

Oakdene Farm

Cattyside Walk

Channels Wood

Bradley Hall

Bradley Farm

Bradley Park

Tenter Hills

NE42

Stanleyburn Bridge

B6399

West Wood

Bradley Fell

KYO CL

Fell Farm

B6317

A695

1 MORGY HILL E
2 MORGY HILL W
3 CLIFFORD GDNS
4 GEORGE ST
5 LLOYD ST
6 EMMA VIEW
7 DAVID TERR
8 CATHERINE VIEW
9 CLAUDE ST
10 BENJAMIN ST
11 DICK ST
12 SCOTT S AVE
13 BRADLEY VIEW
14 FELL VIEW W
15 FELL VIEW
16 MOUNT VIEW

SUNNYGILL TERR
GREENSIDE RD

CROFT VILLAS

Stanleyburn Wood

Coalway Plantation

KYO BDE LA

Jacky's Plantation

ELLISON TERR 1
MELDON TERR 2
STANHOPE ST 3
ROCKWOOD TERR 4
NELSON ST 5
CHARLIE ST 6
FRANK ST 7
BUDDLE GDNS 8
ORCHARD ST 9

Greenside Prim Sch

B6315

Hag Hill

Halliwell Dene

Hazel Plantation

12   13

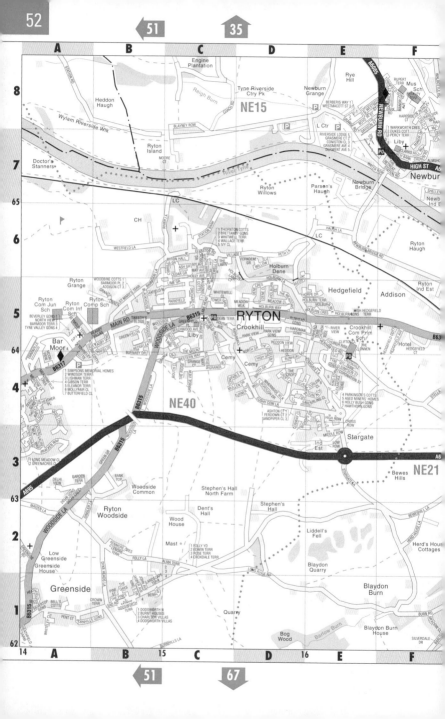

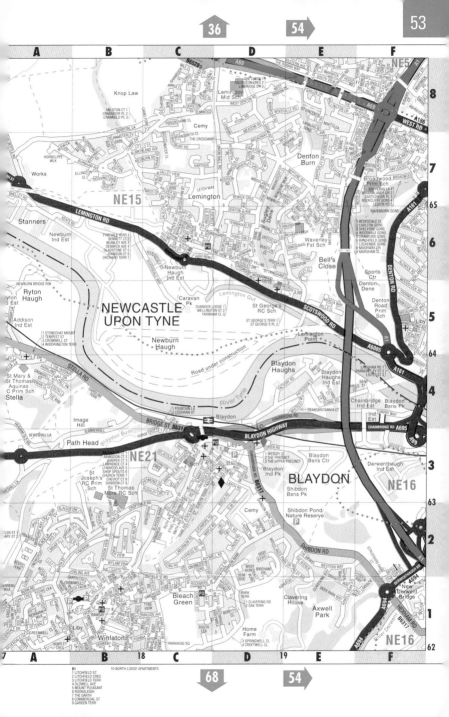

NEWCASTLE UPON TYNE

NE15

NE21

BLAYDON

NE16

B1
1 LITHFIELD ST
2 LITHFIELD CRES
3 LITHFIELD TERR
4 OLDWELL AVE
5 MOUNT PLEASANT
6 ROCKSLEIGH
7 THE GARTH
8 COMMERCIAL ST
9 GARDEN TERR

10 NORTH LODGE APARTMENTS

NE5
Fenham
NE4
NE15
Benwell
Old Benwell
West Gate Com Coll
Newcastle General H
Delaval
Paradise
South Benwell
Elswic
Scotswood
NE21
River Tyne
Derwent Haugh
Metro Ret Pk
Gateshead Metro Ctr
The Metro Ctr
NE11
Dunston
NE16
Swalwell

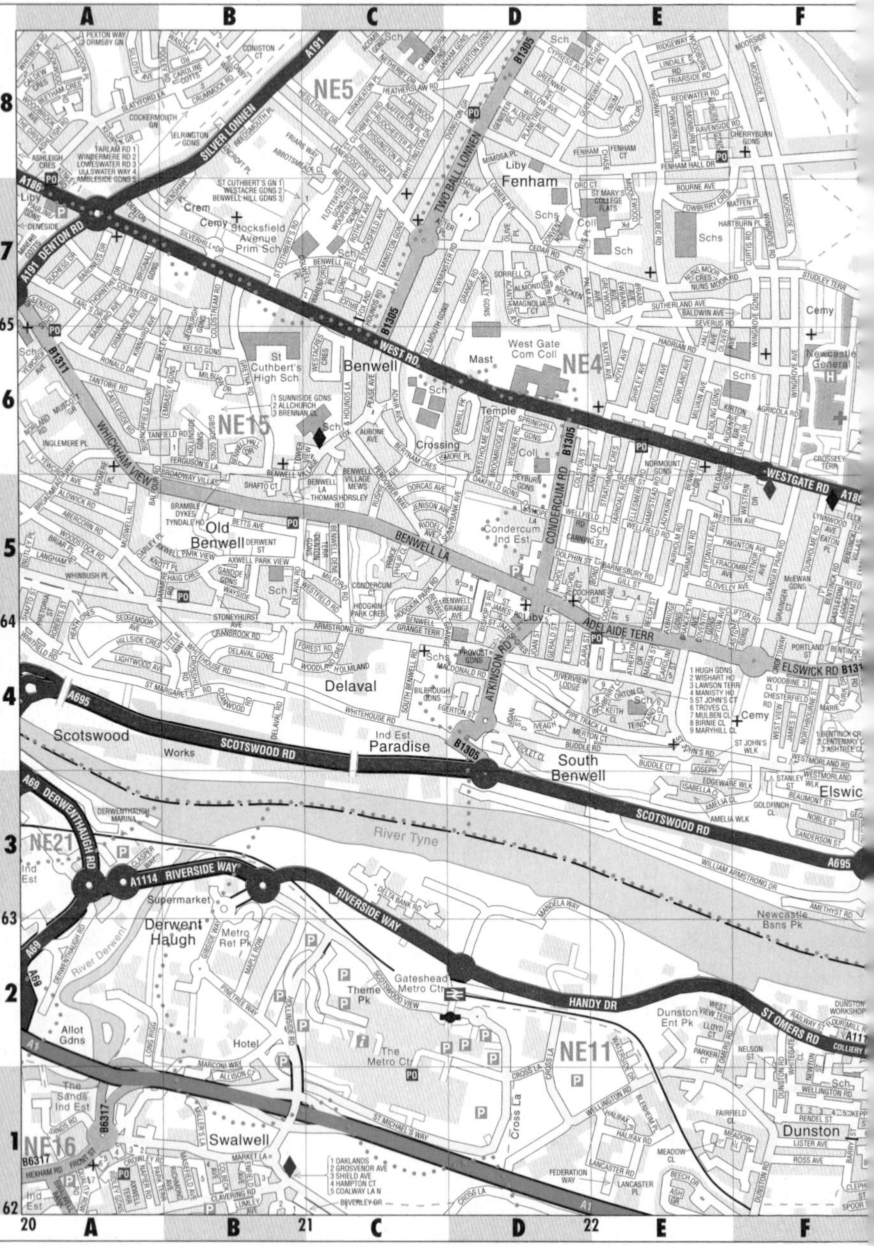

WEST RD
BENWELL LA
WESTGATE RD
ELSWICK RD
SCOTSWOOD RD
RIVERSIDE WAY
HANDY DR
ST OMERS RD
DENTON RD

A1
1 LYNDHURST TERR
2 CROWLEY
3 SPENCERS BANK
4 HOOD ST
5 BREWERY LA
6 BREWERY BANK
7 JUBILEE TERR

D5
1 DOLPHIN CT
2 BOND ST
3 NICHOL ST
4 ST JAMES LODGE
5 ATKINSON TERR
6 ST JAMES GDNS
7 DAVID ADAMS HO
8 BENWELL GRANGE CL
9 BENWELL GRANGE

E5
1 TIVERTON AVE
2 NORMOUNT AVE
3 ADELAIDE HO
4 CLENNEL HO
5 THE ADELAIDE CTR

F1
1 BAKER GDNS
2 FOWLER GDNS
3 KELVIN GDNS
4 TYNDAL GDNS
5 PARSONS GDNS
6 JOHNSON ST
7 RUSKIN AVE
8 KINGSLEY PL

C1
1 OAKLANDS
2 GROSVENOR AVE
3 SHIELD AVE
4 HAMPTON CT
5 COALWAY LA N
6 BEVERLEY DR

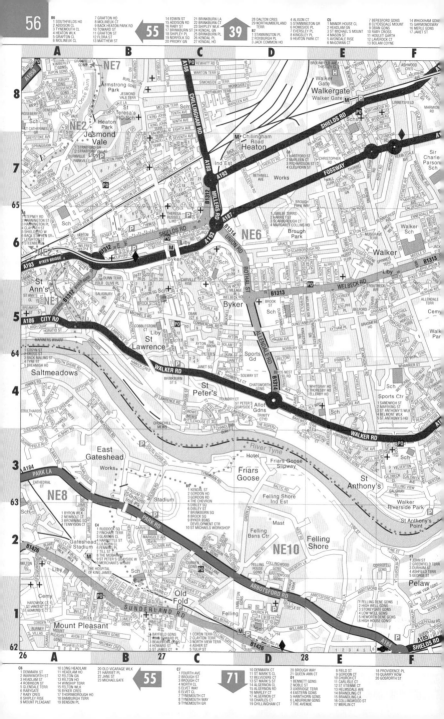

B6
1 SOUTHFIELDS HO
2 ADDISON CL
3 TYNEMOUTH CL
4 HEATON WLK
5 GRAFTON CL
6 MOLINEUX CL

7 GRAFTON HO
8 MOLINEUX CT
9 BACK HEATON PARK RD
10 TOWARD ST
11 GRAFTON ST
12 FLORA ST
13 MATTHEW ST

14 EDWIN ST
15 ADDISON RD
16 RABY ST
17 BRINKBURN ST
18 SHIPLEY ST
19 NORFOLK SQ
20 PRIORY GN

21 BRINKBURN LA
22 BRINKBURN CT
23 SHIPLEY WLK
24 KENDAL GN
25 BRINKBURN PL
26 KENDAL PL
27 KENDAL HO

28 DALTON CRES
29 NORTHUMBERLAND TERR

4 ALISON CT
5 STANNINGTON GR
6 HOMESIDE PL
7 EVERSLEY PL
8 KINGSLEY PL
9 HEATON PARK CT

C5
1 MANOR HOUSE CL
2 HEADLAM GN
3 ST MICHAEL'S MOUNT
4 MASON ST
5 AVONDALE RISE
6 McGOWAN CT

7 BERESFORD GDNS
8 CLYDESDALE MOUNT
9 DEAN GDNS
10 RABY CROSS
11 HOULET GARTH
12 LAVEROCK CT
13 BOLAM COYNE

14 WHICKHAM GDNS
15 GARMONDSWAY
16 MERLE GDNS
17 JANET ST

B7
1 STANNINGTON PL
2 ROXBURGH ST
3 JACK COMMON HO

B9
1 KENDAL ST
2 GORDON HO
3 GLANMIN LA
4 THE CHEVRON
5 DIBLEY SQ
6 DIBLEY ST
7 BRINKBURN SQ
8 BROCK SQ
9 BYKER BSNS DEVELOPMENT CTR
10 ST MICHAELS WORKSHOP

C4
1 RUDDOCK SQ
2 FINCHAM TERR
3 ALBANY SQ
4 HARBUTTLE ST
5 LILBURN ST
6 FENWICK PL
7 TELL ST
8 THE MORNING
9 ST PETER'S QUAYSIDE W
10 MERCHANTS WHARF

C6
1 DENMARK ST
2 WARKWORTH ST
3 HEADLAM ST
4 ROBINSON ST
5 GLENDALE TERR
6 RABYGATE
7 RABY CRES
8 SHIPLEY RISE
9 MOUNT PLEASANT

10 LONG HEADLAM
11 HEADLAM HO
12 FELTON GR
13 FELTON HO
14 WINSHIP TERR
15 FELTON WLK
16 BYKER CRES
17 THORNBROUGH HO
18 BAMBURGH TERR
19 BENSON PL

20 OLD VICARAGE WLK
21 HARRIET PL
22 JANE ST
23 MICHAELGATE

C7
1 FOURTH AVE
2 BROUGH ST
3 BROUGH CT
4 NORTH CL
5 ELVET WAY
6 ELVET CL
7 ALGERNON CT
8 TYNEMOUTH WAY
9 TYNEMOUTH GR

10 DENMARK CT
11 ST MARK'S CL
12 BELVEDERE CT
13 ST MARK'S ST
14 ALGERNON CL
15 ALGERNON HO
16 MARLEY CT
17 ALGERNON CT
18 CHARLES CT
19 CHILLINGHAM CT

20 BROUGH WAY
21 QUEEN ANN CT

D1
1 BENNETT GDNS
2 NOBLE ST
3 UXBRIDGE TERR
4 EASTERN GDNS
5 HAWTHORN GDNS
6 LABURNUM GDNS
7 THE AVENUE

8 FIELD ST
9 GORDON CT
10 CHURCH CT
11 CARLISLE CT
12 ST ETIENNE CT
13 HELMSDALE AVE
14 BRANDLING CT
15 BRANDLING LA
16 COLLINGWOOD ST
17 MERLIN CT

18 PROVIDENCE PL
19 QUARRY ROW
20 GOSFORTH ST

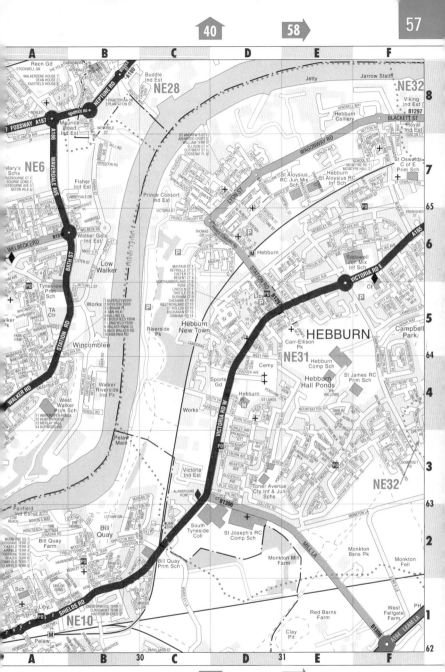

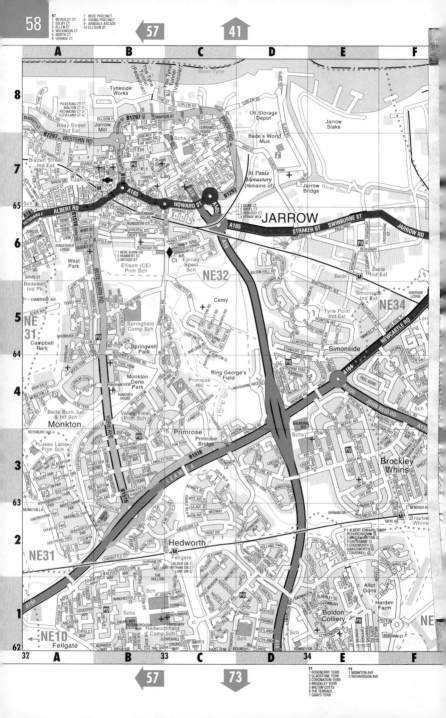

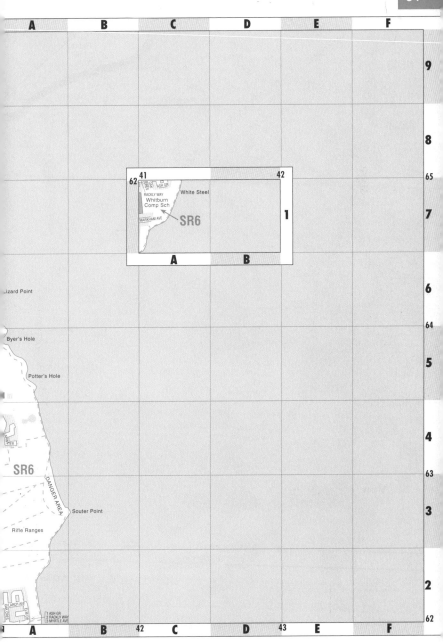

A   B   C   D   E   F

9

8

65

41   42
62 ASH GR
RACKLY WAY   White Steel
Whitburn
Comp Sch
SR6
MARKHAM AVE

1

7

A   B

Lizard Point

6

64

Byer's Hole

5

Potter's Hole

PTER

4

63

SR6

DANGER AREA

Souter Point

3

Rifle Ranges

LARCH AVE

1 ASH GR
2 RACKLY WAY
3 MYRTLE AVE

2

62

A   B   42   C   D   43   E   F

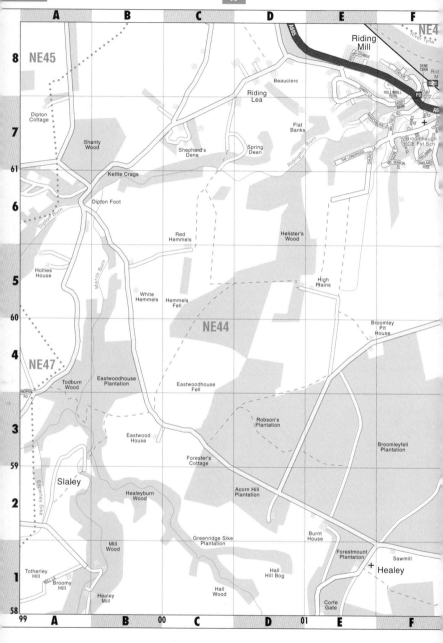

NE4

NE45

Riding Mill

8

Beauclerc

Riding Lea

Dipton Cottage

Flat Banks

7

Shanty Wood

Shepherd's Dene

Spring Dean

Ridingmill Burn

Kettle Crags

61

Dipton Foot

6

Red Hemmels

Helister's Wood

Dipton Burn

Hollies House

High Plains

5

White Hemmels

Hemmels Fell

Broomley Pit House

60

NE44

4

NE47

Todburn Wood

Eastwoodhouse Plantation

Eastwoodhouse Fell

NORUM RD

Robson's Plantation

3

Eastwood House

Broomleyfell Plantation

Forester's Cottage

59

Slaley

Healeyburn Wood

Acorn Hill Plantation

Esperley Sike

2

Burnt House

Greenridge Sike Plantation

Mill Wood

Forestmount Plantation

Sawmill

1

Totherley Hill

Healey

Broomy Hill

Healey Mill

Hall Wood

Hall Hill Bog

Corfe Gate

58

A B C D E F

8

7

61

6

5

60

4

3

59

2

1

58

River Tyne

Sewage Wks

Styford Bridge

Megsmill Plantation

Bywell Castle (remains of)

Bywell

Hotel Broomhaugh

River Tyne

Water Flat

Bywell Hall

1 ST JAMES TERR
2 THE OLD ORCHARD
3 THE SQUARE
4 FORD TERR

Low Shilford

A695

Shilford Middle Wood

Shilford East Wood

Shilford West Wood

Juniperhill Wood

Smithy Burn

Broomleyhope Wood

Roe House

High Shilford
High Shilford Fell

West Broomley

Broomley

Hall Woods

NE44

Pasture House

West Oak

NE43

Broomley Grange

Broomley Fell Farm

Gallaw Hill Farm

Brookside Farm

Bank Foot

Brookside

roomleyfell Plantation

B6309

Broomley Fell Wood

Hadley Burn

B6309

Sandyford Cottage

New Frizzle Close

Wheelbirks

Fell House

Penn's Hill

Wood Cottage

Lingey Field

Fotherley Gill

A68

03

04

A B C D E F

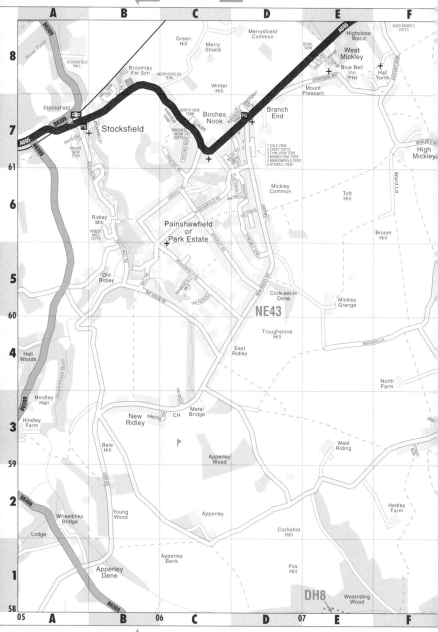

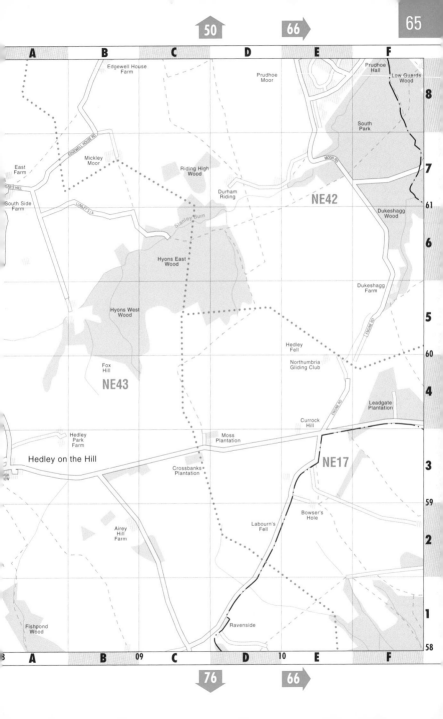

Edgewell House Farm

Prudhoe Moor

Prudhoe Hall

Low Guards Wood

South Park

East Farm

Mickley Moor

Riding High Wood

Durham Riding

NE42

Dukeshagg Wood

South Side Farm

EDGEWELL HOUSE RD

LUMLEY'S LA

Stanley Burn

Hyons East Wood

Dukeshagg Farm

MOOR RD

ENGINE RD

Hyons West Wood

Hedley Fell

Northumbria Gliding Club

Fox Hill

NE43

Leadgate Plantation

Hedley Park Farm

Moss Plantation

Currock Hill

Hedley on the Hill

Crossbanks Plantation

NE17

HIGH VIEW

Airey Hill Farm

Labourn's Fell

Bowser's Hole

Fishpond Wood

Ravenside

A   B   C   D   E   F

Frenches
Close

Halliwell
Dene

KYO BOG LA

BRADLEY FELL RD

West Kyo
Farm

CONWELL LA

ROCKWOOD HILL RD

Kyo Hall

STONEYWAITES 1
MILTON ST 2
APPLEDORE CL 3

ROCKWOOD HILL
EST

LESTER AVE
LONG ROW CL

SUNNY BRAE 1
SILVERTOP TERR 2

WHITEFIELD CLOSE

B6315

8

Low Guards
Wood

North
View

Kyo
Wood

BUCK'S NOOK LA

KYO LA

NE42

7

The
Guards

Buck's
Nook

Coalburns

NE40

JUBILEE
COTTS

61

Guards
Wood

PH

Coal Burn

Barlow Burn

6

Duke's
Hagg

Penny
Hill

Pennyhill
Plantation

Coalburn
Farm

LEAD RD

Coalburn
Plantation

Strothers
Farm

Clinty
Wood

Pennyhill
Plantation

Coalburn
Edge

Horsegate
Plantation

SNOWDON TERR
CO-OPERATIVE
TERR

BELLE

SPEN RD

STROTHERS RD

5

Clinty Burn

Horsegate
Edge

HORSEGATE LA

STROTHERS TERR

SPEN RD

60

Washwell
Hill

CLAYTON TERRACE RD

TOWNELEY
TERR

NE39

High
Spen

4

Boundary
House

Shop
Plantation

Horse
Gate

CH

Bail
Hill

Miller's
Wood

ROBERT TERR COTTS 1
ROBERT TERR 2
JOHNSON TERR 3
ETHEL TERR 4
HUGAR RD 5

THE GRANARIES

BUTE DR

PH

LEADGATE
COTTS

The Bairns
(PH)

Masts

BUTE RD

NORTH VIEW

B6

Leadgate

NE17

Broomfield

Heavy
Gate

High Spen
Prim Sch

3

GREENSIDE RD

59

Ashtree

Green
Head

Broomfield
House

DERWENT
VIEW

Chopwellgate
Cottage

2

NORTH TERR

GREENHEAD
TERR

RAMSAY RD

HALL ROAD
BOWLS

CLAYTON TERRACE RD

HALL RD

MEADOW
BROOK
DR

1 TYNE ST
2 TEE ST
3 BLYTH ST
4 SEVERN ST
5 THAMES ST
6 WANSBECK ST

Chopwell
Wood

X P

Chopwell
Wood Wks

Newhouse
Farm

Chopwell

WHITTONSTALL TERR

PRINC
ST

PO

Liby

WHEAT RD

SOUTH RD

DERWENT
TER

TAY ST

MERCER RD

TIMBER RD

EAST ST

1

WHITTONSTALL TERR 1
RAVENSIDE TERR 1
HOLLINGS 3
BROAD OAK TERR 4
HAVELOCK TERR 5.

WILLIAM ST

ELIZABETH
ST

SCOT TERR

6 JOSEPH TERR
7 BECONSFIELD TERR
8 DISRAELI TERR
9 HILLFORD TERR
10 NELSON TERR
11 FREDERICK ST

58

11   A   B   12   C   D   13   E   F

A B 15 C D 16 E F

8 7 61 6 5 60 4 3 59 2 1 58

Greenside

Reeley Mires
Farm

BURNMILLS LA

Brockwell

Little
Brockwell

SILVERDALE DR 1
WAVERLEY CL 2
HARTSIDE CRES 3
WEST LA 4

SELBY'S
GRAVE

NE40

Reeley Mires
West Wood

Chicken's
Wood

Barlow Burn

BARLOW LA

Barlow
Letch

NE21

Reeley Mires
Wood

North
Farm

Norman's
Riding
Wood

Water Gate
Sewage Works

Ricklees
Farm

Barlow Gill
Wood

The Black
Horse
(PH)

South
Farm

GARESFIELD LA

Winlaton
Care Village

Spenside
Farm

Barlow

Martin's
Wood

BARLOW CRES

Pawston
Birks

BARLOW FELL RD

Barlow Fell

Lillycrook
Hill

STROTHERS RD

PAWSTON RD

High
Thornley

ASHTREE LA

COLLINGDON GN

WEST HIGH HORSE CL

WISHART TERR

HIGH SPEN CT

Spen
Banks

Sherburn Tower
Farm

FELLSIDE LA

SPEN BURN

PINEA CL

SCHOOL LA

Hookergate
Comp Sch

Sherburn Green
Wood

Sch

Sch

NE39

CORBITT TERR

A694 HOOKERGATE RD

THORNLEY VIEW

BURNOP TERR

Low Spen

ROBSON TERR

SPEN LA

WOOD TERR

Low Spen
Farm

Low Spen Burn

CARNFORTH
GDNS

BROCKWELL DR

ROLAND BURN RD

NORWOOD CRES

STATION RD A6314 ECCANBAUGH RD

Hooker
Gate

WILLS MORRIS AVE

NORTH
VIEW W

NORTH
VIEW

THE GREEN

BARKWOOD RD

Rowlands Gill

PH

P

Cemy

St Joseph's RC
Sch

A J COOK'S COTTS

HILLCROFT

SOUTH
VIEW W

COWELL GR

DENE VIEW

SMAILES LA

REDSTART

Liby

PO

PO

Highfield
Com Prim Sch

Highfield

VICTORIA
TERR

WOODSIDE WK

SOUTH SHERBURN

WAGTAIL WAY

MIDDLETON
AVE

MANOR RD

STRATHMORE AVE

PO

BURNOPFIELD RD B6314

GLENDLE
RIDGE

LOW WEST
AVE

RIDGE
WAY

Beda Hills

A694 DIPWOOD RD

STRATHMORE RD B6315

AGED MINERS' HOMES

Derwent
Bridge

River Derwent

BLAYS BANK

B6314

Pallis Burn

ALBERT ST

ALEXANDRA ST

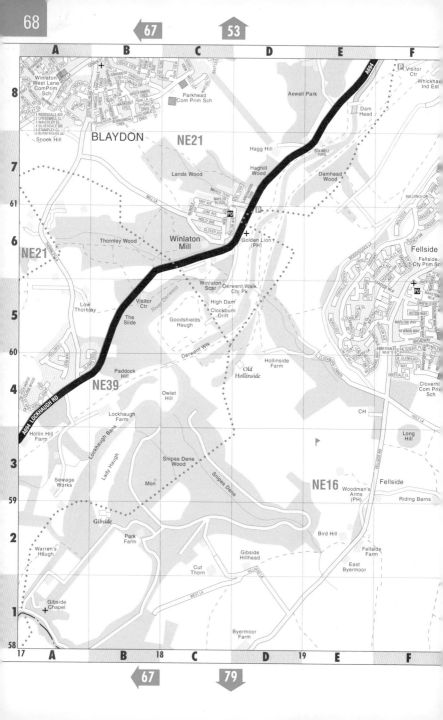

BLAYDON

NE21

NE21

Winlaton West Lane ComPrim Sch

1 REDESDALE AVE
2 CRESSWELL CL
3 WAVERLEY CL
4 SILVERDALE DR
5 STAMPLEY CL
6 BURNTHOUSE LA

Snook Hill

Parkhead Com Prim Sch

Axwell Park

Visitor Ctr

Whickham Ind Est

Dam Head

Hagg Hill

Haghill Wood

Sha Well Turn

Damhead Wood

BULLFINCH DR

Lands Wood

MILL LA

MAY AVE

JUNE AVE

HOLLY AVE

CLOVER AVE

MANOR TERR

NAYLOR BLDGS

PO

Thornley Wood

Winlaton Mill

Golden Lion (PH)

Fellside

Fellside Cty Prim Sch

CASTLE WLK

PO

Winlaton Scar

Derwent Walk Cty Pk

WOODBINE LA

OAKFIELD RD

ASTON WAY

MARLOW WAY

NEWMIN WAY

BROADWAY

Low Thornley

Visitor Ctr

The Slide

High Dam

Clockburn Drift

Goodshields Haugh

River Derwent

CLOCKBURN

ENNERDALE WLK

FAIRSQUARE PL

ROMSIDE LA

GLENHURST

DEEPDALE CL

NE21

60

Derwent Wlk

Hollinside Farm

Old Hollinside

CLOCKBURN LONNEN

Cloverhi Com Pri Sch

NE39

Paddock Hill

Lockhaugh Farm

Owlet Hill

CH

HOLL LA

FELLSIDE RD

Long Hill

A694 LOCKHAUGH RD

Hollin Hill Farm

Lockhaugh Bank

Lady Haugh

Snipes Dene Wood

Snipes Dene

NE16

Fellside

Woodman's Arms (PH)

Riding Barns

Sewage Works

Mon

Gibside

Park Farm

Bird Hill

Fellside Farm

Warren's Haugh

Gibside Hillhead

East Byermoor

Cut Thorn

HILL LA

WEST LA

Gibside Chapel

Byermoor Farm

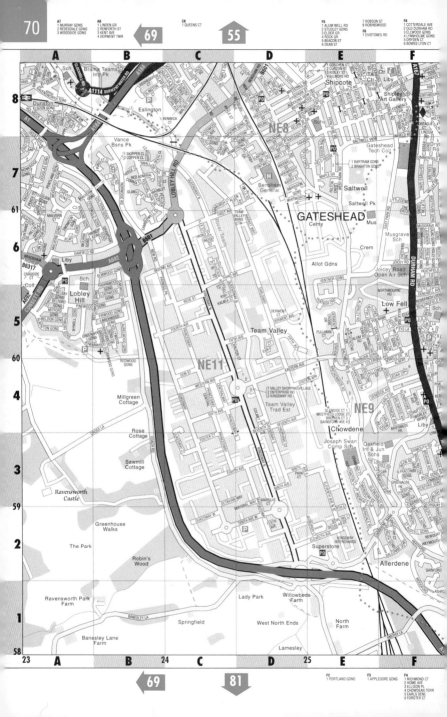

A7 1 Murray Gdns 2 Redesdale Gdns 3 Woodside Gdns
A8 1 Linden Gr 2 Renforth St 3 Kent Ave 4 Derwent Twr
C8 1 Queens Ct
F5 1 Alum Well Rd 2 Studley Gdns 3 Elder Gr 4 Rock Gr 5 Beacon St 6 Dean St
F6 1 Evistones Rd
7 Robson St 8 Robinswood
F8 1 Cotterdale Ave 2 Old Durham Rd 3 Ellwood Gdns 4 Lynnholme Gdns 5 Dryden Ct 6 Bowes Lyon Ct

F2 1 Portland Gdns
F3 1 Appledore Gdns
F4 1 Richmond Ct 2 Home Ave 3 Ellison Pl 4 Chowdean Terr 5 Earls Dene 6 Forster Ct

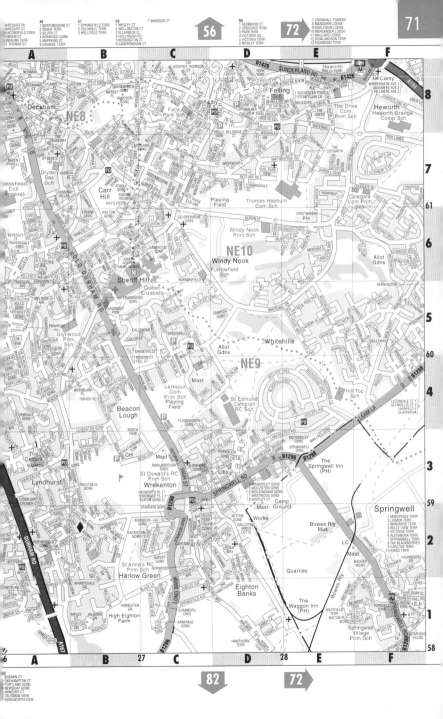

A0
1 NORTHBOURNE ST
2 HARCOURT ST
3 BEACONSFIELD CRES
4 ROBSON ST
5 BONFAUNS TERR
6 ST THOMAS ST

C7
1 SPRINGFIELD TERR
2 COLDWELL TERR
3 SILVER CT

C8
1 WESLEY CT
2 WELLINGTON TERR
3 ELLERBECK CL
4 HOLLYBUSH RD
5 KENSINGTON CT
6 SANDRINGHAM CT

7 WINDSOR CT

D8
1 REDMAYNE CT
2 CROUDACE ROW
3 PARK ROW
4 VICTORIA SQ
5 VICTORIA TERR
6 MORLEY TERR

7 CROWHALL TOWERS
8 MANDARIN LODGE
9 HARLEQUIN LODGE
10 MERGANSER LODGE
11 MALLARD LODGE
12 ROWLANDSON TERR
13 RICHMOND TERR

A2
1 BODMIN CT
2 OKEHAMPTON CT
3 PORTLAND GDNS
4 NEWQUAY GDNS
5 HANOVER CT
6 TALISMAN VIEW
7 KENILWORTH VIEW

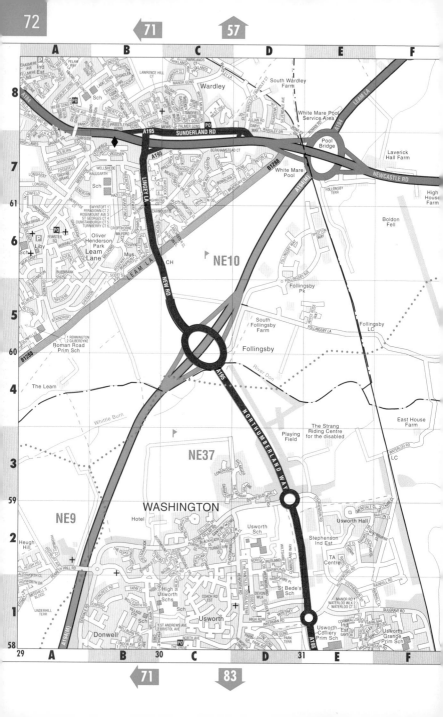

A B C D E F

8

NEW RD B1298

B1298

Boldon North Bridge

NE35
Boldon Comp Sch

West Boldon

Cleadon Lane Ind Est

SOUTH END 1
WINDSOR DR 2
GROSVENOR DR 3

East Boldon

Boldon Flats

WHITBURN RD

SR6

7

WESTERN TERR

FRONT ST

South Boldon

East Boldon Jun Sch

East Boldon City Inf Sch

STATION RD

B1299

East Boldon

Flats Bridge

1 CROSSWAYS
2 STATION TERR
3 STRUAN TERR
4 BEDE TERR

BLUE HOUSE

61

A184 ADDISON RD

1 CLAREMOUNT CT
2 EVEREST GR
3 PENNINE GR

1 ST NICHOLAS RD
2 AVONDALE GDNS
3 AVONDALE TERR
4 HAMILTON TERR
5 THREE RIVERS CT
6 THE FAIRWAYS
7 MANSION HO

Cemy

SUNDERLAND RD

Low House Farm

B7 1 GRANGE TERR
2 ASHLEIGH VILLAS
3 BIRCHWOOD
4 FERNDALE AVE
5 THE TERRACE
6 ST CHAD'S VILLAS
7 BEATRICE GDNS

Stadiu

6

Turner's Hill

Belle Vue Villa

South Lodge

NE36

Field House

Pla Fi

5

Boldon Hills

A4 1 BARROW ST
2 BERWICK AVE
3 BRADMAN SQ
4 KING CHARLES CT
5 KING HENRY CT

Quarry Hill

Mundles

60

St John Bosco RC Prim Sch

Downhill

Community North Sports Complex

Hylton Red House Sch

FONTBURN 1
ROTHLEY CT 2
WOODFORD CL 3
WOOLWICH CL 4
WHITCHURCH CL 5

Witherwa

Witherwack Prim Sch

4

YORK RD

1 KINGSWAY SQ
2 KILLARNEY AVE
3 KESTREL SQ
4 KESTEVEN SQ

1 KENLEY RD
2 KNAREBOROUGH SQ
3 REEDLING CT

1 RANGOON RD
2 RAWMARSH RD
3 RAMILLIES SQ
4 ROCKINGHAM SQ
5 RAEBURN RD
6 REVELSTOKE RD
7 ROCKINGHAM RD

Hylton Red House

RUTHERGLEN SQ

Cemy

Allot Gdns

Playing Fields

Marley Pots

3

SR5

PICKERSGILL RD

1 KIDDERMINSTER SQ
2 KINGSLAND SQ
3 KINGSWOOD SQ

A4 1 BAYSWATER SQ
2 BURKE ST
3 DODDS CT
4 BRENTFORD SQ
5 BALMORAL CT
6 CLOVELLY SQ

Maplewood Sch

Sch

Coll

59

CHELMSFORD RD

CHEADLE RD

CRAMLEIGH RD

Hylton Castle

Liby

B1 1 SHEPPARD TERR
2 STANLEY ST
3 ASHWOOD GR
4 JOYCE TERR
5 THE GROVE
6 THOMPSON CRES
7 PARKHOUSE AVE
8 JENNIFER AVE

C1 1 WREN GR
2 THRUSH GR
3 EAST VIEW S
4 CASTLE ST S
5 BARRON ST S
6 CHAFFINCH RD
7 THE VILLAS

1 REDBURN AVE
2 SHINCLIFFE AVE

Hylton Dene

North Hylton Road Ind Est

Hylton Red House Prim Sch

NORTH HYLTON RD

F2 1 THE POPLARS
2 GROSVENOR ST
3 WALTER THOMAS ST
4 FLORENCE CRES
5 ELMWOOD SQ
6 CARLISLE TERR
7 FITZROY TERR
8 PINEWOOD SQ

Southwick Ind Est

2

COOK SQ

CHISWICK RD

Sch

Hylton Castle

Castletown

North View

Plumtree Ave

RIVERBANK RD

RIVERSIDE RD

Coll

1

Castle View Sch

The Briars

PO

CASTLE VIEW

DENE MEWS
CASTLE...

Hylton Dene Burn

Weardale Way

WESSINGTON WAY

Hylton Park

Alexandra Ave

Business & Innovation Ctr

58

CRICKLEWOOD...

NORTH VIEW

River Wear

DEAN TERR
CLOCKWELL ST

SR4

35 A 36 B C D 37 E F

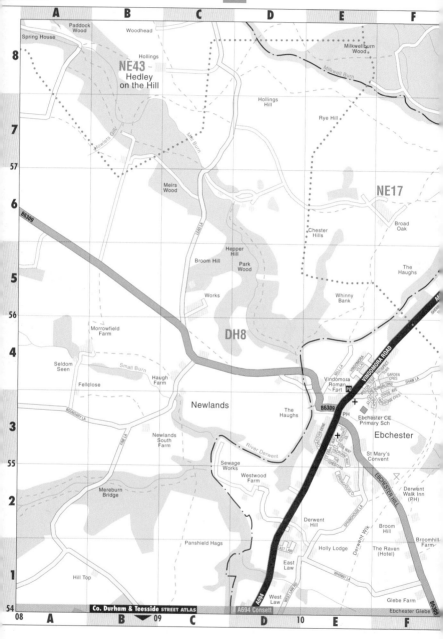

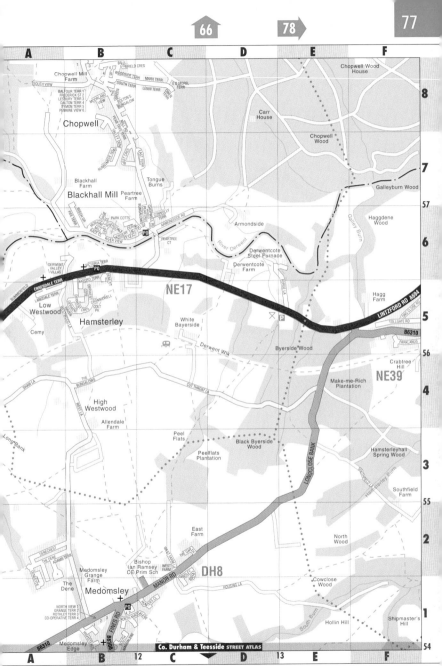

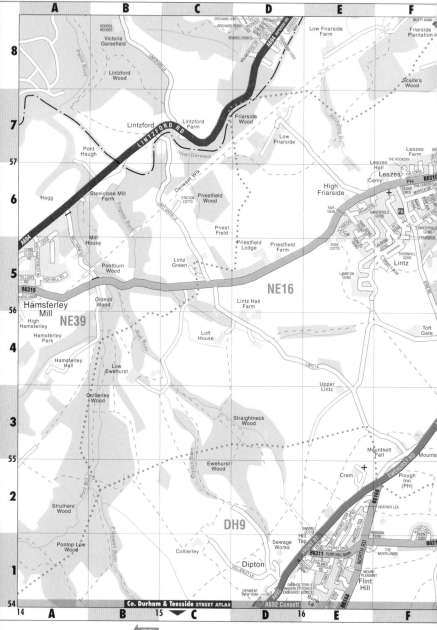

A   **B**   **C**   **D**   **E**   **F**

8

7

57

6

5

56

4

3

55

2

1

54

SCHOOL HOUSES

Victoria Garesfield

Lintzford Wood

ORCHARD AVE
ORCHARD TERR
BOWES LYON CL

Low Friarside Farm

BUSTY BANK
Friarside Plantation

Scaife's Wood

Palle Burn

Lintzford

Lintzford Farm

LINTZFORD RD

Pont Haugh

Friarside Wood

Low Friarside

River Derwent

The Rookery
Leazes Farm
THE COPES
B6310

Leazes Hall
Cemy
Leazes
PH
PO

Hagg

Steelclose Mill Farm

Derwent Wlk

STATION COTTS

Priestfield Wood

High Friarside

CEDAR CRES
MYRTLE GR

GARESFIELD GDNS

Lintz Green La

Fofbods Burn

Priest Field

Mill House

Priestfield Lodge

Priestfield Farm

ROSE COTTS

THORNHILL GDNS
PRIESTFIELD GDNS
FRIARSIDE

Lintz

A694

LONG CLOSE RD
LODGE

High Hackett Rd

MILL LANE RD

Pontburn Wood

Lintz Green

LAMBTON GDNS

Hamsterley Mill

TOLLGATE RD
B6310
PARKLANDS

Oldmill Wood

NE16

Lintz Hall Farm

Toft Gate

High Hamsterley

NE39

Loft House

Hamsterley Park

Red Burn

Hamsterley Hall

Low Ewehurst

Collierley Wood

Straightneck Wood

Upper Lintz

LINTZ LA

Mountsett Fell

Mounts

Pont Burn

Struthers' Wood

Dipton Burn

Ewehurst Wood

Crem

EWEHURST RD

Plough Inn (PH)

B6168

HEATHER LEA

THE MOORLANDS

Pontop Low Wood

Pikewell Burn

Collierley

DH9

Sewage Works

Hill Top

SAWMILL COTTS

FIRST CRES

B6311

FLINT HILL BANK

ROBSON TERR

B631

NORTH RD

MOUNT PLEASANT

Dipton

COLLIERLEY LA

DERWENT VIEW TERR

IVANHOE TERR 1
WAVERLEY TERR 2
EWEHURST GDNS 3

A692

Bone La

PALMER RD

B6168

Flint Hill

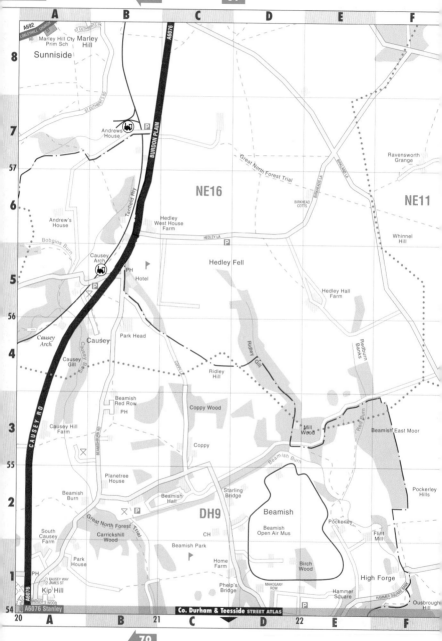

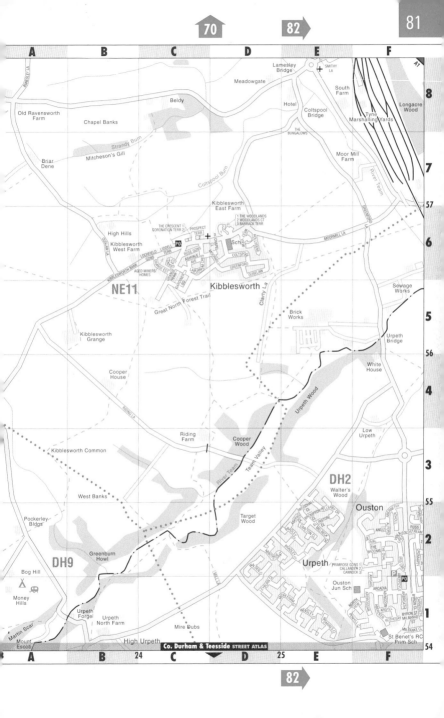

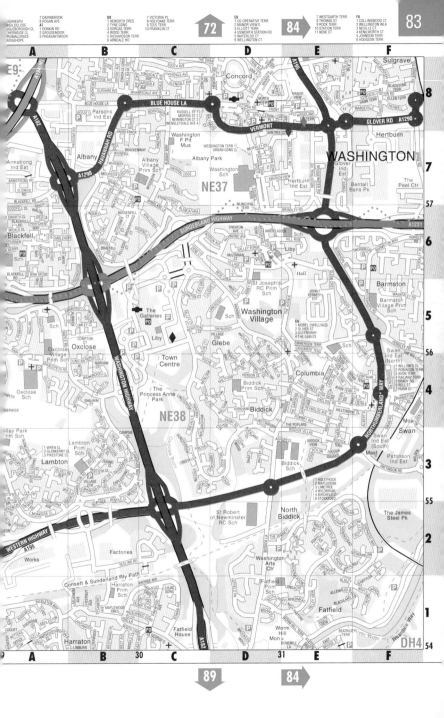

72
84
89
84

D8
1 HEWORTH CRES
2 TYNE GDNS
3 DORCAS TERR
4 WOOD TERR
5 RICHARDSON CT
6 ARNDALE HO

7 VICTORIA PL
8 HOLYOAKE TERR
9 TEES TERR
10 FRANKLIN CT

E8
1 CO-OPERATIVE TERR
2 MANOR VIEW E
3 ELLIOTT TERR
4 USWORTH STATION RD
5 WATERLOO CT
6 WELLINGTON CT

7 WESTGARTH TERR
8 THOMAS ST
9 ROCK TERR
10 STATION TERR
11 NENE CT

F8
1 COLLINGWOOD CT
2 WELLINGTON WLK
3 NEVILLE CT
4 KENILWORTH CT
5 JOHNSON TERR
6 HODGSON TERR

E4
1 MODEL DWELLINGS
2 OLIVER ST
3 QUEENSWAY
4 THE GABLES

1 WILLOW'S S
2 ROBINSON TERR
3 AVON TERR
4 RAILWAY TERR
5 BRADY SQ
6 BELL CT
7 HUGH ST

1 HOLLYHOCK
2 MAPLEDENE
3 LIMETREE
4 WILDBRIAR
5 BIRCHFIELD
6 STOCKFOLD

Concord
Sulgrave
BLUE HOUSE LA
VERMONT
GLOVER RD A1290
Hertburn
WASHINGTON
Albany
Albany Park
Washington F Pit Mus
Albany Village Prim Sch
Washington Sch
NE37
The Peel Ctr
Bentall Bsns Pk
Glover Ind Est
Hertburn Ind Est
Blackfell
SUNDERLAND HIGHWAY
A1231
Barmston
Barmston Village Prim Sch
St Joseph's RC Prim Sch
Hall
Washington Village
JOHN F KENNEDY
Liby
The Galleries
Oxclose
Oxclose Village Prim Sch
Oxclose Sch
Liby
Glebe
Town Centre
Columbia
Swan Ind Est (North)
The Princess Anne Park
Biddick Prim Sch
Biddick
NE38
Swan Ind Est (South)
Swan
Mus
Pattinson Ind Est
Lambton
Lambton Prim Sch
Oxclose Burn
Biddick View
Biddick Sch
North Biddick
The James Steel Pk
WESTERN HIGHWAY
A195
Works
Factories
St Robert of Newminster RC Sch
Consett & Sunderland Rly Path
Harraton Prim Sch
Washington Arts Ctr
Fatfield Prim Sch
Fatfield
Harraton
Fatfield House
Worm Hill Mon
Wearside Way
DH4

E9
A182
A1290
A195
NORTHUMBERLAND WAY
WASHINGTON HIGHWAY

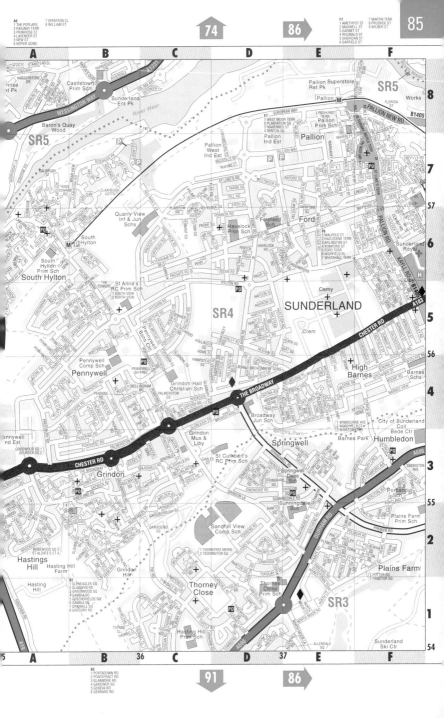

85 75

SR4

Sunderland Royal

SR2

SR3

SUNDERLAND

Hendon

Grangetown

85 92

B3
1 HEATHERLEA GDNS
2 GREENRIGG GDNS
3 PEMBERTON GDNS
4 PINESWAY

C4
1 AVENUE TERR
2 BROOKSIDE TERR
3 BROOK SIDE LODGE
4 BROOKSIDE GDNS
5 HUMBLEDON VIEW
6 ASHBROOKE MOUNT

D4
1 TOWER PL
2 HENDON BURN AVE W
3 ATHOL PK
4 JUNIPER CL
5 VILLETTE BROOK ST
6 HENDON VALLEY CT
7 ERNEST ST
8 ROWLANDSEN TERR
9 TAYLOR GDNS

F2
1 WESTHOLME TERR
2 HOLYROOD RD
3 WINDSOR TERR
4 WESTMINSTER CT
5 RYHOPE ST
6 OCEAN RD N
7 OCEAN RD S
8 STOCKTON TERR
9 HEMMING ST
10 CARNEGIE ST

	A	B	C	D	E	F	
		Maud's Hole					8
	Hudson Dock						7
	SR1	North East Pier					
							57
				Roker Pier	59		6
	Dock	South West Breakwater			10		
	Sewage Works			North Pier	9		5
				SR1			
				41 A	58 B 42		56
							4
	PROMENADE						3
							55
	LC						2
	1 ST AIDAN'S AVE 2 ASKRIGG AVE						
	MILLTHORP CL						1
	SR2						
	RYHOPE RD A1018	Salterfen Rocks					54
	A	B 42	C	D 43	E	F	

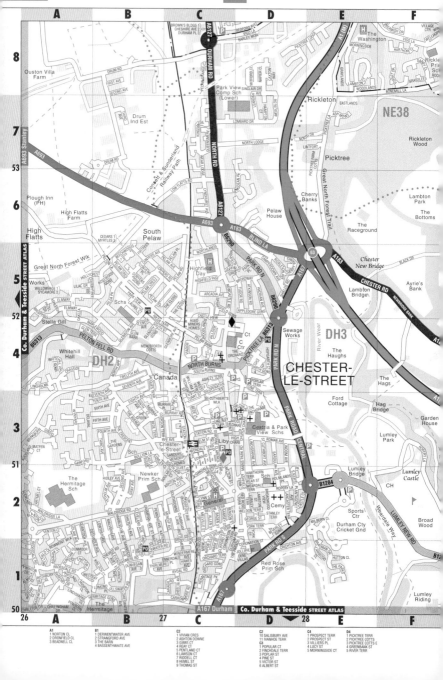

A1
1 NORTON CL
2 DRONFIELD CL
3 BEADNELL CL

B1
1 DERWENTWATER AVE
2 STRANGFORD AVE
3 THE BARN
4 BASSENTHWAITE AVE

C2
1 VIVIAN CRES
2 ASHTON DOWNIE
3 GIBBS CT
4 REAY CT
5 PENTLAND CT
6 LAWSON CT
7 RIDDELL CT
8 HEMEL ST
9 THOMAS ST

C2
10 SALISBURY AVE
11 IVANHOE TERR
C3
1 POPULAR CT
2 FINCHDALE TERR
3 POPLAR ST
4 PINE ST
5 VICTOR ST
6 ALBERT ST

C4
1 PROSPECT TERR
2 PROSPECT ST
3 VILLIERS PL
4 LUCY ST
5 MORNINGSIDE CT

D4
1 PICKTREE TERR
2 PICKTREE COTTS
3 PICKTREE COTTS E
4 GREENBANK ST
5 RIVER TERR

A B C D E F

Penshaw

Penshaw
Park

NE38

North Belt

Biddick Gill
Wood

1 CHANDLERS FORD
2 LADYWOOD PK
3 BISHOPDALE

Three Acre
Clump

HARRATON
TERR

Virginia
Water

New
Bridge

Shepherd's
Gill

Lambton Park

Biddick
Hall

Lambton
Castle

Scorer's
Wood

Sheep
Hill

Biddick Woods

Shiney Row

Lamb
Bridge

DH3

The
Grange

The
Paddocks

Bowes
House

THE AVENUE

GAINSBOROUGH CRES 1
BURNDEN GR 2
PADDOCK CL 3
GOLF COURSE RD 4

Kennel
Field

Weardale Way

DH4

Kennel
Pond

Bowes House
Farm

Wapping
Bridge

South Belt

ESTATE
HOUSES

County Show Ground
(Agricultural)

CHESTER RD

VIOLET TERR 1
2 ROSE CRES
3 MOOR CT

Bournmoor
Prim Sch

Burnside

HOUGHTON
GATE

CASTLEREIGH CL 1
CASTLEMAIN CL 2

PH

Bournmoor

ELLESMERE

New
Lambton

Primrose Hill

HIGH PRIMROSE HILL 4
ARLINGTON CL 5

WEST
VIEW

1 NORTH VIEW
2 LANGTON TERR
3 AGED MINERS' HOMES

Lumley Park
Wood

The Manor
House

Lumley
Forge Bridge

Weardale Way

Floater's
Mill Bridge

PH

Lumley Park Burn

Brecon Hill

B1284

Sch

Castle Dene

LUMLEY NEW RD

AGED MINERS' HOMES 1
TWIKLER TERR 2
PEAR TREE TERR 3

Lumley
Thicks

NORHAM CT 1
DUNSTANBURGH CT 2
APPLESBY CT 3

YANTALLON

Woodstone
Village

AVENUE VIVIAN

RAVENSWORTH

PO

Great Lumley

Woodstone
Farm House

BRIARWOOD ST 1
SCHOOL TERR 2
GILL CRESCENT N 3
GILL CRESCENT S 4
MORTON GRANGE TERR 5
WOODLANDS 6
NORTON CRES 7

EWE HILL TERR W 1
EWE HILL TERR 2

A B 30 C D 31 E F 50

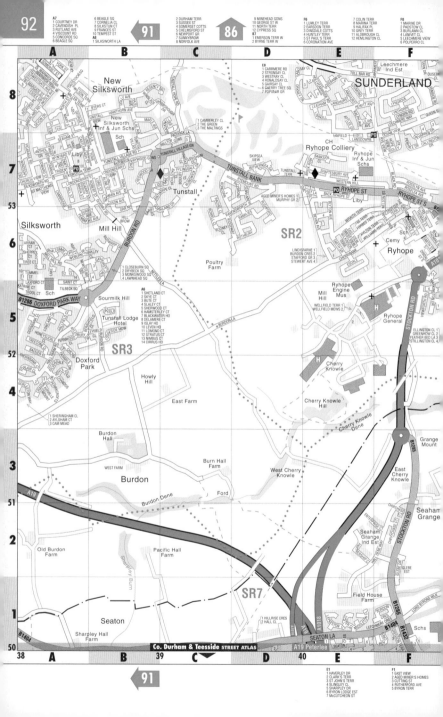

Ryhope
Nook

1 TOLL BAR RD
2 MARINE DR
3 LEICHMERE WAY
4 QUEEN ST
5 LADOCK ST
6 POLPERRO CL

Maiden's
Flat

CLIFF
VIEW

THE VILLAGE

PO

A6
1 FLORALIA AVE
2 GREY TERR
3 GORDON TERR
4 KILBURN CL
5 ERNEST TERR
6 RICHARDSON TERR
7 FAWCETT TERR
8 THOMPSON TERR
9 CRANSTON PL
10 ROBSON PL
11 ARTHUR ST
12 MOIR TERR
13 CHARLES ST
14 JOHN ST

SR2

Pincushion

Hallwell Banks

Ryhope Dene
House
(Convent)

Ryhope Dene

SR7

Hall
Farm

Seaham
Hall

LC

LORD BYRONS WLK

Seaham Dene

1 BURNWAY
2 NEWLANDS RD W
3 NEWARK CRES
4 NAVENBY CL

1 SUTHERLAND ST
2 EMBANKMENT RD

SEAHAM

THE
CASTLEREAGH
HOMES

Seaham
Sch

Northlea

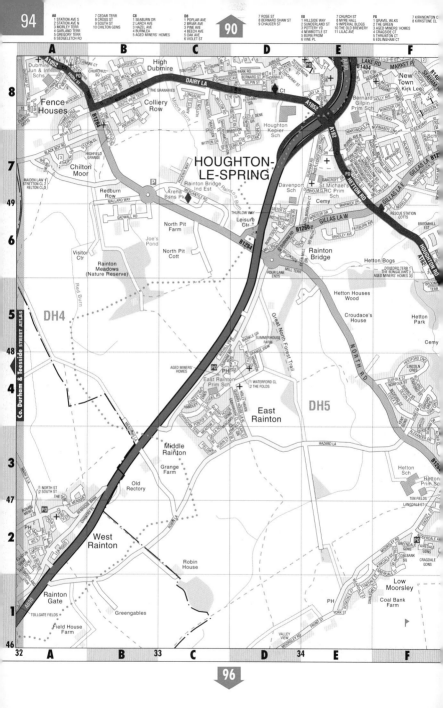

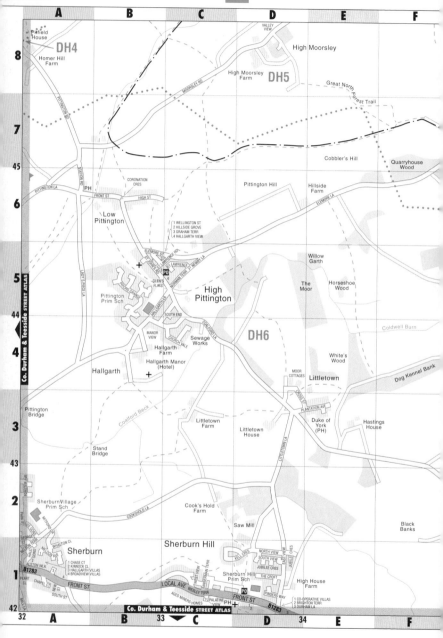

A   B   C   D   E   F

8

Pitfield
House

DH4

Homer Hill
Farm

High Moorsley

High Moorsley
Farm

DH5

Great North
Forest Trail

7

45

Cobbler's Hill

Quarryhouse
Wood

6

Coronation
Cres

Pittington Hill

Hillside
Farm

Low
Pittington

FRONT ST

HIGH ST

PH

PITTINGTON LA

BEACON RD

MOORSLEY RD

VALLEY
VIEW

ELEMORE LA

1 WELLINGTON ST
2 HILLSIDE GROVE
3 GRAHAM TERR
4 HALLGARTH VIEW

Willow
Garth

5

LADY'S PIECE LA

ELEMORE ST

LAWRENCE

NORMAN TERR

NEWRY LA

PO

GLEN'S
FLATS

Pittington
Prim Sch

PLOUG

PIONE GRANT

HALLGARTH LA

SOUTH END

High
Pittington

The
Moor

Horseshoe
Wood

44

MANOR
VIEW

CHURCH LA

COAL FOOT LA

Sewage
Works

DH6

Coldwell Burn

4

Hallgarth
Farm

Hallgarth Manor
(Hotel)

White's
Wood

Hallgarth

MOOR
COTTAGES

Littletown

Dog Kennel Bank

3

Pittington
Bridge

Coalford Beck

Littletown
Farm

Littletown
House

PLANTATION AVE

JOSSEY LA

LITTLETOWN LA

Duke of
York
(PH)

Hastings
House

Stand
Bridge

43

2

FORSTER AVE

COOKSHOLD LA

Cook's Hold
Farm

Saw Mill

Black
Banks

SherburnVillage
Prim Sch

WITHERWACK

HOUSE LA

1

George Cl

WHITTON CL

Sherburn

B1283

PEART
CL

CHAPEL LA

SOUTH ST

PEART CL

MILL LA

1 CHASE CT
2 KINNOCK CL
3 HALLGARTH VILLAS
4 BROADVIEW VILLAS

FRONT ST

Sherburn Hill

LOCAL AVE

WESLEY TERR

WESTERN VIEW

AGED MINERS HOMES

PALATINE
VIEW

PH

BELL CRES

NORTH VIEW

SOUTH VIEW

EAST VIEW

JUBILEE CRES

Sherburn Hill
Prim Sch

PO

THE CROFT

CINDERS WAY

JUBILEE CRES

High House
Farm

1 CO-OPERATIVE VILLAS
2 BRIGHTON TERR
3 DURHAM LA

B1283

42

32   A   B   33   C   D   34   E   F

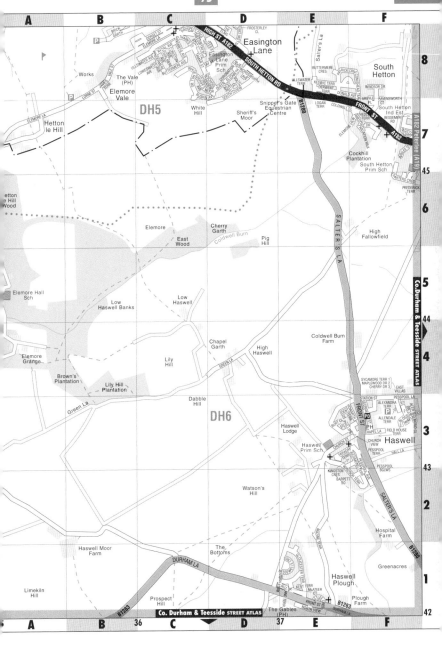

A B C D E F

95

8

Works

FROSTERLEY CL

Easington Lane

The Vale (PH)

Elemore Vale

DH5

Hetton le Hill

White Hill

Sheriff's Moor

Snippet's Gate Equestrian Centre

South Hetton

BUTTERMERE CRES

KESWIC TERR

DERWENT TERR

WINDSOR DR

DONALD AVE

RAVENSWORTH

South Hetton Ind Est

BESSEMER RD

Cockhill Plantation

South Hetton Prim Sch

CHITERS CREEK

FREDERICK TERR

A182 Peterlee (A19)

7

45

6

Elemore

Cherry Garth

Coldwell Burn

East Wood

Pig Hill

High Fallowfield

Elemore Hall Sch

Low Haswell Banks

Low Haswell

Coldwell Burn Farm

Co.Durham & Teesside STREET ATLAS

5

44

Elemore Grange

Lily Hill

Chapel Garth

GREEN LA

High Haswell

SYCAMORE TERR 1
MAPLEWOOD DR 2
CHERRY DR 3

EAST VILLAS

4

Brown's Plantation

Lily Hill Plantation

Green La

Dabble Hill

DH6

Haswell Lodge

Haswell Prim Sch

STATION ST

ALEXANDRA TERR

PO

ALLENDALE TERR

CHURCH VIEW

PESSPOOL TERR

FIELD HOUSE TERR

Haswell

HALL LA

PESSPOOL BGLWS

FRONT ST

3

43

Watson's Hill

KINGSTON CRES

BARPET SQ

PESSPOOL TERR

2

Haswell Moor Farm

The Bottoms

DURHAM LA

Hospital Farm

Greenacres

B1280

SALTER'S LA

1

Limekiln Hill

Prospect Hill

B1283

KENT TERR

McATEER

FRONT ST

SOUTH VIEW

Haswell Plough

Plough Farm

DURHAM LA

B1280

The Gables (PH)

Co. Durham & Teesside STREET ATLAS

42

A 36 B C 37 D E F

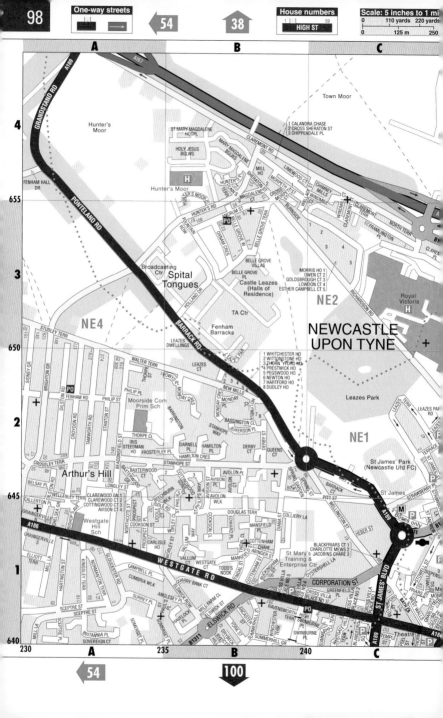

54
98

One-way streets

House numbers
1 HIGH ST 59

Scale: 5 inches to 1 mi
0   110 yards   220 yards
0   125 m   250

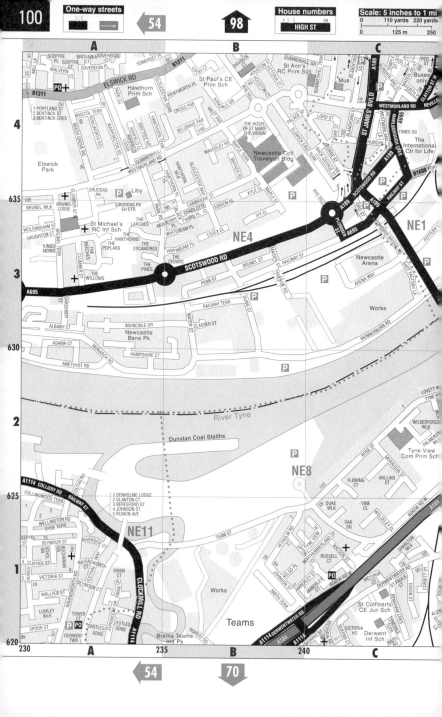

1 PORTLAND ST
2 BENTINCK ST
3 BENTINCK CRES

Elswick
Park

CRUDDAS
PK

CRUDDAS PK
SH CTR

St Michael's
RC Inf Sch

THE
LARCHES

THE
HAWTHORNS
THE
POPLARS

THE
SYCAMORES

THE
BEECHES

THE
WILLOWS

THE
PINES

THE
CEDARS

SCOTSWOOD RD

NE4

Hawthorn
Prim Sch

St Paul's CE
Prim Sch

St Ann's
RC Prim Sch

Mus

WESTMORLAND RD

St James's RC Prim Sch

THE HOSPL
OF ST MARY
THE VIRGIN

Newcastle Coll
Trevelyan Bldg

TIMES SQ
The
International
Ctr for Life

NE1

Newcastle
Arena

ARENA WAY

Works

A695

Newcastle
Bsns Pk

Railway Terr

River Tyne

Dunstan Coal Staiths

Wilberforce
Wlk

Tyne View
Com Prim Sch

NE8

1 DENHOLME LODGE
2 GLANTON CT
3 BERESFORD ST
4 JOHNSON ST
5 RUSKIN AVE

NE11

St Cuthberts
CE Jun Sch

Works

Teams

Derwent
Inf Sch

Brama Teams
Ind Pk

54
70

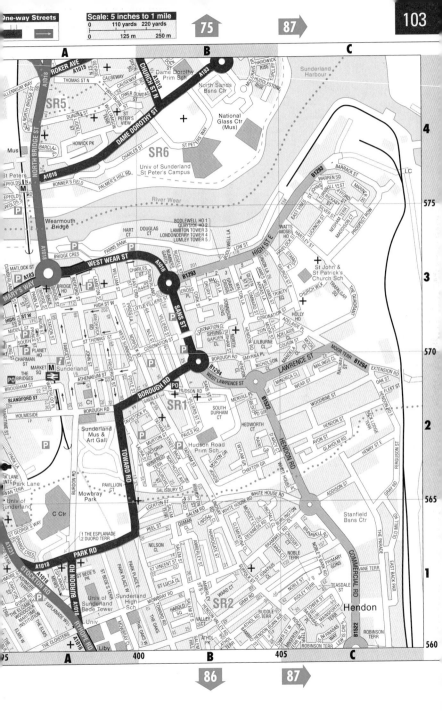

Scale: ⅝ inches to 1 mile

½   1 mile

½   1   1½   2 km

58

A   B   C   D   E   F

HOLY ISLAND

44   Snipe Pt.   Coves Haven   Keel Head   44   8

Snook Pt.   (Lindisfarne)   The Links   Emmanuel Head

Beal Pt.   56

Causeway

Beal Sands   Holy Island Sands   The Basin   Holy Island

42   LINDISFARNE CASTLE (N.T.)   42   7

The Cages   LINDISFARNE PRIORY   The Harbour   Castle Pt.

08   10   12   14

Ho.

Marshall Meadows Bay

lows

St. John's Haven

54

Needles Eye

Steps of Grace

drum

Brotherston's Hole   Sharper's Hd.

ields

BERWICK

BERWICK-   Bucket Rocks

ON-TWEED   Royal   BARRACKS MUSEUM

Border Bri.   **BERWICK-upon-Tweed**

Pier

Tweedmouth

Sandstell Pt.   52

Spittal

Prior   Bear's Hd.

East Ord   Park

Highcliffe   Huds Hd.   5

Prior Ho.

Ord   Redshin Cove

50

A1   Deputy Row   Borewell

Scremerston   Saltpan Rocks   4

Unthank Square   Inlandpasture   Near Skerrs

Old Colliery Row

Unthank   Far Skerrs   48

Blue Ho.

r Dean   Scremerston Hill   Scremerston Town Fm.   3

Oxford   Cheswick Sands

Cat Inn

Nth. Ancroft   Cheswick Ho.   Cheswick   46

dean   Golf Course

Allerdean Greens   Cheswick Blds.

Longdike   Windmill Hill

Ancroft   E. Ancroft   Broom Ho.   North Low   Goswick   2

Berryburn   Bridge Mill   Goswick Sands

Dean   A1   Haggerston   HOLY ISLAND

Berringtonlaw   Castle   The Mead   44

rington Burn   Berrington   New Haggerston   Brockmill   Snook Pt.   1

Beal Pt.

UMBERLAND   Beal   Causeway   Holy Islands Sands

South Low   Beal Sands   42

Low Lynn   West Mains Inn

A   00   B   02   108   C   04   D   06   E   08   F   10

Bowsden   Old Dryburn   Lowick Mill   Mt. Hooley   Fenhamhill   The Cages

dside   Kentstone   Granary Pt.

Dry   Burn   Hunting Hall   Fenham

Barmoor Hill   The Low

625   West   B6353   Fenwick   Fenwick Granary

Eelwell

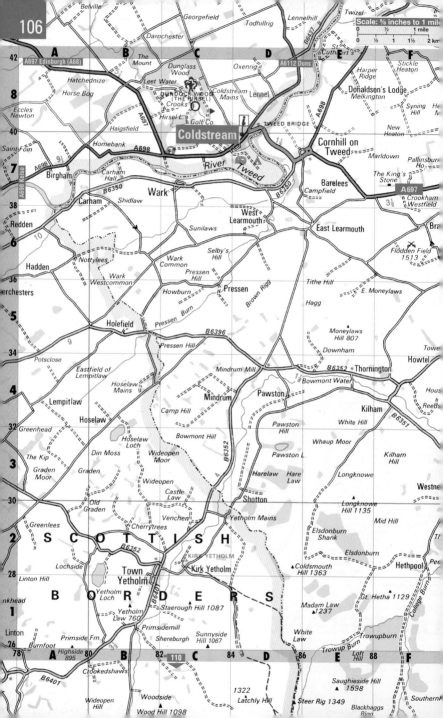

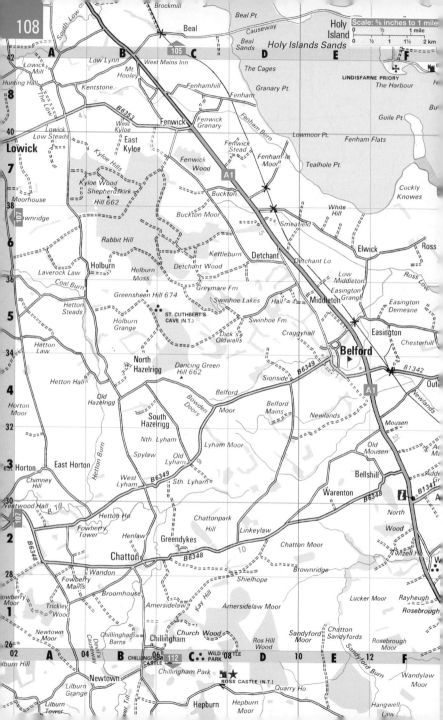

Brockmill
Beal Pt.
Beal
Causeway
Beal Sands
Beal Pt.
Holy Island
Holy Islands Sands

42
A
South Low
Low Lynn
B
105
West Mains Inn
C
Fenhamhill
D
The Cages
E
F
LINDISFARNE PRIORY
The Harbour

Lowick Mill
Mt Hooley
Fenham
Granary Pt.

8
Hunting Hall
The Low
Kentstone
B6353
4½
Fenwick
Fenwick Granary
Fenham Burn
Guile Pt.
Bu

40
Lowick Low Steds
West Kyloe
East Kyloe
Fenwick Stead
Fenham-le-Moor
Lowmoor Pt.
Fenham Flats

Lowick
Kyloe Hills
Fenwick Wood
Tealhole Pt.

7
Moorhouse
Kyloe Wood
Shepherdskirk
Hill 662
Buckton
White Hill
Cockly Knowes

38
107
ownridge
Buckton Moor
A1
Ross

6
Rabbit Hill
Kettleburn
Detchant
Smeafield
Elwick
Ross Low

Holburn
Detchant Wood
Detchant Lo.
Low Middleton

36
Laverock Law
Holburn Moss
Greymare Fm
Middleton
Easington Grange
Easington Demesne

Coal Burn
Greensheen Hill 674
Swinhoe Lakes
Hall
Easington
Chesterhill

5
Hetton Steads
Holburn Grange
ST. CUTHBERT'S CAVE (N.T.)
Swinhoe Fm.
Craggyhall
Belford

34
Hetton Law
Dick's Oldwalls
Sionside
B6349
B1342
Out

North Hazelrigg
Dancing Green Hill 662
Belford
B1342

4
Horton Moor
Hetton Hall
Old Hazelrigg
Bowden Doors
Belford Moor
Belford Mains
Newlands
Newlands
Mousen

32
South Hazelrigg
Nth. Lyham
Spylaw
Lyham Moor
Old Mousen
Add
Ma

3
Horton
East Horton
West Lyham
Old Lyham
Sth. Lyham
Bellshill
B1341

30
Weetwood Hall
107
Hetton Ho.
Fowberry Tower
Henlaw
B6349
Warenton
B6348

2
B6348
Chatton
Chimney Hill
Greendykes
Chattonpark Hill
Linkeylaw
Chatton Moor
North Wood
Twizell Ho.

28
Fowberry Mains
Wandon
Broomhouse
B6348
Shielhope
Brownridge
Lucker Moor
Rayheugh

owberry Moor
Trickley Wood
Amersidelaw
Kay Hill
Amersidelaw Moor
Rosebrough

1
Newtown Moor
Chillingham Barns
Church Wood
Ros Hill Wood
Sandyford Moor
Chatton Sandyfords
Rosebrough Moor

26
02
A
04
B
CHILLINGHAM CASTLE
06
112
C
WILD PARK
08
D
10
E
12
F

burn Hill
Lilburn Grange
Newtown
Devil's Causeway
Chillingham Park
ROSS CASTLE (N.T.)
Quarry Ho.
Sandyford Burn
Wandylaw Moor

Lilburn Tower
Hepburn
Hepburn Moor
Hangwell Law

cale: ⅝ inches to 1 mile

½		1 mile	
½	1	1½	2 km

A B C D E F

42

ISFARNE CASTLE (N.T.)
Castle Pt.
Mouth
ws Hole

8

40

N O R T H U M B E R L A N D

Knivestone
LONGSTONE
LIGHTHOUSE Longstone

7

Clove Car

North Wamses

Big Harcar

South Wamses Roddam and Green

Oxcar or
South
Goldstone

Brownsman

Staple I.

Megstone

Callers Crumstone

38

6

FARNE ISLANDS
Staple Sound

Knoxes Reef Lit. Scarcar

The Kettle

Budle
Bay

Budle Pt.

Inner Sound

The Bush

Harkess
Rocks

Golf Co.

36

CHAPEL & TOWER
Inner Farne

GRACE DARLING
MUSEUM

Islestone

5

Budle

BAMBURGH BAMBURGH
CASTLE

Waren
Mill

B1342 Friary

Greenhill Rocks

B1340

Dukesfield

Greenhill

34

ester

Spindlestone

Glororum

Burton

Monks Ho.

Saddlershall

St Aidan's Dunes

The Tumblers

4

Bradford

New Shoreston

Shoreston
Hall

Crackenpool Burn

Springhill

Seahouses

Braidcarr
Point

erstone

32

stone
nge

Hoppen

Newhouses

Elford

North
Sunderland

Golf Co.

Snook Point

3

Lucker

Pasturehill

Southfield

Annstead

B1340

derstone

Lucker
Sth. Fm.

Burnhouse

Collith Hole

30

Beadnell Haven

Newham
Hall

E. Fleetham

Beadnell

Nacker Hole

2

renford
ORSELAND
ALLERY STUDIO
WO CERAMICS

Coldrife

West
Fleetham

Beadnell Harbour

Henhill

Newham

Swinhoe

28

Birchwood
Hall

Long Nanny

Beadnell
Bay

Newstead

Tughall
Grange

1

CHATHILL

Chathill

Tughall

Newton Links
Ho.

26

BRUNTON

Newton
Links

Snook Pt.

The Nest

Broad
Wood

Crutch
Bog

B1340

A1

A 16 B 18 113 C 20 D 22 E 24 F 26

Commonflat
Wandylaw

Ellingham

Preston

High Newton-
by-the-Sea

Football Hole
Newton Pt.

PRESTON
TOWER

South
Broomfield

Low
Brunton

Newton Hall

St. Mary's or
Newton Haven

Brockdam

Brunton

Low Newton-
by-the-Sea

Brockdam Moor

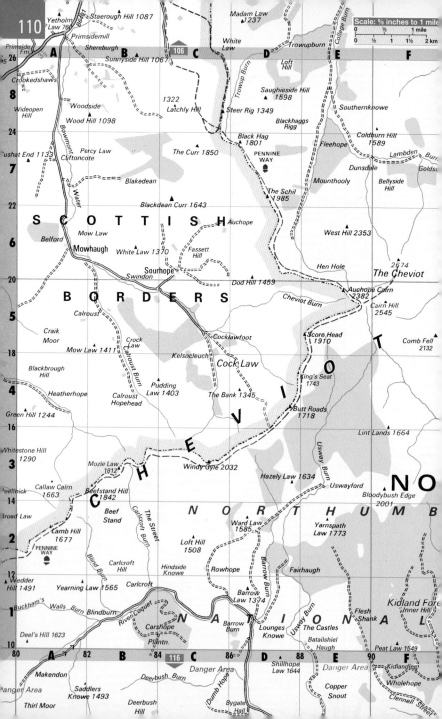

Scale: ⅝ inches to 1 mile

0   ½   1   1½   1 mile
0   ½   1   1½   2 km

SCOTTISH

BORDERS

PENNINE WAY

PENNINE WAY

CHEVIOT

NORTHUMB

NO

NATIONAL

Kidland Fore

Place names (north to south, roughly)

Yetholm Law 760
Staerough Hill 1087
Madam Law 1237
Primsidemill
White Law
Trowupburn
College Burn
Primside Fm
Shereburgh
106
Sunnyside Hill 1067
Crookedshaws
Wideopen Hill
Woodside
Loft Hill
Saughieside Hill 1598
Southernknowe
1322
Latchly Hill
Steer Rig 1349
Coldburn Hill 1589
Wood Hill 1098
Blackhaggs Rigg
Lambden
Cushat End 1133
Percy Law
The Curr 1850
Black Hag 1801
Fleehope
Goldsc
Cliftoncote
Bowmont Water
Dunsdale
Blakedean
PENNINE WAY
Mounthooly
Bellyside Hill
Blackdean Curr 1643
The Schil 1985
Auchope
West Hill 2353
Mow Law
2674
Belford
White Law 1370
Fassett Hill
The Cheviot
Mowhaugh
Sourhope
Hen Hole
Swindon
Dod Hill 1459
Auchope Cairn 2382
Cheviot Burn
Cairn Hill 2545
Calroust
Craik Moor
Score Head 1910
Comb Fell 2132
Mow Law 1411
Crock Law
Cocklawfoot
Calroust Burn
Kelsocleuch
Blackbrough Hill
Cock Law
King's Seat 1743
Heatherhope
Pudding Law 1403
The Bank 1345
Butt Roads 1718
Calroust Hopehead
Green Hill 1244
Lint Lands 1664
Whitestone Hill 1290
Mozie Law 1812
Windy Gyle 2032
Usway Burn
Hazely Law 1634
Peelthick
Callaw Cairn 1663
Uswayford
Broad Law
Beefstand Hill 1842
Bloodybush Edge 2001
Beef Stand
The Street
Carlcroft Burn
Ward Law 1585
Yarnspath Law 1773
Lamb Hill 1677
Loft Hill 1508
PENNINE WAY
Carlcroft Hill
Hindside Knowe
Rowhope
Barrow Burn
Fairhaugh
Wedder Hill 1491
Yearning Law 1565
Carlcroft
Blind Burn
Barrow Law 1374
Flesh Shank
Kidland Fore Inner Hill
Buckham's
Walls Burn
Blindburn
River Coquet
Carshope Plantn.
Barrow Burn
Lounges Knowe
The Castles
Usway Burn
Deel's Hill 1623
Batailshiel Haugh
Peat Law 1549
80
A
82
B
84
116
C
86
D
88
E
90
F
Makendon
Deerbush Burn
Danger Area
Shillhope Law 1644
Danger Area
Kidlandle
Danger Area
Saddlers Knowe 1493
Deerbush Hill
Dumb Hope
Copper Snout
Wholehope
Thirl Moor
Bygate Hall
Clennell Street

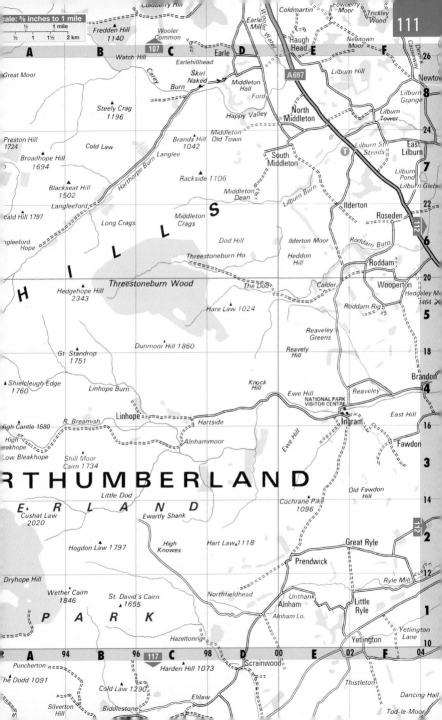

Scale: ⅝ inches to 1 mile

½ · · · 1 mile
½ · 1 · 1½ · 2 km

Coldberry Hill

Coldmartin

Fowberry Moor

Trickley Wood

Fredden Hill 1140

Wooler Common

Earle Mill

Wooler Water

Haugh Head

Newtown Moor

107

Watch Hill

Earlehillhead

Earle

Carey

Skirl Naked

Burn

Middleton Hall

Ford

Happy Valley

A697

North Middleton

Newto

Lilburn Hill

Lilburn Grange

26

8

24

Great Moor

Steely Crag 1196

Preston Hill 1724

Cold Law

Middleton Old Town

Lilburn Tower

Broadhope Hill 1694

Brands Hill 1042

Langlee

South Middleton

Lilburn St Steads

East Lilburn

Langleeford

Blackseat Hill 1502

Rackside 1106

Middleton Dean

Lilburn Burn

T

Ilderton

7

22

Lilburn Pond

Lilburn Glebe

ald Hill 1797

Langleeford Hope

Long Crags

Middleton Crags

Dod Hill

Ilderton Moor

Heddon Hill

Roddam Burn

Roseden

112

6

20

H I L L S

Threestoneburn Ho.

The Dod

Calder

Roddam

Wooperton

Threestoneburn Wood

Hedgehope Hill 2343

Hare Law 1024

Roddam Rig

Hedgeley Me 1464

5

Dunmoor Hill 1860

Reaveley Greens

18

Gt. Standrop 1751

Reavely Hill

Shielcleugh Edge 1760

Linhope Burn

Knock Hill

Ewe Hill

NATIONAL PARK VISITOR CENTRE

Reaveley

Brandon

4

High Cantle 1580

R. Breamish

Linhope

Hartside

Ingram

East Hill

16

High eakhope

Alnhammoor

Ewe Hill

Fawdon

Low Bleakhope

Shill Moor Cairn 1734

3

RTHUMBERLAND

Little Dod

Old Fawdon Hill

14

E R L A N D

Cushat Law 2020

Ewartly Shank

Cochrane Pike 1096

112

2

Hogdon Law 1797

High Knowes

Hart Law 1118

Great Ryle

Dryhope Hill

Prendwick

Ryle Mill

12

Wether Cairn 1846

St. David's Cairn 1655

Northfieldhead

Unthank

Little Ryle

1

P A R K

Alnham

Alnham Lo.

Yetlington Lane

Hazeltonrig

Yetlington

10

Puncherton

117

Scrainwood

94

96

98

00

02

04

A

B

C

D

E

F

Harden Hill 1073

he Dodd 1091

Cold Law 1290

Elilaw

Thistleton

Silverton Hill

Biddlestone

Dancing Hall

Tod-le-Moor

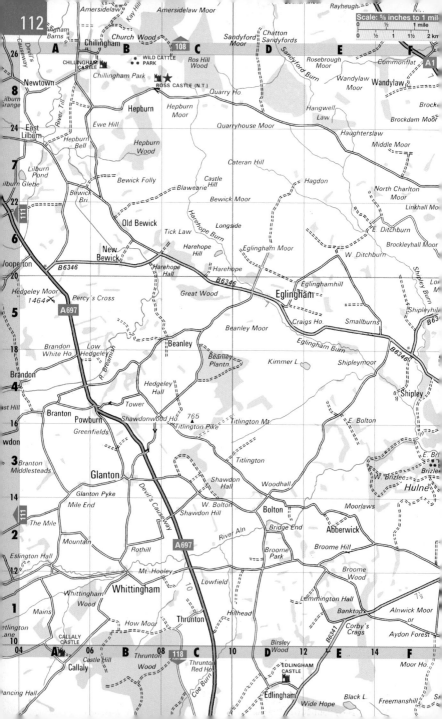

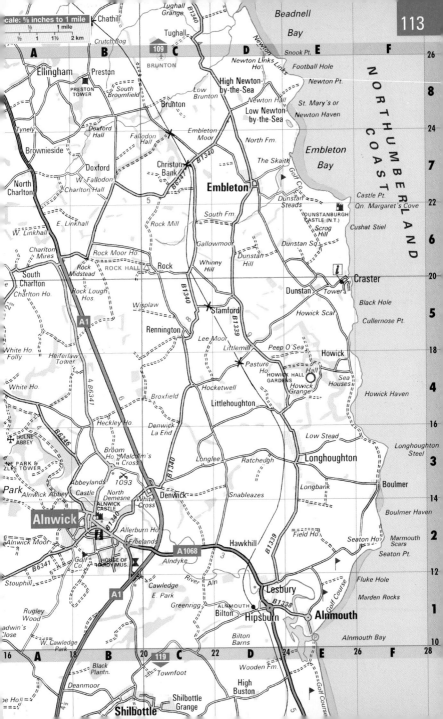

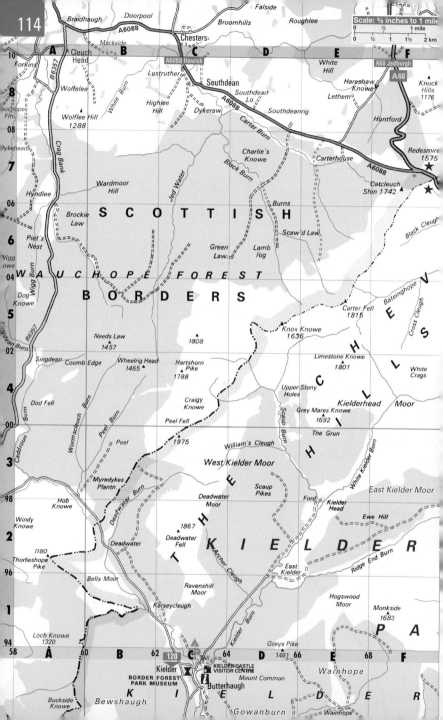

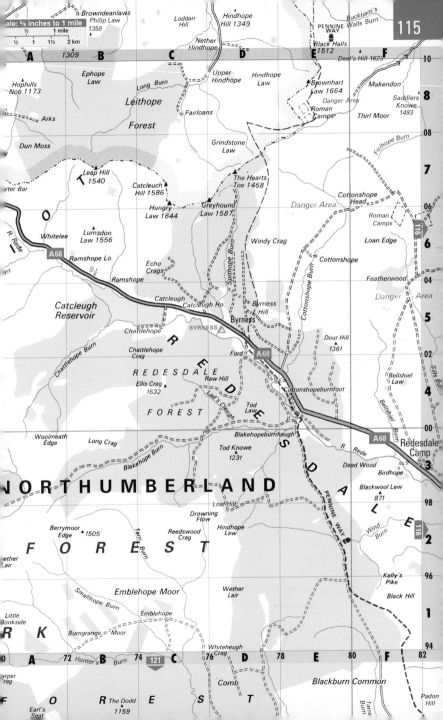

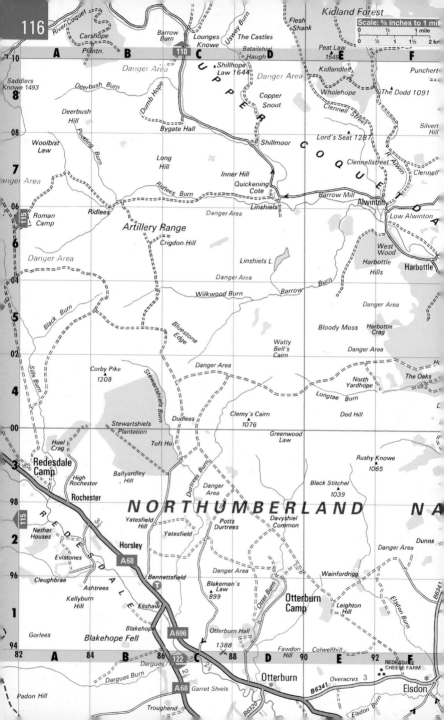

Kidland Forest

River Coquet
Carshope
Plantn.
Saddlers
Knowe 1493
Deerbush Burn
Deerbush
Hill
Woolbist
Law
Danger Area
Roman
Camp
Danger Area
Black Burn
Sills Burn
Huel
Crag
Redesdale
Camp
High
Rochester
Rochester
Nether
Houses
Evistones
Cleughbrae
Kellyburn
Hill
Gorlees
Blakehope Fell
Ashtrees
Padon Hill

Barrow
Burn
Lounges
Knowe
Usway Burn
The Castles
Batailshiel
Haugh
Flesh
Shank
Peat Law
1549
Kidlandlee
Wholehope
Danger Area
Shillhope
Law 1644
Copper
Snout
Clennell Street
Lord's Seat 1287
Clennellstreet
Barrow Mill
Puncherto
The Dodd 1091
Silvert
Hill
Clennell
Alwinton
Low Alwinton
West
Wood
Harbottle
Hills
Harbottle
Dumb Hope
Puddling Burn
Bygate Hall
Long
Hill
Ridlees Burn
Ridlees
Artillery Range
Crigdon Hill
Inner Hill
Quickening
Cote
Shillmoor
Linshiels
Danger Area
Linshiels L.
Danger Area
Wilkwood Burn
Barrow
Burn
Danger Area
Bluestone
Edge
Corby Pike
1208
Stewartshiels Burn
Bloody Moss
Harbottle
Crag
Watty
Bell's
Cairn
Danger Area
Danger Area
North
Yardhope
The Oaks
Ho
Longtae Burn
Stewartshiels
Plantation
Dudlees
Toft Ho
Clemy's Cairn
1076
Dod Hill
Durtrees Burn
Danger Area
Greenwood
Law
Ballyardley
Hill
Rushy Knowe
1065
Danger
Area
Black Stitchel
1039
NORTHUMBERLAND
NA
Yatesfield
Hill
Yatesfield
Potts
Durtrees
Davyshiel
Common
Dunns
Danger Area
Horsley
A68
Bennettsfield
T
Danger Area
Wainfordrigg
Otter Burn
Otterburn
Camp
Leighton
Hill
Elsdon Burn
Blakeman's
Law
899
Elishaw
Blakehope
A696
Otterburn Hall
1388
Fawdon
Hill
Colwellhill
REDESDALE
CHEESE
FARM
Dargues
A68
Garret Shiels
122
Otterburn
Overacres 3
B6341
Elsdon
Elsdon Burn
Dargues Burn
Troughend
B6320
110
115
115
115

A   B   C   D   E   F
10
8
08
7
06
6
04
5
02
4
00
3
98
2
96
1
94
82   84   86   88   90   92

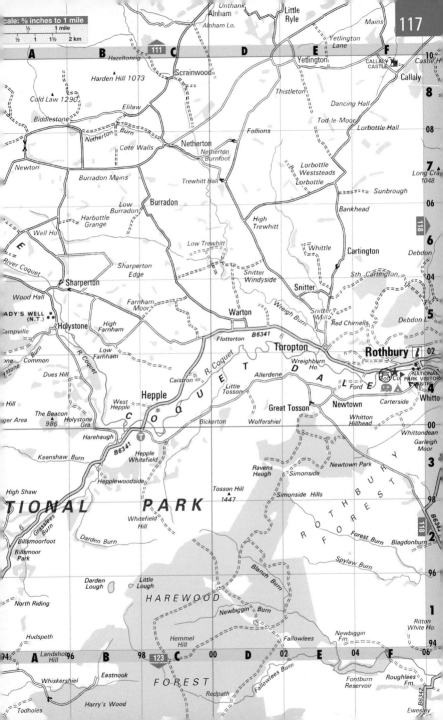

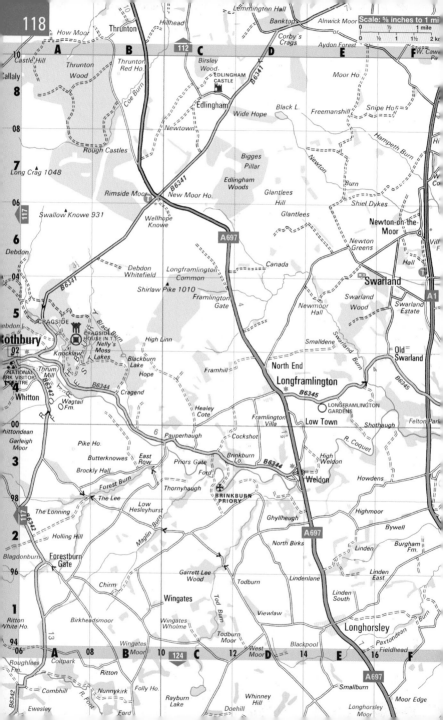

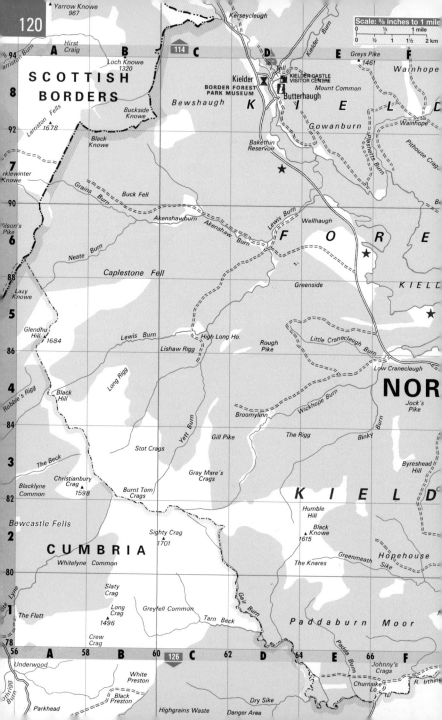

▲ Yarrow Knowe
967

Kerseycleugh

Hirst
Craig

Kielder Burn

A   **B**   114 **C**   **D**   **E** ▲ Greys Pike
1461   **F**

Il   94
arriston Burn   Loch Knowe
1320   Toll   Wainhope

SCOTTISH   Kielder   KIELDER CASTLE
VISITOR CENTRE

8   BORDERS   BORDER FOREST
PARK MUSEUM   Butterhaugh

Bewshaugh   **K**   Mount Common   **Y**   **E**   **L**   **D**

Larriston
Fells   Buckside
Knowe   Gowanburn   Wainhope

92   Larriston
1678   Pithouse Crag

Black
Knowe   Bakethin
Reservoir   ★   Plashetts Burn

rklewinter
Knowe

7   Grains Burn   Buck Fell   Lewis Burn   Wellhaugh

90

Akenshawburn   Akenshaw Burn   **F**   **O**   **R**   **E**

Wilson's
Pike   Neate Burn   **6**   ★   **KIELD**

88   Caplestone Fell   Greenside   **KIELD**

Lazy
Knowe

5   ★

Glendhu
Hill
1684   Lewis Burn   High Long Ho.   Rough
Pike   Little Cranecleugh Burn

86   Lishaw Rigg   Low Cranecleugh

Robbie's Rigg   Long Rigg   **NOR**

4   Black
Hill   Jock's
Pike

84   Yett Burn   Broomylinn   Wickhope Burn   Binky   Burn   Byreshead
Hill

The Beck   Stot Crags   Gill Pike   The Rigg

3   Christianbury
Crag
1598   Gray Mare's
Crags   **K**   **I**   **E**   **L**   **D**

Blacklyne
Common   Burnt Tom
Crags   Humble
Hill

82

Bewcastle Fells   Sighty Crag
1701   ▲ Black
Knowe
1615   Hopehouse

2   CUMBRIA   The Knares   Greenmeath
Sike

80   Whitelyne Common

Lyne   Slaty
Crag   **1**   Long
Crag
1496   Greyfell Common   Tarn Beck   Gair Burn   Paddaburn Moor

The Flatt   Crew
Crag   Johnny's
Crags

78   **A**   58   **B**   60   126 **C**   62   **D**   64   **E**   66   **F**

56

Underwood   Pedile Burn   R. Irthing

rigg Burn   White
Preston   Churnsike
Lo.

Parkhead   Black
Preston   Highgrains Waste   Dry Sike
Danger Area

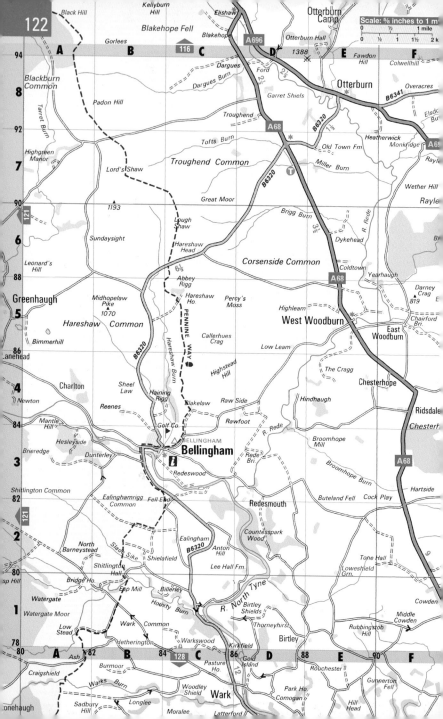

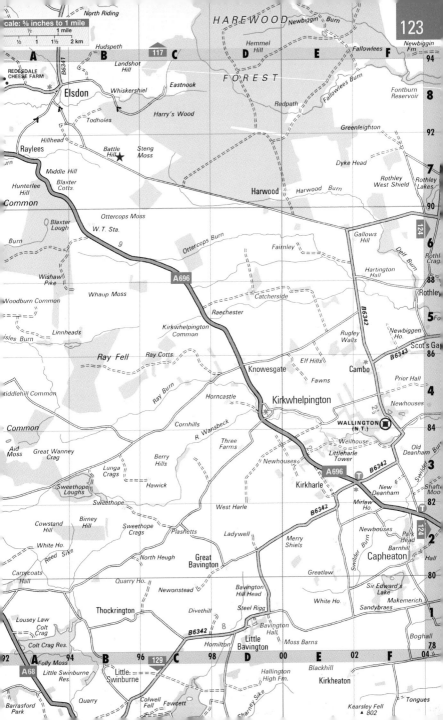

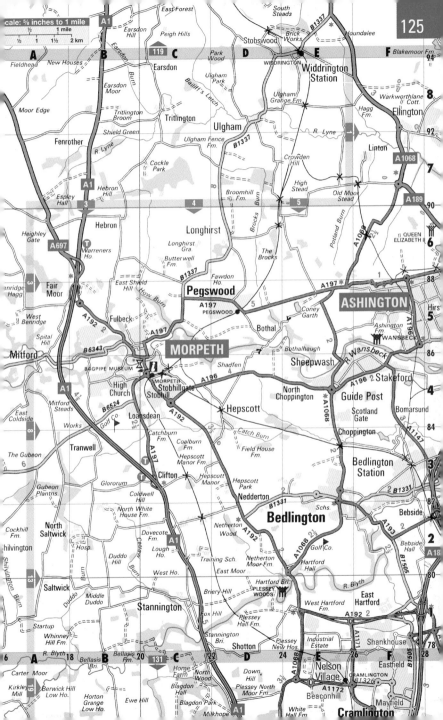

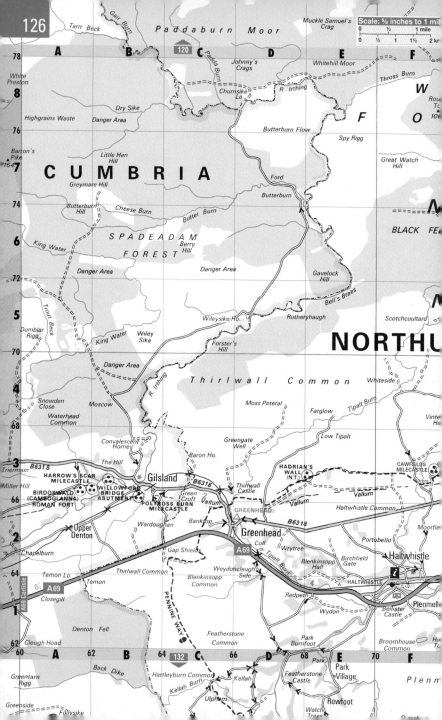

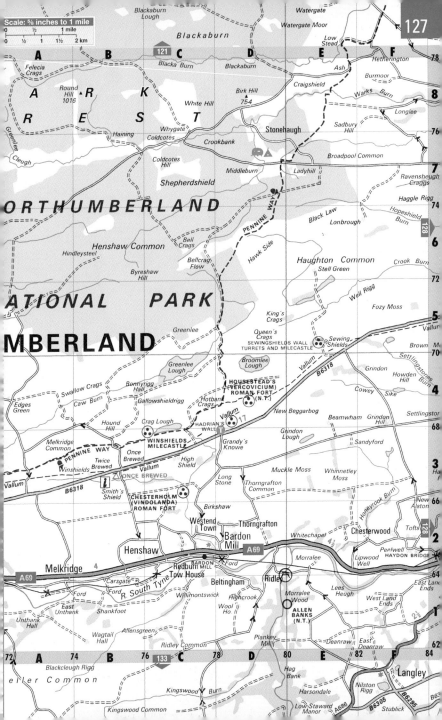

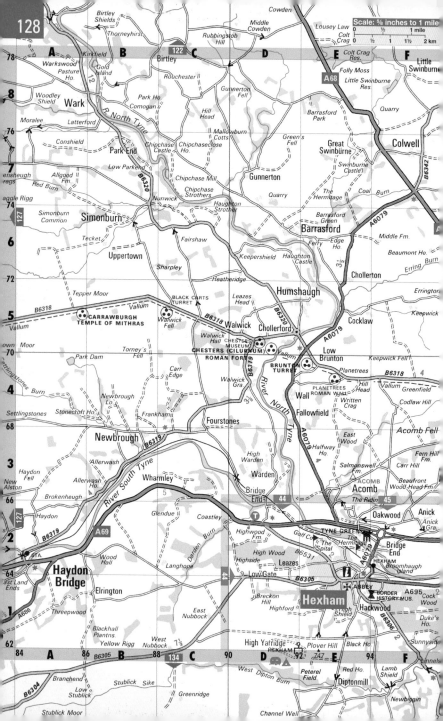

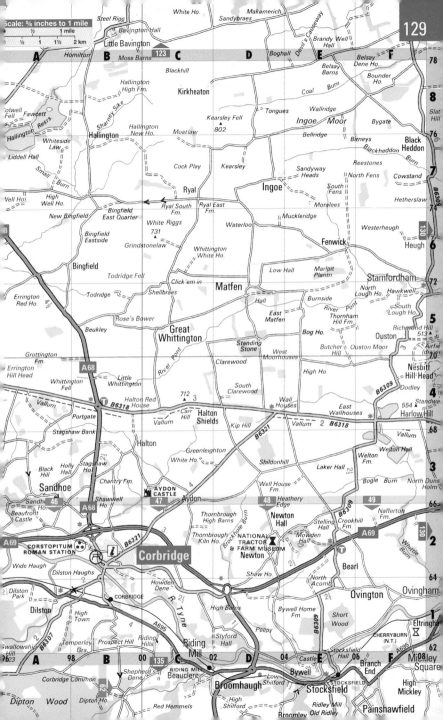

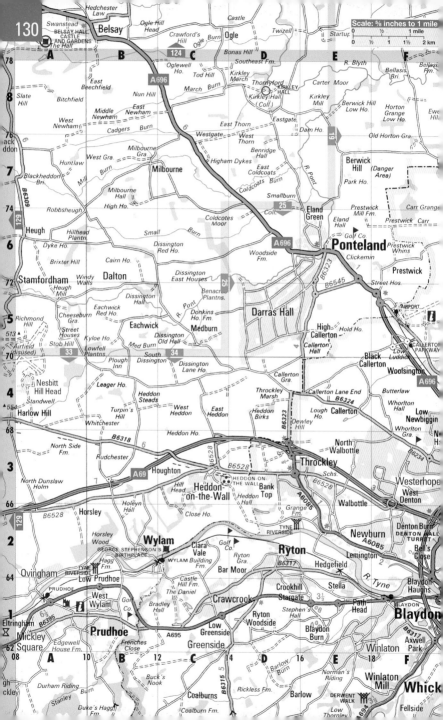

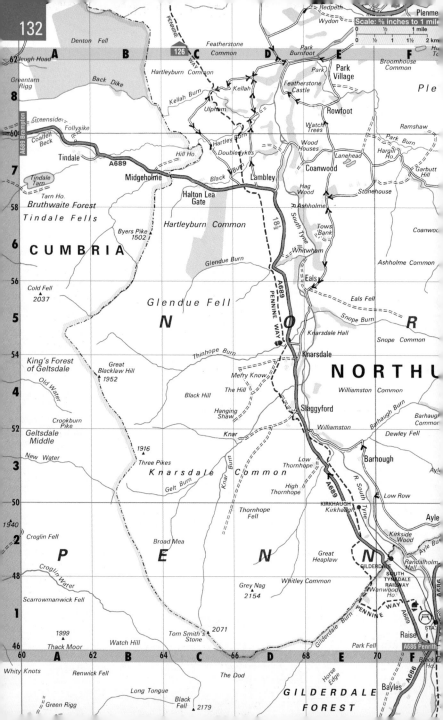

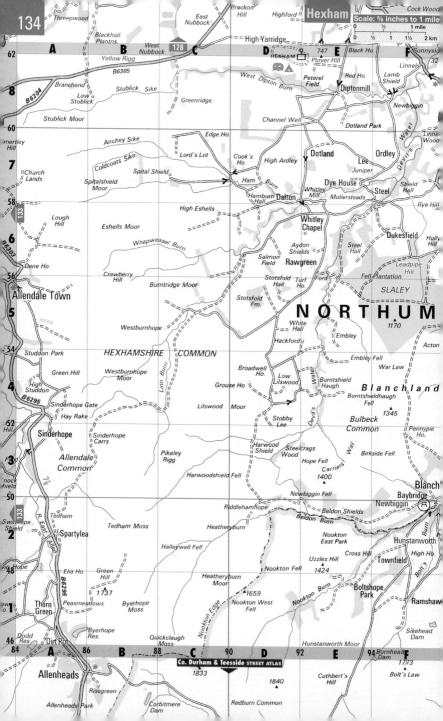

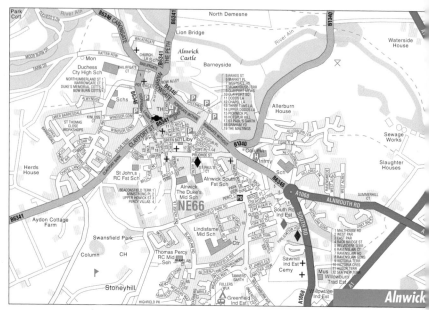

Alnwick

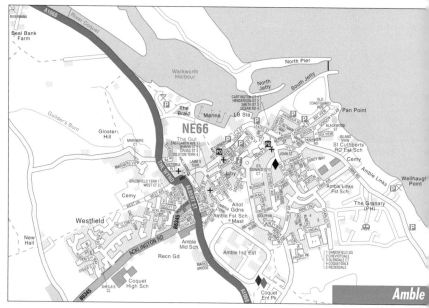

Amble

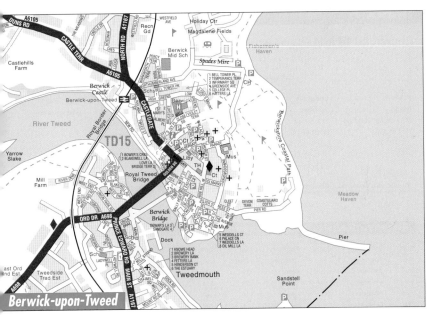

Berwick-upon-Tweed

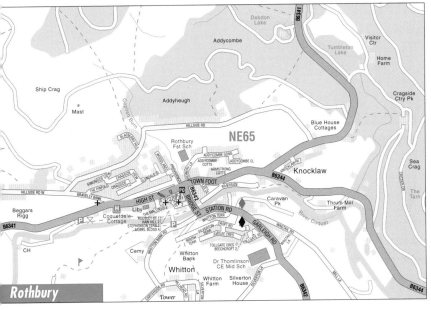

Rothbury

Index

Church Rd 6 Beckenham BR2..........53 C6

Place name	Location number	Locality, town or village	Postcode district	Page and grid square
May be abbreviated on the map	Present when a number indicates the place's position in a crowded area of mapping	Shown when more than one place has the same name	District for the indexed place	Page number and grid reference for the standard mapping

Public and commercial buildings are highlighted in **magenta. Places of interest** are highlighted in blue with a star*

Abbreviations used in the index

Acad	Academy	Comm	Common	Gd	Ground	L	Leisure	Prom	Prom
App	Approach	Cott	Cottage	Gdn	Garden	La	Lane	Rd	Road
Arc	Arcade	Cres	Crescent	Gn	Green	Liby	Library	Recn	Recreation
Ave	Avenue	Cswy	Causeway	Gr	Grove	Mdw	Meadow	Ret	Retail
Bglw	Bungalow	Ct	Court	H	Hall	Meml	Memorial	Sh	Shopping
Bldg	Building	Ctr	Centre	Ho	House	Mkt	Market	Sq	Square
Bsns, Bus	Business	Ctry	Country	Hospl	Hospital	Mus	Museum	St	Street
Bvd	Boulevard	Cty	County	HQ	Headquarters	Orch	Orchard	Sta	Station
Cath	Cathedral	Dr	Drive	Hts	Heights	Pal	Palace	Terr	Terrace
Cir	Circus	Dro	Drove	Ind	Industrial	Par	Parade	TH	Town Hall
Cl	Close	Ed	Education	Inst	Institute	Pas	Passage	Univ	University
Cnr	Corner	Emb	Embankment	Int	International	Pk	Park	Wk, Wlk	Walk
Coll	College	Est	Estate	Intc	Interchange	Pl	Place	Wr	Water
Com	Community	Ex	Exhibition	Junc	Junction	Prec	Precinct	Yd	Yard

Index of localities, towns and villages

A

Abberwick 112 E2
Acklington 119 C4
Acomb 45 A8
Acomb 128 E3
Adderstone 108 F3
Akeld 107 C2
Allanton 104 A7
Allendale Town 133 F5
Allensford 135 F2
Alnham 111 D1
Alnmouth 113 E1
Alnwick 113 B2
Alston 132 F1
Alwinton 116 F7
Amble 119 E6
Ancroft 105 B2
Annitsford 22 B1
Ashington 6 B3
Aydon 129 C3
Ayle 132 F2

B

Backworth 30 C4
Bamburgh 109 B5
Bardon Mill 127 C2
Bareless 106 E7
Barhough 132 E3
Barlow 67 C6
Barrasford 128 D6
Baybridge 134 F3
Beadnell 109 E2
Beal 105 E1
Beamish 80 D2
Beanley 112 C5
Bearsbridge 133 D6
Bebside 16 E7
Bedlington 11 A1
Belford 108 E4
Bellingham 122 B3
Bellshill 108 F3
Belsay 124 D1
Beltingham 127 D1
Berrington 105 B1
Berwick-upon-Tweed ..105 A6
Biddick Hall 59 B2

Bilton 113 D1
Bingfield 129 A6
Birgham 106 A7
Birling 119 D7
Birtley 82 D4
Birtley 122 D1
Black Heddon 129 F7
Blackhall Mill 77 B7
Blagill 133 A1
Blanchland 135 A3
Blaydon 53 E3
Blyth 17 C7
Bolam 124 C3
Boldon Colliery 58 E1
Bolton 112 D2
Boltshope Park 134 F1
Bothal 5 B2
Boulmer 113 F3
Bournmoor 89 D3
Bowsden 107 E8
Brandon 112 A4
Branton 112 A4
Branxton 106 F6
Brockley Whins 58 F3
Broomhill 119 D4
Brownieside 113 A7

Brunswick Village 28 A6
Brunton 113 C8
Budle 109 A5
Burdon 92 B3
Burnopfield 79 A6
Burnside 90 B3
Burradon 117 C7
Butterhaugh 120 D8
Byermoor 79 D7
Byrness 115 D5
Bywell 63 F8

C

Callaly 117 F8
Cambo 123 F4
Cambois 12 C5
Capheaton 123 F2
Carham 106 A7
Carr Shield 133 E1
Carterway Heads 135 E3
Cartington 117 E6
Castle Heaton 107 A8
Castleside 135 F2
Catton 133 F6

Causey Park Bridge ...119 A1
Charlton 122 A4
Chathill 109 C1
Chatton 108 B2
Chester le Street 88 D4
Chesterhope 122 F4
Chesterwood 127 F2
Cheswick 105 C3
Chillingham 108 B1
Chirnside 104 A8
Chollerford 128 D5
Chollerton 128 E6
Choppington 10 E5
Chopwell 66 B3
Christon Bank 113 C7
Clappers 104 E7
Cleadon 60 B1
Coanwood 132 E7
Cocklaw 128 E5
Coldstream 106 D7
Colwell 128 F7
Corbridge 47 B5
Cornhill-on-Tweed ..106 C7
Coupland 107 B3
Cramlington 21 F5
Craster 113 E5

Crawcrook 51 E4
Cresswell 2 A7
Crookham 107 A7
Crookham Eastfield 107 A7

D

Dalton 130 B5
Dalton 134 D7
Denwick 113 C3
Detchant 108 D6
Dinnington 27 B7
Dipton 78 D1
Diptonmill 134 E8
Doddington 107 E4
Donaldson's Lodge 106 E8
Dotland 134 E7
Doxford 113 B7
Druridge 119 E2
Duddo 104 D1
Dudley 29 A7
Dukesfield 134 F6
Dunstan 113 E5
Dunston 54 F1
Dye House 134 E7

E

Eachwick 130 B5
Eals 132 E6
Earle 107 E1
Earsdon 31 A5
Earsdon 125 C8
Easington 108 F5
Easington Lane 97 D8
East Boldon 74 D7
East Cramlington 22 E5
East Hartford 16 B3
East Horton 108 A3
East Kyloe 108 B7
East Learmouth 106 E6
East Lilburn 112 A7
East Ord 105 A5
East Rainton 94 D4
East Sleekburn 12 A3
East Thirston 119 A3
East Woodburn 122 F5
Ebchester 76 F3
Edlingham 118 C8
Edmundbyers 135 C2
Eglingham 112 D5
Elford 109 C3
Ellingham 113 A8
Ellington 1 D4
Elrington 128 B1
Elsdon 123 A8
Elwick 108 E6
Embleton 113 D7
Eshott 119 B2
Etal 107 B7

F

Fallowfield 128 E4
Falstone 121 C5
Fawdon 111 F3
Felkington 104 E2
Felton 119 A4
Fence Houses 94 A8
Fenrother 125 A8
Fenton 107 D4
Fenwick 108 C8
Fenwick 129 E6
Fishwick 104 C5
Ford 107 C6
Fordhill 107 C6
Forestburn Gate 118 A2
Foulden 104 D7
Fourstones 128 C3

G

Gateshead 55 E2
Gateshead 101 C2
Gilsland 126 B3
Glanton 112 B3
Goswick 105 D2
Great Bavington 123 D2
Great Lumley 89 C1
Great Ryle 111 F2
Great Swinburne 128 E7
Great Tosson 117 E4
Great Whittington 129 C5
Greendykes 108 C2
Greenhaugh 121 F5
Greenhead 126 C2
Greenside 52 A1
Grindon 104 C2
Guide Post 10 F6
Gunnerton 128 D7
Guyzance 119 B6

H

Hadden 106 A6
Hadston 119 E4
Haggerston 105 C1
Hallington 129 B7
Halton 129 B3
Halton Lea Gate 132 C7
Halton Shields 129 C4
Haltwhistle 126 F2
Hamsterley 77 B5
Hamsterley Mill 78 A5
Harbottle 116 F6
Harlow Hill 33 A5
Harnham 124 B2
Hartburn 124 C5
Harwood 123 E7
Haswell 97 F3
Haugh Head 107 F1
Hauxley 119 F5
Hawkhill 113 D2
Haydon Bridge 128 A2
Hazlerigg 28 A4
Healeyfield 135 F2
Hebburn 57 E5
Heddon-on-the-Wall 34 F2
Hedley on the Hill 65 A3
Hedworth 58 C2
Helm 119 A2
Henshaw 127 C2
Hepburn 112 B8
Hepple 117 C4
Hepscott 9 F5
Hethpool 106 F2
Hetton le Hole 95 B4
Heugh 130 A6
Hexham 44 E2
High Angerton 124 C4
High Buston 119 C8
High Hauxley 119 E5
High Newton-by-the-Sea 113 D8
High Pittington 96 C5
High Spen 66 F4
Highcliffe 105 B5
Highfields 105 A7
Hipsburn 113 D1
Holburn 108 B6
Holefield 106 B5
Holy Island 105 F1
Holystone 117 A5
Holywell 23 F2
Horncliffe 104 D4
Horndean 104 B4
Horsley 50 D8
Horsley 116 B2
Horsleyhope 135 F1
Hoselaw 106 B4
Houghton-le-Spring 94 D7
Howick 113 E4
Howtel 106 F4
Humbleton 107 D2
Humshaugh 128 D5
Hunstanworth 134 F2
Hutton 104 C6

I

Ilderton 111 E6
Ingoe 129 D7
Ingram 111 E4

J

Jarrow 58 D6

K

Kibblesworth 81 D5
Kielder 120 D8
Kilham 106 F4
Killingworth 29 D3
Kiln Pit Hill 135 E5
Kimmerston 107 C5
Kirk Yetholm 106 C2
Kirkharle 123 E3
Kirkheaton 129 C8
Kirknewton 107 A3
Kirkwhelpington 123 D4
Knarsdale 132 D4
Knowesgate 123 D4

L

Ladykirk 104 B3
Lamberton 104 F8
Lambley 132 D7
Lanehead 121 F4
Langley 133 F8
Lanton 107 B3
Lee 134 F7
Lempitlaw 106 A4
Lennel 106 D8
Lesbury 113 D1
Limestone Brae 133 D2
Linhope 111 C4
Lint 107 B6
Linton 1 B3
Little Bavington 123 D1
Little Ryle 111 E1
Little Swinburne 128 F8
Littlehoughton 113 D4
Longbenton 39 C8
Longframlington 118 D4
Longhorsley 118 E1
Longhoughton 113 E3
Longhurst 4 F7
Longwitton 124 B6
Low Angerton 124 C4
Low Brunton 128 E4
Low Newton-by-the-Sea 113 D8
Low Town 118 D4
Lowick 107 F7
Lucker 109 A3
Lynmouth 2 B2

M

Mardon 107 A6
Matfen 129 D5
Medburn 130 C5
Medomsley 77 B1
Meldon 124 D3
Melkridge 127 A1
Mickley Square 49 E1
Middleton 108 E5
Middleton 124 B4
Midgeholme 132 B7
Milbourne 130 B7
Milfield 107 B4
Mindrum 106 D4
Mitford 3 A8
Molesden 124 F4
Moorside 135 F2
Morpeth 8 F8
Mowhaugh 110 A6
Muggleswick 135 E2

N

Nedderton 15 B8
Nesbit 107 E4
Netherton 117 C7
Netherwitton 124 C7
New Bewick 112 B6
New Hartley 23 D6
New Herrington 90 E6
New Silksworth 92 B8
Newbiggin 134 F2
Newbiggin-by-the-Sea 7 E3
Newbottle 90 E3
Newbrough 128 B3
Newburn 52 F7
Newcastle-upon-Tyne 55 C6
Newcastle-upon-Tyne 98 C3
Newham 109 B2
Newlands 76 C3
Newton 48 C6
Newton 117 E4
Newton Underwood 124 F5
Newton-on-the-Moor 118 F6
Newtown 107 D3
Newtown 112 A8
Ninebanks 133 D4
Norham 104 C3
North Charlton 113 A7
North Hazelrigg 108 B4
North Middleton 111 E8
North Shields 41 F4
North Sunderland 109 D3
North Togston 119 D5

O

Oakwood 45 E8
Ogle 124 E1
Old Bewick 112 B6
Ordley 134 F7
Otterburn 122 E8
Otterburn Camp 116 D1
Ouston 81 F2
Ouston 129 F5
Ouston 133 C4
Outchester 108 F4
Ovingham 50 B5
Ovington 49 C4

P

Park End 128 B7
Park Village 132 E8
Pawston 106 D4
Paxton 104 D6
Pegswood 4 E4
Penshaw 90 C7
Pigdon 124 F6
Plenmeller 126 F1
Ponteland 25 D6
Powburn 112 B4
Prendwick 111 E2
Pressen 106 C5
Preston 113 B8
Prior Park 105 A5
Prudhoe 50 D1

R

Radcliffe 119 E5
Raise 132 F1
Ramshaw 134 F1
Rawgreen 134 E6
Raylees 123 A7
Red Row 119 D3
Redburn 127 C2
Redesdale Camp 116 A3
Redesmouth 122 D3
Rennington 113 C5
Riding Mill 62 E8
Ridley 127 D1
Ridsdale 122 F4
Rochester 116 A3
Rock 113 C6
Roddam 111 F6
Roseden 111 F6
Ross 108 F6
Rothbury 117 F4
Rothley 124 A6
Rowfoot 132 E8
Rowlands Gill 67 E2
Ruffside 135 B3
Ryal 129 C7
Ryhope 92 F6
Ryton 52 D5

S

Sandhoe 129 A3
Scot's Gap 124 A5
Scrainwood 117 C8
Scremerston 105 B4
Seaham 93 C1
Seahouses 109 D3
Seaton 92 B1
Seaton Burn 21 B1
Seaton Delaval 23 C2
Seaton Sluice 24 C5
Seghill 22 F1
Sharperton 117 A5
Sherburn 96 A1
Sherburn Hill 96 C1
Shilbottle 119 A8
Shilbottle Grange 119 B8
Shilvington 124 F2
Shiney Row 90 B5
Shipley 112 F4
Shiremoor 30 F3
Shoresdean 104 E3
Shoreswood 104 D3
Shotleyfield 135 F4
Shotton 20 E8
Shotton 106 D3
Silksworth 91 F7
Simonburn 128 B6
Sinderhope 134 A3
Slaggyford 132 D4
Slaley 62 A2
Slaley 135 A6
Snitter 117 E5
Snods Edge 135 F4
Sourhope 110 C6
South Broomhill 119 D3
South Charlton 113 A6
South Hazelrigg 108 B4
South Hetton 97 F8
South Middleton 111 D7
South Shields 42 E4
Southdean 114 C8
Spartylea 134 A2
Spittal 105 B5
Springwell 71 F2
Stakeford 11 B7
Stamford 113 D5
Stamfordham 130 A5
Stannersburn 121 C5
Stannington 14 D3
Stanton 124 E7
Steel 134 F7
Stobswood 119 C1
Stocksfield 64 B7
Stonehaugh 127 D8
Strothers Dale 135 A6
Sunderland 86 E6
Sunderland 102 C3
Sunniside 69 A2
Swarland 118 F5
Swinhoe 109 D2

T

Tanfield 79 D3
Tanfield Lea 79 D1
Tantobie 79 B2
Thockrington 123 B1
Thorn Green 134 A1
Thorngrafton 127 D2
Thornington 106 F4
Thornley Gate 133 F6
Thornton 104 E3
Throckley 35 D1
Throphill 124 E4
Thropton 117 E5
Thrunton 112 C1
Tindale 132 A7
Togston 119 D4
Tow House 127 C2
Town Yetholm 106 B1
Townfield 134 F2
Tritlington 125 C8
Tughall 109 D1
Tweedmouth 105 A6
Tynemouth 42 B8

U

Ulgham 125 D8
Upper Denton 126 A2
Uppertown 128 B6
Upsettlington 104 B3
Urpeth 81 E2

W

Walbottle 35 F2
Wall 128 D4
Wall Houses 129 D4
Wallsend 40 D2
Walwick 128 D5
Wandylaw 112 F8
Warden 128 D3
Warenford 108 F2
Warenton 108 E3
Wark 106 C7
Wark 128 A8
Warkworth 119 D6
Warren Mill 109 A5
Warton 117 D5
Washington 83 F7
Weldon 118 D3
West Allerdean 104 F3
West Boldon 74 A8
West Chevington 119 C2
West Fleetham 109 C2
West Horton 108 A3
West Learmouth 106 D6
West Rainton 94 B2
West Sleekburn 11 D7
West Thirston 119 A3
West Woodburn 122 E5
Westend Town 127 C2
Westnewton 107 A3
Whalton 124 E2
Wharmley 128 B3
Whickham 69 B7
Whitburn 60 E1
Whiteleas 59 D3
Whitfield 133 C7
Whitley Bay 31 E6
Whitley Chapel 134 E6
Whitsome 104 A5
Whitsomehill 104 A4
Whittingham 112 B1
Whitton 117 F4
Whittonstall 135 F6
Widdrington 119 D1
Widdrington Station 125 E8
Wide Open 28 C5
Wingates 118 B1
Winlaton Mill 68 C6
Wooler 107 E2
Woolsington 36 E8
Wooperton 111 F6
Wylam 51 A5

Y

Yarrow 121 B5
Yeavering 107 B3
Yetlington 117 E8

A

A J Cook's Cotts NE39 .67 B2
Abbay St SR5 .75 A1
Abbey Cl Whitley Bay NE25 .31 D4
Washington NE38 .83 D5
Abbey Ct NE8 .101 C1
Abbey Dr Burnside DH4 .90 C2
Tynemouth NE30 .42 D8
Jarrow NE32 .58 C7
Newcastle-upon-Tyne NE5 .36 B4
Abbey Gate NE61 .8 D7
Abbey Mdws NE61 .8 D7
Abbey Rd NE38 .83 D5
Abbey Terr
Shiremoor NE27 .30 E3
[8] Morpeth NE61 .3 F1
Abbey View Hexham NE46 .45 C4
[7] Morpeth NE61 .3 F1
Abbeyfields Fst Sch NE61 .8 E8
Abbeyvale Dr NE6 .57 B7
Abbot Ct NE8 .101 C3
Abbot's Way NE61 .8 E8
Abbots Cl NE62 .11 B8
Abbots Way
[2] Whickham NE16 .69 B7
Tynemouth NE29 .41 E8
Abbotsfield Cl SR3 .91 F5
Abbotsford Gr SR2 .102 C1
Abbotsford Pk NE25 .31 F4
Abbotsford Rd NE10 .56 D1
Abbotsford Terr NE2 .99 A4
Abbotside Cl DH2 .81 D2
Abbotside Pl NE5 .36 D2
Abbotsmeade Cl NE5 .54 C8
Abbs St SR5 .75 D1
Abercorn Pl NE28 .40 E6
Abercorn Rd
Newcastle-upon-Tyne NE15 .54 A5
Sunderland SR3 .91 D8
Abercrombie Pl [2] NE5 .37 B2
Aberdare Rd SR3 .91 E7
Aberdeen DH2 .81 F1
Aberdeen Ct NE3 .37 D8
Aberdeen Dr NE32 .58 E3
Aberdeen Tower SR3 .91 E8
Aberfoyle DH2 .81 F1
Abernethy DH2 .81 F2
Abersford Cl NE5 .36 B3
Abigail Ct NE3 .38 E5
Abingdon DH2 .81 F1
Abingdon Ct
Blaydon NE21 .53 C3
Newcastle-upon-Tyne NE3 .37 D7
Abingdon Rd NE6 .57 B7
Abingdon Sq NE23 .16 C1
Abingdon St SR4 .85 F5
Abingdon Way NE35 .73 E7
Abinger St NE4 .98 B1
Aboyne Sq SR3 .85 D1
Acacia Ave DH4 .90 A1
Acacia Gr Hebburn NE31 .57 E4
South Shields NE34 .59 F5
Acacia Rd NE10 .56 B2
Acacia Terr NE63 .6 D3
Acanthus Ave NE4 .54 D7
Acer Ct SR2 .86 D4
Acer Dr DH6 .97 F3
Acklam Ave SR2 .87 A1
Acomb Ave
Seaton Delaval NE25 .23 D2
Wallsend NE28 .40 D7
Acomb Cl NE61 .9 C5
Acomb Cres NE3 .38 A8
Acomb Ct
Killingworth NE12 .29 D3
Bedlington NE22 .11 A1
Gateshead NE9 .71 B2
Sunderland SR2 .86 F1
Acomb Dr NE41 .51 A7
Acomb Gdns NE5 .37 C1
Acorn Ave Bedlington NE22 .15 F8
Gateshead NE8 .70 C8
Acorn Rd NE2 .38 E2
Acorn Sq NE42 .50 D2
Acreford Ct NE62 .10 E6
Acton Dr NE29 .41 D8
Acton Pl NE7 .39 B2
Acton Rd NE5 .53 F8
Ada St South Shields NE33 .42 D1
Newcastle-upon-Tyne NE6 .56 E6
Adair Ave NE15 .54 C6
Adair Way NE31 .58 A5
Adams Terr DH8 .77 A2
Adderlane Fst Sch NE42 .50 E3
Adderlane Rd NE42 .50 E3
Adderstone Ave NE23 .22 B5
Adderstone Cres NE2 .38 F2
Adderstone Gdns NE29 .31 B1
Addington Cres NE29 .41 E6
Addington Dr Blyth NE24 .17 E5
Wallsend NE28 .40 D7
Addison Cl [2] NE6 .56 B6
Addison Ct
[7] Wallsend NE28 .41 A1
Ryton NE40 .52 B5
Addison Gdns NE10 .72 B8
Addison Ind Est NE21 .53 A5
Addison Rd
Newcastle-upon-Tyne, Lemington NE15 .53 D7
West Boldon NE36 .74 A7
Addison Rd *continued*
[15] Newcastle-upon-Tyne NE6 .56 B6
Addison St
North Shields NE29 .42 A4
Sunderland SR2 .103 C2
Addison Wlk NE34 .59 A3
Addycombe Terr NE6 .39 C1
Adelaide Cl SR1 .103 C3
Adelaide Ct NE8 .101 B3
Adelaide Ctr The [5] NE4 .54 E5
Adelaide Ho [3] NE4 .54 E5
Adelaide Pl SR1 .103 C3
Adelaide St DH3 .88 C2
Adelaide Terr NE4 .54 E4
Adeline Gdns NE3 .38 A3
Adelphi Cl NE29 .41 C8
Adelphi Pl NE6 .56 E5
Aden Tower SR3 .91 E8
Admington Ct NE62 .10 F7
Admiral Way SR3 .91 C5
Admirals House [9] NE30 .42 D7
Adolphus St SR6 .60 F1
Affleck St NE8 .101 B2
Afton Ct NE34 .59 C5
Afton Way NE3 .37 E6
Agar Rd SR3 .91 D8
Aged Miners' Cotts NE43 .64 F8
Aged Miners' Homes
Chester le Street DH2 .88 C4
Great Lumley DH3 .89 B1
Bournmoor DH4 .89 E2
[5] Houghton-le-Spring DH4 .94 C8
East Rainton DH5 .94 C4
Hetton le Hole DH5 .95 A2
Hetton le Hole DH5 .94 F6
[3] Houghton-le-Spring, New Town DH5 .94 F8
Sherburn Hill DH6 .96 C1
Kibblesworth NE11 .81 C6
Brunswick Village NE13 .28 A6
Burnopfield NE16 .79 A6
Sunniside NE16 .69 A1
Annitsford NE23 .22 B1
Cramlington NE23 .21 F7
Dudley NE23 .29 A6
Cambois NE24 .12 D4
New Hartley NE25 .23 E6
Shiremoor NE27 .30 F3
South Shields NE34 .60 A7
Boldon Colliery NE35 .58 D1
High Spen NE39 .67 A4
Rowlands Gill NE39 .67 F1
Ryton NE40 .52 E4
Prudhoe NE42 .50 B1
[2] Newcastle-upon-Tyne NE5 .36 E3
Stakeford NE62 .11 C8
Ashington NE63 .6 A4
Ashington NE63 .6 F5
Newbiggin-by-the-Sea NE64 .7 D3
Ryhope SR2 .92 E7
New Silksworth SR3 .86 A1
Sunderland SR5 .74 E2
[2] Seaham SR7 .92 F1
Aged Mineworkers Homes
Throckley NE15 .35 B2
Longhurst NE61 .5 B7
Agincourt
Killingworth NE12 .29 D4
Hebburn NE31 .57 D7
Agnes Maria St NE3 .38 A5
Agricola Ct [1] NE33 .42 C4
Agricola Gdns NE28 .40 D7
Agricola Rd NE4 .54 F6
Aidan Ave NE26 .24 B6
Aidan Cl
Brunswick Village NE13 .28 A6
Wallsend NE27 .30 C1
Aidan Ct Jarrow NE32 .58 D6
Longbenton NE7 .39 C5
Aidan Gr NE61 .1 E4
Aidan Wlk NE3 .38 E5
Aiden Way DH5 .95 A5
Ailesbury St SR4 .102 A3
Ainderby Rd NE15 .35 B2
Ainsdale Gdns NE5 .36 C2
Ainslie Pl NE5 .37 C2
Ainsworth Ave NE34 .59 A3
Ainthorpe Cl SR3 .92 B7
Ainthorpe Gdns NE7 .39 C4
Aintree Cl
Washington NE37 .83 D7
Ashington NE63 .6 C2
Aintree Gdns NE8 .70 C7
Aintree Rd SR3 .91 D8
Airedale NE28 .39 F5
Airedale Gdns DH5 .94 F2
Airey Terr
Newcastle-upon-Tyne NE6 .57 A5
Gateshead NE8 .101 A1
Aireys Cl DH4 .94 C8
Airport Freightway NE13 .26 E2
Airport Ind Est NE3 .37 D6
Airville Mount SR3 .92 A4
Aisgill Cl NE23 .22 B6
Aisgill Dr NE5 .36 C1
Aiskell St SR4 .102 A2
Akeld Cl NE23 .22 B5
Akeld Ct NE3 .38 E4
Akeman Way NE34 .59 B5
Akenside Hill NE1 .101 B4
Akenside Terr NE2 .99 C4
Akhurst Sch NE2 .38 F2
Alamein Ave DH5 .94 F8
Alanbrooke Row NE31 .57 C3
Alansway Gdns [9] NE33 .59 D8
Albany Ave NE12 .39 D7
Albany Ct NE4 .100 A3
Albany Gdns [1] NE26 .32 B4
Albany Ho SR5 .75 C1
Albany Mews NE3 .38 A2
Albany Rd NE8 .56 A3
Albany St E NE33 .59 D8
Albany St W NE33 .59 D8
Albany Village Prim Sch NE37 .83 C7
Albany Way NE37 .83 C7
Albatross Way NE24 .17 E3
Albemarle Ave NE2 .38 D3
Albemarle St [4] NE33 .42 C3
Albert Ave NE28 .40 B2
Albert Ct SR2 .102 B1
Albert Dr NE9 .70 F4
Albert Edward Terr NE35 .58 E2
Albert Pl Washington NE38 .83 F4
Gateshead NE9 .70 F4
Albert Rd Bedlington NE22 .11 E2
Seaton Sluice NE26 .24 D6
Jarrow NE32 .58 A6
Sunderland SR4 .102 A3
Albert St
[6] Chester le Street DH3 .88 C3
Newcastle-upon-Tyne NE2 .99 C2
Blyth NE24 .17 E8
Hebburn NE31 .57 D6
Rowlands Gill NE39 .67 A1
Albert Terr
Longbenton NE12 .29 C1
[4] Whitley Bay NE26 .32 B4
Albion Ct
[10] South Shields NE33 .42 C4
Newcastle-upon-Tyne NE6 .56 B5
Albion Gdns NE16 .78 F5
Albion House [3] NE29 .42 A5
Albion Pl SR1 .102 C2
Albion Rd NE29,NE30 .42 A6
Albion Rd W NE29 .42 A5
Albion Ret Ctr NE24 .17 D8
Albion Row
Newcastle-upon-Tyne NE6 .56 B6
Newcastle-upon-Tyne, St Lawrence NE6 .56 B5
Albion St Gateshead NE10 .71 D6
Sunderland SR4 .85 A6
Albion Terr
[8] North Shields NE29 .42 A6
Hexham NE46 .45 A5
Lynmouth NE61 .2 A3
Albion Way
Cramlington NE23 .16 D1
Blyth NE24 .17 C7
Albury Park Rd NE30 .42 C7
Albury Pl NE16 .69 A5
Albury Rd NE2 .38 D3
Albyn Gdns SR3 .86 A3
Alcester Cl NE62 .10 F7
Alconbury Cl NE24 .17 E5
Alcroft Cl NE5 .36 B3
Aldborough St NE24 .17 E7
Aldbrough Cl [11] SR2 .92 F6
Aldbrough St NE34 .59 A5
Aldeburgh Ave NE15 .53 C8
Aldenham Gdns NE30 .32 C1
Aldenham Rd SR3 .91 E8
Aldenham Tower SR3 .91 E8
Alder Ave NE4 .54 D8
Alder Cl Hetton le Hole DH5 .94 F3
Morpeth NE61 .9 A8
Alder Cres DH9 .78 F2
Alder Ct NE25 .31 E4
Alder Gr NE25 .31 E6
Alder Rd Wallsend NE28 .40 E6
Shiremoor NE29 .41 B7
Alder St SR5 .74 B1
Alder Way NE12 .29 C4
Alderley Cl NE35 .58 E1
Alderley Dr NE12 .29 F4
Alderley Rd NE9 .70 E5
Alderley Way NE23 .16 D1
Alderney Gdns NE5 .36 C2
Aldershot Rd SR3 .91 D7
Aldershot Sq SR3 .91 D7
Aldertone Ct NE62 .10 F7
Alderwood
Washington NE38 .89 B8
Ashington NE63 .6 C2
Alderwood Cres NE6 .39 F1
Alderwyk NE10 .72 B6
Aldwick Rd NE15 .54 A5
Aldwych Dr NE29 .41 B7
Aldwych Ho NE33 .42 B2
Aldwych Rd SR3 .91 D7
Aldwych Sq SR3 .91 D6
Aldwych St NE33 .42 E2
Alemouth Rd NE46 .45 B5
Alexander Dr DH5 .94 F3
Alexander Terr
Hazlerigg NE13 .28 A5
Sunderland SR6 .75 D3
Alexandra Ave SR5 .74 F1
Alexandra Cres NE46 .44 F5
Alexandra Dr NE16 .69 C8
Alexandra Gdns
North Shields NE29 .41 E6
Ryton NE40 .52 E4
Alexandra Pk SR2 .86 C4
Alexandra Rd
Newcastle-upon-Tyne NE6 .39 B1
Morpeth NE61 .9 A8
Ashington NE63 .6 F3
Gateshead NE8 .101 B1
Alexandra St
Wallsend NE28 .40 C2
Rowlands Gill NE39 .67 A1
Alexandra Terr
Penshaw DH4 .90 B8
Haswell DH6 .97 F3
Sunniside NE16 .69 C2
[3] Whitley Bay NE26 .32 B4
Stocksfield NE43 .64 D7
Hexham NE46 .44 F5
Newcastle-upon-Tyne NE5 .36 F3
Springwell NE9 .71 F1
Alexandra Way NE23 .22 B5
Alford DH2 .81 F2
Alford Gn NE12 .39 C7
Alfred Ave NE22 .11 B1
Alfred St Blyth NE24 .17 E6
Hebburn NE31 .57 D5
Newcastle-upon-Tyne NE6 .56 E6
Algernon NE12 .29 D5
Algernon Cl [14] NE6 .56 C7
Algernon Ct [17] NE6 .56 C7
Algernon Ind Est NE27 .30 F1
Algernon Pl NE26 .32 B4
Algernon Rd
Newcastle-upon-Tyne, Lemington NE15 .53 C6
[15] Newcastle-upon-Tyne, Heaton NE6 .56 C7
Algernon Terr
Tynemouth NE30 .42 C8
Wylam NE41 .51 A6
Algiers Rd SR3 .91 C7
Alice St Blaydon NE21 .53 B1
South Shields NE33 .59 C8
Sunderland SR2 .102 C1
Alice Well Villas SR4 .84 B3
Aline St SR3 .92 B7
Alison Ct [4] NE6 .56 B7
Alison Dr NE36 .74 D7
All Saints CE Inf Sch NE34 .59 C5
All Saints CE Jun Mix Sch NE34 .59 B4
All Saints Ct NE29 .41 D6
All Saints Dr DH5 .95 A5
All Saints Ho SR6 .75 D1
Allan Rd NE64 .7 D5
Allandale Ave NE12 .39 D7
Allanville NE12 .29 C5
Allchurch NE15 .54 B6
Allchurch Dr NE63 .7 A3
Allen Ave NE11 .70 D7
Allen Banks (N.T.)* NE47 .127 E1
Allen Dr NE46 .45 B4
Allen St DH3 .88 C2
Allendale Ave NE28 .40 B4
Allendale Cres
Penshaw DH4 .90 B8
Shiremoor NE27 .31 A3
Stakeford NE62 .6 A1
Allendale Dr NE34 .60 A8
Allendale Pl NE30 .42 D7
Allendale Rd Blyth NE24 .17 F6
Hexham NE46 .44 F4
Newcastle-upon-Tyne NE6 .56 D5
Sunderland SR3 .91 D8
Allendale Sq SR3 .91 E8
Allendale St DH5 .95 A2
Allendale Terr
Haswell DH6 .97 F3
Newcastle-upon-Tyne NE6 .56 F5
Allenhead NE38 .83 E1
Allenheads
Seaton Delaval NE25 .23 C4
Newcastle-upon-Tyne NE5 .36 E1
Allensgreen NE23 .22 B6
Allerdean Cl
Newcastle-upon-Tyne NE15 .53 B7
Seaton Delaval NE25 .23 D2
Allerdene Wlk NE16 .69 B6
Allerhope NE23 .22 B5
Allerton Gdns NE6 .39 D2
Allerton Pl NE16 .68 F5
Allerwash NE5 .36 E1
Allery Banks NE61 .9 A8
Allgood Terr NE22 .11 B1
Allhusen Terr NE8 .56 B1
Alliance Pl SR4 .102 B3
Alliance St SR4 .102 B3
Allingham Ct NE7 .39 E3
Allison Ct NE11 .54 B1
Alloa Rd SR3 .91 D8
Allonby Way NE5 .54 B8
Alloy Terr NE39 .67 C1
Allwork Terr NE16 .69 B7
Alma Pl Whitley Bay NE26 .32 C4
North Shields NE29 .42 A6
Alma St SR4 .85 A7
Alma Terr NE40 .52 C2
Almond Cl DH6 .97 F3
Almond Cres NE8 .70 C8
Almond Dr SR5 .85 A8
Almond Pl NE4 .54 D7
Almshouses NE15 .52 F7
Aln Ave NE3 .38 A7
Aln Cres NE3 .38 A7
Aln Ct
Newcastle-upon-Tyne NE15 .53 C6
Ellington NE61 .1 E5
Aln Gr NE15 .53 C7
Aln St Hebburn NE31 .57 D6
Ashington NE63 .6 F5
Aln Wlk NE3 .38 A6
Alnham Ct NE3 .37 E7
Alnham Gr NE5 .36 C2
Alnmouth Ave NE29 .41 D4
Alnmouth Dr NE3 .38 E4
Alnmouth Terr NE46 .44 F8
Alnwick Ave
Whitley Bay NE26 .32 A5
North Shields NE29 .41 D4
Alnwick Castle* NE66 .113 B
Alnwick Cl
Chester le Street DH2 .88 A1
Whickham NE16 .69 A7
Alnwick Ct NE38 .83 B5
Alnwick Dr NE22 .10 D1
Alnwick Gr NE32 .58 B2
Alnwick Rd
South Shields NE34 .59 C6
Sunderland SR3 .91 E8
Alnwick Sq SR3 .91 E8
Alnwick St Newburn NE15 .52 F8
Wallsend NE28 .40 C2
Alnwick Terr NE13 .28 C7
Alpine Ct DH2 .88 C3
Alpine Gr NE36 .74 B7
Alpine Way SR3 .86 A3
Alresford NE12 .29 D4
Alston Ave
East Cramlington NE23 .22 D5
Newcastle-upon-Tyne NE6 .56 E6
Alston Cl Wallsend NE28 .41 A4
Tynemouth NE29 .41 C7
Alston Cres SR6 .75 C4
Alston Gdns NE15 .35 D3
Alston Gr NE26 .24 B7
Alston Rd
New Hartley NE25 .23 D6
Washington NE38 .84 B6
Alston St NE8 .101 A1
Alston Wlk DH6 .96 A1
Alstone Ct NE62 .10 F7
Altan Pl NE12 .39 B7
Altrincham Tower SR3 .91 E8
Alum Well Rd
Gateshead NE9 .70 E5
[1] Gateshead, Low Fell NE9 .70 F5
Alverston Cl NE15 .53 C8
Alverstone Ave NE9 .70 E4
Alverstone Rd SR3 .91 D7
Alverthorpe St NE33 .59 D8
Alveston Cl NE62 .10 F7
Alwin NE38 .83 A1
Alwin Cl DH4 .89 E3
Alwinton Ave NE29 .41 D8
Alwinton Cl Blyth NE24 .17 C8
Newcastle-upon-Tyne NE5 .37 A4
Alwinton Dr DH2 .88 A1
Alwinton Gdns NE11 .70 A5
Alwinton Rd NE27 .31 A3
Alwinton Sq [7] NE63 .6 F2
Alwinton Terr NE3 .38 D5
Amalfi Tower SR3 .91 E8
Amara Sq SR3 .91 E8
Ambassadors Way NE29 .41 B8
Amber Ct NE24 .17 C6
Ambergate Cl NE5 .37 A3
Amberley Chase NE12 .29 E4
Amberley Cl NE28 .41 A3
Amberley Ct NE8 .100 C1
Amberley Gdns NE7 .39 C2
Amberley Prim Sch NE12 .29 E4
Amberley St
Gateshead NE8 .100 C1
Sunderland SR2 .103 B1
Amberley St S SR2 .103 B1
Amberley Way NE24 .17 E5
Amberley Wlk NE16 .69 B5
Amberly Gr NE16 .69 A5
Amble Ave
Whitley Bay NE25 .32 B4
South Shields NE34 .60 B8
Amble Cl Blyth NE24 .17 C5
North Shields NE29 .41 E4
Amble Gr NE2 .56 A7
Amble Pl NE12 .29 F1
Amble Tower SR3 .91 E8
Amble Way NE3 .38 B6
Ambleside NE15 .35 E3
Ambleside Ave NE34 .59 E6
Ambleside Cl NE25 .23 D3
Ambleside Gdns
Newcastle-upon-Tyne NE5 .54 B8
Gateshead NE9 .71 A4
Ambleside Terr SR6 .75 C4
Ambridge Way
Seaton Delaval NE25 .23 A4
Newcastle-upon-Tyne NE3 .37 F5
Ambrose Pl NE6 .57 B6
Ambrose Rd SR3 .91 D8
Amec Dr NE28 .41 A1
Amec Way NE28 .40 E1
Amelia Cl NE4 .54 E3
Amelia Gdns SR3 .91 C7
Amelia Wlk NE4 .54 E3
Amen Cnr NE1 .101 B4
Amersham Pl [1] NE5 .37 B2
Amersham Rd NE24 .17 E4
Amesbury Cl NE5 .36 B3
Amethyst Rd NE4 .100 A2
Amethyst St [1] SR4 .85 F7
Amherst Rd NE3 .37 E6
Amos Ayre Pl NE34 .58 F5
Amsterdam Rd SR3 .91 E8
Amy St SR5 .75 B2
Ancaster Ave NE12 .39 B6
Ancaster Rd NE16 .68 F6
Anchorage The
Chester le Street DH3 .88 D3
Penshaw DH4 .90 B6
Ancona St SR4 .85 F7
Ancroft Ave NE29 .41 F7
Ancroft Pl
Newcastle-upon-Tyne NE5 .54 B8
Ashington NE63 .6 F1

Ancroft Rd NE25 ....23 B3
Ancroft Way NE3 ....37 F8
Ancrum St NE2 ....98 B3
Ancrum Way NE16 ....68 F5
Anderson St NE33 ....42 D3
Andover Pl NE28 ....40 E6
Andrew Rd SR3 ....91 D7
Andrews House Sta*
NE16 ....80 B7
Anfield Ct NE3 ....37 E5
Anfield Rd NE3 ....37 E5
Angel of the North (mon)*
NE9 ....82 A8
Angerton Ave
Shiremoor NE27 ....30 F2
Tynemouth NE30 ....32 A1
Angerton Gdns NE5 ....54 D8
Angerton Terr NE23 ....28 F8
Angle Terr NE28 ....40 F2
Anglesey Gdns NE5 ....36 C2
Anglesey Pl NE4 ....98 B1
Anglesey Rd SR3 ....91 D7
Anglesey Sq SR3 ....91 D7
Angram Dr SR2 ....87 A1
Angram Wlk 1 NE5 ....36 C1
Angrove Gdns SR4 ....85 F5
Angus DH2 ....81 F2
Angus Cl NE12 ....29 C3
Angus Cres NE29 ....41 D3
Angus House NE4 ....54 E4
Angus Rd NE8 ....70 C8
Angus Sq SR3 ....91 D7
Ann St Blaydon NE21 ....53 C3
Shiremoor NE27 ....30 E4
Hebburn NE31 ....57 C7
Gateshead NE8 ....101 C2
Ann Wlk NE6 ....57 A4
Ann's Row NE24 ....12 E1
Anne Dr NE12 ....40 A8
Annfield Rd NE23 ....16 B2
Annie St SR6 ....75 E4
Annitsford Dr NE23 ....29 B8
Annitsford Rd NE23 ....22 E1
Annville Cres NE6 ....57 A4
Anscomb Gdns NE7 ....39 A3
Anson Cl NE33 ....59 B8
Anson Pl NE5 ....36 F3
Anson St NE8 ....56 B1
Anstead Cl NE23 ....22 B6
Anthony Rd SR3 ....91 D8
Anton Pl NE23 ....22 B5
Antonine Wlk NE15 ....34 F2
Antrim Cl NE5 ....37 C3
Antwerp Rd SR3 ....91 C7
Apperley NE5 ....36 E1
Apperley Ave NE3 ....37 C4
Apperley Rd NE43 ....64 C6
Appian Pl Throckley NE15 ....35 E2
Gateshead NE9 ....71 B7
Apple Cl NE15 ....53 C8
Apple Ct NE25 ....23 D6
Appleby Ct
Bournmoor DH4 ....89 D1
North Shields NE29 ....41 F5
Appleby Gdns
Wallsend NE28 ....41 A4
Gateshead NE9 ....71 A3
Appleby Pk NE29 ....41 F6
Appleby Rd SR3 ....91 D7
Appleby Sq SR3 ....91 D7
Appleby St NE29 ....42 A4
Appledore Cl NE40 ....66 E8
Appledore Gdns
Chester le Street DH3 ....88 D5
1 Gateshead NE9 ....70 F3
Appledore Rd NE24 ....17 E5
Appleforth Ave SR2 ....87 A1
Appleton Cl NE11 ....70 A8
Appletree Dr NE42 ....50 D3
Appletree Gardens Fst Sch
NE25 ....31 E4
Appletree Gdns
Whitley Bay NE25 ....31 E3
Newcastle-upon-Tyne NE6 ....39 F1
Appletree La NE45 ....47 A5
Appletree Rise NE45 ....47 A5
Applewood NE12 ....29 F3
Appley Terr SR6 ....75 E2
Apsley Cres NE3 ....37 E5
Aqua Terr NE64 ....7 D4
Aquila Dr NE15 ....34 E2
Arbroath DH2 ....81 F1
Arbroath Rd SR3 ....91 D8
Arcade The 2 NE30 ....42 D7
Arcadia DH2 ....81 F1
Arcadia Ave DH3 ....88 C5
Arcadia Terr NE24 ....17 E6
Archbishop Runcie CE Fst
Sch NE3 ....38 D5
Archbold Terr NE2 ....99 B3
Archer Rd SR3 ....91 D8
Archer Sq SR3 ....91 D8
Archer St NE28 ....40 E3
Archer Villas NE28 ....40 D3
Archibald Fst Sch NE3 ....38 C5
Archibald St NE3 ....38 C5
Arcot Ave
Cramlington NE23 ....21 E8
Whitley Bay NE25 ....31 E3
Arcot Dr Whitley Bay NE25 ....31 E3
Newcastle-upon-Tyne NE5 ....53 F8
Arcot Terr 5 NE24 ....17 D8
Arden Ave NE3 ....28 B1
Arden Cl NE28 ....40 D7
Arden Cres NE5 ....37 D1
Arden Sq SR3 ....91 E8
Ardrossan DH2 ....81 F1
Ardrossan Rd SR3 ....91 D7
Arena Bsns Pk DH4 ....94 C7
Arena Way NE4 ....100 C3
Argus Cl NE11 ....70 B7
Argyle Ct DH9 ....80 A1
Argyle House Sch SR2 ....102 C1
Argyle Pl South Hetton DH6 ....97 F7
Tynemouth NE29 ....42 A8
Argyle Sq SR2 ....102 C1
Argyle St
Newcastle-upon-Tyne NE1 ....99 B1
Blyth NE24 ....12 E1
Tynemouth NE30 ....42 D8
Hebburn NE31 ....57 D7
Sunderland SR2 ....102 C1
Argyle Terr
Tynemouth NE29 ....42 A8
Hexham NE46 ....45 B4
Newbiggin-by-the-Sea NE64 ....7 D4
Argyll DH2 ....81 F1
Ariel St NE63 ....6 E3
Arisaig DH2 ....81 F1
Arkle Rd SR3 ....91 D7
Arkle St Hazlerigg NE13 ....28 A4
Gateshead NE8 ....70 C8
Arklecrag NE37 ....83 C6
Arkleside Pl NE5 ....36 D1
Arkwright St NE8 ....70 D7
Arlington Ave NE3 ....37 F3
Arlington Cl DH4 ....89 E3
Arlington Ct NE3 ....38 A3
Arlington Gr
Whickham NE16 ....69 A6
Cramlington NE23 ....16 B2
Arlington Rd NE31 ....57 F4
Arlington St 3 SR4 ....85 F6
Armitage Gdns NE9 ....71 C1
Armondside Rd NE17 ....77 C6
Armstrong Ave
South Shields NE34 ....59 E6
Newcastle-upon-Tyne NE6 ....39 B1
Armstrong Cl NE46 ....44 F3
Armstrong Dr NE12 ....29 B2
Armstrong Ind Est NE37 ....83 A7
Armstrong Rd
Newcastle-upon-Tyne NE15,
NE4 ....54 B5
Wallsend NE28 ....41 A1
Washington NE37 ....83 A7
Armstrong St
Woolsington NE5 ....36 B7
Gateshead NE8 ....70 D7
Armstrong Terr
South Shields NE33 ....59 C8
Morpeth NE61 ....9 A8
Arn Dr SR2 ....92 F8
Arncliffe Ave SR4 ....85 E4
Arncliffe Gdns NE5 ....36 C2
Arndale Arc 9 NE32 ....58 B7
Arndale Ho
Newcastle-upon-Tyne NE3 ....37 E5
6 Washington NE37 ....83 D8
Arndale House
11 Birtley DH3 ....82 C4
Longbenton NE12 ....39 A6
Arnold Rd SR3 ....91 D8
Arnold St NE35 ....73 F8
Arnside Wlk NE5 ....36 C2
Arran Ct SR3 ....92 A6
Arran Dr NE32 ....58 E3
Arran Gdns NE10 ....71 C7
Arran Pl NE29 ....41 C8
Arras La SR1 ....103 B3
Arrol Pk SR4 ....102 B2
Arrow Cl NE12 ....29 B2
Arthington Way NE34 ....59 E5
Arthur Ave SR2 ....93 A6
Arthur Cook Ave NE16 ....69 C6
Arthur St Blyth NE24 ....17 E8
Jarrow NE32 ....58 B6
Gateshead NE8 ....101 C2
11 Ryhope SR2 ....93 A6
Whitburn SR6 ....60 F4
Arthur Terr SR6 ....60 F3
Arundel Cl
Brunswick Village NE13 ....28 A5
Bedlington NE22 ....11 C3
Arundel Ct NE3 ....37 C7
Arundel Dr
Newcastle-upon-Tyne NE15 ....53 E7
Whitley Bay NE25 ....31 C4
Arundel Gdns
Gateshead NE9 ....71 A5
Sunderland SR3 ....91 C7
Arundel Rd SR3 ....91 D8
Arundel Sq NE63 ....6 C3
Arundel Wlk NE16 ....69 A5
Asama Ct NE4 ....100 A3
Ascham House Sch NE3 ....38 C4
Ascot Cl NE28 ....40 D6
Ascot Cres NE8 ....70 C7
Ascot Ct
Newcastle-upon-Tyne NE3 ....37 C7
Sunderland SR3 ....91 D7
Ascot Gdns NE34 ....59 D7
Ascot Wlk NE3 ....37 C7
Ascott Gr NE63 ....6 D2
Ash Ave NE13 ....27 C7
Ash Banks NE61 ....9 A7
Ash Cl NE46 ....44 E3
Ash Ct NE29 ....31 E1
Ash Gr Dunston NE11 ....54 E1
Wallsend NE28 ....40 D1
Ryton NE40 ....52 C6
Morpeth NE61 ....8 E7
Whitburn SR6 ....61 A2
Ash Mdws NE38 ....88 E7
Ash Sq NE38 ....83 E4
Ash St Blaydon NE21 ....53 C1
Ash St *continued*
Mickley Square NE43 ....64 E8
Ash Terr DH9 ....79 B2
Ash Tree Dr NE22 ....10 F2
Ashberry Gr SR6 ....75 D1
Ashbourne Ave NE6 ....56 F6
Ashbourne Cl NE27 ....30 C5
Ashbourne Cres NE63 ....6 C3
Ashbourne Rd NE32 ....58 C5
Ashbrooke NE25 ....31 E5
Ashbrooke Cl NE25 ....31 E5
Ashbrooke Cres SR2 ....86 D4
Ashbrooke Cross SR2 ....86 C3
Ashbrooke Dr NE20 ....25 E7
Ashbrooke Gdns NE28 ....40 E3
Ashbrooke Mount 6
SR2 ....86 C4
Ashbrooke Range SR2 ....86 D3
Ashbrooke Rd SR2 ....86 C4
Ashbrooke St NE3 ....37 E3
Ashbrooke Terr SR2 ....86 D4
Ashburn Rd NE28 ....40 E6
Ashburne Ct SR2 ....86 D4
Ashburton Rd NE3 ....38 A4
Ashbury NE25 ....31 C6
Ashby St SR2 ....86 F3
Ashcroft Dr NE12 ....39 E7
Ashdale Penshaw DH4 ....89 E8
Ponteland NE20 ....25 C3
Ashdale Cres NE5 ....36 D1
Ashdown Cl NE12 ....39 B7
Ashdown Rd SR3 ....91 D7
Ashdown Way NE12 ....39 B7
Asher St NE10 ....56 C1
Ashfield NE32 ....58 D2
Ashfield Ave NE16 ....69 C8
Ashfield Cl NE4 ....100 A4
Ashfield Ct NE39 ....67 A4
Ashfield Gdns NE28 ....40 A3
Ashfield Gr
Whitley Bay NE26 ....32 A7
6 North Shields NE29 ....42 A6
Ashfield Lodge NE4 ....100 A4
Ashfield Pk NE16 ....69 B8
Ashfield Rd
Whickham NE16 ....69 B5
Newcastle-upon-Tyne NE3 ....38 A4
Ashfield Rise NE16 ....69 B5
Ashfield Terr
Chester le Street DH3 ....88 D2
4 Gateshead NE10 ....56 F1
Ryton NE40 ....52 C5
Ashford NE9 ....71 A1
Ashford Cl Blyth NE24 ....17 E5
Tynemouth NE29 ....31 F1
Ashford Gr NE5 ....36 B4
Ashford Rd SR3 ....91 D7
Ashgill NE37 ....83 B6
Ashgrove Ave NE34 ....59 F4
Ashgrove Terr Birtley DH3 ....82 B5
Gateshead NE8 ....101 B1
Ashill Ct SR2 ....86 D4
Ashington Alexandra Fst Sch
NE63 ....6 F3
Ashington Alexandra Mid Sch
NE63 ....6 E4
Ashington Central Fst Sch
NE63 ....6 D3
Ashington Comm High Sch
NE63 ....6 B3
Ashington Dr NE62 ....11 A8
Ashington Hawthorn Fst Sch
NE63 ....6 D1
Ashington Hirst Park Mid Sch
NE63 ....6 E3
Ashington Hospl NE63 ....6 C3
Ashington Rd NE61 ....1 D4
Ashington Seaton Hirst Com
Mid Sch NE63 ....7 A2
Ashington Wansbeck Fst Sch
NE63 ....6 A4
Ashkirk Annitsford NE23 ....29 A8
Sunderland SR3 ....91 E8
Ashkirk Cl DH2 ....88 A1
Ashkirk Way NE25 ....23 D2
Ashleigh DH2 ....88 A5
Ashleigh Cl NE21 ....53 E1
Ashleigh Cres NE5 ....54 A8
Ashleigh Gdns SR6 ....60 A2
Ashleigh Gr
Longbenton NE12 ....39 D7
Newcastle-upon-Tyne NE2 ....38 D2
Tynemouth NE30 ....42 C8
Sunderland SR6 ....75 E4
Ashleigh Rd NE5 ....54 A8
Ashleigh Sch NE30 ....42 B5
Ashleigh Special Sch
NE30 ....42 A6
Ashleigh Villas 2 NE36 ....74 D7
Ashley Cl Killingworth NE12 ....29 F4
Washington NE38 ....83 D3
Ashley Gdns NE62 ....11 A8
Ashley Rd NE34 ....59 C6
Ashley Road Cty Prim Sch
NE34 ....59 C6
Ashley Terr DH3 ....88 C4
Ashmead Cl NE12 ....29 E4
Ashmore St SR2 ....103 A1
Ashmore Terr SR2 ....103 A1
Asholme NE5 ....36 E1
Ashridge Cl NE34 ....60 B5
Ashridge Ct NE10 ....72 C7
Ashton Cl NE5 ....36 B4
Ashton Ct NE40 ....52 D4
Ashton Downe 2 DH2 ....88 C2
Ashton Rise DH2 ....88 C2
Ashton Way
Whitley Bay NE26 ....31 E7
Ashton Way *continued*
Sunderland SR3 ....91 C6
Ashtree Cl
Rowlands Gill NE39 ....67 F3
Newcastle-upon-Tyne NE4 ....54 F4
Ashtree Gdns NE25 ....31 E3
Ashtree La NE21,NE39 ....67 B5
Ashtrees Gdns NE9 ....70 F7
Ashvale Ave NE11 ....81 C6
Ashwell Rd SR3 ....91 D7
Ashwood Ave SR5 ....74 F2
Ashwood Cl
Longbenton NE12 ....39 E8
Cramlington NE23 ....16 C2
Ashwood Cres NE6 ....39 F1
Ashwood Croft NE31 ....57 D7
Ashwood Gdns NE9 ....71 A2
Ashwood Gr
Wide Open NE13 ....28 B5
4 Sunderland SR5 ....74 B1
Ashwood Rd NE46 ....45 C4
Ashwood St SR2 ....102 B1
Ashwood Terr SR2 ....102 B1
Askern Ave SR2 ....87 A1
Askew Rd NE8 ....101 B3
Askew Rd W NE8 ....100 C1
Askrigg Ave
Wallsend NE28 ....40 D7
Sunderland SR2 ....86 F1
Askrigg Cl DH2 ....81 E2
Askrigg Wlk 2 NE5 ....36 C1
Aspen Ct SR3 ....91 E6
Aspen Terr NE5 ....37 E1
Aspen Way NE24 ....17 D4
Aspenlaw NE9 ....71 C4
Aspley Cl SR3 ....92 A6
Association Rd 4 SR6 ....75 E2
Aster Pl NE4 ....54 C7
Aster Terr DH4 ....90 B4
Astley Com High Sch
NE25 ....23 C3
Astley Ct NE12 ....29 D3
Astley Dr NE26 ....31 E8
Astley Gdns
Seaton Delaval NE25 ....23 C3
Seaton Sluice NE26 ....24 B7
Astley Gr NE26 ....24 B7
Astley Rd NE25 ....23 C4
Astley St NE23 ....16 B3
Aston Sq SR3 ....91 D7
Aston St NE33 ....59 D7
Aston Way NE16 ....68 F5
Aston Wlk NE6 ....57 A6
Athelhampton NE38 ....84 A5
Athenaeum Rigg SR2 ....93 A7
Athenaeum St SR1 ....103 A2
Atherton Dr
Fence Houses DH4 ....94 A7
Newcastle-upon-Tyne NE4 ....54 E4
Atherton House NE4 ....54 E4
Athlone Ct NE24 ....17 E8
Athlone Pl DH3 ....82 D1
Athol Gdns
Whitley Bay NE25 ....31 D3
Ryhope SR2 ....93 A6
Athol Gn NE11 ....100 A1
Athol Gr SR3 ....92 A7
Athol House NE20 ....25 F6
Athol Pk 8 SR2 ....86 E4
Athol Rd SR2 ....103 B1
Athol St NE11 ....100 A1
Athol Terr SR2 ....103 B1
Atholl DH2 ....81 F2
Atholl Gdns NE9 ....71 B7
Atkin St NE12 ....29 B5
Atkinson Gdns NE29 ....42 A3
Atkinson Ho Sch NE23 ....22 F2
Atkinson Rd
Chester le Street DH3 ....88 D5
Newcastle-upon-Tyne NE4 ....54 D4
Sunderland SR6 ....75 E4
Atkinson Road Prim Sch
NE4 ....54 D4
Atkinson St NE28 ....40 B1
Atkinson Terr
Wallsend NE28 ....40 B1
5 Newcastle-upon-Tyne
NE4 ....54 D5
Atkinson's Bldgs SR4 ....102 B3
Atlantis Rd SR3 ....91 C8
Atley Way NE23 ....15 E2
Attlee Cl NE23 ....29 B5
Attlee Cres DH6 ....97 E1
Attlee Gr SR2 ....92 E8
Attlee Terr NE64 ....7 F5
Attwood Gr SR5 ....75 B2
Aubone Ave NE15 ....54 C6
Auburn Cl NE28 ....41 A2
Auburn Ct NE28 ....41 B2
Auburn Gdns NE4 ....54 E8
Auburn Pl NE61 ....8 E8
Auckland DH2 ....88 A3
Auckland Ave NE34 ....60 B6
Auckland Rd NE31 ....57 F7
Auckland Terr NE32 ....58 E4
Auden Gr NE4 ....54 E6
Audland Wlk 3 NE5 ....36 C1
Audley Ct NE2 ....38 F2
Audley Gdns SR3 ....86 B3
Audley Rd NE3 ....38 E4
Audouins Row NE8 ....70 E8
August Pl NE33 ....42 D1
Augusta Ct NE28 ....40 E6
Augusta Sq SR3 ....91 D7
Augustus Dr NE22 ....10 E2
Austen Ave NE34 ....59 B4
Austin Sq SR5 ....75 B2
Austral Pl NE13 ....28 A5
Australia Gr NE34 ....58 F3
Australia Tower SR3 ....91 E8
Austwick Wlk 4 NE5 ....36 C1
Autumn Cl NE38 ....83 D6
Avalon Dr NE15 ....53 E8
Avalon Rd SR3 ....91 D8
Avebury Ave NE62 ....11 A7
Avebury Dr NE38 ....83 E5
Avebury Pl NE23 ....16 C1
Avenue Cres NE25 ....23 C4
Avenue Rd
Seaton Delaval NE25 ....23 C3
Gateshead NE8 ....70 F8
Avenue Terr
Seaton Delaval NE25 ....23 D3
1 Sunderland SR2 ....86 C4
Avenue The
Chester le Street DH2 ....88 B3
Birtley DH3 ....82 C4
Bournmoor DH3 ....89 E6
Hetton le Hole DH5 ....95 B4
7 Gateshead, Felling NE10 ....56 D1
Blaydon NE21 ....53 E2
Seaton Delaval NE25,NE26 ....23 E5
Seaton Sluice NE26 ....24 A6
Whitley Bay NE26 ....32 A5
Wallsend NE28 ....40 B1
Washington NE38 ....83 E5
Rowlands Gill NE39 ....67 F1
Corbridge NE45 ....46 F6
Morpeth NE61 ....8 F6
Gateshead, Carr Hill NE9 ....71 B7
Sunderland SR2 ....103 A1
Avenue Vivian
Fence Houses DH4 ....90 A1
Great Lumley DH4 ....89 F1
Aviemore Rd NE36 ....74 B7
Avis Ave NE64 ....7 C3
Avison Ct NE4 ....98 B2
Avison Pl NE4 ....98 B2
Avison St NE4 ....98 B2
Avocet Cl NE24 ....17 E3
Avolon Ct NE4 ....98 B2
Avolon Pl NE4 ....98 B2
Avolon Wlk NE4 ....98 B2
Avon Ave
North Shields NE29 ....41 E4
Hedworth NE32 ....58 C2
Avon Cl Wallsend NE28 ....40 D6
Rowlands Gill NE39 ....67 F3
Avon Cres DH4 ....94 A8
Avon Ct NE25 ....23 D6
Avon Rd NE31 ....57 F4
Avon St Gateshead NE8 ....56 A1
Sunderland SR2 ....103 C2
Avon Terr
Washington NE38 ....83 E4
Washington NE38 ....83 F4
Avondale SR4 ....85 A5
Avondale Ave
Penshaw DH4 ....90 B7
Longbenton NE12 ....39 D8
Blyth NE24 ....16 E8
Avondale Cl 1 NE24 ....16 F8
Avondale Ct NE3 ....38 D4
Avondale Gdns
West Boldon NE36 ....74 A7
Ashington NE63 ....7 A2
Avondale Ho NE6 ....56 C5
Avondale Rd
Ponteland NE20 ....25 A2
Newcastle-upon-Tyne NE6 ....56 C5
Avondale Rise 5 NE6 ....56 C5
Avondale Terr
Chester le Street DH3 ....88 C3
West Boldon NE36 ....74 A7
Gateshead NE8 ....101 B1
Avonlea Way NE5 ....37 C3
Avonmouth Rd SR3 ....91 D7
Avonmouth Sq SR3 ....91 D7
Awnless Ct NE34 ....59 C5
Axbridge Cl NE62 ....11 A7
Axbridge Gdns NE4 ....54 E5
Axford Terr NE17 ....77 B6
Axminster Cl NE23 ....16 D1
Axwell Dr NE24 ....17 B7
Axwell Park Cl 3 NE16 ....69 A7
Axwell Park Rd NE21 ....53 E1
Axwell Park View NE15 ....54 B5
Axwell Terr NE16 ....54 A1
Axwell View
Whickham NE16 ....69 A7
Blaydon NE21 ....53 C1
Aycliffe Ave NE9 ....71 E4
Aycliffe Cres NE9 ....71 D4
Aycliffe Pl NE9 ....71 E4
Aydon Ave NE45 ....47 A6
Aydon Castle* NE45 ....129 C3
Aydon Cl NE30 ....32 C1
Aydon Cres NE45 ....47 B6
Aydon Dr NE45 ....47 A6
Aydon Gdns NE45 ....47 A6
Aydon Gr Jarrow NE32 ....58 B3
Corbridge NE45 ....47 A6
Aydon Ho SR3 ....91 E7
Aydon Rd NE45 ....47 C7
Aydon Rd Est NE45 ....47 A6
Aydon Wlk NE5 ....36 E1
Aylesbury Dr SR3 ....92 A5
Aylesbury Pl NE12 ....39 B7
Aylesford Sq NE24 ....17 E5
Aylsham Cl NE5 ....36 B4
Aylsham Ct SR3 ....92 A4
Aylyth Pl NE3 ....37 F3
Ayr Dr NE32 ....58 E3

Ayre's Quay Rd SR1 .102 C3
Ayre's Terr NE29 .42 A6
Ayrey Ave NE34 .58 F4
Aysgarth Ave
Wallsend NE28 .40 D7
Sunderland SR2 .86 F2
Aysgarth Gn NE3 .37 F4
Ayton Ave SR2 .87 A1
Ayton Cl Stocksfield NE43 .64 D6
Newcastle-upon-Tyne NE5 .36 E3
Ayton Ct NE22 .10 D2
Ayton Prim Sch NE38 .82 F3
Ayton Rd NE38 .82 F4
Ayton Rise NE6 .56 C5
Ayton St NE6 .56 D5
Azalea Ave SR2 .102 C1
Azalea Terr N SR2 .102 C1
Azalea Terr S SR2 .102 C1

B

Back Albion St SR4 .85 A6
Back Beaumont Terr NE3 .38 D5
Back Bridge St SR1 .103 A3
Back Buttsfield Terr DH4 .90 B8
Back Chapman St NE6 .56 C7
Back Coronation Terr DH5 .95 A2
Back Croft Rd NE24 .17 E7
Back George St NE4 .100 C4
Back Goldspink La NE2 .99 C3
Back Hawthorn Rd W NE3 .38 C4
Back Heaton Park Rd 9 NE6 .56 B6
Back High St NE3 .38 C4
Back Hylton Rd SR4 .102 B3
Back La Great Lumley DH3 .89 A5
Penshaw DH4 .90 B8
Blaydon NE21 .53 B2
Whitley Bay NE25 .31 E5
Back Lodge Terr SR1 .103 C2
Back Maling St NE6 .56 A5
Back Mitford St NE4 .100 B3
Back Mowbray Terr NE62 .10 F7
Back New Bridge St NE1, NE2 .99 C2
Back North Bridge St SR5 .103 A4
Back Percy Gdns NE30 .42 D8
Back Riggs 9 NE61 .3 F1
Back Row Whickham NE16 .69 B7
Hexham NE46 .45 B5
Back Ryhope St SR2 .92 E7
Back Shipley Rd 11 NE30 .42 D7
Back St NE21 .53 B1
Back Stephen St 6 NE6 .56 A6
Back Walker Rd NE6 .57 A4
Back Woodbine St NE8 .101 B1
Backview Ct SR5 .75 C3
Backworth La NE23,NE27 .29 F7
Backworth Park Prim Sch NE27 .30 C5
Backworth Terr NE27 .30 D1
Baden Cres SR5 .74 A3
Baden Powell St NE9 .71 A7
Baden St DH3 .88 C2
Bader Ct NE24 .17 F6
Badger Cl SR3 .92 A5
Badger Mews NE9 .71 F2
Badger's Wood DH9 .80 A1
Badgers Gn NE61 .3 D2
Badminton Cl NE35 .58 E1
Baffin Ct SR3 .91 F6
Baildon Cl NE28 .40 C4
Bailey Green Prim Sch NE12 .29 C4
Bailey Sq SR5 .74 A4
Bailey St DH9 .79 B2
Bailey Way DH5 .95 B2
Bainbridge Ave
South Shields NE34 .58 F4
Sunderland SR3 .86 B3
Bainbridge Holme Cl SR3 .86 B3
Bainbridge Holme Rd SR3 .86 C3
Bainford Ave NE15 .54 A7
Baird Ave NE28 .41 C2
Baird Cl NE37 .72 E2
Baird Ct NE8 .56 B1
Baird St SR5 .74 A3
Baker Gdns
Gateshead NE10 .72 B8
1 Dunston NE11 .54 F1
Baker Sq SR5 .74 A3
Baker St
Houghton-le-Spring DH5 .90 E1
Sunderland SR5 .74 A3
Bakewell Terr NE6 .56 D4
Baldersdale Gdns SR2 .86 B2
Baldwin Ave
East Boldon NE36 .74 E8
Newcastle-upon-Tyne NE4 .54 F7
Balfour Rd NE15 .54 A6
Balfour St
Houghton-le-Spring DH5 .90 E1
2 Blyth NE24 .17 D8
Gateshead NE8 .101 A1
Balfour Terr NE17 .66 B1
Balgonie Cotts NE40 .52 C5
Baliol Rd NE43 .64 D7
Balkwell Ave NE29 .41 D5
Balkwell Gn NE29 .41 E6
Ballast Hill NE24 .17 F8
Ballast Hill Rd NE29 .42 A3
Balliol Ave NE12 .29 C1
Balliol Bsns Pk NE12 .39 A7
Balliol Gdns NE7 .39 B5
Balliol Prim Sch NE12 .39 B6
Balmain Rd NE5 .37 E4
Balmlaw NE9 .71 D4
Balmoral Ave
Newcastle-upon-Tyne NE3 .38 E4
Brockley Whins NE32 .58 E3
Balmoral Cl NE22 .11 C2
Balmoral Cres DH5 .94 F7
Balmoral Ct 5 SR5 .74 A3
Balmoral Dr NE10 .71 C8
Balmoral Gdns
Whitley Bay NE26 .31 F6
Tynemouth NE29 .41 F7
Balmoral St NE28 .40 B2
Balmoral Terr
Newcastle-upon-Tyne, South Gosforth NE3 .38 E4
Newcastle-upon-Tyne, Heaton NE6 .56 B8
Sunderland, Grangetown SR2 .86 F2
Sunderland, East Herrington SR3 .91 C7
Balmoral Way
Gateshead NE10 .71 C8
Blyth NE24 .17 C3
Balroy Ct NE12 .39 E7
Baltic Ctr for Contemporary Art NE8 .101 C4
Baltic Ind Pk NE28 .41 E3
Baltic Rd NE10 .56 D3
Baltimore Ave SR5 .73 E3
Baltimore Ct NE37 .83 C8
Baltimore Sq SR5 .73 F3
Bamborough Ct NE23 .29 A8
Bamborough Terr NE30 .42 A7
Bambro' St SR2 .103 B1
Bamburgh Ave NE33, NE34 .43 A1
Bamburgh Castle* NE69 .109 C5
Bamburgh Cl Blyth NE24 .17 C7
Washington NE38 .83 B5
Bamburgh Cres
Shiney Row DH4 .90 B5
Shiremoor NE27 .30 F3
Bamburgh Ct
Newcastle-upon-Tyne NE7 .38 F5
Gateshead NE8 .70 C7
Bamburgh Dr
Gateshead NE10 .57 B2
Wallsend NE28 .40 F2
Pegswood NE61 .4 F3
Bamburgh Gdns SR3 .86 B3
Bamburgh Gr
Jarrow NE32 .58 B4
South Shields NE34 .60 B8
Bamburgh Ho NE5 .36 E3
Bamburgh Rd
Longbenton NE12 .29 F1
Newcastle-upon-Tyne NE5 .36 E3
Bamburgh Sch NE34 .60 A8
Bamburgh Terr
18 Newcastle-upon-Tyne NE6 .56 C6
Ashington NE63 .6 C3
Bamburgh Wlk NE3 .38 A6
Bamford Terr NE12 .29 F1
Bamford Wlk NE34 .59 D5
Bampton Ave SR6 .75 C5
Banbury NE37 .83 E8
Banbury Ave SR5 .74 A4
Banbury Gdns NE28 .40 D5
Banbury Rd NE3 .37 F6
Banbury Terr NE33,NE34 .59 D8
Banbury Way Blyth NE24 .17 E5
North Shields NE29 .41 D4
Bancroft Terr SR4 .85 F6
Banesley La NE11 .70 B1
Banff St SR5 .74 A4
Bangor Sq NE32 .58 A1
Bank Ave NE16 .69 A7
Bank Ct Blaydon NE21 .53 F4
North Shields NE30 .42 B5
Bank Head NE46 .45 B5
Bank Top Tynemouth NE30 .32 C3
Crawcrook NE40 .51 E3
Greenside NE40 .52 B3
Bank Top Hamlet 4 NE16 .69 A7
Bankdale Gdns NE24 .17 A7
Bankfoot Sta NE3 .37 B6
Bankhead Rd NE15 .35 F1
Bankhead Terr DH4 .94 A8
Bankside NE61 .9 A8
Bankside La NE34 .59 C5
Bankside Rd NE15 .53 F5
Bankside Wlk NE62 .11 B8
Bankwell La NE8 .101 B4
Bannerman Terr DH6 .96 C1
Bannister Dr NE12 .40 A8
Bannockburn NE12 .29 C4
Barbara Priestman Sch SR2 .86 B4
Barbara St SR2 .86 F2
Barbary Dr SR6 .75 F2
Barbondale Lonnen NE5 .36 C2
Barbour Ave NE34 .60 A7
Barclay Pl NE5 .37 B1
Barclay St SR6 .103 A4
Barcusclose La DH9,NE16 .79 D5
Bardolph Rd NE29 .41 D6
Bardon Cl NE5 .36 F4
Bardon Cres NE25 .23 F2
Bardon Ct NE34 .59 E5
Bardsey Pl NE12 .39 B7
Barehirst St NE33 .59 B7
Barents Cl 2 NE5 .36 F2
Baret Rd
Newcastle-upon-Tyne, Walker NE6 .56 F7
Newcastle-upon-Tyne, Walkergate NE6 .56 E8
Barford Ct NE9 .71 A2
Barford Dr DH2 .88 A1
Baring St NE33 .42 D4
Barker St NE2 .99 C2
Barking Cres SR5 .73 F3
Barking Sq SR5 .73 F3
Barkwood Rd NE39 .67 D2
Barley Mow DH3 .88 D8
Barley Mow Prim Schs DH3 .82 D1
Barlow Cres NE21 .67 C6
Barlow Fell Rd NE21 .67 C5
Barlow La NE21 .67 E7
Barlowfield Cl NE21 .68 A8
Barmoor Bank NE61 .9 D5
Barmoor Castle* TD15 .107 E7
Barmoor La NE40 .52 B5
Barmoor Pl NE40 .52 B5
Barmoor Terr NE40 .52 A5
Barmouth Cl NE28 .40 D5
Barmouth Rd NE29 .41 C5
Barmston Cl NE38 .83 F4
Barmston Ct NE38 .83 F4
Barmston La NE38 .84 C6
Barmston Rd NE38 .84 A4
Barmston Village Prim Sch NE38 .83 F5
Barmston Way NE38 .83 F6
Barn The 3 DH2 .88 B1
Barnabas Pl SR2 .103 C1
Barnard Cl NE22 .10 E1
Barnard Cres NE31 .57 E7
Barnard Gn NE3 .37 E7
Barnard Gr NE32 .58 D4
Barnard Pk DH5 .95 A4
Barnard St Blyth NE24 .17 E7
Sunderland SR4 .85 F5
Barnes Jun & Inf Schs SR4 .85 F4
Barnes Park Rd SR4 .86 A4
Barnes St DH5 .95 A4
Barnes View SR4 .85 F4
Barnes' Rd NE33 .59 B8
Barnesbury Rd NE4 .54 E5
Barnett Ct SR5 .75 B2
Barningham NE38 .84 A5
Barningham Cl SR3 .86 B2
Barns Cl NE32 .58 A4
Barnstaple Cl NE28 .40 C5
Barnstaple Rd NE29 .31 D1
Barnston NE63 .7 B3
Barnton Rd NE10 .71 E6
Barnwell Prim Sch DH4 .90 B7
Barnwood Cl NE28 .40 C5
Baron's Quay Rd SR5 .85 B8
Baroness Dr NE15 .54 A7
Baronswood NE3 .38 B5
Barpett Sq DH6 .97 F3
Barr Cl NE28 .40 E5
Barrack Ct NE4 .98 C2
Barrack Rd NE2,NE4 .98 B3
Barrack Row DH4 .90 A6
Barrack St SR1 .103 C4
Barrack Terr NE11 .81 D6
Barracks Museum* TD15 .105 B6
Barras Ave
Annitsford NE23 .22 B1
Blyth NE24 .17 E5
Barras Ave W NE24 .17 D5
Barras Bridge NE1 .99 A2
Barras Dr SR3 .86 B3
Barras Gdns NE23 .22 B1
Barras Mews NE23 .22 F1
Barrasford Cl
Newcastle-upon-Tyne NE3 .38 A4
Ashington NE63 .6 A2
Barrasford Dr NE13 .28 C5
Barrasford Rd NE23 .22 C6
Barrasford St NE28 .41 C1
Barrass Ave NE23 .22 F1
Barrie Sq SR5 .75 B2
Barrington Ave NE30 .31 F2
Barrington Ct
Hetton le Hole DH5 .95 A4
Bedlington NE22 .16 A8
Barrington Dr NE38 .83 D4
Barrington Ind Est NE22 .11 B4
Barrington Pk NE22 .11 F3
Barrington Pl
Newcastle-upon-Tyne NE4 .98 B2
Gateshead NE8 .101 A2
Barrington Rd NE22 .11 B3
Barrington St NE33 .42 C3
Barrington Terr DH5 .95 A5
Barron St S 5 SR5 .74 C1
Barrow St SR5 .73 F4
Barrowburn Pl NE23 .23 A1
Barry St Dunston NE11 .54 F1
Gateshead NE8 .70 D7
Barton Cl Wallsend NE28 .40 D5
Tynemouth NE30 .32 B1
Washington NE37 .72 F2
Barton Ct SR6 .75 C5
Bartram Gdns NE8 .70 E7
Bartram St SR5 .75 C3
Barwell Cl NE28 .40 D5
Barwell Ct NE7 .39 E3
Basil Way NE34 .59 E3
Basildon Gdns NE28 .40 C5
Basingstoke Pl NE12 .39 C7
Baslow Gdns SR3 .86 B3
Bassenfell Ct NE37 .83 B6
Bassenthwaite Ave 4 DH2 .88 B1
Bassington Ave NE23 .21 E7
Bassington Cl NE4 .98 B2
Bassington Dr NE23 .21 E8
Bassington Ind Est NE23 .21 D8
Bassington La NE23 .21 D8
Bat House Rd NE43 .64 B5
Bates La NE21 .53 F2
Bath Cl NE28 .40 E5
Bath La
Newcastle-upon-Tyne NE1, NE4 .98 C1
Blyth NE24 .17 F7
Bath Rd Gateshead NE10 .56 D2
Hebburn NE31 .57 E3
Bath Sq NE32 .58 A1
Bath St NE6 .57 B6
Bath Terr Blyth NE24 .17 F7
Newcastle-upon-Tyne NE3 .38 D5
Tynemouth NE30 .42 D7
Bathgate Ave SR5 .73 F3
Bathgate Cl NE28 .40 E5
Bathgate Sq SR5 .73 F3
Batley St SR5 .73 F3
Battle Hill NE46 .45 B4
Battle Hill Dr NE28 .40 D5
Battle Hill Fst Sch NE28 .40 D5
Baugh Cl NE37 .83 A7
Baulkham Hills DH4 .90 B7
Bavington NE10 .72 A5
Bavington Dr NE5 .37 D1
Bavington Gdns NE30 .32 B1
Bavington Rd NE25 .23 D2
Bawtry Gr NE29 .41 E5
Baxter Ave NE4 .54 E6
Baxter Pl NE25 .23 D3
Baxter Rd SR5 .73 F4
Baxter Sq SR5 .73 F4
Baxter's Bldgs NE25 .23 D3
Baxterwood Ct NE4 .98 A2
Baxterwood Gr NE4 .98 A2
Bay View W NE64 .7 E4
Baybridge Rd NE5 .36 E3
Bayfield Gdns NE8 .56 B1
Baysdale DH4 .89 E8
Bayswater Ave SR5 .74 A3
Bayswater Rd
Newcastle-upon-Tyne NE2 .38 E2
Gateshead NE8 .71 B8
Bayswater Sq 1 SR5 .74 A3
Baytree Gdns NE25 .31 F3
Baywood Gr NE28 .40 C5
Beach Ave NE26 .32 A5
Beach Croft Ave NE30 .32 B1
Beach Rd Tynemouth NE29 .42 A8
South Shields NE33 .42 E3
Beach St SR4 .102 B4
Beach Terr NE64 .7 D3
Beach Way NE30 .32 A1
Beachcross Rd SR4 .102 B1
Beaches The NE4 .100 A3
Beachville St SR4 .102 B1
Beachway NE24 .18 A4
Beacon Ct
Brunswick Village NE13 .28 A6
Gateshead NE9 .71 B5
Beacon Dr
Brunswick Village NE13 .28 A5
Sunderland SR6 .75 F1
Beacon Glade NE34 .60 C6
Beacon Ho 4 NE26 .31 F8
Beacon La NE23 .21 E6
Beacon Lough Rd NE9 .71 A4
Beacon Rise NE9 .71 B5
Beacon St
North Shields NE30 .42 C6
South Shields NE33 .42 D5
Gateshead NE9 .71 A5
Beaconsfield Ave NE9 .71 A5
Beaconsfield Cl NE25 .31 D7
Beaconsfield Cres 3 NE9 .71 A5
Beaconsfield Rd NE9 .70 F5
Beaconsfield St
Blyth NE24 .17 F7
Newcastle-upon-Tyne NE4 .98 A2
Beaconsfield Terr
Birtley DH3 .82 B4
Chopwell NE17 .66 B1
Beaconside NE34 .60 C5
Beadling Gdns NE4 .54 E6
Beadnell Ave NE29 .41 D4
Beadnell Cl
3 Chester le Street DH2 .88 A1
Blaydon NE21 .68 A8
Beadnell Ct NE28 .40 E5
Beadnell Gdns NE27 .30 F3
Beadnell Pl NE2 .99 C2
Beadnell Rd NE24 .17 B5
Beadnell Way NE3 .38 A6
Beagle Sq 6 SR3 .92 A7
Beal Cl NE24 .17 C7
Beal Dr NE12 .29 F1
Beal Gdns NE28 .40 F5
Beal Gn NE5 .37 C4
Beal Rd NE27 .30 F3
Beal Terr NE6 .56 F4
Beal Way NE3 .38 B6
Beaminster Way NE3 .37 C5
Beamish Cl NE28 .40 C5
Beamish Ct NE25 .31 E3
Beamish Gdns NE9 .71 D4
Beamish Open Air Mus* DH9 .80 D2
Beamishburn Rd DH9, NE16 .80 B3
Beamsley Terr NE63 .6 D3
Beanley Ave
Newcastle-upon-Tyne NE15 .53 C6
Hebburn NE31 .57 D4
Beanley Cres NE30 .42 D7
Beanley Pl NE7 .39 A3
Bearl View NE43 .64 E8
Beatrice Ave NE24 .17 B4
Beatrice Gdns
South Shields NE34 .59 F6
7 East Boldon NE36 .74 D7
Beatrice Rd NE6 .39 B1
Beatrice St Ashington NE63 .6 E4
Sunderland SR6 .75 E2
Beatrice Terr
Penshaw DH4 .89 E8
Shiney Row DH4 .90 B6
Beattie St NE34 .59 B5
Beatty Ave
Newcastle-upon-Tyne NE2 .38 E3
Sunderland SR5 .73 F3
Beatty Rd NE22 .16 B8
Beaufort Cl
Shiney Row DH4 .90 B5
Newcastle-upon-Tyne NE5 .37 D3
Beaufort Gdns NE28 .40 C5
Beaufront Ave NE46 .45 D4
Beaufront Cl NE10 .72 B6
Beaufront Gdns NE5 .37 C1
Beaufront Terr
Jarrow NE32 .58 B3
South Shields NE33 .59 C8
Beauly NE38 .83 D3
Beaumaris Gdns SR3 .91 C7
Beaumaris Way NE5 .37 B4
Beaumont Ct NE25 .31 D6
Beaumont Dr
Whitley Bay NE25 .31 D7
Washington NE38 .83 D5
Beaumont Manor NE24 .16 F7
Beaumont St Blyth NE24 .17 D8
North Shields NE29 .42 A5
Newcastle-upon-Tyne NE4 .54 F3
Hexham NE46 .45 B5
Sunderland SR2 .86 E4
Sunderland, Southwick SR5 .75 A2
Beaumont Terr
Brunswick Village NE13 .28 A6
Newcastle-upon-Tyne, Gosforth NE3 .38 D5
Jarrow NE32 .58 A5
Prudhoe NE42 .50 A2
Newcastle-upon-Tyne, Westerhope NE5 .36 F3
Beaumont Way NE42 .50 B1
Bebdon Ct NE24 .17 C6
Bebside Furnace Rd NE22,NE24 .16 D8
Bebside Rd NE24 .16 C7
Beckenham Ave NE36 .74 D8
Beckenham Cl NE36 .74 E8
Beckenham Gdns NE28 .40 C4
Beckett St NE8 .56 A4
Beckfoot Cl NE5 .37 B1
Beckford NE38 .84 A4
Beckford Cl NE28 .40 C5
Beckside Gdns NE5 .36 B1
Beckwith Rd SR3 .91 C8
Beda Cotts DH9 .79 A2
Beda Hill NE21 .53 C3
Bedale Cl NE28 .40 C5
Bedale Cres SR5 .74 A3
Bedale Ct
South Shields NE34 .59 A5
Gateshead NE9 .71 B2
Bedale Dr NE25 .31 F3
Bedale Gn NE5 .37 D3
Bedale St DH5 .95 A2
Bedburn NE38 .82 F1
Bedburn Ave SR5 .74 C2
Bede Burn Jun & Inf Sch NE32 .58 A4
Bede Burn Rd NE32 .58 B5
Bede Burn View NE32 .58 B5
Bede Cl NE12 .40 C8
Bede Com Prim Sch NE10 .56 B2
Bede Cres Wallsend NE28 .40 E3
Washington NE38 .83 D6
Bede Ct
Chester le Street DH3 .88 C3
Tynemouth NE30 .32 C3
Gateshead NE8 .56 A2
Bede Ho 9 SR3 .91 D7
Bede Ind Est NE32 .58 E6
Bede Precinct 7 NE32 .58 B7
Bede St SR6 .75 E2
Bede Sta NE32 .58 E6
Bede Terr
Chester le Street DH2 .88 B3
Jarrow NE32 .58 C5
East Boldon NE36 .74 E7
Bede Wlk
Newcastle-upon-Tyne NE3 .38 E5
Hebburn NE31 .57 F5
Bede's World (Mus)* NE32 .58 D7
Bedeburn Foot NE5 .36 F5
Bedeburn Rd NE5 .36 F5
Bedesway NE32 .58 E6
Bedewell Ind Pk NE31 .58 A5
Bedewell Jun Mix & Inf Sch NE31 .57 F6

Bedford Ave Birtley DH3 ...82 D1
Chester le Street DH3 .....88 D8
Wallsend NE28 ....40 A3
South Shields NE33 ....42 C1
Bedford Ct NE30 ....42 B5
Bedford Pl
Newcastle-upon-Tyne NE5 ..36 C1
Gateshead NE8 ....101 B2
New Silksworth SR3 ....92 A8
Bedford St
Hetton le Hole DH5 ....94 F4
North Shields NE29,NE30 ...42 B5
Sunderland SR1 ....103 A3
Bedford Way NE29 ....42 B5
Bedlington Bank NE22, NE24 ....16 A7
Bedlington West End Fst Sch NE22 ....10 E1
Bedlingtonshire High Sch NE22 ....11 D2
Beech Ave
4 Houghton-le-Spring DH4 .94 D8
Dinnington NE13 ....27 B7
Whickham NE16 ....69 C8
Cramlington NE23 ....22 D5
Newcastle-upon-Tyne NE3 ..37 F6
Hexham NE46 ....44 E5
Morpeth NE61 ....9 C7
Whitburn SR6 ....60 F1
Beech Cl NE3 ....28 C1
Beech Ct Ponteland NE20 ..25 A1
North Shields NE29 ....41 F6
Tynemouth NE29 ....31 E1
Newcastle-upon-Tyne NE3 ..38 C4
Beech Dr Dunston NE11 ..54 E1
Corbridge NE45 ....47 B6
Ellington NE61 ....1 D5
Beech Gdns NE9 ....70 F6
Beech Gr Longbenton NE12 .39 D6
Blackhall Mill NE17 ....77 B6
Bedlington NE22 ....11 A1
Whitley Bay NE26 ....31 F5
Wallsend NE28 ....40 B2
South Shields NE34 ....59 F4
Prudhoe NE42 ....50 B2
Springwell NE9 ....71 F1
Beech Gr S NE42 ....50 B2
Beech Grove Ct NE40 .....51 F4
Beech Grove Rd NE4 ....100 A4
Beech Grove Terr NE40 ...51 F4
Beech Grove Terr S NE40 .51 F4
Beech Hill NE46 ....44 E5
Beech Sq NE38 ....83 E4
Beech St Sunniside NE16 ...69 B2
Jarrow NE32 ....58 A7
Newcastle-upon-Tyne NE4 ..54 E5
Mickley Square NE43 ......64 E8
Gateshead NE8 ....56 B1
Beech Terr
Burnopfield NE16 ....79 C6
Blaydon NE21 ....53 C2
Ashington NE63 ....6 E2
Beech Way NE12 ....29 C4
Beechburn Wlk NE4 ....98 A1
Beechcroft NE3 ....38 B2
Beechcroft Ave NE3 ......38 A3
Beecher St NE24 ....17 B8
Beeches The
Longbenton NE12 ....39 D6
Ponteland NE20 ....25 D6
Stannington NE61 ....14 C4
Beechfield Gdns NE28 ....40 A3
Beechfield Rd NE3 ....38 B4
Beechlea NE61 ....14 C3
Beecholm Ct SR2 ....86 D3
Beechway Gateshead NE10 .71 F5
Ashington NE63 ....7 A3
Beechwood Ave
Whitley Bay NE25 ....31 D4
Newcastle-upon-Tyne NE3 ..38 E6
Ryton NE40 ....52 C5
Stakeford NE62 ....11 A8
Gateshead NE9 ....71 A3
Beechwood Cl NE32 ......58 D6
Beechwood Cres SR5 .....74 F2
Beechwood Gdns NE11 ...70 B5
Beechwood Pl NE20 ......25 E7
Beechwood St SR2 ......102 B1
Beechwood Terr
Burnside DH4 ....90 C2
Sunderland SR2 ....102 B1
Beechwoods DH2 ....88 B5
Beeston Ave SR5 ....73 F3
Beetham Cres NE5 ....54 A8
Beethoven St 10 NE33 ....42 D2
Begonia Cl NE31 ....57 E3
Beldene Dr SR4 ....85 E4
Belford Ave NE27 ....30 F3
Belford Cl Wallsend NE28 ..40 D5
Sunderland SR2 ....86 D3
Belford Gdns NE11 ....70 A5
Belford Rd SR2 ....86 E3
Belford Terr
Tynemouth NE30 ....42 A7
Newcastle-upon-Tyne NE6 ..56 E5
Sunderland SR2 ....86 E3
Belfry The DH4 ....90 A4
Belgrade Cres SR5 ....73 F4
Belgrade Sq SR5 ....73 F3
Belgrave Cres NE24 ......17 F6
Belgrave Ct NE10 ....71 D8
Belgrave Gdns
South Shields NE34 ....59 F6
Ashington NE63 ....7 A2
Belgrave Par NE4 ....100 B4
Belgrave Terr
Gateshead NE10 ....71 D7
South Shields NE33 ....42 D3

Bell Gr NE12 ....29 B4
Bell House Rd
Sunderland SR5 ....75 A5
Sunderland, High Southwick SR5 ....75 B3
Bell Rd NE41 ....51 B6
Bell St Penshaw DH4 ......90 B8
North Shields NE30 ....42 B5
Hebburn NE31 ....57 D6
Washington NE38 ....83 F4
Sunderland SR4 ....85 F6
Bell View NE42 ....50 F3
Bell's Cotts NE40 ....52 A1
Bell's Ct NE1 ....99 B1
Bell's Hill NE61 ....13 D3
Bell's Pl NE22 ....16 A8
Bellamy Cres SR5 ....73 F3
Bellburn Ct NE23 ....22 D8
Belle Gr W NE2 ....98 B3
Belle Grove Pl NE2 ....98 B3
Belle Grove Terr NE2 .....98 B3
Belle Grove Villas NE2 ....98 B3
Belle View Terr NE9 ......71 E1
Belle Vue NE39 ....66 F5
Belle Vue Ave NE3 ....38 D5
Belle Vue Bank NE9 ......70 E5
Belle Vue Cres
South Shields NE33 ....59 B6
Sunderland SR2 ....86 C4
Belle Vue Dr SR2 ....86 C4
Belle Vue Gr NE9 ....70 F5
Belle Vue Pk SR2 ....86 C4
Belle Vue Pk W SR2 ......86 C4
Belle Vue Rd SR2 ....86 C4
Belle Vue St NE30 ....32 C3
Belle Vue Terr
4 North Shields NE29 .....42 A4
Crawcrook NE40 ....51 F4
Gateshead NE9 ....70 E5
Belle Vue Villas NE36 .....74 C7
Bellerby Dr DH2 ....81 E2
Bellevue Cres NE23 ......16 B2
Bellfield Ave NE3 ....37 F6
Bellgreen Ave NE3 ....28 D1
Bellingham Cl NE28 ......40 D4
Bellingham Ct
Bedlington NE22 ....11 A1
8 Newcastle-upon-Tyne NE3 ....37 D5
Bellingham Dr NE12 ......40 A8
Bellingham Ho SR4 ......85 B4
Bellister Gr NE5 ....54 C7
Bellister Rd NE29 ....41 D6
Belloc Ave NE34 ....59 B3
Bells Cl
Newcastle-upon-Tyne NE15 .53 E5
2 Blyth NE24 ....16 F8
Bellsburn Ct NE63 ....6 B2
Bellshill Cl NE28 ....40 E6
Bellway Ind Est NE12 .....39 F7
Belmont NE10 ....72 A5
Belmont Ave NE25 ....31 D4
Belmont Cl NE28 ....40 E5
Belmont Cotts NE5 ....36 F3
Belmont Rd SR4 ....85 F5
Belmont Rise DH5 ....95 A1
Belmont St NE6 ....56 F3
Belmont Terr NE9 ....71 E1
Belmont Wlk NE6 ....56 F3
Belmount Ave NE3 ....28 D1
Belper Cl NE28 ....40 C5
Belsay NE38 ....82 F4
Belsay Ave Hazlerigg NE13 .28 A4
Whitley Bay NE25 ....32 B4
South Shields NE34 ....60 A7
Belsay Cl Wallsend NE28 ...40 C5
Pegswood NE61 ....4 F3
Belsay Ct NE24 ....17 C7
Belsay Gdns
Dunston NE11 ....70 A5
Newcastle-upon-Tyne NE3 ..37 F8
Sunderland SR4 ....85 F5
Belsay Gr NE22 ....11 C3
Belsay Hall Castle and Gardens* NE20 ....124 C1
Belsay Ho 7 SR3 ....91 D7
Belsay Pl NE4 ....98 A2
Belsfield Gdns NE32 ......58 B4
Belsize Pl NE6 ....56 F8
Beltingham NE5 ....36 E1
Belvedere NE29 ....41 F7
Belvedere Ave NE25 ......31 F4
Belvedere Ct 12 NE6 ......56 C7
Belvedere Gdns NE12 ....39 D6
Belvedere Parkway NE3 ..37 D6
Belvedere Rd SR2 ....102 C1
Belvedere Ret Pk NE3 ....37 C6
Bemersyde Dr NE2 ....38 E3
Benbrake Ave NE29 ......31 E1
Bendigo Ave NE34 ....58 F3
Benedict Biscop C of E Prim Sch SR3 ....91 D5
Benedict Rd SR6 ....75 F2
Benfield Comp Sch NE6 ..39 E1
Benfield Gr NE26 ....24 B7
Benfield Rd NE6 ....39 E1
Benfleet Ave SR5 ....73 F3
Benjamin Rd NE28 ....41 A3
Benjamin St 10 NE40 .....51 F3
Bennett Ct
Newcastle-upon-Tyne NE15 .53 C6
Sunderland SR2 ....86 E3
Bennett Gdns 1 NE10 ....56 D1
Bennett's Wlk NE61 ....9 A8
Benridge Bank DH4 ....94 A2
Benridge Pk NE24 ....17 B3
Bensham Ave NE8 ....101 A1
Bensham Cres NE8 ......100 C1

Bensham Ct
South Shields NE34 ....59 C5
Gateshead NE8 ....101 A1
Bensham General Hospl NE8 ....70 D7
Bensham Rd
Gateshead NE8 ....101 B3
Gateshead, Bensham NE8 .101 A1
Gateshead, Windmill Hills NE8 ....101 B2
Bensham St NE35 ....58 F1
Benson Cl NE46 ....44 E4
Benson Pl 19 NE6 ....56 C6
Benson Rd NE6 ....56 D6
Benson St DH3 ....88 C2
Bentall Bsns Pk NE37 .....83 F7
Bentinck Cres
Newcastle-upon-Tyne NE4 ..54 F4
Pegswood NE61 ....4 E3
Bentinck Rd NE4 ....54 F5
Bentinck St NE4 ....54 F4
Bentinck Villas NE4 ....54 F5
Benton Ave SR5 ....73 F4
Benton Bank NE2 ....39 A1
Benton Cl NE7 ....39 B5
Benton Hall Wlk NE7 .....39 D2
Benton La NE12 ....39 B7
Benton Lodge Ave NE7 ...39 B5
Benton Park Prim Sch NE7 ....39 B4
Benton Park Rd NE7 .....39 A5
Benton Rd Shiremoor NE27 .30 E1
Biddick Hall NE34 ....59 C2
Newcastle-upon-Tyne NE7 ..39 B3
Benton Square Ind Est NE12 ....30 B1
Benton Sta NE12 ....39 D6
Benton Terr NE2 ....99 C3
Benton Way
Wallsend NE28 ....40 B1
Wallsend NE28 ....57 B8
Bents Cotts App NE33 ....42 E2
Bents Park Rd NE33 ......42 E3
Bents The SR6 ....75 F7
Benwell Dene Terr NE15 ..54 C5
Benwell Gr NE4 ....54 E5
Benwell Grange 9 NE15 .54 D5
Benwell Grange Ave NE15 ....54 D5
Benwell Grange Cl 8 NE15 ....54 D5
Benwell Grange Rd NE15 .54 C5
Benwell Grange Terr NE15 ....54 C5
Benwell Hall Dr NE15 ....54 B6
Benwell Hill Gdns NE5 ...54 C7
Benwell Hill Rd NE5 ......54 C7
Benwell La
Newcastle-upon-Tyne NE15 .54 C5
Newcastle-upon-Tyne, Old Benwell NE15 ....54 B5
Benwell Village NE15 .....54 B6
Benwell Village Mews NE15 ....54 C6
Berberis Way NE15 ....52 E8
Beresford Ave NE31 ......57 E3
Beresford Gdns 7 NE6 ...56 C5
Beresford Pk SR2 ....102 C1
Beresford Rd
Seaton Sluice NE26 ....24 D5
Tynemouth NE30 ....32 A3
Beresford St NE11 ......100 A1
Bergen Cl NE29 ....41 B4
Bergen Sq SR5 ....73 F4
Bergen St SR5 ....73 F4
Berkdale Rd NE9 ....70 E2
Berkeley Cl
Killingworth NE12 ....29 E4
Boldon Colliery NE35 ......58 E2
Sunderland SR3 ....91 C7
Berkeley Sq NE3 ....38 B7
Berkely St NE33 ....42 D2
Berkhamstead Ct NE10 ...72 C7
Berkley Ave NE21 ....53 E2
Berkley Cl NE28 ....40 C5
Berkley Rd NE29 ....41 D6
Berkley St NE15 ....52 F8
Berkley Terr NE15 ....52 F8
Berkley Way NE31 ....57 F8
Berkshire Cl NE5 ....36 F2
Bermondsey St NE2 ......99 C2
Bernard Gilpin Prim Sch DH5 ....94 E8
Bernard Shaw St 8 DH4 .94 D8
Bernard St
Houghton-le-Spring DH4 ....94 D8
Newcastle-upon-Tyne NE6 ..57 B4
Berrington Dr NE5 ....37 B3
Berrishill Gr NE25 ....31 C6
Berry Cl Wallsend NE28 ...40 C5
Newcastle-upon-Tyne NE6 ..57 A6
Berry Hill NE40 ....52 B1
Berryfield Cl SR3 ....92 A5
Berryhill Cl NE21 ....53 D1
Berrymoor NE63 ....6 E4
Bertha Terr DH4 ....90 D4
Bertram Cres NE15 ....54 C6
Bertram St 2 Birtley DH3 .82 C4
South Shields NE33 ....59 C8
Bertram Terr
Pegswood NE61 ....4 F4
Ashington NE63 ....6 D3
Berwell Roman Temple* NE15 ....54 D6
Berwell Vallum Crossing* NE15 ....54 D6
Berwick NE38 ....82 F4
Berwick Castle* TD15 ...105 A6

Berwick Cl NE15 ....53 A7
Berwick Ct NE20 ....25 F7
Berwick Dr NE28 ....40 D5
Berwick Hill Rd NE20 .....25 F8
Berwick Sq SR5 ....73 F3
Berwick Terr NE29 ....41 D4
Besford Gr SR1 ....103 B2
Bessemer Rd DH6 ....97 F7
Bessie Terr NE21 ....53 A2
Best View 3 DH4 ....90 B6
Bet's La NE61 ....13 D8
Bethnell Ave NE6 ....56 D7
Betts Ave NE15 ....54 B5
Beumaris DH4 ....89 D3
Bevan Ave SR2 ....92 E6
Bevan Ct NE12 ....38 F6
Bevan Gdns NE10 ....72 A8
Beverley Cl NE3 ....28 B2
Beverley Cres NE9 ....71 A6
Beverley Ct
1 Jarrow NE32 ....58 B7
Washington NE37 ....83 D7
Gateshead NE9 ....71 A6
Beverley Dr
Whickham NE16,NE21 ......69 C8
Blaydon NE21 ....67 F8
Stakeford NE62 ....6 A1
Beverley Gdns
Chester le Street DH3 .....88 D2
Tynemouth NE30 ....32 C2
Ryton NE40 ....52 A5
Beverley Pk NE25 ....31 E4
Beverley Pl NE28 ....40 F3
Beverley Rd
Whitley Bay NE25 ....31 F4
Gateshead NE9 ....71 A6
Sunderland SR2 ....86 F2
Beverley Terr
Walbottle NE15 ....36 A2
Tynemouth NE30 ....32 C3
Newcastle-upon-Tyne NE6 ..57 A5
Beverley Villas NE30 ......32 C3
Beweshill Cres NE21 ......53 A1
Beweshill La NE21 ....53 A3
Bewick Cres NE15 ....53 D7
Bewick Ct NE1 ....99 B2
Bewick Garth NE43 ....49 E1
Bewick La NE42 ....50 B4
Bewick Pk NE28 ....40 F5
Bewick Rd NE8 ....101 B1
Bewick St
Newcastle-upon-Tyne NE1 .101 A4
South Shields NE33 ....59 C8
Bewicke Lodge NE28 .....41 A2
Bewicke Rd NE28 ....41 A1
Bewicke Rd Ind Est NE28 .41 A1
Bewicke St NE28 ....41 B1
Bewley Gdns NE28 ....40 D5
Bexhill Prim Sch SR5 .....73 F3
Bexhill Rd SR5 ....73 F3
Bexhill Sq Blyth NE24 .....17 E5
Sunderland SR5 ....73 F4
Bexley Ave NE15 ....54 B6
Bexley Pl NE16 ....69 A5
Bexley St SR4 ....85 F6
Bickerton Wlk 2 NE5 .....36 E1
Bickington Ct DH4 ....90 C3
Bicknell Ho NE6 ....56 C5
Biddick Hall Cty Inf Sch NE34 ....59 A3
Biddick Hall Cty Jun Sch NE34 ....59 B4
Biddick Hall Dr NE34 .....59 B4
Biddick La NE38 ....83 D2
Biddick Prim Sch NE38 ...83 D4
Biddick Sch NE38 ....83 E3
Biddick Terr NE38 ....83 E3
Biddick View NE38 ....83 E3
Biddick Villas NE38 ....83 E3
Biddlestone Cres NE29 ...41 D5
Biddlestone Rd NE6 ......39 C1
Bideford Gdns
Whitley Bay NE26 ....32 A6
Jarrow NE32 ....58 E5
South Shields NE34 ....43 A1
Gateshead NE9 ....70 F3
Bideford Gr NE16 ....69 A5
Bideford Rd NE3 ....37 E4
Bideford St SR2 ....86 F2
Big Waters Nature Reserve* NE13 ....28 A7
Bigbury Cl DH4 ....90 C4
Bigg Mkt NE1 ....99 A1
Bigges Gdns NE28 ....39 F4
Bilbrough Gdns NE4 ......54 D4
Bill Quay Prim Sch NE10 .57 C2
Billy Mill Ave NE29 ....41 E6
Billy Mill La NE29 ....41 D8
Bilsdale SR6 ....75 F7
Bilsdale Pl NE12 ....38 F6
Bilsmoor Ave NE7 ....39 B2
Bilton Hall Rd NE32 ......58 D6
Binchester St NE34 ....59 A5
Bingfield Gdns NE5 ......37 C1
Bingley Cl NE28 ....40 E5
Bingley St SR5 ....73 F3
Bink Moss NE37 ....83 A6
Binsby Gdns NE9 ....71 B2
Binswood Ave NE5 ....37 C2
Birch Ave Gateshead NE10 .72 A7
Whitburn SR6 ....60 F1
Birch Cl NE46 ....44 E3
Birch Cres Burnside DH4 ...90 C2
Burnopfield NE16 ....79 A6
Birch Ct Prudhoe NE42 ....50 A2
Silksworth SR3 ....91 E6
Birch Gr Wallsend NE28 ...40 C5
Jarrow NE32 ....58 A7

Birch Rd NE21 ....53 D3
Birch St NE32 ....58 A7
Birch Terr NE6 ....57 A5
Bircham Dr NE21 ....53 D1
Birches Nook Cotts NE43 .64 C7
Birches Nook Rd NE43 ...64 C7
Birches The NE16 ....69 C3
Birchfield NE16 ....69 B5
Birchfield Gdns
Newcastle-upon-Tyne NE15 .53 E7
Gateshead NE9 ....71 A2
Birchfield Rd SR2 ....86 B4
Birchfleld NE38 ....83 E2
Birchgate Cl NE21 ....53 A1
Birchington Ave NE33 ....59 D7
Birchtree Gdns NE25 .....31 F3
Birchvale Ave NE5 ....37 B2
Birchwood 3 NE36 ....74 D7
Birchwood Ave
Wide Open NE13 ....28 C5
Whickham NE16 ....69 A5
Newcastle-upon-Tyne NE7 ..39 C3
Birchwood Cl NE23 ....22 F1
Bird St NE30 ....42 C6
Birdhill Pl NE34 ....59 C5
Birdoswald (Camboglanna) Roman Fort* CA6 .....126 A3
Birds Nest Rd
Newcastle-upon-Tyne NE6 ..56 D4
Newcastle-upon-Tyne NE6 ..56 E4
Birkdale Whitley Bay NE25 .31 D5
South Shields NE33 ....42 E1
Birkdale Ave SR6 ....75 E7
Birkdale Cl Wallsend NE28 .40 C4
Washington NE37 ....72 B2
Newcastle-upon-Tyne NE7 ..39 C4
Birkdale Dr DH4 ....90 A4
Birkdene NE43 ....64 D6
Birkhead Cotts NE11 .....80 E6
Birkheads La NE11 ....80 E6
Birkland La DH9,NE11, NE16 ....80 E7
Birks Rd NE15 ....35 B5
Birkshaw Wlk 1 NE5 .....36 E1
Birling Pl 4 NE5 ....37 D2
Birnam Gr NE32 ....58 E2
Birney Edge NE20 ....25 C1
Birnham Pl NE3 ....37 F3
Birnie Cl NE4 ....54 E4
Birrell Sq SR5 ....73 F4
Birrell St SR5 ....73 F4
Birtley Ave
Tynemouth NE30 ....42 D8
Sunderland SR5 ....73 F4
Birtley Cl NE3 ....38 A4
Birtley East Cty Prim Sch DH3 ....82 C6
Birtley Golf Course DH3 ..82 D2
Birtley La DH3 ....82 D3
Birtley RC Inf Sch DH3 ...82 C5
Birtley RC Jun Sch DH3 ..82 C4
Birtley Villas 1 DH3 ......82 C5
Birtwistle Ave NE31 ......57 D3
Biscop Terr NE32 ....58 C4
Bishop Cres NE32 ....58 C8
Bishop Harland C of E Prim Sch SR5 ....74 C3
Bishop Ian Ramsey CE Prim Sch DH8 ....77 C1
Bishop Morton Gr SR1 ..103 B2
Bishop Ramsay Ct NE34 ..60 A6
Bishop Rock Dr NE12 .....39 A6
Bishop's Ave NE4 ....98 A1
Bishop's Rd NE15 ....54 D5
Bishopdale Penshaw DH4 ..89 E8
Wallsend NE28 ....39 F5
Bishopdale Ave NE24 .....17 A6
Bishopdale House NE4 ....54 E4
Bishops Cl NE28 ....40 E2
Bishops Ct NE5 ....53 F8
Bishops Dr NE40 ....52 D4
Bishops Mdw NE22 ....10 F1
Bishops Way SR3 ....91 E5
Bishopton St Blyth NE24 ...17 E6
Sunderland SR2 ....103 B1
Bishopton Way NE46 .....44 E3
Bisley Dr NE34 ....59 D7
Bittern Cl NE28 ....41 A6
Biverfield Rd NE42 ....50 E3
Black Boy Rd DH4 ....94 A7
Black Boy Yd NE1 ....99 A1
Black Carts Turret* NE47 ....128 C5
Black Dr DH3 ....89 B5
Black La Blaydon NE21 ....53 A2
Gateshead NE9 ....71 C1
Black Middens Bastle House* NE48 ....121 E7
Black Rd Hebburn NE31 ...57 F6
Ryhope SR2 ....92 F7
Blackberries The NE9 .....71 F1
Blackburn Gn NE10 ......71 C7
Blackcap Cl NE38 ....82 F3
Blackclose Bank NE63 .....6 D1
Blackclose Est NE63 ....6 D1
Blackdene NE63 ....6 B2
Blackdown Cl NE12 ......39 A6
Blackett Cotts NE41 ......51 A6
Blackett Pl NE1 ....99 A1
Blackett St
Newcastle-upon-Tyne NE1 ..99 A1
Hebburn NE31,NE32 ....57 F8
Blackett Terr SR4 ....102 A2
Blackfell Prim Sch NE37 .83 A6
Blackfell Rd NE37 ....82 F6

Blackfriars Ct NE1 98 C1
Blackfriars Mus* NE1 98 C1
Blackfriars Way NE12 39 A6
Blackheath Cl NE37 72 C2
Blackheath Ct NE3 37 B5
Blackhill Ave NE28 40 F6
Blackhill Cres NE9 71 D4
Blackhouse La NE40 52 B5
Blackpool Par NE31 58 A3
Blackrow La
Heddon-on-the-Wall NE15 35 A4
Gateshead NE9 71 A3
Blackstone Ct NE21 53 A2
Blackthorn Cl NE16 69 A2
Blackthorn Dr NE28 40 C5
Blackthorn Pl NE4 100 B3
Blackthorn Way
Fence Houses DH4 90 A2
Blyth NE24 17 C4
Ashington NE63 6 B2
Blackthorne NE10 71 F5
Blackwater Ho 7 SR3 92 A6
Blackwell Ave NE6 57 A6
Blackwood Rd SR5 74 A3
Bladen St NE32 58 A7
Bladen Street Ind Est NE32 58 A7
Blagdon Ave NE34 59 E8
Blagdon Cl
Newcastle-upon-Tyne NE1 99 C1
Morpeth NE61 8 E8
Blagdon Cres NE23 21 E8
Blagdon Ct NE22 11 C2
Blagdon Dr NE24 17 C3
Blagdon St NE1 99 C1
Blagdon Terr
Seaton Burn NE13 28 B8
Cramlington NE23 22 B6
Blake Ave NE16 69 B7
Blake Wlk NE8 56 A2
Blakelaw Rd
7 Newcastle-upon-Tyne NE5 37 B2
Newcastle-upon-Tyne NE5 37 C2
Blakemoor Pl NE5 37 C1
Blanche Terr DH9 79 B2
Blanchland NE38 83 E1
Blanchland Ave
Wide Open NE13 28 B6
Newcastle-upon-Tyne NE15 53 C7
Blanchland Cl NE28 40 D5
Blanchland Dr
Seaton Delaval NE25 23 F2
Sunderland SR5 75 C3
Blanchland Terr NE30 42 B7
Blandford Rd NE29 41 D8
Blandford Sq NE1 100 C4
Blandford St
Newcastle-upon-Tyne NE1 100 C4
Sunderland SR1 103 A2
Blandford Way NE28 40 D5
Blaxton Pl NE16 68 F5
Blaydon Ave SR5 74 A4
Blaydon Bank NE21 53 C2
Blaydon Bsns Ctr NE21 53 E3
Blaydon Bsns Pk NE21 53 F4
Blaydon Haughs Ind Est NE21 53 E4
Blaydon Highway NE21 53 D3
Blaydon Ind Pk NE21 53 D3
Blaydon West Prim Sch NE21 53 C3
Blaykeston Cl SR7 92 E1
Blayney Row NE15 52 C8
Bleachfeld NE10 71 F6
Bleasdale Cres DH4 90 B7
Blencathra
Tynemouth NE30 32 A2
Washington NE37 83 C6
Blenheim NE12 29 D4
Blenheim Ct NE24 17 D3
Blenheim Dr NE22 11 C2
Blenheim Gdns NE61 4 E4
Blenheim Pl NE11 54 E1
Blenkinsop Ct NE34 59 B3
Blenkinsop Gr NE32 58 B3
Blenkinsop St 5 NE28 40 B2
Bletchley Ave SR5 73 F4
Blezard Ct NE21 53 E4
Blind La
Chester le Street DH3 88 D6
Burnside DH4 90 B3
New Silksworth SR3 92 B7
Blindy La DH5 95 C1
Bloomfield Ct SR6 75 F2
Bloomfield Dr DH5 94 D3
Bloomsbury Ct NE3 38 B4
Blossom Gr DH4 90 B4
Blossomfield Way DH6 97 F3
Blount St NE6 56 D6
Blucher Rd
Killingworth NE12 29 C2
North Shields NE29 41 F3
Blucher Terr NE15 36 B1
Blue Anchor Ct NE8 101 B4
Blue House Ct NE37 83 B8
Blue House La
Washington NE37 83 C8
Cleadon SR5,SR6 75 A6
Blue House Rd NE31 57 D3
Blue Quarries Rd NE9 71 B6
Blue Row NE15 34 F2
Blue Top Cotts NE23 22 D6
Bluebell Cl Wylam NE41 51 B7
Gateshead NE9 71 B5
Bluebell Dene NE5 37 A5
Bluebell Way NE34 59 B5
Blueburn Dr NE12 29 F3
Blumer St DH4 94 A8
Blyth Bebside Mid Sch NE24 16 F8
Blyth Cl NE23 28 F8
Blyth Com Coll (North Side) NE24 17 A7
Blyth Com Coll (South Side) NE24 17 D5
Blyth Community Hospl NE24 17 D8
Blyth Ct
Newcastle-upon-Tyne NE15 53 C7
South Shields NE34 59 C5
Blyth Dr NE61 9 E1
Blyth Horton Grange Fst Sch NE24 16 F8
Blyth Rd NE26 24 E2
Blyth Sq SR5 74 A3
Blyth St Chopwell NE17 66 C1
Seaton Delaval NE25 23 C3
Sunderland SR5 74 A4
Blyth Terr NE63 6 E4
Blythswood NE2 99 B4
Blyton Ave
South Shields NE34 58 F5
Ryhope SR2 92 E6
Bodlewell Ho SR1 103 B3
Bodlewell La SR1 103 B3
Bodley Cl NE3 37 D5
Bodmin Cl NE28 40 E5
Bodmin Ct 1 NE9 71 A2
Bodmin Rd NE29 41 C8
Bodmin Sq SR5 74 A4
Bodmin Way NE3 37 F6
Bog Houses NE23 16 C2
Bognor St SR5 73 F4
Bohemia Terr NE24 17 E6
Boker La NE35 74 B8
Bolam NE38 82 F4
Bolam Ave Blyth NE24 17 D7
Tynemouth NE30 32 A1
Bolam Coyne 13 NE6 56 C5
Bolam Ct NE15 35 D1
Bolam Dr NE63 6 E2
Bolam Gdns NE28 41 B3
Bolam Gr NE30 32 A1
Bolam Lake* NE20 124 B3
Bolam Pl NE22 11 C2
Bolam Rd NE12 29 C3
Bolam St
Newcastle-upon-Tyne NE6 56 C5
Gateshead NE8 70 B8
Bolam Street Prim Sch NE6 56 C5
Bolam Way
Seaton Delaval NE25 23 C3
Newcastle-upon-Tyne NE6 56 C5
Boland Rd NE61 2 A3
Bolbec Rd NE4 54 E7
Bolburn NE10 72 A7
Boldon Bsns Pk NE35 73 E7
Boldon C of E Prim Sch NE36 73 F7
Boldon Cl NE28 40 D5
Boldon Comp Sch NE35 74 B8
Boldon Dr NE36 74 A7
Boldon Gdns NE9 71 C3
Boldon La
South Shields NE34 59 B5
East Boldon NE35,NE36 59 C1
Cleadon SR6 59 F1
Bolingbroke Rd NE29 41 D6
Bolingbroke St
4 South Shields NE33 42 D2
Newcastle-upon-Tyne NE6 56 A7
Bollihope Dr SR3 86 B2
Bolsover St NE63 6 D3
Bolsover Terr
Pegswood NE61 4 F4
Ashington NE63 6 D3
Bolton's Bglw NE17 77 B8
Bomont Dr NE23 22 D8
Bonaventure DH4 90 C8
Bonchester Cl NE22 10 F2
Bonchester Ct NE28 40 E5
Bonchester Pl NE23 22 D8
Bond Cl SR5 75 C1
Bond Ct NE4 54 E5
Bond St 2 NE4 54 D5
Bondene Ave NE10 71 E8
Bondene Ave W NE10 71 E8
Bondene Way NE23 16 B2
Bondfield Cl NE28 40 F3
Bondfield Gdns NE10 72 A8
Bondgate Cl NE46 45 B4
Bondgate Ct NE46 45 B4
Bondicar Terr NE24 17 E7
Bondicarr Pl 1 NE5 37 D1
Bonemill La
Chester le Street NE38 88 F8
Washington NE38 89 C8
Bonington Way NE5 37 B2
Bonner's Field SR6 103 A4
Bonnivard Gdns NE23 23 A1
Bonsall Ct NE34 59 D5
Booth St Gateshead NE10 71 D8
Sunderland SR4 102 A2
Booths Rd NE63 6 A4
Bootle St SR5 74 A3
Bordeaux Cl SR3 91 E6
Border Forest Park Museum* NE48 120 D8
Border History & Tourist Ctr NE46 45 B5
Border Rd NE28 40 B1
Boreham Cl NE28 40 D5
Borodin Ave SR5 73 F4
Borough Rd
North Shields NE29 42 A5
Jarrow NE32 58 B6
South Shields NE34 60 A5
Sunderland SR1 103 B2
Borrowdale Birtley DH3 82 D1
Whickham NE16 69 D7
Washington NE37 83 C8
Borrowdale Ave
Blyth NE24 17 A8
Newcastle-upon-Tyne NE6 56 F7
Sunderland SR6 75 D5
Borrowdale Cl NE36 74 C8
Borrowdale Cres
Penshaw DH4 90 A8
Blaydon NE21 68 B8
Borrowdale Gdns NE9 71 B3
Borrowdale St DH5 95 A2
Boscombe Dr NE28 40 C4
Boston Ave
Washington NE38 83 D6
Newcastle-upon-Tyne NE7 39 B5
Boston Cl NE28 40 D5
Boston Cres SR5 73 E4
Boston Ct NE12 39 F8
Boston St SR5 73 F4
Bosun's Way NE10 57 A2
Boswell Ave NE34 59 B3
Bosworth NE12 29 D4
Bosworth Gdns NE6 39 D2
Bothal Ave NE62 10 E7
Bothal Bank NE61 5 C2
Bothal Cl Blyth NE24 17 C7
Pegswood NE61 4 E3
Bothal Cotts NE63 5 F4
Bothal Mid Sch NE63 5 F4
Bothal St NE6 56 D6
Bothal Terr
Stakeford NE62 11 B8
Ashington NE63 5 F4
Bottle Bank NE8 101 B4
Bottlehouse St NE6 56 C4
Boulby Cl SR3 92 C7
Boulmer Ave NE23 16 B2
Boulmer Cl NE3 37 F8
Boulmer Ct DH2 88 C2
Boulmer Gdns NE13 28 B6
Boulsworth Rd NE29 31 E1
Boult Terr DH4 90 B6
Boundary Dr NE61 9 A7
Boundary Gdns NE7 39 A3
Boundary La DH8 76 A3
Boundary St SR5 75 C2
Boundary Way NE26 24 D6
Bourn Lea DH4 90 A5
Bourne Ave NE4 54 E7
Bournemouth Ct NE28 40 E5
Bournemouth Gdns
Whitley Bay NE26 32 A6
Newcastle-upon-Tyne NE5 36 F3
Bournemouth Par NE31 58 A3
Bournemouth Rd NE29 41 C5
Bournmoor Prim Sch DH4 89 E3
Bourtree Cl NE28 40 C4
Bowbank Cl SR3 86 B2
Bowburn Ave SR5 74 C2
Bowburn Cl NE10 72 C7
Bower St SR6 75 D4
Bower The NE32 73 B8
Bowes Ave DH5 95 B1
Bowes Cl NE16 69 B2
Bowes Cres NE16 79 D8
Bowes Ct NE3 38 E5
Bowes Ho 8 SR3 91 D7
Bowes Lea DH4 89 F4
Bowes Lyon Cl NE39 78 D8
Bowes Lyon Ct 6 NE9 70 F8
Bowes Rly* NE9 82 E8
Bowes Rly Mus* NE9 71 E2
Bowes St Blyth NE24 17 E6
Newcastle-upon-Tyne NE3 38 E5
Bowes Wlk NE12 39 C7
Bowesville NE16 79 B5
Bowfell Ave NE5 37 D3
Bowfell Cl NE5 37 D3
Bowfell Gdns NE62 11 A8
Bowfield Ave NE3 28 C1
Bowler's Hill NE43 64 F7
Bowlynn Cl SR3 91 E6
Bowman Dr NE23 29 B8
Bowman Pl NE33 42 C1
Bowman Sq NE63 6 D2
Bowman St SR6 60 F1
Bowmont NE61 1 E5
Bowmont Wlk DH2 88 A1
Bowness Ave NE28 40 E6
Bowness Cl NE36 74 C7
Bowness Pl NE9 71 B4
Bowness Rd
Whickham NE16 69 D7
Newcastle-upon-Tyne NE5 37 A1
Bowness St SR5 74 A4
Bowness Terr NE28 40 E5
Bowsden Ct NE3 38 E5
Bowsden Terr NE3 38 E5
Bowtrees SR2 86 D3
Boxlaw NE9 71 C5
Boyd Cres NE28 40 C2
Boyd Rd NE28 40 D2
Boyd St Newburn NE15 52 E8
Newcastle-upon-Tyne NE2 99 C2
Boyd Terr
Newcastle-upon-Tyne NE15 36 B1
Newcastle-upon-Tyne, Westerhope NE5 36 F3
Boyne Ct NE24 17 E8
Boyne Gdns NE27 30 E3
Boystones Ct NE37 83 B6
Brabourne St NE34 59 C6
Brack Terr NE10 57 B2
Bracken Ave NE28 40 C5
Bracken Cl NE13 27 B6
Bracken Dr NE11 69 F6
Bracken Pl NE4 54 D7
Bracken Ridge NE61 3 C1
Bracken Way NE40 52 A3
Brackenburn Cl DH4 90 C1
Brackendene Dr NE9 70 E5
Brackenfield Rd NE3 38 B4
Brackenlaw NE9 71 C3
Brackenridge NE16 78 E6
Brackenside NE3 28 C1
Brackenway NE37 83 B7
Brackenwood Gr SR2 86 C2
Brackley NE37 72 E1
Brackley Gr NE29 41 D4
Bracknell Cl SR3 92 C8
Bracknell Gdns NE5 36 C1
Bradbury Cl NE10 72 D7
Bradbury Ct NE25 23 D6
Bradbury Pl NE25 23 D6
Bradford Ave
Wallsend NE28 40 D5
Sunderland SR5 74 A4
Bradley Ave
Houghton-le-Spring DH5 94 E6
South Shields NE34 60 A6
Bradley Cl DH2 81 E2
Bradley Fell La NE41 51 C2
Bradley Fell Rd NE40, NE42 66 C8
Bradley Rd NE42 50 F3
Bradley Terr DH5 95 C1
Bradley View 13 NE40 51 F3
Bradman Dr DH3 88 E1
Bradman Sq 3 SR5 74 A4
Bradman St SR5 74 A4
Bradshaw Sq SR5 74 A3
Bradshaw St SR5 74 A3
Bradwell Rd NE3 37 E5
Bradwell Way DH4 90 C4
Brady & Martin Ct NE1 99 B2
Brady Sq NE38 83 F4
Brady St SR4 85 F7
Brae The SR2 102 B2
Braebridge Pl NE3 37 F3
Braefell Ct NE37 83 B6
Braemar Ct NE10 57 B2
Braemar Dr NE34 60 A8
Braemar Gdns
Whitley Bay NE25 31 C4
Sunderland SR3 86 B3
Sunderland SR3 91 C6
Braeside Dunston NE11 69 F7
Sunderland SR2 86 B4
Braeside Cl NE30 32 A3
Brahman Ave NE29 41 D4
Braintree Gdns NE3 37 F4
Brama Teams Ind Est NE8 70 B8
Bramble Dykes NE15 54 B6
Bramblelaw NE9 71 C4
Brambling Lea NE22 11 C2
Bramhall Dr NE38 89 B8
Bramham Ct NE34 59 E5
Bramhope Gn NE9 71 B2
Bramley Cl SR4 85 A3
Bramley Ct NE7 39 E3
Brampton Ave NE6 56 F4
Brampton Ct NE23 22 C8
Brampton Gdns
Throckley NE15 35 E2
Wallsend NE28 41 A4
Gateshead NE9 71 A3
Brampton Pl NE29 41 E5
Brampton Rd NE34 59 A5
Bramwell Ct NE3 38 E5
Bramwell Rd SR2 103 B1
Brancepeth Ave
Fence Houses DH4 90 A1
Newcastle-upon-Tyne NE4 54 E5
Brancepeth Cl NE15 53 C7
Brancepeth Rd
Hebburn NE31 57 F7
Washington NE38 83 A4
Brancepeth Terr NE32 58 B3
Branch End Terr NE43 64 D7
Branch St NE21 53 B1
Brand Ave NE4 54 E7
Brandling Ct
14 Gateshead NE10 56 D1
South Shields NE34 60 A4
Brandling Dr NE3 28 D1
Brandling La 15 NE10 56 D1
Brandling Mews NE3 28 D1
Brandling Pk NE2 99 A4
Brandling Pl NE10 56 D1
Brandling Pl S NE2 99 B4
Brandling Prim Sch NE10 56 D1
Brandling St
Gateshead NE8 101 C4
Sunderland SR6 75 E2
Brandling St S SR6 75 E1
Brandling Terr 3 NE30 42 B6
Brandon Ave NE27 30 E3
Brandon Cl
Houghton-le-Spring DH4 94 D7
Blaydon NE21 68 A8
Blyth NE24 17 B8
Brandon Gdns NE9 71 D3
Brandon Gr NE2 99 C3
Brandon Rd
North Shields NE29 41 D6
Newcastle-upon-Tyne NE3 37 F6
Brandy La NE37 83 B7
Brandywell NE10 71 F6
Brannen St NE29 42 A5
Bransdale DH4 89 E8
Bransdale Ave SR6 75 F7
Branston St SR5 75 B2
Branton Ave NE31 57 D3
Brantwood Ave NE25 31 D4
Branxton Cres NE6 56 F5
Bray Cl NE28 40 D5
Braydon Dr NE29 41 E3
Brayside NE32 58 D1
Breamish NE61 1 E5
Breamish Dr NE38 88 F8
Breamish Ho NE1 56 A5
Breamish St
Newcastle-upon-Tyne NE1 56 A5
Jarrow NE32 58 A5
Brearley Way NE10 71 C8
Brecken Ct NE9 70 E4
Breckenbeds Rd NE9 70 E4
Breckon Cl NE63 6 E1
Brecon Cl NE5 37 B4
Bredon Cl NE38 83 B3
Brendale Ave NE5 36 E3
Brenkley Ave NE27 30 F2
Brenkley Cl NE13 27 B7
Brenkley Ct NE13 28 B8
Brenkley Way NE13 21 B1
Brenlynn Cl SR3 91 E6
Brennan Cl
Newcastle-upon-Tyne NE15 54 B6
Ashington NE63 7 A3
Brentford Ave SR5 74 A3
Brentford Sq 4 SR5 74 A3
Brentwood Ave
Newcastle-upon-Tyne NE2 38 E2
Newbiggin-by-the-Sea NE64 7 D5
Brentwood Cl NE25 23 E2
Brentwood Gdns
Whickham NE16 69 B5
Newcastle-upon-Tyne NE2 38 D2
Sunderland SR3 86 B3
Brentwood Gr NE28 40 D1
Brentwood Pl 6 NE33 42 D2
Brentwood Rd DH4 90 A5
Brett Cl NE7 39 D3
Brettanby Gdns NE40 52 C6
Brettanby Rd NE10 71 C7
Bretton Gdns NE7 39 C2
Brettonby Ave NE43 64 D7
Brewer Terr SR2 93 A6
Brewer's La NE28,NE29 41 C3
Brewery Bank 6 NE16 54 A1
Brewery La
Gateshead NE10 56 D2
5 Whickham NE16 54 A1
Ponteland NE20 25 E6
South Shields NE33 42 B2
Brewery St 3 NE24 17 F8
Brewhouse Bank NE30 42 C6
Briar Ave
2 Houghton-le-Spring DH4 94 D8
Whitley Bay NE26 32 A6
Briar Cl Great Lumley DH4 89 E1
Shiney Row DH4 89 F4
Blaydon NE21 53 A2
Wallsend NE28 40 C5
Briar Ct NE26 32 A5
Briar Edge NE12 39 D8
Briar Field NE38 83 D1
Briar La NE15 35 E1
Briar Pl NE15 54 A5
Briar Rd NE39 67 D2
Briar Terr NE16 79 C6
Briar Wlk NE15 54 A5
Briardale Dinnington NE13 27 B7
Bedlington NE22 10 E1
Briardale Rd NE24 17 A8
Briardene
Burnopfield NE16 78 E6
Ashington NE63 6 B2
Briardene Cl SR3 91 C6
Briardene Cres NE3 38 A3
Briardene Dr NE10 72 D8
Briarfield Rd NE3 38 B4
Briarhill DH2 88 A5
Briarlea NE61 9 E4
Briars The SR5 74 B1
Briarside NE5 37 A3
Briarsyde NE12 39 E6
Briarsyde Cl NE16 68 E5
Briarwood NE23 29 B8
Briarwood Ave NE3 38 E6
Briarwood Cres
3 Dunston NE11 69 F8
Newcastle-upon-Tyne NE6 39 F1
Briarwood Rd NE24 17 F6
Briarwood St DH4 89 E1
Briary The NE15 35 C2
Brick Garth DH5 95 C1
Brick Row SR2 92 E7
Bridekirk NE37 83 C7
Bridge Cotts NE23 29 B8
Bridge Cres SR1 103 A3
Bridge End Ind Est NE46 45 C6
Bridge House SR1 103 A3
Bridge Pk NE3 38 C8
Bridge Rd NE61 2 A2
Bridge Rd S NE29 41 E3
Bridge St
Seaton Burn NE13 28 B8
Blaydon NE21 53 C4
Blyth NE24 17 F7
Blyth NE24 17 F8

Bridge St *continued*
Morpeth NE61 8 F8
Newbiggin-by-the-Sea NE64 7 E4
Gateshead NE8 101 B4
Sunderland SR1 103 A3
Bridge Terr
Bedlington NE22 11 C3
Shiremoor NE27 30 F4
Stakeford NE62 11 B8
Bridges The SR1 103 A2
Bridgewater Cl
Newcastle-upon-Tyne NE15 53 C7
Wallsend NE28 40 C4
Bridgewater Rd NE37 83 E7
Bridle Path
East Boldon NE36 74 C7
Sunderland SR3 91 C8
Bridle The NE27 31 B2
Bridlington Ave NE9 70 F3
Bridlington Cl NE28 40 D5
Bridlington Par NE31 58 A3
Bridport Rd NE29 31 D1
Brier Dene Cres NE26 31 F8
Brierdene Cl NE26 31 F8
Brierdene Ct NE26 31 E8
Brierdene Rd NE26 24 F1
Brierdene View NE26 31 E8
Brierfield Gr SR4 85 D4
Brierley Cl NE24 17 B7
Brierley Rd NE24 17 B7
Briermede Ave NE9 70 F4
Briermede Pk NE9 70 F4
Briery Hill La NE61 14 C3
Briery Vale Cl SR2 102 C1
Briery Vale Rd SR2 86 C4
Brieryside NE5 37 D2
Brigham Ave NE3 37 E3
Brigham Pl NE33 42 C3
Bright St
South Shields NE33 42 E2
Sunderland SR6 75 E1
Brightlea DH3 82 E5
Brightman Rd NE29 42 A6
Brighton Ave Prim Sch
NE8 101 A1
Brighton Cl NE28 40 E5
Brighton Gdns NE8 70 E7
Brighton Gr
Whitley Bay NE26 31 F6
North Shields NE29 41 F6
Newcastle-upon-Tyne NE4 98 A2
Brighton Par NE31 58 A3
Brighton Rd NE8 70 E8
Brighton Terr DH6 96 D1
Brignall Gdns NE15 54 A7
Brignall Rise SR3 86 B2
Brigside Cotts NE13 28 C8
Brindley Rd NE37 83 E6
Brinkburn
Chester le Street DH2 88 A3
Washington NE38 83 E2
Brinkburn Ave
Whickham NE16 69 B8
Cramlington NE23 22 C6
Blyth NE24 17 F6
Newcastle-upon-Tyne NE3 38 B6
Gateshead NE8 70 E8
Brinkburn Cl
Blaydon NE21 68 A8
Newcastle-upon-Tyne NE6 56 B6
Brinkburn Comp Sch
NE34 59 D6
Brinkburn Cres
Burnside DH4 90 C1
Ashington NE63 6 E4
Brinkburn Ct
8 North Shields NE30 42 B6
22 Newcastle-upon-Tyne NE6 56 B6
Brinkburn Gdns NE62 11 A8
Brinkburn La 21 NE6 56 B6
Brinkburn Pl 25 NE6 56 B6
Brinkburn Priory* NE65 118 C3
Brinkburn Sq 7 NE6 56 B5
Brinkburn St
North Shields NE28 41 C1
South Shields NE34 59 B6
17 Newcastle-upon-Tyne NE6 56 B6
Newcastle-upon-Tyne, St Lawrence NE6 56 B5
Sunderland SR4 102 A1
Brinkburn St S NE6 56 C4
Brisbane Ave NE34 58 F3
Brisbane Ct NE8 101 B3
Brisbane St SR5 74 A3
Brislee Ave NE30 42 C7
Brislee Gdns NE3 37 E4
Bristlecone SR3 91 E5
Bristol Ave
Washington NE37 83 B8
Sunderland SR5 73 F4
Bristol Dr NE28 40 D5
Bristol St NE25 23 D6
Bristol Terr NE4 100 A4
Bristol Wlk NE25 23 D6
Britannia Ct NE4 100 A4
Britannia Pl NE4 98 A1
Britannia Rd SR3 92 A7
Britannia Terr DH4 94 A8
Brittania Ho NE28 40 F1
Brixham Ave NE9 70 F3
Brixham Cres NE32 58 D5
Brixham Gdns SR3 86 B3
Broad Chare NE1 101 B4
Broad Garth NE1 101 B4
Broad Landing NE33 42 B3
Broad Meadows
Newcastle-upon-Tyne NE3 37 F3
Sunderland SR2 102 B1
Broad Oak Terr NE17 66 B1
Broadbank NE10 72 B8
Broadfield Pl NE34 59 D5
Broadgates NE46 45 B4
Broadlands SR6 75 A7
Broadlea NE10 72 B8
Broadmayne Ave SR4 85 D4
Broadmayne Gdns SR4 85 D4
Broadmead Way NE15 54 A5
Broadmeadows
Washington NE38 83 E2
Sunderland SR3 91 B6
Broadoak NE10 57 B1
Broadpark NE10 72 B8
Broadpool Gn NE16 69 C6
Broadpool Terr NE16 69 C6
Broadsheath Terr SR5 74 F2
Broadside NE10 72 B8
Broadstairs Ct SR4 85 D4
Broadstone Gr NE5 36 C1
Broadstone Way NE28 40 C4
Broadview Villas DH6 96 A1
Broadwater NE10 57 B1
Broadway
Chester le Street DH3 88 D5
Newcastle-upon-Tyne NE15 53 D7
Whickham NE16 69 A4
Ponteland NE20 25 C3
Blyth NE24 17 E6
Guide Post NE62 10 F7
Gateshead NE9 71 B7
Broadway Circ NE24 17 E7
Broadway Cl NE30 32 B3
Broadway Cres NE24 17 E6
Broadway E NE3 38 C7
Broadway East Fst Sch
NE3 38 D7
Broadway Gdns NE46 44 F5
Broadway Jun Sch SR4 85 D4
Broadway The
Houghton-le-Spring DH4 94 E8
Tynemouth NE30 32 B2
Sunderland, Grindon SR4 85 B3
Sunderland, Springwell SR4 85 D4
Sunderland, Castletown SR5 85 A8
Broadway Villas NE15 54 B6
Broadway W NE3 38 B7
Broadwell Ct NE3,NE7 38 F4
Broadwood Prim Sch
NE15 53 F7
Broadwood Rd NE15 53 F7
Broadwood View DH3 88 D2
Brock Farm Ct NE30 42 B6
Brock La NE22,NE62 11 F5
Brock Sq 8 NE6 56 B5
Brock St NE6 56 B5
Brockenhurst Dr SR4 85 A2
Brockhampton Cl NE35 58 E2
Brockley Ave NE34 59 B4
Brockley St SR5 74 A3
Brockley Terr 4 NE35 58 E1
Brockley Whins Sta NE32 58 F2
Brockwade NE10 71 F4
Brockwell Cl NE21 53 A1
Brockwell Ct NE24 17 C5
Brockwell Ctr The NE23 22 B8
Brockwell Dr NE39 67 E3
Brockwell Mid Sch NE23 22 B8
Brockwell Rd NE38 82 F5
Brockwell St NE24 17 C4
Brockwood Cl NE63 6 B1
Brodie Cl NE34 59 C4
Brodrick Cl NE3 37 D5
Brodrick St 18 NE33 42 D3
Brokenheugh NE5 36 F1
Bromarsh Ct SR6 75 F1
Bromford Rd NE3 37 D5
Bromley Ave NE25 31 E4
Bromley Ct NE3 37 D7
Bromley Gdns Blyth NE24 17 E5
Wallsend NE28 40 D5
Brompton Cl DH2 81 E2
Brompton Terr DH4 90 D4
Bromsgrove Cl NE28 40 E5
Bronte St NE8 56 B1
Brook Ct Bedlington NE22 11 A1
Bedlington NE22 16 A8
Brook Side Lodge 3
SR2 86 C4
Brook St Whitley Bay NE26 32 B6
Newcastle-upon-Tyne NE6 56 D5
Brookbank Cl SR3 91 F5
Brooke Ave
Whickham NE16 69 A8
West Boldon NE35 74 B8
Brooke St SR5 102 C4
Brooke's Wlk NE34 59 A2
Brookfield NE3 38 B2
Brookfield Cres NE5 36 C1
Brookfield Terr NE10 57 B2
Brookland Dr NE12 29 E3
Brookland Rd SR4 85 F6
Brookland Terr NE29 31 B1
Brooklands NE20 25 A3
Brooklands Way NE35 73 D8
Brookside
Houghton-le-Spring DH5 94 D6
Annitsford NE23 29 A7
Brookside Ave
Brunswick Village NE13 28 A6
Blyth NE24 17 B7
Brookside Cres NE5 37 D1
Brookside Gdns 4 SR2 86 C4
Brookside Terr 2 SR2 86 C4
Brookside Wood NE38 83 D1
Brooksmead NE28 40 A4
Brookvale Ave NE3 38 A4
Broom Cl Whickham NE16 69 C6
Blaydon NE21 68 B8
Morpeth NE61 9 C7
Broom Ct NE9 82 F8
Broom Gn NE16 69 C6
Broom La NE16 69 C6
Broom Terr
Burnopfield NE16 79 C6
Whickham NE16 69 C6
Broom Wood Ct NE42 50 B1
Broome Cl NE3 37 F6
Broomfield NE32 58 C2
Broomfield Ave
Wallsend NE28 40 C5
Newcastle-upon-Tyne NE6 39 E1
Broomfield Cres NE17 77 B8
Broomfield Rd NE3 38 B4
Broomhaugh CE Fst Sch
NE44 62 F7
Broomhaugh Cl NE46 45 C4
Broomhill Est DH5 94 F6
Broomhill Gdns NE5 37 D1
Broomhill Rd NE42 50 E3
Broomhill Terr DH5 94 F5
Broomhouse La NE42 50 D3
Broomhouse Rd NE42 50 F3
Broomlaw NE9 71 C4
Broomlea NE29 31 B1
Broomlea Ct NE21 53 C3
Broomlee NE63 6 E2
Broomlee Cl NE7 39 D3
Broomlee Rd NE12 29 D3
Broomley Ct NE3 37 F7
Broomley Fst Sch NE43 64 B8
Broomley Wlk NE3 37 F7
Broomridge Ave NE15 54 D6
Brooms The DH2 81 F2
Broomshields Ave SR5 75 B3
Broomshields Cl SR5 75 B3
Broomy Hill Rd NE15 35 D2
Broomylinn Pl NE23 22 C8
Brotherlee Rd NE3 37 F7
Brough Ct 3 NE6 56 C7
Brough Gdns NE28 41 A4
Brough Park Way NE6 56 D7
Brough St 2 NE6 56 C7
Brough Way 20 NE6 56 C7
Brougham St SR1 103 A2
Broughton Rd NE33 42 D2
Brow The NE6 56 C5
Brown Cres NE9 71 C1
Brown's Bldgs DH3 82 C1
Browne Rd SR6 75 E3
Browning Cl NE34 59 B3
Browning Sq NE8 56 A2
Brownlow Cl NE7 39 E3
Brownlow Rd NE34 59 C6
Brownrigg Dr NE23 22 C5
Brownriggs Ct NE37 83 B6
Brownsea Pl NE9 71 A7
Browntop Pl NE34 59 C5
Broxbourne Terr SR4 102 A2
Broxburn Cl NE28 40 E5
Broxburn Ct NE5 37 C3
Broxholm Rd NE6 39 B1
Bruce Cl Whiteleas NE34 59 C4
Newcastle-upon-Tyne NE5 36 F2
Bruce Gdns NE5 54 C7
Brumell Dr NE61 3 D1
Brumwell Ct NE43 64 B7
Brundon Ave NE26 31 F7
Brunel Dr SR6 75 F2
Brunel Lodge NE4 100 A3
Brunel St
Newcastle-upon-Tyne NE4 100 B3
Gateshead NE8 70 D8
Brunel Terr NE4 100 A3
Brunel Wlk NE4 100 A3
Brunswick Gr NE13 28 A6
Brunswick Ind Est NE13 27 F6
Brunswick Park Ind Est
NE13 28 A6
Brunswick Pl NE1 99 A2
Brunswick Rd
Shiremoor NE27 30 F2
Sunderland SR5 74 A4
Brunswick Sq NE27 30 F2
Brunswick St NE33 42 C1
Brunton Ave
Wallsend NE28 41 B3
Newcastle-upon-Tyne NE3 37 F6
Brunton Cl NE27 30 F2
Brunton Gr NE3 37 F6
Brunton La Hazlerigg NE13 27 E2
Newcastle-upon-Tyne, Kingston Park NE3 37 C7
Newcastle-upon-Tyne, Brunton Park NE3,NE13 28 B2
Brunton Rd NE3 37 C7
Brunton St NE29 41 D3
Brunton Terr SR4 102 A2
Brunton Turret* NE46 128 E4
Brunton Way
Gateshead NE10 57 B2
Cramlington NE23 16 B2
Brussels Rd
Wallsend NE28 40 B1
Sunderland SR4 85 D7
Bryan's Leap NE16 79 A7
Bryden Ct NE34 59 D5
Bryers St SR6 60 F1
Buchanan Gn NE11 100 A1
Buchanan St NE31 57 D5
Buck's Nook La NE40 66 C7
Buckingham SR3 91 E8
Buckingham Cl 1 SR6 75 F8
Buckingham St NE4 98 B1
Buckland Cl Burnside DH4 90 C2
Washington NE38 83 D3
Buckthorne Gr NE7 39 C3
Buddle Ct NE4 54 E4
Buddle Rd NE4 54 D4
Buddle St NE28 40 C1
Buddle Terr
4 Shiremoor NE27 30 E1
Sunderland SR2 103 B1
Bude Ct NE28 40 C4
Bude Gdns NE9 70 F3
Bude Gr NE29 31 D1
Budle Cl Blyth NE24 17 C7
Newcastle-upon-Tyne NE3 38 A6
Budleigh Rd NE3 37 F5
Budworth Ave NE26 24 D5
Bugatti Ind Pk NE29 41 C5
Buller's Gn NE61 3 E1
Bullfinch Dr NE16 69 A7
Bullion La DH2 88 B3
Bullion La Sch DH2 88 B3
Bulman's La NE29 42 A8
Bulmer Ho NE34 60 A7
Bulmer Rd NE34 60 A7
Bungalows The
Birtley DH3 82 B6
Hetton le Hole DH5 94 F6
Ebchester DH8 76 F4
Gateshead NE10 71 E8
Kibblesworth NE11 81 E8
Medomsley NE17 77 B4
Wallsend NE28 40 F3
Bunyan Ave NE34 59 A3
Burdale Ave NE5 37 A1
Burdon Ave
Houghton-le-Spring DH5 95 A8
Cramlington NE23 21 F7
Burdon Cl SR6 59 E1
Burdon Cres Ryhope SR2 92 E6
Cleadon SR6 59 E1
Seaham SR7 92 F1
Burdon La SR2,SR3 92 C5
Burdon Lodge NE16 69 C2
Burdon Main Row NE29 42 A4
Burdon Pk NE16 69 C2
Burdon Plain NE16 80 B7
Burdon Rd
Sunderland SR1, SR2 103 A1
Burdon SR3 92 B5
New Silksworth SR3 92 B6
Cleadon SR6 59 E1
Burdon St NE29 41 D3
Burdon Terr
Newcastle-upon-Tyne NE2 99 B4
Bedlington NE22 10 F1
Burford Ct NE7 39 A4
Burford Gdns SR3 86 B3
Burghley Gdns NE61 4 E4
Burghley Rd NE10 71 C6
Burgoyne Ct NE37 83 D8
Burke St 2 SR5 74 A3
Burlawn Cl 3 SR2 92 F8
Burleigh St 9 NE33 42 D2
Burlington Cl SR2 103 C1
Burlington Ct
Newcastle-upon-Tyne NE2 38 F2
Wallsend NE28 40 E7
Burlington Gdns NE6 56 B8
Burlison Gdns NE10 56 C2
Burn Ave
2 Longbenton NE12 39 D8
1 Wallsend NE28 40 B2
Burn Closes Cres NE28 40 E3
Burn Crook DH5 94 D6
Burn Heads Rd NE31 57 D4
Burn La Hetton le Hole DH5 95 A3
Hexham NE46 45 A6
Burn Park Rd
Houghton-le-Spring DH4 94 D8
Sunderland SR2 102 B1
Burn Prom 5 DH4 94 E8
Burn Rd NE21 53 A1
Burn Terr Shiney Row DH4 90 B6
Wallsend NE28 40 F2
Hebburn NE31 57 C2
Burn View Annitsford NE23 29 B8
Hedworth NE32 73 D8
Burnaby Dr NE40 52 B4
Burnaby St SR4 102 A1
Burnbank Gateshead NE10 72 A6
Seaton Burn NE13 28 B8
5 Sunderland SR5 75 B2
Burnbank Ave NE25 31 B5
Burnbridge NE13 28 B8
Burnden Gr DH4 90 A5
Burnet Cl NE28 40 C5
Burnet Ct NE63 6 B1
Burney Villas NE8 56 A1
Burnfoot NE42 50 A4
Burnfoot Terr NE26 32 C4
Burnfoot Way NE3 37 E3
Burnhall Dr SR7 93 A1
Burnham Ave NE15 53 B7
Burnham Cl
1 Penshaw DH4 90 B6
Blyth NE24 17 E5
Burnham Gr
East Boldon NE36 74 D7
Newcastle-upon-Tyne NE6 56 E4
Burnham St NE34 59 C6
Burnhills Gdns NE40 52 A1
Burnhills La NE40 67 B8
Burnhope Dr SR5 75 B3
Burnhope Gdns NE9 71 D3
Burnhope Rd NE38 83 E6
Burnland Terr NE46 44 F5
Burnlea 4 DH4 94 C8
Burnlea Gdns NE23 23 B2
Burnley St NE21 53 C2
Burnmoor Gdns NE9 71 D3
Burnop Terr NE39 67 A2
Burnopfield Gdns NE15 54 A6
Burnopfield Prim Sch
NE16 79 A6
Burnopfield Rd NE39 67 F1
Burns Ave N DH5 94 E7
Burns Ave Blyth NE24 17 C5
West Boldon NE35 74 B8
Burns Ave S DH5 94 E7
Burns Cl West Rainton DH4 94 A2
Whickham NE16 69 B5
Biddick Hall NE34 59 B3
Burns Cres NE16 69 A8
Burns St NE32 58 B7
Burnside Gateshead NE10 71 E7
Newcastle-upon-Tyne NE2 98 B3
Ponteland NE20 25 B3
Bedlington NE22 11 D3
Jarrow NE32 58 C4
East Boldon NE36 74 E7
Ovington NE42 49 D4
Hexham NE46 44 F2
Morpeth NE61 4 A1
Ashington NE63 7 A3
Burnside Ave
Burnside DH4 90 C1
Annitsford NE23 29 B8
Burnside Cl
Whickham NE16 69 A4
Seghill NE23 22 E1
Blyth NE24 17 B8
Ovingham NE42 50 A4
Burnside Comm High Sch
NE28 40 D2
Burnside Cotts
Annitsford NE23 29 C8
Mickley Square NE43 49 E1
Burnside Fst Sch NE23 16 C1
Burnside Prim Sch DH4 90 D1
Burnside Rd
Newcastle-upon-Tyne NE3 38 C7
Tynemouth NE30 32 B3
Rowlands Gill NE39 67 D2
Burnside The NE5 36 E1
Burnside View NE23 22 E1
Burnstones NE5 36 E1
Burnt House Rd NE25 31 E3
Burnt Houses NE40 52 B1
Burnthouse Cl NE21 68 A8
Burnthouse La
Whickham NE16 69 A5
Whickham NE16 69 A6
Whickham, Whickham Fell NE16 69 A4
Burntland Ave SR5 74 F2
Burnville NE6 56 A7
Burnville Rd SR4 102 B1
Burnville Rd S SR4 102 B1
Burnway Washington NE37 83 B8
Seaham SR7 93 A1
Burradon Farm Cotts
NE23 29 D7
Burradon Prim Sch NE23 29 C5
Burradon Rd NE23 29 C7
Burrow St 5 NE33 42 C3
Burscough Cres SR6 75 D2
Burstow Ave NE6 56 E3
Burswell Ave NE46 44 F5
Burswell Villas NE46 44 F5
Burt Ave NE29 41 E5
Burt Cl DH6 97 E3
Burt Cres NE23 29 B8
Burt Memorial Homes
NE62 10 E5
Burt Rd NE22 11 E3
Burt St NE24 17 E8
Burt Terr Walbottle NE15 36 A2
Morpeth NE61 9 A8
Burtree NE38 83 B3
Burwell Ave NE5 53 F8
Burwood Cl NE6 57 A4
Burwood Rd
Tynemouth NE29 41 C8
Newcastle-upon-Tyne NE6 56 F3
Business & Innovation Ctr
SR5 74 F1
Buston Terr NE2 38 F1
Busty Bank
Burnopfield NE16 79 B7
Burnopfield NE16,NE39 79 A8
Butcher's Bridge Rd
NE32 58 B4
Butcher's La NE61 4 F5
Bute Ct 3 SR3 92 A6
Bute Dr NE39 66 F4
Bute Rd N NE39 66 F4
Bute Rd S NE39 66 F3
Bute St DH9 79 A2
Buteland Rd NE15 53 F7
Buteland Terr NE64 7 D4
Butsfield Gdns SR3 86 B2
Butterburn Cl NE7 39 E4
Butterfield Cl NE40 51 F4
Buttermere
Gateshead NE10 72 A8
Cleadon SR6 60 A1
Buttermere Ave
Easington Lane DH5 97 C8
Whickham NE16 69 D7
Buttermere Cl
Chester le Street DH2 88 C2

Buttermere Cl *continued*
Killingworth NE12 ....29 C3
3 Newcastle-upon-Tyne NE5 ....37 B1
Buttermere Cres
South Hetton DH6 ....97 E8
Blaydon NE21 ....68 B8
Buttermere Gdns
South Shields NE34 ....59 E6
Gateshead NE9 ....71 A5
Buttermere Rd NE30 ....32 A2
Buttermere St SR2 ....86 E2
Buttermere Way NE24 ....12 B1
Butterwell Dr NE61 ....4 E3
Buttsfield Terr DH4 ....90 B8
Buxton Cl Wallsend NE28 ....40 D5
Jarrow NE32 ....58 C5
Buxton Gdns
Newcastle-upon-Tyne NE5 ....36 F3
Sunderland SR3 ....86 B3
Buxton Gn NE5 ....36 F3
Buxton Rd NE32 ....58 C5
Buxton St NE1 ....99 C1
By-Way The NE15 ....35 D1
Byer Sq DH5 ....95 A6
Byer St DH5 ....95 A6
Byermoor RC Prim Sch NE16 ....79 D7
Byers Ct SR3 ....92 B8
Byeways The NE12 ....39 B6
Byewell Gr NE27 ....31 A3
Byewell View NE43 ....64 D7
Bygate Cl NE3 ....37 E3
Bygate Rd NE25 ....31 E4
Byker Bank NE6 ....56 A5
Byker Bldgs NE6 ....56 A6
Byker Bridge NE1,NE6 ....56 A6
Byker Bsns Development Ctr 9 NE6 ....56 B5
Byker Cres 16 NE6 ....56 C6
Byker Metro Sta NE6 ....56 C6
Byker Prim Sch NE6 ....56 B5
Byker Terr NE6 ....56 F6
Byland Cl DH4 ....90 C2
Byland Ct NE38 ....83 C5
Byland Rd NE12 ....38 F6
Bylands Gdns SR3 ....86 B3
Byony Toft SR2 ....93 A7
Byrne Terr W 2 SR3 ....92 B7
Byrness NE5 ....36 E1
Byrness Cl NE3 ....37 C4
Byrness Ct NE28 ....40 E5
Byrness Row NE23 ....22 C8
Byron Ave Blyth NE24 ....17 C6
6 Wallsend NE28 ....41 A1
Hebburn NE31 ....57 F6
West Boldon NE35 ....74 A8
Byron Cl NE62 ....10 E7
Byron Ct Whickham NE16 ....69 A8
Newcastle-upon-Tyne NE5 ....36 C2
Byron Lodge Est 6 SR7 ....92 E1
Byron Pl NE63 ....6 F2
Byron Rd SR5 ....75 A2
Byron St Ouston DH2 ....81 F1
Newcastle-upon-Tyne NE2 ....99 B2
4 South Shields NE33 ....59 D8
Sunderland SR5 ....75 C1
Byron Terr
Houghton-le-Spring DH5 ....94 E7
5 Seaham SR7 ....92 F1
Byron Wlk NE8 ....56 A2
Bywell Ave
Newcastle-upon-Tyne, Denton Burn NE15 ....53 E7
Newcastle-upon-Tyne, Fawdon NE3 ....37 F8
South Shields NE34 ....60 A7
Hexham NE46 ....45 D4
Sunderland SR5 ....75 C3
Bywell Cl NE40 ....51 E3
Bywell Gdns
Dunston NE11 ....70 A5
Gateshead NE9 ....71 B6
Bywell Rd Ashington NE63 ....6 D2
Cleadon SR6 ....74 F8
Bywell St NE6 ....56 D5
Bywell Terr NE32 ....58 B3

C

Cadehill Rd NE43 ....64 C6
Cadlestone Ct NE23 ....22 D8
Caedmon Prim Sch NE8 ....101 B1
Caer Urfa Cl NE33 ....42 C4
Caernarvon Cl NE5 ....37 B4
Caernarvon Dr SR3 ....91 C6
Caesar's Wlk 3 NE33 ....42 C4
Cairncross SR5 ....74 A1
Cairnglass Gn NE23 ....22 D8
Cairngorm Ave NE38 ....83 A2
Cairnhill Terr DH4 ....90 D4
Cairns Rd SR5 ....75 C4
Cairns Sq SR5 ....75 C4
Cairns Way NE3 ....37 F7
Cairnside SR3 ....91 C7
Cairnside S SR3 ....91 B7
Cairnsmore Cl
Cramlington NE23 ....22 B4
Newcastle-upon-Tyne NE6 ....57 B8
Cairnsmore Dr NE38 ....83 B3
Cairo St SR2 ....86 F3
Caithness Rd SR5 ....73 F2
Caithness Sq SR5 ....73 F2
Calais Rd SR5 ....73 F1
Calandra Chase NE2 ....98 B4
Caldbeck Ave NE6 ....56 F3
Caldbeck Cl NE6 ....56 F3
Calder Ct 13 SR3 ....91 F6
Calder Gn NE32 ....58 C2
Calder Wlk
Sunniside NE16 ....69 A2
Sunniside NE16 ....69 A3
Calderbourne Ave SR6 ....75 E4
Calderdale NE28 ....39 F5
Calderdale Ave NE6 ....56 F7
Calderwood Cres NE9 ....71 A3
Caldew Cres NE5 ....54 A8
Caldew Ct DH5 ....95 B2
Caldwell Rd NE3 ....37 F8
Caledonia St NE6 ....57 A4
Caledonian Rd SR5 ....73 F3
Caledonian St NE31 ....57 D7
Calf Cl Dr NE32 ....58 B2
Calf Close Wlk NE32 ....58 C2
Calfclose La NE32 ....58 C2
California NE21 ....53 B1
California Gdns 13 NE61 ....9 A8
Callaley Ave NE16 ....68 F6
Callaly Ave NE23 ....22 C6
Callaly Castle* NE66 ....117 F8
Callaly Cl NE61 ....4 F3
Callaly Way NE6 ....56 D4
Callander DH2 ....82 A2
Callendar Ct NE9 ....71 C5
Callerdale Rd NE24 ....17 A7
Callerton NE12 ....29 D5
Callerton Ave NE29 ....41 C6
Callerton Cl
Cramlington NE23 ....22 C6
5 Ashington NE63 ....6 F2
Callerton Ct NE20 ....25 E4
Callerton La NE5,NE15, NE20 ....25 E3
Callerton Lane End Cotts NE5 ....35 E7
Callerton Parkway Sta NE13 ....26 E1
Callerton Pl NE4 ....98 A1
Callerton Rd NE15 ....35 E2
Callerton View NE5 ....36 B4
Callington Cl DH4 ....89 E2
Callington Dr SR2 ....92 F7
Callum Dr NE34 ....60 A8
Calow Way NE16 ....68 F5
Calthwaite Cl SR5 ....74 B2
Calver Ct NE34 ....59 E5
Calvus Dr NE15 ....34 F2
Cam Mead SR3 ....92 A4
Camberley Cl SR3 ....92 C8
Camberley Rd NE28 ....41 A4
Camberwell Cl NE11 ....70 B6
Camberwell Way SR3 ....91 D5
Cambo Ave
Bedlington NE22 ....11 C1
Whitley Bay NE25 ....31 D3
Cambo Cl Blyth NE24 ....17 C7
Wallsend NE28 ....40 D6
Newcastle-upon-Tyne NE3 ....38 D5
Cambo Dr NE23 ....22 C6
Cambo Gn NE5 ....37 C2
Cambo Pl NE30 ....32 A1
Cambois Fst Sch NE24 ....12 C4
Camborne Gr NE8 ....101 C1
Camborne Pl NE8 ....101 C1
Cambourne Ave SR6 ....75 E4
Cambria Gn SR4 ....85 A6
Cambria St SR4 ....85 A6
Cambrian St NE32 ....58 B7
Cambrian Way NE38 ....83 B3
Cambridge Ave
Longbenton NE12 ....39 D8
Whitley Bay NE26 ....32 A5
Wallsend NE28 ....40 A3
Hebburn NE31 ....57 F5
Washington NE37 ....83 B8
Cambridge Cres DH4 ....90 A6
Cambridge Pl DH3 ....82 C1
Cambridge Rd
Stakeford NE62 ....11 A7
New Silksworth SR3 ....92 A7
Cambridge St NE4 ....100 B4
Cambridge Terr NE8 ....101 B1
Camden Sq NE30 ....42 B5
Camden St
Newcastle-upon-Tyne NE1, NE2 ....99 B2
North Shields NE30 ....42 B5
Sunderland SR5 ....75 A1
Camelford Ct NE15 ....53 C8
Cameron Cl NE34 ....59 C3
Cameron Rd NE42 ....50 D2
Camerton Pl NE28 ....40 E7
Camilla Rd NE15 ....34 F2
Camilla St NE8 ....101 C1
Camp Terr NE29 ....42 A6
Campbell Park Rd NE31 ....57 F5
Campbell Pl NE4 ....98 A1
Campbell Rd SR5 ....73 F2
Campbell Sq SR5 ....73 F2
Campbell St NE31 ....57 E7
Campbell Terr DH5 ....95 B1
Camperdown NE5 ....36 F1
Camperdown Ave
Chester le Street DH3 ....88 D5
Killingworth NE12 ....29 B4
Camperdown Ind Est NE12 ....29 B5
Campion Gdns NE10 ....71 D5
Campion Way NE63 ....6 C2
Campsie Cl NE38 ....83 B3
Campsie Cres NE30 ....32 A1
Campus Martius NE15 ....34 E2
Campville NE29 ....42 A6
Camsey Cl NE12 ....38 F7
Camsey Pl NE12 ....38 F7
Canberra Ave NE25 ....31 D3
Canberra Dr NE34 ....58 F4
Canberra Rd SR4 ....85 D4
Candelford Cl NE7 ....39 D3
Candlish St NE33 ....42 D2
Canning St Hebburn NE31 ....57 E5
Newcastle-upon-Tyne NE4 ....54 E5
Canning Street Prim Sch NE4 ....54 D5
Cannock NE12 ....29 D4
Cannock Dr NE7 ....39 A4
Cannon St NE8 ....101 B4
Canon Cockin St SR2 ....86 F4
Canon Gr NE32 ....58 C7
Canon Savage Dr NE46 ....44 E4
Canonbie Sq NE23 ....22 D8
Canonsfield Cl
Newcastle-upon-Tyne NE15 ....36 B3
Silksworth SR3 ....91 F5
Canterbury Ave NE28 ....40 D6
Canterbury Cl
Longbenton NE12 ....39 A7
Ashington NE63 ....6 F2
Canterbury Ho SR5 ....73 F4
Canterbury Rd SR5 ....74 A3
Canterbury St
South Shields NE33 ....59 D8
Newcastle-upon-Tyne NE6 ....56 D6
Canterbury Way
Wide Open NE13 ....28 B5
Hedworth NE32 ....58 A1
Capercaillie Lodge NE23 ....22 B1
Capetown Rd SR5 ....73 F2
Capetown Sq SR5 ....73 F2
Caplestone Cl NE38 ....83 B3
Capstan La NE9 ....71 C2
Captains Row The NE33 ....59 B8
Captains Wharf NE33 ....42 C3
Capulet Gr NE34 ....59 A5
Capulet Terr SR2 ....86 E4
Caradoc Cl NE38 ....83 B3
Caragh Rd DH2 ....88 C1
Caraway Wlk NE34 ....59 E2
Carden Ave NE34 ....60 B5
Cardiff Sq SR5 ....73 F1
Cardigan Gr NE30 ....32 A3
Cardigan Rd SR5 ....73 F2
Cardigan Terr NE6 ....56 B7
Cardinal Cl
Longbenton NE12 ....39 A6
Newcastle-upon-Tyne NE15 ....36 B3
Cardinals Cl 5 SR3 ....91 F5
Cardonnel St NE29 ....42 A4
Cardwell St SR6 ....75 E1
Careen Cres SR3 ....91 B7
Carew Ct NE23 ....22 B5
Carham Ave NE23 ....22 C6
Carham Cl
Newcastle-upon-Tyne NE3 ....38 D6
Corbridge NE45 ....47 B5
Caris St NE8,NE9 ....71 A8
Carisbrooke NE22 ....11 A2
Carisbrooke Ct SR1 ....102 B2
Carlcroft Pl NE23 ....22 C5
Carley Hill Prim Sch SR5 ....75 B3
Carley Hill Rd SR5 ....75 B3
Carley Rd SR5 ....75 B2
Carlingford Rd DH2 ....88 B1
Carliol Pl NE1 ....99 B1
Carliol Sq NE1 ....99 B1
Carliol St NE1 ....99 B1
Carlisle Cl NE27 ....30 C1
Carlisle Cres DH4 ....90 B7
Carlisle Ct 11 NE10 ....56 D1
Carlisle Ho
Newcastle-upon-Tyne NE4 ....98 A1
4 Sunderland SR3 ....91 D7
Carlisle Lea NE61 ....9 B7
Carlisle Pl NE9 ....71 B4
Carlisle St NE10 ....56 D1
Carlisle Terr
3 Shiremoor NE27 ....30 E1
6 Sunderland SR5 ....74 F2
Carlisle Way NE27 ....30 C1
Carlow Dr NE62 ....11 D8
Carlton Ave NE24 ....17 C3
Carlton Cl Urpeth DH2 ....81 E2
Newcastle-upon-Tyne NE3 ....38 A3
Carlton Cres SR3 ....91 C7
Carlton Ct NE11 ....70 C5
Carlton Gdns NE15 ....53 E7
Carlton Gr NE63 ....6 F1
Carlton Ho NE64 ....7 E5
Carlton Rd NE12 ....39 D6
Carlton St NE24 ....17 F7
Carlton Terr Blyth NE24 ....17 D8
North Shields NE29 ....41 F5
Gateshead NE9 ....70 F5
Springwell NE9 ....71 F1
Carlyle Cres NE16 ....69 A8
Carlyle Ct 4 NE28 ....41 A1
Carlyle St 1 NE28 ....41 A1
Carlyon St SR2 ....103 A1
Carmel Gr NE23 ....16 A1
Carnaby Cl NE42 ....50 D3
Carnaby Rd NE6 ....56 F4
Carnation Ave DH4 ....89 E3
Carnation Terr 5 NE16 ....69 B7
Carnegie Cl NE34 ....59 C4
Carnegie St 10 SR2 ....86 F2
Carnforth Cl NE28 ....40 E7
Carnforth Gdns
Rowlands Gill NE39 ....67 E3
Gateshead NE9 ....71 B4
Carnforth Gn NE3 ....37 E4
Carnoustie Ouston DH2 ....82 A1
Washington NE37 ....72 C3
Carnoustie Cl NE7 ....39 C4
Carnoustie Ct
Gateshead NE10 ....72 B6
Whitley Bay NE25 ....31 C5
Carnoustie Dr NE34 ....59 F3
Carol Gdns NE7 ....39 B3
Carol St SR4 ....102 B3
Caroline Cotts NE5 ....54 B8
Caroline Gdns NE28 ....41 A3
Caroline St
Hetton le Hole DH5 ....95 A4
Jarrow NE32 ....58 A7
Newcastle-upon-Tyne NE4 ....54 E4
Caroline Terr NE21 ....53 B4
Carolyn Cl NE12 ....39 C6
Carolyn Cres NE26 ....31 E7
Carolyn Way NE26 ....31 E7
Carpenter St NE33 ....42 B2
Carr Hill Rd N10,NE9 ....71 B7
Carr Hill Sch NE9 ....71 B7
Carr St Blyth NE24 ....17 C4
Hebburn NE31 ....57 D7
Carrawburgh Temple of Mithras* NE47 ....128 A5
Carrfield NE20 ....25 F7
Carrfield Rd NE3 ....37 F5
Carrhouse La SR7 ....95 F4
Carrick Dr NE24 ....17 D4
Carrigill Pl NE12 ....39 A6
Carrington Cl NE23 ....22 F1
Carrmere Rd SR2 ....86 E1
Carrock Ct SR3 ....91 F6
Carroll Wlk NE34 ....59 A2
Carrowmore Rd DH2 ....88 C1
Carrs Cl NE42 ....50 F3
Carrsfield NE45 ....47 A5
Carrsyde Cl NE16 ....68 F5
Carsdale Rd NE3 ....37 D5
Cartington Ave NE27 ....30 F2
Cartington Ct NE3 ....37 E7
Cartington Rd NE29 ....41 E5
Cartington Terr NE6 ....39 C1
Cartmel Ct DH2 ....88 A2
Cartmel Gn NE5 ....37 A1
Cartmel Gr NE8 ....70 D7
Cartmel Pk NE10 ....57 A1
Cartwright Rd SR5 ....74 B1
Carville Fst Sch NE28 ....57 B8
Carville Gdns NE28 ....57 B8
Carville Rd NE28 ....40 B1
Carville Rise NE6 ....56 C6
Carville St NE10 ....56 B2
Carville Station Cotts NE28 ....40 C1
Carvoran 4 NE28 ....40 F4
Carwarding Pl NE5 ....37 C2
Caseton Cl NE25 ....31 C6
Caspian Cl NE32 ....58 C5
Caspian Rd SR5 ....73 F1
Caspian Sq SR5 ....73 F1
Castellian Rd SR5 ....74 C1
Casterton Gr NE5 ....36 B3
Castle Bank NE61 ....9 A8
Castle Cl
Chester le Street DH3 ....88 D2
Hetton le Hole DH5 ....95 B2
Whickham NE16 ....69 A7
7 Newcastle-upon-Tyne NE3 ....37 D5
Prudhoe NE42 ....50 C3
Morpeth NE61 ....8 F8
Castle Ct NE20 ....25 E6
Castle Dene Gr DH4 ....94 D8
Castle Farm Cotts NE7 ....38 E3
Castle Farm Mews NE2 ....38 E3
Castle Farm Rd NE2,NE7 ....38 F4
Castle Farm Tennis Ctr NE7 ....38 F4
Castle Garth NE1 ....101 B4
Castle Gn 10 SR3 ....91 D7
Castle Lea NE42 ....50 B3
Castle Leazes (Halls of Residence) NE2 ....98 B3
Castle Mdws NE61 ....8 E7
Castle Mews SR3 ....91 D7
Castle Rd
Washington NE38 ....83 A5
Prudhoe NE42 ....50 B3
Castle Riggs DH2 ....88 B3
Castle Sq Backworth NE27 ....30 B5
Morpeth NE61 ....9 A8
Castle St Hazlerigg NE13 ....28 A4
Morpeth NE61 ....9 A8
Sunderland SR1 ....102 C3
Castle St S 4 SR5 ....74 C1
Castle Terr NE63 ....6 E4
Castle View
Chester le Street DH3 ....88 C5
Penshaw DH4 ....90 B8
Ovingham NE42 ....50 B4
Prudhoe NE42 ....50 C3
Sunderland SR5 ....74 B1
Castle View Sch SR5 ....74 A1
Castle Wlk NE61 ....9 A7
Castledale Ave NE24 ....17 A6
Castledene Ct
Newcastle-upon-Tyne NE3 ....38 F4
Sunderland SR5 ....74 A2
Castlefields DH4 ....89 D3
Castleford Rd SR5 ....73 F2
Castlegate Gdns NE8 ....100 A1
Castlemain Cl DH4 ....89 D3
Castlenook Pl NE15 ....53 F7
Castlereagh Homes The SR7 ....93 D1
Castlereagh St SR3 ....92 A7
Castlereigh Cl DH4 ....89 D
Castles Gn NE12 ....29 F
Castleside Rd NE15 ....54 A
Castleton Ct
Newcastle-upon-Tyne NE2 38
Cramlington NE23 16
Castleton Gr NE2 ....38 F
Castleton Lodge NE4 54
Castleton Rd NE32 ....58 C
Castletown Prim Sch SR5 ....85 E
Castletown Rd SR5 ....74 D
Castletown Way SR5 ....74 D
Castleway Dinnington NE13 ....27 E
Pegswood NE61 ....4 F
Castlewood Cl NE5 ....36 D
Catchside Cl NE16 ....69 A
Cateran Way NE23 ....22 C
Catharine St W SR4 ....102 A
Cathedral Ct NE8 ....56 A
Cathedral View DH4 ....90 D
Catherine Cookson Ct NE33 ....42 E
Catherine Rd DH4 ....90 D
Catherine St 3 NE33 ....42 D
Catherine View 8 NE40 ....51 F
Catholic Row NE22 ....15 E
Catkin Wlk NE40 ....52 A
Cato Sq SR5 ....75 A
Cato St SR5 ....75 A
Catrail Pl NE23 ....22 C
Cattle Market NE46 ....45 E
Catton Gr NE16 ....69 E
Catton Pl NE28 ....40 E
Cauldwell Ave
Whitley Bay NE25 ....31 D
South Shields NE34 ....59 E
Cauldwell Cl NE25 ....31 E
Cauldwell La NE25 ....31 E
Cauldwell Pl NE34 ....59 E
Cauldwell Villas NE34 ....59 E
Causeway Gateshead NE9 ....71 B
Sunderland SR6 ....103 A
Causeway The
Throckley NE15 ....35 D
Gateshead NE9 ....71 A
Causey Arch* DH9 ....80 A
Causey Arch Sta* NE16 ....80 B
Causey Bank NE1 ....99 B
Causey Brae NE46 ....44 F
Causey Hill Rd
Hexham NE46 ....44 F
Hexham NE46 ....45 B
Causey Hill Way NE46 ....44 E
Causey Pk NE46 ....44 F
Causey Rd DH9,NE16 ....80 A
Causey St NE3 ....38 C
Causey Way Tanfield DH9 ....80 A
Hexham NE46 ....44 F
Cavalier Way SR3 ....91 F
Cavendish Gdns NE63 ....6 D
Cavendish Pl
Burnopfield NE16 ....79 A
Newcastle-upon-Tyne NE2 ....38 F
New Silksworth SR3 ....91 F
Cavendish Rd NE2 ....38 F
Cavendish Sq NE61 ....4 E
Cavendish Terr NE63 ....6 D
Caversham Rd NE5 ....36 B
Cawburn Cl NE7 ....39 E
Cawdell Ct NE30 ....42 B
Cawfields Milecastle* NE49 ....126 F
Cawnpore Sq SR4 ....85 E
Cawthorne Terr NE16 ....79 A
Caxton Way DH3 ....88 D
Caxton Wlk NE34 ....59 A
Caynham Cl NE29 ....41 E
Cayton Gr NE5 ....36 B
Cecil Ct Ponteland NE20 ....25 F
Wallsend NE28 ....57 B
Cecil St NE29 ....42 A
Cecil Terr NE46 ....45 B
Cedar Cl Bedlington NE22 ....10 F
Whitley Bay NE25 ....31 F
Cedar Cres Dunston NE11 ....69 F
Burnopfield NE16 ....78 F
Gateshead NE9 ....70 F
Cedar Ct NE29 ....31 E
Cedar Gr Wallsend NE28 ....40 D
Hebburn NE31 ....57 E
South Shields NE34 ....59 F
Ryton NE40 ....52 C
Whitburn SR6 ....60 F
Cedar Rd Blaydon NE21 ....53 C
Newcastle-upon-Tyne NE4 ....54 D
Cedar Terr
Fence Houses DH4 ....90 A
Washington NE38 ....83 C
Ashington NE63 ....6 E
Cedar Way NE12 ....29 E
Cedars DH2 ....88 B
Cedars Cres SR2 ....86 E
Cedars Ct SR2 ....86 D
Cedars Gn NE9 ....71 A
Cedars Pk SR2 ....86 E
Cedars Specl Sch The NE9 ....71 A
Cedars The Penshaw DH4 ....90 B
Whickham NE16 ....69 B
Newcastle-upon-Tyne NE4 ....100 B
Gateshead NE9 ....71 C
Sunderland SR2 ....86 D
Cedartree Gdns NE25 ....31 E
Cedarway NE10 ....71 E
Cedarwood DH4 ....89 E
Cedarwood Ave NE6 ....40 A
Cedarwood Gr SR2 ....86 D

Cedric Cres SR2 86 B4
Celadon Cl NE15 53 C8
Celandine Cl NE3 38 D7
Celandine Ct NE63 6 B1
Celandine Way NE10 71 E5
Cellar Hill Terr DH4 90 D2
Celtic Cl SR6 59 E1
Celtic Cres SR6 59 E1
Cemetery App NE34 59 E8
Cemetery Rd Jarrow NE32 58 C5
Gateshead NE8 101 C1
Centenary Ave NE34 60 A6
Centenary Cotts NE22 15 F8
Centenary Ct NE4 54 F4
Central Arc NE1 99 A1
Central Ave
North Shields NE29 41 E5
South Shields NE34 59 F6
Guide Post NE62 10 E7
Whitburn SR6 60 E1
Central Gdns NE34 59 F6
Central Newcastle High Sch
NE2 99 B4
Central Newcastle High Sch
The NE3 38 C4
Central Sq NE8 101 C3
Central Way SR4 85 E8
Centralway NE11 70 C4
Centurian Way NE22 10 E2
Centurion Rd NE15 53 F8
Centurion Way
Heddon-on-the-Wall NE15 34 E2
Gateshead NE9 71 B6
Ceolfrid Terr NE32 58 C4
Cestria Cty Prim Sch
DH3 88 D3
Chacombe NE38 83 D3
Chadderton Dr NE5 36 B3
Chadwick St NE28 40 B1
Chadwick Wlk NE8 101 A2
Chaffinch Ct NE63 6 B2
Chaffinch Rd 6 SR5 74 C1
Chaffinch Way NE12 29 C4
Chainbridge Ind Est
NE21 53 F4
Chainbridge Rd
Blaydon NE21 53 D3
Blaydon, Derwenthaugh
NE21 53 F4
Chainbridge Road Ind Est
NE21 53 F4
Chalfont Gr SR4 85 A2
Chalfont Rd NE6 56 F4
Chalford Rd 1 SR5 75 B2
Challoner's Gdns NE61 3 E1
Chamberlain St
Blyth NE24 17 F6
Crawcrook NE40 51 F4
Chambers Cres NE9 71 C1
Chancery La NE24 17 D7
Chandler Ct NE2 38 F2
Chandlers Ford DH4 89 F8
Chandlers Quay NE6 56 C4
Chandless St NE8 101 C3
Chandos SR3 92 A4
Chandos St NE8 70 F8
Chandra Pl 3 NE5 37 B2
Chantry Cl SR3 91 E5
Chantry Dr NE13 28 B6
Chantry Est NE45 46 F6
Chantry Pl
West Rainton DH4 94 A2
3 Morpeth NE61 9 A8
Chapel & Tower* 109 D5
Chapel Ave NE16 79 B6
Chapel Cl
Kibblesworth NE11 81 D6
Newcastle-upon-Tyne NE3 28 D1
Chapel Ct Sherburn DH6 96 A1
Seaton Burn NE13 28 B8
Chapel House Dr NE5 36 C1
Chapel House Gr NE5 36 C1
Chapel House Mid Sch
NE5 36 B2
Chapel House Rd NE5 36 C1
Chapel La Haswell DH6 97 F3
Whitley Bay NE25 31 E4
Wylam NE41 51 A6
Chapel Park Mid Sch
NE5 36 C3
Chapel Pl NE13 28 B8
Chapel Rd NE32 58 B7
Chapel Row Birtley DH3 82 E3
Penshaw DH4 90 C5
Mickley Square NE43 49 E1
Chapel St
Hetton le Hole DH5 95 B4
Tantobie DH9 79 B2
North Shields NE29 41 E5
Chapel View
Brunswick Village NE13 28 A6
Rowlands Gill NE39 67 E3
Chapelville NE13 28 B8
Chapman St SR6 75 E4
Chapter Row NE33 42 C3
Chapwell Woods Rd
NE39 67 A3
Chare The NE1 99 A2
Chareway NE46 45 A6
Chareway La NE46 45 A6
Charlbury Cl NE9 71 F1
Charlcote Cres NE36 74 D7
Charles Ave
Longbenton NE12 39 D8
Whitley Bay NE26 32 B5
Shiremoor NE27 30 F4
Newcastle-upon-Tyne NE3 37 E6
Charles Baker Wlk NE34 60 B7
Charles Ct 18 NE6 56 C7
Charles Dr NE23 29 B8
Charles Perkins Memorial
Cottage Homes DH3 82 C3
Charles St Newbottle DH4 90 D4
Hazlerigg NE13 28 A4
West Boldon NE35 73 F8
Pegswood NE61 4 F3
Gateshead NE8 101 C2
Sunderland SR1 103 B3
13 Ryhope SR2 93 A6
Sunderland, Monkwearmouth
SR6 103 A4
Charleswood NE3 38 D8
Charlie St NE40 51 F1
Charlotte Cl NE4 100 B3
Charlotte Mews NE1 98 C1
Charlotte Sq NE1 98 C1
Charlotte St
Wallsend NE28 40 C2
North Shields NE30 42 B6
South Shields NE33 42 C2
Crawcrook NE40 51 E3
Charlton Cl NE46 44 F2
Charlton Ct NE25 31 E3
Charlton Gdns NE61 9 B7
Charlton Gr SR6 75 A8
Charlton Rd SR5 75 C3
Charlton St
Newcastle-upon-Tyne NE15 53 D6
Blyth NE24 17 D7
Ashington NE63 6 C4
Charlton Villas NE40 52 B1
Charlton Wlk NE8 100 C1
Charman St SR1 103 A3
Charminster Gdns NE6 39 C1
Charnwood Ave NE12 39 A6
Charnwood Ct NE33 42 E2
Charnwood Gdns NE9 71 B5
Charter Dr SR3 91 C7
Charters Cres DH6 97 F7
Chase Ct DH6 96 A1
Chase Farm Dr NE24 16 F7
Chase Mdws NE24 16 F6
Chase Mews NE24 16 F7
Chase Sch NE16 69 B7
Chase The
Killingworth NE12 29 A2
North Shields NE29 41 F6
Washington NE38 82 F1
Hexham NE46 44 F3
Chasedale Cres NE24 17 A7
Chatham Cl NE25 23 D1
Chatham Rd SR5 74 A2
Chathill Cl
Whitley Bay NE25 31 D5
Morpeth NE61 9 B6
Chathill Terr NE6 56 F5
Chatsworth Cres SR4 86 A4
Chatsworth Ct 8 NE33 42 D3
Chatsworth Dr NE22 11 C3
Chatsworth Gdns
Whitley Bay NE25 31 E3
Newcastle-upon-Tyne,
Westerhope NE5 36 F3
Newcastle-upon-Tyne, Walker
NE6 56 D4
Chatsworth Pl NE16 69 A5
Chatsworth Rd NE32 58 C5
Chatsworth St SR4 102 A1
Chatsworth St S SR4 86 A4
Chatterton St SR5 75 A2
Chatton Ave
Cramlington NE23 22 C6
South Shields NE34 60 B8
Chatton Cl
Chester le Street DH2 88 A1
Morpeth NE61 9 C5
Chatton St NE28 41 C1
Chatton Wynd NE3 38 A7
Chaucer Ave NE34 59 A3
Chaucer Cl NE8 56 A2
Chaucer Rd NE16 69 B8
Chaucer St 9 DH4 94 D8
Chaytor Gr SR1 103 B2
Chaytor St NE32 58 B8
Cheadle Ave
Cramlington NE23 16 A1
Wallsend NE28 40 E6
Cheadle Rd SR5 74 A2
Cheam Cl NE16 69 B5
Cheam Rd SR5 74 A2
Cheddar Gdns NE9 70 F3
Cheldon Cl NE25 31 C6
Chelford Cl NE28 40 E7
Chelmsford Gr NE2 56 A7
Chelmsford Rd SR5 74 A2
Chelmsford Sq SR5 74 A3
Chelmsford St 5 SR3 92 A8
Chelsea Gdns NE8 71 B8
Chelsea Gr NE4 98 A1
Cheltenham Ct NE63 6 C2
Cheltenham Dr NE35 58 E2
Cheltenham Rd SR5 74 A2
Cheltenham Sq SR5 74 A2
Cheltenham Terr NE6 56 B7
Chelton Cl NE13 28 B4
Chepstow Gdns NE8 70 D7
Chepstow Rd NE15 53 F6
Chepstow St SR4 102 B2
Cherribank SR2 92 E6
Cherry Banks DH3 88 D5
Cherry Blossom Way
NE37 73 B1
Cherry Cotts DH9 79 B2
Cherry Dr DH6 97 F3
Cherry Gr
Killingworth NE12 29 C4
Cherry Gr continued
Prudhoe NE42 50 B3
Cherry Knowle Hospl
SR2 92 E4
Cherry Tree Dr NE22 10 F1
Cherry Tree Gdns NE15 50 C8
Cherry Tree La NE41 51 A6
Cherry Tree Sq 6 SR2 92 E8
Cherry Tree Wlk NE31 57 E4
Cherry Trees NE24 17 D6
Cherry Way
Fence Houses DH4 90 B1
Killingworth NE12 29 C4
Cherryburn Cotts NE43 49 E2
Cherryburn Gdns NE4 54 E8
Cherrytree Cl NE12 29 F2
Cherrytree Ct NE22 11 D2
Cherrytree Dr NE16 69 C8
Cherrytree Gdns
Whitley Bay NE25 31 F3
Gateshead NE9 71 A4
Cherrytree Rd DH2 88 A5
Cherrywood NE6 39 E1
Cherrywood Gdns SR3 92 B7
Cherwell NE37 83 F8
Cherwell Sq NE12 29 C1
Chesham Gdns NE5 36 B2
Chesham Gn NE3 37 F5
Cheshire Ave DH3 82 C1
Cheshire Cl NE63 6 A4
Cheshire Ct NE31 57 D5
Cheshire Gdns NE28 40 A3
Cheshire Gr NE34 60 B7
Chesils The NE12 39 A5
Chesmond Dr NE21 53 C3
Chessar Ave NE5 37 B2
Chester Ave NE28 40 F3
Chester Cl NE20 25 B4
Chester Cres
Newcastle-upon-Tyne NE2 99 C3
Sunderland SR1 102 B2
Chester Ct NE12 39 B6
Chester Gdns NE34 59 E7
Chester Gr Seghill NE23 22 E1
Blyth NE24 17 C6
Chester Mews SR4 102 B2
Chester Oval SR2 102 B2
Chester Pl NE8 101 B2
Chester Rd
Chester le Street DH3 88 F5
Bournmoor DH3,DH4 89 D3
Penshaw DH4 90 B7
Shiney Row DH4 90 B7
Sunderland, High Barnes
SR1 SR2,SR4 85 F5
Sunderland SR1,SR4 102 B2
Sunderland, Grindon SR4 85 B3
Chester Sq NE61 2 A3
Chester St Newbottle DH4 90 D2
Newcastle-upon-Tyne NE2 99 C3
Sunderland SR4 102 A2
Chester St E SR4 102 B2
Chester St W SR4 102 A2
Chester Terr SR1 102 B2
Chester Terr N SR4 102 B2
Chester Way NE32 58 A1
Chester-le-Street CE Jun
Sch DH2 88 B5
Chester-le-Street General
Hospl DH3 88 C2
Chester-le-Street Sta
DH3 88 C3
Chesterfield Rd NE4 54 F4
Chesterhill NE23 22 B5
Chesterholm (Vindolanda)
Roman Fort* NE47 127 C3
Chesters 5 NE28 40 F4
Chesters (Cilurnum) Roman
Fort* NE46 128 D5
Chesters Ave NE12 39 A5
Chesters Dene DH8 76 E3
Chesters Gdns NE40 51 E4
Chesters Museum*
NE46 128 D5
Chesters Pk NE9 70 F6
Chesters The
Ebchester DH8 76 E3
Whitley Bay NE25 31 E6
Newcastle-upon-Tyne NE5 36 C1
Chesterton Rd NE34 59 B3
Chesterwood Dr NE28 40 A2
Chesterwood Terr NE10 57 B1
Chestnut Ave
Whickham NE16 69 B5
Blyth NE24 12 D1
Whitley Bay NE25 31 F4
Washington NE38 83 B1
Newcastle-upon-Tyne NE5 37 E2
Chestnut Cl
Killingworth NE12 29 B4
Hedworth NE32 58 D1
Chestnut Cres SR5 74 F3
Chestnut Gdns NE8 70 C8
Chestnut Gr NE34 59 F4
Chestnut St
Wallsend NE28 40 C1
Ashington NE63 6 D3
Chestnut Terr DH4 90 C3
Cheswick Dr NE3 38 D6
Chevin Cl NE28,NE6 40 B1
Chevington NE10 72 A5
Chevington Cl NE61 4 E3
Chevington Gdns 6 NE5 37 D1
Chevington Gr NE25 31 D7
Cheviot Cl
Tynemouth NE29 31 F2
Washington NE37 83 A6
Ellington NE61 1 D4
Cheviot Ct Blaydon NE21 53 C3
Whitley Bay NE26 32 C4
Morpeth NE61 9 A6
Cheviot Cty Jun Mix Sch
NE34 60 A8
Cheviot Fst Sch NE5 37 A4
Cheviot Gdns NE11 70 A7
Cheviot Gn NE11 70 A8
Cheviot Gr NE61 4 E3
Cheviot Grange NE23 29 C6
Cheviot La SR2 92 E7
Cheviot Mount NE6 56 C6
Cheviot Rd
Chester le Street DH2 88 B1
Blaydon NE21 53 C1
Hebburn NE32 58 A4
South Shields NE34 60 A7
South Shields NE34 60 A8
Cheviot St SR43 85 F7
Cheviot View
Longbenton NE12 39 C6
Brunswick Village NE13 28 A6
Ponteland NE20 26 A5
Seghill NE23 22 F1
Whitley Bay NE26 32 B5
Prudhoe NE42 50 E2
Ashington NE63 6 E5
Cheviot Way
Hexham NE46 45 A4
Stakeford NE62 11 B8
Chevron The 4 NE6 56 B5
Chevychase Ct SR7 92 F2
Chevyside Mid Sch NE5 37 A4
Cheyne Rd NE42 50 C2
Cheyne The SR3 92 A5
Chichester Ave NE23 21 F8
Chichester Cl
Newcastle-upon-Tyne NE3 37 D8
Ashington NE63 7 A2
Gateshead NE8 101 B2
Chichester Gr NE22 10 F2
Chichester Pl NE33 59 C8
Chichester Rd
South Shields NE33 42 D1
Sunderland SR6 75 E4
Chichester Rd E NE33 42 D1
Chichester Sta NE33 59 C8
Chichester Way NE32 58 B1
Chick's La 4 SR6 75 F8
Chicken Rd NE28 40 A4
Chigwell Cl DH4 90 B7
Chilcote NE10 71 D7
Chilcrosse NE10 71 F6
Chilham Ct
Tynemouth NE29 41 B8
Washington NE38 83 B4
Chillingham Castle*
NE66 112 B8
Chillingham Cl NE24 17 B5
Chillingham Cres NE63 6 C3
Chillingham Ct 19 NE6 56 C7
Chillingham Dr
Chester le Street DH2 88 A1
North Shields NE29 41 D4
Chillingham Ind Est NE6 56 C7
Chillingham Rd NE6 56 C8
Chillingham Road Prim Sch
NE6 56 C8
Chillingham Road Sta
NE6 56 D7
Chillingham Terr NE32 58 D4
Chilside Rd NE10 71 D7
Chiltern Ave DH2 88 B2
Chiltern Cl
Washington NE38 83 B3
Ashington NE63 6 F1
Chiltern Dr NE12 29 B1
Chiltern Gdns NE11 70 B7
Chiltern Rd NE29 31 F2
Chilton Gdns 10 DH4 94 A8
Chilton St 1 SR5 75 C1
Chimney Mills NE2 98 C4
China St SR2 86 E4
Chingford Cl DH4 90 C7
Chip The NE61 8 F5
Chipchase NE38 82 F4
Chipchase Ave NE23 22 B6
Chipchase Cl
Bedlington NE22 10 D1
Pegswood NE61 4 F3
Chipchase Cres NE5 36 E3
Chipchase Ct
Bournmoor DH4 89 D1
New Hartley NE25 23 D6
Seaham SR7 92 F2
Chipchase Terr NE32 58 B3
Chippendale Pl NE2 98 B4
Chirdon Cres NE46 45 C4
Chirnside NE23 22 B4
Chirton Ave
North Shields NE29 41 F5
South Shields NE34 60 C6
Chirton Dean Way NE29 42 A3
Chirton Dene Quays
NE28 41 F2
Chirton Gn Blyth NE24 17 B5
North Shields NE29 41 F5
Chirton Gr NE34 60 C6
Chirton Hill Dr NE29 41 C7
Chirton La NE29 41 E5
Chirton Lodge NE28 41 E5
Chirton St Joseph's RC Sch
NE29 41 E5
Chirton West View NE29 41 F5
Chirton Wynd NE6 56 C5
Chislehurst Rd DH4 90 B7
Chiswick Gdns NE8 71 A8
Chiswick Rd
Seaton Delaval NE25 23 E2
Sunderland SR5 74 A2
Chiswick Sq SR5 74 A2
Chollerford Ave
Whitley Bay NE25 32 B4
North Shields NE29 41 D6
Chollerford Cl NE3 38 A4
Chollerford Mews NE25 23 F2
Chollerton Dr
Longbenton NE12 40 A8
Bedlington NE22 11 A1
Choppington Fst Sch
NE62 10 E5
Choppington Rd
Bedlington NE22,NE62 10 F2
Morpeth NE61 9 B6
Chopwell Gdns NE9 71 D2
Chopwell Prim Sch NE17 66 B1
Chopwell Rd NE17 77 C6
Chopwell Wood Wlks*
NE39 66 F2
Chorley Pl NE6 56 E5
Chowdean Terr 4 NE9 70 F4
Chowdene Bank NE11,
NE9 70 F2
Christ Church CE Prim Sch
Newcastle-upon-Tyne NE2 99 C2
North Shields NE30 42 A6
Christal Terr SR6 75 D3
Christie Terr NE6 56 F5
Christon Cl NE3 38 E5
Christon Rd NE3 38 D5
Christon Way NE10 57 B2
Christopher Rd NE6 56 E7
Chudleigh Gdns NE5 36 B2
Church Ave
Newcastle-upon-Tyne NE3 38 D5
Choppington NE62 10 E5
West Sleekburn NE62 11 D7
Church Bank
Newburn NE15 52 F7
Wallsend NE28 40 D2
Jarrow NE32 58 D7
Sunderland SR5 75 A1
Church Chare
Chester le Street DH3 88 D3
Whickham NE16 69 B7
Ponteland NE20 25 F7
Church Cl Ebchester DH8 76 E3
Dinnington NE13 27 B7
Bedlington NE22 15 F8
Whitley Bay NE25 31 C4
Riding Mill NE44 62 F7
Church Ct
10 Gateshead NE10 56 D1
Bedlington NE22 15 F8
Church Dr NE9 71 A6
Church Flatt NE20 25 F7
Church High Sch NE2 99 B4
Church La
Bedlington NE22 16 A7
Newcastle-upon-Tyne NE3 38 D5
Riding Mill NE44 62 E7
Gateshead NE9 71 B6
Sunderland SR1 102 C2
Whitburn SR6 75 F8
Church Mews NE27 30 C5
Church Pl NE10 56 D1
Church Rd
Hetton le Hole DH5 95 A5
Newburn NE15 52 F7
Backworth NE27 30 C5
Newcastle-upon-Tyne NE3 38 D5
Wylam NE41 51 A6
Stannington NE61 14 C3
Gateshead NE9 71 A5
Church Rise
Whickham NE16 69 B7
Ryton NE40 52 E5
Church Row NE46 45 B5
Church Sq NE61 2 B3
Church St Birtley DH3 82 C4
Penshaw DH4 90 B6
West Rainton DH4 94 A2
7 Houghton-le-Spring DH4,
DH5 94 E8
Haswell DH6 97 E3
Gateshead, Felling NE10 71 D8
Dunston NE11 100 A1
Sunniside NE16 69 A1
Blaydon NE21 53 B1
Cramlington NE23 22 B6
Blyth NE24 17 E8
North Shields NE30 42 B6
Hebburn NE31 57 D7
Newcastle-upon-Tyne NE6 57 A4
Gateshead NE8 101 B4
Sunderland, South Hylton
SR4 85 A6
Sunderland, Southwick SR5 75 B2
Church St E SR1 103 C3
Church St N SR6 103 B4
Church Terr NE21 53 C3
Church Vale DH6 96 C4
Church View Haswell DH6 97 F3
Earsdon NE25 31 A5
Wallsend NE28 40 D2
Boldon Colliery NE35 58 E1
Washington NE37 83 D7
Newbiggin-by-the-Sea NE64 7 C5
New Silksworth SR3 92 A7
Church Way Earsdon NE25 31 A6
North Shields NE29,NE30 42 A6
South Shields NE33 42 C3

Church Wlk
Newcastle-upon-Tyne NE6 57 A5
Morpeth NE61 8 E7
Sunderland SR1 103 C3
Churchburn Dr NE61 8 F6
Churchdown Cl NE35 58 E2
Churcher Gdns NE28 40 A4
Churchill Ave
Whitley Bay NE25 31 F3
Sunderland SR5 75 A2
Churchill Gdns NE2 39 A1
Churchill Mews NE6 56 C4
Churchill Sq DH4 94 B8
Churchill St
Newcastle-upon-Tyne NE1 100 C4
Wallsend NE28 40 F4
Sunderland SR1 103 B2
Churchlands NE46 45 D4
Churchwalk House NE6 57 A5
Churston Cl DH4 90 C4
Chuter Ede Comp Sch NE34 59 B2
Chyll Edge NE61 3 C1
Cicero Terr 4 SR5 75 A2
Cinderford Cl NE35 58 E2
Circle Pl NE46 45 A5
Cirencester St SR4 102 B3
Cirrus Ho 14 SR3 92 A6
Citadel E NE12 29 D3
Citadel W NE12 29 D3
City Hall NE1 99 B2
City of Sunderland Coll SR5 74 E2
City of Sunderland Coll Bede Ctr SR3 85 F3
City of Sunderland Coll Shiney Row Ctr DH4 90 B5
City of Sunderland Coll Tunstall Ctr SR2 86 E2
City Rd NE1 99 C1
City Way SR3 91 C6
Civic Ct NE31 57 F5
Clacton Rd SR5 73 F1
Clanfield Ct NE7 38 F4
Clanny Ho SR4 85 F6
Clanny St Sunderland SR1 102 B2
Sunderland SR1 102 C2
Clanton Cl NE10 72 C7
Clapham Ave NE6 56 D5
Clara Ave NE27 30 F4
Clara St Blaydon NE21 53 B1
Newcastle-upon-Tyne NE4 54 D4
Clarabad Terr NE12 30 A1
Clarance Pl NE3 38 E5
Claremont Ave
Newcastle-upon-Tyne NE15 53 D7
Sunderland SR6 75 E3
Claremont Cres NE26 31 E7
Claremont Ct NE26 31 E8
Claremont Dr DH4 90 A6
Claremont Gdns
Whitley Bay NE26 31 F6
East Boldon NE36 74 D7
Claremont North Avenue Path NE8 101 B2
Claremont Pl
Newcastle-upon-Tyne NE2 98 C3
Gateshead NE8 101 B1
Claremont Rd
Newcastle-upon-Tyne NE2 98 B4
Whitley Bay NE26 31 F7
Sunderland SR6 75 E3
Claremont South Ave NE8 101 B1
Claremont St NE2 98 C3
Claremont Terr
Gateshead NE10 57 B1
Newcastle-upon-Tyne NE2 98 C3
Blyth NE24 17 D7
Sunderland SR2 102 C1
Claremont Wlk NE8 101 A1
Claremount Ct NE36 74 B7
Clarence Cres 2 NE26 32 B4
Clarence Ho NE2 99 C2
Clarence St Tantobie DH9 79 B2
Newcastle-upon-Tyne NE1, NE2 99 C2
Seaton Sluice NE26 24 D5
2 Sunderland SR5 75 A2
Clarence Terr DH3 88 C3
Clarendon Rd NE6 39 C1
Clarendon Sq SR5 75 B3
Clarewood Ave NE34 60 A8
Clarewood Ct NE4 98 B2
Clarewood Gn NE4 98 A2
Clarewood Pl NE5 54 C8
Clark's Terr 2 SR7 92 E1
Clarke Terr NE10 71 C8
Clarke's Terr NE23 29 A6
Clarks Field NE61 8 E8
Clarks Hill Wlk NE15 52 F7
Clasper Ct 11 NE33 42 C4
Clasper St NE4 100 B3
Clasper Way NE16 54 A3
Claude St
Hetton le Hole DH5 95 A3
9 Crawcrook NE40 51 F3
Claudius Ct 4 NE33 42 C4
Claverdon St NE5 36 B4
Clavering Pl NE1 101 A4
Clavering Rd
Whickham NE16 54 B1
Blaydon NE21 53 C1
Clavering Sq NE11 69 F8
Clavering St NE28 41 B1
Clavering Way NE21 53 E2
Claverley Dr NE27 30 C5
Claxheugh Cotts SR4 85 B7
Claxheugh Rd SR4 85 B7
Claymere Rd SR2 86 E1
Claypath NE10 71 F4
Claypath La NE33 42 D2
Claypath Rd DH5 95 B2
Claypath St 4 NE6 56 A6
Claypool Ct NE34 59 C5
Clayside House 3 NE33 42 D1
Clayton Park Sq NE2 99 B4
Clayton Rd NE2 99 B4
Clayton St
Newcastle-upon-Tyne NE1 99 A1
Bedlington NE22 11 D3
Dudley NE23 28 F8
Jarrow NE32 58 B7
Clayton St W NE1 100 C4
Clayton Terr
Heddon-on-the-Wall NE15 34 F2
Gateshead NE8 56 C1
Clayton Terrace Rd
High Spen NE13,NE39 66 D4
Chopwell NE17 66 C2
Clayworth Rd NE3 28 B1
Cleadon CE Inf Sch SR6 60 B1
Cleadon Gdns
Wallsend NE28 41 A5
Gateshead NE9 71 D3
Cleadon Hill Dr NE34 60 A4
Cleadon Hill Rd NE34 60 B4
Cleadon La SR6 60 C1
Cleadon Lane Ind Est NE36 74 E8
Cleadon Lea SR6 59 F1
Cleadon Mdws SR6 60 A2
Cleadon Old Hall SR6 60 A1
Cleadon St NE6 56 E6
Cleadon Twrs NE34 60 B4
Cleadon Village Cty Jun Mix Sch SR6 59 F1
Cleasby Gdns NE9 70 F6
Cleasewell Terr NE62 11 A7
Cleaside Ave NE34 60 A4
Cleaswell Hill NE62 10 F7
Cleaswell Hill Special Sch NE62 10 F7
Cleehill Dr NE29 31 F1
Cleeve Ct NE38 83 C5
Cleghorn St 4 NE6 56 C8
Clematis Cres NE9 71 D2
Clement Ave NE22 11 C1
Clement St NE9 70 F5
Clementina Cl SR2 103 B1
Clennel Ave NE31 57 D5
Clennel Ho 4 NE4 54 E5
Clent Way NE12 39 A6
Clephan St NE11 54 F1
Clervaux Terr NE32 58 C6
Cleveland Ave
Chester le Street DH2 88 B2
North Shields NE29 41 F6
Newbiggin-by-the-Sea NE64 7 D4
Cleveland Cres NE29 42 A6
Cleveland Ct Jarrow NE32 58 A7
9 South Shields NE33 42 C4
Cleveland Dr NE38 83 B3
Cleveland Gdns
Wallsend NE28 41 B3
Newcastle-upon-Tyne NE7 39 A3
Cleveland Rd
North Shields NE29 42 A6
Sunderland SR4 85 F5
Cleveland St 3 NE33 42 D4
Cleveland Terr
North Shields NE29 42 A6
Newbiggin-by-the-Sea NE64 7 D4
Cleveland View SR6 75 E6
Cliff Rd SR2 93 A6
Cliff Row NE26 32 C4
Cliff Terr SR2 93 A6
Cliff View SR2 93 A6
Cliffe Ct SR6 75 F4
Cliffe Pk SR6 75 F4
Clifford Gdns 3 NE40 51 F3
Clifford Rd NE6 56 D5
Clifford St
Chester le Street DH3 88 C1
Blaydon NE21 53 C3
North Shields NE30 42 C6
Newcastle-upon-Tyne NE6 56 B6
Sunderland SR4 102 A2
Clifford Terr
Chester le Street DH3 88 C2
Crawcrook NE40 51 F3
Cliffside NE34 60 C6
Clifton Ave Wallsend NE28 40 B2
South Shields NE34 59 E7
Clifton Cl Ryton NE40 52 E4
Stakeford NE62 11 A8
Clifton Ct NE3 37 D7
Clifton Gdns Blyth NE24 17 D4
North Shields NE29 41 E3
Gateshead NE9 70 F7
Clifton Gr NE25 31 E6
Clifton La NE61 9 B2
Clifton Rd
Cramlington NE23 22 C5
Newcastle-upon-Tyne NE4 54 F5
Sunderland SR6 75 E4
Clifton Terr
Longbenton NE12 39 D7
Whitley Bay NE26 32 B5
South Shields NE33 59 C8
Clifton Wlk NE5 36 B2
Cliftonbourne Ave SR6 75 E4
Cliftonville Ave NE4 54 E5
Cliftonville Gdns NE26 32 A6
Climbing Tree Wlk NE61 4 E3
Clintburn Ct NE23 22 C8
Clinton Pl Hazlerigg NE3 28 B2
Sunderland SR3 91 C6
Clipsham Cl NE12 39 B6
Clipstone Ave NE6 56 E3
Clipstone Cl NE15 35 C2
Clive Pl NE6 56 B5
Clive St North Shields NE29 42 B5
9 South Shields NE34 59 A4
Clockburn Lonnen NE16 68 E4
Clockburnsyde Cl NE16 68 E5
Clockmill Rd NE11,NE8 100 A1
Clockstand Cl 8 SR6 75 E2
Clockwell St SR5 74 F1
Cloggs The NE20 25 F7
Cloister Ave NE34 59 A5
Cloister Ct NE8 101 C3
Cloister Garth NE7 38 F5
Cloister Wlk NE32 58 C7
Cloisters The
South Shields NE34 59 F7
Newcastle-upon-Tyne NE7 38 F5
Sunderland SR2 103 A1
Close NE1 101 A4
Close E The DH2 88 C5
Close St
Sunderland, Millfield SR4 102 A3
4 Sunderland, Southwick SR5 75 B1
Close The
Chester le Street DH2 88 C5
Houghton-le-Spring DH5 94 F8
Burnopfield NE16 79 C7
Ponteland NE20 25 E5
Blaydon NE21 53 A1
Seghill NE23 22 F1
Blyth NE24 12 E1
Prudhoe NE42 50 E3
Newcastle-upon-Tyne NE5 53 E8
Stannington NE61 14 C3
Cleadon SR6 59 F1
Closeburn Sq SR3 92 B6
Closefield Gr NE25 31 E4
Cloth Mkt NE1 99 A1
Clough Dene
Tantobie DH9 79 B2
Tantobie, Pickering Nook NE16 79 A3
Clough La NE1 99 A1
Clousden Dr NE12 29 E1
Clousden Grange NE12 29 E1
Clovelly Ave NE4 54 E5
Clovelly Gdns
Bedlington NE22 15 F8
Whitley Bay NE26 32 A6
Clovelly Pl Ponteland NE20 25 C2
Jarrow NE32 58 E5
Clovelly Sq 6 SR5 74 A3
Clover Ave
Shiney Row DH4 90 B4
Gateshead NE10 56 B2
Winlaton Mill NE21 68 C6
Clover Hill NE16 69 B2
Cloverdale NE22 10 E1
Cloverdale Gdns
Whickham NE16 69 B5
Newcastle-upon-Tyne NE7 39 B3
Cloverfield Ave NE3 37 F6
Cloverhill NE32 58 C1
Cloverhill Ave NE31 57 D3
Cloverhill Cl NE23 22 A1
Cloverhill Com Prim Sch NE16 68 F4
Cloverhill Dr NE40 52 A4
Clumber St NE4 100 A3
Clumber St N NE4 100 A3
Clyde Ave NE31 57 E3
Clyde Ct 10 SR3 91 F6
Clyde St Chopwell NE17 66 C1
Gateshead NE8 71 A8
Clydedale Ave NE12 39 D8
Clydesdale Ave DH4 90 B7
Clydesdale Mount 8 NE6 56 C5
Clydesdale Rd NE6 56 C5
Clydesdale St DH5 95 A2
Clyvedon Rise NE34 60 A3
Co-operative Bldgs NE25 23 D3
Co-operative Cres NE10 71 C7
Co-operative St DH3 88 C4
Co-operative Terr
Great Lumley DH4 89 F1
Medomsley DH8 77 B1
Gateshead NE10 71 C7
Longbenton NE12 30 A1
Brunswick Village NE13 28 A6
Burnopfield NE16 79 B6
Backworth NE27 30 E3
11 Shiremoor NE27 30 E1
1 Washington NE37 83 E8
High Spen NE39 66 F5
Pegswood NE61 4 F3
Sunderland SR4 102 A1
Co-operative Villas DH6 96 D1
Coach La
Brunswick Village NE13 27 E4
Hazlerigg NE13 28 B4
Dinnington NE13,NE3 27 E4
North Shields NE29 42 A5
Newcastle-upon-Tyne NE7 39 C4
Coach Open NE28 41 B1
Coach Rd
Kibblesworth NE11 70 B3
Throckley NE15 35 C1
Wallsend NE28 40 C1
Coach Rd *continued*
Washington NE37 72 C2
Coach Rd Est NE37 72 C1
Coach Road Gn NE10 56 C2
Coal La NE42 49 D4
Coalbank Rd DH5 94 F2
Coalbank Sq DH5 94 F2
Coaley La DH4 90 C3
Coalford La DH6 96 C4
Coalway Dr NE16 69 B8
Coalway La
Whickham NE16 69 B7
Greenside NE40, NE41 51 D1
Coalway La N NE16 54 B1
Coanwood Dr NE23 22 C5
Coanwood Gdns NE11 70 B5
Coanwood Rd NE15 54 B4
Coanwood Way NE16 69 B3
Coast Rd
Shiremoor NE28,NE29 41 C6
Wallsend NE28,NE29 40 C4
Tynemouth NE29 41 C6
South Shields NE34,SR6 60 D6
Newcastle-upon-Tyne NE7 39 E2
Coates Endowed Mid Sch NE20 25 E7
Coatsworth Ct NE8 101 B2
Coatsworth Rd NE8 101 B1
Cobalt Cl NE15 53 C8
Cobbett Cres NE34 59 B3
Cobbler's La NE43 49 B8
Cobblestone Ct NE6 56 B5
Cobden Rd NE23 22 C4
Cobden St
4 Wallsend NE28 40 B2
Gateshead NE8 56 A1
Cobden Terr NE8 56 A1
Cobham Pl NE6 57 A4
Cobham Sq SR5 75 B2
Coble Dene NE29 41 E2
Coble Landing NE33 42 B3
Coburg St Blyth NE24 17 F7
North Shields NE30 42 B6
Gateshead NE8 101 C2
Coburn Cl NE23 29 C5
Cochran St NE21 53 C4
Cochrane Ct NE4 54 E5
Cochrane Park Ave NE7 39 C2
Cochrane St NE4 54 E5
Cochrane Terr NE13 27 B7
Cockburn Terr NE29 41 D3
Cockermouth Gn NE5 54 A8
Cockermouth Rd SR5 73 F2
Cockshaw NE46 45 A5
Cockshaw Ct NE46 45 A5
Cockshaw Terr NE46 45 A5
Cockshoot Dean NE42 50 D3
Cohen Ct NE8 70 E8
Cohort Cl DH8 76 E3
Colbeck Ave NE16 54 B1
Colbeck Terr 3 NE30 42 D7
Colbourne Ave NE23 15 E1
Colbourne Cres NE23 15 E1
Colbury Cl NE23 16 A2
Colby Ct NE4 100 B4
Colchester St NE34 59 A5
Colchester Terr SR4 85 F5
Coldbeck Ct NE23 22 C5
Coldingham Gdns NE5 37 D2
Coldside Gdns NE5 36 B3
Coldstream DH2 82 A2
Coldstream Ave SR5 75 B2
Coldstream Cl DH4 90 B5
Coldstream Dr NE21 68 A8
Coldstream Gdns NE28 41 A3
Coldstream Rd NE15 54 B7
Coldstream Way NE29 41 C8
Coldwell Cl DH6 97 F7
Coldwell La NE10 71 C7
Coldwell Park Ave NE10 71 D7
Coldwell Park Dr NE10 71 D7
Coldwell Rd NE42 50 F3
Coldwell St NE10 71 D8
Coldwell Terr 2 NE10 71 C7
Cole Gdns NE10 72 A8
Colebridge Cl NE5 37 C3
Colebrooke DH3 82 D2
Colegate NE10 71 F7
Colegate Com Prim Sch NE10 71 F7
Colegate W NE10 71 F7
Colepeth NE10 71 E7
Coleridge Ave
South Shields NE33 42 E1
Gateshead NE9 70 E4
Coleridge Rd SR5 74 B2
Coleridge Sq NE31 57 E6
Coley Gn NE5 36 B4
Coley Hill Cl NE5 36 C4
Coley Terr SR6 75 E3
Colgrove Pl NE3 37 E5
Colgrove Way NE3 37 F5
Colima Ave SR5 85 C8
Colin Pl NE6 57 A8
Colin Terr 7 SR2 92 F6
College Burn Rd SR3 91 E5
College Dr NE33 59 E8
College La
Newcastle-upon-Tyne NE1 99 B2
Longbenton NE7 39 C6
College Pl NE63 6 E2
College Rd Hebburn NE31 57 D2
Ashington NE63 6 E2
College St NE1 99 B2
College View 4 SR5 75 C1
Collier Cl NE15 35 D1
Collierley La DH9 78 D1
Colliery La
Hetton le Hole DH5 95 B2
Newcastle-upon-Tyne NE4 98 B1
Colliery Rd NE11 54 F2
Collin Ave NE34 60 B5
Collingdon Gn NE39 67 A4
Collingdon Rd NE39 67 A4
Collingwood Ave NE28 40 B4
Collingwood Cl NE23 21 F8
Collingwood Cotts NE20 25 B7
Collingwood Cres NE20 25 D4
Collingwood Ct 1 NE37 83 F8
Collingwood Ctr NE29 31 F1
Collingwood Dr
Shiney Row DH4 90 A6
Hexham NE46 44 F2
Collingwood Gdns NE10 56 D2
Collingwood Ho
North Shields NE29 41 F5
South Shields NE33 42 E5
Collingwood Mansions NE29 42 B4
Collingwood Pl NE62 11 A7
Collingwood Prim Sch NE29 41 D5
Collingwood Rd
Earsdon NE25 31 A5
Newbiggin-by-the-Sea NE64 7 D5
Collingwood St
Hetton le Hole DH5 95 A6
Newcastle-upon-Tyne NE1 101 A4
16 Gateshead NE10 56 D1
Hebburn NE31 58 A6
South Shields NE33 59 C8
3 Sunderland SR5 75 B2
Collingwood Terr
Dunston NE11 100 A1
1 Newcastle-upon-Tyne NE2 38 F1
Blyth NE24 17 E7
Whitley Bay NE26 32 C4
Tynemouth NE30 42 D7
Collingwood View NE29 41 F5
Collywell Bay Rd NE26 24 D5
Collywell Ct NE26 24 D6
Colman Ave NE34 59 A5
Colmet Ct NE11 70 D4
Colnbrook Cl NE3 37 D7
Colomba Wlk NE3 38 E5
Colombo Rd SR5 73 F1
Colston St NE4 54 D6
Colston Way NE25 31 D7
Colt Pk NE17 77 B5
Coltere Ave NE36 74 E7
Colton Gdns NE9 71 A3
Coltpark NE5 36 F1
Coltpark Pl NE23 22 B5
Coltsfoot Gdns NE10 71 C5
Coltspool NE11 81 D6
Columba St SR5 75 B2
Columbia Grange NE3 37 E5
Columbia Terr NE24 17 E6
Colwell Pl NE5 54 B7
Colwell Rd
Shiremoor NE27 30 F2
Tynemouth NE29 31 F1
Ashington NE63 6 F1
Colwyn Par NE31 58 A2
Colwyne Pl NE5 37 B2
Combe Dr NE15 53 B7
Comet Row NE12 29 C2
Comet Sq SR3 92 A7
Comical Cnr NE33 42 B4
Comma Ct NE11 70 B7
Commercial Rd
Blyth NE24 17 E8
Newcastle-upon-Tyne, South Gosforth NE3 38 E5
Jarrow NE32 58 C8
South Shields NE33 42 B1
Newcastle-upon-Tyne, Byker NE6 56 C5
Sunderland SR2 86 F4
Commercial St 8 NE21 53 B1
Commissioners' Wharf NE29 42 A2
Compton Ave NE34 59 D7
Compton Ct NE38 83 B5
Compton Rd NE29 41 F5
Concord Ho NE5 36 F2
Concorde Sq 5 SR3 92 A7
Concorde Way NE32 58 B6
Condercum Ct NE15 54 C5
Condercum Ind Est NE4 54 D5
Condercum Rd NE4 54 D5
Cone St NE33 42 B2
Cone Terr DH3 88 D4
Conewood House NE3 37 F6
Conhope La NE15,NE4 54 D5
Conifer Cl NE21 68 B8
Conifer Ct NE12 39 F8
Coniscliffe Ave NE3 37 F4
Conishead Terr DH6 97 F8
Coniston Birtley DH3 82 D2
Gateshead NE10 72 A8
Coniston Ave
Easington Lane DH5 97 C8
Whickham NE16 69 D7
Newcastle-upon-Tyne NE2 38 E2
Hebburn NE31 57 F4
Newbiggin-by-the-Sea NE64 7 C3
Sunderland SR5 75 C4
Coniston Cl
Chester le Street DH2 88 C2
Killingworth NE12 29 C3
Newburn NE15 52 E7
Coniston Cres NE21 68 B8
Coniston Ct NE5 54 B8

Coniston Dr NE32 58 D3
Coniston Gdns NE9 71 B5
Coniston Pl NE9 71 B5
Coniston Rd Blyth NE24 12 A1
Wallsend NE28 41 A4
Tynemouth NE30 32 A2
Connaught Cl DH4 90 C5
Connaught Gdns NE12 39 D7
Connaught Terr NE32 58 B6
Conningsby Cl NE3 38 D8
Conniscliffe Ct NE46 44 F3
Conniscliffe Rd NE46 44 F3
Connolly Terr NE17 77 C6
Consett Rd NE11 70 A5
Constable Cl NE40 52 C4
Constable Gdns NE34 59 C3
Constables Garth 6 DH3 82 C4
Content St NE21 53 C1
Convent Rd NE4 54 D7
Conway Cl
Bedlington NE22 10 D1
Ryton NE40 52 D4
Conway Dr NE7 39 A4
Conway Gdns
Wallsend NE28 40 A4
Sunderland SR3 91 C7
Conway Gr NE26 24 B7
Conway Rd SR5 73 F2
Conway Sq Gateshead NE9 71 A8
Sunderland SR5 73 F2
Conyers Ave DH2 88 B5
Conyers Gdns DH2 88 B5
Conyers Pl DH2 88 B5
Conyers Rd
Chester le Street DH2 88 C5
Newcastle-upon-Tyne NE6 56 C6
Cook Cl NE33 59 B8
Cook Gdns NE10 72 B8
Cook Sq SR5 74 A2
Cooks Wood NE38 83 D3
Cookshold La
Sherburn DH6 96 B2
Sherburn Hill DH6 96 B2
Cookson Cl
Newcastle-upon-Tyne NE4 98 B1
Corbridge NE45 46 F6
Cookson House NE33 42 C3
Cookson St NE4 98 A1
Cookson Terr DH2 88 B3
Cookson's La NE1 101 A4
Coomassie Rd NE24 17 E7
Coomside NE23 22 C4
Cooper St SR6 75 E1
Coopies Field NE61 9 B8
Coopies Haugh NE61 9 C7
Coopies La NE61 9 B7
Coopies Lane Ind Est
NE61 9 C7
Coopies Way NE61 9 C7
Copland Terr NE2 99 C2
Copley Ave NE34 59 C2
Copley Dr SR3 86 B2
Copper Chare NE61 3 F1
Copper Cl NE11 70 B7
Copperas La NE15 53 F7
Coppergate Ct NE31 57 F7
Coppice The NE26 24 C6
Coppice Way NE2 99 C2
Coppy La DH9 80 C4
Copse The Prudhoe NE42 50 E2
Burnopfield NE16 78 F6
Blaydon NE21 53 F2
Newcastle-upon-Tyne NE3 38 D8
Washington NE37 72 B2
Coptleigh DH5 95 A7
Coquet NE38 82 F1
Coquet Ave Blyth NE24 17 E5
Whitley Bay NE26 32 A5
Newcastle-upon-Tyne NE3 38 B6
South Shields NE34 60 B8
Coquet Bldgs NE15 36 B1
Coquet Dr NE61 1 E5
Coquet Gr NE15 35 C2
Coquet Ho 16 SR3 91 F6
Coquet Park Fst Sch
NE26 32 A6
Coquet St
Newcastle-upon-Tyne NE1 56 A6
Chopwell NE17 66 C1
Hebburn NE31 57 D6
Jarrow NE32 58 A5
Ashington NE63 6 E4
Coquet Terr Dudley NE23 28 F8
Newcastle-upon-Tyne NE6 56 B8
Coquetdale Ave NE6 57 A6
Coquetdale Cl NE61 4 E3
Coquetdale Pl NE22 11 C1
Coquetdale Villas 5 SR6 75 E2
Corbiere Cl SR3 91 E6
Corbitt St NE8 100 C1
Corbridge Ave NE13 28 B6
Corbridge CE Fst Sch
NE45 47 A6
Corbridge Cl NE28 40 E6
Corbridge Mid Sch NE45 46 F7
Corbridge Rd
Hexham NE46 45 D4
Newcastle-upon-Tyne NE6 56 C6
Corbridge St NE6 56 B6
Corby Gate SR2 86 D4
Corby Gdns NE6 56 F6
Corby Hall Dr SR2 86 D4
Corchester La NE46,NE45 46 C7
Corchester Rd NE22 10 F2
Corchester Twrs NE45 46 E7
Corchester Wlk NE7 39 C4
Corfu Rd SR5 74 A2
Corinthian Sq SR5 74 A2
Cork St SR1 103 B3
Cormorant Cl Blyth NE24 17 F4
4 Washington NE38 82 F3
Ashington NE63 6 E1
Corn Mill Dr DH5 94 D6
Cornbank Cl SR3 92 A5
Corndean NE38 84 A4
Cornel Mews NE7 39 C3
Cornel Rd NE7 39 C3
Cornelia Cl 7 SR3 92 A7
Corney St NE33 59 B7
Cornfields The NE31 57 E6
Cornforth Cl
Gateshead NE10 72 C6
Ashington NE63 6 B2
Cornhill Hedworth NE32 58 C1
Newcastle-upon-Tyne NE5 36 F1
Cornhill Ave NE3 37 F7
Cornhill Cres NE29 41 D7
Cornhill Rd
Cramlington NE23 22 C6
6 Sunderland SR5 75 B2
Cornmill* TD12 107 B7
Cornmoor Gdns NE16 69 B5
Cornmoor Rd NE16 69 B6
Cornthwaite Dr SR6 75 E8
Cornwall Rd NE31 57 F3
Cornwallis Sq NE33 42 B1
Cornwallis St 13 NE33 42 C3
Cornwell Cres NE22 16 B8
Cornwell Ct NE7 38 F4
Coronation Ave
Sunniside NE16 69 B2
6 Ryhope SR2 92 F6
Coronation Bglws NE3 38 D5
Coronation Cl SR1 103 B3
Coronation Cotts NE61 2 A3
Coronation Cres
Burnside DH4 90 C2
Whitley Bay NE25 31 F4
Coronation Gn DH5 97 D8
Coronation Rd
Sunniside NE16 69 B2
Seaton Delaval NE25 23 C3
Newcastle-upon-Tyne NE5 36 B3
Coronation St
Chester le Street DH3 88 D1
Annitsford NE23 22 B1
Blyth NE24 17 E6
Wallsend NE28 40 C2
North Shields NE29 42 A4
South Shields NE33 42 C2
Ryton NE40 52 E4
Newbiggin-by-the-Sea NE64 7 E5
Sunderland SR1 103 B3
Coronation Terr
Chester le Street DH3 88 C2
Hetton le Hole DH5 95 A2
Kibblesworth NE11 81 C6
Tynemouth NE29 31 B1
3 Boldon Colliery NE35 58 E1
Ashington NE63 6 E1
Sunderland SR4 85 B6
Corporation Rd SR2 86 F4
Corporation St NE4 98 C1
Corporation Yd NE61 3 F1
Corpus Christie RC Prim Sch
NE8 70 E8
Corrighan Terr DH5 94 C4
Corrofell Gdns NE10 56 F1
Corry Ct SR4 85 E4
Corsair NE16 68 F6
Corsenside NE5 36 F1
Corstopitum 3 NE28 40 F4
Corstopitvm Roman Fort*
NE45 46 E6
Corstorphine Town NE33 42 B1
Cortina Ave SR4 85 D4
Corvan Terr DH9 79 A2
Cosford Ct NE3 37 C7
Cossack Terr SR4 85 E7
Cosser St NE24 17 B4
Cosserat Pl NE31 57 D7
Coston Dr NE33 42 C3
Cosyn St NE6 56 A5
Cotehill Dr NE20 25 B4
Cotehill Rd 2 NE5 37 B1
Cotemede NE10 72 A5
Cotfield Wlk NE8 101 A1
Cotgarth The NE10 71 E7
Cotherstone Ct SR3 86 B2
Cotman Gdns NE34 59 D2
Cotswold Ave
Chester le Street DH2 88 B1
Longbenton NE12 29 B1
Cotswold Cl NE38 83 B4
Cotswold Dr
Whitley Bay NE25 31 F3
Ashington NE63 6 F1
Cotswold Gdns
Dunston NE11 70 A7
Newcastle-upon-Tyne NE7 39 A3
Cotswold La NE35 58 F2
Cotswold Rd
Tynemouth NE29 31 E2
Sunderland SR5 74 A2
Cotswold Sq SR5 74 A3
Cottage La NE5 37 D1
Cottenham Chare NE4 98 B1
Cottenham St NE4 98 B1
Cotter Riggs Pl NE5 36 B2
Cotter Riggs Wlk NE5 36 B2
Cotterdale NE28 39 F5
Cotterdale Ave 1 NE8 70 F8
Cottersdale Gdns NE5 36 B3
Cottinglea NE61 3 F2
Cottingvale NE61 3 F2
Cottingwood Ct NE4 98 B2
Cottingwood Gdns
Newcastle-upon-Tyne NE4 98 B2
Morpeth NE61 3 F1
Cottingwood Gn NE24 17 C3
Cottingwood La NE61 3 F2
Cottonwood
Shiney Row DH4 89 F6
Silksworth SR3 91 E5
Coulson Park Fst Sch
NE63 6 F2
Coulthards La NE8 101 C3
Coulthards Pl NE8 56 A4
Coulton Dr NE36 74 D7
Council Ave DH4 90 B6
Council Rd NE63 6 C4
Council Terr NE37 83 D7
Counden Rd 4 NE5 36 E3
Countess Ave NE26 32 A5
Countess Dr NE15 54 A7
Coupland Gr NE32 58 B3
Coupland Rd NE63 6 C3
Court Rd NE22 10 F1
Court The NE16 69 C6
Courtfield Rd NE6 56 F8
Courtney Ct NE3 37 C7
Courtney Dr SR3 91 F8
Cousin St SR1 103 C2
Coutts Rd NE6 56 E8
Cove The DH4 90 B6
Coventry Gdns
North Shields NE29 41 E4
Newcastle-upon-Tyne NE4 54 E4
Coventry Way NE32 58 B1
Coverdale Gateshead NE10 72 A6
Wallsend NE28 39 F5
Coverdale Ave Blyth NE24 17 A7
Washington NE37 83 C8
Coverley Rd SR5 74 B2
Covers The
Longbenton NE12 39 E6
Wallsend NE28 40 B3
Morpeth NE61 9 A7
Cow La NE45 46 F7
Cowan Cl NE21 53 A4
Cowan Terr SR2 103 A2
Cowans Ave NE12 29 C4
Cowdray Ct NE3 37 C7
Cowdray Rd SR5 74 B2
Cowell Gr NE39 67 C2
Cowen Gdns NE9 71 A1
Cowen Rd NE21 53 D3
Cowen St Blaydon NE21 68 B8
Newcastle-upon-Tyne NE6 56 F6
Cowen Terr NE39 67 F3
Cowgarth NE46 45 A5
Cowgate NE1 99 B1
Cowgate L Ctr NE5 37 D3
Cowgate Prim Sch NE4 54 D8
Cowley Cres DH5 94 C4
Cowley Pl NE24 17 B8
Cowley Rd NE24 12 B1
Cowpath Gdns NE10 57 B2
Cowpen Rd NE24 17 C8
Cox Chare NE1 99 C1
Coxfoot Cl NE34 59 C5
Coxgreen Rd DH4 84 B2
Coxlodge Rd NE3 38 A5
Coxlodge Terr NE3 38 A5
Coxon St Gateshead NE10 57 B2
Sunderland SR2 103 B1
Coxon Terr NE8 56 C1
Crabtree Rd NE43 64 C7
Cradock Ave NE31 57 D4
Craggyknowe NE37 82 F6
Craghall Dene NE2 38 E4
Craghall Dene Ave NE2 38 E4
Cragleas NE16 79 A4
Cragside
Chester le Street DH2 88 A4
Brunswick Village NE13 28 B6
Cramlington NE23 22 C4
Whitley Bay NE26 31 E7
South Shields NE34 60 B5
Corbridge NE45 47 B7
Cragside* NE65 118 A5
Newcastle-upon-Tyne NE7 39 B3
Cragside Ave NE29 41 D8
Cragside Ct
4 Houghton-le-Spring DH5 94 F8
Dunston NE11 70 A6
Cragside Cty Prim Sch
NE7 39 A3
Cragside Fst Sch NE23 22 B4
Cragside Gdns
Dunston NE11 70 A5
Killingworth NE12 29 F4
Wallsend NE28 40 F3
Cragside Ho 5 SR3 91 D7
Cragside House (N.T.)*
NE65 118 A5
Cragside Rd NE37 83 A7
Cragston Ave NE5 37 C3
Cragston Cl NE5 37 C2
Cragton Gdns NE24 17 B7
Craig Cres NE23 29 A8
Craig St 1 DH3 82 C4
Craigavon Rd SR5 74 B2
Craigend NE23 22 B5
Craighill 1 DH4 90 A6
Craiglands The SR3 86 C3
Craigmill Pk NE24 17 A8
Craigmillar Ave NE5 37 C3
Craigmillar Cl NE5 37 C3
Craigmont Ct NE12 39 D6
Craigshaw Rd SR5 73 F3
Craigshaw Sq SR5 73 F3
Craigwell Dr SR3 92 A4
Craik Ave NE34 59 B5
Crake Way NE38 82 F2
Cramer St NE8 101 C1
Cramilngton Terr 10
NE27 30 E1
Cramlington Beacon Hill Fst
Sch NE23 21 E6
Cramlington Com High Sch
NE23 22 A4
Cramlington Rd SR5 73 F2
Cramlington Sq SR5 73 F2
Cramlington Sta NE23 21 F7
Cramlington Terr NE24 17 C4
Cramond Ct NE9 70 E3
Cramond Way NE23 22 B4
Cranberry Rd SR5 74 B2
Cranberry Sq SR5 74 A2
Cranborne SR3 91 C6
Cranbourne Gr NE30 32 B3
Cranbrook Ave NE3 38 C7
Cranbrook Ct NE3 37 E7
Cranbrook Dr NE42 50 B2
Cranbrook Rd NE15 54 B4
Cranemarsh Cl NE63 6 C1
Craneshaugh Cl NE46 45 E4
Cranesville NE9 71 C5
Craneswater Ave NE26 24 F1
Cranfield Pl NE15 53 C7
Cranford Gdns NE15 53 E7
Cranford St NE34 59 C6
Cranford Terr SR4 102 A1
Cranham Cl NE12 29 F4
Cranlea NE3 37 C6
Cranleigh Ave NE3 37 C7
Cranleigh Gr NE42 50 D3
Cranleigh Pl NE25 31 D6
Cranleigh Rd SR5 74 A2
Cranshaw Pl NE23 22 C5
Cranston Pl 9 SR2 93 A6
Crantock Rd NE3 37 F5
Cranwell Ct NE3 37 C7
Cranwell Dr NE13 28 B6
Craster Ave
Longbenton NE12 29 F1
Shiremoor NE27 30 F3
South Shields NE34 60 B8
Craster Cl Blyth NE24 17 C7
Whitley Bay NE25 31 D7
Craster Gdns NE28 40 F3
Craster Rd NE29 41 D5
Craster Sq NE3 38 A6
Craster Terr NE7 39 B2
Crathie DH3 82 C7
Craven Ct SR6 75 F1
Crawcrook La NE40, NE41 51 D5
Crawcrook Terr NE40 51 E3
Crawford Cotts NE61 4 A1
Crawford Ct SR3 91 F6
Crawford Pl NE25 31 E4
Crawford St NE24 12 D1
Crawford Terr
Newcastle-upon-Tyne NE6 56 F5
Morpeth NE61 4 A1
Crawhall Cres NE61 8 E7
Crawhall Cty Fst Sch
NE23 22 A5
Crawhall Rd NE1 99 C1
Crawley Ave NE31 57 D3
Crawley Gdns NE16 69 C7
Crawley Rd NE28 40 B1
Crawley Sq NE31 57 D3
Craythorne Gdns NE6 39 D2
Creeve lea NE38 83 C3
Creighton Ave NE3 37 E4
Creland Way NE5 37 C3
Crescent Ave NE46 44 F5
Crescent The
Chester le Street DH2 88 B3
Newbottle DH4 90 D4
Shiney Row DH4 90 A5
Hetton le Hole DH5 95 A3
5 Dunston NE11 69 F8
Kibblesworth NE11 81 C6
Newcastle-upon-Tyne,
Kenton Bankfoot NE13 37 B6
9 Throckley NE15 35 D2
Sunniside NE16 69 B2
Whickham NE16 69 C6
Ponteland NE20 25 A3
Seghill NE23 22 F1
Whitley Bay NE26 32 B4
Wallsend NE28 40 B3
Tynemouth NE30 42 C8
Jarrow NE32 58 A4
South Shields NE34 59 F5
High Spen NE39 66 F3
Rowlands Gill NE39 67 F2
Ryton NE40 52 D5
Wylam NE41 51 B5
Morpeth NE61 8 F6
Newcastle-upon-Tyne NE7 39 B5
New Silksworth SR3 86 A1
Cleadon SR6 74 F8
Crescent Vale NE26 32 A4
Crescent Way NE12 39 E8
Crescent Way N NE12 39 E8
Crescent Way S NE12 39 E8
Creslow NE10 71 F6
Cressbourne Ave SR6 75 E4
Cresswell Ave
Longbenton NE12 29 F1
Seaton Sluice NE26 24 C6
Tynemouth NE29 41 F7
Cresswell Cl Blaydon NE21 68 A8
Whitley Bay NE25 31 E3
Cresswell Dr Blyth NE24 17 C5
Newcastle-upon-Tyne NE3 37 E7
Cresswell Home Farm Cotts
NE61 2 B4
Cresswell Rd
Wallsend NE28 40 A1
Ellington NE61 1 E6
Cresswell St NE6 56 D6
Cresswell Terr
Ashington NE63 6 C4
Sunderland SR2 102 C1
Crest The Dinnington NE13 27 B7
Bedlington NE22 10 E1
Seaton Sluice NE26 24 E4
Cresthaven NE10 71 E6
Crichton Ave DH3 88 D1
Cricket Terr NE16 79 A6
Cricklewood Dr DH4 90 B6
Cricklewood Rd SR5 74 A1
Criddle St NE8 56 A4
Crieff Gr NE32 58 D3
Crieff Sq SR5 73 F2
Crigdon Hill NE5 36 F1
Crighton NE38 83 A5
Crimdon Gr DH4 94 C7
Crimea Rd SR5 73 F2
Crindledykes NE38 83 E2
Cripps Ave NE10 72 B8
Crocus Cl NE21 53 A2
Croft Ave Longbenton NE12 39 E7
Wallsend NE28 40 C2
Sunderland SR4 102 A2
Croft Cl NE40 52 D4
Croft Cotts NE43 64 D7
Croft Ho NE42 50 A4
Croft House Sch NE46 44 F5
Croft Rd NE24 17 E7
Croft St NE1 99 B1
Croft Terr Horsley NE15 50 C8
Jarrow NE32 58 B6
2 Hexham NE46 45 A4
Croft The
Sherburn Hill DH6 96 D1
Killingworth NE12 29 E4
Newcastle-upon-Tyne NE3 38 A4
Ryton NE40 52 D4
Croft View NE40 51 E3
Croft Villas 2 NE40 51 E3
Croft's La NE15 50 C8
Croftdale Rd NE21 53 B2
Crofter Cl NE23 22 A1
Crofthead Dr NE23 22 B4
Crofton Fst Sch NE24 17 E6
Crofton Mill Ind Est NE24 17 F7
Crofton St Blyth NE24 17 E7
South Shields NE34 59 C6
Crofton Way NE15 53 B7
Crofts Ave NE45 47 B5
Crofts Cl NE45 47 B5
Crofts Pk NE61 9 E5
Crofts The NE20 25 F6
Crofts Way NE45 47 A6
Croftside DH3 82 C5
Croftside Ave 2 SR6 75 F8
Croftside Ho 4 SR3 91 F5
Croftsway NE4 54 F4
Croftwell Cl NE21 53 D1
Cromarty St SR6 75 D2
Cromdale Pl NE5 37 B1
Cromer Ave NE9 70 F3
Cromer Ct NE9 71 A3
Cromer Gdns
Newcastle-upon-Tyne NE2 38 E3
Whitley Bay NE26 32 A6
Crompton Rd NE6 56 B8
Cromwell Ave NE21 53 B2
Cromwell Ct NE21 53 A4
Cromwell Pl NE21 53 A1
Cromwell Rd
Gateshead NE10 57 B2
Whickham NE16 69 C8
Cromwell St Ryton NE21 53 A4
Gateshead NE8 56 A1
Sunderland SR4 102 A3
Cromwell Terr
North Shields NE29 41 F6
Gateshead NE8 101 A1
Crondall St NE33 59 D7
Cronin Ave NE34 59 B4
Cronniewell NE17 77 B5
Crookham Gr NE61 9 B5
Crookham Way NE23 22 C4
Crookhill Com Prim Sch
NE40 52 E5
Crookhill Terr NE40 52 E4
Cropthorne NE10 72 B6
Crosby Gdns NE9 71 B3
Crosland Pk NE23 15 F2
Cross Ave NE28 39 F4
Cross Camden La NE29,
NE30 42 B5
Cross Carliol St NE1 99 B1
Cross Dr NE40 52 C6
Cross Keys La NE9 70 F5
Cross La Dunston NE11 54 D2
Kibblesworth NE11 70 B4
Cross Morpeth St NE2 98 B4
Cross Par NE4 100 B4
Cross Pl SR1 103 B3
Cross Rigg Cl DH4 90 A7
Cross Row Ryton NE40 52 E4
Gateshead NE8 56 B1
Cross Sheraton St NE2 98 B4
Cross St
8 Fence Houses DH4 94 A8
Houghton-le-Spring DH4 90 D1
High Pittington DH6 96 D3
Newcastle-upon-Tyne NE1 98 C1

Cross St *continued*
Newcastle-upon-Tyne, St Ann's NE6 56 A5
Gateshead NE8 101 C1
Cross Terr NE39 67 D1
Cross Vale Rd SR2 86 C4
Cross Villa Place No 1 NE4 98 C1
Cross Villa Place No 2 NE4 98 C1
Cross Villa Place No 3 NE4 98 C1
Cross Villa Place No 4 NE4 98 B1
Cross Villa Place No 5 NE4 98 B1
Cross Way The NE61 8 F6
Crossbank Rd NE5 37 D3
Crossbrook Rd 2 NE5 37 D2
Crossby Ct SR2 103 C1
Crossfell NE20 25 C4
Crossfell Gdns NE62 11 A8
Crossfield Pk NE10 71 C6
Crossfield Terr NE6 57 A4
Crossgate NE33 42 C2
Crossgate Rd DH5 95 A2
Crossgill NE37 83 B7
Crosshill Rd NE15 54 B4
Crosslaw NE5 36 F1
Crosslea Ave SR3 86 B3
Crossley Terr
Longbenton NE12 29 F1
Newcastle-upon-Tyne NE4 98 A2
Crossway
Newcastle-upon-Tyne NE2 38 E3
Tynemouth NE30 42 C8
South Shields NE34 60 A5
Guide Post NE62 10 F7
Gateshead NE9 71 B6
Crossway Ct NE5 37 F3
Crossway The
Newcastle-upon-Tyne, Lemington NE15 53 D7
Newcastle-upon-Tyne, Kenton NE3 37 F4
Crossway Villas NE9 71 A6
Crossways Hedworth NE32 58 C1
East Boldon NE36 74 E7
New Silksworth SR3 91 F7
Crossways The NE13 28 A4
Crosthwaite Gr SR5 74 A1
Croudace Row 2 NE10 71 D8
Crow Bank NE28 40 C2
Crow Hall La NE23 21 F7
Crow Hall Rd NE23 15 F1
Crow La SR3 91 B7
Crowhall La NE10 71 D8
Crowhall Towers 7 NE10 71 D8
Crowley 2 NE16 54 A1
Crowley Ave NE16 69 C8
Crowley Gdns NE21 53 C2
Crowley Rd NE16 54 A1
Crown And Anchor Cotts NE15 50 C8
Crown Rd SR5 75 A1
Crown St Blyth NE24 17 F7
7 Morpeth NE61 9 A8
Crown Terr NE40 52 B1
Crowther Ind Est
Birtley NE37 82 F4
Washington NE38 82 F5
Crowther Rd NE38 82 F5
Crowtree L Ctr SR1 102 C2
Crowtree Rd SR1 102 C3
Croxdale Ct NE34 59 A5
Croxdale Gdns NE10 57 B2
Croxdale Terr
Gateshead NE10 57 B2
Greenside NE40 52 C1
Croydon Rd NE4 98 A2
Crozier St SR5 75 C1
Cruddas Pk NE4 100 A4
Cruddas Pk Sh Ctr NE4 100 A4
Crudwell Cl NE35 58 E2
Crummock Ave SR6 75 C4
Crummock Rd NE5 54 B8
Crumstone Ct NE12 29 E4
Crusade Wlk NE32 58 A5
Cty Cricket Gd NE2 99 C4
Cuba St SR2 86 E4
Cuillin Cl NE38 83 B3
Culford Pl NE28 40 E6
Cullercoats Prim Sch NE30 32 C3
Cullercoats Rd SR5 73 F1
Cullercoats Sq SR5 73 F1
Cullercoats St NE6 56 E6
Cullercoats Sta NE30 32 C3
Culloden Wlk NE12 29 D4
Culzean Ho 6 SR3 91 D7
Cumberland Ave
Bedlington NE22 10 E1
Newbiggin-by-the-Sea NE64 7 D4
Cumberland Pl
Birtley DH3 82 D1
South Shields NE34 60 B7
Cumberland Rd
Shiremoor NE29 41 B7
New Silksworth SR3 92 A8
Cumberland St
Wallsend NE28 40 C2
Wallsend, Willington Quay NE28 41 B1
Sunderland SR1 103 A3
Cumberland Way NE37 72 D2
Cumberland Wlk NE7 39 B4
Cumbria Wlk NE4 98 A1
Cumbrian Ave
Chester le Street DH2 88 C2
Sunderland SR6 75 C5
Cummings St NE24 17 E8
Curlew Cl
Longbenton NE12 39 A7
Washington NE38 83 A2
Ryton NE40 52 E4
Ashington NE63 11 E8
Curlew Hill NE61 3 D2
Curlew Rd Jarrow NE32 58 C8
Jarrow NE32 58 D8
Curlew Way NE24 17 E4
Curly Kews NE61 8 E8
Curran House NE32 58 C8
Curren Gdns NE10 56 C2
Curtis Rd NE4 54 F7
Curzon Pl 6 NE5 37 B2
Curzon Rd W NE28 40 B1
Curzon St NE8 70 E8
Cushat Cl NE6 56 C5
Cushy Cow La NE40 52 D4
Cut Bank NE1 56 A5
Cut Throat La NE17,NE39 77 C4
Cuthbert Ct NE32 58 E6
Cuthbert St
Sunniside NE16 69 A1
Hebburn NE31 57 D7
Gateshead NE8 101 A2
Cuthbert Wlk NE3 38 E5
Cuthbertson Cl SR6 75 E5
Cutting St 3 SR7 92 F1
Cygnet Cl
Newcastle-upon-Tyne NE5 36 D4
Ashington NE63 11 D8
Cyncopa Way NE5 37 D2
Cypress Ave NE4 54 D8
Cypress Cres
Dunston NE11 70 A7
Blyth NE24 17 E7
Cypress Dr NE24 17 E7
Cypress Gdns
Killingworth NE12 29 C4
Blyth NE24 17 E7
Cypress Gr NE40 52 C6
Cypress Rd Blaydon NE21 53 C2
Gateshead NE9 71 D2
Cypress Sq 11 SR3 92 A8
Cyprus Gdns NE9 71 A6

D

D'arcy Ct SR1 103 B2
Dachet Rd NE25 31 D7
Dacre Rd SR6 75 D4
Dacre St
South Shields NE33 59 C8
Morpeth NE61 3 F1
Daffodil Cl NE21 53 B2
Dahlia Ct SR4 102 B3
Dahlia Pl NE4 54 D7
Dahlia Way NE31 57 E4
Dainton Cl DH4 90 C4
Dairnbrook 7 NE37 83 A6
Dairy La DH4 94 C8
Daisy Cotts 9 DH3 82 C4
Dale Rd NE25 31 D4
Dale St Cambois NE24 12 E1
South Shields NE33 42 D3
Crawcrook NE40 51 F4
Dale Terr SR6 75 E3
Dale Top NE25 23 F1
Dale View NE43 64 D7
Dale View Gdns NE40 51 F3
Dalegarth Gr SR6 75 C5
Dales The NE5 37 E2
Dalla St SR4 85 A7
Dalmahoy NE37 72 D3
Dalmatia Terr NE24 17 E6
Dalston Pl NE24 17 E4
Dalton Ave NE61 2 A3
Dalton Cl NE23 22 B6
Dalton Cres 28 NE6 56 B6
Dalton Ct NE28 39 F5
Dalton Pl
Newcastle-upon-Tyne NE5 36 C3
Sunderland SR4 102 B2
Dalton St
Newcastle-upon-Tyne NE6 56 B5
Newcastle-upon-Tyne NE6 56 B6
Dalton Terr NE17 77 B8
Dalton Way DH4 90 A7
Daltons La NE33 42 B2
Dame Allan's Boys Sch NE4 54 E7
Dame Allan's Girls Sch NE4 54 E7
Dame Dorothy Cres SR6 75 E1
Dame Dorothy Prim Sch SR6 103 B4
Dame Dorothy St SR6 103 A4
Dame Flora Robson Ave NE34 58 F4
Damside NE61 9 A8
Danby Cl Washington NE38 88 F8
New Silksworth SR3 92 B6
Danby Gdns NE6 39 D1
Danville Rd SR6 75 E4
Darden Cl NE12 29 F4
Darden Lough NE5 36 F1
Darenth St NE34 59 C6
Darien Ave SR6 75 D4
Dark La NE61 4 A1
Darley Ct 15 SR3 91 F6
Darley Pl NE15 54 A5
Darnell Pl NE4 98 B2
Darnley Rd NE63 6 C3
Darras Ct NE33 42 D1
Darras Dr NE29 41 C7
Darras Hall Fst Sch NE20 25 C3
Darras Mews NE20 25 C4
Darras Rd NE20 25 D4
Darrell St NE13 28 A6
Dartford Cl NE25 23 E3
Dartford Rd
South Shields NE33 42 F2
Sunderland SR6 75 D4
Dartmouth Ave NE9 70 F2
Darvall Cl NE25 31 D7
Darwin Cres NE3 37 F3
Darwin St SR5 74 F2
Daryl Cl NE21 53 A1
Daryl Way NE10 72 D8
Davenport Dr NE3 28 B1
Davenport Sch DH5 94 D7
David Adams Ho 7 NE15 54 D5
David Gdns SR6 75 F3
David St NE28 40 B2
David Terr 7 NE40 51 F3
Davidson Cotts NE2 38 E3
Davidson Rd NE10 57 B2
Davidson St NE10 71 D8
Davison Ave
Whitley Bay NE26 31 F6
New Silksworth SR3 92 B7
Davison St Newburn NE15 52 E8
Blyth NE24 17 E8
Boldon Colliery NE35 58 E1
Davison Terr 3 SR5 75 A2
Davy Bank NE28 40 D1
Dawlish Cl NE29 41 D8
Dawlish Gdns NE9 70 F3
Dawlish Pl NE5 36 C3
Dawson Pl NE61 3 F1
Dawson Sq 4 NE30 42 D7
Dawson Terr SR4 85 A7
Daylesford Dr NE3,NE7 38 F4
Daylesford Rd NE23 16 A2
Dayshield NE5 36 F1
De Merley Rd NE61 3 F1
De Mowbray Way NE61 3 D2
De Walden Sq NE61 4 E3
De Walden Terr NE61 4 F3
Deacon Cl NE15 36 B2
Deacon Ct NE12 39 A7
Deaconsfield Cl SR3 91 F5
Deadridge La NE45 47 B7
Deal Cl NE24 17 E4
Dean House NE6 57 A8
Dean Rd
South Shields NE33 59 B7
South Shields, Dean NE33 59 C8
Dean St
Newcastle-upon-Tyne NE1 99 B1
Hexham NE46 45 C5
Gateshead NE9 71 A5
Dean Terr
South Shields NE33 59 B7
Ryton NE40 52 C5
Sunderland SR5 75 A1
Dean View Dr NE24 17 B8
Deanery St NE22 10 F1
Deanham Gdns NE5 54 D8
Deans Ave NE64 7 C5
Deans Cl 1 NE16 69 B7
Deansfield Cl SR3 91 F5
Deansfield Gr NE15 36 B3
Dearham Gr NE23 16 A2
Debdon Gdns NE6 39 D1
Debdon Pl NE23 22 B6
Debdon Rd NE63 6 F2
Debussy Ct NE32 58 C6
Deckham St NE8 71 A8
Deckham Terr NE8,NE9 71 A8
Dee Rd NE31 57 F3
Dee St NE32 58 C7
Deel Ho 2 SR3 91 D7
Deepbrook Rd 5 NE5 37 C1
Deepdale Wallsend NE28 39 F5
Washington NE38 83 A1
Deepdale Cl NE16 68 F4
Deepdale Cres NE5 37 E2
Deepdale Gdns NE12 29 C3
Deepdale Gn NE5 37 E2
Deepdale Rd NE30 32 B2
Deepdale St DH5 95 A2
Deepdene Gr SR6 75 E5
Deepdene Rd SR6 75 D5
Deer Bush NE5 36 F1
Deer Park Way NE21 53 E1
Deerbolt Pl NE12 39 C7
Deerfell Cl NE63 6 B2
Deerness Rd SR2 103 B1
Dees Ave NE28 40 B3
Defender Ct SR5 85 C8
Defoe Ave NE34 59 C3
Deighton Wlk NE5 36 F1
Delacour Rd NE21 53 C3
Delamere Cres NE23 16 A2
Delamere Ct 8 SR3 92 A6
Delamere Rd NE3 37 F5
Delaval DH2 88 A3
Delaval Ave
Seaton Delaval NE25 23 C3
North Shields NE29 41 E6
Delaval Com Mid Sch NE24 17 D5
Delaval Com Prim Sch NE15 54 B5
Delaval Cres NE24 17 B4
Delaval Ct
Killingworth NE12 29 E1
Delaval Ct *continued*
Bedlington NE22 11 C2
15 South Shields NE33 42 D1
Delaval Gdns
Newcastle-upon-Tyne NE15 54 B4
Blyth NE24 17 B4
Delaval Rd
Newcastle-upon-Tyne, Delaval NE15 54 B4
Newcastle-upon-Tyne, Old Benwell NE15 54 B5
Whitley Bay NE26 32 C4
Delaval St NE24 17 B4
Delaval Terr Blyth NE24 17 E8
Newcastle-upon-Tyne NE3 38 A4
Delaval Trad Est NE25 23 C5
Delhi Cres NE40 52 A3
Delhi Gdns NE40 52 A3
Delhi View NE40 52 A3
Dell The Newbottle DH4 90 D3
Morpeth NE61 3 E3
Dellfield Dr SR4 85 A4
Demesne Dr NE22 15 F8
Demesne The NE63 7 B2
Dempsey Rd NE13 28 B4
Denbeigh Pl NE12 39 C7
Denbigh Ave
Wallsend NE28 41 A3
Sunderland SR6 75 D4
Denbigh Community Prim Sch NE28 41 A3
Denby Cl NE23 16 A2
Dene Ave
Houghton-le-Spring DH5 95 A7
Killingworth NE12 29 A2
Brunswick Village NE13 28 A6
Newcastle-upon-Tyne, Denton Burn NE15 53 D7
Newcastle-upon-Tyne, South Gosforth NE3 38 E4
Rowlands Gill NE39 67 D1
Hexham NE46 45 C4
Dene Bank View NE3 37 E3
Dene Cl Ryton NE40 52 D5
Ovingham NE42 50 B5
Riding Mill NE44 62 F8
Newcastle-upon-Tyne NE7 39 A1
Dene Cres
Whitley Bay NE26 31 F6
Wallsend NE28 40 D2
Newcastle-upon-Tyne NE3 38 E4
Rowlands Gill NE39 67 D1
Ryton NE40 52 D5
Dene Ct Birtley DH3 82 C7
Hamsterley NE17 77 B6
Washington NE38 83 C6
Newcastle-upon-Tyne NE7 39 B1
Dene Garth NE42 50 A5
Dene Gdns
Houghton-le-Spring DH5 94 F7
Gateshead NE10 57 B1
Newcastle-upon-Tyne NE15 53 D6
Whitley Bay NE25 31 E5
Dene Gr Seghill NE23 23 B2
Newcastle-upon-Tyne NE3 38 E4
Prudhoe NE42 50 B3
Dene Head Cotts NE15 35 E2
Dene La Cleadon SR6 75 C7
Sunderland SR6 75 D4
Dene Mews SR5 74 C1
Dene Pk Ponteland NE20 25 B3
Hexham NE46 45 C4
Sunderland SR5 74 C1
Dene Rd Blaydon NE21 53 D3
Tynemouth NE30 42 C8
Rowlands Gill NE39 67 D1
Wylam NE41 51 B7
Guide Post NE62 10 E7
Sunderland SR5 74 C1
Dene Side NE21 53 D2
Dene St Hetton le Hole DH5 95 B6
Holywell NE25 23 F2
Prudhoe NE42 50 E3
New Silksworth SR3 86 A1
Sunderland SR4 85 F7
Dene Terr Newburn NE15 52 F8
Blaydon NE21 53 B2
Newcastle-upon-Tyne NE3 38 E4
Jarrow NE32 58 A4
Ovington NE42 49 D4
Riding Mill NE44 62 F8
Dene Terrace E NE41 51 A7
Dene Terrace W NE41 51 A7
Dene The
West Rainton DH4 94 A2
Medomsley DH8 77 A2
Whitley Bay NE25 31 E5
Wylam NE41 51 B6
Dene View
Burnopfield NE16 79 A6
Bedlington NE22 11 C1
Newcastle-upon-Tyne NE3 38 E4
High Spen NE39 67 A3
Rowlands Gill NE39 67 C2
Ellington NE61 1 E4
Ashington NE63 6 B3
Dene View Cres SR4 85 B6
Dene View Ct NE24 17 B7
Dene View Dr NE24 17 B8
Dene View E NE22 11 C1
Dene View W NE22 16 B8
Dene Villas DH3 88 D1
Denebank NE25 31 E5
Deneburn NE10 72 A7
Denecrest DH8 77 A2
Denecroft NE41 51 A6
Deneford NE9 71 A1
Deneholm
Whitley Bay NE25 31 E5
Wallsend NE28 40 D3
Denelands NE46 45 C5
Deneside Dunston NE11 69 F7
Newcastle-upon-Tyne, Denton Burn NE15 54 A7
Seghill NE23 23 A2
Hedworth NE32 58 C1
South Shields NE34 60 C6
Newcastle-upon-Tyne, Newbiggin Hall Est NE5 36 F4
Deneside Ave NE9 70 F4
Deneside Cl NE15 35 D2
Deneside Ct NE2 56 A8
Denesyde DH8 77 A2
Deneway NE39 68 A4
Denewell Ave
Newcastle-upon-Tyne NE7 39 A3
Gateshead NE9 70 F5
Denewood NE12 29 E2
Denewood Ct NE28 41 A2
Denham Ave SR6 75 D4
Denham Dr NE25 23 D2
Denham Gr NE21 67 F8
Denham Wlk NE5 36 C3
Denhill Pk NE15 54 D6
Denholm Ave NE23 16 A2
Denholme Lodge NE11 100 A1
Denmark Ct 10 NE6 56 C7
Denmark St
1 Newcastle-upon-Tyne NE6 56 C6
Gateshead NE8 101 C2
Dennison Cres DH3 82 C6
Denshaw Cl NE23 16 B2
Dent Cl DH6 97 E3
Dent St Blyth NE24 17 F6
Sunderland SR6 75 D4
Dentdale DH4 89 E8
Denton Ave
Newcastle-upon-Tyne NE15 53 D6
North Shields NE29 41 C6
Denton Chare NE1 101 A4
Denton Ct NE5 54 A7
Denton Gate NE5 37 A3
Denton Gdns NE15 54 C5
Denton Gr NE5 37 A3
Denton Park Ho NE5 36 E2
Denton Park Mid Sch NE5 36 F2
Denton Park Sh Ctr NE5 36 E2
Denton Rd NE15 53 F6
Denton Road Prim Sch NE15 53 F5
Denton View NE21 53 B2
Denver Gdns NE6 56 E5
Denway Gr NE26 24 B7
Denwick Ave NE15 53 C6
Denwick Terr NE30 42 C7
Depot Rd NE6 56 D7
Deptford Rd
Gateshead NE8 56 A4
Sunderland SR4 102 B3
Deptford Terr SR4 102 A4
Derby Cres NE31 57 D5
Derby Ct NE4 98 B2
Derby Gdns NE28 40 A3
Derby St Jarrow NE32 58 C7
South Shields NE33 42 C2
Newcastle-upon-Tyne NE4 98 B2
Sunderland SR2 102 C2
Derby Terr NE33 42 D2
Dereham Cl NE26 24 D5
Dereham Ct NE5 37 B4
Dereham Rd NE26 24 D5
Dereham Terr NE62 11 C8
Dereham Way NE29 41 B8
Derry Ave SR6 75 E4
Derwent Ave
Gateshead NE11 70 D5
Newburn NE15 52 E7
Hebburn NE31 57 E3
Rowlands Gill NE39 67 E1
Derwent Cote NE17 77 B5
Derwent Cres
Whickham NE16 69 B8
Hamsterley NE17 77 B5
Derwent Crook Dr NE9 70 E5
Derwent Ct NE11 70 D5
Derwent Gdns
Wallsend NE28 41 A4
Gateshead NE9 71 A5
Derwent Haven NE17 77 B5
Derwent Inf Sch NE8 100 C1
Derwent Rd
Seaton Sluice NE26 24 C6
Tynemouth NE30 32 B2
Hexham NE46 45 C4
Derwent St Penshaw DH4 90 B6
Hetton le Hole DH5 95 B2
Newcastle-upon-Tyne NE15 54 B5
Blackhall Mill NE17 77 C6
Chopwell NE17 66 B1
Sunderland SR1 102 C2
Derwent Terr
South Hetton DH6 97 E8
Burnopfield NE16 79 B7
Washington NE38 83 E4
Derwent Tower NE11 100 A1
Derwent Valley Villas NE17 77 A6
Derwent View
Burnopfield NE16 79 B6
Chopwell NE17 66 C2
Blaydon NE21 53 B1
Derwent View Terr DH9 78 D1

Derwent Walk Cty Pk*
NE16,NE21,NE39 ... 68 C5
Derwent Way
Killingworth NE12 ... 29 C3
Blaydon NE21 ... 53 E1
Derwentcote Steel Furnace*
NE17 ... 77 E6
Derwentdale Gdns NE7 ... 39 B3
Derwenthaugh Ind Est
NE16 ... 53 F3
Derwenthaugh Marina
NE21 ... 54 A3
Derwenthaugh Rd NE21 ... 54 A3
Derwentwater Ave 1
DH2 ... 88 B1
Derwentwater Ct NE8 ... 101 A1
Derwentwater Gdns
NE16 ... 69 D7
Derwentwater Rd
Newbiggin-by-the-Sea NE64 ... 7 C3
Gateshead NE8 ... 100 C1
Derwentwater Terr NE33 ... 59 C8
Deuchar Ho NE2 ... 99 C3
Deuchar St NE2 ... 99 C4
Devon Ave NE16 ... 69 C7
Devon Cl NE63 ... 5 F4
Devon Cres DH3 ... 82 B6
Devon Dr SR3 ... 92 A8
Devon Gdns
South Shields NE34 ... 60 B7
Gateshead NE9 ... 70 F7
Devon Rd Tynemouth NE29 ... 31 D1
Hebburn NE31 ... 57 F3
Devon St Penshaw DH4 ... 90 C6
Hetton le Hole DH5 ... 94 F4
Devon Wlk NE37 ... 72 D1
Devonport DH4 ... 90 C3
Devonshire Dr NE27 ... 30 C1
Devonshire Gdns NE28 ... 40 A3
Devonshire Pl NE2 ... 38 F1
Devonshire St
South Shields NE33 ... 59 B7
Sunderland SR5 ... 75 C1
Devonshire Terr
Newcastle-upon-Tyne NE2 ... 99 A3
6 Whitley Bay NE26 ... 32 B4
Devonshire Tower 1
SR5 ... 75 D1
Devonworth Pl NE24 ... 17 A7
Dewberry Cl NE24 ... 17 C4
Dewhurst Terr NE16 ... 69 B2
Dewley NE23 ... 22 B5
Dewley Ct NE23 ... 22 B5
Dewley Pl NE5 ... 36 E4
Dewley Rd NE5 ... 37 B1
Dewsgreen NE23 ... 22 B6
Dexter Way NE10 ... 71 C8
Deyncourt NE20 ... 25 D2
Deyncourt Cl NE20 ... 25 D1
Diamond Ct NE3 ... 37 D5
Diamond Hall Jun & Inf Sch
SR4 ... 85 F7
Diamond Sq 3 NE46 ... 45 B4
Diamond St NE28 ... 40 B2
Diana St NE4 ... 98 B1
Dibley Sq 5 NE6 ... 56 B5
Dibley St 6 NE6 ... 56 B5
Dick St 11 NE40 ... 51 F3
Dickens Ave
Whickham NE16 ... 69 A8
Biddick Hall NE34 ... 59 B3
Dickens St
Houghton-le-Spring DH4 ... 94 D8
Sunderland SR5 ... 75 A1
Dickens Wlk NE5 ... 36 C3
Dickson Dr NE46 ... 44 E3
Didcot Ave NE29 ... 41 E4
Didcot Way NE36 ... 73 E7
Dillon St NE32 ... 58 A5
Dilston Ave
Whitley Bay NE25 ... 32 B4
Hexham NE46 ... 45 D4
Dilston Cl Shiremoor NE27 ... 30 F2
Washington NE38 ... 83 A4
Pegswood NE61 ... 5 A3
Dilston Dr
Newcastle-upon-Tyne NE5 ... 36 E3
Ashington NE63 ... 6 D2
Dilston Gdns SR4 ... 85 F5
Dilston Haugh Cotts
NE45 ... 46 D4
Dilston Rd NE4 ... 98 A2
Dilston Terr
Newcastle-upon-Tyne NE3 ... 38 E4
Jarrow NE32 ... 58 C3
Dimbula Gdns NE7 ... 39 D2
Dinmont Pl NE23 ... 22 B5
Dinnington Fst Sch NE13 ... 27 C7
Dinsdale Ave NE28 ... 40 C4
Dinsdale Cotts 3 SR2 ... 92 F6
Dinsdale Pl NE2 ... 99 C3
Dinsdale Rd
Newcastle-upon-Tyne NE2 ... 99 C3
2 Sunderland SR6 ... 75 E2
Dinsdale St SR2 ... 92 F6
Dinsdale St S SR2 ... 92 F6
Dipe La NE36 ... 74 B7
Dipton Ave NE4 ... 54 E4
Dipton Cl NE46 ... 45 E4
Dipton Gdns SR3 ... 86 B2
Dipton Gr NE23 ... 22 B6
Dipton Rd NE25 ... 31 D7
Dipwood Rd NE39 ... 67 E1
Dipwood Way NE39 ... 78 D8
Discovery Ct SR3 ... 91 F7
Dishforth Gn NE9 ... 71 B1
Dispensary La NE1 ... 99 A1
Disraeli St
Fence Houses DH4 ... 94 B8
Blyth NE24 ... 17 D8
Blyth NE24 ... 17 E8
Disraeli Terr NE17 ... 66 B1
Dissington Pl
Whickham NE16 ... 69 A5
Newcastle-upon-Tyne NE5 ... 54 C8
Ditchburn Terr SR4 ... 85 F8
Dixon Ave DH8 ... 76 F4
Dixon Pl NE11 ... 69 F8
Dixon Rd DH5 ... 94 D6
Dixon St
South Shields NE33 ... 42 C1
Gateshead NE8 ... 100 C1
Dixon's Sq SR6 ... 103 A4
Dobson Cl NE4 ... 100 B3
Dobson Cres NE6 ... 56 C4
Dock Rd NE29 ... 42 A4
Dock Rd S NE29 ... 42 A3
Dock St South Shields NE33 ... 59 B7
Sunderland SR6 ... 75 E1
Dockendale La NE16 ... 69 C7
Dockendale Mews NE16 ... 69 C7
Dockwray Cl NE30 ... 42 C6
Dockwray Sq NE30 ... 42 B5
Dod Law* NE71 ... 107 F3
Doddfell Cl NE37 ... 83 A6
Doddington Cl NE15 ... 53 B7
Doddington Dr NE23 ... 22 B6
Doddington Villas NE10 ... 71 C7
Dodds Ct 3 SR5 ... 74 A3
Dodds Farm NE3 ... 38 A5
Dodds Terr DH3 ... 82 C6
Dodsworth N NE40 ... 52 B1
Dodsworth Terr NE40 ... 52 B1
Dodsworth Villas NE40 ... 52 B1
Dog Bank NE1 ... 101 B4
Dogger Bank NE61 ... 3 E1
Dolphin Ct 1 NE4 ... 54 D5
Dolphin Quay NE29 ... 42 B5
Dolphin St NE4 ... 54 D5
Dolphin Villas NE13 ... 28 B4
Dominies Cl NE39 ... 67 F3
Don Dixon Dr NE32 ... 58 B1
Don Gdns
West Boldon NE36 ... 73 F7
Washington NE37 ... 72 D1
Don Rd NE32 ... 58 D7
Don St NE11 ... 70 C4
Don View NE36 ... 74 A7
Donald Ave DH6 ... 97 F8
Donald St NE3 ... 38 E5
Doncaster Rd NE2 ... 99 C3
Doncrest Rd NE37 ... 72 B1
Donkin Rd NE37 ... 82 F7
Donkin Terr
North Shields NE30 ... 42 C7
Crawcrook NE40 ... 51 E3
Donkins St NE35 ... 58 E1
Donnington Ho 1 SR3 ... 91 D7
Donnington Cl SR5 ... 74 A1
Donnington Ct NE3,NE7 ... 38 F4
Donnison Gdns SR1 ... 103 B3
Donridge NE37 ... 72 B1
Donside NE10 ... 71 F4
Donvale Rd NE37 ... 72 A1
Donwell Cty Jun Sch
NE37 ... 72 C1
Dorcas Ave NE15 ... 54 C5
Dorcas Terr 3 NE37 ... 83 D8
Dorchester Cl NE5 ... 36 B3
Dorchester Ct NE25 ... 23 C6
Dorchester Gdns NE9 ... 70 F2
Dorking Ave NE29 ... 41 E4
Dorking Cl NE24 ... 17 E4
Dorking Rd SR6 ... 75 E4
Dornoch Cres NE10 ... 71 E6
Dorrington Rd NE3 ... 37 E7
Dorset Ave Birtley DH3 ... 82 D1
Wallsend NE28 ... 40 A3
Hebburn NE31 ... 57 F5
South Shields NE34 ... 60 B7
Sunderland SR6 ... 75 E4
Dorset Cl NE63 ... 5 F4
Dorset Gr NE29 ... 31 D1
Dorset Rd
Newcastle-upon-Tyne NE15 ... 53 F6
Gateshead NE8 ... 56 A4
Dorset St DH5 ... 97 C8
Dotland Cl NE46 ... 45 E4
Double Row NE25 ... 23 B5
Douglas Ave NE3 ... 38 A4
Douglas Bader Ho NE24 ... 17 F6
Douglas Cl NE34 ... 59 C4
Douglas Ct
Gateshead NE11 ... 70 E2
Sunderland SR1 ... 103 B3
Douglas Gdns NE11 ... 70 A7
Douglas Par NE31 ... 58 A2
Douglas Rd SR6 ... 75 E4
Douglas St
7 Wallsend NE28 ... 40 B2
Wallsend, Willington Quay
NE28 ... 41 A1
Douglas Terr
Penshaw DH4 ... 90 C8
Washington NE37 ... 72 D1
Newcastle-upon-Tyne NE4 ... 98 B1
Doulting Cl NE12 ... 39 B6
Dove Ave NE32 ... 58 C3
Dove Cl NE12 ... 29 C4
Dove Ct 8 Birtley DH3 ... 82 C5
Tynemouth NE30 ... 32 C3
Dove Row NE30 ... 32 C3
Dovecote Cl NE25 ... 31 C6
Dovecote Rd NE12 ... 39 E7
Dovecrest Ct 7 NE28 ... 40 F4
Dovedale Ave NE24 ... 17 A8
Dovedale Ct NE34 ... 59 A5
Dovedale Gdns
Newcastle-upon-Tyne NE7 ... 39 B3
Gateshead NE9 ... 71 A4
Dovedale Rd SR6 ... 75 C5
Dover Cl Bedlington NE22 ... 10 D1
Newcastle-upon-Tyne NE5 ... 36 C3
Dovercourt Rd NE6 ... 57 A4
Dowling Ave NE25 ... 31 F4
Downe Cl NE24 ... 17 F4
Downend Rd NE5 ... 36 E3
Downfield NE37 ... 72 D3
Downham NE5 ... 36 F1
Downham Ct NE33 ... 42 C1
Downhill Cty Inf Sch
NE34 ... 60 B7
Downhill La
Hedworth NE36 ... 73 D4
West Boldon NE37 ... 73 F5
Downhill Prim Sch SR5 ... 74 B4
Downing Dr NE61 ... 8 E7
Downs La DH5 ... 95 B5
Downs Pit La DH5 ... 95 C5
Downswood NE12 ... 29 F3
Doxford Ave DH5 ... 94 F6
Doxford Gdns 4 NE5 ... 37 D1
Doxford Park Way SR3 ... 91 E6
Doxford Pl NE23 ... 22 B5
Doxford Terr DH5 ... 94 F6
Dr Henry Russell Ct
NE15 ... 54 A5
Dr Pit Cotts NE22 ... 10 F1
Drake Cl NE33 ... 59 B8
Drawback Cl NE42 ... 50 D2
Drayton Rd
Newcastle-upon-Tyne NE3 ... 37 E4
Sunderland SR6 ... 75 D4
Drey The NE20 ... 25 B3
Drive Com Prim Sch The
NE10 ... 71 E8
Drive The Birtley DH3 ... 82 D1
Gateshead, Felling NE10 ... 71 E8
Whickham NE16 ... 69 C6
Wallsend NE28 ... 40 B2
Newcastle-upon-Tyne, Gosforth
NE3 ... 38 C3
Tynemouth NE30 ... 42 D8
Washington NE37 ... 72 C1
Newcastle-upon-Tyne, East
Denton NE5 ... 54 A8
Newcastle-upon-Tyne NE7 ... 39 B4
Gateshead, Saltwell NE9 ... 70 F6
Drivecote NE10 ... 71 E8
Dronfield Cl 2 DH2 ... 88 A1
Drove Rd NE15 ... 35 B3
Drum Ind Est DH2 ... 88 B7
Drum Rd DH2,DH3 ... 88 B8
Drumaldrace 5 NE37 ... 83 A6
Drummond Cres NE34 ... 58 F5
Drummond Rd NE3 ... 37 F4
Drummond Terr NE30 ... 42 B6
Drumoyne Cl SR3 ... 91 B6
Drumoyne Gdns NE25 ... 31 D3
Drumsheugh Pl NE5 ... 37 B2
Druridge Ave SR6 ... 75 E5
Druridge Bay* NE61 ... 119 E4
Druridge Cres Blyth NE24 ... 17 B5
South Shields NE34 ... 60 B8
Druridge Dr Blyth NE24 ... 17 B5
Newcastle-upon-Tyne NE5 ... 37 D2
Drury La
Newcastle-upon-Tyne NE1 ... 99 A1
Tynemouth NE29 ... 41 C7
Sunderland SR1 ... 103 B3
Drybeck Ct
Cramlington NE23 ... 22 D8
Newcastle-upon-Tyne NE4 ... 98 B1
Drybeck Sq SR3 ... 92 B6
Drybeck Wlk NE23 ... 22 D8
Dryborough St SR4 ... 102 B3
Dryburgh NE38 ... 83 D5
Dryburgh Cl NE29 ... 41 E8
Dryden Cl NE34 ... 59 B2
Dryden Ct 5 NE9 ... 70 F8
Dryden Rd NE9 ... 70 F7
Dryden Road Hospl NE9 ... 70 F8
Dryden Sec Sch NE9 ... 71 A7
Dryden St SR5 ... 75 A2
Drysdale Cres NE13 ... 28 A6
Drysdale Ct NE13 ... 28 B6
Dubmire Cotts DH4 ... 94 A8
Dubmire Ct DH4 ... 94 A8
Dubmire Ind Est DH4 ... 90 B1
Dubmire Jun & Inf Schs
DH4 ... 94 A8
Duchess Cres NE32 ... 58 B3
Duchess Cres E NE32 ... 58 B3
Duchess Dr NE15 ... 54 A7
Duchess St NE26 ... 32 A5
Duckets Dean NE42 ... 50 D3
Duckpool La NE16 ... 69 C7
Duckpool La N NE16 ... 69 C8
Duddon Pl NE9 ... 71 B4
Dudley Ave SR6 ... 75 D4
Dudley Bsns Ctr NE23 ... 22 A2
Dudley Ct NE23 ... 22 A6
Dudley Dr NE23 ... 29 A8
Dudley Gdns SR3 ... 91 C7
Dudley House NE4 ... 98 B2
Dudley La
Seaton Burn NE13,NE23 ... 28 D8
Cramlington NE23 ... 22 A4
Dudley Lane Cotts NE13 ... 28 C8
Dugdale Ct 6 NE3 ... 37 D5
Dugdale Rd NE3 ... 37 D5
Duke of Northumberland Ct
NE28 ... 40 E5
Duke St
Newcastle-upon-Tyne NE1 ... 100 C4
Gateshead NE10 ... 57 A1
Whitley Bay NE26 ... 32 A5
North Shields NE29 ... 42 B4
Ashington NE63 ... 6 C4
Sunderland SR4 ... 102 A2
Duke St N SR6 ... 75 D2
Duke Wlk NE8 ... 100 C1
Duke's Ave NE31 ... 57 D4
Duke's Gdns NE24 ... 17 C8
Dukes Cott NE15 ... 52 F7
Dukes Ct NE42 ... 50 E4
Dukes Dr NE3 ... 28 B1
Dukes Mdw NE13 ... 36 E8
Dukes Rd NE46 ... 44 E5
Dukes Way NE42 ... 50 E4
Dukesfield NE23 ... 22 B6
Dukesway NE11 ... 70 C4
Dukesway Ct NE11 ... 70 C3
Dukesway W NE11 ... 70 C2
Dulverston Cl NE5 ... 36 C3
Dulverton Ave NE33 ... 59 D7
Dulverton Ct NE2 ... 38 F2
Dumas Wlk NE5 ... 36 C3
Dumfries Cres NE32 ... 58 E3
Dun Cow St SR1 ... 102 C3
Dunbar Cl NE5 ... 36 C3
Dunbar St SR4 ... 85 F5
Dunblane Cres NE5 ... 36 F1
Dunblane Dr NE24 ... 17 E4
Dunblane Rd SR6 ... 75 E4
Dunbreck Gr SR4 ... 86 A4
Duncan Gdns NE61 ... 8 F7
Duncan St
Newcastle-upon-Tyne NE6 ... 57 A5
Gateshead NE8 ... 56 B1
Sunderland SR4 ... 85 F7
Dunces Hos NE61 ... 9 D7
Dundas St SR6 ... 103 A4
Dundas Way NE10 ... 71 C8
Dundee Cl NE5 ... 36 C3
Dundee Ct NE32 ... 58 E3
Dundock Wood (The
Hirsel)* TD12 ... 106 C8
Dundrennan NE38 ... 83 C3
Dunelm SR2 ... 86 B4
Dunelm Cl 5 DH3 ... 82 C4
Dunelm Dr
Houghton-le-Spring DH4 ... 94 D7
West Boldon NE36 ... 74 B8
Dunelm Rd DH5 ... 94 F4
Dunelm S SR4 ... 86 B4
Dunelm St NE33 ... 42 D2
Dunford Gdns NE5 ... 36 D4
Dunholm Cl DH5 ... 94 E7
Dunholme Rd NE4 ... 54 F5
Dunira Cl NE2 ... 38 F2
Dunkeld Cl NE24 ... 17 E4
Dunkirk Ave DH5 ... 94 F7
Dunlin Cl NE40 ... 52 E4
Dunlin Ct NE61 ... 2 A3
Dunlin Dr Blyth NE24 ... 17 E4
Washington NE38 ... 82 F3
Dunlop Cl NE7 ... 39 C4
Dunlop Cres NE34 ... 60 A6
Dunmoor Cl NE3 ... 38 A4
Dunmoor Ct DH2 ... 88 A1
Dunmore Ave SR6 ... 75 E4
Dunmorlie St NE6 ... 56 D6
Dunn Ave SR3 ... 86 A1
Dunn St NE4 ... 100 B3
Dunn St Prim Sch NE32 ... 58 C7
Dunn Terr NE6 ... 56 B6
Dunn's Terr NE2 ... 98 B4
Dunne Rd NE21 ... 53 E4
Dunning St SR1 ... 102 C3
Dunnlynn Cl SR3 ... 91 E6
Dunnock Dr
Sunniside NE16 ... 69 A3
Washington NE38 ... 82 F2
Dunnock Lodge NE15 ... 53 D6
Dunnykirk Ave 2 NE3 ... 37 D5
Dunsdale Dr NE23 ... 22 D8
Dunsdale Rd NE25 ... 23 E2
Dunsgreen NE20 ... 25 E5
Dunsgreen Ct NE20 ... 25 E5
Dunsley Gdns NE13 ... 27 B7
Dunslow Croft NE15 ... 33 C1
Dunsmuir Gr NE8 ... 70 D8
Dunstable Pl NE5 ... 36 B3
Dunstan Cl DH2 ... 88 A1
Dunstan Wlk NE5 ... 36 F1
Dunstanburgh Castle (N.T.)*
NE66 ... 113 E6
Dunstanburgh Cl
Bedlington NE22 ... 10 D1
Washington NE38 ... 83 B4
Newcastle-upon-Tyne NE6 ... 56 D5
Dunstanburgh Ct
Bournmoor DH4 ... 89 D1
Gateshead NE10 ... 72 B7
Dunstanburgh Rd NE6 ... 56 D5
Dunster Ho 3 SR3 ... 91 D7
Dunston Bank NE11 ... 69 F7
Dunston Ent Pk NE11 ... 54 E2
Dunston Hill Com Prim Sch
NE11 ... 69 F8
Dunston Hill Hospl NE11 ... 69 D7
Dunston Pl NE24 ... 17 B8
Dunston Rd NE11 ... 54 F1
Dunston Riverside Prim Sch
NE11 ... 54 F1
Dunston Sta NE11 ... 70 A8
Dunston Workshops
NE11 ... 54 F2
Dunvegan DH3 ... 82 E2
Dunvegan Ave DH2 ... 88 B1
Dunwoodie Terr NE46 ... 45 A5
Duoro Terr SR2 ... 103 A1
Durant Rd NE1 ... 99 B2
Durban St NE24 ... 17 D8
Durham Ave NE37 ... 83 B8
Durham Cl NE22 ... 10 D2
Durham Ct NE31 ... 57 D5
Durham Cty Cricket Gd
DH3 ... 88 E2
Durham Dr NE32 ... 58 B2
Durham Gr NE32 ... 58 B2
Durham Ho SR5 ... 73 F4
Durham La Haswell DH6 ... 97 C1
Sherburn Hill DH6 ... 96 D1
Durham Pl Birtley DH3 ... 82 D1
Gateshead NE8 ... 101 C1
Durham Rd Birtley DH3 ... 82 C3
Chester le Street DH3 ... 88 C1
Chester le Street, Barley Mow
DH3 ... 88 C8
East Rainton DH5 ... 94 C4
Houghton-le-Spring DH5 ... 90 F3
Houghton-le-Spring DH5 ... 94 E7
Cramlington NE23 ... 16 C1
Gateshead NE8,NE9 ... 70 F6
Gateshead NE9 ... 82 B8
Sunderland SR3 ... 85 E2
Durham St
Fence Houses DH4 ... 94 A8
3 Gateshead NE10 ... 56 F1
Wallsend NE28 ... 40 C2
Newcastle-upon-Tyne NE4 ... 54 F5
Durham St W NE28 ... 40 C2
Durham Terr SR3 ... 86 A1
Duxfield Rd NE7 ... 39 B3
Dwyer Cres SR2 ... 92 F6
Dyer Sq SR5 ... 75 B2
Dyke Heads La NE40 ... 52 B1
Dykefield Ave NE3 ... 37 E7
Dykelands Rd SR6 ... 75 E5
Dykelands Way NE34 ... 58 F3
Dykenook Cl NE16 ... 69 A4
Dykes Way NE10 ... 71 D5
Dymock Ct NE3 ... 37 B5

E

E D Morel Terr NE17 ... 77 C8
Eaglescliffe Dr NE7 ... 39 D2
Eaglesdene DH5 ... 95 A4
Ealing Ct NE3 ... 37 B6
Ealing Dr NE30 ... 32 C1
Ealing Sq
Cramlington NE23 ... 21 D6
Sunderland SR5 ... 75 A3
Eardulph Ave DH3 ... 88 D3
Earl Grey Way NE29 ... 41 F3
Earl St SR4 ... 102 B2
Earl's Dr NE15 ... 54 A7
Earl's Gdns NE24 ... 17 C8
Earlington Ct NE12 ... 29 E1
Earls Ct Gateshead DH98 ... 70 D5
Prudhoe NE42 ... 50 E4
Sunderland SR5 ... 75 A4
Earls Dene 5 NE9 ... 70 F4
Earls Dr NE9 ... 70 F4
Earls Gn DH5 ... 94 D3
Earlston St SR5 ... 75 A4
Earlston Way NE23 ... 16 C2
Earlsway DH98,NE11,NE82 ... 70 D5
Earlswood Ave NE9 ... 70 F4
Earlswood Gr NE24 ... 17 D3
Earlswood Pk NE9 ... 70 F4
Earnshaw Way NE25 ... 31 D7
Earsdon Cl NE5 ... 37 A1
Earsdon Ct NE25 ... 31 D4
Earsdon Rd
Houghton-le-Spring DH5 ... 94 F8
Earsdon NE25 ... 31 C4
Whitley Bay NE25 ... 31 C4
Shiremoor NE27 ... 30 E4
Newcastle-upon-Tyne NE3 ... 37 E3
Earsdon Terr
9 Shiremoor NE27 ... 30 E1
2 Ryhope SR2 ... 92 F6
Earsdon View NE27 ... 30 F4
Earth Balance* NE22 ... 11 C5
Easby Cl NE3 ... 38 D8
Easby Rd NE38 ... 83 D4
Easdale Ave NE3 ... 28 C1
Easedale NE26 ... 24 C6
Easedale Gdns NE9 ... 71 B3
Easington Ave
Cramlington NE23 ... 16 C2
Gateshead NE9 ... 71 C3
Easington Lane Prim Sch
DH5 ... 97 D8
Easington St SR5 ... 102 C4
Easington St N SR5 ... 102 C4
East Acre NE21 ... 53 D1
East Acres NE13 ... 27 C8
East Ave Longbenton NE12 ... 39 D6
Whitley Bay NE25 ... 31 E5
South Shields NE34 ... 60 A6
Washington NE38 ... 83 B1
East Back Par SR2 ... 103 C1
East Bailey NE12 ... 29 F3
East Benton Cotts NE12 ... 39 E5
East Boldon Inf Sch
NE36 ... 74 D7
East Boldon Jun Sch
NE36 ... 74 D7
East Boldon Rd SR6 ... 59 F1
East Boldon Sta NE36 ... 74 E8

East Bridge St DH4 83 E1
East Cl NE34 60 A6
East Cleft Rd SR2 102 B2
East Cres NE22 11 D2
East Cross St SR1 103 A3
East Dr Blyth NE24 17 C4
Cleadon SR6 74 F8
East End NE26 24 E4
East Farm Ct NE16 69 C3
East Farm Terr NE23 22 B6
East Fields SR6 75 F8
East Ford Rd NE62 11 C8
East Forest Hall Rd NE12 39 E8
East Front NE2 99 B4
East Gate Morpeth NE61 9 A6
Gateshead NE8 101 C3
East George Potts St 13 NE33 42 D1
East George St NE30 42 C6
East Gr SR4 85 B5
East Grange
Holywell NE25 23 F2
Sunderland SR5 75 C3
East Hartford Sch NE23 16 B3
East Herrington Prim Sch SR3 91 C7
East Hill Rd NE8 56 B1
East Holborn NE33 42 B2
East Law DH8 76 D1
East Lea Blaydon NE21 68 C8
Newbiggin-by-the-Sea NE64 7 E5
East Loan NE61 4 A2
East Moffett St 11 NE33 42 D1
East Moor Rd SR4 85 F7
East Oakwood NE46 45 E8
East Par NE26 32 B5
East Park Gdns NE21 53 C1
East Park Rd NE9 70 F6
East Park View NE24 18 A7
East Pastures NE63 6 B2
East Percy St NE30 42 C6
East Rainton Prim Sch DH5 94 C4
East Riggs NE22 15 F8
East Sea View NE64 7 F5
East St Chopwell NE17 66 D1
Tynemouth NE30 42 E7
Hebburn NE31 57 F7
9 South Shields NE33 42 C3
High Spen NE39 66 F4
Mickley Square NE43 49 F1
Gateshead NE8 101 C3
Whitburn SR6 75 F8
East Stainton St 10 NE33 42 D1
East Stevenson St 12 NE33 42 D1
East Tanfield Sta DH9 79 E2
East Terr Chopwell NE17 77 C7
Stakeford NE62 11 C7
East Thorp NE5 36 F5
East View
Sherburn Hill DH6 96 D1
Wide Open NE13 28 B7
Burnopfield NE16 79 A6
Blaydon NE21 53 D3
Bedlington NE22 11 D3
Seghill NE23 22 F1
New Hartley NE25 23 C5
Hebburn NE31 57 D4
West Boldon NE35 73 F8
Rowlands Gill NE39 67 C2
Crawcrook NE40 51 E6
Morpeth NE61 9 A8
Stakeford NE62 11 C7
Ryhope SR2 92 E6
Sunderland, Castletown SR5 74 C1
Sunderland, Roker SR6 75 E3
1 Seaham SR7 92 F1
East View Ave NE23 22 B6
East View S 3 SR5 74 C1
East View Terr
Gateshead NE10 71 F6
Whickham NE16 69 B8
Dudley NE23 29 A8
East Villas DH6 97 F4
East Vines SR1 103 C3
East Woodlands NE46 45 D4
Eastbourne Ave
Newcastle-upon-Tyne NE6 57 A6
Gateshead NE8 70 E8
Eastbourne Ct NE6 57 A6
Eastbourne Gdns
Cramlington NE23 21 D6
Whitley Bay NE26 32 A6
Newcastle-upon-Tyne NE6 57 A6
Eastbourne Gr 12 NE33 42 D3
Eastbourne Par NE31 58 A2
Eastbourne Sq SR5 75 A4
Eastburn Gdns NE10 57 B2
Eastcheap NE6 39 C1
Eastcliffe Ave NE3 38 A3
Eastcombe Cl NE35 58 E2
Eastcote Terr NE6 56 F4
Easten Terr NE28 41 C1
Easterfield Ct NE61 4 A1
Eastern Ave NE11,NE9 70 D4
Eastern Gdns 4 NE10 56 D1
Eastern Way
Ponteland NE20 25 D3
Newcastle-upon-Tyne NE5 37 D2
Eastfield Ave
Whitley Bay NE25 31 D4
Newcastle-upon-Tyne NE28, NE6 57 A8
Eastfield House NE6 57 A8
Eastfield Rd
Longbenton NE12 39 D6
South Shields NE34 59 F8
Eastfield St SR4 85 F5
Eastfield Terr NE12 39 D6
Eastfields NE46 45 D4
Eastgarth NE5 37 A5
Eastgate Hexham NE46 45 B4
Choppington NE62 10 F5
Eastgate Bank NE43 64 F8
Eastgate Gdns NE4 54 E4
Eastgreen NE62 10 F5
Eastlands Blaydon NE21 53 B1
Chester le Street NE38 88 E7
Newcastle-upon-Tyne NE7 39 A3
Eastlea Fst Sch NE23 22 C8
Eastleigh Cl NE35 73 E8
Easton Holmes NE22 11 C2
Eastward Gn NE25 31 D4
Eastway NE34 60 B5
Eastwood Ave NE24 17 D3
Eastwood Cl NE23 29 C5
Eastwood Ct NE12 39 D7
Eastwood Gdns
Gateshead, Old Fold NE10 56 C2
Newcastle-upon-Tyne NE3 37 F4
Gateshead, Low Fell NE9 71 A6
Eastwood Grange Ct NE46 45 E4
Eastwood Grange Rd NE46 45 E4
Eastwood Mid Sch NE42 50 F3
Eastwood Pl NE23 16 C2
Eastwood Villas NE42 50 F4
Eastwoods Rd NE42 50 F3
Eaton Pl NE4 54 F5
Eavers Ct NE34 59 C5
Ebba Wlk NE3 38 D5
Ebchester Ave NE9 71 D3
Ebchester CE Primary Sch DH8 76 E3
Ebchester Ct NE3 37 C5
Ebchester Hill DH8 76 F2
Ebchester St NE34 59 A5
Ebdon La SR6 75 D4
Ebor St South Shields NE34 59 A4
Newcastle-upon-Tyne NE6 56 C8
Eccles Ct NE27 30 C5
Eccles Terr 2 NE27 30 E1
Eccleston Cl NE27 30 C4
Eccleston Rd NE33 42 E2
Ecgfrid Terr NE32 58 C4
Eddison Rd NE38 83 F4
Eddleston NE38 83 A1
Eddleston Ave NE3 38 A3
Eddrington Gr NE5 36 C2
Ede Ave Dunston NE11 69 F8
South Shields NE34 60 B7
Eden Ave NE16 79 A6
Eden Cl NE5 36 C2
Eden Ct Bedlington NE22 16 A8
5 Wallsend NE28 40 B1
Eden Dale NE40 51 F4
Eden Gr NE61 9 A6
Eden House Rd SR2,SR4 102 B1
Eden Pl NE30 32 A1
Eden St NE28 40 B1
Eden St W SR1 102 C3
Eden Terr Penshaw DH4 90 B6
Lynmouth NE61 2 A3
Sunderland SR2 102 B1
Eden Vale SR2 102 B1
Eden Wlk NE32 58 C3
Edenbridge Cres NE12 39 B7
Edendale Ave Blyth NE24 17 B8
Newcastle-upon-Tyne NE6 57 A6
Edendale Ct Blyth NE24 17 B8
1 South Shields NE34 59 A4
Edendale Ho NE24 17 B7
Edendale Terr NE8 70 F8
Edengarth NE30 32 A2
Edgar St NE3,NE7 38 F5
Edge Hill NE20 25 C1
Edge Mount NE12 29 E4
Edgecote NE37 83 F8
Edgefield Ave NE3 37 F5
Edgefield Dr NE23 16 C2
Edgehill NE61 9 B6
Edgehill Cl NE20 25 C1
Edgeware Ct SR5 75 A3
Edgeware Wlk NE4 54 E3
Edgewell Ave NE42 50 B1
Edgewell Grange NE42 50 C2
Edgewell House Rd NE42, NE43 65 B8
Edgewell Rd NE42 50 B1
Edgewood Ponteland NE20 25 D2
Hexham NE46 45 D4
Edgewood Ave NE22 11 C1
Edgeworth Cl NE35 58 E2
Edgeworth Cres SR6 75 D2
Edgmond Ct SR2 92 E8
Edgware Rd NE8 71 A8
Edhill Ave NE34 59 A4
Edhill Gdns NE34 58 F4
Edinburgh Ct NE3 37 D8
Edinburgh Dr NE22 10 E2
Edinburgh Rd NE32 58 E4
Edinburgh Sq 3 SR5 75 A3
Edington Gdns NE40 51 E6
Edington Gr NE30 32 A1
Edington Rd NE30 32 A1
Edison Gdns NE8 70 E7
Edith Ave NE21 53 C2
Edith Moffat House 7 NE29 42 A6
Edith St Tynemouth NE30 42 C8
Edith St *continued*
Jarrow NE32 58 A7
Sunderland SR2 86 E4
Sunderland, Southwick SR5 75 C2
Edith Terr Newbottle DH4 90 D3
5 Whickham NE16 69 A7
Edlingham Castle* NE66 118 C8
Edlingham Cl NE3,NE7 38 F4
Edlingham Ct 6 DH5 94 F8
Edmonton Sq 1 SR5 75 A3
Edmund Pl NE9 70 F5
Edna Terr NE5 37 A3
Edward Burdis St SR5 75 B2
Edward Pl NE4 98 B1
Edward Rd Birtley DH3 82 B5
Bedlington NE22 11 D3
Wallsend NE28 40 F3
Edward St
Chester le Street DH3 88 C3
Hetton le Hole DH5 95 A4
Burnopfield NE16 79 A4
Blyth NE24 17 D7
Newcastle-upon-Tyne NE3 38 C5
Hebburn NE31 57 C6
Crawcrook NE40 51 E3
Morpeth NE61 9 A8
Pegswood NE61 4 F3
New Silksworth SR3 92 A7
Edward's Wlk NE1 99 A2
Edwards Rd NE26 32 C4
Edwin Gr NE28 41 A3
Edwin St
Houghton-le-Spring DH5 90 E1
Brunswick Village NE13 28 A6
14 Newcastle-upon-Tyne NE6 56 B6
Sunderland SR4 85 E7
Edwin Terr NE40 52 C2
Edwin's Ave S NE12 39 E8
Edwina Gdns NE29 41 E7
Edwins Ave NE12 39 E8
Egerton Rd NE34 59 C6
Egerton St
Newcastle-upon-Tyne NE4 54 D4
Sunderland SR2 103 B1
Eggleston Dr SR3 86 A2
Egham Rd NE5 36 C2
Eglesfield Rd NE33 59 C8
Eglingham Ave NE30 32 C1
Eglingham Cl NE61 9 B6
Eglingham Way NE61 9 B6
Eglington Tower 2 SR5 75 D1
Eglinton St SR5 75 C1
Eglinton St N SR5 75 C1
Egremont Dr NE9 71 A6
Egremont Gdns NE9 71 A6
Egremont Pl NE26 32 B4
Egremont Way NE23 16 C2
Egton Terr DH3 82 C5
Eider Cl NE24 17 E3
Eighteenth Ave NE24 17 D5
Eighth Ave
Chester le Street DH2 88 B3
Gateshead NE11 70 D3
Blyth NE24 17 D6
Newcastle-upon-Tyne NE6 56 C8
Morpeth NE61 9 B7
Ashington NE63 6 E2
Eighth Row NE63 6 B4
Eighton Terr NE9 71 E3
Eilansgate NE46 45 A5
Eilansgate Terr NE46 45 A5
Eilanville NE46 45 A5
Eishort Way NE12 39 B6
Eland Cl NE3 37 D5
Eland Edge NE20 25 F6
Eland La NE20 25 F7
Elberfeld Ct NE32 58 B6
Elder Gdns NE9 71 C1
Elder Gr
South Shields NE34 59 F3
3 Gateshead NE9 70 F5
Elder Sq NE63 6 E2
Elderwood Gdns NE11 70 B5
Eldon Ct 1 NE28 41 B1
Eldon Gdn NE1 99 A2
Eldon La NE1 99 A1
Eldon Pl
Newcastle-upon-Tyne NE1 99 A3
Newcastle-upon-Tyne, Lemington NE15 53 D7
Eldon Rd
Newcastle-upon-Tyne NE15 53 D7
Hexham NE46 45 D4
Eldon Square Sh Ctr NE1 99 A2
Eldon St Wallsend NE28 41 B2
South Shields NE33 42 B1
Gateshead NE8 56 A2
Sunderland SR4 102 A2
Eleanor St
Tynemouth NE30 32 C3
South Shields NE33 42 D3
Eleanor Terr
2 Whickham NE16 69 A7
Crawcrook NE40 52 A4
Electric Cres DH4 90 D4
Elemore Hall Sch DH6 97 A5
Elemore La
Easington Lane DH5 97 A7
High Pittington DH6 96 E6
Elemore St DH6 96 B5
Elemore View DH6 97 F7
Elenbel Ave NE22 11 C1
Eleventh Ave
Chester le Street DH2 88 B3
Gateshead NE11 70 E2
Blyth NE24 17 E6
Eleventh Ave *continued*
Morpeth NE61 9 B7
Eleventh Ave N NE11 70 E3
Eleventh Row NE63 6 B4
Elford Cl NE25 31 D5
Elfordleigh DH4 90 C4
Elgar Ave 3 NE5 36 C2
Elgin Ave NE28 40 F4
Elgin Cl Bedlington NE22 11 D2
Cramlington NE23 21 D6
Tynemouth NE29 41 C8
Elgin Ct NE10 57 B2
Elgin Gdns NE6 56 F6
Elgin Pl DH3 82 D2
Elgin Rd NE9 71 B8
Elgin St NE32 58 E4
Elgy Rd NE3 38 B3
Elisabeth Ave DH3 82 B6
Elizabeth Cres NE23 29 A8
Elizabeth Ct NE12 30 A1
Elizabeth Diamond Gdns NE33 59 B8
Elizabeth Dr NE12 40 A8
Elizabeth Rd NE28 41 A2
Elizabeth St
Houghton-le-Spring DH5 90 E1
Chopwell NE17 66 B1
East Cramlington NE23 22 F5
7 South Shields NE33 42 D2
Newcastle-upon-Tyne NE6 56 A6
Sunderland, Castletown SR5 74 B1
Sunderland, Monkwearmouth SR5 75 C3
Elizabeth Woodcock Maritime Inst The SR2 103 A1
Ell-Dene Cres NE10 71 E7
Ellen Ct 3 NE32 58 B7
Ellen Terr NE37 83 F8
Ellerbeck Cl 3 NE10 71 C8
Ellerby Ho NE6 56 E4
Ellersmere Gdns NE30 32 B2
Ellerton Way
Gateshead NE10 71 C8
Cramlington NE23 16 C2
Ellesmere DH4 89 D3
Ellesmere Ave
Newcastle-upon-Tyne, South Gosforth NE3 38 E4
Newcastle-upon-Tyne, Westerhope NE5 37 A2
Newcastle-upon-Tyne, Walkergate NE6 56 E8
Ellesmere Ct SR2 86 E1
Ellesmere Gdns NE62 11 C8
Ellesmere Rd NE4 54 E5
Ellesmere Terr SR6 75 E3
Ellington Cl Urpeth DH2 81 E2
Newcastle-upon-Tyne NE15 53 B7
Ryhope SR2 92 F5
Ellington Fst Sch NE61 1 E5
Ellington Terr NE63 5 F4
Elliot Cl DH4 90 B7
Elliot Ct NE61 9 B7
Elliot Gdns NE34 59 D2
Elliot Rd NE10 56 B1
Elliott Dr NE10 71 D8
Elliott St NE24 17 C4
Elliott Terr
3 Washington NE37 83 E8
Newcastle-upon-Tyne NE4 98 A1
Ellis Rd SR5 75 A3
Ellis Sq Pegswood NE61 4 F3
Sunderland SR5 75 B3
Ellison (C of E) Prim Sch NE32 58 B6
Ellison Pl
Newcastle-upon-Tyne NE1 99 B2
Jarrow NE32 58 B8
3 Gateshead NE9 70 F4
Ellison Rd NE11,NE8 69 F8
Ellison St Hebburn NE31 57 C7
Hebburn NE31 57 D6
10 Jarrow NE32 58 B7
Gateshead NE8 101 C3
Ellison Terr NE40 51 F1
Ellwood Gdns 3 NE9 70 F8
Elm Ave Dunston NE11 69 F7
Dinnington NE13 27 B7
Whickham NE16 69 C8
South Shields NE34 59 F4
Elm Bank Rd NE41 51 B5
Elm Cl Cramlington NE23 16 C2
Hexham NE46 44 E3
Elm Croft Rd NE12 39 E7
Elm Ct NE16 69 B5
Elm Dr Bedlington NE22 15 F8
Whitburn SR6 61 A2
Elm Gr Killingworth NE12 29 D1
Burnopfield NE16 78 F6
Newcastle-upon-Tyne NE3 37 F7
South Shields NE34 59 F4
Elm Pl DH4 90 D3
Elm Rd Ponteland NE20 26 A5
Blaydon NE21 53 D2
Shiremoor NE29 41 B8
Elm St
Chester le Street DH3 88 C3
Seaton Burn NE13 28 C8
Sunniside NE16 69 B2
Jarrow NE32 58 A7
Mickley Square NE43 64 E8
Elm St W NE16 69 B2
Elm Terr Birtley DH3 82 B5
Tantobie DH9 79 B2
Elm Trees NE24 17 D6
Elmfield Cl SR3 91 C6
Elmfield Gdns
Whitley Bay NE25 31 D3
Elmfield Gdns *continued*
Wallsend NE28 39 F4
Newcastle-upon-Tyne NE3 38 B4
Elmfield Gr NE3 38 B4
Elmfield Pk NE3 38 B3
Elmfield Rd
Walbottle NE15 35 E2
Newcastle-upon-Tyne NE3 38 C3
Hebburn NE31 57 F3
Elmfield Terr
Gateshead NE10 57 B2
Hebburn NE31 57 F4
Elms The
Easington Lane DH5 97 D8
Ellington NE61 1 D4
Sunderland SR2 103 A1
Elms W SR2 103 A1
Elmsford Gr NE12 39 B6
Elmsleigh Gdns SR6 60 A2
Elmtree Gdns NE25 31 E3
Elmtree Gr NE3 38 B3
Elmtrees NE3 38 B3
Elmway DH2 88 A5
Elmwood NE15 53 C8
Elmwood Ave
Wide Open NE13 28 C5
Wallsend NE28 40 F2
Sunderland SR5 74 F3
Elmwood Cres NE6 39 F1
Elmwood Dr NE20 25 E7
Elmwood Gdns NE11 70 B6
Elmwood Gr NE26 32 A6
Elmwood Rd NE25 31 E4
Elmwood Sq 5 SR5 74 F2
Elmwood St
Great Lumley DH4 89 E1
Sunderland SR2 102 B1
Elrick Cl NE5 36 C2
Elrington Gdns NE5 54 B8
Elsdon Ave NE25 23 D3
Elsdon Cl NE24 17 C7
Elsdon Ct NE16 69 A5
Elsdon Dr
Longbenton NE12 39 F8
Ashington NE63 6 C3
Elsdon Gdns NE11 70 A8
Elsdon Pl 7 NE29 42 A4
Elsdon Rd Whickham NE16 69 A6
Newcastle-upon-Tyne NE3 38 C5
Elsdon St NE29 42 A4
Elsdon Terr
4 Wallsend NE28 40 B1
North Shields NE29 41 D4
Elsdonburn Rd SR3 91 E5
Elsham Gn NE3 37 E6
Elsing Cl NE5 37 B4
Elstob Pl
Newcastle-upon-Tyne NE6 56 E4
Sunderland SR2 86 A2
Elston Cl NE5 36 C2
Elstree Ct NE3 37 B7
Elstree Gdns NE24 17 D3
Elstree Sq SR5 75 A3
Elswick East Terr NE4 100 B4
Elswick Rd
Washington NE37 83 A7
Newcastle-upon-Tyne NE4 100 A4
Elswick Row NE4 98 B1
Elswick St NE4 98 B1
Elswick Way NE34 59 A6
Elswick Way Ind Est NE34 59 A6
Elsworth Gn NE5 37 C3
Elterwater Rd DH2 88 B1
Elton St E NE28 40 B1
Elton St W NE28 40 B1
Eltringham Cl NE28 40 A2
Eltringham Cotts NE43 49 F1
Eltringham Rd NE42 50 A2
Elvaston Dr NE46 45 B3
Elvaston Gr NE46 45 B3
Elvaston Park Rd NE46 45 A3
Elvaston Rd Ryton NE40 52 C6
Hexham NE46 45 B4
Elvet Cl
Brunswick Village NE13 28 B6
6 Newcastle-upon-Tyne NE6 56 C7
Elvet Ct NE6 56 C7
Elvet Gn
Chester le Street DH2 88 C2
Hetton le Hole DH5 95 A1
Elvet Way 5 NE6 56 C7
Elvington St SR6 75 E3
Elwin Cl NE26 24 D5
Elwin Pl NE26 24 D5
Elwin Terr SR2 102 C2
Ely Cl NE12 39 D4
Ely St NE8 101 B1
Ely Way NE32 58 B1
Elysium La NE8 101 A1
Embankment Rd SR7 93 B1
Embassy Gdns NE15 54 B6
Emblehope NE37 83 A6
Emblehope Dr NE3 38 A4
Emblehope Ho SR3 91 E8
Embleton Ave
Wallsend NE28 40 E5
Newcastle-upon-Tyne NE3 38 A6
South Shields NE34 60 B8
Embleton Cres NE29 41 C8
Embleton Dr
Chester le Street DH2 88 A1
Blyth NE24 17 C5
Embleton Gdns
Gateshead NE10 56 D1
5 Newcastle-upon-Tyne NE5 37 D1

Embleton Rd
Gateshead NE10 57 B2
Tynemouth NE29 41 C8
Emden Rd NE3 37 F6
Emerson Pl NE27 30 E3
Emily Davison Ave NE61 8 E8
Emily St Newbottle DH4 90 D4
Newcastle-upon-Tyne NE6 56 E6
Gateshead NE8 56 B1
Emlyn Rd NE34 59 C6
Emma Ct SR2 103 B1
Emma View 6 NE40 51 F3
Emmanuel Cty Tech Coll NE11 70 A5
Emmaville NE40 52 A4
Emmaville Prim Sch NE40 51 F4
Emmbrook Cl DH5 94 D4
Emmerson Rd NE64 7 D5
Emmerson Terr NE38 83 E5
Emmerson Terr W 1 SR3 92 B7
Emperor Way SR3 91 C5
Empress Rd NE6 57 B4
Empress St 3 SR5 75 C1
Emsworth 4 SR5 75 A3
Emsworth Rd SR5 75 A3
Enderby Dr NE46 44 E3
Enderby Rd SR4 102 B3
Enfield Ave NE16 54 B1
Enfield Gdns NE16 69 B5
Enfield Rd NE9 70 F8
Enfield St SR4 85 F7
Engel St NE39 67 B2
Engine Inn Rd NE28 40 F4
Engine La NE9 70 F4
Engine Rd
Hedley on the Hill NE17 65 E4
Prudhoe NE42 65 F5
Englefeld NE10 71 F4
Englefeld Cl NE3 37 D7
Englemann Way SR3 91 E5
English Martyrs Prim Sch SR5 74 E2
English Martyrs' RC Prim Sch NE5 54 C8
Enid Ave SR6 75 D3
Enid St NE13 28 A4
Ennerdale Birtley DH3 82 D2
Washington NE37 83 C7
Sunderland SR2 86 C4
Ennerdale Cres
Penshaw DH4 90 A8
Blaydon NE21 68 B8
Ennerdale Gdns
Wallsend NE28 41 A4
Gateshead NE9 71 A5
Ennerdale Pl DH2 88 C1
Ennerdale Rd Blyth NE24 16 F8
Tynemouth NE30 32 A2
Newcastle-upon-Tyne NE6 56 F6
Ennerdale St DH5 94 F2
Ennerdale Terr NE17 77 A5
Ennerdale Wlk NE16 68 F5
Ennis Cl NE62 11 D8
Ennismore Ct NE12 39 D6
Enslin St NE6 56 F3
Enterprise Ct
Cramlington NE23 15 F1
Seaham SR7 92 F2
Enterprise Ho NE11 70 D4
Epinay Specl Sch NE32 58 C6
Epinay Wlk NE32 58 C6
Epping Ct NE23 21 D6
Epping Sq 5 SR5 75 A3
Eppleton Prim Sch DH5 95 A6
Eppleton Row DH5 95 B4
Eppleton Terr E DH5 95 B4
Eppleton Terr W DH5 95 B4
Epsom Cl NE29 41 F4
Epsom Ct NE3 37 C7
Epsom Dr NE63 6 C2
Epsom Sq 6 SR5 75 A3
Epsom Way NE24 17 D3
Epwell Gr NE23 16 C2
Equitable St NE28 40 B1
Erick St NE1 99 B1
Erin Sq SR5 75 B3
Erith Terr SR4 85 F6
Ermine Cres NE9 71 B6
Ermyn Way NE34 59 B5
Ernest St
West Boldon NE35 74 A8
7 Sunderland SR2 86 E4
Ernest Terr
Chester le Street DH3 88 C2
5 Ryhope SR2 93 A6
Ernwill Ave SR5 74 B1
Errington Cl NE20 25 C2
Errington Pl NE42 50 C2
Errington Rd NE20 25 B2
Errington Terr NE12 29 E1
Errol Pl DH3 82 D2
Erskine Ct NE2 38 F2
Erskine Rd NE33 42 D2
Erskine Way NE33 42 D2
Esdale SR2 92 E6
Esher Ct NE3 37 C7
Esher Gdns NE24 17 D3
Esher Pl NE23 21 D6
Eshmere Cres NE5 36 C3
Eshott Cl
Newcastle-upon-Tyne, Fawdon NE3 38 A6
Newcastle-upon-Tyne, East Denton NE5 37 A1
Eshott Ct NE5 37 A1
Esk Ct 12 SR3 91 F6
Esk St N10,NE9 71 B7
Eskdale Birtley DH3 82 E1
Penshaw DH4 90 A8
Eskdale Ave Blyth NE24 17 A8
Wallsend NE28 40 C5
Eskdale Cres NE37 72 B1
Eskdale Ct NE34 59 C6
Eskdale Dr NE32 58 D3
Eskdale Gdns NE9 71 A3
Eskdale Mans NE2 99 B4
Eskdale Rd SR6 75 F6
Eskdale St
Hetton le Hole DH5 94 F2
South Shields NE34 59 C5
Eskdale Terr
Newcastle-upon-Tyne NE2 99 B4
Tynemouth NE26 32 C4
Eslington Ct NE8 70 B8
Eslington Ho NE2 99 B4
Eslington Mews NE63 6 F4
Eslington Rd NE2 99 B3
Eslington Terr NE2 99 B4
Esmaralda Gdns NE23 22 F1
Esplanade NE26 32 B5
Esplanade Ave NE26 32 B5
Esplanade Mews SR2 103 A1
Esplanade Pl NE26 32 B5
Esplanade The SR2 103 A1
Esplanade W SR2 103 A1
Espley Cl NE12 40 A8
Espley Ct NE3 37 E7
Essen Way SR3 86 B3
Essex Cl
Newcastle-upon-Tyne NE4 100 B3
Ashington NE63 6 A4
Essex Dr NE37 72 D1
Essex Gdns Wallsend NE28 40 E3
South Shields NE34 60 C7
Gateshead NE9 70 F7
Essex Gr SR3 92 A8
Essex St DH5 94 F4
Estate Houses DH4 89 E4
Esther Cambell Ct NE2 98 C3
Esther Sq NE38 83 E4
Esthwaite Ave DH2 88 B1
Eston Ct Blyth NE24 17 B8
Wallsend NE28 39 F5
Eston Gr SR5 75 C3
Estuary Way SR4 85 B7
Etal Ave Whitley Bay NE25 32 B4
North Shields NE29 41 D4
Etal Castle* TD12 107 B7
Etal Cl NE27 30 F3
Etal Cres Shiremoor NE27 30 F3
Jarrow NE32 58 E4
Etal Ct 2 NE29 42 A6
Etal Ho NE63 6 F4
Etal La NE5 37 B3
Etal Pl NE3 38 A7
Etal Rd NE24 17 B3
Etal Way NE5 37 B4
Ethel Ave Blaydon NE21 53 C2
Ryhope SR2 93 A6
Ethel St Dudley NE23 29 A6
Newcastle-upon-Tyne NE4 54 D4
Ethel Terr
South Shields NE34 59 B5
High Spen NE39 66 F3
7 Hexham NE46 45 A4
Sunderland SR5 74 B1
Etherley Rd NE6 56 D7
Etherstone Ave NE7 39 C3
Eton Cl NE23 16 C2
Eton Sq NE31 57 F6
Ettrick Cl NE12 29 C4
Ettrick Gdns
Gateshead NE8 71 B8
Sunderland SR4 85 F4
Ettrick Gr SR3 85 F4
Ettrick Lodge NE3 38 D4
Ettrick Rd NE32 58 A5
European Way SR4 85 E8
Euryalus Ct NE33 42 F1
Eustace Ave NE29 41 E5
Euston Ct SR5 75 A4
Eva St NE15 53 C6
Evanlade NE10 72 B6
Evelyn St SR2 102 B1
Evelyn Terr NE21 53 C3
Evenwood Gdns NE9 71 B5
Ever Ready Ind Est DH9 79 D2
Everard St NE23 16 B3
Everest Gr NE36 74 B7
Everest Sq SR5 75 A4
Eversleigh Pl NE15 35 E2
Eversley Cres SR5 75 B3
Eversley Pl Wallsend NE28 40 F3
7 Newcastle-upon-Tyne NE6 56 B7
Everton La SR5 75 A3
Evesham SR4 85 A6
Evesham Ave NE26 31 F6
Evesham Cl NE35 58 F1
Evesham Garth NE3 37 E3
Evesham Pl NE23 21 D7
Evistones Gdns NE6 56 E3
Evistones Rd NE9 71 A7
Ewart Cres NE34 58 E4
Ewart Ct NE3 38 A7
Ewbank Ave NE4 54 E7
Ewe Hill Cotts DH4 89 F1
Ewe Hill Terr DH4 89 F1
Ewe Hill Terr W DH4 89 F1
Ewehurst Cres DH9 78 E1
Ewehurst Gdns DH9 78 E1
Ewehurst Par DH9 78 E2
Ewehurst Rd DH9 78 E2
Ewehurst Terr DH9 78 E2
Ewen Ct NE29 41 B8
Ewesley NE38 89 A8
Ewesley Cl NE5 37 A1
Ewesley Gdns NE13 28 B6
Ewesley Rd SR4 85 F5
Ewing Rd SR4 102 A1
Exchange Bldgs NE26 32 B5
Exebly Cl NE3 38 D8
Exeter Cl
Cramlington NE23 21 E7
Ashington NE63 7 A2
Exeter Ct NE31 57 D5
Exeter Rd Wallsend NE28 40 A5
Tynemouth NE29 31 C1
Exeter St
Newcastle-upon-Tyne NE6 57 A4
Gateshead NE8 101 C1
Sunderland SR4 85 F7
Exeter Way NE32 58 B2
Exmouth Rd NE29 41 C5
Exmouth Sq SR5 75 A3
Exmouth St 2 SR5 75 A3
Extension Rd SR1 103 C2
Eyemouth Ct NE34 59 A5
Eyemouth La SR5 75 A4
Eyemouth Rd NE29 41 C5

F

Faber Rd SR5 75 A3
Factory Rd NE21 53 D4
Fair Gn NE25 31 C4
Fair View
West Rainton DH4 94 A2
Burnopfield NE16 78 E6
Prudhoe NE42 50 C2
Fairburn Ave
Houghton-le-Spring DH5 94 E6
Newcastle-upon-Tyne NE7 39 C4
Fairdale Ave NE7 39 C4
Fairfield Longbenton NE12 38 F6
Hexham NE46 44 F4
Fairfield Ave
3 Longbenton NE12 39 D8
Whickham NE16 69 A5
Blyth NE24 17 D4
Fairfield Cl NE11 54 E1
Fairfield Cres NE46 45 E8
Fairfield Dr
Whitley Bay NE25 31 D4
Tynemouth NE30 32 B2
Ashington NE63 7 A2
Whitburn SR6 60 F2
Fairfield Gn NE25 31 C4
Fairfield Ind Est NE10 57 A2
Fairfield Rd NE2 38 D1
Fairfield Terr NE10 57 B2
Fairfields NE40 52 B5
Fairgreen Cl SR3 91 F5
Fairhaven NE9 71 F2
Fairhaven Ave NE6 57 A6
Fairhill Cl NE7 39 C4
Fairholm Rd NE4 54 E5
Fairholme Ave NE34 59 F6
Fairholme Rd SR3 86 C3
Fairisle DH2 82 A1
Fairlands E SR6 75 D2
Fairlands W SR6 75 D2
Fairlawn Gdns SR4 85 E4
Fairles St NE33 42 D4
Fairmead Way SR4 85 A6
Fairmile Dr SR3 92 A4
Fairmont Way NE7 39 C4
Fairney Cl NE20 25 F6
Fairney Edge NE20 25 F6
Fairnley Wlk NE5 37 A2
Fairspring NE5 37 A2
Fairview Ave NE34 59 F7
Fairview Gn NE7 39 C4
Fairville Cl NE23 16 B2
Fairville Cres NE7 39 C4
Fairway Morpeth NE61 8 F5
Stakeford NE62 11 A8
Fairway Cl NE3 38 B8
Fairway The Ryton NE21 53 A4
Newcastle-upon-Tyne NE3 38 B8
Washington NE37 72 D3
Fairways Whitley Bay NE25 31 D5
1 New Silksworth SR3 92 B7
Fairways Ave NE7 39 C4
Fairways The NE36 74 A7
Fairwood Rd NE46 45 D4
Fairy St DH5 95 A4
Falcon Ct NE63 6 B1
Falcon Hill NE61 8 D7
Falcon Pl NE12 39 A7
Falcon Terr NE41 51 B6
Falcon Way NE34 59 B4
Falconar St NE2 99 B2
Falconar's Ct NE1 99 A1
Faldonside NE6 39 D2
Falkirk NE12 29 D4
Falkland Ave
Newcastle-upon-Tyne NE3 37 F3
Hebburn NE31 57 E6
Falkland Rd SR4 85 E6
Falla Park Com Prim Sch NE10 71 C8
Falla Park Cres NE10 71 C8
Falla Park Rd NE10 71 C8
Falloden Ave NE3 37 F8
Fallodon Gdns NE5 37 D2
Fallodon Rd NE29 41 D5
Fallow Park Ave NE24 17 C6
Fallow Rd NE34 60 D6
Fallowfeld NE10 72 A7
Fallowfield Ave NE3 37 F6
Fallowfield Way
Washington NE38 83 E2
Ashington NE63 6 B2
Falmouth Dr NE32 58 D5
Falmouth Rd
North Shields NE29 41 C5
Tynemouth NE29 41 D8
Newcastle-upon-Tyne NE6 56 B7
Sunderland SR4 85 E7
Falmouth Sq SR4 85 E6
Falmouth Wlk NE23 22 A8
Falsgrave Pl NE16 68 F5
Falstaff Rd NE29 41 D6
Falston Rd NE24 17 C5
Falstone Gateshead NE10 72 A5
Washington NE38 83 F2
Falstone Ave
Newcastle-upon-Tyne NE15 53 E8
South Shields NE34 60 A6
Falstone Cl NE12 40 A8
Falstone Cres NE63 6 E1
Falstone Sq NE3 38 A6
Falstone Way NE46 44 F3
Faraday Cl NE38 84 B5
Faraday Gr Gateshead NE8 70 E7
Sunderland SR4 85 F6
Faraday Terr DH6 97 E3
Farbridge Cres DH8 76 F3
Farding Lake Ct NE34 60 C6
Farding Sq NE34 60 C6
Fareham Gr NE35 73 D8
Fareham Way NE23 22 B7
Farlam Ave NE30 32 A1
Farlam Rd NE5 54 B8
Farleigh Ct NE29 41 B8
Farm Cl Sunniside NE16 69 B2
Washington NE37 72 B1
Farm Hill Rd SR6 60 A2
Farm St SR5 75 B1
Farn Ct NE3 37 D8
Farnborough Cl NE23 22 B8
Farnborough Dr SR3 92 B8
Farndale NE28 39 F5
Farndale Ave
Stakeford NE62 11 A8
Sunderland SR6 75 F6
Farndale Cl
Dinnington NE13 27 B7
Blaydon NE21 67 F8
Farndale Ct NE24 17 D4
Farndale Rd NE4 54 E5
Farne Ave
Newcastle-upon-Tyne NE3 38 A7
South Shields NE34 60 B8
Ashington NE63 6 D2
Farne Fst Sch NE5 37 A3
Farne Rd NE27 30 F3
Farne Sq SR4 85 D7
Farne Terr NE6 56 E6
Farnham Cl NE15 53 D6
Farnham Gr NE24 17 D4
Farnham Rd NE34 59 C6
Farnham St NE15 53 D6
Farnham Terr SR4 85 F4
Farnley Rd NE6 39 C1
Farnon Rd NE3 38 A5
Farnsworth Ct NE2 38 F2
Farquhar St 4 NE2 38 F1
Farrfeld NE10 71 F4
Farrier Cl NE38 83 E2
Farriers Ct NE22 11 C5
Farringdon Comm Sch SR3 91 D7
Farringdon Inf Sch SR3 91 D8
Farringdon Jun Sch SR3 91 D8
Farringdon Rd NE30 32 A2
Farringdon Row SR4 102 C3
Farrington Ave SR3 91 C8
Farrow Dr SR6 60 E1
Farthings The NE37 72 B2
Fatfield Pk NE38 83 D1
Fatfield Prim Sch NE38 83 D1
Fatfield Rd NE38 83 E4
Fatherly Terr DH4 94 B8
Faversham Ct NE3 37 D7
Faversham Pl NE23 22 B8
Fawcett St SR1 103 A2
Fawcett Terr 7 SR2 93 A6
Fawcett Way NE33 42 C3
Fawdon Cl NE3 37 F8
Fawdon Gr NE61 4 D3
Fawdon La NE3 37 F7
Fawdon Park Ctr NE3 37 F6
Fawdon Park Rd NE3 37 F6
Fawdon Pl NE29 41 C6
Fawdon Sta NE3 37 F6
Fawdon Wlk NE3 37 D7
Fawlee Gn NE5 37 C4
Fawn Rd SR4 85 C6
Feather Bed La SR2 93 A6
Featherstone NE38 82 F5
Featherstone Gr
Bedlington NE22 10 E2
Jarrow NE32 58 A3
Featherstone St SR6 75 F2
Federation Terr DH9 79 B2
Federation Way NE11 54 E1
Fee Terr SR2 92 E6
Feetham Ave NE12 40 A8
Feetham Ct NE12 30 A1
Felixstowe Dr NE7 39 D3
Fell Bank DH3 82 D4
Fell Cl Birtley DH3 82 E3
Sunniside NE16 69 B2
Washington NE37 83 B7
Fell Ct NE9 71 B5
Fell Dyke Com Prim Sch NE9 71 D3
Fell Rd Springwell NE9 71 F1
Sunderland SR4 85 D7
Fell Sq SR4 85 D7
Fell Terr NE16 79 B6
Fell View High Spen NE39 67 A3
15 Crawcrook NE40 51 F3
Fell View W 14 NE40 51 F3
Fell Way The NE5 36 D1
Fellcross DH3 82 C5
Felldyke NE10 71 F5
Fellgate Ave NE32 58 C1
Fellgate Cty Inf Sch NE32 58 B1
Fellgate Cty Jun Mix Sch NE32 58 B1
Fellgate Gdns NE10 72 C8
Fellgate Sta NE32 58 C2
Felling Bsns Ctr NE10 56 D2
Felling Dene Gdns NE10 56 E1
Felling House Gdns NE10 56 D2
Felling Shore Ind Est NE10 56 D3
Felling Sta NE10 56 D1
Felling View NE6 56 F3
Fellmere Ave NE10 72 A8
Fells Rd NE11 70 D7
Fellsdyke Ct NE9 71 C6
Fellside Birtley DH3 82 D3
Ponteland NE20 25 B1
South Shields NE34 60 B5
Fellside Ave NE16 69 B3
Fellside Cl NE20 25 B1
Fellside Com Prim Sch NE16 69 A6
Fellside Ct
Whickham NE16 69 A7
Washington NE37 83 B6
Fellside Rd
Byermoor NE16 79 C8
Sunniside NE16 68 F3
Fellside The NE3 37 F4
Felsham Sq SR4 85 E7
Felstead Cres SR4 85 D7
Felstead Pl NE24 17 D4
Felstead Sch SR4 85 D6
Felstead Sq SR4 85 D6
Felthorpe Ct NE5 37 B4
Felton Ave
Whitley Bay NE25 32 B4
Newcastle-upon-Tyne NE3 38 A6
South Shields NE34 60 A7
Felton Cl Shiremoor NE27 30 F3
Morpeth NE61 9 B6
Felton Cres NE8 70 E7
Felton Dr NE12 29 F1
Felton Gn 12 NE6 56 C6
Felton Ho 13 NE6 56 C6
Felton Terr NE63 6 D2
Felton Wlk 15 NE6 56 C6
Fence Houses Woodlea Prim Sch DH4 89 E1
Fence Rd DH3 89 E5
Fencer Ct NE3 38 C8
Fencer Hill Park NE3 38 C8
Fenham Chase NE4 54 E8
Fenham Ct NE4 54 E8
Fenham Hall Dr NE4 54 E8
Fenham Rd
Newcastle-upon-Tyne NE4 98 A2
Lynmouth NE61 1 F3
Fenkle St NE1 99 A1
Fennel NE9 71 C4
Fennel Gr NE34 59 E3
Fenning Pl 6 NE6 56 C4
Fenside Rd SR2 92 F8
Fenton Cl DH2 88 A2
Fenton Sq SR4 85 D6
Fenton Terr DH4 90 D6
Fenton Wlk NE5 37 A2
Fenwick Ave Blyth NE24 17 D5
South Shields NE34 59 A5
Fenwick Cl Penshaw DH4 90 B8
3 Newcastle-upon-Tyne NE2 38 F1
Fenwick Gr Hexham NE46 45 A5
Morpeth NE61 4 A1
Fenwick St DH4 90 B8
Fenwick Terr
2 Newcastle-upon-Tyne NE2 38 F1
North Shields NE29 42 A6
Fenwicks St NE35 58 E1
Ferdown Ct NE40 52 D4
Ferguson Cres NE13 28 A4
Ferguson St SR2 103 C2
Ferguson's La NE15 54 B6
Fern Ave
Newcastle-upon-Tyne, Jesmond NE2 38 F1
Cramlington NE23 16 B2
North Shields NE29 41 F6
Newcastle-upon-Tyne, Fawdon NE3 38 A7
Sunderland SR5 75 A2
Whitburn SR6 60 F2
Fern Ct NE62 10 E7
Fern Dene Rd NE8 70 E8
Fern Dr Annitsford NE23 29 B8
Cleadon SR6 59 F1
Fern Gdns NE9 70 F6
Fern St SR4 102 B3
Fern Terr DH9 78 F1
Fernbank NE26 24 C6
Fernclough NE9 71 C5

Ferndale Ave
Wallsend NE28 40 C2
Newcastle-upon-Tyne NE3 28 D1
4 East Boldon NE36 74 D7
Ferndale Cl NE24 17 A8
Ferndale Gr NE36 74 D7
Ferndale La NE36 74 D7
Ferndale Rd DH4 90 A8
Ferndale Terr
Springwell NE9 71 F1
Sunderland SR4 85 E8
Ferndene NE28 40 E4
Ferndene Cres SR4 85 F6
Ferndene Ct NE3 38 D4
Ferndene Gr Ryton NE40 52 D6
Newcastle-upon-Tyne NE7 39 C3
Ferndown Ct NE10 72 B7
Ferngrove NE32 73 C8
Fernhill Ave NE16 69 A7
Fernlea NE23 29 B8
Fernlea Cl NE38 83 E2
Fernlea Gdns NE40 52 A4
Fernlea Gn NE3 37 F5
Fernley Villas NE23 22 D6
Fernsway SR3 86 B3
Fernville Ave NE16 69 B2
Fernville Rd NE3 38 B3
Fernville St SR4 102 B1
Fernway NE61 9 B8
Fernwood NE2 99 B4
Fernwood Ave NE3 38 D6
Fernwood Cl SR3 92 A5
Fernwood Rd
Newcastle-upon-Tyne, Lemington NE15 53 D6
Newcastle-upon-Tyne, Jesmond NE2 99 B4
Ferrand Dr DH4 94 D8
Ferriby Cl NE3 38 D8
Ferrisdale Way NE3 37 F7
Ferry Landing NE42 49 F3
Ferry St Jarrow NE32 58 B8
South Shields NE33 42 B3
Ferryboat La
Sunderland, Castletown SR5 85 A7
Sunderland, Hylton Castle SR5 73 F2
Ferrydene Ave NE3 37 F4
Festival Cotts NE12 29 B5
Festival Park Dr NE11 70 B7
Festival Way NE11,NE8 100 A1
Fetcham Ct NE3 37 C7
Fewster Sq NE10 72 A6
Field Cl NE2 99 C2
Field Fare Ct NE16 79 C5
Field House Rd NE8 70 E7
Field House Terr DH6 97 F3
Field La NE10 72 A8
Field Sq SR4 85 D6
Field St
8 Gateshead NE10 56 D1
Newcastle-upon-Tyne NE3 38 E5
Field Terr
4 Throckley NE15 35 D2
Jarrow NE32 58 B5
Fieldfare Cl 2 NE38 82 F3
Fieldfare Ho 9 NE24 17 F8
Fieldhouse Cl NE61 9 F5
Fieldhouse La NE61 9 E5
Fielding Ct NE34 59 A3
Fielding Pl NE9 71 B8
Fieldside East Rainton DH5 94 C3
Whitburn SR6 60 E1
Fife Ave
Chester le Street DH2 88 C3
Brockley Whins NE32 58 E3
Fife St NE8 56 A1
Fife Terr NE17 77 B6
Fifteenth Ave NE24 17 D6
Fifth Ave
Chester le Street DH2 88 B3
Gateshead DH98,NE11 70 D5
Blyth NE24 17 D6
Newcastle-upon-Tyne NE6 56 C7
Morpeth NE61 9 B7
Ashington NE63 6 E3
Fifth Row NE61 1 A3
Filey Cl NE23 22 B8
Filton Cl NE23 22 B8
Finchale NE38 83 C3
Finchale Cl
Houghton-le-Spring DH4 94 D8
Dunston NE11 69 F6
Sunderland SR2 103 B1
Finchale Gdns
Throckley NE15 35 D3
Gateshead NE9 71 C2
Finchale Rd NE31 57 E3
Finchale Terr
Great Lumley DH4 89 E1
Jarrow NE32 58 D4
2 Newcastle-upon-Tyne NE6 56 C4
Finchdale Cl NE29 41 F4
Finchdale Terr
2 Chester le Street DH3 88 C3
Newcastle-upon-Tyne NE6 56 C5
Finchley Cres NE6 57 A8
Finchley Ct NE6 57 A8
Findon Gr NE29 41 E4
Fine La DH8 76 B3
Fines Rd DH8 77 B1
Finsbury Ave NE6 56 E6
Finsbury St 2 SR5 75 C1
Finsmere Pl 1 NE5 37 B1
Finstock Ct NE7 38 F4
Fir Gr South Shields NE34 59 F5
Ellington NE61 1 D4
Fir St NE32 58 A7
Fir Terr NE16 79 B6
Firbank Ave NE30 32 B2
Firbanks NE32 58 D1
Firfield Com Sch NE5 37 D2
Firfield Rd NE5 37 D2
Firs The NE3 38 B4
First Ave
Chester le Street DH2 88 B8
Gateshead NE11 70 C6
Blyth NE24 17 D6
North Shields NE29 41 C4
Newcastle-upon-Tyne NE6 56 C7
Morpeth NE61 9 B7
Ashington NE63 6 E4
First Row Ellington NE61 1 E4
Linton NE61 1 A3
Ashington NE63 6 A4
First St NE8 101 A1
Firth Sq SR4 85 D7
Firtree Ave
Longbenton NE12 29 D1
Washington NE38 83 C1
Newcastle-upon-Tyne NE6 40 A1
Firtree Cres NE12 29 C1
Firtree Gdns NE25 31 F3
Firtree Rd NE16 69 A6
Firtrees
Chester le Street DH2 88 B5
Gateshead NE10 71 E5
Firtrees Ave NE28 41 B3
Firwood Cres NE39 67 A3
Firwood Gdns NE11 70 B5
Fisher Ind Est NE6 57 B7
Fisher La
Cramlington NE13 21 B5
Cramlington NE13,NE23 21 B5
Fisher Rd NE27 30 B6
Fisher St NE6 57 B7
Fisherwell Rd NE10 57 A1
Fitzpatrick Pl NE33 42 E2
Fitzroy Terr 7 SR5 74 F2
Fitzsimmons Ave NE28 40 B3
Flag Ho NE33 42 E1
Flag Lo NE33 42 E1
Flagg Ct NE33 42 D3
Flaunden Cl NE34 60 B5
Flax Sq SR4 85 C7
Flaxby Cl NE3 38 D8
Fleet St SR1 103 C2
Fleming Bsns Ctr NE2 99 B4
Fleming Ct NE8 100 C2
Fleming Gdns NE10 71 D7
Fletcher Cres DH4 90 E6
Fletcher Terr DH4 90 D4
Flexbury Gdns
Gateshead, Mount Pleasant NE10 71 C8
Newcastle-upon-Tyne NE15 53 E7
Gateshead, Lyndhurst NE9 71 A2
Flint Hill Bank DH9 78 E1
Flock Sq SR4 85 D7
Flodden NE12 29 D4
Flodden Rd SR4 85 D6
Flodden St NE6 56 D5
Flora St 12 NE6 56 B6
Floral Dene SR4 85 A6
Floralia Ave 1 SR2 93 A6
Florence Ave NE9 71 A6
Florence Cres 4 SR5 74 F2
Florence St NE21 53 B1
Florida St SR4 85 F8
Flotterton Gdns NE5 54 C7
Flour Mill Rd NE11 54 F2
Fold The Burnopfield NE16 79 A7
Whitley Bay NE25 31 E5
Newcastle-upon-Tyne NE6 57 A8
New Silksworth SR3 92 B5
Folds The
Fence Houses DH4 94 B8
East Rainton DH5 94 D4
Folldon Ave SR6 75 D3
Follingsby Ave NE10 72 D6
Follingsby Dr NE10 72 C7
Follingsby La NE10 72 E5
Follingsby Pk NE10 72 D5
Follingsby Way NE10 72 D6
Follonsby Terr NE10 72 E7
Folly La NE40 52 B2
Folly The NE36 74 A7
Folly Yd NE40 52 C2
Font Side NE61 3 A1
Fontaine Rd SR1 102 C3
Fontburn NE61 1 E6
Fontburn Cres NE63 6 F3
Fontburn Ct
North Shields NE29 41 D4
Sunderland SR5 74 F4
Fontburn Gdns NE61 8 E7
Fontburn Pl NE7 39 A5
Fontburn Rd
Bedlington NE22 11 C1
Seaton Delaval NE25 23 D3
Fontburn Terr NE30 42 B6
Fonteyn Pl NE23 16 B2
Fontwell Dr NE8 70 D7
Forbeck Rd SR4 85 D6
Forber Ave NE34 60 B6
Forbes Terr SR2 92 E6
Ford Ave
North Shields NE29 41 D4
Ashington NE63 6 D2
Sunderland SR4 85 A6
Ford Cres Shiremoor NE27 30 E3
Ford Cres *continued*
Jarrow NE32 58 B3
Sunderland SR4 85 A6
Ford Dr NE24 17 C7
Ford Gr NE3 38 B7
Ford Oval SR4 85 B7
Ford Pk NE62 11 C8
Ford St
Newcastle-upon-Tyne NE6 56 A5
Gateshead NE8 56 B1
Ford Terr Wallsend NE28 40 F2
Riding Mill NE44 63 A8
Guide Post NE62 10 F7
5 Sunderland SR4 85 F6
Ford The NE42 50 D3
Ford View NE23 22 A1
Fordenbridge Cres SR4 85 E6
Fordenbridge Rd SR4 85 D6
Fordenbridge Sq SR4 85 E6
Fordfield Rd SR4 85 D6
Fordhall Dr SR4 85 E6
Fordham Rd SR4 85 E6
Fordham Sq SR4 85 E6
Fordland Pl SR4 85 F6
Fordley Com Prim Sch NE23 29 A8
Fordmoss Wlk NE5 37 A2
Fore St
Newcastle-upon-Tyne NE2 56 A8
Hexham NE46 45 B5
Forest Ave NE12 39 E8
Forest Dr NE38 88 F8
Forest Hall Prim Sch NE12 29 D1
Forest Hall Rd NE12 29 E1
Forest Hall St Mary's RC Sch NE12 29 D1
Forest Rd
Newcastle-upon-Tyne NE15 54 C4
South Shields NE33 42 C2
Sunderland SR4 85 D6
Forest Rd Ind Est NE33 42 C2
Forest Way NE23 22 F1
Forestborn Ct 5 NE5 36 F2
Forfar St SR6 75 D2
Forge Cl NE17 77 B6
Forge La Bournmoor DH3 89 B2
Hamsterley Mill NE17 77 E5
Forge Rd NE11,NE8 70 A8
Forge Wlk NE15 35 F1
Forres Pl NE23 22 B8
Forrest Rd NE28 40 A1
Forster Ave Sherburn DH6 96 A2
Bedlington NE22 10 E1
South Shields NE34 59 E6
Forster Ct 6 NE9 70 F4
Forster St
Newcastle-upon-Tyne NE1 99 C1
Blyth NE24 17 F7
Sunderland SR6 75 E1
Forsyth Rd NE2 38 E1
Forsyth St NE29 31 B1
Fort Sq 2 NE33 42 C4
Fort St NE33 42 D4
Forth Banks NE1 101 A4
Forth Ct
South Shields NE34 59 C5
7 Silksworth SR3 91 F6
Forth La NE1 101 A4
Forth Pl NE1 100 C4
Forth St
Newcastle-upon-Tyne NE1 101 A4
Chopwell NE17 66 C1
Fortrose Ave SR3 86 A3
Forum Ct NE22 10 F1
Forum The
Newcastle-upon-Tyne NE15 53 F7
2 Wallsend NE28 40 B1
Forum Way NE23 22 A6
Foss Way Ebchester DH8 76 E3
South Shields NE34 59 B5
Fossdyke NE10 71 F5
Fosse Law NE15 35 E1
Fosse Terr NE9 71 B6
Fossefeld NE10 72 A7
Fossway NE6 56 E7
Foster Ct NE11 70 C3
Foster St
Newcastle-upon-Tyne, Low Walker NE6 57 B6
Newcastle-upon-Tyne, Wincomblee NE6 57 B5
Foundary Ct NE6 56 C4
Foundry Ct NE6 56 C4
Foundry La NE6 56 A6
Fountain Cl NE22 10 F1
Fountain Gr NE34 59 F8
Fountain Head Bank NE26 24 C6
Fountain La NE21 53 C3
Fountain Row NE2 98 B3
Fountains Cl
Dunston NE11 69 F6
Washington NE38 83 D4
Fountains Cres
Burnside DH4 90 C2
Hebburn NE31 57 E3
Four Lane Ends
Hetton le Hole DH5 95 B2
Houghton-le-Spring DH5 94 D6
Four Lane Ends Sta NE7 39 C5
Fouracres Rd NE5 37 E2
Fourstones NE5 37 A2
Fourstones Cl NE3 37 D5
Fourstones Rd SR4 85 E6
Fourteenth Ave NE24 17 D6
Fourth Ave
Chester le Street DH2 88 B3
Fourth Ave *continued*
Gateshead NE11 70 C5
Blyth NE24 17 D6
1 Newcastle-upon-Tyne NE6 56 C7
Morpeth NE61 9 B7
Ashington NE63 6 D3
Fourth Row NE61 1 A4
Fourth St NE8 101 A1
Fowberry Cres NE4 54 E7
Fowberry Rd NE15 53 F4
Fowler Cl DH4 90 C4
Fowler Gdns 2 NE11 54 F1
Fowler St NE33 42 C3
Fox and Hounds La NE15 54 C6
Fox and Hounds Rd NE5 54 C7
Fox Ave NE34 59 A4
Fox Covert La NE20 25 D6
Fox Lea Wlk NE23 22 E1
Fox St SR2 102 B1
Foxcover NE63 6 F1
Foxcover La SR3 91 B7
Foxcover Rd
Sunderland SR3 91 A8
Penshaw SR4 84 F2
Foxglove Cl NE24 17 C4
Foxglove Ct NE34 59 B4
Foxhill Cl NE63 6 B1
Foxhills Cl NE38 83 E2
Foxhills Covert NE16 68 E5
Foxhills The NE16 68 E6
Foxholmes NE32 73 D8
Foxhunters Light Ind Site NE25 31 F3
Foxhunters Rd NE25 31 F3
Foxlair Cl SR3 92 A4
Foxley NE37 83 E8
Foxley Cl NE12 29 F4
Foxton Ave
Newcastle-upon-Tyne NE3 37 F7
Tynemouth NE30 32 B3
Foxton Cl NE29 41 E3
Foxton Ct SR6 60 A1
Foxton Gn NE3 37 E5
Foxton Hall NE37 72 D3
Foxton Way NE10 57 B2
Foyle St SR1 103 A2
Framlington Pl NE2 98 C3
Frances St Blaydon NE21 53 A2
9 New Silksworth SR3 92 A7
Frances Ville NE62 10 E4
Francis St SR6 75 D2
Frank Pl NE29 42 A6
Frank St Wallsend NE28 40 B1
Greenside NE40 51 F1
Sunderland SR5 75 B2
Frankham St 1 NE5 36 F2
Frankland Dr NE25 31 E3
Franklin Ct 10 NE37 83 D8
Franklin St
South Shields NE33 42 C2
Sunderland SR4 102 A3
Franklyn Ave NE26 24 B7
Fraser Cl NE33 59 B8
Frazer Terr NE10 57 B2
Freda St SR5 74 F1
Frederick Gdns DH4 90 A7
Frederick Rd SR1 103 A3
Frederick St
Chopwell NE17 77 B8
South Shields NE33 42 C1
Sunderland SR1 103 A2
Sunderland, South Hylton SR4 85 A6
Frederick Terr
Hetton le Hole DH5 95 B1
South Hetton DH6 97 F6
3 Whitburn SR6 60 F1
Freehold Ave NE62 10 F7
Freehold St 5 NE24 17 F8
Freeman Hospl NE7 39 A4
Freeman Rd NE3,NE7 38 F4
Freeman Way
Whitley Bay NE26 31 E7
Ashington NE63 6 F1
Freesia Grange NE38 83 E3
Freezemoor Rd DH4 90 D6
Fremantle Rd NE34 60 B5
French St NE24 17 E8
Frenchman's Row NE15 35 B2
Frenchman's Way NE34 60 B8
Frensham NE38 84 A4
Frenton Cl NE5 36 C2
Friar Rd SR4 85 D6
Friar Sq SR4 85 D6
Friar Way NE32 58 C7
Friar's Row NE16 78 F5
Friarage Ave SR6 75 D3
Friars NE1 98 C1
Friars Dene Rd NE10 56 C2
Friars Gate NE61 8 D7
Friars St NE1 98 C1
Friars Way NE5 54 C8
Friarsfield Cl SR3 91 E5
Friarside Cres NE39 78 D8
Friarside Gdns
Burnopfield NE16 78 F6
Whickham NE16 69 A6
Friarside Rd NE4 54 E8
Friary Gdns NE10 56 C1
Frobisher Ct SR3 91 F6
Frobisher St NE31 58 A6
Frome Gdns NE9 70 F2
Frome Pl NE23 22 B8
Frome Sq SR4 85 C6
Front Rd SR4 85 D6
Front St
Chester le Street DH3 88 C3
Front St *continued*
Fence Houses DH4 94 A8
Newbottle DH4 90 D4
Hetton le Hole DH5 95 A3
Hetton le Hole, Low Moorsley DH5 94 E1
Haswell DH6 97 F3
High Pittington DH6 96 B6
Sherburn DH6 96 A1
Sherburn Hill DH6 96 D1
South Hetton DH6 97 F7
Tanfield DH9 79 D3
Tantobie DH9 79 B2
Killingworth NE12,NE23 29 B5
Dinnington NE13 27 B7
Burnopfield NE16 79 B6
Burnopfield, Hobson NE16 79 A4
Burnopfield, Lintz NE16 78 E6
Whickham NE16 69 B7
Whickham, Swalwell NE16 54 A1
Blaydon NE21 53 B1
Annitsford NE23 22 B1
Cramlington NE23 22 B6
Seghill NE23,NE13 22 F2
Bebside NE24 16 E7
Earsdon NE25 31 A5
Whitley Bay NE25,NE26 31 E4
North Shields NE29 41 E5
Tynemouth, Preston NE29 42 A8
Tynemouth NE30 42 D7
Tynemouth, Cullercoats NE30 32 C3
Boldon Colliery NE35 58 E1
East Boldon NE36 74 C7
Washington NE37 83 D8
Prudhoe, Hagg Bank NE41 50 F5
Prudhoe NE42 50 D2
Corbridge NE45 46 F5
Ellington NE61 1 C5
Guide Post NE62 10 E7
Newbiggin-by-the-Sea NE64 7 E4
Longbenton NE7,NE12 39 C5
Cleadon SR6 60 A1
Whitburn SR6 75 F8
Front St E Penshaw DH4 90 B8
Bedlington NE22 16 A8
Front St W Penshaw DH4 90 B8
Bedlington NE22 15 F8
Front Street Com Prim Sch NE16 69 A7
Frosterley Cl DH5 97 D8
Frosterley Gdns SR3 86 B2
Frosterley Pl NE4 98 A2
Frosterley Wlk NE16 69 B3
Froude Ave NE34 59 C3
Fuchsia Gdns NE31 57 E3
Fuchsia Pl NE5 37 D2
Fulbrook Cl NE23 16 B2
Fulbrook Rd NE3 37 F5
Fuller Rd SR2 86 E4
Fullerton Pl NE9 71 A8
Fulmar Dr Blyth NE24 17 E3
Washington NE38 82 F3
Fulmar Wlk SR6 60 F2
Fulwell Ave NE34 60 B7
Fulwell Gn NE5 37 B1
Fulwell Inf Sch SR6 75 D4
Fulwell Prim Jun Mix Sch SR6 75 E4
Fulwell Rd SR6 75 D2
Furnace Bank NE22 11 D1
Furness Ct 1 SR3 91 F6
Furrowfield NE10 71 C6
Furrowfield Jun Sch DH3 82 D3
Furrowfield Sch NE10 71 C6
Furzefield Rd NE3 38 B4
Fyling Ho 3 SR3 91 F5
Fylingdale Dr SR3 92 C7

G

Gables Ct SR4 85 C3
Gables The
Newcastle-upon-Tyne NE13 37 B6
3 Blyth NE24 17 D8
4 Washington NE38 83 E4
Gadwall Rd DH4 94 B6
Gainers Terr NE28 57 C8
Gainford
Chester le Street DH2 88 A3
Gateshead NE9 70 F2
Gainsborough Ave
Whiteleas NE34 59 D2
Washington NE38 83 E4
Gainsborough Cl NE25 31 C7
Gainsborough Cres
Shiney Row DH4 90 A5
Gateshead NE9 71 B7
Gainsborough Pl NE23 22 B3
Gainsborough Rd SR4 85 C2
Gainsborough Sq SR4 85 C2
Gainsbro Gr NE4 54 F6
Gainsford Ave NE9 70 E4
Gairloch Cl NE23 16 B1
Gairloch Dr NE38 83 A3
Gairloch Rd SR4 85 C3
Gairsay Cl 5 SR2 92 E8
Galashiels Gr DH4 90 B5
Galashiels Rd SR4 85 C3
Galashiels Sq SR4 85 C3
Galen Ho NE1 99 A1
Gallalaw Terr NE3,NE7 38 F5
Gallant Terr NE28 41 C1
Galleries The NE38 83 C5
Galley's Gill Rd SR1 102 C3

Galloping Green Cotts
NE9 .... 71 D2
Galloping Green Rd NE9 .71 D2
Gallowgate NE1 .... 98 C1
Gallowhill La NE15,NE42 ..50 B7
Gallows Bank NE46 ....45 B3
Galsworthy Rd
Biddick Hall NE34 ....59 B3
Whiteleas NE34 ....59 C3
Sunderland SR4 ....85 C3
Galway Rd SR4 ....85 B3
Galway Sq SR4 ....85 B3
Gambia Rd 4 SR4 ....85 B2
Gambia Sq 6 SR4 ....85 B2
Ganton Ave NE23 ....22 B4
Ganton Cl NE37 ....72 C2
Ganton Ct NE34 ....59 F3
Gaprigg Ct NE46 ....45 B4
Gaprigg La NE46 ....45 A4
Garasdale Cl NE24 ....17 D4
Garcia Terr SR6 ....75 E4
Garden City Villas NE63 ....6 D3
Garden Cl NE13 ....28 B8
Garden Cres DH8 ....76 F4
Garden Croft NE12 ....39 E8
Garden Dr NE31 ....57 D4
Garden Est DH5 ....95 B4
Garden House Est NE40 ..51 E4
Garden La
South Shields NE33 ....42 C2
Cleadon SR6 ....74 F8
Garden Pk 9 NE28 ....40 F4
Garden Pl Penshaw DH4 ...90 B7
Sunderland SR1 ....102 C3
Garden St Newbottle DH4 ..90 D3
Blaydon NE21 ....53 C3
Newcastle-upon-Tyne NE3 ..38 C4
Garden Terr
Newbottle DH4 ....90 D3
9 Blaydon NE21 ....53 B1
Earsdon NE25 ....31 A5
Crawcrook NE40 ....51 F4
Crawcrook, Ryton Woodside
NE40 ....52 A3
Hexham NE46 ....45 A5
Gardener St NE4 ....100 A3
Gardens The
Chester le Street DH2 ......88 B3
Whitley Bay NE25 ....31 F4
Washington NE38 ....83 E4
Gardiner Rd SR4 ....85 B3
Gardiner Sq
Kibblesworth NE11 ....81 C6
4 Sunderland SR4 ....85 B3
Gardner Pk NE29 ....41 F5
Gardner Pl NE29 ....42 B5
Garesfield Gdns
Burnopfield NE16 ....78 F6
Rowlands Gill NE39 ....67 E3
Garesfield Golf Course
NE17 ....66 D4
Garesfield La NE21,NE39 ..67 E6
Gareston Cl NE24 ....17 B7
Garfield St 6 SR4 ....85 F7
Garforth Cl NE23 ....22 A4
Garland Terr 6 DH4 ......94 A8
Garleigh Cl NE12 ....29 F3
Garmondsway 15 NE6 .....56 C5
Garner Cl NE5 ....36 D3
Garnet St 3 SR4 ....85 F7
Garrett Cl NE28 ....40 F3
Garrick Cl NE29 ....41 C7
Garrick St NE33 ....59 C8
Garrigill NE38 ....83 F1
Garsdale DH3 ....82 E1
Garsdale Ave NE37 ....83 C8
Garsdale Rd NE26 ....24 E1
Garside Ave DH3 ....82 C6
Garsin Cl NE7 ....39 E3
Garth Cotts NE46 ....45 A4
Garth Cres Blaydon NE21 ..53 B1
South Shields NE34 ....43 A1
Garth Farm Rd NE21 ......53 B1
Garth Heads NE1 ....99 C1
Garth Sixteen NE12 ......29 D4
Garth The Medomsley DH8 .77 C3
7 Blaydon NE21 ....53 B1
Newcastle-upon-Tyne, Kenton
NE3 ....37 F4
Newcastle-upon-Tyne, West
Denton NE5 ....36 E1
Garth Thirty Three NE12 ..29 D3
Garth Thirty Two NE12 ....29 E3
Garth Twenty NE12 ....29 E3
Garth Twenty Five NE12 ..29 F3
Garth Twenty Four NE12 ..29 F3
Garth Twenty One NE12 ..29 E4
Garth Twenty Seven
NE12 ....29 F3
Garth Twenty Two NE12 ...29 E3
Garthfield Cl NE5 ....37 A3
Garthfield Cnr NE5 ......37 A3
Garthfield Cres NE5 .....37 A3
Gartland Rd SR4 ....85 B3
Garvey Villas N10,NE9 ....71 C6
Garwood St NE33 ....59 B8
Gas House La NE61 ....4 A1
Gas La NE21 ....53 C4
Gaskell Ave NE34 ....59 B3
Gatacre St NE24 ....17 E8
Gateley Ave NE24 ....17 D4
Gatesgarth NE9 ....71 A5
Gatesgarth Gr SR6 ....75 E5
Gateshead Highway
NE8 ....101 C2
Gateshead International Stad
(Athletics Gd) NE10 .....56 C3
Gateshead Jewish Boys Sch
NE8 ....101 B1
Gateshead Jewish Prim Sch
NE8 ....101 B1
Gateshead Jewish Teachers
Training Coll NE8 ....101 B1
Gateshead Library* NE8 ..70 F8
Gateshead Metro Ctr Sta
NE11 ....54 D2
Gateshead Rd NE16 ......69 C3
Gateshead Sta NE8 ......101 B3
Gateshead Stadium Sta
NE8 ....56 A2
Gateshead Talmudical Coll
NE8 ....101 B1
Gateshead Tech Coll NE9 .70 F7
Gateshead Tech Coll
(Annexe) NE9 ....71 A7
Gatwick Ct NE3 ....37 C7
Gatwick Rd SR4 ....85 B3
Gaughan Cl NE6 ....56 F3
Gaweswell Terr DH4 .....90 D4
Gayhurst Cres SR3 ....92 B6
Gayton Rd NE37 ....72 E1
Geddes Rd SR4 ....85 B3
Gellesfield Chare NE16 ...69 B4
Gelt Cres DH5 ....95 B2
General Graham St SR4 .102 A1
General Havelock Rd
SR4 ....85 E6
General's Wood The
NE38 ....89 B8
Geneva Rd 5 SR4 ....85 B3
Genister Pl NE4 ....54 D8
Geoffrey St
Whiteleas NE34 ....59 C3
Whitburn SR6 ....60 F1
George Pl NE1 ....99 A2
George Rd
Bedlington NE22 ....11 D2
Wallsend NE28 ....57 B8
George Scott St NE33 ....42 D4
George Smith Gdns
NE10 ....56 C2
George Sq 6 NE30 ....42 B6
George St Birtley DH3 ....82 B4
Chester le Street DH3 .....88 D2
Hetton le Hole DH5 ....95 A5
Haswell DH6 ....97 F3
Sherburn DH6 ....96 A1
Newcastle-upon-Tyne NE1,
NE4 ....100 C4
5 Gateshead NE10 ....56 F1
Brunswick Village NE13 ...28 A6
Whickham NE16 ....69 A7
Blaydon NE21 ....53 D3
Blyth NE24 ....17 E6
Wallsend NE28 ....41 B1
Newcastle-upon-Tyne, Coxlodge
NE3 ....38 A5
North Shields NE30 ....42 B6
4 Crawcrook NE40 ....51 F3
Walbottle NE5 ....35 F2
Ashington NE63 ....6 E4
Ryhope SR2 ....93 A6
New Silksworth SR3 ....92 A8
George St N SR6 ....103 A4
George St W 10 SR3 .....92 A8
George Stephenson High Sch
NE12 ....29 D3
George Stephenson Way
NE29 ....42 A3
George Stephenson's
Cottage* NE41 ....51 D7
George's View NE23 ......29 A7
Georges Rd
Newcastle-upon-Tyne NE4 ..54 F4
Newcastle-upon-Tyne, Elswick
NE4 ....54 F3
Georgian Ct
Longbenton NE12 ....29 B1
Sunderland SR4 ....86 A4
Gerald St Whiteleas NE34 .59 C3
Newcastle-upon-Tyne NE4 ..54 D4
Gerrard Cl
Cramlington NE23 ....22 B4
Whitley Bay NE26 ....24 E1
Gerrard Rd
Whitley Bay NE26 ....24 F1
6 Sunderland SR4 ....85 B3
Gertrude St DH4 ....90 D2
Gibbon's Wlk NE34 ......59 A2
Gibbs Ct 3 DH2 ....88 C2
Gibside DH2 ....88 A3
Gibside Chapel* NE16 ....68 A1
Gibside Cres NE16 ....79 D8
Gibside Ct NE11 ....69 F6
Gibside Gdns NE15 ......54 B6
Gibside Terr NE16 ....79 B6
Gibside View NE21 ....68 B8
Gibside Way NE11 ....54 B2
Gibson Ct NE35 ....73 F8
Gibson Fields NE46 ......45 B4
Gibson Ho 5 NE46 ....45 A4
Gibson Pl NE46 ....45 A5
Gibson St
Newcastle-upon-Tyne NE1 ..99 C1
Wallsend NE28 ....40 F5
Newbiggin-by-the-Sea NE64 ..7 D4
Gibson Terr NE40 ....52 A4
Gifford Sq SR4 ....85 C4
Gilberdyke NE10 ....72 A5
Gilbert Rd SR4 ....85 B2
Gilbert Sq SR4 ....85 B2
Gilbert St NE33 ....59 C8
Gilderdale DH4 ....89 E8
Gilderdale Way NE23 .....22 A3
Giles Pl NE46 ....45 A5
Gilesgate NE46 ....45 A5
Gilesgate Rd DH5 ....95 B1
Gilhurst Grange SR1 ....102 B2
Gill Bridge Ave SR1 .....102 C3
Gill Burn NE39 ....67 E3
Gill Crescent N DH4 ......89 E1
Gill Crescent S DH4 ......89 E1
Gill Ct NE13 ....28 A6
Gill Rd SR1 ....102 C3
Gill Side Gr SR6 ....75 E2
Gill St NE4 ....54 E5
Gillas La DH5 ....95 A7
Gillas La E DH5 ....94 F7
Gillas La W DH5 ....94 E6
Gillas Lane Inf Sch DH5 ..94 F7
Gillhurst Ho SR1 ....102 B3
Gillies St NE6 ....56 D6
Gilliland Cres DH3 ......82 C6
Gillingham Rd SR4 ....85 C3
Gillside Ct NE34 ....59 A5
Gillwood Ct DH4 ....90 A6
Gilmore Cl NE5 ....36 D3
Gilmore Ho NE8 ....70 E8
Gilpin St DH4 ....94 D8
Gilsland Ave NE28 ....40 F3
Gilsland Gr NE23 ....16 B1
Gilsland St SR4 ....102 A2
Gilwell Way NE3 ....28 B1
Gingler La NE40 ....52 A2
Girtin Rd NE34 ....59 D2
Girvan Terr DH5 ....95 B1
Girvan Terr W DH5 ....95 B1
Gisburn Ct NE23 ....16 B1
Gishford Way NE5 ....37 B2
Givens St SR6 ....75 E2
Glade The Walbottle NE15 ..36 A2
Hedworth NE32 ....73 B8
Gladeley Way NE16 ......69 B2
Gladewell Ct NE62 ....10 E7
Gladstonbury Pl NE12 ....39 C7
Gladstone Ave NE26 ......31 F6
Gladstone Pl NE2 ....99 B3
Gladstone St
Fence Houses DH4 ....94 B8
Newcastle-upon-Tyne NE15 ..53 C6
Blyth NE24 ....17 D8
3 Wallsend NE28 ....41 B1
Hebburn NE31,NE32 ....58 A6
Morpeth NE61 ....9 B8
Sunderland SR6 ....75 D1
Gladstone Terr
Birtley DH3 ....82 B4
Penshaw DH4 ....89 F8
Newcastle-upon-Tyne NE2 ..99 B3
Bedlington NE22 ....11 A1
7 Whitley Bay NE26 ......32 B4
2 Boldon Colliery NE35 ...58 E1
Washington NE37 ....83 F8
Gateshead NE8 ....101 C1
Gladstone Terr W NE8 ...101 B1
Gladwyn Rd 2 SR4 ....85 B2
Gladwyn Sq SR4 ....85 B2
Glaholm Rd SR2 ....103 C2
Glaisdale Ct NE34 ....59 A4
Glaisdale Dr SR6 ....75 E6
Glaisdale Rd NE7 ....39 A5
Glamis Ave
Newcastle-upon-Tyne NE3 ..28 C1
Sunderland SR4 ....85 C4
Glamis Cres NE39 ....68 B4
Glamis Ct NE34 ....59 F3
Glamis Terr NE16 ....69 A1
Glamis Villas DH3 ....82 C6
Glanmore Rd 3 SR4 ......85 B3
Glantlees NE5 ....37 A2
Glanton Ave NE25 ....23 C3
Glanton Cl
Chester le Street DH2 ......88 A2
3 Newcastle-upon-Tyne
NE6 ....56 C4
Morpeth NE61 ....9 B5
Glanton Ct NE11 ....100 A1
Glanton Ho NE24 ....17 B8
Glanton Rd
Tynemouth NE29 ....41 D7
Hexham NE46 ....45 D4
Glanton Sq SR4 ....85 C3
Glanton Wynd NE3 ....38 B7
Glanville Cl NE11 ....70 B7
Glanville Rd SR3 ....91 D5
Glasbury Ave SR4 ....85 C4
Glasgow Rd NE32 ....58 E3
Glassey Terr NE22 ....11 D1
Glasshouse St NE6 ......56 C4
Glastonbury NE38 ....83 D4
Glastonbury Gr NE2 .....38 F2
Glazebury Way NE23 .....16 B1
Glebe Ave
Longbenton NE12 ....39 D7
Whickham NE16 ....69 B7
Glebe Cl Ponteland NE20 ..25 E7
Newcastle-upon-Tyne NE5 ..36 D3
Glebe Cres
Longbenton NE12 ....29 D1
Washington NE38 ....83 E6
Glebe Ct NE22 ....10 F1
Glebe Dr SR7 ....92 F2
Glebe Est SR7 ....92 F2
Glebe Farm NE62 ....10 F8
Glebe Mews NE22 ....10 F1
Glebe Rd Longbenton NE12 .29 D1
Bedlington NE22 ....10 F1
Glebe Rise NE16 ....69 B7
Glebe Sch The NE12 .....29 D2
Glebe St NE4 ....54 E6
Glebe Terr
2 Houghton-le-Spring DH4 .90 D1
1 Dunston NE11 ....69 F8
Glebe Terr continued
Longbenton NE12 ....29 D1
Choppington NE62 ....10 E4
Glebe The NE61 ....14 C4
Glebe Village Prim Sch
NE38 ....83 D5
Glebe Villas NE12 ....29 C1
Glebe Wlk NE16 ....69 B7
Glebelands NE45 ....47 A6
Glen Ave NE43 ....64 C7
Glen Barr DH2 ....88 B4
Glen Cl NE39 ....67 E3
Glen Ct NE31 ....57 D5
Glen Luce Dr SR2 ....86 F2
Glen Path SR2 ....86 D3
Glen St NE31 ....57 D5
Glen Terr
Chester le Street DH2 ......88 A4
Washington NE38 ....83 E4
Hexham NE46 ....44 F5
Glen The SR2 ....86 D3
Glen Thorpe Ave SR6 ....75 E2
Glen's Flats DH6 ....96 B5
Glenallen Gdns NE30 ....32 C1
Glenavon Ave DH2 ....88 B4
Glenbrooke Terr NE9 ....70 F4
Glenburn Cl NE38 ....82 F3
Glencarron Cl NE38 .....83 A3
Glencoe NE12 ....29 D4
Glencoe Ave
Chester le Street DH2 ......88 B4
Cramlington NE23 ....22 B3
Glencoe Rd SR4 ....85 B2
Glencoe Rise NE39 ......67 C1
Glencoe Sq SR4 ....85 B3
Glencoe Terr NE39 ......67 C1
Glencourse NE36 ....74 E7
Glendale Ave
Whickham NE16 ....69 A6
Blyth NE24 ....16 E8
Whitley Bay NE26 ....32 A7
Wallsend NE28 ....40 B4
North Shields NE29 ....41 F6
Newcastle-upon-Tyne NE3 ..38 A4
Washington NE37 ....83 C8
Stakeford NE62 ....11 A8
Glendale Cl Blaydon NE21 ..67 F8
Newcastle-upon-Tyne NE5 ..36 D3
Sunderland SR3 ....91 C6
Glendale Gdns
Stakeford NE62 ....11 A8
Gateshead NE9 ....71 B5
Glendale Gr NE29 ....41 F6
Glendale Rd
Shiremoor NE27 ....31 A3
Ashington NE63 ....7 A2
Glendale Terr 5 NE6 ....56 C6
Glendford Pl NE24 ......17 D4
Glendower Ave NE29 ....41 D6
Glendyn Cl NE7 ....39 A1
Gleneagle Cl NE5 ....36 D3
Gleneagles
Whitley Bay NE25 ....31 D6
South Shields NE33 ....42 F1
Gleneagles Cl NE7 ......39 C5
Gleneagles Ct NE25 .....31 D6
Gleneagles Dr NE37 .....72 C2
Gleneagles Rd
Gateshead NE9 ....70 E3
Sunderland SR4 ....85 B2
Gleneagles Sq 1 SR4 ....85 B2
Glenesk Gdns SR2 ....86 C2
Glenesk Rd SR2 ....86 C3
Glenfield Ave NE23 .....16 B1
Glenfield Rd
Longbenton NE12 ....39 B7
Longbenton NE12 ....39 C7
Glengarvan Cl NE38 .....83 A3
Glenholme Cl NE38 .....82 F3
Glenhurst Dr
Whickham NE16 ....68 F4
Newcastle-upon-Tyne NE5 ..36 D3
Glenhurst Gr NE34 ......59 F6
Glenkerry Cl NE38 ......83 A3
Glenleigh Dr SR4 ....85 C4
Glenluce Ct NE23 ....22 B4
Glenluce Dr NE23 ....22 B3
Glenmoor NE31 ....57 D7
Glenmore Ave DH2 ......88 C4
Glenmuir Ave NE23 .....22 A3
Glenorrin Cl NE38 ....83 A3
Glenridge Ave NE6 ......39 B1
Glenroy Gdns DH2 ......88 B4
Glenshiel Cl NE38 ....83 A3
Glenside Hedworth NE32 ...58 C2
Ellington NE61 ....1 E5
Glenside Ct NE9 ....70 E4
Glenthorn Rd NE2 ....38 E2
Glenthorne Rd 1 SR6 ....75 E2
Glenuce DH3 ....82 E3
Glenwood NE63 ....6 C2
Glenwood Wlk NE5 ......36 D3
Gloria Ave NE25 ....23 D6
Glossop St NE39 ....66 F4
Gloucester Ave SR6 .....75 E4
Gloucester Ct NE3 ......37 C8
Gloucester Pl NE34 .....60 A5
Gloucester Rd
Shiremoor NE29 ....41 B7
Newcastle-upon-Tyne NE4 ..98 A1
Gloucester St NE25 .....23 D6
Gloucester Terr
Haswell DH6 ....97 E1
Newcastle-upon-Tyne NE4 .100 A4
Gloucester Way
Hedworth NE32 ....58 B2
Newcastle-upon-Tyne NE4 .100 B4
Glover Ind Est NE37 ....83 E7
Glover Rd
Washington NE37 ....83 F8
Sunderland SR4 ....85 B2
Glover Sq SR4 ....85 B2
Glynfellis NE10 ....71 F4
Glynfellis Ct NE10 .....71 F5
Glynn House NE4 ....54 E4
Glynwood Cl NE23 ......16 B1
Glynwood Com Prim Sch
NE9 ....71 A5
Glynwood Gdns NE9 ....71 A5
Goalmouth Cl 6 SR6 ....75 E2
Goathland Ave
Longbenton NE12 ....39 C6
Newcastle-upon-Tyne NE12 .39 C7
Goathland Cl SR3 ....92 C7
Goathland Dr SR3 ....92 B6
Goathland Prim Sch
NE12 ....39 C6
Godfrey Rd SR4 ....85 B3
Gofton Wlk NE5 ....37 A2
Goldcrest Rd NE38 .....82 F3
Goldfinch Cl NE4 ....54 F4
Goldlynn Dr SR3 ....91 E6
Goldsbrough Ct NE2 ....98 C3
Goldsmith Rd SR4 ......85 B2
Goldspink La NE2 ......56 A7
Goldstone Ct NE12 .....29 E4
Goldthorpe Cl NE23 ....16 B1
Golf Course Rd DH4 ....90 A4
Gompertz Gdns NE33 ...59 B8
Gooch Ave NE22 ....11 A4
Goodrich Cl DH4 ....90 C5
Goodwood NE12 ....29 E3
Goodwood Ave NE8 .....70 C8
Goodwood Cl NE5 ......36 D3
Goodwood Ct NE63 ....6 D2
Goodwood Rd SR4 .....85 A3
Goodwood Sq SR4 .....85 A3
Goole Rd SR4 ....85 C3
Goose Hill NE61 ....9 A8
Gordon Ave
Newcastle-upon-Tyne NE3 ..38 C4
Sunderland SR5 ....85 A8
Gordon Ct 9 NE10 ......56 D1
Gordon Dr NE36 ....74 D7
Gordon Ho 2 NE6 ......56 B5
Gordon Rd Blyth NE24 ...17 F6
South Shields NE34 ....59 C6
3 Newcastle-upon-Tyne
NE6 ....56 B5
Sunderland SR4 ....85 B2
Gordon Sq
Whitley Bay NE26 ....32 C4
Newcastle-upon-Tyne NE6 ..56 B5
Gordon St NE33 ....59 D8
Gordon Terr
Bedlington NE22 ....16 A8
Whitley Bay NE26 ....32 C5
Prudhoe NE42 ....50 D2
Stakeford NE62 ....11 C7
3 Ryhope SR2 ....93 A6
Sunderland SR5 ....75 A2
Gordon Terrace W NE62 ..11 C7
Gorleston Way SR3 .....92 A4
Gorse Ave NE34 ....60 A5
Gorse Hill Way NE5 ....37 C3
Gorse Rd SR2 ....103 A1
Gorsedene Ave NE26 ....24 F1
Gorsedene Rd NE26 .....24 F1
Gorsehill NE9 ....71 C5
Gorseway NE61 ....8 D7
Goschen St Blyth NE24 ...17 D8
Gateshead NE8 ....70 D8
Sunderland SR5 ....75 A2
Gosforth Ave NE34 .....59 C3
Gosforth Bsns Pk NE12 ..38 F7
Gosforth Cen Mid Sch
NE3 ....38 D6
Gosforth Ctr NE3 ....38 C4
Gosforth East Mid Sch
NE3 ....38 D7
Gosforth High Sch NE3 ..38 C6
Gosforth Park Fst Sch
NE3 ....38 D7
Gosforth Park Villas
NE13 ....28 C4
Gosforth Park Way NE12 ..38 F7
Gosforth St
20 Gateshead NE10 ....56 D1
Newcastle-upon-Tyne NE2 ..99 C2
Sunderland SR6 ....75 E1
Gosforth Terr
Gateshead NE10 ....56 F1
Newcastle-upon-Tyne NE3 ..38 E5
Gosforth West Mid Sch
NE3 ....38 B5
Gosport Way NE24 .....17 D4
Gossington NE38 ....84 A5
Gossipgate Gallery*
CA9 ....133 A1
Goswick Ave NE7 ....39 B3
Goswick Dr NE3 ....37 F8
Goundry Ave SR2 ......93 A6
Gourock Sq SR4 ....85 A3
Gowan Terr NE2 ....38 F1
Gowanburn
Cramlington NE23 ....22 A3
Washington NE38 ....83 F2
Gower Rd SR5 ....75 A2
Gower St NE6 ....57 A4
Gower Wlk NE10 ....71 C8
Gowland Ave NE4 ......54 E6
Grace Darling Museum*
NE69 ....109 B5

Grace Gdns NE28 ....40 A4
Grace St Dunston NE11 ....69 F8
Newcastle-upon-Tyne, Byker NE6 ....56 C6
Newcastle-upon-Tyne, Walker NE6 ....56 D6
Gracefield Cl NE5 ....36 D3
Gradys Yd NE15 ....35 D3
Grafton Cl 5 NE6 ....56 B6
Grafton House 7 NE6 ....56 B6
Grafton Rd NE26 ....32 C4
Grafton St
11 Newcastle-upon-Tyne NE6 ....56 B6
Sunderland SR4 ....102 B3
Gragareth Way NE37 .....83 A6
Graham Ave NE16 ....69 B8
Graham Park Rd NE3 .....38 C3
Graham Rd NE31 ....57 D5
Graham St NE33 ....42 D2
Graham Terr DH6 ....96 B5
Grahamsley St NE8 .....101 C2
Grainger Ct NE4 ....54 F5
Grainger Mkt NE1 ....99 A1
Grainger Park Rd NE4 ....54 F5
Grainger St NE1 ....99 A1
Graingerville N NE4 ......98 A1
Graingerville S NE4 ......98 A1
Grampian Ave DH2 ....88 B2
Grampian Cl NE29 ....31 F1
Grampian Gdns NE11 .....70 B6
Grampian Gr NE36 ....74 B7
Grampian Pl NE12 ....29 B1
Granaries The
Fence Houses DH4 ....94 B8
High Spen NE39 ....66 F4
Penshaw SR4 ....84 F3
Granby Cl Sunniside NE16 ..69 B3
Sunderland SR3 ....86 B3
Granby St NE16 ....69 B2
Grand Par NE30 ....32 D1
Grandstand Rd NE2 ......38 B2
Grange Ave
Fence Houses DH4 ....90 A1
Longbenton NE12 ....39 E6
Bedlington NE22 ....11 E3
Shiremoor NE27 ....30 F4
Grange Cl Blyth NE24 .....17 D4
Whitley Bay NE25 ....31 D4
Wallsend NE28 ....40 C2
Tynemouth NE30 ....32 B2
Grange Cres
Gateshead NE10 ....72 A7
Ryton NE40 ....52 C4
Sunderland SR2 ....103 A1
Grange Ct Gateshead NE10 .72 A7
6 Jarrow NE32 ....58 B7
Ryton NE40 ....52 C4
Prudhoe NE42 ....50 D2
Morpeth NE61 ....9 A7
Grange Dr NE40 ....52 C4
Grange Est NE11 ....81 C6
Grange Farm Dr NE16 ....69 A5
Grange Fst Sch NE3 ......38 B6
Grange La NE16 ....69 B5
Grange Lonnen NE40 .....52 B5
Grange Nook NE16 ....69 A5
Grange Park Ave
Bedlington NE22 ....11 E3
Sunderland SR5 ....75 C3
Grange Park Prim Sch SR5 ....75 C2
Grange Pk NE25 ....31 D4
Grange Pl NE32 ....58 B7
Grange Rd
Gateshead NE10 ....72 A7
Newburn NE15 ....52 E8
Ponteland NE20 ....25 F7
Newcastle-upon-Tyne, Gosforth NE3 ....38 C7
Jarrow NE32 ....58 B7
Newcastle-upon-Tyne, Fenham NE4 ....54 D7
Ryton NE40 ....52 C5
Morpeth NE61 ....9 A6
Sunderland SR5 ....85 A8
Grange Rd W NE32 ....58 B7
Grange St S SR2 ....86 F2
Grange Terr
Prudhoe NE42 ....50 D2
Medomsley DH8 ....77 B1
Kibblesworth NE11 ....81 C6
1 East Boldon NE36 ......74 D7
6 Gateshead NE9 ....71 A8
Sunderland SR2 ....103 A1
2 Sunderland, Southwick SR5 ....75 B2
Grange The
Bedlington NE22 ....10 A1
East Boldon NE36 ....74 D7
Grange View
Newbottle DH4 ....90 D3
East Rainton DH5 ....94 D5
Ryton NE40 ....52 C4
Sunderland SR5 ....75 C3
Grange Villas NE28 ......40 C2
Grange Wlk 3 NE16 ......69 A5
Grangemere Cl SR2 ......86 F1
Grangetown Prim Sch SR2 ....86 F3
Grangeway NE29 ....31 F1
Grangewood Cl DH4 .....90 A5
Grangewood Ct 3 DH4 ...90 A6
Grant St NE32 ....58 A7
Grantham Dr NE9 ....70 E4
Grantham Pl NE23 ....22 A4
Grantham Rd
Newcastle-upon-Tyne NE2 ..99 C3
Sunderland SR6 ....75 E2
Grantham St NE24 ....17 F6
Granville Ave
Longbenton NE12 ....29 E1
Seaton Sluice NE26 ....24 D5
Granville Cres NE12 ......39 E7
Granville Ct NE2 ....99 C4
Granville Dr
Shiney Row DH4 ....90 C5
Longbenton NE12 ....39 E7
Newcastle-upon-Tyne NE5 ..36 D3
Granville Gdns
Newcastle-upon-Tyne NE2 ..56 A8
Stakeford NE62 ....11 A8
Granville Lodge NE12 ....39 E8
Granville Rd
Newcastle-upon-Tyne, Jesmond NE2 ....99 C4
Newcastle-upon-Tyne, Gosforth NE3 ....38 D7
Granville St
Gateshead NE8 ....101 C1
Sunderland SR4 ....102 B3
Grasmere Birtley DH3 .....82 E2
Cleadon SR6 ....60 A1
Grasmere Ave
Easington Lane DH5 ....97 C8
Gateshead NE10 ....71 F8
Newburn NE15 ....52 E7
Hedworth NE32 ....58 D3
Newcastle-upon-Tyne NE6 ..56 F5
Grasmere Cres
5 Penshaw DH4 ....90 B6
Blaydon NE21 ....68 B8
Whitley Bay NE26 ....31 F7
Sunderland SR5 ....75 C3
Sunderland, Monkwearmouth SR5 ....75 C2
Grasmere Ct
Killingworth NE12 ....29 C3
Newburn NE15 ....52 E7
Grasmere Gdns
South Shields NE34 ....59 E6
Washington NE38 ....83 E4
Grasmere Ho NE6 ....56 E5
Grasmere Pl NE3 ....38 C7
Grasmere Rd
Chester le Street DH2 ......88 B1
Whickham NE16 ....69 C7
Wallsend NE28 ....40 A1
Hebburn NE31 ....57 F4
Grasmere St NE8 ....101 B1
Grasmere St W NE8 .....101 B1
Grasmere Terr
Washington NE38 ....83 E5
Newbiggin-by-the-Sea NE64 ..7 D4
Grasmere Way NE24 ......17 A8
Grasmoor Pl NE15 ....53 B7
Grassbanks NE10 ....72 A6
Grassholm Pl NE12 ....39 A7
Grassholme Mdws SR3 ....86 B2
Grassington Dr NE23 .....22 A4
Grasslees NE38 ....88 F8
Grasswell Dr NE5 ....37 D3
Gravel Wlks DH5 ....90 F1
Gravesend Rd SR4 ....85 B2
Gravesend Sq SR4 ....85 C2
Gray Ave
Chester le Street DH2 ......88 B2
Wide Open NE13 ....28 C7
Gray Ct SR2 ....86 D4
Gray Rd Sunderland SR2 ..103 B1
Sunderland SR2 ....103 C2
Gray St NE24 ....12 E1
Gray's Wlk NE34 ....59 A2
Graylands NE38 ....88 E8
Grayling Ct SR3 ....91 C5
Grayling Rd NE11 ....70 B7
Grays Cross SR1 ....103 B3
Grays Terr 7 NE35 ....58 E1
Graystones NE10 ....72 B6
Great Lime Rd
Killingworth NE12 ....29 D1
Wide Open NE12,NE13, NE23 ....29 A5
Killingworth NE12,NE3 .....29 A3
Great North Rd
Newcastle-upon-Tyne, West Jesmond NE2 ....38 D2
Newcastle-upon-Tyne, Gosforth NE3 ....38 C7
Stannington NE61 ....9 A2
Greathead St NE33 ....59 B7
Grebe Cl Blyth NE24 ......17 E5
Ashington NE63 ....6 E1
Grebe Ct NE2 ....38 F1
Greely Rd NE5 ....36 F2
Green Acres
Ponteland NE20 ....25 C1
Morpeth NE61 ....8 E7
Green Ave DH4 ....90 D4
Green Bank NE46 ....45 C4
Green Cl Whitley Bay NE25 .31 D4
Tynemouth NE30 ....32 B1
Stannington NE61 ....14 C4
Green Cres NE23 ....28 F8
Green Gr NE40 ....52 B3
Green Hill Wlk NE34 ......60 C6
Green La Haswell DH6 .....97 B3
Gateshead, Felling NE10 ....56 D2
Gateshead, Pelaw NE10 ....57 A1
Killingworth NE12 ....29 E2
Woolsington NE13 ....36 F8
Dudley NE23 ....28 F8
South Shields NE34 ....59 B4
Green La *continued*
East Boldon NE36 ....74 E6
Morpeth NE61 ....4 B1
Stannington NE61 ....13 D2
Stannington, Duddo Hill NE61 ....13 D5
Ashington NE63 ....6 C3
Seaton SR7 ....95 F6
Morpeth, Stobhillgate NE61 ..9 B7
Green Lane Gdns NE10 ...56 C2
Green Pk NE28 ....39 E3
Green Sq NE25 ....31 D4
Green St SR1 ....103 A3
Green Terr SR1 ....102 C2
Green The
Chester le Street DH2 ......88 B3
Houghton-le-Spring DH5 ...90 F1
Gateshead NE10 ....71 E8
Walbottle NE15 ....35 F1
Chopwell NE17 ....77 B8
Ponteland NE20 ....25 F7
Whitley Bay NE25 ....31 E6
Newcastle-upon-Tyne NE3 ..37 F3
Rowlands Gill NE39 ....67 C2
Ovington NE42 ....49 C4
Sunderland SR1 ....102 C2
New Silksworth SR3 ....92 C7
Sunderland, Southwick SR5 .75 A1
Green Way NE25 ....31 D4
Green's Pl NE33 ....42 C4
Green-Fields NE40 ....52 B5
Greenacre Pk NE9 ....70 E3
Greenacres Cl NE40 ....52 A3
Greenbank Blaydon NE21 ..53 C2
Jarrow NE32 ....58 B7
Greenbank Dr SR4 ....85 A5
Greenbank St 4 DH3 ....88 D4
Greenbank Villas NE32 ....58 B7
Greenbourne Gdns NE10 .71 C7
Greencroft NE63 ....6 C2
Greencroft Ave
Corbridge NE45 ....47 A6
Newcastle-upon-Tyne NE6 ..57 A8
Greendale Cl NE24 ....17 A8
Greendale Gdns DH5 .....94 F2
Greendyke Ct NE5 ....37 A5
Greener Ct NE42 ....50 B1
Greenesfield Bsns Ctr NE8 ....101 B3
Greenfield Ave NE5 ....37 A2
Greenfield Dr NE62 ....10 E6
Greenfield Pl
Newcastle-upon-Tyne NE4 ..98 C1
Ryton NE40 ....52 D5
Greenfield Rd NE3 ....28 B1
Greenfield Terr 2 NE10 ...56 F1
Greenfields DH2 ....82 A2
Greenfields Com Prim Sch NE13 ....28 C6
Greenfields Specl Sch NE31 ....58 A6
Greenfinch Cl NE38 ....82 F3
Greenford NE11 ....81 D6
Greenford La DH2,NE11 ...81 F6
Greenford Rd NE6 ....57 A4
Greenhaugh NE12 ....29 B1
Greenhaugh Rd NE25 .....31 B5
Greenhead NE38 ....82 F4
Greenhead Rd NE17 ......66 B3
Greenhead Terr NE17 .....66 B2
Greenhill View NE5 ....37 E2
Greenhills NE12 ....29 D5
Greenholme Cl NE23 ......16 B1
Greenhow Cl SR2 ....92 F5
Greenlands NE32 ....58 C2
Greenlands Ct NE25 ......23 D4
Greenlaw NE5 ....53 E8
Greenlaw Rd NE23 ....22 A3
Greenlea NE29 ....31 B1
Greenlea Cl
High Spen NE39 ....67 A3
Sunderland SR4 ....85 C3
Greenlee NE63 ....6 E2
Greenlee Dr NE7 ....39 D3
Greenock Rd SR4 ....85 B2
Greenrigg Blaydon NE21 ...53 D1
Seaton Sluice NE26 ....24 C6
Greenrigg Gdns 2 SR3 ...86 B3
Greenriggs Ave NE3 ....28 D1
Greenrising NE42 ....49 D4
Greenshields Rd SR4 ......85 B2
Greenshields Sq 5 SR4 ...85 B2
Greenside NE34 ....60 B6
Greenside Ave
Brunswick Village NE13 ....28 A6
Wallsend NE28 ....40 F3
Greenside Cres NE15 ......54 A7
Greenside Ho NE24 ....17 B8
Greenside Prim Sch NE40 ....51 F1
Greenside Rd
Crawcrook NE40 ....51 F2
Crawcrook NE40 ....51 F3
Greentree Sq NE5 ....37 B2
Greenway
Newcastle-upon-Tyne, Fenham NE4 ....54 D8
Newcastle-upon-Tyne, Westerhope NE5 ....36 D4
Greenway The SR4 ....85 C4
Greenwell Cl NE21 ....53 A1
Greenwell Dr NE42 ....50 D3
Greenwell Terr NE40 ......51 E4
Greenwich Pl NE8 ....56 A4
Greenwood NE12 ....29 F3
Greenwood Ave
Bedlington NE22 ....11 D3
Newcastle-upon-Tyne NE6 ..40 A1
Greenwood Gdns
Gateshead NE10 ....56 D2
Dunston NE11 ....70 B5
Greenwood Rd SR4 ....85 B3
Greenwood Sq 3 SR4 ....85 B2
Greetlands Rd SR2 ....86 C2
Gregory Rd 8 SR4 ....85 B2
Gregory Terr DH4 ....90 A1
Gregson Terr SR7 ....92 F1
Grenada Cl NE26 ....31 F8
Grenada Dr NE26 ....31 F8
Grenada Pl NE26 ....31 F8
Grenfell Sq 7 SR4 ....85 B2
Grenville Ct
Ponteland NE20 ....25 A4
Cramlington NE23 ....22 A5
Grenville Dr NE3 ....28 B1
Grenville Terr NE1 ....99 C1
Grenville Way NE26 ....31 E7
Grenwood Ave DH4 ....94 C8
Gresford St NE33 ....59 C6
Gresham Cl NE23 ....22 B4
Greta Ave DH4 ....90 A6
Greta Gdns NE33 ....59 D8
Greta Terr SR4 ....102 A1
Gretna Dr NE32 ....58 F2
Gretna Rd NE15 ....54 B6
Gretton Pl NE7 ....39 A3
Grey Ave NE23 ....22 A3
Grey Lady Wlk NE42 .....50 D3
Grey Pl 10 NE61 ....9 A8
Grey St
Houghton-le-Spring DH4 ...90 D1
Newcastle-upon-Tyne NE1 ..99 A1
Brunswick Village NE13 ....28 A6
Wallsend NE28 ....40 C2
North Shields NE30 ....42 B6
Grey Terr 10 SR2 ....92 F6
Grey's Ct NE1 ....99 A1
Greybourne Gdns SR2 ....86 C2
Greyfriars La NE12 ....39 A6
Greystead Cl NE5 ....36 D3
Greystead Rd NE25 ....31 B5
Greystoke Ave
Whickham NE16 ....69 B5
Newcastle-upon-Tyne NE2 ..56 A7
Sunderland SR2 ....86 C2
Greystoke Gdns
Whickham NE16 ....69 B5
Newcastle-upon-Tyne NE2 ..56 A8
10 Morpeth NE61 ....3 F1
Gateshead NE9 ....71 B2
Sunderland SR2 ....86 C3
Greystoke Pk NE3 ....38 C8
Greystoke Pl NE23 ....22 A3
Greystoke Wlk 2 NE16 ...69 A5
Greystone Pl SR5 ....75 A2
Greywood Ave NE4 ....54 E7
Grieve St NE24 ....12 D1
Grieves' Row NE23 ....22 A1
Griffith Terr 7 NE27 ......30 E1
Grimsby St NE24 ....17 E6
Grindleford Ct NE34 ......59 E5
Grindon Ave SR4 ....85 B5
Grindon Cl
Cramlington NE23 ....22 A3
Whitley Bay NE25 ....31 E2
Grindon Ct SR4 ....85 C3
Grindon Gdns SR4 ....85 C3
Grindon Hall Christian Sch SR4 ....85 C4
Grindon Inf Sch SR4 ......85 B2
Grindon La
Sunderland, Springwell SR3, SR4 ....85 D3
Sunderland, South Hylton SR4 ....85 B5
Grindon Mus* SR4 ....85 C3
Grindon Pk SR4 ....85 C3
Grindon Terr SR4 ....102 A1
Grinstead Cl NE34 ....59 F7
Grisedale Gdns NE9 ......71 A3
Grizedale NE37 ....83 B6
Grizedale Ct SR6 ....75 C5
Groat Mkt NE1 ....99 A1
Grosvenor Ave
Whickham NE16 ....69 B8
Newcastle-upon-Tyne NE2 ..38 F1
Grosvenor Cl NE23 ....22 A3
Grosvenor Cres NE31 .....57 F4
Grosvenor Ct NE5 ....36 D3
Grosvenor Dr
Whitley Bay NE26 ....32 A4
South Shields NE34 ....59 F8
Cleadon SR6 ....74 E8
Grosvenor Gdns
Newcastle-upon-Tyne NE2 ..56 A8
Wallsend NE28 ....41 A3
South Shields NE34 ....59 F6
Grosvenor Mews
1 North Shields NE29 .....42 A6
4 South Shields NE33 .....59 E8
Grosvenor Pl
Newcastle-upon-Tyne NE2 ..38 F1
North Shields NE29 ....42 A6
Grosvenor Rd
Newcastle-upon-Tyne NE2 ..38 F1
South Shields NE33 ....59 E8
Grosvenor St SR5 ....75 A2
Grosvenor Villas NE2 .....38 F1
Grosvenor Way NE5 ....36 D3
Grotto Gdns NE34 ....60 D6
Grotto Rd NE34 ....60 D6
Grousemoor 2 NE37 .....83 A7
Grousemoor Dr NE63 ......6 C1
Grove Ave NE3 ....38 D4
Grove Cotts 8 DH3 ......82 C4
Grove Rd Walbottle NE15 ...35 F2
Grove Rd *continued*
Gateshead NE9 ....71 A6
Grove Terr
Burnopfield NE16 ....79 B6
Sunniside NE16 ....69 B1
Grove The
Houghton-le-Spring DH5 ....94 D6
Longbenton NE12 ....39 D6
Whickham NE16 ....69 C6
Newcastle-upon-Tyne, Jesmond NE2 ....38 F2
Ponteland NE20 ....25 D5
Whitley Bay NE25 ....31 F4
Newcastle-upon-Tyne, Gosforth NE3 ....38 D4
Hedworth NE32 ....73 B8
Rowlands Gill NE39 ....67 F1
Stocksfield NE43 ....64 C3
Newcastle-upon-Tyne, West Denton NE5 ....36 D1
Ryhope SR2 ....92 F6
Sunderland, Ashbrooke SR2 .86 D4
6 Sunderland, Castletown SR5 ....74 B1
Guardian Ct NE26 ....32 C4
Guardians Ct NE20 ....25 F7
Gubeon Wood NE61 ....8 C2
Guelder Rd NE7 ....39 C3
Guernsey Rd SR4 ....85 B2
Guernsey Sq SR4 ....85 B2
Guessburn NE43 ....64 B6
Guide Post Mid Sch NE62 ....10 F7
Guide Post Ringway Fst Sch NE62 ....10 F8
Guildford Pl NE6 ....56 B7
Guildford Sq NE61 ....2 A3
Guildford St SR2 ....86 E4
Guillemot Cl NE24 ....17 E5
Guillemot Row NE12 ....29 C4
Guisborough Dr NE29 .....41 B8
Guisborough St SR4 ......85 F5
Gullane NE37 ....72 D3
Gullane Cl NE10 ....57 C2
Gunn St NE11 ....69 F8
Gunnerston Gr 1 NE3 ....37 D5
Gunnerton Cl NE23 ....22 B4
Gunnerton Pl NE29 ....41 D6
Gut Rd NE28 ....40 F1
Guyzance Ave NE3 ....38 B6
Gypsies Green Sports Gd NE33 ....42 F2

H

Hackwood Pk NE46 ....45 B3
Hackworth Gdns NE41 ....51 B6
Hackworth Way NE29 .....41 F3
Haddington Rd NE25 ......31 D7
Haddon Cl NE25 ....31 B5
Haddon Gn NE25 ....31 B5
Haddricksmill Ct NE3 .....38 E4
Haddricksmill Rd NE2, NE3 ....38 E4
Hadleigh Ct 9 DH4 ....90 B6
Hadleigh Rd SR4 ....85 D5
Hadrian Ave DH3 ....88 D5
Hadrian Ct
Killingworth NE12 ....29 E3
Ponteland NE20 ....25 B1
Hadrian Gdns NE21 ....53 D1
Hadrian Ho 2 NE15 ....35 D2
Hadrian Hospl NE28 ....40 C4
Hadrian Jun Mixed & Inf Sch NE33 ....42 C4
Hadrian Lodge NE34 ......58 F5
Hadrian Park Fst Sch NE28 ....40 E
Hadrian Park Mid Sch NE28 ....40 E
Hadrian Pl Walbottle NE15 .35 E2
Gateshead NE9 ....71 B7
Hadrian Rd Blyth NE24 ....17 C
Wallsend NE28 ....40 D
Jarrow NE32 ....58 D4
Newcastle-upon-Tyne NE4 ..54 E6
Hadrian Road Sta NE28 ...40 E2
Hadrian St SR4 ....102 A3
Hadrian's Wall (N.T.)* NE47 ....127 D
Hadrian's Wall (N.T.)* NE49 ....126 D
Hadrians Ct NE11 ....70 D3
Hadrians Way DH8 ....76 E
Hadstone Pl 3 NE5 ....37 C1
Hagg Bank Cotts NE41 ....50 F5
Haggerston Cl NE5 ....37 B4
Haggerston Cres NE5 .....37 B4
Haggerston Ct NE5 ....37 B4
Haggerston Terr NE32 ....58 E4
Haggerstone Dr SR5 ......85 A8
Haggie Ave NE28 ....40 D
Hahnemann Ct SR5 ....75 B
Haig Ave NE25 ....31 F
Haig Cres NE15 ....54 B
Haig Rd NE22 ....16 B
Haig St NE11 ....69 F
Haigh Terr NE9 ....71 C
Hailsham Ave NE12 ....39 C
Haininghead NE38 ....83 E
Hainingwood Terr NE10 ...57 B
Haldane Ct NE2 ....99 B
Haldane St NE63 ....6 C
Haldane Terr NE2 ....99 B
Halewood Ave NE3 ....37 E
Half Fields Rd NE21 ....53 B

Half Moon La
Tynemouth NE30 . . . . .42 D7
Gateshead NE8 . . . . .101 B2
Half Moon St NE62 . . . . . . .11 B8
Halidon Rd SR2 . . . . .86 D1
Halidon Sq SR2 . . . . .86 D1
Halifax Pl Dunston NE11 . . .54 E1
9 Sunderland SR2 . . . . .92 F6
Halifax Rd NE11 . . . . .54 E1
Halkirk Way NE23 . . . . .16 A1
Hall Ave NE4 . . . . .54 E6
Hall Cl West Rainton DH4 . . .94 A2
Seaton SR7 . . . . .92 D1
Hall Dene Way SR7 . . . . . . .92 F2
Hall Dr NE12 . . . . .29 C5
Hall Farm Cl NE43 . . . . .64 B8
Hall Farm Rd SR3 . . . . .92 A5
Hall Garth NE3 . . . . .38 C8
Hall Gdns Sherburn DH6 . . .96 A1
Gateshead NE10 . . . . .71 D7
Seaton Sluice NE26 . . . . . . .24 A6
West Boldon NE36 . . . . .74 A7
Hall Gn NE24 . . . . .17 B7
Hall La West Rainton DH4 . .94 A2
Houghton-le-Spring DH5 . . . .94 F7
Haswell DH6 . . . . .97 F3
Hall Pk NE21 . . . . .53 A4
Hall Rd Chopwell NE17 . . . . .66 C2
Hebburn NE31 . . . . .57 E5
Washington NE37 . . . . .83 E8
Hall Road Bglws NE17 . . . .66 B2
Hall Terr Gateshead NE10 . .57 B2
Blyth NE24 . . . . .17 E8
Hall View SR6 . . . . .75 F8
Halleypike C NE7 . . . . .39 D3
Hallfield Cl SR3 . . . . .92 A5
Hallgarth NE10 . . . . .72 A7
Hallgarth Ct SR6 . . . . .75 F1
Hallgarth La DH6 . . . . .96 B5
Hallgarth Rd NE21 . . . . . . .53 B2
Hallgarth View DH6 . . . . . .96 C5
Hallgarth Villas DH6 . . . . .96 A1
Hallgate NE46 . . . . .45 B5
Halling Cl NE6 . . . . .57 A4
Hallington Dr NE25 . . . . . .23 D3
Hallington Mews NE12 . . . .29 C3
Halliwell St DH4 . . . . .90 D1
Hallorchard Rd NE46 . . . . .45 B5
Hallow Dr NE15 . . . . .35 D1
Hallside Rd NE24 . . . . .17 B6
Hallstile Bank NE46 . . . . . .45 B5
Hallwood Cl NE22 . . . . .15 A8
Halstead Pl 2 NE33 . . . . . .42 D1
Halstead Sq SR4 . . . . .85 D5
Halterburn Cl NE3 . . . . . . .38 A4
Halton Cl NE43 . . . . .64 D6
Halton Dr Wide Open NE13 .28 C6
Backworth NE27 . . . . .30 D3
Hamar Cl NE29 . . . . .41 C4
Hambard Way NE38 . . . . . .83 D4
Hambledon Ave DH2 . . . . .88 B2
Hambledon Ave NE30 . . . . .32 A3
Hambledon Cl NE35 . . . . . .73 E8
Hambledon Gdns NE7 . . . .39 A3
Hambledon St NE24 . . . . . .17 D8
Hambleton Ct NE63 . . . . .6 F1
Hambleton Gn NE9 . . . . . . .71 B1
Hambleton Rd NE38 . . . . . .83 B3
Hamilton Cres
Tynemouth NE29 . . . . .41 C8
Newcastle-upon-Tyne NE4 . .98 B2
Hamilton Ct SR6 . . . . .75 F2
Hamilton Dr NE26 . . . . .31 F8
Hamilton Pl NE4 . . . . .98 B2
Hamilton Terr
West Boldon NE36 . . . . .74 A7
9 Morpeth NE61 . . . . .9 A8
Hamilton Way 2 NE26 . . . .31 F8
Hammer Square Bank
DH9 .80 F1
Hampden Rd SR6 . . . . .75 E2
Hampden St NE33 . . . . .59 C8
Hampshire Ct NE4 . . . . . .100 A2
Hampshire Gdns NE28 . . . .40 E4
Hampshire Pl NE37 . . . . . . .72 D1
Hampshire Way NE34 . . . . .60 C7
Hampstead Cl NE24 . . . . . .17 C3
Hampstead Gdns NE32 . . .58 D2
Hampstead Rd
Newcastle-upon-Tyne NE4 . .54 E5
Sunderland SR4 . . . . .85 D4
Hampstead Sq SR4 . . . . . . .85 C4
Hampton Cl NE23 . . . . .22 D7
Hampton Ct
Chester le Street DH3 . . . . .88 D7
Whickham NE16 . . . . .54 B1
Hampton Dr
Gateshead NE10 . . . . .71 C8
Whitley Bay NE25 . . . . .31 C4
Hampton Rd NE30 . . . . .32 A2
Hamsterley Cres
Newcastle-upon-Tyne NE15 .53 B7
Gateshead NE9 . . . . .71 C3
Hamsterley Ct 6 SR3 . . . . .92 A6
Hamsterley Dr NE12 . . . . . .29 C4
Hanby Gdns SR3 . . . . .86 A3
Hancock Mus* NE2 . . . . . . .99 A3
Hancock St NE1,NE2 . . . . . .99 A3
Handel St NE33 . . . . .42 D2
Handley Cres DH5 . . . . . . .94 C4
Handley Cross DH8 . . . . . . .77 C2
Handy Dr NE11 . . . . .54 E2
Hangmans La SR3,SR7 . . . .91 E3
Hanlon Ct Hebburn NE32 . . .57 F7
Jarrow NE32 . . . . .58 A8
Hann Terr NE37 . . . . .83 F8
Hannington Pl 3 NE6 . . . . .56 A6
Hannington St 2 NE6 . . . . .56 A6
Hanover Cl 2 NE5 . . . . . . .36 C2
Hanover Ct
Annitsford NE23 . . . . .22 B1
5 Gateshead NE9 . . . . .71 A2
Hanover Dr NE21 . . . . .53 A1
Hanover Gdns 3 NE28 . . . .41 A1
Hanover House NE32 . . . . .58 B4
Hanover Pl
Cramlington NE23 . . . . .16 A2
Sunderland SR4 . . . . .102 B4
Hanover Sq NE1 . . . . .101 A4
Hanover St NE1 . . . . .101 A4
Hanover Wlk
Blaydon NE21 . . . . .68 A8
1 Newcastle-upon-Tyne
NE5 .36 C2
Harbord Terr NE26 . . . . . . .23 F5
Harbottle Ave
Shiremoor NE27 . . . . .31 A2
Newcastle-upon-Tyne NE3 . .38 A6
Harbottle Cres NE32 . . . . .58 B2
Harbottle Ct NE6 . . . . .56 C4
Harbottle St 4 NE6 . . . . . .56 C4
Harbour Dr NE33 . . . . .42 E4
Harbour The DH4 . . . . .90 B6
Harbour View
Cambois NE22 . . . . .12 B3
South Shields NE33 . . . . . . .42 D5
Sunderland SR6 . . . . .75 F2
Harcourt Pk 1 NE9 . . . . . . .71 A5
Harcourt Rd SR2 . . . . .86 D1
Harcourt St 2 NE9 . . . . . . .71 A5
Hardgate Rd SR2 . . . . .86 D1
Hardie Ave NE16 . . . . .69 A8
Hardie Dr NE36 . . . . .74 B7
Hardman Gdns NE40 . . . . .52 D5
Hardwick Ct NE8 . . . . .56 A1
Hardwick Pl NE3 . . . . .38 A3
Hardwick Rise SR6 . . . . . .103 B4
Hardy Ave NE34 . . . . .59 B3
Hardy Ct 5 NE30 . . . . .42 B6
Hardy Gr NE28 . . . . .40 A5
Hardy Sq SR5 . . . . .75 A2
Hardyards Ct NE34 . . . . . . .59 C5
Harebell Rd NE9 . . . . .71 C4
Harehills Ave NE5 . . . . . . .37 D3
Harehills Tower NE3 . . . . .37 E3
Harelaw Dr NE63 . . . . .6 B1
Harelaw Gr NE5 . . . . .36 D1
Hareshaw Rd NE25 . . . . . . .31 B5
Hareside NE23 . . . . .22 A5
Hareside Cl NE15 . . . . .52 F8
Hareside Ct NE15 . . . . .52 F8
Hareside Wlk NE15 . . . . . .52 F8
Harewood Cl
Whickham NE16 . . . . .69 A4
Whitley Bay NE25 . . . . .31 B4
Harewood Cres NE25 . . . . .31 B4
Harewood Ct NE25 . . . . . . .31 B4
Harewood Dr NE22 . . . . . . .11 C2
Harewood Gdns
Pegswood NE61 . . . . .4 E4
Sunderland SR3 . . . . .86 A3
Harewood Gn NE9 . . . . . . .71 B2
Harewood Rd NE3 . . . . . . .38 C6
Hareydene NE5 . . . . .36 F5
Hargill Dr NE38 . . . . .83 A1
Hargrave Ct NE24 . . . . . . .17 C6
Harland Way NE38 . . . . . . .83 D5
Harle Cl NE5 . . . . .36 E1
Harle Rd NE27 . . . . .30 D3
Harle St NE28 . . . . .40 B2
Harlebury NE27 . . . . .30 C1
Harlequin Lodge 9
NE10 . . . . .71 D8
Harleston Way NE10 . . . . .71 E6
Harley Terr NE3 . . . . .38 D5
Harlow Ave
Backworth NE27 . . . . .30 D3
Newcastle-upon-Tyne NE3 . .37 F7
Harlow Cl NE23 . . . . .16 A1
Harlow Green Com Inf Sch
NE9 .71 A2
Harlow Green Jun Sch
NE9 .71 A2
Harlow Green La NE9 . . . .71 A2
Harlow Pl NE7 . . . . .39 B3
Harlow St SR4 . . . . .102 B2
Harnham Ave NE29 . . . . . .41 D5
Harnham Gdns NE5 . . . . . .37 C1
Harnham Gr NE23 . . . . . . .22 A5
Harold Sq SR2 . . . . .103 B1
Harold St NE32 . . . . .58 C7
Harper St NE24 . . . . .17 D7
Harperley Dr SR3 . . . . .86 B2
Harperley La DH9 . . . . . . .79 B1
Harraby Gdns NE9 . . . . . . .71 B3
Harras Bank DH3 . . . . .82 C3
Harraton Prim Sch NE38 . .83 B1
Harraton Terr
12 Birtley DH3 . . . . .82 C4
Bournmoor DH3 . . . . .89 C7
Harriet Pl 21 NE6 . . . . .56 C6
Harriet St Blaydon NE21 . . .53 C2
Newcastle-upon-Tyne NE6 . .56 D6
Harrington Gdns NE62 . . . .11 C8
Harrington St 6 NE28 . . . .40 B2
Harriot Dr NE12 . . . . .29 B2
Harrison Ct Birtley DH3 . . .82 C3
Annitsford NE23 . . . . .29 B8
Harrison Gdns NE8 . . . . . .70 D7
Harrison Pl NE2 . . . . .99 B3
Harrison Rd NE28 . . . . .41 A3
Harrogate St SR2 . . . . . . .103 B1
Harrow Cres DH4 . . . . .90 A6
Harrow Gdns NE13 . . . . . . .28 C5
Harrow Sq SR4 . . . . .85 D5
Harrow St NE27 . . . . .30 E4
Harrow's Scar Milecastle*
CA6 . . . . .126 A3
Hart Ct SR1 . . . . .103 A3
Hart Sq SR4 . . . . .85 E5
Hart Terr SR6 . . . . .75 F6
Hartburn NE10 . . . . .72 A6
Hartburn Dr NE5 . . . . .36 D3
Hartburn Pl NE4 . . . . .54 F7
Hartburn Rd NE30 . . . . . . .32 A1
Hartburn Terr NE25 . . . . . .23 D3
Hartburn Wlk NE3 . . . . . . .37 D5
Hartford NE12 . . . . .29 D5
Hartford Bank NE23 . . . . . .15 C4
Hartford Bridge Farm
NE22 . . . . .15 C5
Hartford Cres
Bedlington NE22 . . . . .15 E8
Ashington NE63 . . . . .6 D2
Hartford Ct NE22 . . . . .15 E8
Hartford Dr NE22 . . . . .15 C5
Hartford House NE4 . . . . .98 B2
Hartford Rd
Bedlington NE22 . . . . .15 D6
Nedderton NE22 . . . . .15 D6
Newcastle-upon-Tyne NE3 . .38 D7
South Shields NE34 . . . . . . .59 A5
Sunderland SR4 . . . . .85 D5
Hartford Rd E NE22 . . . . . .15 F8
Hartford St 1 NE6 . . . . . . .56 C8
Harforth Cres NE10 . . . . . .57 C1
Harthope NE61 . . . . .1 E5
Harthope Ave SR5 . . . . . . .74 C3
Harthope Cl NE38 . . . . .88 F8
Harthope Dr NE29 . . . . . . .41 E3
Hartington Rd NE30 . . . . .32 B2
Hartington St
Newcastle-upon-Tyne NE4 . .98 A1
Gateshead NE8 . . . . .101 C1
Sunderland SR6 . . . . .75 E1
Hartington Terr NE33 . . . .59 D8
Hartland Dr DH3 . . . . .82 D3
Hartlands NE22 . . . . .15 E8
Hartleigh Pl NE24 . . . . . . .17 B7
Hartley Ave NE26 . . . . .31 E5
Hartley Ct
Brunswick Village NE13 . . . .27 F5
New Hartley NE25 . . . . .23 D6
Hartley Gdns NE25 . . . . . .23 C3
Hartley Ho NE26 . . . . .31 F5
Hartley La Holywell NE25 . .31 B7
Whitley Bay NE25,NE26 . . . .24 C2
Hartley Sq NE26 . . . . .24 D4
Hartley St
Seaton Delaval NE25 . . . . . .23 C3
Sunderland SR1 . . . . .103 C3
Hartley St N NE25 . . . . . . .23 C3
Hartley Terr NE24 . . . . . . .17 C4
Hartleyburn Ave NE31 . . . .57 D3
Hartoft Cl DH4 . . . . .90 D3
Harton Comp Sch NE34 . . .60 A6
Harton Cty Inf Sch NE34 . .60 B6
Harton Gr NE34 . . . . .59 E7
Harton House Rd NE34 . . .59 F7
Harton House Rd E NE34 .60 A7
Harton Jun Mix Sch
NE34 . . . . .60 A6
Harton La NE34 . . . . .59 D6
Harton Quay NE33 . . . . . . .42 B2
Harton Rise NE34 . . . . .60 A7
Harton View NE36 . . . . . . .74 A7
Hartside Birtley DH3 . . . . .82 D1
Newcastle-upon-Tyne NE15 .53 C7
Hartside Cres
Blaydon NE21 . . . . .68 A8
Cramlington NE23 . . . . .16 A2
Backworth NE27 . . . . .30 D4
Hartside Gdns
Easington Lane DH5 . . . . . . .95 C1
Newcastle-upon-Tyne NE2 . .38 F1
Hartside Pl NE3 . . . . .28 C1
Hartside Rd SR4 . . . . .85 D4
Hartside Sq SR4 . . . . .85 D4
Harvest Cl SR3 . . . . .91 F5
Harvey Cl
Washington NE38 . . . . .82 F5
Ashington NE63 . . . . .7 A3
Harvey Combe NE12 . . . . . .29 B3
Harvey Cres NE10 . . . . .72 B8
Harwood Cl
Cramlington NE23 . . . . .22 A5
Washington NE38 . . . . .83 A1
Harwood Ct SR6 . . . . .75 E1
Harwood Dr NE12 . . . . .30 A3
Hascombe Cl NE25 . . . . . . .31 D6
Haslemere Dr SR3 . . . . . . .86 A3
Hassop Way NE22 . . . . . . .10 F2
Hasting Hill Prim Sch
SR3 .85 C1
Hastings Ave
Longbenton NE12 . . . . .39 D7
Seaton Sluice NE26 . . . . . . .24 B7
Whitley Bay NE26 . . . . .24 F1
Newcastle-upon-Tyne NE3 . .37 D7
Hastings Ct
Bedlington NE22 . . . . .11 C2
New Hartley NE25 . . . . .23 D6
Hastings Dr NE30 . . . . .42 C8
Hastings Gdns NE25 . . . . .23 D6
Hastings Par NE31 . . . . . . .58 A3
Hastings St
Cramlington NE23 . . . . .22 C5
Sunderland SR2 . . . . .86 E3
Hastings Terr
Cramlington NE23 . . . . .16 D1
New Hartley NE25 . . . . .23 D7
Sunderland SR2 . . . . .86 F3
Haswell Cl NE10 . . . . .72 D7
Haswell Gdns NE30 . . . . . .42 A6
Haswell Prim Sch DH6 . . .97 E3
Hatfield Ave NE31 . . . . . . .57 F6
Hatfield Dr NE23 . . . . .23 A2
Hatfield Gdns
Whitley Bay NE25 . . . . .31 B5
Sunderland SR3 . . . . .86 A3
Hatfield Sq 11 NE33 . . . . . .42 D3
Hathaway Gdns SR3 . . . . . .86 A3
Hathersage Gdns NE34 . . .59 D5
Hatherton Ave NE30 . . . . . .32 B3
Hathery La NE24 . . . . .16 D5
Haugh La
Ryton, Ryton Haugh NE21 . .53 A5
Ryton NE21,NE40 . . . . .52 E6
Hexham NE46 . . . . .45 B5
Haughs The NE42 . . . . .50 D3
Haughton Cres
Hedworth NE32 . . . . .58 B2
Newcastle-upon-Tyne NE5 . .36 E1
Haughton Ct NE4 . . . . . . .100 A3
Haughton Terr NE24 . . . . . .17 E7
Hautmont Rd NE31 . . . . . . .57 F4
Hauxley NE12 . . . . .29 D5
Hauxley Dr
Cramlington NE23 . . . . .16 A1
Newcastle-upon-Tyne NE3 . .37 F7
Hauxley Gdns NE5 . . . . . . .37 D2
Havanna NE12 . . . . .29 D5
Havannah Cres NE13 . . . . .27 B6
Havannah Rd NE37 . . . . . . .83 B7
Havant Gdns NE13 . . . . . . .28 B7
Havard Rd NE3 . . . . .37 E6
Havelock Cl NE8 . . . . .101 B2
Havelock Cres NE22 . . . . . .11 F3
Havelock Ct SR4 . . . . .85 D6
Havelock Ho SR4 . . . . .85 D6
Havelock Mews NE22 . . . . .11 F3
Havelock Pl NE4 . . . . .98 B1
Havelock Prim Sch SR4 . . .85 D6
Havelock Rd NE27 . . . . . . .30 D3
Havelock St Blyth NE24 . . .17 E8
South Shields NE33 . . . . . . .42 B1
South Shields NE33 . . . . . . .42 C1
Sunderland SR1 . . . . .103 C3
Havelock Terr
Tantobie DH9 . . . . .79 B2
Chopwell NE17 . . . . .66 B1
Jarrow NE32 . . . . .58 B5
Gateshead NE8 . . . . .101 B2
Sunderland SR2 . . . . .102 B1
Haven Ct Blyth NE24 . . . . . .17 C6
Sunderland SR6 . . . . .75 F1
Haven The Penshaw DH4 . . .90 B6
North Shields NE29 . . . . . . .42 A3
Prudhoe NE42 . . . . .50 D2
Haven View NE64 . . . . .7 E4
Havercroft NE10 . . . . .72 B7
Haverley Dr SR7 . . . . .92 E1
Haversham CL NE7 . . . . . . .39 A5
Haversham Pk SR5 . . . . . . .75 C5
Hawarden Cres SR4 . . . . .102 A1
Hawes Ave DH2 . . . . .88 C1
Hawes Ct SR6 . . . . .75 C5
Hawesdale Cres NE21 . . . .68 B8
Haweswater Cl NE34 . . . . .59 D6
Haweswater Cres NE64 . . . .7 C4
Hawick Cres NE6 . . . . .56 B4
Hawk Terr DH3 . . . . .82 E2
Hawkesley Rd SR4 . . . . . . .85 D5
Hawkey's La NE29 . . . . . . .41 F6
Hawkhills Terr DH3 . . . . . .82 C5
Hawkhurst NE38 . . . . .83 E2
Hawkins Ct SR3 . . . . .91 F6
Hawks Rd NE8 . . . . .101 C4
Hawks St NE8 . . . . .56 A4
Hawksbury NE16 . . . . .69 A7
Hawksfeld NE10 . . . . .71 E4
Hawkshead Ct NE3 . . . . . . .37 D7
Hawkshead Pl NE9 . . . . . . .71 B4
Hawksley NE5 . . . . .36 F2
Hawksmoor Cl NE63 . . . . . . .6 C1
Hawkwell Rise NE15 . . . . . .35 D1
Hawsker Cl SR3 . . . . .92 C7
Hawthorn Ave
Brunswick Village NE13 . . . .28 A6
New Silksworth SR3 . . . . . . .92 B8
Hawthorn Cl NE16 . . . . .69 B5
Hawthorn Cres NE38 . . . . .83 C1
Hawthorn Dr
Dunston NE11 . . . . .69 F8
Hedworth NE32 . . . . .58 D2
Hawthorn Gdns
5 Gateshead NE10 . . . . .56 D1
Whitley Bay NE26 . . . . .31 F5
Tynemouth NE29 . . . . .41 F7
Newcastle-upon-Tyne NE3 . .37 F4
Ryton NE40 . . . . .52 E4
Hawthorn Gr NE28 . . . . . . .40 B2
Hawthorn Mews NE3 . . . . .38 C4
Hawthorn Pl
Killingworth NE12 . . . . .29 C4
Newcastle-upon-Tyne NE4 .100 B4
Hawthorn Prim Sch
NE4 . . . . .100 A4
Hawthorn Rd
Blaydon NE21 . . . . .53 C1
Newcastle-upon-Tyne NE3 . .38 C4
Ashington NE63 . . . . .6 E3
Hawthorn Rd W NE3 . . . . . .38 C4
Hawthorn St
Burnside DH4 . . . . .90 C2
Jarrow NE32 . . . . .58 A7
Walbottle NE5 . . . . .35 F2
Sunderland SR4 . . . . .102 A2
Hawthorn Terr
Chester le Street DH3 . . . . .88 D2
Newcastle-upon-Tyne NE4 .100 A4
Crawcrook NE40 . . . . .51 E3
Hawthorn Terr *continued*
Gateshead NE9 . . . . .71 D1
Sunderland SR6 . . . . .75 E6
Hawthorn Villas NE23 . . . .22 D6
Hawthorn Way NE20 . . . . .25 D3
Hawthorn Wlk NE4 . . . . . .100 B4
Hawthorne Ave
Hebburn NE31 . . . . .57 F6
South Shields NE34 . . . . . . .59 F4
Hawthorne Gdns NE9 . . . . .70 F6
Hawthorne Rd NE24 . . . . . .17 F7
Hawthorne Terr DH9 . . . . .79 D3
Hawthorns The
East Boldon NE36 . . . . .74 D7
Newcastle-upon-Tyne NE4 .100 A3
Gateshead NE9 . . . . .71 D1
Hay St SR5 . . . . .102 C4
Haydock Dr NE10 . . . . .72 C7
Haydon NE38 . . . . .83 E1
Haydon Cl NE3 . . . . .37 F8
Haydon Dr NE25 . . . . .31 F3
Haydon Gdns NE27 . . . . . . .30 D4
Haydon Rd NE63 . . . . .6 D2
Haydon Sq SR4 . . . . .85 D5
Hayes Wlk NE13 . . . . .28 B6
Hayfield La NE16 . . . . .69 B6
Hayhole Rd NE29 . . . . .41 E2
Haylands Sq NE34 . . . . . . .59 D5
Hayleazes Rd NE15 . . . . . .53 F7
Haymarket NE1 . . . . .99 A2
Haymarket La NE1 . . . . . . .99 A2
Haymarket Sta NE1 . . . . . .99 A2
Haynyng The NE10 . . . . . . .71 E7
Hayricks The DH9 . . . . . . .79 D4
Hayton Ave NE34 . . . . .60 A5
Hayton Cl NE23 . . . . .22 C7
Hayton Rd NE30 . . . . .32 A2
Hayward Ave NE25 . . . . . . .23 D3
Hazard La
Hetton le Hole DH5 . . . . . . .94 E3
West Rainton DH5 . . . . .94 E3
Hazel Ave
3 Houghton-le-Spring DH4 .94 C8
Tynemouth NE29 . . . . .41 F7
New Silksworth SR3 . . . . . . .92 B8
Hazel Gr
Chester le Street DH2 . . . . . .88 A5
Killingworth NE12 . . . . .29 B2
Burnopfield NE16 . . . . .79 C6
South Shields NE34 . . . . . . .59 F4
Ellington NE61 . . . . .1 E5
Hazel Rd Blaydon NE21 . . . .53 D2
Gateshead NE8 . . . . .70 C8
Hazel St NE32 . . . . .58 A7
Hazel Terr DH4 . . . . .90 C2
Hazeldene
Whitley Bay NE25 . . . . .31 E5
Hedworth NE32 . . . . .73 C8
Hazeldene Ave NE3 . . . . . .37 C5
Hazeldene Ct NE30 . . . . . . .42 C7
Hazeley Gr 4 NE3 . . . . . . .37 D5
Hazeley Way NE3 . . . . .37 D5
Hazelgrove NE10 . . . . .72 B7
Hazelmere Ave
Bedlington NE22 . . . . .10 E1
Newcastle-upon-Tyne NE3 . .28 D1
Hazelmere Cres NE23 . . . .22 C8
Hazelmere Dene NE23 . . . .22 E1
Hazelmoor NE31 . . . . .57 D7
Hazelwood NE12 . . . . .29 F3
Hazelwood Ave
Newcastle-upon-Tyne NE2 . .38 E2
Newbiggin-by-the-Sea NE64 . .7 D5
Sunderland SR5 . . . . .74 F2
Hazelwood Cl NE9 . . . . . . .71 D2
Hazelwood Com Prim Sch
NE13 . . . . .28 B5
Hazelwood Gdns NE38 . . . .83 C1
Hazelwood Terr NE28 . . . . .41 A3
Hazledene Terr 2 SR4 . . . .85 F6
Hazlitt Ave NE34 . . . . .59 B3
Hazlitt Pl NE23 . . . . .23 A1
Headlam Gn 2 NE6 . . . . . . .56 C5
Headlam Ho 11 NE6 . . . . . .56 C6
Headlam St 3 NE6 . . . . . . .56 C6
Headlam View NE28 . . . . . .41 A2
Healey Dr SR3 . . . . .86 B2
Heartsbourne Dr NE34 . . . .59 F3
Heath Cl NE11 . . . . .70 B7
Heath Cres NE15 . . . . .54 A4
Heath Grange DH5 . . . . . . .90 E1
Heath Sq SR4 . . . . .85 E5
Heathcote Gn NE5 . . . . . . .37 B3
Heathdale Gdns NE7 . . . . .39 B3
Heather Cl SR6 . . . . .60 A2
Heather Dr DH5 . . . . .95 A5
Heather Gr NE10 . . . . .56 B2
Heather Lea DH9 . . . . .78 E2
Heather Lea La NE42 . . . . .50 D3
Heather Pl
Newcastle-upon-Tyne NE4 . .54 E8
Crawcrook NE40 . . . . .52 A4
Heather Terr NE16 . . . . . . .79 B6
Heatherdale Terr NE9 . . . .71 B3
Heatherlaw
Washington NE37 . . . . .82 F6
Gateshead NE9 . . . . .71 C5
Heatherlea Gdns 1 SR3 . . .86 B3
Heatherlee Gdns NE62 . . . .11 A8
Heatherslaw Light Railway*
TD12 . . . . .107 B7
Heatherslaw Rd NE5 . . . . . .54 C8
Heatherwell Gn NE10 . . . . .71 C7
Heathery La NE3 . . . . .38 E7
Heatheryhill NE46 . . . . . . .44 A4

Heathfield Morpeth NE61 ...9 B6
Sunderland SR2 ...86 C2
Heathfield Cres NE5 ...37 D3
Heathfield Farm NE40 ...52 A1
Heathfield Gdns NE40 ...52 A1
Heathfield Pl NE3 ...28 D1
Heathfield Rd NE9 ...70 F6
Heathway NE32 ...58 C2
Heathwell Gdns NE16 ...69 B8
Heathwell Rd NE15 ...53 F7
Heathwood Ave 1 NE16 ...69 A7
Heaton Cl NE6 ...56 B7
Heaton Gdns NE34 ...59 C2
Heaton Gr NE6 ...56 B7
Heaton Hall Rd NE6 ...56 B7
Heaton Manor Sch (Lower) NE7 ...39 A2
Heaton Manor Sch (Upper) NE7 ...39 C4
Heaton Park Ct 9 NE6 ...56 B7
Heaton Park Rd NE6 ...56 B7
Heaton Park View NE6 ...56 B7
Heaton Pl NE6 ...56 B6
Heaton Rd NE6 ...56 B7
Heaton Terr
North Shields NE29 ...41 E6
Newcastle-upon-Tyne NE6 ...56 A6
Heaton Wlk 4 NE6 ...56 B6
Hebburn Comp Sch NE31 ...57 E4
Hebburn Hospl NE31 ...57 D4
Hebburn St Aloysius RC Inf Sch NE31 ...57 E7
Hebburn Sta NE31 ...57 D6
Heber St NE1 ...98 C1
Hebron Ave NE61 ...4 E4
Hebron Pl NE63 ...6 F3
Hebron Way NE23 ...22 A5
Hector St NE27 ...30 F4
Heddon Ave NE13 ...28 A4
Heddon Banks NE15 ...34 E1
Heddon Cl
Newcastle-upon-Tyne NE3 ...38 A6
Ryton NE40 ...52 D5
Heddon View
Blaydon NE21 ...53 B2
Ryton NE40 ...52 D5
Heddon Way NE34 ...59 B6
Heddon-on-the-Wall St Andrew's CE Fst Sch NE15 ...34 E2
Hedge Cl NE11 ...70 B7
Hedgefield Ave NE21 ...52 F5
Hedgefield Cotts NE21 ...52 F5
Hedgefield Ct NE21 ...52 F5
Hedgefield Gr NE24 ...17 C3
Hedgefield View NE23 ...22 A1
Hedgehope 6 NE37 ...83 A6
Hedgehope Rd NE5 ...37 A4
Hedgelea NE40 ...52 B5
Hedgelea Rd DH5 ...94 C3
Hedgeley Rd
Tynemouth NE29 ...41 D7
Hebburn NE31 ...57 E6
Newcastle-upon-Tyne NE5 ...53 E8
Hedgeley Terr NE6 ...56 F6
Hedgerow Mews NE63 ...6 B2
Hedley Ave NE24 ...17 F6
Hedley Cl 7 NE33 ...42 C4
Hedley Ct NE24 ...17 F6
Hedley La NE11,NE16 ...80 C6
Hedley Pl NE28 ...40 B1
Hedley Rd
Seaton Delaval NE25 ...23 E2
North Shields NE29 ...41 F3
Wylam NE41 ...51 B6
Hedley St
Newcastle-upon-Tyne NE3 ...38 C5
5 South Shields NE33 ...42 C4
Gateshead NE8 ...70 D8
Hedley Terr
Newcastle-upon-Tyne NE3 ...38 C5
Ryhope SR2 ...93 A6
Hedworth Ave NE34 ...59 A4
Hedworth Ct SR1 ...103 B2
Hedworth La
Hedworth NE32 ...58 D2
Boldon Colliery NE35 ...58 E1
Hedworth Lane Prim Sch NE35 ...58 D1
Hedworth Pl NE9 ...71 C3
Hedworth St DH3 ...88 C3
Hedworth Terr DH4 ...90 B6
Hedworth View NE32 ...58 D3
Hedworthfield Comp Sch NE32 ...58 B1
Hedworthfield Prim Sch NE32 ...58 D1
Heighley St NE15 ...53 F5
Helen St Blaydon NE21 ...53 A2
Sunderland SR6 ...75 E4
Helena Ave NE26 ...32 B5
Hellpool La NE46 ...44 F5
Helmdon NE37 ...83 E8
Helmsdale Ave 13 NE10 ...56 D1
Helmsdale Rd SR4 ...85 D5
Helmsley Cl DH4 ...90 A6
Helmsley Ct SR5 ...74 E3
Helmsley Dr NE28 ...40 F2
Helmsley Gn NE9 ...71 B2
Helmsley Rd NE2 ...99 C3
Helston Ct NE15 ...53 B7
Helvellyn Ave NE38 ...83 A3
Helvellyn Rd SR2 ...86 D2
Hemel St 8 DH3 ...88 C2
Hemlington Cl 12 SR2 ...92 F6
Hemming St 9 SR2 ...86 F2
Hemsley Rd NE34 ...43 A1
Hencotes NE46 ...45 A4
Hencotes Ct 4 NE46 ...45 A4
Hencotes Mews 8 NE46 ...45 A4
Henderson Ave NE16 ...69 A8
Henderson Cl NE46 ...44 F3
Henderson Ct NE29 ...41 F3
Henderson Gdns NE10 ...72 B8
Henderson Rd
Wallsend NE28 ...40 B3
Wallsend, Battle Hill NE28 ...40 B4
South Shields NE34 ...58 F4
Sunderland SR4 ...85 F6
Henderson's Bldgs NE64 ...7 E5
Hendersyde Cl NE5 ...37 B3
Hendon Burn Ave SR2 ...103 B1
Hendon Burn Ave W 2 SR2 ...86 E4
Hendon Cl
North Shields NE29 ...42 A3
Sunderland SR1 ...103 B2
Hendon Gdns NE32 ...58 D2
Hendon Ho NE63 ...6 A4
Hendon Rd
Gateshead NE8,NE9 ...71 B8
Sunderland SR1 ...103 B3
Sunderland, Hendon SR1, SR2 ...103 C2
Hendon Rd E SR1 ...103 C2
Hendon St SR1 ...103 C2
Hendon Valley Ct 6 SR2 ...86 E4
Hendon Valley Rd SR2 ...103 B1
Henley Cl NE23 ...22 D7
Henley Gdns NE28 ...41 B4
Henley Rd
Tynemouth NE30 ...32 C1
Sunderland SR4 ...85 D5
Henley Sq NE61 ...2 A3
Henley Way NE35 ...73 E8
Henlow Rd NE15 ...53 C7
Henry Nelson St NE33 ...42 D4
Henry Robson Way NE33 ...42 C2
Henry Sq NE2 ...99 C2
Henry St Shiney Row DH4 ...90 B6
Hetton le Hole DH5 ...95 A5
Houghton-le-Spring DH5 ...90 E1
North Shields NE29 ...42 A4
Newcastle-upon-Tyne NE3 ...38 C5
South Shields NE33 ...42 D4
Henry St E SR2 ...103 C2
Henry Terr DH4 ...89 F2
Hensby Ct NE5 ...37 B4
Henshaw Ct NE63 ...6 B2
Henshaw Gr NE25 ...23 F2
Henshaw Pl NE5 ...54 B7
Henshelwood Terr 2 NE2 ...38 E1
Henson Cl NE38 ...83 D4
Hepburn Gdns NE10 ...56 C1
Hepburn Gr SR5 ...73 F1
Hepple Ct NE24 ...17 C6
Hepple Rd NE64 ...7 C3
Hepple Way NE3 ...38 A6
Hepscott Dr NE25 ...31 D6
Hepscott Terr NE33 ...59 D8
Hepscott Wlk NE61 ...4 E3
Herbert St NE8 ...56 A1
Herbert Terr SR5 ...75 B5
Herd Cl NE21 ...53 A1
Herd House La NE21 ...52 F2
Herdinghill NE37 ...82 F6
Herdlaw NE23 ...22 A6
Hereford Ct
Newcastle-upon-Tyne NE3 ...37 D8
Sunderland SR2 ...86 D1
Hereford Rd SR2 ...86 D1
Hereford Sq SR2 ...86 D1
Hereford Way NE32 ...58 B2
Hermiston NE25 ...31 E5
Hermitage Gdns DH2 ...88 B1
Hermitage Pk DH3 ...88 C1
Hermitage Sch The DH2 ...88 A2
Heron Cl Blyth NE24 ...17 E4
Washington NE38 ...83 A2
Ashington NE63 ...6 E1
Heron Dr NE33 ...42 C4
Heron Pl NE12 ...39 A7
Herrick St NE5 ...37 A3
Herring Gull Cl NE24 ...17 E3
Herrington Mews DH4 ...90 E6
Herrington Rd SR3,DH4 ...91 B6
Hersham Cl NE3 ...37 D7
Hertburn Gdns NE37 ...83 D7
Hertburn Ind Est NE37 ...83 E7
Hertford NE9 ...70 F2
Hertford Ave NE34 ...60 C7
Hertford Cl NE25 ...31 D6
Hertford Cres DH5 ...94 F4
Hertford Gr NE23 ...22 C7
Hesket Ct NE3 ...37 E7
Hesleyside 6 NE63 ...6 F2
Hesleyside Dr NE5 ...54 C8
Hesleyside Rd NE25 ...31 B5
Hessewelle Cres DH6 ...97 E1
Hester Ave NE25 ...23 D6
Hester Bglws NE25 ...23 D6
Hester Gdns NE25 ...23 E6
Heswall Rd NE23 ...16 A2
Hetton Lyons Country Park* DH5 ...95 C4
Hetton Lyons Ind Est DH5 ...95 B3
Hetton Lyons Prim Sch DH5 ...95 A2
Hetton Prim Sch DH5 ...94 F3
Hetton Rd DH5 ...94 E7
Hetton Sch DH5 ...94 F3
Heugh Hill NE9 ...72 A2
Hewitson Terr NE10 ...71 C8
Hewitt Ave SR2 ...92 E8
Hewley Cres NE15 ...35 D1
Heworth Burn Cres NE10 ...71 E8
Heworth Cres 1 NE37 ...83 D8
Heworth Ct NE34 ...59 A5
Heworth Dene Gdns NE10 ...56 E1
Heworth Gr NE37 ...83 C8
Heworth Grange Comp Sch NE10 ...71 F8
Heworth Rd NE37 ...72 D1
Heworth Sta (British Rail & Metro) NE10 ...71 F8
Heworth Way NE10 ...72 A8
Hewson Pl NE9 ...71 B6
Hexham NE38 ...82 F4
Hexham Abbey NE46 ...45 B5
Hexham Ave
Cramlington NE23 ...22 D7
Hebburn NE31 ...57 E3
Newcastle-upon-Tyne NE6 ...56 F5
Hexham Cl NE29 ...41 C7
Hexham Ct NE11 ...69 F6
Hexham East Fst Sch NE46 ...45 C4
Hexham General Hospl NE46 ...45 C4
Hexham Hackwood Park Sch NE46 ...45 B3
Hexham Mid Sch NE46 ...45 B4
Hexham Old Rd NE21, NE40 ...52 E5
Hexham Priory Sch NE46 ...45 C4
Hexham Race Course NE46 ...44 D1
Hexham Rd
Heddon-on-the-Wall NE15 ...34 E2
Throckley NE15 ...35 C2
Whickham NE16 ...54 A1
Sunderland SR4 ...85 D5
Hexham Sta NE46 ...45 C5
Hextol Cres NE46 ...45 A4
Hextol Gdns NE15 ...53 F7
Hextol Terr NE46 ...44 F4
Heybrook Ave NE29 ...41 F8
Heyburn Gdns NE15 ...54 D5
Hi-Tec Village NE35 ...73 D7
Hibernia Rd NE6 ...57 A4
Hibernian Rd NE32 ...58 B7
Hickling Ct NE5 ...37 C4
Hickstead Cl NE28 ...40 E7
Hickstead Gr NE23 ...22 D7
Hiddleston Ave NE7 ...39 B5
High Axwell NE21 ...53 D2
High Back Cl NE32 ...58 A4
High Barnes Terr SR4 ...102 A1
High Bridge NE1,NE99 ...99 A1
High Burswell NE46 ...44 F5
High Chare DH3 ...88 D3
High Cl NE42 ...50 F3
High Croft NE37 ...72 C1
High Croft Cl NE31 ...57 D4
High Dene NE7 ...39 B1
High Dewley Burn NE15 ...35 D3
High Downs Sq DH5 ...95 A5
High Farm Mid Sch NE28 ...40 B5
High Flatworth NE29 ...41 B4
High Friar La NE1 ...99 A1
High Gate The NE3 ...37 E4
High Gr NE40 ...52 D4
High Hamsterley Rd NE39 ...78 A5
High Hedgefield Terr NE21 ...52 E5
High Heworth La NE10 ...71 E7
High Horse Cl NE39 ...68 A4
High Horse Close Wood NE39 ...68 A4
High House Cl NE61 ...8 D8
High House Gdns NE10 ...56 E1
High La DH4 ...90 F4
High Lane Row NE31 ...57 F7
High Lanes NE10 ...71 F7
High Laws NE3,NE7 ...38 F4
High Level Rd NE8 ...101 B3
High Market NE63 ...6 A4
High Mdw NE34 ...59 F8
High Meadow NE34 ...59 F8
High Meadows NE3 ...37 E3
High Mill Rd NE39 ...78 A5
High Moor Ct NE5 ...37 E2
High Moor Pl NE34 ...59 C5
High Pasture NE38 ...83 E1
High Pk NE61 ...9 A7
High Primrose Hill DH4 ...89 D3
High Quay
Newcastle-upon-Tyne NE1 ...56 A5
Blyth NE24 ...17 F8
High Rd The NE34 ...60 A6
High Reach NE10 ...57 A2
High Ridge NE13 ...28 B4
High Row
Great Lumley DH4 ...89 E1
Newcastle-upon-Tyne NE15 ...53 C6
Washington NE37 ...72 D1
Ryton NE40 ...52 E4
High Sandgrove SR6 ...60 A1
High Shaw NE42 ...50 B1
High Spen Ct NE39 ...67 A4
High Spen Prim Sch NE39 ...66 F3
High St
Easington Lane DH5 ...95 C1
High Pittington DH6 ...96 B6
Gateshead, Felling NE10 ...71 D8
Newburn NE15 ...52 F7
High St *continued*
Blyth NE24 ...17 D7
Blyth NE24 ...17 E7
Newcastle-upon-Tyne NE3 ...38 C4
Jarrow NE32 ...58 C7
Jarrow NE32 ...58 D7
Choppington NE62 ...10 E6
Guide Post NE62 ...10 E7
Newbiggin-by-the-Sea NE64 ...7 F5
Gateshead NE8 ...101 C3
Gateshead, Wrekenton NE9 ...71 C3
Sunderland SR4 ...85 A6
High St Cuthbert's Ave 10 NE46 ...45 A4
High St E Wallsend NE28 ...40 C1
Sunderland SR1 ...103 B3
High St W
Newcastle-upon-Tyne NE28, NE6 ...40 A1
Wallsend NE28,NE6 ...40 A1
Sunderland SR1 ...103 A3
High Stobhill NE61 ...9 A6
High Swinburne Pl NE4 ...98 B1
High Usworth Cty Inf Sch NE37 ...72 C1
High Usworth Cty Jun Sch NE37 ...72 C1
High View Ponteland NE20 ...25 D2
Wallsend NE28 ...40 B3
Hedley on the Hill NE43 ...64 F3
High View N NE28 ...40 B4
High Well Gdns NE10 ...56 E1
High West St NE8 ...101 C2
Higham Pl NE1 ...99 B2
Highburn NE23 ...22 A5
Highbury Gateshead NE10 ...71 E8
Newcastle-upon-Tyne NE2 ...38 D2
Whitley Bay NE25 ...31 E5
Highbury Ave NE9 ...72 A2
Highbury Cl NE9 ...72 A2
Highbury Pl NE29 ...41 F6
Highcliffe Gdns NE8 ...71 A8
Highcroft Dr SR6 ...60 E1
Highcroft Pk SR6 ...60 F1
Highcross Rd NE30 ...32 A3
Highfield Birtley DH3 ...82 C6
Sunniside NE16 ...69 B3
Prudhoe NE42 ...50 D2
Highfield Ave NE12 ...39 D8
Highfield Cl NE5 ...36 F3
Highfield Cres DH3 ...88 C5
Highfield Ct NE10 ...71 E7
Highfield Cty Inf Sch NE34 ...43 A1
Highfield Day Hospl DH3 ...88 C5
Highfield Dr
Fence Houses DH4 ...94 B7
South Shields NE34 ...59 F8
Ashington NE63 ...7 A2
Highfield Gdns DH3 ...88 C5
Highfield Grange DH4 ...94 B7
Highfield Jun & Inf Schs NE39 ...67 C2
Highfield La NE42 ...50 C1
Highfield Pl
Brunswick Village NE13 ...28 A5
6 Sunderland SR4 ...85 F6
Highfield Rd
Shiney Row DH4 ...90 A6
South Shields NE33,NE34 ...59 F8
Rowlands Gill NE39 ...67 C1
Newcastle-upon-Tyne NE5 ...36 F3
Gateshead NE8 ...56 A1
Highfield Rise DH3 ...88 C5
Highfield Terr
Prudhoe NE42 ...50 B2
Newcastle-upon-Tyne NE6 ...57 A4
Highfields Mid Sch NE42 ...50 C2
Highford Gdns NE61 ...8 E7
Highford La NE46 ...44 E4
Highgate Gdns NE32 ...58 D2
Highgate Rd SR4 ...85 D5
Highgreen Chase NE16 ...69 A4
Highgrove NE5 ...36 D2
Highheath 1 NE37 ...83 A6
Highland Rd NE5 ...37 D3
Highlaws Gdns NE9 ...71 B2
Highmoor NE61 ...8 D7
Highridge DH3 ...82 C5
Highside Dr SR3 ...86 A3
Highstead Ave NE23 ...16 A1
Highsteads DH8 ...77 B1
Hightree Cl SR3 ...91 F5
Highwell La 4 NE5 ...36 E1
Highwood Rd NE15 ...53 F7
Highworth Dr
Newcastle-upon-Tyne NE7 ...39 D3
Springwell NE9 ...71 F1
Hilda Pk DH2 ...88 B5
Hilda St Gateshead NE8 ...101 A1
Sunderland SR6 ...75 D3
Hilda Terr
Chester le Street DH2 ...88 B4
7 Throckley NE15 ...35 D2
Hilden Bldgs NE7 ...39 C2
Hilden Gdns NE7 ...39 C2
Hill Ave NE23 ...23 A2
Hill Brow SR3 ...92 B6
Hill Crest Gateshead NE10 ...71 E6
Burnopfield NE16 ...79 B6
Hill Crest Gdns NE2 ...38 E4
Hill Croft NE15 ...33 C1
Hill Dyke NE9 ...71 C2
Hill Gate NE61 ...9 A8
Hill Head Dr NE5 ...36 D1
Hill Head Rd NE5 ...36 D2
Hill House Rd NE15 ...35 C2
Hill La DH4 ...84 C1
Hill Park Rd NE32 ...58 C5
Hill Pk NE20 ...25 D2
Hill Rise Washington NE38 ...83 E6
Crawcrook NE40 ...51 F3
Hill St Jarrow NE32 ...58 A7
South Shields NE33 ...42 B1
Corbridge NE45 ...46 F5
New Silksworth SR3 ...92 A7
Hill Terr DH4 ...90 E6
Hill The NE42 ...50 B4
Hill Top Birtley DH3 ...82 D4
Blaydon NE21 ...53 B1
Hill Top Ave NE9 ...71 B5
Hill Top Cl NE62 ...10 F8
Hill Top Gdns NE9 ...71 A5
Hill Top Sch NE10 ...71 E4
Hill View Gdns SR3 ...86 B3
Hill View Inf Sch SR2 ...86 D2
Hill View Jun Sch SR2 ...86 D2
Hill View Rd SR2 ...86 D2
Hill View Sq SR2 ...86 D2
Hillary Ave NE12 ...39 E8
Hillcrest Whitley Bay NE25 ...31 E5
Hedworth NE32 ...58 D2
South Shields NE34 ...60 B5
Prudhoe NE42 ...50 D2
Ashington NE63 ...7 A2
Sunderland SR3 ...91 B8
Hillcrest Ave NE62 ...10 F8
Hillcrest Ct NE42 ...50 D2
Hillcrest Dr Dunston NE11 ...69 E7
Hexham NE46 ...45 C4
Hillcrest Sch NE23 ...22 B6
Hillcroft 4 Birtley DH3 ...82 C5
Rowlands Gill NE39 ...67 C2
Gateshead NE9 ...71 A6
Hillfield NE25 ...31 D5
Hillfield Gdns SR3 ...86 B3
Hillfield St NE8 ...101 B2
Hillford Terr NE17 ...66 B1
Hillgate NE8 ...101 B4
Hillhead Gdns NE11 ...70 A6
Hillhead La NE16 ...68 D2
Hillhead Parkway NE5 ...36 C2
Hillhead Way NE5 ...36 E3
Hillheads Ct NE25 ...32 A4
Hillheads Rd NE25,NE26 ...32 A4
Hillingdon Gr SR4 ...85 A2
Hillrise Cres SR7 ...92 D1
Hills Ct NE21 ...53 E4
Hills St NE8 ...101 B3
Hillsden Rd NE25 ...31 D7
Hillside Birtley DH3 ...82 D4
Chester le Street DH3 ...88 C4
Dunston NE11 ...69 F7
Killingworth NE12 ...29 E2
Ponteland NE20 ...25 C1
Blaydon NE21 ...53 B2
South Shields NE34 ...60 B4
West Boldon NE36 ...74 A7
Morpeth NE61 ...8 F7
Ashington NE63 ...6 C4
Sunderland SR3 ...86 C3
Hillside Ave NE15 ...53 F8
Hillside Cl NE39 ...67 E3
Hillside Cres NE15 ...54 A4
Hillside Dr SR6 ...60 E1
Hillside Gdns SR3 ...86 C3
Hillside Grove DH6 ...96 B5
Hillside Pl NE9 ...71 A6
Hillside Rd NE46 ...45 D4
Hillside Way DH4 ...90 E1
Hillsleigh Rd NE5 ...37 D2
Hillsview Ave NE3 ...37 E5
Hillthorne Cl NE38 ...83 E4
Hilltop Gdns SR3 ...92 C7
Hilltop Ho NE5 ...37 A2
Hillview SR3 ...91 B7
Hillview Cres DH4 ...90 D3
Hillview Gr DH4 ...90 D3
Hillview Rd DH4 ...90 D3
Hilton Ave NE5 ...37 B2
Hilton Cl NE23 ...16 A2
Hilton Prim Sch NE5 ...37 B2
Hind St SR1 ...102 C2
Hindley Cl NE40 ...51 E3
Hindley Gdns NE4 ...54 D7
Hindmarch Dr NE35,NE36 ...74 B7
Hindson's Cres N DH4 ...90 A5
Hindson's Cres S DH4 ...90 A5
Hinkley Cl SR3 ...92 B6
Hippingstones La NE45 ...46 F6
Hipsburn Dr SR3 ...86 A3
Hiram Dr NE36 ...74 D7
Hirst Head NE22 ...11 A1
Hirst High Sch NE63 ...6 F2
Hirst Terr N NE22 ...11 A1
Hirst Villas NE22 ...11 B1
Histon Ct NE5 ...37 B3
Histon Way NE5 ...37 B3
Hither Gn NE32 ...58 D2
Hobart NE26 ...31 F7
Hobart Ave NE34 ...58 F3
Hodgkin Park Cres NE15 ...54 C5
Hodgkin Park Rd NE15 ...54 C5
Hodgson Terr 6 NE37 ...83 F8
Hodgson's Rd NE24 ...12 D1
Hodkin Gdns NE9 ...71 B6
Hogarth Cotts NE22 ...16 A8
Hogarth Dr NE38 ...83 E3
Hogarth Rd NE34 ...59 C2
Holbein Rd NE34 ...59 C3
Holborn Pl NE5 ...36 E1
Holborn Rd SR4 ...85 D5
Holborn Sq SR4 ...85 D4
Holburn Cl NE40 ...52 D5
Holburn Cres NE40 ...52 E5
Holburn Gdns NE40 ...52 E5

Holburn La NE40 .52 D6
Holburn Lane Ct NE40 .52 D6
Holburn Terr NE40 .52 E5
Holburn Way NE40 .52 D5
Holburn Wlk NE40 .52 E5
Holden Pl NE5 .37 D2
Holder House La NE34 .59 E3
Holder House Way NE34 .59 E2
Holderness Rd
Wallsend NE28 .41 B3
Newcastle-upon-Tyne NE6 .39 B1
Hole La Sunniside NE16 .69 B3
Whickham NE16 .68 F4
Holeyn Hall Rd NE41 .51 A7
Holeyn Rd NE15 .35 C1
Holland Dr NE2 .98 B3
Holland Park Dr NE32 .58 D2
Holland Pk NE28 .39 E3
Holley Park Prim Sch
NE38 .83 A3
Hollinghill Rd NE25 .23 E2
Hollings Cres NE28 .40 B4
Hollings Terr NE17 .66 A1
Hollingside Way NE34 .59 D5
Hollington Ave NE12 .39 B6
Hollington Cl NE12 .39 B6
Hollinhill NE39 .68 A5
Hollinhill La NE39 .67 F4
Hollinhill Rd NE37 .83 E7
Hollinhill Terr NE44 .62 F8
Hollinside Cl NE16 .69 A5
Hollinside Gdns NE15 .54 B6
Hollinside Rd
Whickham NE11 .54 B2
Sunderland SR4 .85 D4
Hollinside Sq SR4 .85 C5
Hollinside Terr NE39 .67 D2
Hollon St NE61 .3 E1
Hollow The NE32 .58 B2
Hollowdene DH5 .95 A3
Hollows The NE63 .7 B2
Holly Ave
Houghton-le-Spring DH5 .94 F8
Dunston NE11 .69 F7
Longbenton NE12 .29 D1
Newcastle-upon-Tyne, Jesmond
NE2 .38 F1
Winlaton Mill NE21 .68 C6
Earsdon NE25 .31 B5
Whitley Bay NE26 .32 A5
Wallsend NE28 .40 C1
Newcastle-upon-Tyne, Fawdon
NE3 .37 F6
South Shields NE34 .60 A5
Ryton NE40 .52 C6
Morpeth NE61 .8 E7
Newbiggin-by-the-Sea NE64 .7 C5
New Silksworth SR3 .92 B8
Whitburn SR6 .75 F8
Holly Ave W NE2 .38 E1
Holly Bush Gdns NE40 .52 E4
Holly Cl NE12 .29 C4
Holly Cres NE38 .83 C1
Holly Ct
Newcastle-upon-Tyne NE5 .37 B2
Sunderland SR4 .102 A2
Holly Gdns NE9 .70 F6
Holly Gr NE42 .50 B3
Holly Haven DH5 .94 D4
Holly Hill NE10 .71 D8
Holly Ho SR1 .103 C3
Holly Mews NE26 .32 A5
Holly Park View NE10 .71 D8
Holly Rd NE29 .41 F7
Holly St Jarrow NE32 .58 A7
Ashington NE63 .6 D3
Holly Terr NE16 .79 C5
Holly View NE10 .71 C8
Hollybush Rd 4 NE10 .71 C8
Hollycarrside Rd SR2 .92 E8
Hollycrest DH2 .88 B5
Hollydene
Kibblesworth NE11 .81 D6
Rowlands Gill NE39 .67 F2
Hollyhock Hebburn NE31 .57 E3
Washington NE38 .83 E2
Hollymount Sq NE22 .16 A8
Hollymount Terr NE22 .16 A8
Hollys The DH3 .82 B7
Hollywell Gr NE13 .36 F8
Hollywell Rd NE29 .41 D6
Hollywood Ave
Newcastle-upon-Tyne, Gosforth
NE3 .38 D6
Newcastle-upon-Tyne, Walkerville
NE6 .40 A1
Sunderland SR5 .74 F2
Hollywood Cres NE3 .38 D6
Hollywood Gdns NE11 .70 B5
Holm Gn NE25 .31 D4
Holman Ct NE33 .42 C2
Holmcroft NE64 .7 E5
Holmdale NE63 .6 C2
Holme Ave
Whickham NE16 .69 B7
Newcastle-upon-Tyne NE6 .39 F1
Holme Gdns
Wallsend NE28 .41 A2
Sunderland SR3 .86 B3
Holme Rise NE16 .69 B7
Holmesdale Rd NE5 .37 D1
Holmeside SR1 .103 A2
Holmewood Dr NE39 .78 D8
Holmfield Ave NE34 .59 E7
Holmland NE15 .54 C4
Holmlands NE25 .31 E5
Holmlands Cl NE25 .31 E5
Holmlands Pk DH3 .88 D2
Holmlands Pk N SR2 .86 C4
Holmlands Pk S SR3 .86 C4
Holmside Ave NE11 .70 A8
Holmwood Ave
Whitley Bay NE25 .31 D4
Newbiggin-by-the-Sea NE64 .7 D5
Holmwood Gr NE2 .38 D2
Holwick Cl NE38 .83 A2
Holy Cross RC Prim Sch
NE28 .40 F4
Holy Island NE46 .45 A5
Holy Jesus Bglws NE2 .98 B4
Holyfields NE27 .30 E2
Holylake Sq SR4 .85 D5
Holyoake Gdns
Birtley DH3 .82 C4
Gateshead NE9 .70 F8
Holyoake St NE42 .50 D3
Holyoake Terr 8 NE37 .83 D8
Holyrood Rd 2 SR2 .86 F2
Holystone Ave Blyth NE24 .17 C5
Whitley Bay NE25 .32 B4
Newcastle-upon-Tyne NE3 .38 B6
Holystone Cl
Burnside DH4 .90 B2
Blyth NE24 .17 B5
Holystone Cres NE7 .39 B2
Holystone Ct NE8 .101 A1
Holystone Dr NE27 .30 C2
Holystone Gdns NE29 .41 D8
Holystone Grange NE27 .30 C1
Holystone Prim Sch
NE27 .30 C2
Holystone St NE31 .57 D6
Holystone Way NE12,
NE27 .40 C8
Holywell Ave
Holywell NE25 .23 F2
Whitley Bay NE26 .31 F6
Newcastle-upon-Tyne NE6 .56 E3
Holywell Cl Blaydon NE21 .53 D1
Holywell NE25 .23 F2
Newcastle-upon-Tyne NE4 .98 B2
Holywell Dene Rd NE25 .23 F2
Holywell La NE16 .69 B3
Holywell Mews NE26 .31 F6
Holywell Terr NE27 .30 D1
Holywell Village Fst Sch
NE25 .23 F2
Home Ave 2 NE9 .70 F4
Home Farm Cl NE63 .5 F4
Home Pk NE28 .39 E3
Homedale Prudhoe NE42 .50 E2
Hexham NE46 .45 C4
Homedale Pl NE42 .50 E1
Homedowne House NE3 .38 C5
Homeforth House NE3 .38 C5
Homeside Pl 6 NE6 .56 B7
Homestall Cl NE34 .59 D5
Honeycomb Cl 7 SR3 .91 F5
Honeycrook Dr NE7 .39 E3
Honeysuckle Ave NE34 .59 B5
Honeysuckle Cl SR3 .92 A5
Honister Ave NE2 .38 E3
Honister Cl NE15 .53 D7
Honister Dr SR5 .75 C3
Honister Pl NE15 .53 D7
Honister Rd NE30 .32 B2
Honister Way NE24 .17 C3
Honiton Cl DH4 .90 C4
Honiton Ct NE3 .37 B6
Honiton Way NE29 .41 B8
Hood Cl SR5 .75 C1
Hood St
Newcastle-upon-Tyne NE1 .99 A1
4 Whickham NE16 .54 A1
Morpeth NE61 .3 F1
Hookergate Comp Sch
NE39 .67 B3
Hookergate La NE39 .67 A2
Hope Shield NE38 .82 F1
Hope St Jarrow NE32 .58 C7
South Shields NE34 .59 B5
Sunderland SR1 .102 C2
Hope View SR2 .92 F7
Hopedene NE10 .72 A5
Hopgarth Ct DH3 .88 D4
Hopgarth Gdns DH3 .88 D4
Hopkins Ct SR4 .85 F7
Hopkins Wlk NE34 .59 A2
Hopper Pl NE8 .101 C3
Hopper Rd NE10 .71 C7
Hopper St
8 Wallsend NE28 .40 B2
5 North Shields NE29 .41 F5
Gateshead NE8 .101 C3
Horatio St
Newcastle-upon-Tyne NE1 .56 A5
Sunderland SR6 .75 E1
Hornbeam Pl NE4 .100 B3
Horncliffe Gdns NE16 .69 C8
Horncliffe Pl NE15 .35 B2
Horncliffe Wlk NE15 .53 A7
Horning Ct NE5 .37 B4
Hornsea Cl NE13 .28 B5
Hornsey Cres DH5 .95 B1
Hornsey Terr DH5 .95 B1
Horse Crofts NE21 .53 C3
Horsegate Bank NE17,
NE40 .66 D5
Horsham Gdns SR3 .86 A3
Horsham Gr NE29 .41 E4
Horsley Ave
Shiremoor NE27 .30 F2
Crawcrook NE40 .51 E3
Horsley Cl NE62 .10 F8
Horsley Ct NE3 .37 E6
Horsley Gdns
Dunston NE11 .70 A8
Seaton Delaval NE25 .23 F2
Horsley Gr SR3 .86 A3
Horsley Hill Rd NE33 .42 E1
Horsley Hill Sq NE34 .60 B7
Horsley Rd
Washington NE38 .84 A5
Ovingham NE42 .50 A5
Newcastle-upon-Tyne NE7 .39 B2
Horsley Terr
12 Tynemouth NE30 .42 D7
Newcastle-upon-Tyne NE6 .56 F5
Horsley Vale NE34 .60 A8
Horsley View NE42 .50 F3
Horsley Wood Cotts
NE15 .50 D7
Horton Ave
Bedlington NE22 .15 F8
Shiremoor NE27 .30 F2
Whiteleas NE34 .59 D3
Horton Cres NE13 .27 B7
Horton Dr NE23 .16 B2
Horton Pl NE24 .17 B4
Horton Rd NE22,NE24 .16 C5
Horton St NE24 .17 F7
Hortondale Gr NE24 .17 B7
Horwood Ave NE5 .36 E2
Hospital Dr NE31 .57 D4
Hospital La NE15 .53 B8
Hospital Of King James The
NE8 .56 B1
Hospl of St Mary the Virgin
The NE4 .100 B4
Hotch Pudding Pl NE5 .36 F1
Hotspur Ave
Bedlington NE22 .15 F8
Whitley Bay NE25 .32 A4
South Shields NE34 .59 F7
Hotspur Prim Sch NE2 .56 A6
Hotspur Rd NE28 .40 A5
Hotspur St
Tynemouth NE30 .42 D8
Newcastle-upon-Tyne NE6 .56 A7
Houghton Ave
Tynemouth NE30 .32 B3
Newcastle-upon-Tyne NE5 .37 E3
Houghton Cut DH5 .90 E1
Houghton Ent Ctr DH5 .94 E8
Houghton Enterprise Ctr
DH5 .94 E8
Houghton Gate DH3 .89 B3
Houghton Kepier Sch
DH4 .94 D8
Houghton Rd
Newbottle DH4 .90 D3
Hetton le Hole DH5 .95 A4
Houghton Rd W DH5 .95 A4
Houghton St SR4 .102 A2
Houghtonside DH4 .90 E1
Houlet Garth 11 NE6 .56 C5
Houlsyke Cl SR3 .92 C7
Houndelee Pl NE5 .37 C1
Houndslow Dr NE63 .6 B2
Hounslow Gdns NE32 .58 D2
House of Hardy Museum*
NE66 .113 B2
House Terr NE37 .83 D8
Housing La DH8,DH9 .77 D1
Housteads (Vercovium)
Roman Fort (N.T.)*
NE47 .127 D4
Housteads 6 NE28 .40 F4
Houston Ct NE4 .100 B4
Houston St NE4 .100 B4
Houxty Rd NE25 .31 B5
Hovingham Gdns SR3 .86 A3
Howard Cl NE27 .30 C1
Howard Ct NE30 .42 B5
Howard Gr NE61 .4 E3
Howard Pl NE3 .38 C5
Howard Rd NE61 .4 A1
Howard St
Newcastle-upon-Tyne NE1 .99 C1
Gateshead, Windy Nook
NE10 .71 C6
North Shields NE30 .42 B5
Jarrow NE32 .58 C6
Gateshead, Mount Pleasant
NE8 .56 B1
3 Sunderland SR5 .75 D1
Howard Terr
High Spen NE39 .66 F4
1 Morpeth NE61 .3 F1
Howardian Cl NE38 .83 B3
Howarth St SR4 .102 A2
Howarth Terr DH6 .97 F3
Howat Ave NE5 .37 E1
Howburn Cres NE61 .4 E3
Howdene Rd NE15 .53 F6
Howdon Green Ind Est
NE28 .41 B2
Howdon La NE28 .41 A2
Howdon Rd NE28,NE29 .41 E3
Howdon Sta NE28 .41 A2
Howe Sq SR4 .85 C5
Howe St Hebburn NE31 .58 A6
Gateshead NE8 .56 A1
Howick Ave NE3 .38 A7
Howick Hall Gardens*
NE66 .113 E4
Howick Pk SR6 .103 A4
Howlett Hall Rd NE15 .53 F6
Howley Ave SR5 .74 C2
Hownam Cl NE3 .38 A4
Hoy Cres SR7 .92 F1
Hoylake Ave NE7 .39 C5
Hoyle Ave NE4 .54 E6
Hoyle Fold SR3 .92 A4
Hubert St NE35 .73 F8
Hucklow Gdns NE34 .59 D5
Huddart Terr 2 DH3 .82 C5
Huddleston Rd NE6 .56 D7
Huddlestone Rise SR6 .103 B4
Hudleston NE26 .32 C4
Hudshaw Gdns NE46 .45 D4
Hudson Ave
Bedlington NE22 .11 B1
Annitsford NE23 .29 B8
Hudson Rd SR1 .103 B2
Hudson Road Prim Sch
SR1 .103 B2
Hudson St
North Shields NE30 .42 C6
South Shields NE33 .59 B6
Gateshead NE8 .101 B3
Hugar Rd NE39 .67 A3
Hugh Ave NE27 .30 F4
Hugh Gdns NE4 .54 E4
Hugh St Wallsend NE28 .40 B1
Washington NE38 .83 F4
Sunderland SR6 .75 E4
Hull St NE4 .54 F5
Hulne Abbey* NE66 .113 A3
Hulne Ave NE30 .42 D7
Hulne Park & Brizlee Tower*
NE66 .112 F3
Hulne Terr NE15 .53 C6
Humber Ct 11 SR3 .91 F6
Humber Gdns NE8 .56 B1
Humber St NE17 .66 C1
Humbert St NE32 .58 B6
Humbledon Pk SR3 .86 A3
Humbledon View 5 SR2 .86 C4
Hume St
Newcastle-upon-Tyne NE6 .56 A5
Sunderland SR4 .102 A2
Humford Gn NE24 .16 F7
Humford Way NE22 .16 A7
Humsford Gr NE23 .22 C8
Humshaugh Cl NE12 .40 A8
Humshaugh Rd NE29 .41 C6
Hunn's Buildings NE62 .10 E5
Hunstanton Ct NE9 .70 E3
Hunt Lea NE16 .68 E5
Huntcliffe Ave SR6 .75 E6
Huntcliffe Gdns NE6 .39 D1
Hunter Ave NE24 .17 F6
Hunter Cl NE36 .74 D6
Hunter House NE6 .57 A4
Hunter St Shiney Row DH4 .90 A5
South Shields NE33 .42 D1
Hunter Terr SR2 .86 E3
Hunter's Moor Cl NE2 .98 B4
Hunter's Moor Hospl
NE2 .98 B4
Hunter's Pl NE2 .98 B4
Hunter's Rd
Newcastle-upon-Tyne,
Spital Tongues NE2 .98 B3
Newcastle-upon-Tyne,
South Gosforth NE3 .38 F5
Hunters Cl
Medomsley DH8 .77 C1
North Shields NE29 .41 D3
Hunters Ct Wallsend NE28 .40 C2
Newcastle-upon-Tyne NE3 .38 E5
Hunters Hall Rd SR4 .102 B1
Hunters Lodge NE28 .40 C2
Huntingdon Cl NE3 .37 D8
Huntingdon Gdns SR3 .86 A3
Huntingdon Pl NE30 .42 D7
Huntington Dr NE23 .22 D7
Huntley Cres NE21 .68 A8
Huntley Sq SR4 .85 D5
Huntley Terr 4 SR2 .92 F6
Huntly Rd NE25 .31 D7
Hurst Terr NE6 .56 E6
Hurstwood Rd SR4 .86 A4
Hurworth Ave NE34 .60 B7
Hurworth Pl NE32 .58 B6
Hutton Cl
Chester le Street DH3 .88 E1
Houghton-le-Spring DH4 .94 C8
Washington NE38 .82 F5
Hutton St
Newcastle-upon-Tyne NE3 .38 A5
Boldon Colliery NE35 .58 F1
Sunderland SR4 .102 B1
Hutton Terr
Newcastle-upon-Tyne NE2 .99 C3
Gateshead NE9 .70 F4
Huxley Cl NE34 .59 B2
Huxley Cres NE8 .70 D7
Hyacinth Ct SR4 .102 B3
Hyde Pk NE28 .39 F3
Hyde St
South Shields NE33 .42 D2
Sunderland SR2 .86 F4
Hyde Terr NE3 .38 D5
Hydepark St NE8 .70 D8
Hylton Ave NE34 .60 B7
Hylton Bank SR4 .85 B6
Hylton Castle* SR5 .74 B2
Hylton Castle Jun Sch
SR5 .74 A2
Hylton Castle Rd SR5 .74 B1
Hylton Cl NE22 .10 D1
Hylton Ct NE38 .83 B5
Hylton Grange SR5 .84 F8
Hylton La NE36,SR5 .74 A5
Hylton Park SR5 .74 E1
Hylton Park Rd SR5 .74 E1
Hylton Rd Jarrow NE32 .58 B4
Sunderland SR4 .85 D5
Hylton Red House Prim Sch
SR5 .74 D2
Hylton Red House Sch
SR5 .74 E4
Hylton St Newbottle DH4 .90 D2
17 North Shields NE29 .42 A5
Gateshead NE8 .56 B1
Sunderland SR4 .102 A2
Hylton Terr
6 North Shields NE29 .42 A5
Ryhope SR2 .92 E6
Hylton Wlk SR4 .85 A5
Hymers Ave NE34 .58 F4
Hyperion Ave NE34 .59 A5

I

Ilderton Pl NE5 .53 E8
Ilex St NE11 .70 C6
Ilford Ave NE23 .16 A1
Ilford Pl NE8,NE9 .71 A8
Ilford Rd
Newcastle-upon-Tyne NE2 .38 D3
Wallsend NE28 .40 F3
Ilford Road Sta NE2 .38 D3
Ilfracombe Ave NE4 .54 E5
Ilfracombe Gdns
Whitley Bay NE26 .31 F6
Gateshead NE9 .70 F3
Ilminster Ct NE3 .37 C6
Imeary Gr 9 NE33 .42 D1
Imeary St NE33 .42 D1
Imperial Bldgs 9 DH4 .94 E8
Inchberry Cl NE4 .54 E4
Inchcliffe Cres NE5 .37 C2
Indigo St NE11 .70 C6
Industrial Rd NE37 .83 E7
Industry Rd NE6 .39 D2
Ingham Gr NE23 .16 A1
Ingham Grange NE33 .42 E1
Ingham Pl NE2 .99 C2
Ingham Terr NE41 .51 B6
Ingleborough Cl 3 NE37 .83 A6
Ingleborough Dr NE40 .52 D4
Ingleby Terr Lynmouth NE61 .2 A3
Sunderland SR4 .102 A1
Ingleby Way NE24 .17 D3
Inglemere Pl NE15 .54 A6
Ingleside Whickham NE16 .68 F6
South Shields NE34 .60 B6
Ingleton Ct SR4 .102 B1
Ingleton Dr NE15 .35 B2
Ingleton Gdns NE24 .17 C3
Inglewood Cl NE24 .16 F7
Inglewood Pl NE3 .28 C1
Ingoe Ave NE3 .37 F7
Ingoe Cl NE24 .17 C7
Ingoe St
Newcastle-upon-Tyne NE15 .53 C6
North Shields NE28 .41 C2
Ingoldsby Ct SR4 .85 E4
Ingram Ave NE3 .37 F8
Ingram Cl
Chester le Street DH2 .88 A1
Wallsend NE28 .40 F5
Ingram Dr Blyth NE24 .17 B7
Newcastle-upon-Tyne NE5 .36 D4
Ingram Terr NE6 .57 A6
Inkerman Rd NE37 .72 D1
Inkerman St SR5 .75 A1
Innesmoor NE31 .57 D7
Inskip Terr NE8 .70 F8
Institute Rd NE63 .6 B4
International Ctr for Life The
NE1 .100 C4
Inverness Rd NE32 .58 E2
Inverness St SR6 .75 D2
Invertay NE3 .38 E5
Invincible Dr NE4 .100 A3
Iolanthe Cres NE6 .56 E7
Iolanthe Terr NE33 .42 E1
Iona Pl NE6 .57 A6
Iona Rd
Gateshead N10,NE9 .71 B7
Brockley Whins NE32 .58 E3
Irene Ave SR2 .86 F1
Iris Cl NE21 .53 A2
Iris Cres DH2 .81 F2
Iris Pl NE4 .54 D7
Iris St NE11 .70 C6
Iris Steedman House
NE4 .98 A2
Iris Terr Bournmoor DH4 .89 E3
Crawcrook NE40 .51 F3
Iroko St NE11 .70 C6
Ironside St DH5 .90 E1
Irthing NE61 .1 E5
Irthing Ave NE6 .56 D4
Irton St NE3 .38 C5
Irvine Ho 7 NE12 .39 D8
Irwin Ave NE28 .40 C3
Isabella Cl NE4 .54 E3
Isabella Rd NE24 .17 C6
Isabella Wlk NE15 .35 D1
Islay Ho 9 SR3 .92 A6
Ivanhoe NE25 .31 E5
Ivanhoe Cres SR2 .86 B4
Ivanhoe Terr
11 Chester le Street DH3 .88 C2
Dipton DH9 .78 E1
Ivanhoe View NE9 .71 B2
Iveagh Cl NE4 .54 D4
Iveson Rd NE46 .44 E3
Ivor St SR2 .87 A2

Ivy Ave Ryton NE40 52 C6
Newbiggin-by-the-Sea NE64 7 C5
Ivy Cl
Newcastle-upon-Tyne NE4 100 B3
Ryton NE40 52 C6
Ivy La NE9 71 A3
Ivy Pl DH9 79 C3
Ivy Rd Longbenton NE12 39 E8
Newcastle-upon-Tyne, Gosforth NE3 38 C4
Newcastle-upon-Tyne, Walkergate NE6 56 F8
Ivy Road Prim Sch NE12 39 E8
Ivy St Gateshead NE11 70 C6
Seaton Burn NE13 28 C8
Ivy Terr DH4 90 B6
Ivymount Rd NE6 39 B1
Ixia St NE11 70 C6

J

Jack Common Ho 3 NE6 56 B7
Jack's Terr NE34 59 C5
Jackson Ave NE20 25 F7
Jackson Rd NE41 51 B6
Jackson St
Newcastle-upon-Tyne NE6 56 F6
Gateshead NE8 101 C3
Sunderland SR4 102 A1
Jackson St W NE30 42 B6
Jackson Terr 8 NE61 9 A8
Jacobins Chare NE4 98 C1
Jacques St SR4 85 F8
Jacques Terr DH2 88 B4
Jade Cl NE15 53 C8
James Armitage St SR5 75 B2
James Ave NE27 30 F4
James Mather St NE33 42 D3
James St Tanfield Lea DH9 79 F1
10 Whickham NE16 69 A7
Newcastle-upon-Tyne, Elswick NE4 54 F4
Newcastle-upon-Tyne, Westerhope NE5 36 F2
Sunderland SR5 75 A2
James Steel Pk* NE38 84 A2
James Terr
Fence Houses DH4 94 A8
Easington Lane DH5 97 B8
Wallsend NE28 40 B1
James Williams St SR1 103 B3
Jameson Dr NE45 47 B7
Jane Eyre Terr NE8 56 B1
Jane St Hetton le Hole DH5 95 A6
22 Newcastle-upon-Tyne NE6 56 C6
Jane Terr NE6 57 A4
Janet Sq NE6 56 C5
Janet St
17 Newcastle-upon-Tyne, St Lawrence NE6 56 C5
Newcastle-upon-Tyne, St Peters NE6 56 C4
Janus Cl NE5 36 C4
Jarrow Rd NE32,NE34 58 F6
Jarrow St Peter's C of E Prim Sch NE32 58 C7
Jarrow Sta NE32 58 B7
Jasmin Ave NE5 36 C4
Jasmine Cl NE6 39 E1
Jasmine Ct Ashington NE63 6 C1
Sunderland SR4 102 B3
Jasmine Terr DH3 82 D4
Jasmine Villas 7 NE16 69 A7
Jasper Ave NE40 52 B1
Jedburgh Cl
Tynemouth NE29 41 E8
Newcastle-upon-Tyne NE5 36 C4
Gateshead NE8 101 C1
Jedburgh Ct NE11 70 E2
Jedburgh Gdns NE15 54 B7
Jedburgh Rd DH4 90 B6
Jedmoor NE31 57 D7
Jefferson Cl SR5 75 C4
Jefferson Pl NE4 98 B2
Jellicoe Rd NE6 56 E3
Jenifer Gr NE7 39 A4
Jenison Ave NE15 54 C5
Jennifer Ave 9 SR5 74 B1
Jersey Sq NE61 2 A3
Jervis St NE31 57 F6
Jesmond Dene Rd
Newcastle-upon-Tyne, Jesmond NE2 38 F2
Newcastle-upon-Tyne, West Jesmond NE2 38 D3
Jesmond Gdns
Newcastle-upon-Tyne NE2 38 F1
Biddick Hall NE34 59 C3
Jesmond Park Ct NE7 39 B1
Jesmond Pk E NE7 39 B1
Jesmond Pk W NE7 39 A2
Jesmond Pl 1 NE2 38 E1
Jesmond Rd NE2 99 C4
Jesmond Rd W NE2 99 B3
Jesmond Sta NE2 99 C3
Jesmond Terr NE26 32 B4
Jesmond Vale NE2 56 A7
Jesmond Vale La NE6 56 B8
Jesmond Vale Terr NE6 56 B8
Jessel St NE9 70 F4
Jetty The NE10 57 A2
Jeycroft Ct NE30 42 B5
Joan Ave SR2 86 F1
Joan St NE4 54 D4
Joannah St SR5 75 C3
Jobling Ave NE21 53 B2
Jobling Cres NE61 9 B6
Joel Terr NE10 57 B2
John & Margaret Common Homes for Aged Miners 5 NE24 16 F8
John Ave NE40 52 B1
John Brown Ct NE22 10 F1
John Candlish Rd SR4 102 A3
John Clay St
3 South Shields NE33 42 D1
5 South Shields, Dean NE33 59 D8
John Dobson St NE1, NE99 99 B2
John F Kennedy Est NE38 83 E5
John F Kennedy Prim Sch NE38 83 E5
John Reid Rd NE34 59 C4
John Spence Community High Sch NE29 42 A8
John St Prudhoe NE42 50 E3
Fence Houses DH4 94 A8
Hetton le Hole DH5 95 A3
Houghton-le-Spring DH5 94 F8
1 Gateshead, Pelaw NE10 56 F1
Blyth NE24 17 B8
Earsdon NE25 31 A5
Wallsend NE28 40 B2
Newcastle-upon-Tyne NE3 38 A5
Tynemouth NE30 32 C3
West Boldon NE35 73 F8
Pegswood NE61 4 F3
Ashington NE63 6 C4
Gateshead, Old Fold NE8 56 B1
Sunderland SR1 103 A3
14 Ryhope SR2 93 A6
Sunderland, South Hylton SR4 85 A7
John Taylor Ct SR5 75 A3
John Wesley Ct NE42 50 D2
John Williamson St NE33 59 C7
Johnson St
6 Dunston NE11 54 F1
Newcastle-upon-Tyne NE15 53 C6
South Shields NE33 59 C7
Gateshead NE8 100 B1
Sunderland SR1 102 C3
Johnson Terr
5 Washington NE37 83 F8
High Spen NE39 66 F4
Johnsons Villas NE62 10 B7
Johnston Ave NE31 57 D3
Joicey Aged Miners Homes 7 DH4 90 B6
Joicey Rd NE9 70 F6
Joicey Road Open Air Sch NE9 70 F6
Joicey St NE10 57 A1
Jolliffe St DH3 88 D1
Jonadab Rd NE10 57 A2
Jonadab St NE10 57 A1
Jones St 3 DH3 82 C4
Jonquil Cl NE5 36 C4
Joseph Cl NE4 54 E4
Joseph Hopper Aged Miners' Homes DH3 82 C7
Joseph Hopper Meml Homes NE9 71 C6
Joseph Swan Comp Sch NE9 70 E3
Joseph Terr NE17 66 B1
Jowett Sq SR5 75 A2
Joyce Cl NE10 72 D8
Joyce Terr 5 SR5 74 B1
Jubilee Ave NE9 71 C1
Jubilee Bldgs 2 NE46 45 B4
Jubilee Cotts
Houghton-le-Spring DH4 94 D8
Greenside NE40 66 D7
Lynmouth NE61 2 A3
Jubilee Cres
Sherburn Hill DH6 96 D1
Newcastle-upon-Tyne NE3 38 A5
Jubilee Ct Annitsford NE23 22 B1
Blyth NE24 17 D6
Hebburn NE31 58 A6
Jubilee Est NE63 6 D1
Jubilee Ho DH5 95 C1
Jubilee Ind Est NE63 6 D1
Jubilee Rd
Newcastle-upon-Tyne NE1 99 C1
Blyth NE24 17 E6
Newcastle-upon-Tyne, Coxlodge NE3 38 B5
Ovington NE42 49 C4
Jubilee Sq
Easington Lane DH5 95 C1
South Hetton DH6 97 F7
Jubilee St 3 NE28 40 B2
Jubilee Terr Tantobie DH9 79 A2
Seaton Burn NE13 28 B8
7 Whickham NE16 54 A1
Bedlington NE22 11 D2
Washington NE38 84 A2
Crawcrook NE40 51 E3
Newbiggin-by-the-Sea NE64 7 E4
Jubilee Terrs NE6 56 D6
Julian Ave
South Shields NE33 42 D4
Newcastle-upon-Tyne NE6 56 E7
Julian Rd NE10 72 D8
Julian St NE33 42 D4
Juliet Ave NE29 41 D6
Juliet St NE63 6 E4
Julius Caesar St 5 SR5 75 A2
Julius Ct NE33 42 C4
June Ave NE21 68 C6
Juniper Cl Blyth NE24 17 C4
Newcastle-upon-Tyne NE3 28 D1
4 Sunderland SR2 86 E4
Juniper Ct NE21 53 C3
Juniper Wlk NE5 36 D4
Jutland Ave NE31 57 E6

K

Kalmia St NE11 70 C5
Kane Gdns NE10 71 C6
Kateregina DH3 82 D4
Katherine St NE63 6 E4
Katrine Cl DH2 88 B1
Katrine Ct SR3 92 A5
Kay's Cotts NE10 71 C7
Kayll Rd SR4 85 F6
Kearsley Cl NE25 23 D3
Kearton Ave NE5 36 C3
Keats Ave Blyth NE24 17 C5
West Boldon NE35 74 B8
Sunderland SR5 75 A2
Keats Gr NE63 6 F3
Keats Rd NE15 53 A6
Keats Wlk
Biddick Hall NE34 59 A3
Gateshead NE8 56 A2
Keeble Ct NE63 7 B3
Keebledale Ave NE6 56 F7
Keele Dr NE23 21 D6
Keelman's La SR4 85 C7
Keelman's Rd SR4 85 B7
Keelmans Terr NE24 17 E8
Keelmen's Hospl NE1 99 C1
Keighley Ave SR5 74 B4
Keighley Sq SR5 74 A4
Keir Hardie Ave NE10 72 A8
Keir Hardie Ct NE64 7 E5
Keir Hardie St
Fence Houses DH4 94 B8
Rowlands Gill NE39 67 B2
Keir Hardie Terr DH3 82 B6
Keir Hardie Way SR5 75 C1
Keith Cl NE4 54 E4
Keith Sq SR5 74 B4
Keldane Gdns NE4 54 E6
Kelfield Gr NE23 16 B2
Kelham Sq SR5 74 A4
Kell Cres DH6 96 C1
Kell's Way NE39 67 E1
Kellfield Ave NE9 71 A6
Kellfield Rd NE9 71 A5
Kells Gdns NE9 71 A5
Kells La NE9 70 F5
Kellsway NE10 71 F5
Kellsway Ct NE10 71 F5
Kelly Rd NE31 57 E3
Kelsey Way NE23 16 B2
Kelso Cl NE5 36 C4
Kelso Dr NE29 41 E8
Kelso Gdns
Newcastle-upon-Tyne NE15 54 B6
Bedlington NE22 11 C1
Wallsend NE28 41 A4
Kelso Gr DH4 90 A6
Kelso Pl NE8 100 B1
Kelson Way NE5 36 C4
Kelston Way NE5 37 C2
Kelvin Gdns 3 NE11 54 F1
Kelvin Gr
Newcastle-upon-Tyne NE2 99 C3
Tynemouth NE29 42 A8
South Shields NE33 42 F1
Gateshead NE8 70 D8
Cleadon SR6 59 E1
Sunderland SR6 75 E2
Kelvin Grove Com Prim Sch NE8 70 E8
Kelvin Pl NE12 30 A1
Kemble Cl NE23 16 B2
Kemble Sq SR5 74 B4
Kempton Gdns NE8 70 C7
Kendal DH3 82 E2
Kendal Ave Blyth NE24 17 D6
Tynemouth NE30 32 B2
Kendal Cres NE9 71 B5
Kendal Dr
Cramlington NE23 22 C8
East Boldon NE36 74 C8
Kendal Gdns NE28 41 A4
Kendal Gn 24 NE6 56 B6
Kendal House 27 NE6 56 B6
Kendal Pl 26 NE6 56 B6
Kendal St 1 NE6 56 B5
Kendale Wlk NE5 36 E3
Kendor Gr NE61 8 F6
Kenilworth NE12 29 D4
Kenilworth Ct
4 Washington NE37 83 F8
Newcastle-upon-Tyne NE4 100 A4
Kenilworth Rd
Whitley Bay NE25 31 F4
Newcastle-upon-Tyne NE4 100 A4
Ashington NE63 6 C3
Kenilworth Sq SR5 74 C4
Kenilworth View 7 NE9 71 A2
Kenley Rd
Newcastle-upon-Tyne NE5 54 A8
Sunderland SR5 74 C4
Kenmoor Way NE5 36 C3
Kenmore Cres NE40 52 B2
Kennersdene NE30 42 C8
Kennet Ave NE32 58 C3
Kennet Sq SR5 74 B4
Kennford NE9 71 A2
Kennington Gr NE6 56 E5
Kensington Ave NE3 38 C7
Kensington Cl NE25 31 F5
Kensington Cotts NE61 9 B8
Kensington Ct
5 Gateshead NE10 71 C8
South Shields NE33 59 E8
Kensington Gdns
Whitley Bay NE25 31 F5
Wallsend NE28 39 E3
1 North Shields NE30 42 B6
Kensington Gr NE30 42 B7
Kensington Terr
2 Dunston NE11 69 F8
Newcastle-upon-Tyne NE2 99 A3
Kensington Villas 5 NE5 36 E3
Kent Ave 3 Dunston NE11 70 A8
Wallsend NE28 40 F2
Hebburn NE31 57 D5
Kent Cl NE63 6 A4
Kent Ct NE3 37 D8
Kent Gdns DH5 94 F4
Kent Pl NE34 60 A6
Kent St NE32 58 A6
Kent Terr DH6 97 E1
Kentchester Rd SR5 74 C4
Kentmere DH3 82 E1
Kentmere Ave
Newcastle-upon-Tyne NE6 56 F7
Sunderland SR6 75 C5
Kentmere Cl NE23 23 A2
Kenton Ave NE3 38 A3
Kenton Bank NE5 37 C5
Kenton Bar Prim Sch NE5 37 D4
Kenton Cres NE3 37 F4
Kenton Ct NE33 42 D1
Kenton Gr SR6 75 D1
Kenton La NE3 37 E4
Kenton Lodge (Residential Special Sch) NE3 38 B2
Kenton Park Sh Ctr NE3 38 A4
Kenton Rd
Tynemouth NE29 41 C7
Newcastle-upon-Tyne NE3 38 A3
Kenton Sch NE5 37 E4
Kentucky Rd SR5 74 A4
Kenwood Gdns NE9 71 A2
Kenya Rd SR5 74 C4
Kepier Chare Prim Sch NE40 51 F3
Kepier Gdns 6 SR4 85 A6
Keppel St Dunston NE11 54 F1
3 South Shields NE33 42 C3
Kepwell Bank Top NE42 50 C3
Kepwell Bk NE42 50 D3
Kepwell Ct NE42 50 D3
Kepwell Rd NE42 50 C2
Kerby Cl NE34 58 F4
Kerry Cl NE24 17 E8
Kerry Sq SR5 74 B4
Kesteven Sq SR5 74 B4
Keston Dr NE23 16 B2
Kestrel Cl NE38 83 A2
Kestrel Ct 13 DH3 82 C4
Kestrel Dr NE63 6 B1
Kestrel Lodge Flats 6 NE33 42 D3
Kestrel Mews NE16 69 A7
Kestrel Pl NE12 39 A7
Kestrel Sq SR5 74 B4
Kestrel St NE11 70 C6
Kestrel Way
North Shields NE29 42 A3
South Shields NE34 59 B4
Keswick Ave SR6 75 D4
Keswick Dr NE30 32 B2
Keswick Gdns NE28 41 A3
Keswick Gr NE5 54 A8
Keswick St NE8 101 B1
Keswick Terr DH6 97 E8
Kettering Pl NE23 22 C8
Kettering Sq SR5 74 B4
Kettlewell Terr 7 NE30 42 B6
Ketton Cl NE12 39 B6
Kew Gdns NE26 31 F6
Keyes Gdns NE2 38 E3
Kibblesworth Bank NE11 81 B6
Kibblesworth Prim Sch NE11 81 D6
Kidd Sq SR5 74 B4
Kidderminster Dr NE5 36 C3
Kidderminster Rd SR5 74 B3
Kidderminster Sq SR5 74 B3
Kidland Cl NE63 6 F4
Kidlandlee Gn NE5 37 A4
Kidlandlee Pl NE5 37 A4
Kidsgrove Sq SR5 74 B3
Kielder NE38 82 F4
Kielder Ave NE23 21 D6
Kielder Castle Visitor Centre* NE48 120 D8
Kielder Cl
Killingworth NE12 29 C4
Blyth NE24 17 B5
Newcastle-upon-Tyne NE5 37 A4
Kielder Dr NE63 6 C3
Kielder Gdns Jarrow NE32 58 B3
Stakeford NE62 6 A1
Kielder Pl NE25 31 B5
Kielder Rd
Newcastle-upon-Tyne NE15 53 C7
Earsdon NE25 31 B5
Kielder Terr NE30 42 B6
Kielder Way NE3 38 B7
Kilburn Cl 4 SR2 93 A6
Kilburn Gdns NE29 41 D
Kilburn Gn NE9 71 B
Kilburne Cl NE7 39 E
Kildale DH4 89 E
Kildare Sq SR5 74 B
Killarney Ave SR5 74 E
Killarney Sq SR5 74 B
Killiebrigs NE15 34 E
Killin Cl NE5 36 C
Killingworth Ave NE27 30 E
Killingworth Ctr The NE12 29 D
Killingworth Dr
Killingworth NE12 29 B
Sunderland SR3,SR4 85 E
Killingworth La NE27 30 A
Killingworth Mid Sch NE12 29 D
Killingworth Pl NE1 99 A
Killingworth Rd
Killingworth NE12 29 E
Newcastle-upon-Tyne NE3, NE7 38 F
Killingworth Way NE12, NE27 29 D
Killowen St NE9 70 E
Kiln Rise NE16 69 A
Kilnshaw Pl NE3 28 D
Kilsyth Ave NE29 31 E
Kilsyth Sq SR5 74 B
Kimberley NE38 84 A
Kimberley Ave NE29 41 E
Kimberley Gdns
Newcastle-upon-Tyne NE2 56 A
Stocksfield NE43 64 C
Kimberley St Blyth NE24 17 D
Sunderland SR4 85 F
Kimberley Terr NE24 17 E
Kinfauns Terr 5 NE9 71 A
King Charles Ct 4 SR5 74 A
King Charles Twr NE2 99 C
King Edward Inf Sch NE30 42 B
King Edward Jun Sch NE30 42 B
King Edward Pl NE8 56 B
King Edward Rd
Tynemouth NE30 42 C
Ryton NE40 52 E
Newcastle-upon-Tyne NE6 39 B
Sunderland SR4 85 B
King Edward St
Tanfield Lea DH9 79 C
Gateshead NE8 56 B
King Edward VI Sch The NE61 3 F
King George Ave NE11 69 F
King George Rd
Newcastle-upon-Tyne NE3 37 E
South Shields NE34 59 E
King George V Comp Sch NE34 59 E3
King George's Rd NE64 7 D5
King Henry Ct 5 SR5 74 A4
King James Ct SR5 74 A4
King James St NE8 101 C
King John St NE6 56 B8
King John Terr NE6 56 B8
King John's Ct NE20 25 A4
King St Birtley DH3 82 B4
Newcastle-upon-Tyne NE1 101 B4
Gateshead, Pelaw NE10 57 A1
Blyth NE24 17 E8
North Shields NE30 42 B6
South Shields NE33 42 C
Newbiggin-by-the-Sea NE64 7 E5
Gateshead, Bensham NE8 70 C8
Sunderland SR1 103 A3
Sunderland, Fulwell SR6 75 D4
King's Ave NE61 3 F1
King's Dr Whitley Bay NE26 32 A4
Greenside NE40 52 B1
King's Gdns NE24 17 C8
King's Pl SR4 102 A3
King's Rd
Newcastle-upon-Tyne NE1, NE2 99 A2
Bedlington NE22 11 D2
Whitley Bay NE26 31 F6
King's School Tynemouth NE30 42 D7
King's Terr SR4 102 A3
King's Wlk NE1 99 A3
Kingarth Ave SR6 75 E5
Kingdom Pl NE29 42 A3
Kingfisher Cl NE63 11 E8
Kingfisher Lodge NE32 58 A6
Kingfisher Rd NE12 39 A7
Kingfisher Way
Blyth NE24 17 F4
Shiremoor NE28 41 A6
Kingham Ct NE7 38 F4
Kinghorn Sq SR5 74 B4
Kings Ave Hebburn NE31 57 F5
Sunderland SR6 75 E5
Kings Cl NE8 56 B1
Kings Meadow NE32 58 C1
Kings Meadows NE4 100 A3
Kings Pk NE62 10 F5
Kings Rd NE12 29 C1
Kings Rd N NE28 40 B4
Kings Rd S NE28 40 B3
Kings Rd The SR5 75 A2
Kings Terr NE9 71 F1
Kings Wlk NE5 36 C4
Kingsbridge NE12 38 F7
Kingsbridge Cl NE28 41 E4
Kingsclere Ave SR5 74 B3

Kingsclere Sq SR5 ....74 B4
Kingsdale Ave Blyth NE24 .17 A7
Washington NE37 ....83 C8
Kingsdale Rd NE12 ....38 F7
Kingsgate NE46 ....45 A5
Kingsgate Terr NE46 ....45 A5
Kingsland NE2 ....99 B4
Kingsland Sq SR5 ....74 B3
Kingsley Ave
Whitley Bay NE25 ....32 A4
Newcastle-upon-Tyne NE3 ..28 D1
Biddick Hall NE34 ....59 A3
Kingsley Cl [4] SR5 ....75 A1
Kingsley Pl
[8] Dunston NE11 ....54 F1
Whickham NE16 ....69 B8
Wallsend NE28 ....40 F3
[8] Newcastle-upon-Tyne NE6 ....56 B7
Kingsley Rd NE61 ....2 A2
Kingsley Terr
Newcastle-upon-Tyne NE4 ..98 A1
Crawcrook NE40 ....51 E4
Kingsmeadow Com Comp Sch NE11 ....69 E8
Kingsmere DH3 ....88 C7
Kingsmere Gdns NE6 ....57 A4
Kingston Ave NE6 ....56 D4
Kingston Cl NE26 ....31 F8
Kingston Cres DH6 ....97 E3
Kingston Ct
[6] Whitley Bay NE26 ....31 F8
Hebburn NE31 ....57 D5
Kingston Dr NE26 ....31 F8
Kingston Gn NE6 ....56 D5
Kingston Mews DH4 ....90 C5
Kingston Park Ave NE3 ..37 C6
Kingston Park Ctr NE3 ..37 C6
Kingston Park Prim Sch NE3 ....37 C6
Kingston Park Rd NE3, NE13 ....37 F7
Kingston Park Sta NE3 ..37 C6
Kingston Rd NE8 ....71 B8
Kingston Terr SR6 ....75 D2
Kingston Way [3] NE26 ....31 F8
Kingsway
Houghton-le-Spring DH5 ....94 F8
Sunniside NE16 ....69 A2
Ponteland NE20 ....25 E6
Blyth NE24 ....17 E6
Tynemouth NE30 ....42 C8
South Shields NE33 ....42 F2
Newcastle-upon-Tyne NE4 ..54 E8
Kingsway Ave NE3 ....38 C7
Kingsway Fst Sch NE24 ..17 E6
Kingsway Ho NE11 ....70 D4
Kingsway Interchange NE11 ....70 E3
Kingsway N NE11 ....70 C5
Kingsway Rd SR5 ....74 B4
Kingsway S NE11 ....70 D3
Kingsway Sq SR5 ....74 B4
Kingswood Ave NE2 ....38 D3
Kingswood Cl NE35 ....58 E1
Kingswood Dr NE20 ....25 C4
Kingswood Gr SR4 ....85 A2
Kingswood Rd NE23 ....22 C8
Kingswood Sq SR5 ....74 B3
Kinlett NE38 ....84 A5
Kinloch Ct DH2 ....88 B1
Kinloss Sq NE23 ....22 C8
Kinnaird Ave NE15 ....54 A6
Kinnock Cl DH6 ....96 A1
Kinross Cl DH3 ....82 D2
Kinross Ct NE10 ....57 B2
Kinross Dr NE3 ....37 F5
Kinsale Sq SR5 ....74 B4
Kinver Dr NE5 ....36 C3
Kipling Ave
Whickham NE16 ....69 B8
Hebburn NE31 ....57 F6
West Boldon NE35 ....74 B8
Kipling Ct NE16 ....69 B8
Kipling St SR5 ....75 A1
Kipling Wlk NE8 ....56 A2
Kirk St NE6 ....56 C5
Kirk View DH4 ....90 D3
Kirkbride Pl NE23 ....22 C8
Kirkdale Ct [2] NE34 ....59 A4
Kirkdale Gn NE4 ....100 B4
Kirkdale Sq SR5 ....74 B3
Kirkdale St DH5 ....94 F2
Kirkham NE38 ....83 D4
Kirkham Ave NE3 ....37 C7
Kirkharle Dr NE61 ....4 E4
Kirkheaton Pl NE5 ....54 C8
Kirkland Wlk NE27 ....30 E3
Kirklands NE23 ....29 C5
Kirklea Rd DH5 ....94 F8
Kirkleatham Gdns NE6 ..39 D2
Kirkley Ave NE34 ....60 A6
Kirkley Cl NE3 ....38 B6
Kirkley Dr Ponteland NE20 .25 E7
Ashington NE63 ....6 E2
Kirkley Hall* NE20 ....130 D8
Kirkley Lodge NE3 ....38 B6
Kirkley Rd NE27 ....30 F2
Kirklinton Rd NE30 ....32 A2
Kirknewton Cl [7] DH5 ....94 F8
Kirkside DH4 ....90 E6
Kirkston Ave NE15 ....53 D7
Kirkstone DH3 ....82 D2
Kirkstone Ave
Tynemouth NE30 ....32 A2
Hedworth NE32 ....58 D3
Sunderland SR5 ....75 C3
Kirkstone Cl [8] DH5 ....94 F8
Kirkstone Gdns NE7 ....39 A3
Kirkstone Rd NE10 ....71 F8
Kirkwall Cl SR5 ....74 A1
Kirkwood NE23 ....29 C5
Kirkwood Ave SR4 ....85 A2
Kirkwood Dr NE3 ....37 F5
Kirkwood Gdns NE10 ....72 B8
Kirkwood Pl NE3 ....28 B1
Kirton Ave NE4 ....54 E6
Kirton Park Terr NE29, NE30 ....42 A7
Kirton Way NE23 ....22 C8
Kismet St SR5 ....75 A2
Kitchener Rd SR6 ....60 F4
Kitchener St
Gateshead NE9 ....71 A8
Sunderland SR4 ....85 F4
Kitchener Terr
New Herrington DH4 ....90 D6
North Shields NE30 ....42 C7
Jarrow NE32 ....58 B5
Sunderland SR2 ....86 F2
Kittiwake Cl Blyth NE24 ..17 E3
Shiremoor NE28 ....41 A7
Kittiwake Dr NE38 ....82 F3
Kittiwake House NE26 ....32 B5
Kitty Brewster Ind Est NE24 ....12 B1
Kitty Brewster Rd NE24 ..16 F8
Kiwi St NE11 ....70 C5
Knaresborough Cl NE22 ..10 D2
Knaresborough Sq SR5 ..74 C4
Knaresdale DH3 ....82 D1
Knarsdale Ave NE29 ....41 D6
Knarsdale Pl [3] NE5 ....36 E1
Knightsbridge
Newcastle-upon-Tyne NE3 ..38 C6
Sunderland SR3 ....91 E8
Knightside Gdns NE11 ....70 A7
Knightside Wlk NE5 ....36 C3
Knivestone Ct NE12 ....29 E4
Knobbyends La NE21 ....67 F8
Knoll Rise NE11 ....69 F7
Knoll The Ellington NE61 ....1 C5
Sunderland SR2 ....102 B1
Knollside Cl SR3 ....91 F5
Knop Law Fst Sch NE5 ..36 C3
Knott Flats [13] NE30 ....42 D7
Knott Pl NE15 ....54 B5
Knoulberry NE37 ....83 A6
Knoulberry Rd NE37 ....83 A6
Knowle Pl NE12 ....39 B5
Knowledge Hill NE21 ....53 B1
Knowsley Ct NE3 ....37 B5
Knox Cl NE22 ....11 D2
Knox Rd NE22 ....16 B8
Knox Sq SR5 ....75 A2
Knutsford Wlk NE23 ....22 C8
Kramel Fst Sch NE23 ....22 C5
Kristin Ave NE32 ....58 C4
Kyffin View NE34 ....60 B5
Kyle Cl NE4 ....100 B4
Kyle Rd NE8 ....70 C8
Kylins The NE61 ....9 A6
Kyloe Ave NE25 ....23 D2
Kyloe Cl NE3 ....37 E7
Kyloe Pl NE5 ....37 A3
Kyloe Villas NE5 ....37 A3
Kyo Bog La NE41,NE42 ....51 B1
Kyo Cl NE41 ....51 B1
Kyo La NE40 ....66 D7

L

L'Arbre Cres NE16 ....68 F7
La Sagesse High Sch NE2 ....38 E3
Laburnum Ave
Gateshead NE10 ....72 A7
Blyth NE24 ....17 D8
Whitley Bay NE26 ....32 A5
Wallsend NE28 ....40 B2
Washington NE38 ....83 B1
Newcastle-upon-Tyne NE6 ..56 F8
Laburnum Cl SR4 ....85 A6
Laburnum Cres NE11 ....81 C6
Laburnum Ct NE12 ....29 C4
Laburnum Gdns
[6] Gateshead, Felling NE10 .56 D1
Jarrow NE32 ....58 A4
Gateshead, Low Fell NE9 ..70 F6
Laburnum Gr
Sunniside NE16 ....69 B2
Whickham NE16 ....69 A7
Hebburn NE31 ....57 E3
South Shields NE34 ....59 F5
Sunderland SR5 ....85 A8
Cleadon SR6 ....60 A1
Laburnum Rd
Blaydon NE21 ....53 C2
Sunderland SR6 ....75 D3
Laburnum Terr NE63 ....6 D3
Laburnun Ct NE62 ....10 E7
Lacebark Shiney Row DH4 ..89 F6
Silksworth SR3 ....91 E4
Ladock Cl SR2 ....93 A8
Lady Beatrice Terr DH4 ..90 E7
Lady St DH5 ....95 A5
Lady Waterford Hall* TD15 ....107 C6
Lady's Piece La DH6 ....96 A5
Lady's Well (N.T.)* NE65 ....117 A5
Lady's Wlk
South Shields NE33 ....42 C4
Morpeth NE61 ....3 E1
Ladybank NE5 ....36 B4
Ladycutters La NE45 ....46 F3
Ladyhaugh Dr NE16 ....69 A4
Ladykirk Rd NE4 ....54 E5
Ladykirk Way NE23 ....21 E6
Ladyrigg NE20 ....25 D4
Ladysmith St NE33 ....42 D2
Ladywell NE43 ....64 D6
Ladywell Rd NE21 ....53 C2
Ladywell Way NE20 ....25 D7
Ladywood Pk DH4 ....89 F8
Laet St NE29 ....42 B5
Laindon Ave SR6 ....75 D4
Laing Art Gallery & Mus* NE1 ....99 B2
Laing Gr NE28 ....41 B3
Laith Rd NE3 ....37 E5
Lake App NE21 ....53 F1
Lake Ave NE34 ....60 C6
Lake Ct SR3 ....92 A6
Lake Rd DH5 ....94 E8
Lake View NE31 ....57 E4
Lakeside Blaydon NE21 ....53 F1
South Shields NE34 ....60 D6
Laleham Ct NE3 ....37 D7
Lamb St
East Cramlington NE23 ....22 F5
Newcastle-upon-Tyne NE6 ..57 A5
Lamb Terr [6] NE27 ....30 E1
Lambden Cl NE29 ....41 E3
Lambert Rd NE37 ....82 F7
Lambert Sq NE3 ....38 A5
Lambeth Pl NE8 ....71 A8
Lambley Ave NE30 ....32 B2
Lambley Cl NE16 ....69 A2
Lambley Cres NE31 ....57 D3
Lambourn Ave
Longbenton NE12 ....39 C7
North Shields NE29 ....41 E4
Lambourne Cl DH4 ....89 E3
Lambourne Rd SR2 ....86 C3
Lambton Ave NE16 ....69 C8
Lambton Cl NE40 ....51 F4
Lambton Ct
Washington NE38 ....88 E8
Sunderland SR3 ....91 C7
Lambton Dr DH5 ....95 A1
Lambton Gdns NE16 ....78 E5
Lambton Prim Sch NE38 ..83 B3
Lambton Rd
Newcastle-upon-Tyne NE2 ..99 B4
Hebburn NE31 ....57 F7
Lambton St
Chester le Street DH3 ....88 D2
Gateshead NE8 ....101 B3
Sunderland SR1 ....103 A3
Lambton Terr
Penshaw DH4 ....89 F8
Jarrow NE32 ....58 B4
Lambton Tower SR1 ....103 B3
Lampeter Cl NE5 ....37 B4
Lamport St NE31 ....57 C7
Lampton Ct NE22 ....11 C2
Lampton Lea DH4 ....90 A4
Lanark Cl NE29 ....41 C8
Lanark Dr NE32 ....58 E2
Lancaster Ct NE3 ....37 D7
Lancaster Dr NE28 ....40 D7
Lancaster House NE23 ....22 D5
Lancaster Pl NE11 ....54 E1
Lancaster Rd NE11 ....54 E1
Lancaster St NE4 ....98 B1
Lancaster Terr
Chester le Street DH3 ....88 D2
Morpeth NE61 ....4 A1
Lancaster Way NE32 ....58 A1
Lancastrian Rd NE23 ....22 A5
Lancefield Ave NE6 ....56 F4
Lancet Ct NE8 ....101 C2
Lanchester Ave NE9 ....71 E3
Lanchester Cl NE10 ....72 C6
Lanchester Gn NE22 ....10 F2
Lanchester Pk NE38 ....83 E2
Lanchester St NE34 ....59 B5
Lancing Ct NE3 ....37 C7
Landscape Terr NE40 ....52 B1
Landsdowne Gdns NE62 ..11 A8
Landseer Gdns
Whiteleas NE34 ....59 D2
Gateshead NE9 ....71 B7
Landswood Terr NE21 ....68 D7
Lane Cnr NE34 ....59 C5
Lane Head NE40 ....52 C5
Lanercost NE38 ....83 D5
Lanercost Ave NE21 ....53 B2
Lanercost Dr NE5 ....54 C8
Lanercost Gdns
Gateshead NE10 ....71 C6
Throckley NE15 ....35 D2
Lanercost Pk NE23 ....22 D5
Lanercost Rd NE29 ....41 E5
Lanesborough Ct NE3 ....38 A5
Langdale Birtley DH3 ....82 E1
Whitley Bay NE25 ....31 E5
Washington NE37 ....83 C7
Langdale Cl NE12 ....39 A6
Langdale Cres NE21 ....68 B8
Langdale Dr NE23 ....21 E6
Langdale Gdns
Wallsend NE28 ....41 A5
Newcastle-upon-Tyne NE6 ..57 A6
Langdale Rd
Penshaw DH4 ....90 A8
Gateshead NE9 ....71 A5
Langdale St DH5 ....95 A2
Langdale Terr NE17 ....77 A5
Langdale Way NE36 ....74 C7
Langdon Cl NE29 ....31 F1
Langdon Rd NE5 ....36 E2
Langford Dr NE35 ....58 F2
Langham Ave NE29 ....41 C8
Langham Rd NE15 ....54 A5
Langholm Rd
Newcastle-upon-Tyne NE3 ..38 C7
East Boldon NE36 ....74 D8
Langhorn Cl NE6 ....56 B7
Langhurst SR2 ....92 E8
Langleeford Rd NE5 ....37 A4
Langley Ave
Gateshead NE10 ....72 B6
Blyth NE24 ....17 B8
Whitley Bay NE25 ....31 D3
Shiremoor NE27 ....31 A3
Hexham NE46 ....45 D4
Langley Cl NE38 ....83 B4
Langley Fst Sch NE25 ....31 D3
Langley Mere [8] NE12 ....39 D8
Langley Rd
North Shields NE29 ....41 D6
Newcastle-upon-Tyne, West Denton NE5 ....53 F8
Newcastle-upon-Tyne, Walker NE6 ....56 F6
Ashington NE63 ....6 C3
Sunderland SR3 ....86 B2
Langley St DH4 ....90 D6
Langley Tarn [1] NE29 ....42 A4
Langley Terr NE32 ....58 B3
Langport Rd SR2 ....86 D3
Langton Cl SR4 ....102 B2
Langton Ct NE20 ....25 B4
Langton Dr NE23 ....16 C2
Langton St NE8 ....101 C1
Langton Terr
Bournmoor DH4 ....89 E2
Newcastle-upon-Tyne NE7 ..39 B2
Langwell Cres NE63 ....6 C4
Langwell Terr NE61 ....4 F4
Lanivet Cl [4] SR2 ....92 F8
Lannerwood [5] NE29 ....42 A4
Lansbury Cl DH3 ....82 B6
Lansbury Dr DH3 ....82 B5
Lansbury Gdns NE10 ....72 A8
Lansbury Rd NE16 ....69 C6
Lansbury Way SR5 ....74 B1
Lansdowne SR2 ....92 E7
Lansdowne Cres NE3 ....38 C5
Lansdowne Ct NE46 ....44 F3
Lansdowne Gdns NE2 ....56 A8
Lansdowne Pl NE3 ....38 C5
Lansdowne Rd NE12 ....39 D8
Lansdowne St SR4 ....102 B3
Lansdowne Terr
North Shields NE29 ....41 F6
Newcastle-upon-Tyne NE3 ..38 C5
Lansdowne Terr E NE3 ..38 C5
Lansdowne Terr W NE29 ..41 F6
Lanthwaite Rd NE9 ....71 A4
Lanton St DH4 ....90 D6
Lapford Dr NE23 ....16 C1
Lapwing Cl Blyth NE24 ....17 E4
Washington NE38 ....82 F3
Lapwing Ct
Burnopfield NE16 ....79 C5
South Shields NE34 ....59 E5
Larch Ave
Houghton-le-Spring DH4 ....90 D1
South Shields NE34 ....60 A5
Whitburn SR6 ....61 A2
Larch Cl NE9 ....71 D2
Larch Rd NE21 ....53 D3
Larch St NE16 ....69 B2
Larch Terr DH9 ....79 A1
Larches The
Burnopfield NE16 ....79 B7
Newcastle-upon-Tyne NE4 .100 A3
Larchlea NE20 ....25 C2
Larchlea S NE20 ....25 C2
Larchwood NE38 ....83 B1
Larchwood Ave
Wide Open NE13 ....28 C5
Newcastle-upon-Tyne, Fawdon NE3 ....37 F7
Newcastle-upon-Tyne, Walkergate NE6 ....56 E8
Larchwood Dr NE63 ....6 C1
Larchwood Gdns NE11 ....70 B5
Larchwood Gr SR2 ....86 C2
Lark Rise Cl NE7 ....39 D3
Larkfield Cres DH4 ....90 A5
Larkfield Rd SR2 ....86 C3
Larkspur NE9 ....71 C4
Larkspur Com Prim Sch NE9 ....71 C4
Larkspur Rd NE16 ....69 B6
Larkspur Terr NE2 ....38 E1
Larkswood NE34 ....60 B7
Larne Cres NE9 ....71 A5
Larriston Pl NE23 ....21 F6
Lartington Gdns NE3 ....38 F5
Larwood Cl DH3 ....88 E1
Lascelles Ave NE34 ....59 E5
Laski Gdns NE10 ....72 B8
Lassells Rise NE42 ....50 D4
Latimer St NE30 ....42 D8
Latrigg Ct [25] SR3 ....91 F6
Lauderdale Ave NE28 ....40 C4
Launceston Cl NE3 ....37 D8
Launceston Dr SR3 ....91 C7
Laura St SR1 ....103 B2
Laurel Ave
Killingworth NE12 ....30 A1
Newcastle-upon-Tyne NE3 ..38 A7
Laurel Cres Burnside DH4 ..90 C3
Newcastle-upon-Tyne NE6 ..39 F1
Laurel Ct
Chester le Street DH2 ....88 B5
Laurel Ct *continued*
North Shields NE30 ....42 B5
Laurel Dr NE63 ....6 C1
Laurel End NE12 ....30 A1
Laurel Gr SR2 ....86 D2
Laurel Rd NE21 ....53 D2
Laurel St Throckley NE15 ..35 D3
Wallsend NE28 ....40 C1
Laurel Terr
Burnopfield NE16 ....78 F6
Seaton Delaval NE25 ....23 E2
Laurel Way NE40 ....52 A3
Laurel Wlk NE3 ....38 C5
Laurelwood Gdns NE11 ..70 B5
Laurens Ct NE37 ....83 D8
Lavender Ct NE63 ....6 C1
Lavender Gdns
Newcastle-upon-Tyne NE2 ..38 D1
Gateshead NE9 ....70 F6
Lavender Gr SR5 ....74 A1
Lavender La NE34 ....59 B5
Lavender Rd NE16 ....69 A6
Lavender Row NE9 ....71 B5
Lavender St [4] SR4 ....85 A6
Lavender Wlk NE31 ....57 E3
Laverick NE10 ....71 F6
Laverock Ct [12] NE6 ....56 C5
Laverock Hall Rd NE24 ..17 B3
Laverock Pl Blyth NE24 ..17 B3
[3] Newcastle-upon-Tyne NE3 ....37 D5
Lavers Rd DH3 ....82 C5
Lavington Rd NE34 ....59 E8
Lawe Rd NE33 ....42 D4
Lawn Cotts SR3 ....91 F6
Lawn Dr NE36 ....73 F6
Lawn The NE40 ....52 C6
Lawnhead Sq SR3 ....92 B6
Lawns The
Easington Lane DH5 ....95 C1
Whitburn SR6 ....75 F8
Lawnsway NE32 ....58 C1
Lawnswood DH5 ....94 F7
Lawrence Ave
Blaydon NE21 ....53 C3
Whiteleas NE34 ....59 D3
Lawrence Ct
Gateshead NE10 ....72 C8
Blaydon NE21 ....53 C3
Lawrence Hill Ct NE10 ..72 B8
Lawrence St SR1 ....103 C2
Laws St SR6 ....75 D4
Lawson Ave NE32 ....58 D3
Lawson Cres SR6 ....75 D4
Lawson Ct [6] DH2 ....88 C2
Lawson House NE4 ....54 E4
Lawson St Wallsend NE28 ..40 C1
North Shields NE29 ....42 A4
Lawson St W [8] NE29 ....42 A4
Lawson Terr
Hetton le Hole DH5 ....95 B1
Newcastle-upon-Tyne NE4 ..54 E4
Laxford DH3 ....82 D2
Laxford Ct SR3 ....92 A5
Laybourn Gdns [5] NE34 ..59 A4
Layburn Gdns NE15 ....53 E8
Laycock Gdns NE23 ....22 F1
Layfield Rd NE3 ....28 C1
Laygate NE33 ....42 C1
Laygate Lane Prim Sch NE33 ....42 C1
Laygate Pl NE33 ....42 C1
Laygate St NE33 ....42 B1
Lea Ave NE32 ....58 C2
Lea Gn DH3 ....82 E1
Lea Riggs DH4 ....94 A2
Lea View NE34 ....60 B8
Leabank NE15 ....53 D8
Leaburn Terr NE42 ....50 B2
Lead Gate NE15 ....33 C1
Lead La DH8,NE43 ....76 C6
Lead Rd
High Spen NE17,NE40 ....66 D6
Greenside NE40 ....52 B1
Stocksfield NE43 ....64 B2
Leadgate Cotts NE17 ....66 A4
Leafield Cres NE34 ....60 A8
Leagreen Ct NE3 ....38 A6
Leaholme Cres NE24 ....17 C6
Lealholm Rd NE7 ....39 A5
Leam Gdns NE10 ....72 C8
Leam La Gateshead NE10 ..72 B6
Jarrow NE32 ....58 C3
Leamington St SR4 ....102 B1
Leamside Gateshead NE10 ..71 F6
Jarrow NE32 ....58 C4
Leander Ave
Chester le Street DH3 ....88 D7
Stakeford NE62 ....11 B8
Leander Ct NE62 ....11 B8
Leander Dr NE35 ....73 E8
Leaplish NE38 ....83 F2
Leas The DH4 ....90 D3
Leasyde Wlk NE16 ....68 F5
Leatham SR2 ....92 E8
Leaway NE42 ....50 B2
Leazes Arc NE1 ....99 A2
Leazes Cres
Newcastle-upon-Tyne NE1 ..98 C2
Hexham NE46 ....44 F5
Leazes Ct NE4 ....98 B2
Leazes Dwellings NE4 ....98 B3
Leazes La
Newcastle-upon-Tyne NE1 ..99 A2
Corbridge NE45 ....47 A8

Leazes La *continued*
Hexham NE46 ....44 E5
Leazes Par NE2 ....98 B2
Leazes Park Rd NE1 ....99 A2
Leazes Parkway NE15 ....35 D1
Leazes Pk NE46 ....44 E5
Leazes Terr
Newcastle-upon-Tyne NE1 ..98 C2
Corbridge NE45 ....46 F6
Hexham NE46 ....44 F5
Leazes The
Throckley NE15 ....35 C1
Burnopfield NE16 ....78 F6
South Shields NE34 ....59 F6
Sunderland SR1 ....102 B2
Leazes View
Rowlands Gill NE39 ....67 D2
Ovington NE42 ....49 D4
Leazes Villas NE16 ....79 A6
Lecondale NE10 ....71 F5
Lecondale Ct NE10 ....71 F5
Ledbury Rd SR2 ....86 D3
Lee Cl NE38 ....84 B6
Lee St
6 Sunderland, Southwick SR5 ....75 B1
Sunderland, Fulwell SR6 ....75 D4
Lee Terr DH5 ....95 B2
Leechmere Cres SR7 ....92 F1
Leechmere Ind Est SR2 ..86 E1
Leechmere Rd SR2 ....86 D1
Leechmere View 5 SR2 ..92 F8
Leechmere Way SR2 ....92 F8
Leeds St SR6 ....75 E2
Leeholme DH5 ....94 F7
Leeming Gdns NE9 ....71 B6
Legg Ave NE22 ....11 E3
Legges Dr NE13 ....20 D6
Legion Gr NE15 ....53 F7
Legion Rd NE15 ....53 F7
Leicester Cl NE28 ....40 A5
Leicester St NE6 ....56 E5
Leicester Way NE32 ....58 A1
Leighton Rd SR2 ....86 D2
Leighton St
South Shields NE33 ....42 E2
7 Newcastle-upon-Tyne NE6 ....56 A6
Leighton Terr DH3 ....82 B5
Leith Ct NE34 ....59 C5
Leith Gdns DH9 ....79 D1
Leland Pl NE61 ....8 D7
Lemington Fst Sch NE15 .53 D6
Lemington Gdns NE5 ....54 C7
Lemington Mid Sch NE15 ....53 D8
Lemington Rd NE15 ....53 B6
Lemon St NE33 ....59 B6
Lena Ave NE25 ....31 E4
Lenin Terr NE17 ....77 C8
Lenore Terr NE40 ....52 B2
Leominster Rd SR2 ....86 D2
Leopold St NE32 ....58 B6
Lesbury Ave
Shiremoor NE27 ....30 E3
Wallsend NE28 ....40 F3
Stakeford NE62 ....6 A1
Ashington NE63 ....6 D2
Lesbury Chase NE3 ....38 B7
Lesbury Gdns NE13 ....28 C6
Lesbury Rd NE6 ....56 B8
Lesbury St
Newcastle-upon-Tyne NE15 .53 C6
North Shields NE28 ....41 C1
Lesbury Terr NE17 ....77 B8
Lesley Ct NE3 ....38 C5
Leslie Ave NE31 ....57 E5
Leslie Cl NE40 ....52 E4
Leslie Cres NE3 ....38 C3
Leslies View NE61 ....3 E2
Letch Way NE15 ....53 C7
Letchwell Villas NE12 ....29 E1
Leuchars Ct DH3 ....82 C3
Leven Ave DH2 ....88 B1
Leven Ho 10 SR3 ....92 A6
Levens Wlk NE23 ....21 E7
Levisham Cl SR3 ....92 C7
Lewis Cres SR2 ....103 C1
Lewis Dr NE4 ....54 F6
Lewis Gdns NE34 ....59 C3
Leybourne Ave NE12 ....29 D1
Leybourne Dene NE12 ....29 D2
Leybourne Hold DH3 ....82 C6
Leyburn Cl Urpeth DH2 ....81 D1
Houghton-le-Spring DH4 ....90 D1
Leyburn Dr NE7 ....39 A3
Leyburn Gr DH4 ....90 D1
Leyburn Pl DH3 ....82 B6
Leyfield Cl SR3 ....92 B5
Leyton Pl NE8 ....71 B8
Liberty Terr DH9 ....79 B2
Library NE42 ....50 D3
Liburn Cl NE36 ....74 C8
Lichfield Ave NE6 ....56 E4
Lichfield Cl
Newcastle-upon-Tyne NE3 ..37 E7
Ashington NE63 ....6 F2
Lichfield Rd SR5 ....75 A3
Lichfield Way NE32 ....58 A1
Lidcombe Cl SR3 ....92 C7
Liddell Ct SR6 ....75 F2
Liddell St
North Shields NE29,NE30 ..42 B5
Sunderland SR6 ....103 A4
Liddell Terr
Kibblesworth NE11 ....81 C6
Gateshead NE8 ....70 D8
Liddle Ct NE4 ....98 A1
Liddle Rd NE4 ....98 A1
Liddles St NE22 ....11 D3
Lieven St NE13 ....28 A4
Liffey Rd NE31 ....57 F3
Lightbourne Rd NE6 ....57 A6
Lightfoot Sports Ctr The NE6 ....56 F4
Lightwood Ave NE15 ....54 A4
Lilac Ave
11 Houghton-le-Spring DH5 .94 E8
Longbenton NE12 ....39 F8
Blyth NE24 ....17 D8
South Shields NE34 ....60 A5
New Silksworth SR3 ....92 B8
Whitburn SR6 ....60 F3
Lilac Cl NE5 ....36 B4
Lilac Cres NE16 ....79 A6
Lilac Ct Ellington NE61 ....1 E6
Ashington NE63 ....6 C1
Lilac Gdns
Whickham NE16 ....69 A6
Washington NE38 ....83 C1
Gateshead NE9 ....70 F6
Cleadon SR6 ....60 A2
Lilac Gr
Chester le Street DH2 ....88 A5
Sunderland SR6 ....75 D3
Lilac Rd NE6 ....40 A1
Lilac Sq DH4 ....89 E3
Lilac St SR4 ....85 A6
Lilac Wlk NE31 ....57 E3
Lilburn Cl 5 NE6 ....56 C4
Lilburn Gdns NE3,NE7 ....38 F4
Lilburn Pl SR5 ....75 A1
Lilburn Rd NE27 ....30 E2
Lilburn St NE29 ....41 F5
Lilburne Cl SR1 ....103 B3
Lilian Ave Wallsend NE28 ..40 A1
Sunderland SR2 ....92 E8
Lilley Gr SR5 ....74 B1
Lilley Terr NE39 ....67 F3
Lilleycroft NE39 ....67 F2
Lily Ave
Newcastle-upon-Tyne NE2 ..38 E1
Bedlington NE22 ....16 B8
Lily Bank NE28 ....40 C2
Lily Cl NE21 ....53 A2
Lily Cres
Newcastle-upon-Tyne NE2 ..38 E1
Whitburn SR6 ....60 F3
Lily Est NE15 ....35 D3
Lily Gdns DH9 ....78 E1
Lily St SR4 ....102 B3
Lily Terr Newbottle DH4 ....90 D4
Newcastle-upon-Tyne NE5 ..37 A3
Lilywhite Terr DH5 ....95 B1
Lime Ave DH4 ....90 C1
Lime Gr Ryton NE40 ....52 C5
Prudhoe NE42 ....50 B3
Lime St
Newcastle-upon-Tyne NE1, NE6 ....56 A5
Throckley NE15 ....35 D3
Blaydon NE21 ....53 D1
Sunderland SR4 ....102 B3
Limecroft NE32 ....58 C1
Limekiln Ct NE28 ....40 D2
Limekiln Rd NE28 ....40 D2
Limes Ave NE24 ....12 D1
Limes The Penshaw DH4 ....90 B8
Stannington NE61 ....14 C3
Sunderland SR2 ....86 D4
Limestone La NE20 ....25 B7
Limetree NE38 ....83 E2
Limetrees Gdns NE9 ....70 F7
Limewood Ct NE2 ....98 B4
Limewood Gr NE13 ....28 B5
Linacre Cl NE3 ....37 B6
Linbridge Dr NE5 ....36 E1
Linburn NE38 ....89 B8
Lincoln Ave
Wallsend NE28 ....40 A3
New Silksworth SR3 ....92 A8
Lincoln Cres DH5 ....94 F4
Lincoln Ct NE31 ....57 D5
Lincoln Gn NE3 ....28 C1
Lincoln Rd
Cramlington NE23 ....16 C1
South Shields NE34 ....60 B7
Lincoln St
Gateshead NE8 ....101 B1
Sunderland SR4 ....85 F7
Lincoln Way NE32 ....58 B1
Lindale Ave NE16 ....69 A5
Lindale Rd NE4 ....54 E8
Lindean Pl NE23 ....21 F6
Linden NE9 ....71 D4
Linden Ave
Newcastle-upon-Tyne, Gosforth NE3 ....38 C4
Newcastle-upon-Tyne, Fenham NE4 ....54 D7
Linden Cl NE62 ....11 A8
Linden Gdns SR2 ....86 C3
Linden Gr
Houghton-le-Spring DH4 ....94 D8
1 Dunston NE11 ....70 A8
Linden Rd
Longbenton NE12 ....39 D7
Blaydon NE21 ....53 D2
Seaton Delaval NE25 ....23 B3
Newcastle-upon-Tyne NE3 ..38 C4
Sunderland SR2 ....86 C3
Linden Sch NE12 ....39 D8
Linden Terr
Longbenton NE12 ....39 D6
Whitley Bay NE26 ....32 A5
Springwell NE9 ....71 F1
Linden Way
Ponteland NE20 ....25 C3
Ellington NE61 ....1 D5
Gateshead NE9 ....71 D2
Lindfield Ave NE5 ....37 C1
Lindisfarne
Washington NE38 ....83 C4
Ryhope SR2 ....92 E6
Lindisfarne Ave DH3 ....88 D3
Lindisfarne Castle (N.T.)* TD15 ....105 ??
Lindisfarne Cl
Chester le Street DH2 ....88 A1
Burnside DH4 ....90 C2
Newcastle-upon-Tyne, Jesmond NE2 ....38 F2
Newcastle-upon-Tyne, West Denton NE5 ....36 F1
Morpeth NE61 ....9 A6
Pegswood NE61 ....5 A4
Lindisfarne Com Prim Sch NE8 ....56 A2
Lindisfarne Ct NE32 ....58 F6
Lindisfarne Dr NE8 ....101 C2
Lindisfarne Ho 2 NE63 ....6 F2
Lindisfarne La NE61 ....9 A6
Lindisfarne Pl NE28 ....40 D3
Lindisfarne Priory* TD15 ....105 ??
Lindisfarne Rd
Newcastle-upon-Tyne NE2 ..38 F2
Hebburn NE31 ....57 E3
Jarrow NE32 ....58 D4
Lindisfarne Recess NE32 .58 D4
Lindisfarne Terr NE30 ....42 A7
Lindisfarne Wlk NE62 ....10 E7
Lindom Ave DH3 ....88 D3
Lindrick Ct NE10 ....72 C7
Lindsay Ave NE24 ....17 C8
Lindsay Cl SR2 ....103 B1
Lindsay Ct SR6 ....60 F2
Lindsay Rd SR2 ....103 B1
Lindsay St DH5 ....95 B5
Lindsey Cl NE23 ....21 E6
Lindum Rd NE9 ....70 F8
Linfield SR2 ....92 E7
Lingcrest NE9 ....71 C5
Lingdale Ave SR6 ....75 E6
Lingey Gdns NE10 ....72 C8
Lingey House Prim Schs NE10 ....72 B7
Lingey La NE10 ....72 B7
Lingfield DH5 ....94 F7
Lingholme DH2 ....88 A4
Lingmell NE37 ....83 B6
Lingshaw NE10 ....72 B7
Lingside NE32 ....58 C1
Linhope Ave NE3 ....37 F7
Linhope Fst Sch NE5 ....36 F2
Linhope Rd NE5 ....36 F2
Link Ave NE22 ....10 D1
Link Rd Hazlerigg NE13 ....28 A4
Newcastle-upon-Tyne NE5 ..37 E2
Link The NE46 ....44 F5
Links Ave
Whitley Bay NE26 ....31 F7
Tynemouth NE30 ....32 C2
Links Ct NE26 ....32 A7
Links Gn NE3 ....38 D6
Links Rd Blyth NE24 ....17 F4
Seaton Sluice NE24 ....18 A2
Tynemouth NE30 ....32 C2
Links The NE26 ....32 A7
Links View Blyth NE24 ....17 C4
Ashington NE63 ....12 A8
Links Wlk NE5 ....36 F2
Linkway NE32 ....58 D1
Linley Hill NE16 ....68 E4
Linnel Dr NE15 ....53 E7
Linnet Cl NE38 ....83 A3
Linnet Ct NE63 ....6 B2
Linnet Gr SR5 ....74 C1
Linnetsfield NE6 ....56 F8
Linney Gdns NE34 ....59 A4
Linnheads NE42 ....50 B1
Linshiels Gdns 1 NE63 ....6 F2
Linskell SR2 ....92 E8
Linskill Terr NE30 ....42 B7
Linskill Pl
Newcastle-upon-Tyne NE3 ..37 F3
North Shields NE30 ....42 B7
Linskill PRU NE30 ....42 B7
Linskill St NE30 ....42 B5
Linskill Terr NE30 ....42 B7
Linslade Wlk NE23 ....21 F6
Lintfort NE38 ....88 E7
Linthorpe Ct NE34 ....59 A5
Linthorpe Rd
Newcastle-upon-Tyne NE3 ..38 C7
Tynemouth NE30 ....32 B1
Linton NE12 ....29 D5
Linton Fst Sch NE61 ....1 A3
Linton Rd
Whitley Bay NE26 ....24 E1
Gateshead NE9 ....70 F3
Lintonville Rd NE63 ....6 C4
Lintonville Terr NE63 ....6 C5
Lintz Green La NE16,NE39 .78 C6
Lintz La NE16 ....78 E4
Lintz Terr NE16 ....78 F6
Lintzford Gdns
Newcastle-upon-Tyne NE15 .53 E7
Rowlands Gill NE39 ....78 D8
Lintzford La NE39 ....67 B1
Lintzford Rd
Hamsterley Mill NE39 ....78 C7
Rowlands Gill NE39 ....78 C7
Linum Pl NE4 ....54 E8
Linwood Pl NE3 ....28 C1
Lion Wlk NE29 ....42 A3
Lisa Ave SR4 ....85 A5
Lisburn Terr SR4 ....102 A3
Lish Ave NE26 ....32 C4
Lishman Terr NE40 ....52 A4
Lisle Gr NE28 ....41 A3
Lisle Rd NE34 ....60 A6
Lisle St
Newcastle-upon-Tyne NE1 ..99 A2
Wallsend NE28 ....40 B2
Lismor Terr NE9 ....71 F1
Lismore Ave NE33 ....59 D7
Lismore Pl NE15 ....54 D6
Lister Ave Dunston NE11 ..54 F1
Greenside NE40 ....66 F8
Lister Cl DH5 ....94 D6
Lister St NE15 ....53 F5
Listers La NE9 ....71 A8
Litchfield Cres 2 NE21 ..53 B1
Litchfield La NE21 ....53 B1
Litchfield St 1 NE21 ....53 B1
Litchfield Terr 3 NE21 ..53 B1
Little Bedford St NE29, NE30 ....42 B5
Little Dene NE2 ....38 D3
Little Villiers St SR1 ....103 B3
Little Way NE15 ....54 B4
Littleburn Cl DH4 ....90 C2
Littledene NE9 ....70 F7
Littletown La DH6 ....96 D3
Litton Ct 14 SR3 ....91 F6
Littondale NE28 ....39 F4
Liverpool St NE1 ....99 A2
Livingstone Pl 8 NE33 ..42 C4
Livingstone Rd SR1 ....102 C3
Livingstone St 2 NE33 ..42 D4
Livingstone View NE30 ..42 C7
Lizard La NE34,SR6 ....60 E4
Lloyd Ave DH5 ....94 C4
Lloyd Ct NE11 ....54 E2
Lloyd St 5 NE40 ....51 F3
Lobban Ave NE31 ....57 D3
Lobelia Ave NE10 ....56 B2
Lobelia Cl NE5 ....36 B3
Lobley Gdns NE11 ....70 A6
Lobley Hill Prim Sch NE11 ....70 A6
Lobley Hill Rd NE11,NE8 ..70 C7
Lobleyhill Rd
Byermoor NE16 ....79 D8
Sunniside NE16 ....79 D8
Local Ave DH6 ....96 C1
Locarno Pl NE64 ....7 E4
Lochcraig Pl NE23 ....21 F6
Lochfield Gdns NE11 ....81 C6
Lochmaben Terr SR5 ....75 D2
Lockerbie Gdns NE15 ....53 E7
Lockerbie Rd NE23 ....21 F6
Lockhaugh Rd NE39 ....68 A4
Locksley Cl NE29 ....31 B1
Locomotion Way
Killingworth NE12 ....29 B5
North Shields NE29 ....42 A4
Locomotive Ct NE42 ....50 C2
Lodge Cl NE39 ....78 A5
Lodges Rd The NE9 ....70 F3
Lodgeside Mdw SR3 ....92 B5
Lodore Ct 5 SR3 ....91 F6
Lodore Gr NE32 ....58 D3
Lodore Rd NE2 ....38 D3
Lofthill 6 SR3 ....91 E5
Logan Rd NE6 ....39 F1
Logan St DH5 ....95 A3
Logan Terr DH6 ....97 E8
Lola St NE13 ....27 F4
Lombard Dr DH3 ....88 D7
Lombard St
Newcastle-upon-Tyne NE1 .101 B4
Sunderland SR1 ....103 B3
Lomond Cl NE38 ....83 B3
Lomond Ct 11 SR3 ....92 A6
Lomond Pl DH2 ....88 B1
London Ave NE37 ....72 B1
Londonderry St SR3 ....92 A7
Londonderry Terr SR3 ....92 B7
Londonderry Tower SR1 ....103 B3
Londonderry Way DH4 ..90 A7
Long Bank Birtley DH3 ....82 C7
Gateshead NE9 ....71 C1
Long Close Rd NE39 ....77 F5
Long Crag NE37 ....83 A5
Long Dr NE61 ....8 F5
Long Gair NE21 ....68 A8
Long Headlam 10 NE6 ....56 C6
Long Meadow Cl NE40 ....52 A3
Long Pk NE64 ....7 D4
Long Ridge Rd
Blaydon NE21,NE40 ....52 D2
Greenside NE21,NE40 ....52 D2
Long Rigg NE16 ....54 A2
Long Row NE33 ....42 B4
Long Row Cl NE40 ....66 F8
Longacre
Houghton-le-Spring DH4 ....94 C8
Washington NE38 ....83 E1
Longbenton Com Coll NE12 ....39 C7
Longbenton Sta NE12 ....39 A5
Longborough Ct NE7 ....39 A4
Longclose Bank DH8,DH9, NE17,NE39 ....77 E3
Longdean Cl NE31 ....57 C5
Longdean Pk DH3 ....88 D
Longfellow St DH5 ....94 E
Longfield Cl NE34 ....59 D
Longfield Rd SR6 ....75 D
Longfield Terr NE6 ....57 A
Longframlington Gardens* NE65 ....118 E
Longhirst Gateshead NE10 .72 A
Killingworth NE12 ....29 D
Newcastle-upon-Tyne NE5 ..36 F
Longhirst Dr NE13 ....28 B
Longhirst Rd NE61 ....4 F
Longhirst Village NE61 ....4 F
Longlands Dr DH5 ....94 E
Longleat Gdns
10 South Shields NE33 ....42 D
Pegswood NE61 ....4 E
Longley St NE4 ....98 A
Longmeadows
Ponteland NE20 ....25 B
Sunderland SR3 ....91 C
Longniddry NE37 ....72 C
Longniddry Ct NE9 ....70 E
Longridge NE21 ....53 A
Longridge Ave
Washington NE38 ....83 B
Newcastle-upon-Tyne NE7 ..39 D
Longridge Dr NE26 ....31 E
Longridge Sq SR2 ....86 D
Longridge Way
Bedlington NE22 ....11 A
Cramlington NE23 ....21 F
Longrigg NE10 ....72 A
Longrigg Rd NE11 ....54 B
Longriggs The NE44 ....62 E
Longshank La DH3 ....82 A
Longstaff Gdns NE34 ....58 F
Longston Ave NE30 ....32 B
Longstone Ct NE12 ....29 E
Longstone Lighthouse* 109 F
Longstone Sq NE5 ....36 D
Longwood Cl NE16 ....69 B
Lonnen Ave NE4 ....54 D
Lonnen Dr NE16 ....69 A
Lonnen The
South Shields NE34 ....60 B
Ryton NE40 ....52 E
Lonsdale DH3 ....82 E1
Lonsdale Ave Blyth NE24 ..16 E8
Sunderland SR6 ....75 E7
Lonsdale Ct NE34 ....59 A4
Lonsdale Gdns NE28 ....41 A4
Lonsdale Rd SR6 ....75 E2
Lonsdale Terr NE2 ....38 E2
Loraine Terr NE15 ....53 C6
Lord Blyton Prim Sch NE34 ....58 F5
Lord Byrons Wlk SR7 ....93 B1
Lord Gort Cl 1 SR5 ....75 A1
Lord Lawson of Beamish Comp Sch DH3 ....82 D3
Lord Nelson St NE33, NE34 ....59 B6
Lord St
Newcastle-upon-Tyne NE1 .100 C4
South Shields NE33 ....42 E1
New Silksworth SR3 ....92 B7
Lordenshaw NE5 ....36 F2
Lorne St DH5 ....97 B8
Lorne Terr SR2 ....103 A1
Lorrain Rd NE34 ....59 D2
Lort Ho NE2 ....99 C2
Lorton Ave NE30 ....32 A2
Lorton Rd NE9 ....71 A4
Losh Terr NE6 ....56 F5
Lossiemouth Rd NE29 ....41 C5
Lothian Cl DH3 ....82 D1
Lothian Ct NE5 ....37 C3
Lotus Cl NE5 ....36 B3
Lotus Pl NE4 ....54 D7
Loudon St NE34 ....59 C5
Lough Ct NE9 ....71 B5
Loughborough Ave
Tynemouth NE30 ....32 C1
Sunderland SR2 ....86 C3
Loughbrow Pk NE46 ....45 B2
Loughrigg Ave NE23 ....21 F6
Louie Terr NE9 ....71 A5
Louis Ave SR6 ....75 D3
Louise Terr DH3 ....88 C3
Loup St NE21 ....53 C3
Louvain Terr
Hetton le Hole DH5 ....95 A5
Guide Post NE62 ....10 F7
Louvain Terr W DH5 ....95 A5
Lovaine Ave
Whitley Bay NE25 ....32 A4
8 North Shields NE29 ....42 A5
Lovaine Flats NE1 ....99 B2
Lovaine Pl NE29 ....42 A5
Lovaine Pl W 6 NE29 ....41 F5
Lovaine Row NE30 ....42 E8
Lovaine St NE15 ....52 E8
Lovaine Terr NE29 ....42 A6
Love Ave NE23 ....29 B7
Love Avenue Cotts NE23 ..29 B8
Love La NE1 ....99 C1
Loveless Gdns NE10 ....72 B8
Lovett Wlk NE8 ....100 C2
Low Burswell NE46 ....44 F5
Low Chare DH3 ....88 D3
Low Cl NE42 ....50 E3
Low Downs Rd DH5 ....95 A6
Low Farm NE61 ....1 D4
Low Fell Jun & Inf Sch NE9 ....70 F5
Low Flatts Rd DH3 ....88 C6
Low Fold NE6 ....56 B5

Low Friar St NE1 .99 A1
Low Gate Prim Sch NE46 .44 A4
Low Gosforth Ct NE3 .28 D1
Low Haugh NE20 .25 F7
Low Heworth La NE10 .56 F1
Low La NE34 .59 C5
Low Leam Ct NE5 .36 F1
Low Main Pl NE23 .22 B6
Low Mdw SR6 .60 A1
Low Quay NE24 .17 F8
Low Reach NE10 .57 A2
Low Row Blaydon NE40 .52 E3
Sunderland SR1 .102 C2
Low St SR1 .103 B3
Low Stobhill NE61 .9 A7
Low Well Gdns NE10 .56 E1
Low West Ave NE39 .67 D1
Lowbiggin NE5 .36 E5
Lowdham Ave NE29 .41 E4
Lowdon Ct NE2 .98 C3
Lower Crone St NE27 .30 F4
Lower Dundas St SR6 .103 A4
Lower Rudyerd St NE29 .42 B5
Lowerson Ave DH4 .90 A5
Loweswater Ave
Chester le Street DH2 .88 B1
Easington Lane DH5 .97 C8
Loweswater Cl NE24 .11 F1
Loweswater Rd
Newcastle-upon-Tyne NE5 .54 B8
Gateshead NE9 .71 A4
Loweswood Cl NE7 .39 A1
Lowfield Terr NE6 .56 F4
Lowfield Wlk NE16 .69 A6
Lowgate NE15 .35 D1
Lowick Cl DH3 .82 D1
Lowick Ct NE3 .38 E4
Lowland Cl SR3 .92 A5
Lownds Terr NE6 .56 E6
Lowrey's La NE9 .70 F5
Lowry Gdns NE34 .59 D2
Lowry Rd SR6 .75 E5
Lowther Ave DH2 .88 B2
Lowther Cl NE63 .6 F1
Lowther Sq NE23 .21 E6
Lowthian Cres NE6 .56 E5
Lowthian Terr NE38 .83 F4
Lucknow St SR1 .103 C3
Lucock St NE34 .59 B5
Lucy St
4 Chester le Street DH3 .88 C4
Blaydon NE21 .53 D3
Ludlow Ave NE29 .41 E8
Ludlow Ct NE3 .37 E7
Ludlow Dr NE25 .31 B5
Ludlow Rd SR2 .86 D3
Luffness Dr NE34 .59 F3
Luke's La NE10,NE31 .57 F1
Lukes Lane Prim Sch
NE31 .58 A3
Lulsgate SR5 .74 A1
Lulworth Ave NE32 .58 E5
Lulworth Ct SR3 .91 C7
Lulworth Gdns SR2 .86 C3
Lumden's La NE61 .8 F8
Lumley Ave
Whickham NE16 .54 B1
South Shields NE34 .60 B6
Lumley Cl
Chester le Street DH2 .88 B3
Washington NE38 .83 B5
Lumley Cres DH4 .90 C4
Lumley Ct Bedlington NE22 .11 C2
Hebburn NE31 .57 F8
Sunderland SR3 .91 C7
Lumley Gdns
Burnopfield NE16 .78 E5
Gateshead NE8 .56 B1
Lumley New Rd DH3,DH4 .89 C1
Lumley St Newbottle DH4 .90 D2
Sunderland SR4 .102 B2
Lumley Terr
Chester le Street DH3 .88 D2
Jarrow NE32 .58 C4
1 Ryhope SR2 .92 F6
Lumley Tower SR1 .103 B3
Lumley Wlk NE11 .100 A1
Lumley's La NE43 .65 B6
Lumsden's La NE61 .3 F1
Lune Gn NE32 .58 C2
Lunedale Ave SR6 .75 C5
Lunesdale St DH5 .95 A2
Lupin Cl NE5 .36 C4
Luss Ave NE32 .58 E3
Lutterworth Cl NE12 .39 B6
Lutterworth Dr NE12 .39 A6
Lutterworth Rd
Longbenton NE12 .39 B5
Sunderland SR2 .86 C3
Luxembourg Rd SR4 .85 D7
Lychgate Ct NE8 .101 C3
Lydbury Cl NE23 .16 C1
Lydcott NE38 .84 B5
Lyden Gate NE9 .71 A3
Lydford Ct Newbottle DH4 .90 C3
Newcastle-upon-Tyne NE3 .37 C6
Lydford Way DH3 .82 D3
Lydney Cl NE15 .35 C1
Lyn-Thorpe Gr SR6 .75 E3
Lyncroft NE63 .6 C2
Lyncroft Rd NE29 .41 E6
Lyndale NE23 .16 C1
Lynden Gdns NE5 .37 A3
Lynden Rd SR2 .92 F8
Lyndhurst Ave
Chester le Street DH3 .88 C6
Newcastle-upon-Tyne NE2 .38 E2
Gateshead NE9 .71 A4
Lyndhurst Cl NE21 .68 A8
Lyndhurst Cres NE9 .71 A4
Lyndhurst Dr NE9 .71 A3
Lyndhurst Gdns NE2 .38 D2
Lyndhurst Gn NE9 .70 F4
Lyndhurst Gr NE9 .71 A4
Lyndhurst Rd
Longbenton NE12 .39 D7
Whitley Bay NE25 .31 E5
Ashington NE63 .6 F1
Lyndhurst St 3 NE33 .42 D2
Lyndhurst Terr
1 Whickham NE16 .54 A1
Sunderland SR4 .85 E8
Lyndon Cl NE36 .74 B7
Lyndon Dr NE36 .74 B7
Lyndon Gr NE36 .74 B7
Lyndon Wlk NE24 .16 F8
Lyne Terr NE61 .1 F3
Lynemouth Fst Sch NE61 .2 B3
Lynemouth Rd NE61 .1 D4
Lynfield NE26 .31 E7
Lynfield Ct NE5 .37 B3
Lynfield Pl NE5 .37 B3
Lynford Gdns SR2 .86 C3
Lyngrove SR2 .92 F8
Lynholm Gr NE12 .39 D8
Lynmouth Pl NE7 .39 B3
Lynmouth Rd
North Shields NE29 .41 C5
Gateshead NE9 .70 F3
Lynn Rd Wallsend NE28 .40 A1
Tynemouth NE29 .41 D7
Lynn St
Chester le Street DH3 .88 C2
Blyth NE24 .17 D7
Lynndale Ave NE24 .17 A7
Lynnholm Cl NE7 .39 B2
Lynnholme Gdns
4 Gateshead NE9 .70 F8
Gateshead, Deckham NE9 .71 A8
Lynnwood Ave NE4 .54 F5
Lynnwood Terr NE4 .54 F5
Lynthorpe SR2 .92 F8
Lynton Ave NE32 .58 E5
Lynton Ct Newbottle DH4 .90 C3
Newcastle-upon-Tyne NE5 .37 B3
Lynton Pl NE5 .37 B3
Lynton Way NE5 .37 B3
Lynwood Ave
Blaydon NE21 .53 C3
Newbiggin-by-the-Sea NE64 .7 D5
Sunderland SR4 .85 A2
Lynwood Cl NE20 .25 C2
Lyon St NE31 .57 D7
Lyons Ave DH5 .95 B2
Lyons Cotts DH5 .95 B2
Lyons La DH5 .95 C1
Lyons The DH5 .95 B2
Lyric Cl NE29 .41 C8
Lysdon Ave NE25 .23 D6
Lyster Cl SR7 .92 E1
Lytchfield NE10 .72 B7
Lytham Cl
Cramlington NE23 .21 E6
Wallsend NE28 .40 E7
Washington NE37 .72 C2
Lytham Dr NE25 .31 D5
Lytham Gn NE10 .57 B2
Lytham Grange DH4 .90 A4
Lytham Pl NE6 .56 E5
Lythe Way NE12 .39 C6

M

Mabel St NE21 .53 C3
Macadam St NE8 .70 D7
Macdonald Rd NE4 .54 D4
Maclynn Cl SR3 .91 E6
Macmerry Cl SR5 .84 F8
Macmillan Gdns NE10 .72 A8
Maddison Ct SR1 .103 C3
Maddison Gdns NE23 .22 E1
Maddison St NE24 .17 E8
Maddox Rd NE12 .39 D6
Madeira Ave NE26 .31 F7
Madeira Cl NE5 .36 C4
Madeira Terr 8 NE33 .42 D1
Madras St NE34 .59 A4
Mafeking Pl NE29 .31 B1
Mafeking St
Whitley Bay NE26 .32 B5
Newcastle-upon-Tyne NE6 .56 F3
5 Gateshead NE9 .71 A8
Sunderland SR4 .85 F7
Magdalene Ct NE2 .98 B4
Magdelene Pl SR4 .85 F7
Magenta Cres NE5 .36 C4
Magnolia Ct NE4 .54 D7
Magnolia Dr NE63 .6 C1
Magpie Ct NE63 .6 B2
Mahogany Row DH9 .80 D1
Maiden La NE40 .52 A2
Maiden Law DH4 .94 A7
Maiden St NE4 .100 B3
Maiden's Wlk NE46 .45 C4
Maidens Croft NE46 .44 F4
Maidstone Cl SR3 .91 D6
Maidstone Terr DH4 .90 D4
Main Cres NE28 .39 F4
Main Rd Dinnington NE13 .27 C6
Newcastle-upon-Tyne NE3 .37 B6
Ryton NE40 .52 B5
Wylam NE41 .51 B6
Main St Ponteland NE20 .25 E6
Crawcrook NE40 .51 F4
Corbridge NE45 .47 A5
Main St N NE23 .22 F1
Main St S NE23 .22 F1
Mains Park Rd DH3 .88 D3
Mains Pl NE61 .3 F1
Mainsforth Terr SR2 .103 C1
Mainsforth Terr W SR2 .86 E4
Mainstone Cl NE23 .22 A6
Maitland Terr NE64 .7 D4
Makendon St NE31 .57 E7
Makepeace Terr NE9 .71 F1
Malaburn Way 2 SR5 .75 A1
Malaga Cl NE5 .36 B4
Malaya Dr NE6 .57 B5
Malcolm Ct NE25 .31 D4
Malcolm St NE6 .56 A6
Malden Cl NE23 .21 F6
Maling Pk SR4 .85 B7
Maling St NE6 .56 A5
Malings Cl SR1 .103 C2
Mallard Cl
Washington NE38 .82 F4
Ashington NE63 .11 D8
Mallard Ct NE12 .29 C4
Mallard Lodge 11 NE10 .71 D8
Mallard Way
Fence Houses DH4 .94 B7
Blyth NE24 .17 F3
Shiremoor NE28 .41 A6
Mallowburn Cres NE3 .37 C4
Malmo Cl NE29 .41 B5
Malone Gdns DH3 .82 D6
Malory Pl NE8 .101 C2
Maltby Cl
Washington NE38 .83 D4
2 Silksworth SR3 .91 E5
Maltings The SR3 .92 C7
Maltkiln NE46 .45 A4
Malton Cl
Newcastle-upon-Tyne NE15 .53 E6
Blyth NE24 .17 B7
Malton Cres NE29 .41 F4
Malton Ct NE32 .58 A7
Malton Gdns NE28 .40 B4
Malton Gn NE9 .71 B1
Malvern Ave DH2 .88 B2
Malvern Cl NE63 .6 F1
Malvern Ct Dunston NE11 .70 A6
Newcastle-upon-Tyne NE15 .53 B7
Cleadon SR6 .59 F1
Malvern Gdns
Dunston NE11 .70 A7
Sunderland SR6 .75 E3
Malvern Rd
Seaton Sluice NE26 .24 D5
Wallsend NE28 .41 A3
Tynemouth NE29 .41 E8
Washington NE38 .83 B3
Malvern St NE33 .59 C7
Malvins Close Fst Sch
NE24 .17 C7
Malvins Close Rd NE24 .17 C7
Malvins Rd NE24 .17 B8
Manchester St NE61 .3 F1
Mandale Cres NE30 .32 A3
Mandarin Cl NE5 .36 C5
Mandarin Lodge 8 NE10 .71 D8
Mandarin Way NE38 .84 C6
Mandela Cl SR1 .103 C3
Mandela Way NE11 .54 D2
Mandeville NE37 .83 F8
Manet Gdns NE34 .59 D4
Mangrove Cl NE5 .36 C4
Manila St SR2 .86 E4
Manisty Ho NE4 .54 E4
Manley View NE63 .7 A3
Manners Gdns NE25 .23 C4
Manningford Cl NE23 .22 A5
Manningford Dr SR3 .91 E5
Manor Ave Newburn NE15 .52 F8
Longbenton NE7 .39 C5
Manor Chare NE1 .99 B1
Manor Cl
Newcastle-upon-Tyne NE3 .38 D5
Riding Mill NE44 .62 F7
Manor Ct NE33 .42 E1
Manor Dr
Newbiggin-by-the-Sea NE64 .7 E5
Longbenton NE7 .39 C5
Manor Gdns
Gateshead NE10 .72 C8
Longbenton NE7 .39 C5
Manor Gr
New Herrington DH4 .90 F7
Newburn NE15 .52 F7
Longbenton NE7 .39 C5
Manor House Cl 1 NE6 .56 C5
Manor House Farm Cotts
NE5 .37 D4
Manor House Rd NE2 .38 F1
Manor Pk
Washington NE37 .83 D8
Corbridge NE45 .46 F6
Manor Pl NE7 .39 C5
Manor Rd Medomsley DH8 .77 C1
Tynemouth NE30 .42 D7
Washington NE37 .83 D8
Longbenton NE7 .39 C5
Manor Terr Blaydon NE21 .53 A1
Winlaton Mill NE21 .68 C7
Manor View
High Pittington DH6 .96 B4
Washington NE37 .83 E8
Newbiggin-by-the-Sea NE64 .7 E5
Manor View E 2 NE37 .83 E8
Manor Wlk NE7 .39 C5
Manorfields NE12 .39 D6
Manors Sta NE1 .99 B1
Manors Sta (Metro) NE1 .99 B1
Manors The NE42 .50 E3
Manorway
Tynemouth NE30 .42 D8
Hedworth NE32 .58 C2
Mansel Terr NE24 .16 E7
Mansell Pl NE3 .37 E3
Mansfield Cres SR6 .75 E2
Mansfield Ct NE36 .74 A7
Mansfield Pl NE4 .98 B1
Mansfield St NE4 .98 B1
Mansion Ho NE36 .74 A7
Manston Cl SR3 .91 D6
Manx Sq SR5 .75 B3
Maple Ave Dunston NE11 .70 A7
Whitley Bay NE25 .31 F4
New Silksworth SR3 .92 B8
Maple Cl
Newcastle-upon-Tyne NE15 .53 E6
Bedlington NE22 .10 F1
Maple Cres NE24 .16 F8
Maple Ct Killingworth NE12 .29 C4
New Hartley NE25 .23 D6
Maple Gr
Gateshead, Felling NE10 .71 E8
South Shields NE34 .59 F5
Prudhoe NE42 .50 B2
Gateshead, Saltwell NE8 .70 E7
Whitburn SR6 .60 F1
Maple Rd NE21 .53 C2
Maple Row NE11 .54 B2
Maple St Jarrow NE32 .58 A7
Newcastle-upon-Tyne NE4 .100 B4
Ashington NE63 .6 D3
Maple Terr
Shiney Row DH4 .90 A5
Burnopfield NE16 .78 F6
Newcastle-upon-Tyne NE4 .100 B4
Maplebeck Cl SR3 .91 D5
Mapledene NE38 .83 E2
Mapledene Rd NE3 .37 F6
Maplewood
Chester le Street DH2 .88 B4
Newcastle-upon-Tyne NE6 .56 E8
Maplewood Ave SR5 .74 F3
Maplewood Cres NE38 .83 B1
Maplewood Dr DH6 .97 F3
Maplewood Sch SR5 .74 E3
Maplewood St DH4 .89 E1
Mapperley Dr NE15 .53 E7
Marblet Ct NE11 .70 B7
Marbury Cl SR3 .91 D6
March Rd NE23 .29 B7
March Terr NE13 .27 A7
Marchburn La NE44 .62 E7
Marcia Ave SR6 .75 D3
Marconi Way NE11 .54 B2
Marcross Cl NE15 .36 B2
Marcross Dr SR3 .91 E5
Mardale NE37 .83 B7
Mardale Gdns NE9 .71 A3
Mardale Rd NE5 .37 B1
Mardale St DH5 .95 A2
Marden Ave NE30 .32 C3
Marden Bridge Mid Sch
NE25 .32 A4
Marden Cl NE61 .8 D7
Marden Cres NE26 .32 C4
Marden Ct NE26 .24 B7
Marden Farm Dr NE30 .32 B3
Marden High Sch NE30 .32 B1
Marden Rd NE26 .32 A4
Marden Rd S NE25 .32 B4
Marden Terr NE30 .32 C3
Mare Cl NE23 .23 A3
Mareburn Cres NE10 .71 E8
Maree Cl SR3 .91 E5
Margaret Alice St SR4 .85 E7
Margaret Collins House
NE6 .56 D6
Margaret Cotts NE25 .31 F2
Margaret Dr NE12 .40 A8
Margaret Gr NE34 .59 A5
Margaret Rd NE26 .32 C4
Margaret St SR2 .87 A2
Margaret Sutton Sch The
NE34 .59 D6
Margaret Terr
Penshaw DH4 .90 C6
Tanfield Lea DH9 .79 C1
Rowlands Gill NE39 .67 C1
Margate St SR3 .92 A8
Marguerite Ct SR4 .102 B3
Maria St
Newcastle-upon-Tyne NE4 .54 E4
New Silksworth SR3 .92 A7
Marian Ct NE8 .101 A1
Marian Dr NE10 .57 C3
Marian Way
Ponteland NE20 .25 B2
South Shields NE34 .59 F3
Marie Curie Dr NE4 .54 F4
Marigold Ave NE10 .56 B2
Marigold Cres DH4 .89 E3
Marigold Ct SR4 .102 B3
Marigold Wlk NE34 .59 B5
Marina Ave SR6 .75 D3
Marina Ct SR6 .75 D3
Marina Dr
Whitley Bay NE25 .31 C4
South Shields NE33 .42 E3
Marina Gr SR6 .75 D3
Marina Terr
8 Ryhope SR2 .92 F6
Whitburn SR6 .60 F1
Marina View
Wallsend NE28 .40 F2
Hebburn NE31 .57 D6
Marine App NE33 .42 E2
Marine Ave NE26 .31 F5
Marine Dr Jarrow NE31 .58 A3
Sunderland SR2 .93 A8
Marine Gdns NE26 .32 A6
Marine Park Fst Sch
NE26 .32 A6
Marine Park Jun Mix & Inf
Sch NE33 .42 D3
Marine St NE64 .7 E5
Marine Terr NE24 .17 E7
Marine View NE26 .24 C7
Marine Wlk SR6 .75 F2
Mariner Sq SR1 .103 C4
Mariners Point 8 NE30 .42 D7
Mariners Wharf NE1 .56 A5
Mariners' Cotts NE33 .42 E3
Mariners' La NE30 .42 C7
Marion St SR2 .86 E4
Maritime St SR1 .103 A2
Maritime Terr SR1 .102 C2
Maritme Pl 3 NE61 .3 F1
Marius Ave NE15 .34 F2
Mariville E SR2 .93 A5
Mariville W SR2 .93 A5
Marjorie St NE23 .22 F5
Mark Rise DH5 .95 A5
Mark's La DH4 .94 A3
Markby Cl 3 SR3 .91 E5
Market Cres DH4 .90 C6
Market La
Newcastle-upon-Tyne NE1 .99 B1
Dunston NE11,NE16 .69 D8
Market Pl
Houghton-le-Spring DH5 .94 F8
Bedlington NE22 .15 F8
Blyth NE24 .17 E8
Corbridge NE45 .46 F5
Hexham NE46 .45 B5
Market Place Ind Est
DH5 .90 F1
Market Sq Jarrow NE32 .58 B7
Lynmouth NE61 .2 B2
Sunderland SR1 .103 A2
Market St
Hetton le Hole DH5 .95 B4
Newcastle-upon-Tyne NE1 .99 B1
Dudley NE23 .29 A8
Blyth NE24 .17 E8
Hexham NE46 .45 B5
Market Way NE11 .70 D6
Markham Ave SR6 .61 A1
Markham St SR2 .86 F2
Markington Dr SR2 .92 F5
Markle Gr DH5 .94 D5
Marlboro Ave NE16 .69 B8
Marlborough App NE3 .38 C7
Marlborough Ave NE3 .38 C7
Marlborough Cres
Newcastle-upon-Tyne NE1 .100 C4
Gateshead NE9 .71 C3
Marlborough Ct
Houghton-le-Spring DH5 .94 E6
Newcastle-upon-Tyne NE3 .37 D7
Marlborough House
NE26 .31 F6
Marlborough Rd
Washington NE37 .83 F8
Sunderland SR4 .85 A3
Marlborough St N NE33 .59 D8
Marlborough St S NE33 .59 D8
Marlborough Terr NE62 .10 F4
Marleen Ave NE6 .56 C8
Marleen Ct 2 NE6 .56 C8
Marlesford Cl SR3 .91 D6
Marley Cres SR5 .74 F3
Marley Ct 16 NE6 .56 C7
Marley Hill Cty Prim Sch
NE16 .80 A8
Marlfield Ct NE5 .37 B3
Marlow Dr SR3 .91 D5
Marlow Pl NE12 .39 C6
Marlow St NE24 .17 D7
Marlow Way NE16 .68 F5
Marlowe Gdns NE8 .101 C1
Marlowe Pl DH5 .94 F7
Marlowe Wlk NE34 .59 A3
Marmion Rd NE6 .57 A8
Marmion Terr NE25 .31 F4
Marne St DH4 .90 C6
Marondale Ave NE6 .56 F7
Marquis Ave NE5 .36 C4
Marquis Cl NE12 .39 D5
Marquis Ct Prudhoe NE42 .50 E4
Gateshead NE11 .70 D3
Marquisway NE11 .70 D2
Marr Rd NE31 .57 F5
Marsden Ave SR6 .60 F3
Marsden Cl DH4 .94 C8
Marsden Cliffs Nature
Reserve* NE34 .60 E6
Marsden Gr NE9 .71 D3
Marsden La
South Shields NE34 .60 C7
Newcastle-upon-Tyne NE5 .37 A3
Marsden Prim Sch SR6 .60 F3
Marsden Rd
South Shields NE34 .60 A7
Cleadon SR6 .74 F8
Marsden St 6 NE33 .59 D8
Marsden View SR6 .60 F3
Marsh Ct NE11 .70 B7
Marshall St SR6 .75 D4
Marshall Wallis Rd NE33 .59 C8
Marshall's Ct NE1 .99 A1

Marsham Cl
Newcastle-upon-Tyne NE15 .53 E7
Cleadon SR6 .60 A2
Marsham Rd 3 NE5 .36 E3
Marshes' Houses NE62 .11 D7
Marshmont Ave NE30 .32 C1
Marske Terr NE6 .56 E6
Marston NE12 .29 D4
Marston Wlk NE16 .68 F5
Martello Gdns NE7 .39 D2
Martha St DH9 .79 B2
Martin Ct NE38 .82 F2
Martin Rd NE28 .41 A2
Martin Terr 7 SR4 .85 F7
Martindale Ave SR6 .75 C5
Martindale Pk DH5 .94 E8
Martindale Pl NE25 .23 E3
Martindale Wlk NE12 .29 C3
Marwell Dr NE37 .72 E2
Marwood Ct NE25 .31 D6
Marx Terr NE17 .77 C8
Mary Agnes St NE3 .38 A5
Mary Ave DH3 .82 B6
Mary Magdalene Bglws
NE2 .98 B4
Mary St Blaydon NE21 .53 C3
Blaydon, Winlaton NE21 .53 A2
Sunderland SR1 .102 C2
New Silksworth SR3 .92 A8
Mary Terr NE5 .37 A3
Mary Trevelyan Prim Sch
NE4 .100 A3
Mary's Pl NE6 .57 B6
Maryhill Cl NE4 .54 E4
Maryside Pl NE40 .51 F7
Masefield Ave NE16 .54 B1
Masefield Dr NE34 .59 A2
Masefield Pl NE8 .101 C2
Mason Ave NE26 .32 B5
Mason Rd NE28 .40 A4
Mason St
Brunswick Village NE13 .28 A6
4 Newcastle-upon-Tyne
NE6 .56 C5
Mason View NE13 .28 B8
Massingham Way NE34 .59 B5
Mast La NE30 .32 B3
Master Mariners' Homes
NE30 .42 C7
Master's Cres NE42 .50 B2
Matamba Terr SR4 .102 B2
Matanzas St SR2 .86 E3
Matfen Ave
Hazlerigg NE13 .28 A4
Shiremoor NE27 .31 A2
Matfen Cl
Newcastle-upon-Tyne NE15 .53 E6
Blyth NE24 .17 C7
Matfen Ct DH2 .88 A3
Matfen Dr SR3 .91 D6
Matfen Gdns NE28 .40 F5
Matfen Pl
Newcastle-upon-Tyne, Fawdon
NE3 .38 A6
Newcastle-upon-Tyne, Fenham
NE4 .54 F7
Matfen Terr NE64 .7 D3
Mather Rd NE4 .100 B4
Mathesons Gdns NE61 .8 F8
Matlock Gdns NE5 .36 F3
Matlock Rd NE32 .58 C5
Matlock Sq NE61 .2 A2
Matlock St SR1 .103 A3
Matthew Bank NE2 .38 E3
Matthew Rd NE24 .17 F5
Matthew St 13 NE6 .56 B6
Maud St
Newcastle-upon-Tyne NE15 .53 C6
Sunderland SR6 .75 E4
Maud Terr Tanfield DH9 .79 D3
5 Shiremoor NE27 .30 E1
Maud's Terr NE64 .7 E5
Maude Gdns 7 NE28 .40 B1
Maudlin Pl 2 NE5 .37 D1
Maudlin St DH5 .95 B6
Mauds La SR1 .103 B3
Maughan St NE24 .17 F7
Maurice Rd NE28 .57 B8
Maurice Road Ind Est
NE28 .57 B8
Mautland Sq DH4 .90 E1
Mautland St DH4 .90 E1
Maxton Cl SR3 .91 D5
Maxwell NE33 .42 C2
Maxwell Ho NE24 .17 B7
Maxwell St
South Shields NE33 .42 C2
Gateshead NE8 .70 D7
2 Sunderland SR4 .85 F7
Maxwell St Ind Est NE33 .42 C2
May Ave
Winlaton Mill NE21 .68 C7
Ryton NE40 .52 C6
Newbiggin-by-the-Sea NE64 .7 C5
May Gr SR6 .60 F3
May St Birtley DH3 .82 C4
Blaydon NE21 .53 B1
South Shields NE33 .42 D1
Sunderland SR4 .102 B3
Maydown Cl SR5 .84 F8
Mayfair Ct NE31 .57 D5
Mayfair Gdns
Ponteland NE20 .25 F6
South Shields NE34 .59 E7
Gateshead NE8 .71 A8
Mayfair Rd NE2 .38 D2
Mayfield Whickham NE16 .69 B5
Morpeth NE61 .8 E7
Mayfield Ave
Throckley NE15 .35 E1
Cramlington NE23 .22 C6
Mayfield Ct SR6 .75 D3
Mayfield Dr SR6 .75 B8
Mayfield Gdns
Throckley NE15 .35 E1
Wallsend NE28 .40 A3
Jarrow NE32 .58 A6
Mayfield Gr SR4 .85 A2
Mayfield Pl NE13 .28 A5
Mayfield Rd
Newcastle-upon-Tyne NE3 .38 C4
Sunderland SR4 .85 A6
Mayfield Terr NE5 .37 E1
Mayo Dr 1 SR3 .91 E5
Mayoral Way NE11 .70 D3
Maypole Cl 8 SR5 .75 B2
Mayswood Rd SR6 .75 D3
Maytree House NE4 .100 A4
Maywood Cl NE3 .37 E4
Mazine Terr DH6 .97 E2
McAnany Ave NE34 .59 D5
McAteer Ct DH6 .97 E1
McClaren Way DH4 .90 F7
McCracken Cl NE3 .38 C8
McCracken Dr NE13 .28 C7
McCutcheon Ct NE6 .56 E3
McCutcheon St 7 SR7 .92 E1
McErlane Sq NE10 .57 B2
McEwan Gdns NE4 .54 F5
McGowen Ct 6 NE6 .56 C5
McIlvenna Gdns NE28 .40 B4
Mcintyre Hall NE31 .57 F7
Mcintyre Rd NE31 .57 F7
McKendrick Villas NE5 .37 D1
McLennan Ct NE38 .83 D6
McNamara Rd NE28 .40 F3
Mcnulty Ct NE23 .28 F8
Meacham Way NE16 .69 A5
Mead Ave NE12 .39 E8
Mead Cres NE12 .39 F8
Mead Way NE12 .39 F8
Mead Wlk NE6 .56 F6
Meadow Bank Dr NE62 .10 E6
Meadow Brook Dr NE17 .66 C2
Meadow Cl
Houghton-le-Spring DH5 .94 F7
Dunston NE11 .54 E1
Longbenton NE12 .39 B7
Blaydon NE21 .52 F1
Seghill NE23 .22 F2
Ryton NE40 .52 D5
Meadow Ct
Ponteland NE20 .25 E5
Bedlington NE22 .10 E1
Meadow Dr
Seaton Burn NE13 .28 C8
Sunderland, East Herrington
SR3 .91 B6
Sunderland, South Hylton
SR4 .85 A5
Meadow Gdns SR3 .86 B3
Meadow Gr SR4 .85 B5
Meadow Grange DH4 .89 E2
Meadow La Dunston NE11 .54 F1
Crawcrook NE40 .52 A4
Sunderland SR3 .91 B6
Meadow Laws NE34 .60 A4
Meadow Pk NE44 .62 F7
Meadow Rd
Newcastle-upon-Tyne NE15 .53 D8
Whitley Bay NE25 .31 D4
Seaton Sluice NE26 .24 B6
Wallsend NE28 .40 F1
Meadow Rise
Newcastle-upon-Tyne NE5 .37 B4
Gateshead NE9 .71 C5
Meadow St DH5 .94 C3
Meadow Terr DH4 .90 C6
Meadow Vale SR2 .86 C4
Meadow View Dipton DH9 .78 E1
New Hartley NE25 .23 D6
North Shields NE28 .41 E4
Hedworth NE32 .73 D8
Sunderland SR3 .91 B5
Meadow Well Prim Sch
NE29 .41 D4
Meadow Well Sta NE29 .41 E4
Meadow Wlk NE40 .52 D5
Meadowbank NE23 .29 A8
Meadowbrook Dr NE10 .72 C7
Meadowcroft Mews
NE8 .101 A1
Meadowdale Cres
Bedlington NE22 .10 D1
Newcastle-upon-Tyne NE5 .37 D3
Meadowdale Mid Sch
NE22 .10 E1
Meadowfield
Ponteland NE20 .25 E7
Whitley Bay NE25 .31 D5
Ashington NE63 .7 A2
Meadowfield Ave NE3 .38 A6
Meadowfield Cres NE40 .52 A4
Meadowfield Ct NE20 .25 E7
Meadowfield Dr SR6 .60 B1
Meadowfield Est NE9 .71 F1
Meadowfield Gdns NE6 .40 A1
Meadowfield Ind Est
NE20 .25 E6
Meadowfield Pk NE20 .25 E6
Meadowfield Pk S NE43 .64 C5
Meadowfield Rd
Newcastle-upon-Tyne NE3 .38 B4
Meadowfield Rd *continued*
Stocksfield NE43 .64 C5
Meadowfield Terr
Killingworth NE12 .29 F1
Stocksfield NE43 .64 D7
Meadows La DH4,DH5 .94 B3
Meadows The
Bournmoor DH4 .89 D3
West Rainton DH4 .94 A3
Burnopfield NE16 .79 A4
Newcastle-upon-Tyne NE3 .37 F6
Ryton NE40 .52 D5
Meadowside SR2 .86 B4
Meadowsweet Cl NE24 .17 C4
Meadowvale NE20 .25 A2
Meadway Dr NE12 .39 F8
Meal Market NE46 .45 B5
Means Dr NE23 .29 B5
Medburn Ave NE30 .32 C2
Medburn Rd
Newcastle-upon-Tyne NE15 .53 C7
Seaton Delaval NE25 .23 E2
Medham Cl NE10 .71 E6
Medina Cl SR3 .91 E5
Medlar NE9 .71 D4
Medlar Cl DH4 .89 F6
Medomsley Gdns NE9 .71 E4
Medomsly St SR4 .102 A3
Medway NE32 .58 C2
Medway Ave NE31 .57 E3
Medway Cres NE8 .71 B8
Medway Ct NE3 .37 E5
Medway Gdns
Tynemouth NE30 .42 A7
Sunderland SR4 .85 D4
Medway Pl NE23 .16 D1
Medwyn Cl
Bournmoor DH4 .89 E3
Blyth NE24 .17 D5
Megstone Ave NE23 .22 A5
Megstone Ct NE12 .29 E4
Melbeck Dr DH2 .81 E2
Melbourne Cres NE25 .31 E3
Melbourne Ct
Newcastle-upon-Tyne NE1 .99 C1
Gateshead NE8 .101 B3
Melbourne Gdns NE34 .58 F3
Melbourne Pl SR4 .85 E4
Melbourne St NE1 .99 B1
Melbury NE25 .31 D6
Melbury Ct SR6 .75 D3
Melbury Rd NE7 .39 A1
Meldon Ave Sherburn DH6 .96 A1
Newcastle-upon-Tyne NE3 .37 F7
South Shields NE34 .59 E6
Meldon Cl NE28 .40 E3
Meldon Ct NE40 .51 E3
Meldon Gdns
Dunston NE11 .70 A5
Stakeford NE62 .10 F8
Meldon Ho NE24 .17 B8
Meldon Rd SR4 .85 F7
Meldon St NE28 .41 C1
Meldon Terr
Greenside NE40 .51 F1
Newcastle-upon-Tyne NE6 .56 B8
Newbiggin-by-the-Sea NE64 .7 D3
Meldon Way NE21 .67 F8
Melgarve Dr SR3 .91 E5
Melkington Ct NE5 .37 B3
Melkridge Gdns NE7 .39 D3
Melkridge Pl NE23 .22 A5
Mellendean Cl NE5 .37 B3
Melmerby Cl NE3 .38 D7
Melness Rd NE13 .28 A5
Melock Ct NE13 .28 A5
Melrose NE38 .83 D3
Melrose Ave
Bebside NE22 .11 D1
Seaton Delaval NE25 .23 D2
Whitley Bay NE25 .31 F4
Backworth NE27 .30 C5
Tynemouth NE30 .32 A2
Hebburn NE31 .57 E3
Gateshead NE9 .71 A5
Melrose Cl
Newcastle-upon-Tyne NE15 .53 E6
Hazlerigg NE3 .28 B2
Melrose Ct NE22 .11 D2
Melrose Gdns
Newbottle DH4 .90 C3
Wallsend NE28 .41 A4
Sunderland SR6 .75 E3
Melrose Gr NE32 .58 E4
Melrose Terr
Bedlington NE22 .11 D2
Newbiggin-by-the-Sea NE64 .7 D3
Melrose Villas NE22 .11 D2
Melsonby Cl SR3 .91 D6
Meltham Ct NE15 .36 B2
Meltham Dr SR3 .91 E5
Melton Ave NE6 .56 F5
Melton Cres NE26 .24 D5
Melton Dr NE25 .23 D6
Melvaig Cl SR3 .91 E5
Melville Ave NE24 .17 D5
Melville Gdns NE25 .31 C4
Melville Gr NE7 .39 A4
Melville St DH3 .88 C2
Melvin Pl NE5 .37 B2
Melvyn Gdns SR6 .75 E3
Membury Cl 4 SR3 .91 E5
Memorial Sq NE64 .7 D5
Menai Ct 9 SR3 .91 F6
Menceforth Cotts DH2 .88 B4
Mendip Ave DH2 .88 C2
Mendip Cl
Tynemouth NE29 .31 F1
Mendip Cl *continued*
Ashington NE63 .6 E1
Mendip Dr NE38 .83 B3
Mendip Gdns NE11 .70 B6
Mendip Way NE12 .38 F6
Mentieth Cl NE38 .83 B3
Menvill Pl SR1 .103 B2
Mercantile Rd DH4 .94 C7
Merchants Wharf 10 NE6 .56 C4
Mercia Way NE15 .53 E5
Mere Knolls Rd SR6 .75 E4
Meredith Gdns NE8 .101 C1
Meresyde NE10 .72 A7
Meresyde Ct NE10 .72 A7
Merevale Cl NE37 .72 E2
Merganser Lodge 10
NE10 .71 D8
Meridan Way NE7 .39 D3
Meridien Ho 3 NE33 .59 E8
Merlay Dr NE13 .27 B6
Merlay Hall NE6 .57 A4
Merle Gdns
16 Newcastle-upon-Tyne
NE6 .56 C5
Morpeth NE61 .3 D2
Merle Terr SR4 .85 F7
Merley Gate NE61 .9 A6
Merlin Cres NE28 .40 F3
Merlin Ct 17 NE10 .56 D1
Merlin Dr DH3 .88 D7
Merlin Pl NE12 .39 A7
Merlin Way Earsdon NE27 .31 A1
Shiremoor NE27 .41 A8
Merrick Ho 21 SR3 .91 F6
Merrington Cl
New Hartley NE25 .23 D7
Silksworth SR3 .91 D6
Merrion Cl SR3 .91 D6
Merryfield Gdns SR6 .75 E3
Merryshields Terr NE43 .64 C8
Mersey Ct 17 SR3 .91 F6
Mersey Pl NE8 .71 B8
Mersey Rd Hebburn NE31 .57 F3
Gateshead NE8 .71 B8
Mersey St NE17 .66 C1
Merton Ct NE4 .54 D4
Merton Rd NE20 .25 E6
Merton Sq NE24 .17 E8
Merton Way NE20 .25 E6
Methuen St NE9 .71 A8
Methven Way NE23 .16 C2
Metro Ctr The NE11 .54 C2
Metro Ret Pk NE11 .54 B2
Metroland Indoor Theme
Pk* NE11 .54 C2
Mews The
Fence Houses DH4 .94 A7
Newcastle-upon-Tyne NE1 .99 A2
Gateshead NE10 .72 B8
Blaydon NE21 .53 E2
North Shields NE30 .42 A6
Tynemouth NE30 .42 E8
Sunderland SR3 .91 B7
Michaelgate 23 NE6 .56 C6
Mickle Cl NE37 .83 A6
Mickleton Gdns SR3 .86 B2
Micklewood Cl NE61 .4 E6
Mickley Fst Sch NE43 .49 E1
Middle Chare DH3 .88 D3
Middle Cl NE38 .83 B1
Middle Dr
Woolsington NE13 .26 F1
Ponteland NE20 .25 C3
Middle Engine La
Shiremoor NE27,NE28,NE29 .41 A7
Wallsend NE27,NE28,NE29 .40 F5
Middle Farm Ct NE23 .22 B7
Middle Garth 1 NE5 .37 D1
Middle Gate
Newcastle-upon-Tyne NE5 .36 D1
Morpeth NE61 .8 F6
Middle Gn NE25 .31 C4
Middle Row
Great Lumley DH4 .89 E1
Blaydon NE40 .52 E3
Middle St Blyth NE24 .17 B4
Tynemouth NE30 .42 E7
Corbridge NE45 .46 F5
Newcastle-upon-Tyne NE6 .56 F6
Sunderland SR1 .102 C3
Sunderland SR1 .103 A3
Middle St E NE6 .57 A6
Middlebrook NE20 .25 B3
Middlefields Ind Est
NE34 .59 B6
Middleham Cl DH2 .81 E1
Middleham Ct SR5 .74 E3
Middleton Ave
Rowlands Gill NE39 .67 F1
Newcastle-upon-Tyne NE4 .54 E6
Middleton Cl SR7 .92 E1
Middleton Ct NE2 .99 C3
Middleton St NE24 .17 E7
Middlewood Pk NE4 .54 E7
Midfield Dr SR6 .75 E2
Midgley Dr SR3 .91 E5
Midhurst Ave NE34 .60 A8
Midhurst Cl SR3 .91 D6
Midhurst Rd NE12 .39 D7
Midmoor Rd SR4 .85 E7
Midsomer Cl SR3 .91 D5
Midway NE6 .57 A6
Milbanke Cl DH2 .81 F1
Milbanke St DH2 .81 F1
Milbur Cl NE46 .44 F2
Milburn Cl DH3 .88 E2
Milburn Dr NE15 .54 B6
Milburn Rd NE63 .6 D2
Milburn Terr
Shiney Row DH4 .90 B
Stakeford NE62 .11 C
Milcombe Cl SR3 .91 D
Mildmay Rd NE2 .38 D
Mildred St DH5 .90 E
Mile End Rd NE33 .42 C
Milecastle Ct NE5 .36 D
Milecastle Fst Sch NE5 .36 C
Milfield Ave
Shiremoor NE27 .31 A
Wallsend NE28 .40 C
Milford Ct NE10 .72 B
Milford Gdns NE3 .28 B
Milford Rd NE15 .54 C
Military Rd
Heddon-on-the-Wall NE15 .34 C
North Shields NE30 .42 B
Military Vehicle Mus*
NE2 .99 A
Milk Mkt NE1 .99 C
Milkwell NE45 .47 A
Milkwell La NE45 .47 A
Mill Bank SR5 .75 C
Mill Cl North Shields NE29 .41 E
Riding Mill NE44 .62 F
Mill Cres Penshaw DH4 .90 B
Hebburn NE31 .57 C
Mill Ct Bournmoor DH4 .89 E
Hamsterley NE17 .77 B
Ellington NE61 .1 C
Mill Dam NE33 .42 B
Mill Dene View NE32 .58 C
Mill Dyke Cl NE25 .31 C
Mill Farm NE61 .1 C
Mill Farm Cl NE4 .98 B
Mill Farm Rd NE39 .78 A
Mill Gr Tynemouth NE30 .42 C
South Shields NE34 .60 B
Mill Grange NE44 .63 A
Mill Hill DH5 .94 D
Mill Hill Prim Sch SR3 .92 A
Mill Hill Rd
Newcastle-upon-Tyne NE5 .53 F
Silksworth SR3 .92 A
Mill House NE2 .98 B
Mill La Urpeth DH2 .81 D
Sherburn DH6 .96 A
Ebchester DH8 .76 E
Hebburn NE10,NE31 .57 E
Jarrow NE10,NE31 .57 E
Heddon-on-the-Wall NE15 .34 F
Winlaton Mill NE21 .68 B
Seghill NE23 .22 D
North Shields NE29 .42 B
Newcastle-upon-Tyne NE4 .100 A
Slaley NE44 .62 A
Whitburn SR6 .60 F
Mill Pit DH4 .90 B
Mill Race Cl NE17 .77 B
Mill Rd Blackhall Mill NE17 .77 B
Chopwell NE17 .77 B
Gateshead NE8 .101 C
Mill Rise NE3 .38 E
Mill St SR4 .102 B
Mill Terr Shiney Row DH4 .90 B
Houghton-le-Spring DH5 .94 D
Mill View Gateshead NE10 .71 C
West Boldon NE36 .74 A
Mill View Ave SR6 .75 D
Mill View Rise NE42 .50 D
Mill Way NE15,NE42 .50 D
Millais Gdns NE34 .59 C2
Millbank Cres NE22 .11 A1
Millbank Ind Est NE33 .42 C2
Millbank Pl NE22 .16 B8
Millbank Rd
Bedlington NE22 .11 B1
Newcastle-upon-Tyne NE6 .57 A4
Millbank Terr NE22 .11 A1
Millbeck Gr DH5 .94 D6
Millbrook Gateshead NE10 .71 E7
North Shields NE29 .41 E5
Millbrook Rd NE23 .16 D1
Millburn St SR4 .102 B3
Milldale Ave NE24 .17 A7
Milldene Ave NE30 .42 C8
Millennium Bridge*
NE1,NE8 .102 C4
Millennium Way SR5 .102 C4
Miller St NE8 .70 D8
Miller Terr SR3 .92 A8
Miller's La NE16 .54 B1
Millers Hill DH4 .90 C6
Millers Rd NE6 .56 C7
Millfield Bedlington NE22 .16 A7
Seaton Sluice NE26 .24 D5
Millfield Ave NE3 .37 E3
Millfield Cl
Chester le Street DH2 .88 A1
Newburn NE15 .52 F7
Millfield Ct
Whickham NE16 .69 C7
Bedlington NE22 .16 A8
Seaton Sluice NE26 .24 D5
Hexham NE46 .44 F5
Millfield E NE22 .16 A7
Millfield Gdns
Gateshead NE10 .71 C8
Blyth NE24 .12 D1
Tynemouth NE30 .42 C8
Hexham NE46 .44 F5
Millfield Gr NE30 .42 C8
Millfield La NE15 .52 F8
Millfield N NE22 .16 A8
Millfield Rd
Whickham NE16 .69 B6
Riding Mill NE44 .62 F7

Millfield S NE22 16 A7
Millfield Sta SR4 102 B3
Millfield Terr
Hexham NE46 44 F5
Whitburn SR6 60 F2
Millfield W NE22 16 A8
Millford NE10 72 B6
Millgrove View NE3 37 F3
Milling Ct NE8 100 C2
Millom Pl NE9 71 B4
Mills Gdns NE28 40 B3
Millside NE61 8 F8
Millthorp Cl SR2 87 A1
Millview Dr NE30 42 C8
Millway
Seaton Sluice NE26 24 D5
Gateshead NE9 71 A7
Millway Gr NE26 24 D5
Milne Ct NE22 10 F1
Milne Way NE3 37 F6
Milner Cres NE21 53 A1
Milner St NE33 42 E2
Milrig Cl SR3 91 E5
Milsted Cl SR3 91 D5
Milsted Ct NE15 36 B2
Milton Ave
Houghton-le-Spring DH5 94 F7
Hebburn NE31 57 E6
Milton Cl NE2 99 C3
Milton Gn NE2 99 C3
Milton Gr
North Shields NE29 41 F6
Prudhoe NE42 50 B2
Ashington NE63 6 F3
Milton Pl
Newcastle-upon-Tyne NE2 99 C3
North Shields NE29 41 F6
Springwell NE9 71 E1
Milton Rd NE16 69 B8
Milton Sq NE8 56 A2
Milton St Jarrow NE32 58 B8
1 South Shields NE33 59 D8
Greenside NE40 51 E1
Sunderland SR4 102 A3
Milton Terr NE29 41 F6
Milvain Ave NE4 54 E6
Milvain Cl NE8 101 C1
Milvain St NE8 101 C1
Milverton Ct NE3 37 C6
Mimosa Dr NE31 57 E3
Mimosa Pl NE4 54 D8
Minden St NE1 99 B1
Mindrum Terr
North Shields NE29 41 D4
Newcastle-upon-Tyne NE6 56 F5
Mindrum Way NE25 23 D3
Minehead Gdns 9 SR3 92 A8
Miner's Cotts NE16 69 C6
Miners Cotts NE15 54 A7
Minerva Cl NE5 36 C4
Mingarry DH3 82 E2
Mingary Cl DH5 94 C4
Minorca Cl SR1 103 C2
Minorca Pl NE3 37 F3
Minskip Cl SR3 91 E5
Minster Ct NE8 101 C3
Minster Gr NE15 36 B3
Minster Par NE32 58 C7
Minton Ct NE29 41 F4
Minton La NE29 41 F4
Minton Sq 4 SR4 85 E7
Mirk La NE8 101 B4
Mirlaw Rd NE23 21 F5
Mistletoe Rd NE2 38 E1
Mitcham Cres NE7 39 B4
Mitchell Ave
Newcastle-upon-Tyne NE2 38 E2
Whitley Bay NE25 31 D4
Mitchell Dr NE63 7 B3
Mitchell Gdns NE34 59 F7
Mitchell St Birtley DH3 82 C4
Crawcrook NE40 51 E3
Newcastle-upon-Tyne NE6 57 B5
Mitchell Terr DH9 79 B2
Mitchell's Bldgs NE9 72 A1
Mitford Ave Blyth NE24 17 C6
Seaton Delaval NE25 23 C3
Pegswood NE61 4 E4
Mitford Cl
Chester le Street DH3 88 D8
Washington NE38 83 B4
Mitford Dr Sherburn DH6 96 A2
Newcastle-upon-Tyne NE5 36 E3
Ashington NE63 6 D2
Mitford Gdns
Dunston NE11 70 A5
Wide Open NE13 28 C6
Wallsend NE28 40 F5
Stakeford NE62 10 F8
Mitford Pl NE3 38 A6
Mitford Rd
South Shields NE34 59 E6
Morpeth NE61 3 E1
Mitford St
North Shields NE28 41 C2
Sunderland SR6 75 E4
Mitford Terr NE32 58 B2
Mitford Way NE13 27 B7
Mithras Gdns NE15 34 E2
Mitre Ind Est NE33 59 B7
Mitre Pl NE33 59 B7
Moat Gdns NE10 72 C8
Modder St NE6 56 F3
Model Dwellings 1
NE38 83 E4
Model Terr DH4 90 A8
Modigars La NE43 64 F4
Moffat Ave NE32 58 E4
Moffat Cl NE29 41 C8
Moine Gdns SR6 75 E3
Moir Terr 12 SR2 93 A6
Molesdon Cl NE30 32 A1
Molineux Cl 6 NE6 56 B6
Molineux Ct 3 NE6 56 B6
Molineux St NE6 56 B6
Mollyfair Cl NE40 52 A4
Monarch Rd NE4 100 A2
Monarch Terr NE21 53 C2
Monarch Way SR3 91 C5
Monday Cres NE4 98 B2
Monday Pl NE4 98 B2
Monk Ct NE8 101 C2
Monk St
Newcastle-upon-Tyne NE1 98 C1
Sunderland SR6 75 D1
Monk's Terr NE46 45 D4
Monkchester Gn NE6 56 E5
Monkchester Rd NE6 56 E4
Monkdale Ave NE24 17 A6
Monkhouse Ave NE30 32 A1
Monkhouse Prim Sch
NE30 32 B1
Monkridge
Newcastle-upon-Tyne NE15 36 B2
Whitley Bay NE26 31 E7
Monkridge Ct NE3 38 E4
Monkridge Gdns NE11 70 A7
Monks Ave NE25 31 D3
Monks Meadows NE46 45 D4
Monks Park Way NE12 39 A6
Monks Rd NE25 31 C3
Monks Ridge NE61 8 D7
Monks Way NE30 32 C1
Monks Wood NE30 41 F8
Monkseaton Com High Sch
NE25 31 E2
Monkseaton Dr NE25,
NE26 31 E6
Monkseaton Mid Sch
NE25 31 E4
Monkseaton Rd NE25 31 B5
Monkseaton Sta NE25 31 F5
Monkseaton Terr NE63 6 E1
Monksfeld NE10 71 E7
Monksfield Cl 6 SR3 91 F5
Monkside
Cramlington NE23 21 F5
Newcastle-upon-Tyne NE6 56 D8
Monkside Cl NE38 83 A2
Monkstone Ave NE30 42 C8
Monkstone Cl NE30 42 C8
Monkstone Cres NE30 32 C1
Monkstone Grange NE30 32 B1
Monksway NE32 58 E6
Monkswood Sq SR3 92 B6
Monkton NE10 71 F6
Monkton Ave NE34 59 A4
Monkton Bsns Pk NE31 57 F2
Monkton Cty Inf Sch
NE34 59 A3
Monkton Cty Jun Sch
NE34 58 F4
Monkton Hall NE32 57 F4
Monkton La
Jarrow NE31,NE32 57 F2
Hebburn NE32 57 F4
Monkton Rd NE32 58 B7
Monkton Terr NE32 58 C6
Monkwearmouth Hospl
SR5 75 C3
Monkwearmouth Sch
SR6 75 D5
Monkwearmouth Station
Mus* SR5 103 A4
Monmouth Gdns NE28 41 A4
Monroe Pl NE5 37 D2
Mons Ave NE31 57 E6
Montagu Ave NE3 38 A2
Montagu Ct NE3 38 A2
Montagu Prim Schs NE5 37 E2
Montague Ct NE9 70 F8
Montague St
Newcastle-upon-Tyne NE15 53 D6
Sunderland SR6 75 D3
Monterey
Washington NE37 72 D1
Silksworth SR3 91 E5
Montford Cl SR3 91 D5
Montpellier Pl NE3 37 F3
Montpellier Terr SR2 86 E3
Montrose Cl NE25 23 D6
Montrose Cres NE9 71 B7
Montrose Dr NE10 72 C7
Montrose Gdns
Morpeth NE61 8 F7
Sunderland SR3 86 A3
Monument Mall Sh Ctr
NE1 99 A1
Monument Sta NE1 99 A1
Monument Terr
10 Birtley DH3 82 C4
Penshaw DH4 90 A8
Monument View DH4 90 B8
Moonfield NE46 45 B4
Moor Cl Tynemouth NE29 41 C8
Sunderland SR1 103 C3
Moor Cotts DH6 96 D4
Moor Cres NE3 38 C3
Moor Crest Terr 2 NE29 41 F8
Moor Croft NE64 7 E5
Moor Ct Bournmoor DH4 89 E3
Newcastle-upon-Tyne NE3 38 B2
Whitburn SR6 75 E8
Moor Edge Prim Sch
NE12 29 C3
Moor Edge Rd NE27 30 E4
Moor Gdns NE29 41 C8
Moor Grange NE42 50 D1
Moor La Ponteland NE20 25 C4
South Shields NE34 59 E6
Newcastle-upon-Tyne NE5 37 D4
Stannington NE61 14 C6
Whitburn SR6 75 D8
Moor La E NE34 59 F7
Moor Park Ct NE29 41 C7
Moor Park Rd NE29 41 C7
Moor Pl NE3 38 C3
Moor Rd NE42 65 E7
Moor Rd N NE3 38 D4
Moor Rd S NE2,NE3 38 D3
Moor St SR1 103 B3
Moor Terr SR1 103 C3
Moor View
Killingworth NE12 29 C4
Crawcrook NE40 52 A4
Newbiggin-by-the-Sea NE64 7 E5
Whitburn SR6 75 E8
Moor View Cl NE61 4 E3
Moor View Wlk NE12 29 C4
Moorcroft Cl NE15 53 D7
Moorcroft Rd NE15 53 E6
Moordale Ave NE24 17 A6
Moore Ave Dunston NE11 69 F8
South Shields NE34 59 F6
Moore Cres DH3 82 C6
Moore Cres N DH5 94 E7
Moore Cres S DH5 94 E7
Moore Ct NE15 52 B7
Moore St NE8 56 A1
Moorfield NE2 38 D3
Moorfield Gdns SR6 75 A8
Moorfields NE61 9 A6
Moorfoot Ave DH2 88 C2
Moorfoot Gdns NE11 70 A7
Moorhead NE5 37 E1
Moorhead Mews NE5 37 E1
Moorhouse Cl NE34 59 D5
Moorhouse Est NE63 6 F3
Moorhouse Gdns DH5 95 B2
Moorhouse La NE63 6 F3
Moorhouses Rd NE29 41 C7
Moorings The 8 NE6 56 C4
Moorland Ave NE22 11 E3
Moorland Cotts NE22 11 D3
Moorland Cres
Bedlington NE22 11 E3
Newcastle-upon-Tyne NE6 56 E7
Moorland Ct NE22 11 E3
Moorland Dr NE22 11 E3
Moorland View NE17 77 B8
Moorland Villas NE22 11 E3
Moorland Way NE23 15 E1
Moorlands Hedworth NE32 58 D1
Prudhoe NE42 50 E1
Moorlands The DH9 78 E1
Moormill NE11 81 D6
Moormill La NE11 81 E6
Moors Cl DH4 94 B8
Moorsburn Dr DH4 90 C1
Moorsfield DH4 94 B8
Moorside Longbenton NE12 29 B2
Washington NE37 83 B7
Moorside Com Prim Sch
NE4 98 A2
Moorside Community Prim
Sch NE4 98 A2
Moorside Ct NE5 37 E1
Moorside Fst Sch NE64 7 D5
Moorside N NE4 54 F8
Moorside Pl NE4 54 F8
Moorside Rd SR3 91 D5
Moorside S NE4 54 F7
Moorsley Rd DH5 94 F2
Moorvale La NE5 37 E2
Moorview Cres NE5 37 E2
Moorway NE37 83 B6
Moorway Dr NE15 53 E7
Moraine Cres NE17 77 B6
Moralee Cl NE7 39 D3
Moran St SR6 75 D4
Moray Cl DH3 82 D1
Moray St SR6 75 D3
Morcott Gdns NE29 41 F4
Morden St NE1 99 A2
Mordey Cl SR2 103 B1
Morecambe Par NE31 58 A2
Moreland Rd NE34 59 D3
Moreland St SR6 75 D2
Moresby Rd NE23 16 C2
Morgan Bsns Ctr NE12 29 B5
Morgan St SR5 75 B2
Morgans Way NE21 53 A2
Morgy Hill E 2 NE40 51 F3
Morgy Hill W 1 NE40 51 F3
Morland Ave NE38 83 E4
Morland Gdns NE9 71 B7
Morley Ave NE10 57 B2
Morley Hill Rd NE5 53 F8
Morley Pl NE27 30 F4
Morley Terr
Fence Houses DH4 90 A1
6 Gateshead NE10 71 D8
Morningside NE38 88 E8
Morningside Ct 5 DH3 88 C4
Mornington Ave NE3 37 F3
Morpeth Ave
Wide Open NE13 28 C7
Jarrow NE32 58 B3
South Shields NE34 59 E7
Pegswood NE61 4 E3
Morpeth Chantry Mid Sch
NE61 3 E1
Morpeth Cl
Washington NE38 83 A4
Morpeth Cl *continued*
Guide Post NE62 10 E7
Morpeth Collingwood Sch
NE61 9 B7
Morpeth Cottage Hospl
NE61 8 F6
Morpeth Dr SR3 91 D6
Morpeth Fst Sch NE61 9 A8
Morpeth Newminster Mid
Sch NE61 3 E1
Morpeth Rd
Guide Post NE62 10 E7
Ashington NE63 5 F4
Morpeth Rd Fst Sch
NE24 17 D8
Morpeth St NE2 98 B4
Morpeth Sta NE61 9 A7
Morpeth Stobhillgate Fst Sch
NE61 9 B7
Morpeth Terr NE29 41 D4
Morpeth Wansbeck St
Aidan's CE Fst Sch NE61 3 D2
Morris Ave NE34 59 B3
Morris Cres NE35 74 A8
Morris Ct NE23 29 B8
Morris Gdns NE10 72 B8
Morris Ho NE2 98 C3
Morris Rd NE16 69 B8
Morris St Birtley DH3 82 C4
Washington NE37 83 C8
Gateshead NE8 70 C8
Morrison Rd NE61 4 A1
Morrison St NE8 100 C2
Morriss Terr DH5 94 F7
Morrit Ct NE7 39 C5
Morston Dr NE15 53 E6
Mortimer Ave
North Shields NE29 41 D6
Newcastle-upon-Tyne NE5 36 F3
Mortimer Chase NE23 16 C3
Mortimer Comp Sch
NE34 59 D7
Mortimer Prim Sch NE34 59 D7
Mortimer Rd NE33,NE34 59 D7
Mortimer St SR4 85 F7
Mortimer Terr
Seaton Delaval NE25 23 E2
Pegswood NE61 4 F4
Morton Cl NE38 83 D4
Morton Cres
Great Lumley DH4 89 F1
Woolsington NE5 36 B6
Morton Grange Terr DH4 89 E1
Morton St
1 South Shields NE33 42 D4
Newcastle-upon-Tyne NE6 56 D6
Morton Wlk 6 NE33 42 C4
Morval Cl SR3 91 D5
Morven Dr NE10 57 B1
Morven Lea NE21 53 B2
Morven Pl NE63 6 B4
Morven Terr NE63 6 B4
Morwick Cl NE23 22 A5
Morwick Pl 3 NE5 37 D1
Morwick Rd NE29 41 D8
Mosley St NE1 99 B1
Moss Bank NE9 71 B3
Moss Cl NE15 53 C8
Moss Cres NE40 52 A4
Moss Side NE9 71 C3
Mosspool NE21 53 A2
Mostyn Gn NE3 37 F5
Motcombe Way NE23 16 D2
Moulton Ct NE5 37 C2
Moulton Pl NE5 37 C2
Mount Cl
Killingworth NE12 29 D4
Whitley Bay NE25 31 D3
Sunderland SR4 85 B6
Mount Ct DH3 82 D5
Mount Gr Dunston NE11 69 F7
Sunderland SR4 86 A4
Mount La NE9 82 E8
Mount Lonnen NE9 82 E8
Mount Pleasant
Birtley DH3 82 C5
Houghton-le-Spring DH5 94 F8
Dipton DH9 78 E1
5 Blaydon NE21 53 B1
9 Newcastle-upon-Tyne
NE6 56 C6
3 Sunderland SR5 75 A1
Mount Pleasant Bglws 5
DH3 82 C5
Mount Pleasant Ct NE15 35 D2
Mount Pleasant Gdns
NE8 56 A1
Mount Rd Birtley DH3 82 D5
Gateshead NE9 82 E8
Sunderland SR4 85 F4
Mount Terr NE33 42 C2
Mount The Throckley NE15 35 C2
Ryton NE40 52 C5
Mount View
Whickham NE16 69 B8
16 Crawcrook NE40 51 F3
Mount View Terr NE43 64 A7
Mountbatten Ave NE31 57 E4
Mountfield Gdns NE3 37 F5
Mountfield Prim Sch
NE3 37 E5
Mountford Rd NE25 23 D7
Mountside Gdns NE11 69 F7
Mourne Gdns NE11 70 A6
Mowbray Cl SR2 103 A1
Mowbray Cty Jun Mix Sch
NE33 42 F1
Mowbray Mews NE33 42 E2
Mowbray Rd
Longbenton NE12 39 E8
North Shields NE29 41 D6
South Shields NE33 42 E1
Sunderland SR2 103 B1
Mowbray St NE6 56 A7
Mowbray Terr NE62 10 F7
Mowden Hall (Prep Sch)
NE43 48 E7
Moyle Terr NE16 79 A4
Mozart St NE33 42 D2
Muirfield
Whitley Bay NE25 31 D5
South Shields NE33 42 F1
Muirfield Dr
Gateshead NE10 71 E6
Washington NE37 72 C2
Muirfield Rd NE7 39 C5
Mulben Cl NE4 54 E4
Mulberry Cl NE24 17 D4
Mulberry Gdns NE10 56 C2
Mulberry Gr NE16 79 A4
Mulberry Pl NE4 100 B3
Mulberry St NE10 56 C1
Mulcaster Gdns NE28 40 A3
Mulgrave Dr SR6 75 E1
Mulgrave Terr NE8 101 B3
Mulgrave Villas NE8 101 B2
Mull Gr NE32 58 E3
Mullen Dr NE40 52 D4
Mullen Gdns NE28 40 A4
Mullen Rd NE28 40 B4
Mundella Terr NE6 56 B7
Mundle Ave NE21 68 C6
Mundles La NE36 74 D6
Municipal Terr NE38 83 D6
Munslow Rd SR3 91 D8
Murphy Gr SR2 92 E7
Murray Ave DH4 90 A1
Murray Ct DH2 88 B3
Murray Gdns 1 NE11 70 A7
Murray Pl DH2 88 C3
Murray Rd
Chester le Street DH2,DH3 88 C3
Wallsend NE28 40 F3
Murray St NE21 53 C3
Murrayfield NE23 22 F2
Murrayfield Rd NE5 37 D3
Murston Ave NE23 16 C2
Murton La
Easington Lane DH5 95 D1
Tynemouth NE27,NE29 31 B2
Murton St SR1 103 B2
Muscott Gr NE15 54 A6
Musgrave Rd NE9 70 F6
Musgrave Sch NE9 70 F6
Musgrave Terr
Gateshead NE10 57 B2
Washington NE38 83 D6
Newcastle-upon-Tyne NE6 56 E6
Muswell Hill NE15 54 A5
Mutual St NE28 40 B1
Mylord Cres NE12 29 B5
Myre Hall 8 DH5 94 E8
Myrella Cres SR2 86 C2
Myreside Pl NE12 39 B7
Myrtle Ave Dunston NE11 69 F8
Whitburn SR6 60 F1
Myrtle Cres NE12 29 D1
Myrtle Gr Gateshead NE11 70 F5
Burnopfield NE16 78 F6
Newcastle-upon-Tyne NE2 38 E2
Wallsend NE28 40 D1
South Shields NE34 59 F4
Myrtle Rd NE21 53 C1
Myrtle Terr NE63 6 D4
Myrtles DH2 88 B5

N

Nafferton Pl NE5 54 C8
Nailsworth Cl NE35 58 E2
Nairn Cl Birtley DH3 82 D2
Washington NE37 72 C2
Nairn Rd NE23 22 B7
Nairn St NE32 58 E3
Nansen Cl NE5 36 F2
Napier Cl DH3 88 D8
Napier Ct NE16 69 B4
Napier Rd NE16 54 A1
Napier St
Newcastle-upon-Tyne NE2 99 C2
Jarrow NE32 58 B7
South Shields NE33,NE34 59 B6
Napier Way NE21 53 E2
Narvik Way NE29 41 B4
Nash Ave NE34 59 D3
Naters St NE26 32 C4
National Glass Ctr (Mus)*
SR6 103 B4
Natley Ave NE36 74 E7
Navan Cl NE62 11 D8
Navenby Cl
Newcastle-upon-Tyne NE3 38 D8
Seaham SR7 93 A1
Naworth Ave NE30 32 A1
Naworth Dr NE5 36 E3
Naworth Terr NE32 58 D4
Nawton Ave SR5 75 C2
Nayland Rd NE23 22 A7
Naylor Ave NE21 68 C6
Naylor Bldgs NE21 68 C6
Naylor Ct NE21 53 E4
Naylor Pl NE26 24 B7

Neale St Tantobie DH9 ... 79 B2
Prudhoe NE42 ... 50 D3
Sunderland SR6 ... 75 E3
Nearlane Cl NE13 ... 28 C8
Neasdon Cres NE30 ... 32 B1
Neasham Rd SR7 ... 93 A1
Nedderton Cl NE5 ... 36 B4
Needham Pl NE23 ... 22 B7
Neighbourhood Ctr The NE5 ... 37 A5
Neil St DH5 ... 95 C1
Neill Dr NE16 ... 69 B2
Neilson Rd NE10 ... 56 B3
Nell Terr NE39 ... 67 C1
Nellie Gormley House NE12 ... 29 B2
Nelson Ave
Cramlington NE23 ... 21 F8
Newcastle-upon-Tyne NE3 ... 38 A5
South Shields NE33 ... 42 E3
Nelson Cl Ashington NE63 ... 6 E2
Sunderland SR2 ... 103 B1
Nelson Cres NE29 ... 41 D2
Nelson Dr NE23 ... 15 F1
Nelson House 14 NE30 ... 42 D7
Nelson Ind Est NE23 ... 15 E2
Nelson Park Ind Est NE23 ... 15 E1
Nelson Park West NE23 ... 15 D1
Nelson Rd
Cramlington NE23 ... 15 D1
Earsdon NE25 ... 31 B5
Newcastle-upon-Tyne NE6 ... 57 B4
Stakeford NE62 ... 11 A7
Nelson St
Chester le Street DH3 ... 88 C2
Hetton le Hole DH5 ... 95 A3
Newcastle-upon-Tyne NE1 ... 99 A1
Dunston NE11 ... 54 F2
11 South Shields NE33 ... 42 C3
Washington NE38 ... 83 E4
Greenside NE40 ... 51 F1
Gateshead NE8 ... 101 C3
Ryhope SR2 ... 92 F7
Nelson Terr Sherburn DH6 ... 96 A1
Chopwell NE17 ... 66 B1
North Shields NE29 ... 41 D3
Nelson Way NE23 ... 15 E2
Nene Ct 11 NE37 ... 83 E8
Nent Gr NE46 ... 45 C4
Neptune Rd
Newcastle-upon-Tyne, Denton Burn NE15 ... 53 E7
Newcastle-upon-Tyne, Lemington NE15 ... 53 D6
Wallsend NE28 ... 57 B8
Nesburn Rd SR4 ... 102 A1
Nesham Pl DH5 ... 94 F8
Nesham Terr SR1 ... 103 C3
Ness Ct NE21 ... 53 A2
Nest Rd NE10 ... 56 D2
Nether Farm Rd NE10 ... 56 F1
Nether Riggs NE22 ... 15 F8
Netherburn Rd SR5 ... 75 C2
Netherby Dr NE5 ... 54 C8
Netherdale NE22 ... 10 D1
Netherton NE12 ... 29 C4
Netherton Ave NE29 ... 41 D7
Netherton Gdns NE13 ... 28 B6
Netherton Gr NE29 ... 41 D7
Netherton La NE22 ... 10 C1
Netherton Park Assessment Ctr NE61 ... 14 D6
Nettleham Rd SR5 ... 75 C2
Nettles La SR3 ... 92 B6
Nevill Rd NE43 ... 64 D7
Neville Cres DH3 ... 82 C6
Neville Ct 3 NE37 ... 83 F8
Neville Rd
Newcastle-upon-Tyne NE15 ... 53 E7
Sunderland SR4 ... 85 F7
Neville Sq NE61 ... 2 A2
Neville St NE1 ... 101 A4
Neville's Cross Rd NE31 ... 57 F5
Nevinson Ave NE34 ... 59 E3
Nevis Cl NE26 ... 31 E8
Nevis Ct NE26 ... 31 E8
Nevis Gr NE36 ... 74 B7
Nevis Way NE26 ... 31 E7
New Bridge St NE1 ... 99 C1
New Bridge St W NE1, NE99 ... 99 B2
New Delaval Cty Sch NE24 ... 17 B4
New Dr SR7 ... 93 B1
New Durham Rd SR2 ... 102 C2
New Front St DH9 ... 79 D1
New George St NE33 ... 42 C1
New Green St NE33 ... 42 C1
New Hartley Fst Sch NE25 ... 23 D6
New Herrington Ind Est DH4 ... 90 D6
New King St NE64 ... 7 F5
New Mills NE4 ... 98 B2
New Penshaw Prim Sch DH4 ... 90 B8
New Phoenix Yd 1 NE61 ... 9 A8
New Quay NE29 ... 42 B4
New Queen St NE64 ... 7 E5
New Rd Gateshead NE10 ... 72 C5
Dunston NE11 ... 70 B6
Burnopfield NE16 ... 79 B7
West Boldon NE35 ... 74 B8
Washington NE38 ... 89 C8
New Ridley Rd NE43 ... 64 D5
New Seaham Prim Sch SR7 ... 92 F1
New Silksworth Inf Sch SR3 ... 92 B7
New Silksworth Jun Sch SR3 ... 92 B7
New South Terr DH3 ... 82 D4
New St Sherburn DH6 ... 96 A1
5 Sunderland SR4 ... 85 A6
New York Prim Sch NE29 ... 41 C8
New York Rd
Shiremoor NE27 ... 30 E2
Tynemouth NE29 ... 31 B1
New York Way NE27 ... 41 A8
Newark Cres SR7 ... 93 A1
Newark Dr SR6 ... 75 F8
Newark Sq NE29 ... 41 F4
Newarth Cl NE15 ... 53 E7
Newbank Wlk NE21 ... 53 A1
Newbiggin La NE5 ... 36 F4
Newbiggin Mid Sch NE64 ... 7 C4
Newbiggin Rd NE63 ... 6 E1
Newbold Ave SR5 ... 75 C2
Newbold St NE6 ... 56 D5
Newbolt Ct NE8 ... 56 A2
Newbottle Prim Sch DH4 ... 90 D3
Newbottle St DH4 ... 90 E1
Newbridge Ave SR5 ... 75 C2
Newbridge Bank DH3 ... 88 F5
Newbrough Cres NE2 ... 38 E2
Newburgh Ave NE25 ... 23 D2
Newburn Ave SR5 ... 75 C2
Newburn Bridge Rd NE15,NE21 ... 52 E6
Newburn Cres DH4 ... 90 D1
Newburn Ct NE33 ... 42 D1
Newburn Haugh Ind Est NE15 ... 53 C6
Newburn Ind Est NE21 ... 53 A6
Newburn Lane End NE15 ... 35 D2
Newburn Manor Fst Sch NE15 ... 52 F8
Newburn Motor Mus* NE15 ... 52 F8
Newburn Rd
Newburn NE15 ... 52 F8
Throckley NE15 ... 35 E1
Newbury NE12 ... 29 D4
Newbury Ave NE8 ... 70 D8
Newbury Cl NE15 ... 53 D7
Newbury St
South Shields NE33 ... 59 D7
Sunderland SR5 ... 75 D3
Newby La DH6 ... 96 C5
Newby Pl NE9 ... 71 B4
Newcastle Arena NE4 ... 100 C3
Newcastle Bank NE9 ... 82 B7
Newcastle Bsns Pk NE4 ... 100 A3
Newcastle Coll Trevelyan Bldg NE4 ... 100 B4
Newcastle Discovery Mus* NE1 ... 100 C4
Newcastle General Hospl NE4 ... 54 F6
Newcastle International Airport NE13 ... 26 D3
Newcastle Nuffield Hospl The NE2 ... 99 B4
Newcastle Rd Birtley DH3 ... 82 D3
Chester le Street DH3 ... 88 C5
Hedworth NE10,NE36 ... 73 C7
Blyth NE24 ... 17 C4
Jarrow NE34 ... 58 F5
West Boldon NE36 ... 73 E6
Sunderland SR5 ... 75 C3
Newcastle St NE29 ... 42 A5
Newcastle Terr 5 NE30 ... 42 D7
Newcastle Upon Tyne Central Sta NE1 ... 101 A4
Newdene Wlk NE15 ... 53 D7
Newfield Wlk NE16 ... 69 A6
Newgate Sh Ctr NE1 ... 99 A1
Newgate St
Newcastle-upon-Tyne NE1 ... 99 A1
Morpeth NE61 ... 3 F1
Newham Ave NE13 ... 28 A4
Newhaven Ave SR5 ... 75 C2
Newington Ct
Washington NE37 ... 83 C8
Sunderland SR5 ... 75 C1
Newington Rd NE6 ... 56 A6
Newker Prim Sch DH2 ... 88 B2
Newland Ct NE34 ... 59 C5
Newlands NE30 ... 32 A2
Newlands Ave Blyth NE24 ... 17 D5
Whitley Bay NE25 ... 31 D3
Newcastle-upon-Tyne NE3 ... 28 D1
Sunderland SR3 ... 86 B3
Newlands Pl NE24 ... 17 D5
Newlands Prep Sch NE3 ... 38 D4
Newlands Rd
Newcastle-upon-Tyne NE2 ... 38 D3
Blyth NE24 ... 17 D5
Newlands Rd W SR7 ... 93 A1
Newlyn Cres NE29 ... 41 E5
Newlyn Dr
Cramlington NE23 ... 22 B8
Jarrow NE32 ... 58 D6
Newlyn Rd NE3 ... 37 E5
Newman Pl NE8 ... 71 A8
Newman Terr NE8 ... 71 A8
Newman's Way 1 NE46 ... 45 B4
Newmarch St NE32 ... 58 A7
Newmarket Wlk 1 NE33 ... 42 D1
Newmin Way NE16 ... 68 F5
Newminster Cl DH4 ... 90 B2
Newminster Rd NE4 ... 54 D7
Newport Gr 6 SR3 ... 92 A8
Newquay Gdns 4 NE9 ... 71 A2
Newriggs NE38 ... 83 E2
Newsham Cl NE5 ... 36 B4
Newsham Fst Sch NE24 ... 17 C5
Newsham Rd NE24 ... 17 C6
Newstead Ct NE38 ... 83 C5
Newstead Rd DH4 ... 90 C2
Newstead Sq SR3 ... 92 A6
Newsteads Cl NE25 ... 31 D5
Newsteads Dr NE25 ... 31 D5
Newton Ave
Wallsend NE28 ... 40 F3
Tynemouth NE30 ... 32 B3
Newton Cl NE15 ... 53 E7
Newton Gr NE34 ... 59 A5
Newton House NE4 ... 98 B2
Newton Pl NE7 ... 39 B2
Newton Rd NE7 ... 39 B2
Newton St Dunston NE11 ... 54 F2
Gateshead NE8 ... 70 D8
Newton Terr NE43 ... 49 E1
Nichol Ct NE4 ... 54 D5
Nichol St NE4 ... 54 D5
Nicholas Ave SR6 ... 75 F8
Nicholas St DH5 ... 95 B5
Nicholson Cl SR1 ... 103 B2
Nicholson Terr NE12 ... 29 E1
Nidderdale Ave DH5 ... 94 F2
Nidderdale Cl NE24 ... 17 A8
Nidsdale Ave NE6 ... 57 A7
Nightingale Cl SR4 ... 85 B4
Nile Cl NE15 ... 53 C8
Nile Ct NE8 ... 56 A1
Nile St North Shields NE29 ... 42 A5
South Shields NE33 ... 42 B2
Sunderland SR1 ... 103 B3
Nilverton Ave SR2 ... 86 D3
Nimbus Ct 13 SR3 ... 92 A6
Nine Lands DH4 ... 94 C8
Ninth Ave
Chester le Street DH2 ... 88 B3
Gateshead NE11 ... 70 D3
Blyth NE24 ... 17 D6
Newcastle-upon-Tyne NE6 ... 56 C8
Morpeth NE61 ... 9 B7
Ninth Ave E NE11 ... 70 D3
Ninth Row NE63 ... 6 B4
Nissan Way NE37,SR5 ... 84 B7
Nithdale Cl NE6 ... 57 B8
Nixon St NE8 ... 56 A4
Nixon Terr NE24 ... 17 F6
Noble Gdns NE34 ... 58 F4
Noble St
2 Gateshead NE10 ... 56 D1
Newcastle-upon-Tyne NE4 ... 54 F3
Sunderland SR2 ... 103 C1
Noble Terr
11 Morpeth NE61 ... 9 A8
Sunderland SR2 ... 103 C1
Noble's Bank Rd SR2 ... 103 C1
Noel Ave NE21 ... 68 C6
Noel Terr NE21 ... 68 D7
Noirmont Way SR3 ... 91 E6
Nook The
Whitley Bay NE25 ... 31 F4
North Shields NE29 ... 41 F5
Nookside SR4 ... 85 C4
Nookside Ct SR4 ... 85 C4
Nora St South Shields NE34 ... 59 C5
Sunderland SR4 ... 85 F4
Norbury Gr NE6 ... 56 D5
Nordale Way NE24 ... 17 A8
Norfolk Ave Birtley DH3 ... 82 D1
New Silksworth SR3 ... 91 F8
Norfolk Cl Ashington NE63 ... 6 A4
Seaham SR7 ... 93 A1
Norfolk Dr NE37 ... 72 D2
Norfolk Gdns NE28 ... 40 E4
Norfolk Mews 11 NE30 ... 42 A6
Norfolk Pl DH3 ... 82 D1
Norfolk Rd
South Shields NE34 ... 60 C7
Gateshead NE8 ... 56 A4
Norfolk Sq 19 NE6 ... 56 B6
Norfolk St
Hetton le Hole DH5 ... 94 F4
North Shields NE30 ... 42 B5
Sunderland SR1 ... 103 A3
Norfolk Way NE15 ... 53 E7
Norham Ave N NE34 ... 60 A8
Norham Ave S NE34 ... 60 A8
Norham Castle* TD15 ... 104 C3
Norham Cl
Brunswick Village NE13 ... 28 A5
Blyth NE24 ... 17 C7
Norham Com Tech Coll NE29 ... 41 D5
Norham Ct
Bournmoor DH4 ... 89 D1
Washington NE38 ... 83 B4
Norham Dr
Newcastle-upon-Tyne NE5 ... 36 E3
Morpeth NE61 ... 9 B5
Norham Gdns NE62 ... 6 A1
Norham Pl NE2 ... 38 E1
Norham Rd
Whitley Bay NE25,NE26 ... 31 F5
North Shields NE29 ... 41 C5
Newcastle-upon-Tyne NE3 ... 38 B6
Ashington NE63 ... 6 D2
Norham Rd N NE29 ... 41 B7
Norham Terr NE32 ... 58 B3
Norhurst NE16 ... 68 E5
Norland Rd NE15 ... 53 F6
Norley Ave SR5 ... 75 C2
Norma Cres NE26 ... 32 C4
Norman Ave SR3 ... 92 B7
Norman Rd NE39 ... 67 F1
Norman Terr
High Pittington DH6 ... 96 C5
Wallsend NE28 ... 41 B2
Morpeth NE61 ... 9 A8
Normanby Cl SR7 ... 93 A1
Normanby Ct SR6 ... 75 F1
Normandy Cres DH5 ... 94 F8
Normanton Terr NE4 ... 98 A1
Normount Ave 2 NE4 ... 54 E5
Normount Gdns NE4 ... 54 E6
Normount Rd NE4 ... 54 E5
Norseland Gallery Studio Two Ceramics* NE70 ... 108 F2
North App DH2 ... 88 B4
North Ave
Longbenton NE12 ... 39 D6
Newcastle-upon-Tyne, Gosforth NE3 ... 38 C4
South Shields NE34 ... 59 F6
Washington NE37 ... 72 C1
Newcastle-upon-Tyne, Westerhope NE5 ... 36 F2
Guide Post NE62 ... 10 E7
North Balkwell Farm Ind Est NE29 ... 41 B7
North Bank Ct 7 SR5 ... 75 B2
North Bridge St SR5 ... 103 A4
North Burns DH3 ... 88 C4
North Church St 2 NE30 ... 42 B6
North Cl
South Shields NE34 ... 59 F6
Ryton NE40 ... 52 C5
4 Newcastle-upon-Tyne NE6 ... 56 C7
North Cres NE38 ... 83 B1
North Croft NE12 ... 39 E7
North Cross St NE3 ... 38 C5
North Ct 5 NE32 ... 58 B7
North Dr Hebburn NE31 ... 57 C4
Chester le Street NE38 ... 88 E7
Cleadon SR6 ... 59 F1
North Durham St SR1 ... 103 B3
North East Aircraft Mus* SR5 ... 73 E2
North Eastern Ct NE16 ... 69 E8
North Farm NE22 ... 15 A8
North Farm Ave SR4 ... 85 B2
North Farm Rd NE31 ... 57 D5
North Fawdon Prim Sch NE3 ... 37 F7
North Gr Ryton NE40 ... 52 D5
Sunderland SR6 ... 75 E3
North Grange NE20 ... 25 E8
North Guards SR6 ... 75 F8
North Hall Rd SR4 ... 85 D4
North Hylton Rd SR5 ... 74 E2
North Hylton Road Ind Est SR5 ... 74 D2
North Jesmond Ave NE2 ... 38 E2
North King St NE30 ... 42 B6
North La
Hetton le Hole DH5 ... 95 E5
East Boldon NE36 ... 74 C7
North Leech NE61 ... 3 D2
North Leigh DH9 ... 79 D1
North Lodge DH3 ... 88 D7
North Lodge Apartments 10 NE21 ... 53 B1
North Magdalene DH8 ... 77 B1
North Mason Lodge NE13 ... 27 B8
North Mdws NE42 ... 50 B5
North Milburn St SR4 ... 102 B3
North Moor Ct SR3 ... 85 E1
North Moor La SR3 ... 91 E8
North Moor Rd SR3 ... 85 E1
North Par
Whitley Bay NE26 ... 32 B5
Choppington NE62 ... 10 E6
North Pl NE61 ... 3 E1
North Ravensworth St SR4 ... 102 B3
North Rd
Chester le Street DH3 ... 88 C7
Hetton le Hole DH5 ... 94 E4
Houghton-le-Spring DH5 ... 94 E4
Dipton DH9 ... 78 E1
Ponteland NE20 ... 25 E8
Wallsend NE28 ... 40 B2
Tynemouth NE29 ... 42 A8
Boldon Colliery NE35 ... 58 E1
West Boldon NE35,NE36 ... 73 F7
East Boldon NE36 ... 74 C7
Slaley NE47 ... 62 A4
Seaham SR7 ... 93 D1
North Ridge
Bedlington NE22 ... 10 D1
Bedlington NE22 ... 10 E1
Whitley Bay NE25 ... 31 C6
North Row NE42 ... 50 A2
North Sands Bsns Ctr SR6 ... 103 B4
North Seaton Ind Est NE63 ... 6 F1
North Seaton Rd
Ashington NE63 ... 6 D2
Newbiggin-by-the-Sea NE64 ... 7 D3
North Shields Sta NE29 ... 42 A5
North St Birtley DH3 ... 82 E3
Newbottle DH4 ... 90 D4
West Rainton DH4 ... 94 A2
East Rainton DH5 ... 94 D4
Newcastle-upon-Tyne NE1 ... 99 A2
Blaydon NE21 ... 53 A2
Jarrow NE32 ... 58 B7
South Shields NE33 ... 42 C3
New Silksworth SR3 ... 92 A8
North St *continued*
5 Sunderland SR5 ... 75 C1
Cleadon SR6 ... 60 A1
North St E NE1 ... 99 B2
North Terr Chopwell NE17 ... 66 B2
Newcastle-upon-Tyne NE2 ... 98 C3
1 Shiremoor NE27 ... 30 E3
Wallsend NE28 ... 40 E2
Hexham NE46 ... 45 B4
11 New Silksworth SR3 ... 92 A8
North Tyne Ind Est NE12 ... 40 A8
North Tyneside Coll NE28 ... 40 E5
North Tyneside General Hospl NE29 ... 31 E1
North View Ouston DH2 ... 81 F1
Bournmoor DH4 ... 89 E2
Easington Lane DH5 ... 95 C1
Haswell DH6 ... 97 E1
Sherburn Hill DH6 ... 96 D1
Medomsley DH8 ... 77 B1
Whickham NE11 ... 69 A7
4 Longbenton NE12 ... 39 D8
Dinnington NE13 ... 27 B7
Hazlerigg NE13 ... 28 A4
Bedlington NE22 ... 11 D3
Cambois NE24 ... 12 C6
Wallsend NE28 ... 40 C2
Tynemouth, Preston NE29 ... 41 F8
Tynemouth, Cullercoats NE30 ... 32 C4
Jarrow NE32 ... 58 A6
South Shields NE34 ... 59 F8
Washington NE37 ... 83 D8
High Spen NE39 ... 66 F3
Rowlands Gill NE39 ... 67 C2
Crawcrook NE40 ... 51 E7
Ryton NE40 ... 52 A5
Mickley Square NE43 ... 49 E1
Newcastle-upon-Tyne NE6 ... 56 B7
Newcastle-upon-Tyne NE6 ... 56 C7
Stakeford NE62 ... 11 C8
Ashington NE63 ... 6 C4
Newbiggin-by-the-Sea NE64 ... 7 D3
Gateshead NE9 ... 71 B3
Sunderland, South Hylton SR4 ... 85 B5
Sunderland, Castletown SR5 ... 74 C1
Sunderland, Monkwearmouth SR6 ... 75 D3
North View Terr
Fence Houses DH4 ... 94 B8
Prudhoe NE42 ... 50 B2
Stocksfield NE43 ... 64 C7
Gateshead NE8 ... 56 C1
North View W NE39 ... 67 C2
North Villas NE23 ... 22 A1
North Walbottle Rd
Walbottle NE15 ... 36 A2
Newcastle-upon-Tyne NE5 ... 36 B4
Northbourne Ave NE61 ... 3 F2
Northbourne Ho NE9 ... 70 F5
Northbourne Rd NE31, NE32 ... 58 A6
Northbourne St
Newcastle-upon-Tyne NE4 ... 54 F4
Gateshead NE8 ... 70 F8
Northburn Fst Sch NE23 ... 16 A1
Northcote NE16 ... 69 A5
Northcote Ave
Whitley Bay NE25 ... 31 D4
Newcastle-upon-Tyne NE5 ... 36 C1
Sunderland SR1 ... 103 B2
Northcote St
8 South Shields NE33 ... 59 D8
Newcastle-upon-Tyne NE4 ... 98 A1
Northcott Gdns NE23 ... 22 E1
Northdene DH3 ... 82 C7
Northern Counties Sch for the Deaf NE2 ... 38 D1
Northern Terr NE23 ... 22 A1
Northern Way SR5 ... 75 A2
Northfield NE22 ... 12 B4
Northfield Cl NE16 ... 68 F5
Northfield Dr
Killingworth NE12 ... 29 B2
Sunderland SR4 ... 85 B2
Northfield Gdns NE34 ... 59 F8
Northfield Rd
Newcastle-upon-Tyne NE3 ... 38 B4
South Shields NE33 ... 42 F1
Northgate NE12 ... 29 D4
Northgate & Prudhoe NHS Trust Northgate Hospl NE61 ... 3 D4
Northland Cl SR4 ... 85 B2
Northlands
Chester le Street DH3 ... 88 C5
Blaydon NE21 ... 53 B1
Tynemouth NE30 ... 32 B1
Northlands Rd NE61 ... 3 F2
Northlea NE15 ... 53 E8
Northmoor Rd NE6 ... 56 E8
Northolt Ave NE23 ... 22 B7
Northside Pl NE25 ... 23 E2
Northumberland Aged Mineworkers Homes NE23 ... 22 D5
Northumberland Ave
Longbenton NE12 ... 39 D7
Bedlington NE22 ... 10 E1
Wallsend NE28 ... 40 F2
Newcastle-upon-Tyne NE3 ... 38 A3
Newbiggin-by-the-Sea NE64 ... 7 D4
Northumberland Cl NE63 ... 6 A4
Northumberland Coll NE63 ... 6 E2

Northumberland Ct NE31 .57 D5
Northumberland Dock Rd
NE28 ....41 C1
Northumberland Gdns
Newcastle-upon-Tyne, Jesmond Vale NE2 ....56 A8
Newcastle-upon-Tyne, North Wallbottle NE5 ....36 B3
Northumberland National Park Visitor Centre* NE65 ....117 F4
Northumberland National Park Visitor Centre* NE66 ....111 E4
Northumberland Pl
Birtley DH3 ....82 D1
Newcastle-upon-Tyne NE1 ..99 A2
9 North Shields NE30 ....42 A6
Northumberland Rd
Newcastle-upon-Tyne NE1, NE99 ....99 B2
Newcastle-upon-Tyne, Lemington NE15 ....53 C6
Ryton NE40 ....52 C6
Northumberland Sq
Whitley Bay NE26 ....32 A5
4 North Shields NE30 ....42 B6
Northumberland St
Newcastle-upon-Tyne NE1 ..99 A2
Wallsend NE28 ....40 C2
North Shields NE30 ....42 C6
Gateshead NE8 ....100 C1
Northumberland Terr
Wallsend NE28 ....40 F2
Tynemouth NE30 ....42 D7
29 Newcastle-upon-Tyne NE6 ....56 B6
Northumberland Villas
NE28 ....40 E2
Northumberland Way
Washington, Usworth NE10, NE37 ....72 D3
Washington, Columbia NE37, NE38 ....83 F4
Northumbria Lodge NE5 ..37 E1
Northumbria Police Headquarters NE20 ....25 D8
Northumbria Wlk
Newcastle-upon-Tyne, East Denton NE5 ....37 A2
Newcastle-upon-Tyne, West Denton NE5 ....36 F1
Northumbrian Rd NE23 ...22 B6
Northumbrian Way
Killingworth NE12 ....29 C2
North Shields NE29 ....42 A3
Northway Throckley NE15 ..35 D3
Guide Post NE62 ....10 F7
Gateshead NE9 ....71 B7
Northwood Ct SR5 ....75 C2
Norton Ave SR7 ....93 A1
Norton Cl DH2 ....88 A1
Norton Rd SR5 ....75 A3
Norton Way NE15 ....53 E6
Norway Ave SR4 ....85 E4
Norwich Ave NE13 ....28 B5
Norwich Cl NE63 ....7 A2
Norwich Way
Cramlington NE23 ....22 A7
Hedworth NE32 ....58 B1
Norwood Ave
Newcastle-upon-Tyne, Brunton Park NE3 ....28 C1
Newcastle-upon-Tyne, Heaton NE6 ....39 B1
Norwood Cres NE39 ....67 F2
Norwood Ct NE9 ....71 C2
Norwood Gdns 4 NE9 ...71 A8
Norwood Rd
Gateshead NE11 ....70 B7
Newcastle-upon-Tyne NE15 .53 D8
Numbers Garth SR1 ....103 B3
Nun St NE1 ....99 A1
Nuneaton Way NE5 ....36 B4
Nunn St DH4 ....90 A5
Nunnykirk Cl NE42 ....50 A4
Nuns La
Newcastle-upon-Tyne NE1 ..99 A1
Gateshead NE8 ....101 C3
Nuns Moor Cres NE4 ....54 E7
Nuns Moor Rd NE4 ....54 E7
Nunthorpe Ave SR2 ....86 F1
Nunwick Gdns NE29 ....41 C6
Nunwick Way NE7 ....39 D4
Nursery Cl SR3 ....86 A2
Nursery Ct NE17 ....77 B6
Nursery La
Gateshead NE10 ....71 C7
Cleadon SR6 ....60 A1
Nursery Pk NE63 ....6 E1
Nursery Rd SR3 ....86 A2
Nutley Pl NE15 ....54 A5
Nye Baven Ho NE63 ....6 E2
Nye Dene SR5 ....74 B1

O

O'Hanlon Cres NE28 ....40 A4
Oak Ave
5 Houghton-le-Spring DH4 .94 D8
Dunston NE11 ....69 F7
Dinnington NE13 ....27 C7
South Shields NE34 ....60 A5
Oak Cl NE46 ....44 E3
Oak Cres SR6 ....61 A2
Oak Gr Longbenton NE12 ...39 D8
Wallsend NE28 ....40 D1
Oak Rd NE29 ....41 B7
Oak Sq NE8 ....100 C1
Oak St Great Lumley DH4 ..89 E1
Seaton Burn NE13 ....28 C8
1 Throckley NE15 ....35 D2
Jarrow NE32 ....58 A7
Washington NE38 ....83 F4
Mickley Square NE43 ....64 E8
Sunderland SR1 ....103 C2
Oak Terr Tantobie DH9 ....79 B2
Burnopfield NE16 ....79 C6
Blaydon NE21 ....53 C1
Oakapple Cl NE22 ....10 F1
Oakdale NE22 ....15 B8
Oakdale Cl NE15 ....53 D6
Oakdale Terr DH3 ....88 C2
Oakenshaw NE15 ....53 E6
Oakeys Rd DH9 ....79 F1
Oakfield Ave NE16 ....69 B6
Oakfield Cl
Whickham NE16 ....69 B6
Sunderland SR3 ....91 C6
Oakfield Coll NE4 ....54 D6
Oakfield Ct SR3 ....91 C6
Oakfield Dr
Killingworth NE12 ....29 F3
Whickham NE16 ....69 B6
Oakfield Gdns
Newcastle-upon-Tyne NE15 .54 D5
Wallsend NE28 ....39 F3
Oakfield Grange NE13 ....27 B7
Oakfield Inf & Jun Schs NE9 ....70 F3
Oakfield N NE40 ....52 B5
Oakfield Pk NE42 ....50 D2
Oakfield Rd Dunston NE11 .70 A6
Whickham NE16 ....69 A5
Newcastle-upon-Tyne NE3 ..38 B3
Oakfield Terr
Gateshead NE10 ....57 B2
Killingworth NE12 ....29 E1
Newcastle-upon-Tyne NE3 ..38 B4
Oakfield Way NE23 ....22 F1
Oakfields NE16 ....79 B7
Oakham Ave NE16 ....68 F6
Oakham Gdns NE29 ....41 E5
Oakhampton Dr DH4 ....90 C4
Oakhurst Dr NE3 ....38 A3
Oakhurst Terr NE12 ....39 D7
Oakland Rd
Newcastle-upon-Tyne NE2 ..38 D2
Whitley Bay NE25 ....31 D4
Oakland Terr
Lynemouth NE61 ....2 A2
Ashington NE63 ....6 C3
Oaklands Whickham NE16 ..69 C8
Ponteland NE20 ....25 D4
Newcastle-upon-Tyne NE3 ..38 C3
Riding Mill NE44 ....62 F7
Stakeford NE62 ....11 A7
Oaklands Ave NE3 ....38 C3
Oaklands Ct NE20 ....25 D4
Oaklands Rise NE44 ....62 F7
Oaklands Terr SR4 ....102 A1
Oaklea DH2 ....88 A5
Oakleigh Gdns SR6 ....60 A2
Oakley Cl NE23 ....29 B8
Oakley Dr NE23 ....22 D7
Oakley Gardens Specl Sch SR6 ....60 B2
Oakmere Cl 2 DH4 ....90 B6
Oakridge NE16 ....68 F6
Oaks The Penshaw DH4 ....90 B8
High Spen NE39 ....67 A3
Greenside NE40 ....52 B1
Hexham NE46 ....44 F3
Sunderland SR2 ....103 B1
Oaks W The SR2 ....103 B1
Oaktree Ave NE6 ....40 A1
Oaktree Gdns NE25 ....31 E3
Oaktree Terr NE42 ....50 D2
Oakville NE63 ....7 A2
Oakwellgate NE8 ....101 C4
Oakwood Gateshead NE10 ..71 E5
Hebburn NE31 ....57 C7
Oakwood NE46 ....45 E8
Oakwood Ave
Wide Open NE13 ....28 C5
Newbiggin-by-the-Sea NE64 ..7 D5
Gateshead NE9 ....71 A3
Oakwood Bank NE46 ....45 C7
Oakwood Cl NE9 ....71 F1
Oakwood Gdns NE11 ....70 B5
Oakwood Pl 2 NE5 ....37 C1
Oakwood St SR2 ....102 B1
Oakwood Terr NE28 ....41 D2
Oatens Bank NE15 ....33 A2
Oates St SR4 ....102 A2
Oatfield Cl NE63 ....6 B2
Oatlands Rd SR4 ....85 E4
Oban Ave NE28 ....40 F4
Oban Ct NE6 ....56 C5
Oban Gdns 9 NE6 ....56 C5
Oban St Gateshead NE10 ..56 C1
Brockley Whins NE32 ....58 E3
Ocean Rd
South Shields NE33 ....42 D3
Sunderland SR2 ....86 F2
Ocean Rd N 6 SR2 ....86 F2
Ocean Rd S 7 SR2 ....86 F2
Ocean View
Whitley Bay NE26 ....32 B5
Newbiggin-by-the-Sea NE64 ..7 E4
Sunderland SR2 ....92 F8
Ochiltree Ct NE26 ....24 D6
Octavia Cl NE22 ....10 E2
Octavia Ct NE28 ....40 F4
Octavian Way NE11 ....70 C3
Odinel Ct NE42 ....50 D3
Offerton Cl 7 SR4 ....85 A6
Offerton La Penshaw SR4 ..84 F4
Sunderland SR4 ....85 A5
Offerton St SR4 ....102 B2
Office Pl DH5 ....95 A3
Office Row
New Herrington DH4 ....90 E7
Washington NE38 ....83 A1
Ogden St SR4 ....102 B2
Ogle Ave Hazlerigg NE13 ..28 A4
Morpeth NE61 ....8 E8
Ogle Dr NE24 ....17 C7
Ogle Gr NE32 ....58 A3
Oil Mill Rd NE6 ....57 B7
Okehampton Ct 2 NE9 ..71 A2
Okehampton Sq SR5 ....75 A3
Old Brewery Sq NE42 ....49 C4
Old Brewery The 10 DH4 ..94 E8
Old Coastguard Cotts NE30 ....42 E7
Old Coronation St NE33 ..42 C2
Old Course Rd SR6 ....75 A8
Old Durham Rd NE8,NE9 ..71 B6
Old Farm Ct NE16 ....69 B2
Old Fold Rd NE10,NE8 ....56 B2
Old Forge The NE43 ....48 C5
Old Main St NE40 ....51 E3
Old Mill Rd
Sunderland, Hendon SR2 ..103 C1
Sunderland, High Southwick SR5 ....75 A3
Old Orchard The NE44 ....63 A7
Old Rectory Cl DH9 ....79 D4
Old Sawmill NE61 ....8 A8
Old Station Ct NE20 ....25 C3
Old Vicarage Wlk 20 NE6 .56 C6
Old Well La NE21 ....53 B1
Oldfield Rd NE6 ....56 F3
Oldgate NE61 ....8 F8
Oldgate Ct NE61 ....8 F8
Oldstead Gdns SR4 ....85 E4
Oldwell Ave 4 NE21 ....53 B1
Olga Terr NE39 ....67 C1
Olive Gdns NE9 ....71 A6
Olive Pl NE4 ....54 D7
Olive St South Shields NE33 .59 B6
Sunderland SR1 ....102 C2
Oliver Ave NE4 ....54 E6
Oliver Cres DH3 ....82 C6
Oliver St 2 NE38 ....83 E4
Olivers Mill NE61 ....8 F8
Ollerton Dr NE15 ....35 B2
Ollerton Gdns NE10 ....71 C6
Olney Cl NE23 ....22 D7
Olympia Ave NE62 ....10 F7
Olympia Gdns NE61 ....4 A1
Olympia Hill NE61 ....3 F2
Ongar Way NE12 ....39 B7
Onslow Gdns NE9 ....70 F5
Onslow St SR4 ....85 E7
Open The NE1 ....99 A2
Oram Cl NE61 ....9 B8
Orange Gr Whickham NE16 .69 C8
Annitsford NE23 ....22 B1
Orchard Ave NE39 ....67 D1
Orchard Cl
Killingworth NE12 ....29 F2
Sunniside NE16 ....69 B3
South Shields NE34 ....59 B5
Rowlands Gill NE39 ....78 D8
Prudhoe NE42 ....50 D1
Morpeth NE61 ....9 B8
Ashington NE63 ....6 C2
Orchard Cres NE45 ....47 A5
Orchard Ct
Tynemouth NE29 ....42 A8
Ryton NE40 ....52 C5
Greenside NE40,NE41 ....51 F1
Orchard Dene NE39 ....67 D1
Orchard Gdns
Chester le Street DH3 ....88 C1
Wallsend NE28 ....40 A4
Gateshead NE9 ....71 A4
Whitburn SR6 ....75 E8
Orchard Gn NE5 ....37 D4
Orchard Hill NE42 ....50 D3
Orchard Pk 7 DH3 ....82 C4
Orchard Pl NE2 ....38 F1
Orchard Rd
Whickham NE16 ....69 C7
Rowlands Gill NE39 ....67 D1
Orchard Rise NE15 ....53 B7
Orchard St Birtley DH3 ....82 C4
Newcastle-upon-Tyne NE1 .101 A4
Sunderland SR4 ....85 F7
Orchard Terr
Chester le Street DH3 ....88 C1
Newcastle-upon-Tyne NE15 .53 C6
8 Throckley NE15 ....35 D2
Rowlands Gill NE39 ....78 D8
Orchard The
Chester le Street DH3 ....88 D4
Newcastle-upon-Tyne NE15 .53 D6
Whickham NE16 ....69 C7
4 North Shields NE29 ....42 A6
East Boldon NE36 ....74 C7
Wylam NE41 ....51 A6
Hepscott NE61 ....9 E5
Orchard-Leigh NE15 ....53 E6
Orchards The NE24 ....17 B8
Orchid Cl NE34 ....59 B5
Orchid Cres NE10 ....56 C2
Ord Ct NE4 ....54 D7
Ord St NE4 ....100 C3
Ord Terr NE62 ....11 B8
Orde Ave NE28 ....40 E3
Ordley Cl NE15 ....53 E6
Oriel Cl SR6 ....75 D1
Oriole House NE12 ....39 D7
Orkney Dr SR2 ....92 D8
Orlando Rd NE29 ....41 E6
Ormesby Rd SR6 ....75 D3
Ormiscraig NE15 ....53 E6
Ormiston NE15 ....53 E6
Ormonde Ave NE15 ....54 A6
Ormonde St Jarrow NE32 ..58 B7
Sunderland SR4 ....102 A1
Ormsby Gn NE5 ....54 A8
Ormskirk Cl NE15 ....53 D6
Ormskirk Gr NE23 ....22 C7
Ormston St NE23 ....16 B3
Orpen Ave NE34 ....59 C3
Orpine Ct NE63 ....6 C2
Orpington Ave NE6 ....56 E6
Orpington Rd NE23 ....22 C7
Orr Ave SR3 ....92 B6
Orton Cl NE4 ....54 E4
Orwell Cl NE34 ....59 B2
Osbaldeston Gdns NE3 ...38 B3
Osborne Ave
Newcastle-upon-Tyne NE2 ..99 C4
South Shields NE33 ....42 E1
Hexham NE46 ....44 F5
Osborne Cl NE22 ....11 C2
Osborne Ct NE2 ....99 C4
Osborne Gdns
Whitley Bay NE26 ....31 F5
Tynemouth NE29 ....42 A7
Osborne House NE28 ....40 E2
Osborne Rd
Chester le Street DH3 ....88 C3
Newcastle-upon-Tyne NE2 ..38 E2
Sunderland SR5 ....85 A7
Osborne St
South Shields NE33 ....42 E2
Sunderland SR6 ....75 D2
Osborne Terr
Newcastle-upon-Tyne NE2 ..99 B3
Cramlington NE23 ....22 A7
Gateshead NE8 ....101 A1
Osborne Villas NE2 ....99 B4
Osforth Park Way NE3 ....39 A8
Osier Ct NE62 ....11 C7
Oslo Cl NE29 ....41 B4
Osman Cl SR2 ....103 B1
Osprey Dr Blyth NE24 ....17 F5
Shiremoor NE28 ....41 A6
Osprey House 4 NE2 ....38 E1
Osprey Way NE34 ....59 B4
Oswald Rd
Hetton le Hole DH5 ....95 A5
Morpeth NE61 ....4 A2
Newbiggin-by-the-Sea NE64 ..7 D5
Oswald St Whiteleas NE34 .59 C3
Sunderland SR4 ....102 A3
Oswald Terr
Gateshead NE8 ....101 A1
Sunderland, Grangetown SR2 ....86 F2
Sunderland, Castletown SR5 ....74 C1
Oswald Terr S SR5 ....74 C1
Oswald Wlk NE3 ....38 E5
Oswestry Pl NE23 ....22 C7
Oswin Ave NE12 ....39 D8
Oswin Ct NE12 ....29 E1
Oswin Rd NE12 ....29 E1
Oswin Terr NE29 ....41 D5
Otley Cl NE23 ....22 D7
Otter Burn Way NE42 ....50 B1
Otterburn Ave
Earsdon NE25 ....31 B4
Newcastle-upon-Tyne NE3 ..38 A4
Otterburn Cl NE12 ....39 F8
Otterburn Cres DH4 ....90 C1
Otterburn Ct
Whitley Bay NE25 ....31 B4
Gateshead NE8 ....101 A1
Otterburn Dr NE63 ....6 B1
Otterburn Gdns
Dunston NE11 ....70 A7
Whickham NE16 ....69 B7
South Shields NE34 ....59 E6
Gateshead NE9 ....70 E5
Otterburn Gr NE24 ....17 B5
Otterburn Rd NE29 ....41 F7
Otterburn Terr NE2 ....38 E1
Ottercap Cl NE15 ....53 D6
Ottercops NE42 ....50 B1
Otterington NE38 ....84 B4
Ottershaw NE15 ....53 E6
Otto Terr SR2 ....102 B1
Ottovale Cres NE21 ....53 A1
Ottringham Cl NE15 ....53 D6
Oulton Cl
Cramlington NE23 ....22 C7
Newcastle-upon-Tyne NE5 ..37 B4
Our Lady Queen of Peace RC Prim Sch DH4 ....90 A7
Ousby Ct NE3 ....37 D7
Ouse St NE1 ....56 A5
Ouseburn Cl SR2 ....92 F8
Ouseburn Rd
Newcastle-upon-Tyne, St Ann's NE1 ....56 A6
Newcastle-upon-Tyne, Jesmond Vale NE2,NE6 ....56 A8
Ouselaw NE11 ....81 D6
Ouslaw La NE11 ....81 B6
Ouston Cl NE10 ....72 C7
Ouston Inf Sch DH2 ....82 A1
Ouston Jun Sch DH2 ....81 F1
Ouston St NE15 ....53 F5
Outram St DH5 ....90 E1
Oval Park View NE10 ....71 D7
Oval The Ouston DH2 ....81 F2
Houghton-le-Spring DH4 ....94 D8
Longbenton NE12 ....39 E6
Woolsington NE13 ....36 F8
Bedlington NE22 ....11 C1
Blyth NE24 ....17 B3
Washington NE37 ....83 D8
Newcastle-upon-Tyne NE6 ..56 D4
4 Sunderland SR5 ....75 B2
Overdale Ct NE62 ....10 E6
Overdene NE15 ....53 F7
Overfield Rd NE3 ....37 F5
Overhill NE15 ....34 E2
Overhill Terr NE8 ....101 A1
Overton Cl NE15 ....53 D6
Overton Rd NE29 ....41 E8
Ovingham CE Fst Sch NE42 ....50 A3
Ovingham Cl NE38 ....83 F5
Ovingham Gdns NE13 ....28 B6
Ovingham Mid Sch NE42 .50 A3
Ovingham Rd NE41 ....51 A6
Ovington Gr NE5 ....54 D8
Ovington View NE42 ....50 B1
Owen Brannigan Dr NE23 ....29 B7
Owen Ct NE2 ....98 C3
Owen Dr NE35,NE36 ....74 B8
Owen Terr Tantobie DH9 ..79 B2
Chopwell NE17 ....77 C8
Owlet Cl NE21 ....53 A1
Oxberry Gdns NE10 ....71 C7
Oxbridge St SR2 ....86 F2
Oxclose Rd NE38 ....83 E4
Oxclose Sch NE38 ....83 A4
Oxclose Village Prim Sch NE38 ....83 A5
Oxford Ave
Cramlington NE23 ....22 C7
Wallsend NE28 ....40 A3
10 South Shields NE33 ....59 D8
Washington NE37 ....83 B8
Oxford Cl SR3 ....91 F8
Oxford Cres
Hetton le Hole DH5 ....94 F4
Hebburn NE31 ....57 F6
Oxford Pl DH3 ....82 C1
Oxford Rd NE62 ....11 A7
Oxford Sq SR4 ....85 E7
Oxford St
Newcastle-upon-Tyne NE1 ..99 B2
Blyth NE24 ....17 F7
Whitley Bay NE26 ....32 B5
Tynemouth NE30 ....42 D7
South Shields NE33 ....59 D8
Sunderland SR4 ....85 E7
Oxford Terr
Shiney Row DH4 ....90 A6
Gateshead NE8 ....101 B1
Oxford Way NE32 ....58 B1
Oxnam Cres NE2 ....98 B3
Oxted Cl NE23 ....22 D7
Oxted Pl NE6 ....56 E3
Oystershell La NE4 ....98 C1
Oyston St NE33 ....42 C2
Ozanan Cl NE23 ....29 B7

P

Packham Rd SR4 ....85 C5
Paddock Cl
Shiney Row DH4 ....89 F5
Prudhoe NE42 ....50 E2
Cleadon SR6 ....59 E1
Paddock Hill NE20 ....25 F7
Paddock La SR3 ....92 C7
Paddock Rise NE63 ....6 B2
Paddock The
New Herrington DH4 ....90 F7
Gateshead NE10 ....71 F6
Woolsington NE13 ....36 F8
Walbottle NE15 ....35 F1
East Cramlington NE23 ....22 D5
Blyth NE24 ....17 C7
Seaton Delaval NE25 ....23 E3
Stocksfield NE43 ....64 C5
Ashington NE63 ....7 B2
Paddock Wood NE42 ....50 E2
Pader Cl NE13 ....28 B5
Padgate Rd SR4 ....85 C6
Padonhill 5 SR3 ....91 E5
Padstow Cl 2 SR2 ....92 F8
Padstow Ct NE9 ....70 F2
Padstow Rd NE29 ....41 E4
Page Ave NE34 ....59 E7
Page St NE31 ....57 F7
Page's Bldgs NE35 ....73 E8
Paignton Ave
Whitley Bay NE25 ....31 E4
Newcastle-upon-Tyne NE4 ..54 F5
Paignton Sq SR3 ....85 E2
Painshawfield Rd NE43 ..64 C6
Paisley Sq SR3 ....85 E2
Palace Rd NE22 ....11 D2
Palace St NE4 ....100 B4
Palatine View DH6 ....96 C1
Palermo St SR4 ....85 F8
Paley St SR1 ....102 C3
Palgrove Rd SR4 ....85 C5
Palgrove Sq SR4 ....85 C5
Pallinsburn Ct NE5 ....37 B3
Pallion Ind Est SR4 ....85 D7
Pallion New Rd SR4 ....85 F8
Pallion Pk SR4 ....85 F7

Pallion Prim Sch SR4 ....85 E8
Pallion Rd SR4 ....85 F6
Pallion Ret Pk SR4 ....85 E8
Pallion Sta SR4 ....85 E8
Pallion Subway SR4 ....85 F8
Pallion Way SR4 ....85 E7
Pallion West Ind Est SR4 .85 D7
Palm Ave
South Shields NE34 ....60 A5
Newcastle-upon-Tyne NE4 ..54 D7
Palm Ct NE12 ....29 F1
Palm Terr DH9 ....79 C3
Palmer Community Hospl
NE32 ....58 B7
Palmer Cres NE31 ....57 F6
Palmer Gdns NE10 ....72 C8
Palmer Rd DH9 ....78 E1
Palmer St NE32 ....58 A7
Palmer's Hill Rd SR6 ....103 A4
Palmers Gn NE12 ....29 F1
Palmerston Ave NE6 ....56 E7
Palmerston Rd SR4 ....85 B3
Palmerston Sq SR4 ....85 C4
Palmerston St NE33 ....59 C8
Palmerston Wlk NE8 ....101 A2
Palmersville NE12 ....29 F1
Palmersville Sta NE12 ....30 A1
Palmstead Rd SR4 ....85 C5
Palmstead Sq SR4 ....85 C5
Pancras Rd SR3 ....85 E2
Pandon NE1 ....99 B1
Pandon Bank NE1 ....99 B1
Pandon Ct NE2 ....99 C2
Pandon Quays NE1 ....99 C1
Panfield Terr DH4 ....89 E2
Pangbourne Cl NE15 ....53 C8
Pankhurst Gdns NE10 ....72 A8
Pann La SR1 ....103 A3
Panns Bank SR1 ....103 A3
Pantiles The NE37 ....72 D2
Parade Cl NE6 ....57 A5
Parade The
Chester le Street DH3 ....88 D1
Wallsend NE28 ....40 D5
Washington NE38 ....83 E4
Newcastle-upon-Tyne NE6 ..57 A5
Sunderland SR2 ....103 C1
Paradise Row NE23 ....22 B6
Park Ave Dunston NE11 ....69 E7
Blaydon NE21 ....53 C2
Bedlington NE22 ....11 E3
Whitley Bay NE26 ....32 A5
Shiremoor NE27 ....31 A3
Wallsend NE28 ....40 B2
Newcastle-upon-Tyne, Fawdon
NE3 ....37 F7
Newcastle-upon-Tyne, Gosforth
NE3 ....38 B6
North Shields NE30 ....42 C7
South Shields NE34 ....59 F4
Washington NE37 ....83 D8
Prudhoe NE42 ....50 E1
Hexham NE46 ....44 F5
New Silksworth SR3 ....92 B7
Sunderland SR6 ....75 E4
Park Chare NE38 ....83 D5
Park Cl NE4 ....100 A4
Park Cotts NE17 ....77 B6
Park Cres Shiremoor NE27 ....30 F3
North Shields NE30 ....42 B7
Park Cres E NE30 ....42 C7
Park Ct
Gateshead, Team Valley
NE11 ....70 D3
Newcastle-upon-Tyne NE6 ..40 A1
Gateshead NE8 ....101 C3
Park Dr Longbenton NE12 ..39 E8
Whickham NE16 ....69 C8
Blyth NE24 ....17 B4
Newcastle-upon-Tyne NE3 ..28 C1
Morpeth NE61 ....8 F7
Stannington NE61 ....9 E1
Park Field NE40 ....52 C5
Park Field Terr NE26 ....24 C6
Park Gate SR6 ....75 E3
Park Gates NE26 ....32 A5
Park Gr Shiremoor NE27 ..30 F3
Washington NE37 ....72 D1
Park Head Rd NE7 ....39 A1
Park House Gdns DH6 ....96 A2
Park La Blaydon NE21 ....68 B8
Shiremoor NE27 ....30 F2
Prudhoe NE42 ....50 D1
Gateshead NE8 ....56 A3
Sunderland SR1 ....103 A2
Park Lane Intc SR1 ....103 A2
Park Lane Sta SR1 ....103 A2
Park Lea SR3 ....91 B6
Park Lea Rd SR6 ....75 E3
Park Par Whitley Bay NE26 .32 A5
Sunderland SR6 ....75 E2
Park Pl DH3 ....88 D5
Park Pl E SR2 ....103 A1
Park Pl W SR2 ....103 A1
Park Rd
Gateshead NE10,NE8 ....56 B2
Newburn NE15 ....52 F8
Bedlington NE22 ....16 A8
Blyth NE24 ....17 F7
Seaton Delaval NE25 ....23 C3
Whitley Bay NE26 ....32 A6
Shiremoor NE27 ....30 F3
Wallsend NE28 ....40 C1
Hebburn NE31 ....57 E5
Jarrow NE32 ....58 A6

Park Rd *continued*
Rowlands Gill NE39 ....67 D2
Newcastle-upon-Tyne NE4 .100 A3
Lynmouth NE61,NE63 ....2 A2
Ashington NE63 ....6 B3
Sunderland SR2 ....103 A1
Park Rd N DH3 ....88 D4
Park Rd S DH3 ....88 D1
Park Rise NE15 ....53 C7
Park Road Central DH3 ..88 D3
Park Road East NE63 ....6 C4
Park Row
3 Gateshead NE10 ....71 D8
Sunderland SR5 ....75 A1
Park Site NE61 ....9 F5
Park St S SR5 ....74 C1
Park Terr
Newcastle-upon-Tyne NE1,
NE2 ....99 A3
Dunston NE11 ....69 F8
Killingworth NE12 ....29 B2
Burnopfield NE16 ....79 A6
Whickham NE16 ....54 A1
Blaydon NE21 ....53 D2
Bedlington NE22 ....11 D3
Whitley Bay NE26 ....32 A6
Wallsend NE28 ....40 B2
North Shields NE30 ....42 C7
Washington NE37 ....72 D1
Sunderland SR5 ....75 A2
Park View
Chester le Street DH2 ....88 B5
Bournmoor DH3 ....89 D4
Shiney Row DH4 ....90 B6
Hetton le Hole DH5 ....95 A3
Longbenton, Forest Hall
NE12 ....39 D8
Longbenton, West Moor
NE12 ....29 B2
Wide Open NE13 ....28 C6
Burnopfield NE16 ....79 B6
Blaydon NE21 ....68 C8
Blyth NE24 ....17 F7
Seaton Delaval NE25 ....23 D3
Whitley Bay NE26 ....32 A5
Wallsend NE28 ....40 B2
Jarrow NE32 ....58 B4
Newcastle-upon-Tyne NE6 ..57 A5
Ashington NE63 ....6 B4
Park View Cl NE40 ....52 D5
Park View Com Sch DH3 .88 D3
Park View Com Sch (Lower)
DH3 ....88 D7
Park View Ct NE26 ....32 A5
Park View Gdns NE40 ....52 D5
Park Villas Wallsend NE28 ..40 B2
Ashington NE63 ....6 B4
Park Wall Cnr SR3 ....91 B6
Parkdale Rise NE16 ....69 A7
Parker Ave NE3 ....38 B3
Parker Ct NE11 ....54 E2
Parkfield NE32 ....58 C1
Parkgate La NE21 ....68 B8
Parkham Cl NE23 ....16 B1
Parkhead Com Prim Sch
NE21 ....68 C8
Parkhead Gdns NE21 ....68 B8
Parkhead Sq NE21 ....53 C1
Parkhouse Ave SR5 ....85 B8
Parkhurst Rd SR4 ....85 B4
Parkin Gdns NE10 ....71 E7
Parkinson's Cotts NE40 ..52 E4
Parkland Longbenton NE12 .39 D6
Ryton NE21 ....53 A4
Parkland Ave NE21 ....68 B8
Parklands Gateshead NE10 .72 C8
Ponteland NE20 ....25 B2
Hamsterley Mill NE39 ....77 F5
Parklands Ct NE10 ....57 C1
Parklands Way NE10 ....72 C8
Parklea NE26 ....24 C6
Parkmore Rd SR4 ....85 A3
Parks The DH3 ....88 E1
Parkshiel NE34 ....60 A4
Parkside Tanfield Lea DH9 ..79 C1
Dunston NE11 ....69 F8
Throckley NE15 ....35 E1
Bedlington NE22 ....11 E3
Wallsend NE28 ....40 D3
Tynemouth NE30 ....32 D1
Hebburn NE31 ....57 D4
Sunderland SR3 ....91 B6
Parkside Ave
Blaydon NE21 ....53 C1
Newcastle-upon-Tyne NE7 ..39 B5
Parkside Cotts DH9 ....79 C1
Parkside Cres NE30 ....42 D8
Parkside Ct NE26 ....31 F5
Parkside Mid Sch NE23 ..22 B7
Parkside S SR3 ....91 B6
Parkside Specl Sch
Wallsend NE28 ....40 B2
Wallsend, Battle Hill NE28 ..40 A5
Parkside Terr NE28 ....40 A4
Parkstone Cl SR4 ....85 A2
Parkville NE6 ....56 A7
Parkway Whickham NE16 ..68 E6
Washington, Biddick NE38 ..83 C4
Washington, Washington Village
NE38 ....83 D5
Guide Post NE62 ....10 F8
Parkway Sch NE5 ....36 D2
Parkwood Ave NE42 ....50 F3
Parliament St NE31 ....57 C7
Parmontley St NE15 ....53 F5
Parnell St DH4 ....94 B8
Parry Dr SR6 ....60 E1
Parson Rd NE41 ....51 B6

Parson's Ave NE6 ....56 F5
Parsons Ind Est NE37 ....83 B8
Parsons Rd NE37 ....83 B7
Parsons' Gdns 5 NE11 ..54 F1
Partick Rd SR4 ....85 B4
Partick Sq SR4 ....85 C4
Partnership Ct SR7 ....92 E2
Partridge Cl NE38 ....82 F4
Pasteur Rd DH6 ....97 F7
Paston Rd NE25 ....23 D2
Pastures The Blyth NE24 ..17 D4
Stocksfield NE43 ....64 B8
Morpeth NE61 ....8 D7
Pathside NE32 ....58 C2
Patience Ave NE13 ....28 C8
Patina Cl NE15 ....53 C8
Paton Rd SR3 ....85 F2
Paton Sq SR3 ....85 F2
Patrick Cain Ho NE33 ....59 B8
Patrick Cres DH6 ....97 E8
Patrick Terr NE23 ....29 B7
Patterdale Cl NE36 ....74 C7
Patterdale Gdns NE7 ....39 B4
Patterdale Gr SR5 ....75 C4
Patterdale Ho NE24 ....17 A8
Patterdale Rd NE24 ....17 A8
Patterdale St DH5 ....95 A2
Patterdale Terr NE8 ....70 F8
Patterson Cl NE46 ....44 E3
Patterson St NE21 ....53 E4
Pattinson Gdns
Gateshead, Old Fold NE10 ..56 C2
Gateshead, Carr Hill NE9 ..71 B7
Pattinson Ind Est
Washington NE38 ....84 B6
Washington, Swan NE38 ....83 F3
Pattinson Rd NE38 ....84 B4
Patton Way NE61 ....4 E3
Pauline Ave SR6 ....75 D3
Pauline Gdns NE15 ....54 A7
Pauls Gn DH5 ....95 A6
Pauls Rd SR1 ....103 B2
Paulsway NE32 ....58 E6
Pavilion Mews NE2 ....99 C4
Pavilion The NE16 ....53 F1
Pavillion Ct SR1 ....103 A2
Pawston Rd NE21,NE39 ..67 B5
Paxford Cl NE7 ....39 A5
Paxton House* TD15 ....104 D5
Paxton Terr SR4 ....102 A3
Peacehaven Ct NE37 ....72 C2
Peacock Ct NE11 ....70 B7
Peacock St W SR4 ....85 F6
Pear Tree Terr
Great Lumley DH3 ....89 B1
Chopwell NE17 ....77 B8
Peareth Ct NE8 ....101 C3
Peareth Gr SR6 ....75 F3
Peareth Hall Rd NE37,
NE9 ....72 A2
Peareth Rd SR6 ....75 F4
Pearl Rd SR3 ....85 F2
Pearson Pl
North Shields NE30 ....42 B6
Jarrow NE32 ....58 C8
Pearson St NE33 ....42 D4
Pearson's Terr NE46 ....45 A5
Peart Cl DH6 ....96 A1
Peartree Bglws NE17 ....77 C6
Peartree Ct NE17 ....77 C6
Peartree Gdns NE6 ....40 A1
Peary Cl NE5 ....36 F2
Pease Ave NE15 ....54 C6
Peasemoor Rd SR4 ....85 B5
Pebble Beach SR6 ....75 F7
Pecket Cl NE24 ....17 A5
Peddars Way NE34 ....59 B5
Peebles Cl NE29 ....41 C8
Peebles Rd SR3 ....85 E2
Peel Ctr The NE37 ....83 F7
Peel Gdns NE34 ....58 E4
Peel La NE1 ....100 C4
Peel St
Newcastle-upon-Tyne NE1 .100 C4
Sunderland SR2 ....103 B1
Peepy Cotts NE43 ....48 D2
Pegswood Fst Sch NE61 ....4 F4
Pegswood House NE4 ....98 B2
Pegswood Ind Est NE61 ....4 F4
Pegswood Sta NE61 ....4 F3
Pegwood Rd SR4 ....85 C5
Pelaw Ave
Chester le Street DH2 ....88 C5
Newbiggin-by-the-Sea NE64 ..7 D5
Pelaw Bank DH3 ....88 C4
Pelaw Cres DH2 ....88 B5
Pelaw Grange Ct DH3 ....88 C8
Pelaw Ind Est NE10 ....72 A8
Pelaw Inf Sch DH2 ....88 B5
Pelaw Pl DH2 ....88 C5
Pelaw Rd DH2 ....88 C5
Pelaw Sq
Chester le Street DH2 ....88 B5
Sunderland SR4 ....85 C7
Pelaw Sta NE10 ....57 A1
Pelaw Way NE10 ....57 A1
Peldon Cl NE7 ....38 F5
Pelham Ct NE3 ....37 D7
Pelton Fell Rd DH2 ....88 B4
Pelton La DH2 ....88 B5
Pelton Rd SR4 ....85 C4
Peltondale Ave NE24 ....17 A6
Pemberton Bank DH5 ....95 C1
Pemberton Cl 7 SR5 ....75 B1
Pemberton Gdns 3 SR3 ..86 B3
Pemberton St DH5 ....95 A4
Pembridge NE38 ....83 A5

Pembroke Ave
Birtley DH3 ....82 D1
Newcastle-upon-Tyne NE6 ..56 E7
New Silksworth SR3 ....92 A6
Pembroke Ct
Newcastle-upon-Tyne NE3 ..37 D7
Newbiggin-by-the-Sea NE64 ..7 E5
Pembroke Dr NE20 ....25 B4
Pembroke Gdns
Wallsend NE28 ....41 A4
Ashington NE63 ....7 A1
Pembroke Terr NE33 ....59 C7
Pendeford NE38 ....84 A4
Pendle Cl NE38 ....83 B3
Pendle Gn SR4 ....102 A1
Pendleton Dr NE23 ....16 B1
Pendower Hall Sch NE15 .54 C6
Pendower Way NE15 ....54 C5
Penfold Cl NE7 ....39 C4
Penhale Dr SR2 ....92 F7
Penhill Cl DH2 ....81 F1
Penistone Rd SR4 ....85 A4
Penman Pl NE29 ....42 A4
Penman Sq SR4 ....85 C4
Penman St NE29 ....42 A4
Penn Sq SR4 ....85 C6
Penn St NE4 ....100 B3
Pennant Sq SR4 ....85 C6
Pennine Ave DH2 ....88 B2
Pennine Ct 23 SR3 ....91 F6
Pennine Dr NE63 ....6 E1
Pennine Gdns NE11 ....70 A6
Pennine Gr NE36 ....74 B7
Pennine View NE17 ....77 B8
Pennine Way NE12 ....39 A6
Pennycross Rd SR4 ....85 A4
Pennycross Sq SR4 ....85 A5
Pennyfine Cl NE29 ....42 A8
Pennyfine Rd NE16 ....69 C2
Pennygate Sq SR4 ....85 A5
Pennygreen Sq SR4 ....85 A5
Pennymore Sq SR4 ....85 A4
Pennywell Bsns Ctr SR4 ..85 C5
Pennywell Comp Sch
SR4 ....85 B4
Pennywell Ind Est SR4 ..85 A3
Pennywell Rd SR4 ....85 C4
Pennywell Sh Prec SR4 .85 C4
Penrith Ave NE30 ....32 A2
Penrith Gdns NE9 ....71 B4
Penrith Gr NE9 ....71 B4
Penrith Rd Hebburn NE31 ..57 F4
Sunderland SR5 ....75 C4
Penrose Gn NE3 ....37 F5
Penrose Rd SR4 ....85 B4
Pensford Ct NE3 ....37 C6
Penshaw Gn NE5 ....37 D3
Penshaw La DH4 ....90 B8
Penshaw Monument*
SR4 ....84 C1
Penshaw View
Birtley DH3 ....82 E3
Gateshead NE10 ....72 C8
Hebburn NE31 ....57 E4
Jarrow NE32 ....58 B4
Penshaw Way DH3 ....82 E4
Pensher St
Gateshead NE10 ....56 C1
Sunderland SR4 ....102 B2
Pensher St E NE10 ....56 C1
Pent Ct NE40 ....52 A1
Pentland Cl
Cramlington NE23 ....16 B1
Tynemouth NE29 ....31 F1
Washington NE38 ....83 B3
Ashington NE63 ....6 E1
Pentland Ct 5 DH2 ....88 C2
Pentland Gdns NE11 ....70 A7
Pentland Gr NE12 ....29 B1
Pentridge Cl NE23 ....22 C7
Penwood Rd SR4 ....85 C5
Penyghent Way NE37 ....83 A6
Penzance Par NE31 ....58 A2
Penzance Rd SR4 ....85 B4
Peplow Sq SR4 ....85 C7
Peppercorn Ct NE1 ....101 B4
Peragrine CT NE28 ....41 F6
Percival St SR4 ....85 F7
Percy Ave
Whitley Bay NE26 ....32 A5
Tynemouth NE30 ....32 C3
Percy Cl NE46 ....44 F3
Percy Cotts NE25 ....23 E2
Percy Cres NE29 ....41 D3
Percy Ct NE29 ....41 D3
Percy Gardens Cotts
NE30 ....42 D8
Percy Gdns Dunston NE11 .70 A7
Longbenton NE12 ....39 D8
Whitley Bay NE25 ....32 A4
Tynemouth NE30 ....42 E8
Stakeford NE62 ....11 A8
Percy Lonnen NE42 ....50 D3
Percy Main Prim Sch
NE29 ....41 D2
Percy Main Sta NE29 ....41 D3
Percy Park Rd NE30 ....42 D8
Percy Pk NE30 ....42 D8
Percy Rd NE26 ....32 B5
Percy Scott St NE34 ....59 C3
Percy St
Hetton le Hole DH5 ....95 B4
Newcastle-upon-Tyne NE1 ..99 A2
Longbenton NE12 ....29 F1
Newcastle-upon-Tyne, Lemington
NE15 ....53 C6
Cramlington NE23 ....22 C5
Blyth NE24 ....17 F8

Percy St *continued*
Wallsend NE28 ....40 C2
Tynemouth NE30 ....42 E7
Jarrow NE32 ....58 C7
5 South Shields NE33 ....42 D2
Ashington NE63 ....6 E4
Percy St John's C of E Prim
Sch NE29 ....41 E3
Percy St S NE24 ....17 F7
Percy Terr Penshaw DH4 ....90 A8
Newburn NE15 ....52 F7
Whitley Bay NE25 ....31 E5
Newcastle-upon-Tyne NE3 ..38 E5
Sunderland SR2 ....86 E4
4 Whitburn SR6 ....60 F7
Percy Terr S SR2 ....86 F3
Percy Way NE15 ....36 A1
Peregrine Pl NE12 ....39 A7
Perivale Rd SR4 ....85 B4
Perry St NE8,NE9 ....70 F8
Perrycrofts SR3 ....92 A4
Perth Ave NE32,NE34 ....58 E3
Perth Cl Wallsend NE28 ....40 F4
Tynemouth NE29 ....41 C8
Perth Ct Gateshead NE11 ..70 E3
Sunderland SR3 ....85 E1
Perth Gdns NE28 ....40 F4
Perth Rd SR3 ....85 F2
Perth Sq SR3 ....85 F2
Pescott Cl NE46 ....45 B4
Pesspool Ave DH6 ....97 F3
Pesspool Bglws DH6 ....97 F3
Pesspool La DH6 ....97 F3
Pesspool Terr DH6 ....97 F3
Peterborough Cl NE8 ...101 B2
Peterborough Way NE32 .58 B1
Petersfield Rd SR4 ....85 B4
Petersham Rd SR4 ....85 C6
Peth Gn DH5 ....95 B3
Peth Head NE46 ....45 C5
Peth La NE40 ....52 D6
Petherton Ct NE3 ....37 C6
Pethgate Ct 5 NE61 ....9 A8
Petrel Cl 12 NE33 ....42 C4
Petrel Way NE24 ....17 F4
Petteril NE38 ....83 A1
Petworth Cl NE33 ....42 D3
Petworth Gdns NE61 ....4 E4
Pevensey Cl NE29 ....31 F1
Pexton Way NE5 ....54 A8
Pheasantmoor 3 NE37 ..83 A7
Philadelphia Aged Miners
Homes 6 DH4 ....90 B6
Philadelphia Complex
DH4 ....90 D6
Philadelphia La DH4 ....90 C4
Philip Pl NE4 ....98 A2
Philip Sq SR3 ....85 E2
Philip St NE4 ....98 A2
Philiphaugh NE28 ....57 B8
Philipson St NE6 ....56 F6
Phillips Ave NE16 ....69 A8
Phillips Cl DH6 ....97 E3
Phobe Grange Cotts
NE42 ....50 D2
Phoenix Chase NE29 ....41 C8
Phoenix Ct
Tynemouth NE29 ....41 C8
Morpeth NE61 ....8 F8
Phoenix Rd
Washington NE38 ....82 E6
Sunderland SR4 ....85 C6
Phoenix St NE24 ....17 B4
Phoenix Way DH4 ....94 C7
Piccadilly SR3 ....91 E8
Picherwell NE10 ....71 D7
Pickard St SR4 ....102 A3
Pickering Ct NE32 ....58 A7
Pickering Gn NE9 ....71 B2
Pickering Rd SR4 ....85 B3
Pickering Sq SR4 ....85 B4
Pickersgill Ho SR5 ....74 C3
Pickhurst Rd SR4 ....85 B3
Pickhurst Sq SR4 ....85 B3
Picktree Cotts 2 DH3 ....88 D4
Picktree Cotts E 3 DH3 ..88 D4
Picktree Farm Cotts
NE38 ....88 E7
Picktree La
Chester le Street DH3 ....88 D4
Chester le Street, Picktree
DH3,NE38 ....88 E7
Picktree Lodge
Chester le Street DH3 ....88 D8
Birtley NE38 ....82 E1
Picktree Terr 1 DH3 ....88 D4
Pier Par NE33 ....42 E4
Pier Rd NE30 ....42 E7
Pier View SR6 ....75 F2
Pikestone Cl NE38 ....83 A3
Pilgrim Cl SR5 ....75 C1
Pilgrim St
Newcastle-upon-Tyne NE1 ..99 B1
Newcastle-upon-Tyne NE1 .101 B4
Pilgrims Ct NE2 ....99 B4
Pilgrims Way NE61 ....8 D7
Pilgrimsway Jarrow NE32 .58 E6
Gateshead NE9 ....71 B7
Pilton Rd NE5 ....36 F3
Pilton Wlk NE5 ....36 F3
Pimlico Ct NE9 ....70 F4
Pimlico Rd
Hetton le Hole DH5 ....95 B1
Sunderland SR4 ....85 B4
Pinders Way DH6 ....96 D1
Pine Ave
3 Houghton-le-Spring DH4 .94 D8
Dinnington NE13 ....27 C7

Pine Ave *continued*
Newcastle-upon-Tyne NE3 . . 37 F7
South Shields NE34 . . . . 60 A5
Guide Post NE62 . . . . 10 D7
Pine Rd NE21 . . . . 53 C2
Pine St Birtley DH3 . . . . 82 C5
4 Chester le Street DH3 . . . 88 C3
Seaton Burn NE13 . . . . 28 C8
Throckley NE15 . . . . 35 D3
Jarrow NE32 . . . . 58 A6
Greenside NE40 . . . . 52 B1
Sunderland SR4 . . . . 85 F7
Pinedale Dr DH6 . . . . 97 F7
Pinegarth NE20 . . . . 25 C2
Pines The
Newcastle-upon-Tyne NE4 . 100 A3
Greenside NE40 . . . . 52 B1
Pinesway 4 SR3 . . . . 86 B3
Pinetree Gdns NE25 . . . . . . 31 E3
Pinetree Way NE11 . . . . 54 B2
Pinewood NE31 . . . . 57 C7
Pinewood Ave
Wide Open NE13 . . . . 28 C5
Cramlington NE23 . . . . 16 B1
Washington NE38 . . . . 83 C1
Pinewood Cl
Newcastle-upon-Tyne, Kingston Park NE3 . . . . 37 B7
Newcastle-upon-Tyne, Walkerville NE6 . . . . 39 F1
Pinewood Dr NE61 . . . . 3 D2
Pinewood Gdns NE11 . . . . 70 A5
Pinewood Rd SR5 . . . . 74 F2
Pinewood Sq 8 SR5 . . . . . 74 F2
Pinewood St DH4 . . . . 89 E1
Pinewood Villas NE34 . . . . 60 A6
Pink La NE1 . . . . 100 C4
Pinner Pl NE6 . . . . 56 E4
Pinner Rd SR4 . . . . 85 C5
Pintail Ct 10 NE34 . . . . 59 A4
Pioneer Terr NE22 . . . . 11 C2
Pipe Ave NE16 . . . . 78 F6
Pipe Track La NE4 . . . . 54 D4
Piper Rd NE42 . . . . 50 B5
Pipershaw NE37 . . . . 82 F6
Pipewellgate NE8 . . . . 101 B3
Pit Row SR3 . . . . 91 F8
Pitcairn Rd SR4 . . . . 85 C5
Pitt St NE4 . . . . 98 C2
Pittington La DH6 . . . . 96 A6
Pittington Prim Sch DH6 . 96 B5
Pittington Rd DH4,DH5 . . . 96 A7
Plains Farm Prim Sch
SR3 . . . . 85 F2
Plains Rd SR3 . . . . 85 F2
Plaistow Sq SR4 . . . . 85 C6
Plaistow Way NE23 . . . . 16 B1
Plane Tree Ct SR3 . . . . 91 E6
Planesway NE10 . . . . 71 E5
Planet Ho SR1 . . . . 103 A3
Planet Pl NE12 . . . . 29 C2
Planetree Ave NE4 . . . . 54 D8
Planetrees Roman Wall*
NE46 . . . . 128 E4
Plantagenet Ave DH3 . . . . 88 D2
Plantation Ave
High Pittington DH6 . . . . 96 E3
Whickham NE16 . . . . 69 A8
Plantation Gr NE10 . . . . 57 C2
Plantation Rd SR4 . . . . 85 E7
Plantation Sq 2 SR4 . . . . . 85 E7
Plantation St NE28 . . . . 57 B8
Plantation The NE9 . . . . 71 A4
Plantation Wlk DH6 . . . . . . 97 F7
Plawsworth Gdns NE9 . . . . 71 C3
Pleasant Pl 6 DH3 . . . . 82 C5
Plenmeller Pl NE16 . . . . . . 69 A3
Plessey Ave NE24 . . . . 17 F6
Plessey Cres NE25 . . . . 32 B4
Plessey Ct NE24 . . . . 17 B4
Plessey Gdns NE29 . . . . 41 D5
Plessey Rd NE24 . . . . 17 D5
Plessey Rd Fst Sch NE24 . 17 F7
Plessey St NE23 . . . . 16 B3
Plessey Terr NE7 . . . . 39 B2
Plessey Woods Ctry Pk*
NE22 . . . . 15 B4
Plough Rd SR3 . . . . 91 F5
Plover Cl Blyth NE24 . . . . . . 17 E4
5 Washington NE38 . . . . 82 F3
Plover Dr NE16 . . . . 79 C5
Plover Lo DH3 . . . . 82 C6
Ploverfield Cl NE63 . . . . 6 C2
Plummer St NE4 . . . . 100 C3
Plummer Tower Mus*
NE1 . . . . 99 B1
Plumtree Ave SR5 . . . . 74 C2
Plunkett Rd DH9 . . . . 78 E1
Plymouth Sq SR3 . . . . 85 E2
Point Pleasant Ind Est
NE28 . . . . 40 F1
Point Pleasant Terr NE28 . 40 E1
Polden Cres NE29 . . . . 31 F1
Polebrook Rd SR4 . . . . 85 C6
Pollard St NE33 . . . . 42 D3
Polmaise St NE21 . . . . 53 C2
Polmuir Rd SR3 . . . . 85 F2
Polmuir Sq SR3 . . . . 85 E2
Polpero Cl DH3 . . . . 82 D3
Polperro Cl 6 SR2 . . . . 92 F8
Polton Sq SR4 . . . . 85 C6
Poltrossburn Milecastle*
CA6 . . . . 126 B3
Polwarth Cres NE3 . . . . 38 C8
Polwarth Dr NE3 . . . . 28 C1
Polwarth Rd NE3 . . . . 28 C1
Polworth Sq SR3 . . . . 85 F2
Pont Haugh NE20 . . . . 25 F7
Pont St NE63 . . . . 6 D3
Pont View NE20 . . . . 25 F7
Pontdyke NE10 . . . . 71 F4
Pontefract Rd 2 SR4 . . . . . 85 B3
Ponteland Cl
Tynemouth NE29 . . . . 41 C7
Washington NE38 . . . . 82 F4
Ponteland Com High Sch
NE20 . . . . 25 F5
Ponteland Fst Sch NE20 . . 25 F7
Ponteland Mid Sch NE20 . 25 F5
Ponteland Rd
Woolsington NE13 . . . . 37 A7
Heddon-on-the-Wall NE15 . . 35 D5
Newcastle-upon-Tyne, Spital Tongues NE2 . . . . 98 A3
Ponteland NE20 . . . . 26 A5
Newcastle-upon-Tyne, Kenton Bankfoot NE3 . . . . . 37 B6
Newcastle-upon-Tyne, Blakelaw NE5 . . . . 37 D3
Ponthaugh NE39 . . . . 67 F3
Pontop Sq SR4 . . . . 85 C7
Pontop St DH5 . . . . 94 C4
Pontop View NE39 . . . . 67 D2
Poole Cl NE23 . . . . 22 C7
Poole Rd SR4 . . . . 85 C6
Pooley Cl NE5 . . . . 37 B1
Pooley Rd NE5 . . . . 37 B1
Poplar Ave
1 Houghton-le-Spring DH4 . 94 D8
Dinnington NE13 . . . . 27 C7
Burnopfield NE16 . . . . 78 F6
Blyth NE24 . . . . 12 D1
Newcastle-upon-Tyne NE6 . . 39 F1
Poplar Cl NE31 . . . . 57 E3
Poplar Cres Birtley DH3 . . . 82 B5
Dunston NE11 . . . . 69 F7
Gateshead NE8 . . . . 101 B2
Poplar Dr SR6 . . . . 60 F1
Poplar Gr Bedlington NE22 . 11 C1
South Shields NE34 . . . . 59 F5
7 Sunderland SR2 . . . . 92 E8
Poplar Pl NE3 . . . . 38 C5
Poplar Rd NE21 . . . . 53 C1
Poplar St
8 Chester le Street DH3 . . . 88 C3
Throckley NE15 . . . . 35 D3
Ashington NE63 . . . . 6 D4
Poplar Terr DH3 . . . . 88 D4
Poplars The Penshaw DH4 . 90 B8
Easington Lane DH5 . . . . 95 C1
Newcastle-upon-Tyne, Gosforth NE3 . . . . 38 C3
Washington NE38 . . . . 83 D4
Newcastle-upon-Tyne, Elswick NE4 . . . . 100 A3
1 Sunderland, South Hylton SR4 . . . . 85 A6
1 Sunderland, Southwick SR5 . . . . 74 F2
Popplewell Gdns NE9 . . . . 71 A4
Popplewell Terr NE29 . . . . 42 A8
Popular Ct 1 DH3 . . . . 88 C3
Porchester Dr NE23 . . . . . . 22 C7
Porlock Ct NE23 . . . . 16 A1
Porlock Rd NE32 . . . . 58 D5
Portadown Rd 1 SR4 . . . . . 85 B3
Portberry St NE33 . . . . 42 B1
Portberry St Ind Est
NE33 . . . . 59 B8
Portberry Way NE33 . . . . . . 42 B1
Portchester Gr NE35 . . . . . . 73 E8
Portchester Rd SR4 . . . . . . 85 C5
Portchester Sq SR4 . . . . . . 85 C4
Porthcawl Dr NE37 . . . . 72 C2
Portia St NE63 . . . . 6 E4
Portland Cl DH2 . . . . 88 A1
Portland Gdns
Cramlington NE23 . . . . 22 C7
Tynemouth NE30 . . . . 42 A7
1 Gateshead NE9 . . . . 70 F2
Portland Ind Est NE63 . . . . 5 F5
Portland Mews NE2 . . . . . . 99 C3
Portland Rd
Walbottle NE15 . . . . 35 E2
Newcastle-upon-Tyne NE2 . . 99 C2
Sunderland SR3 . . . . 85 F3
Portland Sch SR3 . . . . 85 F3
Portland Sq SR3 . . . . 85 F3
Portland St
Gateshead NE10 . . . . 57 A1
1 Blyth NE24 . . . . 17 D8
Newcastle-upon-Tyne NE4 . . 54 F4
Portland Terr
Newcastle-upon-Tyne NE2 . . 99 C3
Hexham NE46 . . . . 44 F5
Ashington NE63 . . . . 5 F5
Portman Mews NE2 . . . . . . 99 C2
Portman Pl NE6 . . . . 56 E3
Portman Sq SR4 . . . . 85 C5
Portmarnock NE37 . . . . 72 B2
Portmeads Rd DH3 . . . . 82 D4
Portmeads Rise DH3 . . . . . 82 D4
Portobello Ind Est DH3 . . . 82 E4
Portobello La SR5,SR6 . . . . 75 D1
Portobello Prim Sch
DH3 . . . . 82 D2
Portobello Terr DH3 . . . . . . 82 E2
Portobello Way DH3 . . . . . . 82 D4
Portree Cl DH3 . . . . 82 D1
Portree Sq SR3 . . . . 85 E2
Portrush Cl NE37 . . . . 72 C2
Portrush Rd SR4 . . . . 85 C6
Portrush Way NE7 . . . . 39 C5
Portslade Rd SR4 . . . . 85 B4
Portsmouth Rd
North Shields NE29 . . . . 41 C5
Portsmouth Rd *continued*
Sunderland SR4 . . . . 85 B5
Portsmouth Sq SR4 . . . . . . 85 B5
Portugal Pl NE28 . . . . 40 B1
Post Office La NE29 . . . . . . 42 A8
Post Office St 4 NE24 . . . . 17 F8
Postern Cres NE61 . . . . 8 F7
Potland View NE61 . . . . 1 A3
Potter Sq SR3 . . . . 85 F2
Potter St Wallsend NE28 . . . 41 A1
Jarrow NE32 . . . . 58 A7
Potteries The NE33 . . . . . . 42 E1
Pottersway NE9 . . . . 71 B7
Pottery Bank
Newcastle-upon-Tyne NE6 . . 56 F3
Morpeth NE61 . . . . 3 E2
Pottery Bank Ct NE61 . . . . . 3 E2
Pottery La
Newcastle-upon-Tyne NE1 . 100 C3
Sunderland SR4 . . . . 85 A7
Pottery Rd SR5 . . . . 75 A1
Pottery Yd 3 DH4 . . . . 94 E8
Potts St NE6 . . . . 56 C6
Pow Hill* DH8 . . . . 135 C4
Powburn Cl DH2 . . . . 88 A1
Powburn Gdns NE4 . . . . . . 54 E8
Powis Rd SR3 . . . . 85 F2
Powis Sq SR3 . . . . 85 F2
Powys Pl NE4 . . . . 98 B2
Poynings Cl NE5 . . . . 37 C5
Praetorian Dr NE28 . . . . 40 B1
Precinct The
Blaydon NE21 . . . . 53 D3
Sunderland SR2 . . . . 102 B2
Sunderland, Hillview SR2 . . . 86 C2
Prefect Pl NE9 . . . . 71 A7
Premier Rd SR3 . . . . 85 F2
Prendwick Ave NE31 . . . . . . 57 D3
Prendwick Ct NE31 . . . . 57 D3
Prengarth Ave SR6 . . . . 75 D3
Prensgarth Way NE34 . . . . . 58 F3
Prescot Rd SR4 . . . . 85 C6
Press La SR1 . . . . 103 A3
Prestbury Ave NE23 . . . . . . 16 A1
Prestbury Rd SR4 . . . . 85 A3
Prestdale Ave NE24 . . . . . . 17 A7
Presthope Rd SR4 . . . . 85 B4
Prestmede NE10 . . . . 71 E7
Preston Ave NE30 . . . . 42 B7
Preston Ct NE29 . . . . 42 A8
Preston Gate NE29 . . . . 31 F1
Preston Grange Prim Sch
NE29 . . . . 31 E1
Preston North Rd NE29 . . . 31 F1
Preston Pk NE29 . . . . 42 A7
Preston Rd
Tynemouth NE29,NE30 . . . . . 42 A7
Sunderland SR2 . . . . 86 F4
Preston Terr
12 Shiremoor NE27 . . . . 30 E1
1 Tynemouth NE29 . . . . 41 F8
Preston Tower* NE67 . . . . 113 B8
Preston Twrs NE29 . . . . 42 A7
Preston Wood NE30 . . . . . . 32 A1
Prestonhill 7 SR3 . . . . 91 E5
Prestwick NE10 . . . . 71 E5
Prestwick Ave NE29 . . . . . . 41 C6
Prestwick Cl NE37 . . . . 72 C2
Prestwick Dr NE10 . . . . 72 C7
Prestwick Gdns NE3 . . . . . . 37 F4
Prestwick House NE4 . . . . . 98 B2
Prestwick Pit Hos NE20 . . . 26 C3
Prestwick Rd SR4 . . . . 85 C6
Prestwick Terr NE20 . . . . . . 26 C3
Pretoria Ave NE61 . . . . 8 F8
Pretoria Sq SR3 . . . . 85 E2
Pretoria St NE15 . . . . 54 A5
Price St Hebburn NE31 . . . . 57 C7
Morpeth NE61 . . . . 3 E1
Priestclose Cotts NE42 . . . . 50 F2
Priestclose Rd NE42 . . . . . 50 D2
Priestfield Cl SR3 . . . . 91 F5
Priestfield Gdns NE16 . . . . 78 F6
Priestlands Ave 1 NE46 . . . 45 A4
Priestlands Cl NE46 . . . . . . 45 A3
Priestlands Cres NE46 . . . . 45 A4
Priestlands Dr NE46 . . . . . . 45 A4
Priestlands Gr NE46 . . . . . . 45 A3
Priestlands La NE46 . . . . . . 45 A4
Priestlands Rd NE46 . . . . . . 45 A4
Priestley Ct NE34 . . . . 59 A3
Priestley Gdns NE10 . . . . . 72 B7
Priestly Cres SR4 . . . . 102 B4
Priestman Ct SR4 . . . . 85 D6
Priestpopple NE46 . . . . 45 B4
Primary Gdns SR2 . . . . . . 103 C1
Primate Rd SR3 . . . . 85 E2
Primrose Ave NE34 . . . . 59 B5
Primrose Cl NE23 . . . . 29 A8
Primrose Cres
Bournmoor DH4 . . . . 89 E3
Sunderland SR6 . . . . 75 D3
Primrose Ct NE63 . . . . 6 B1
Primrose Gdns
Ouston DH2 . . . . 81 F2
Wallsend NE28 . . . . 40 A4
Primrose Hill NE9 . . . . 71 A5
Primrose Hill Hospl
NE32 . . . . 58 C4
Primrose Hill Terr NE32 . . 58 C3
Primrose Prec SR6 . . . . 75 D3
Primrose St 3 SR4 . . . . 85 A6
Primrose Terr Birtley DH3 . 82 D4
Jarrow NE32 . . . . 58 C4
Prince Albert Terr NE2 . . . . 99 C2
Prince Consort Ind Est
NE31 . . . . 57 C7
Prince Consort La NE31 . . 57 D6
Prince Consort Rd
Hebburn NE31 . . . . 57 C6
Jarrow NE32 . . . . 58 C6
Gateshead NE8 . . . . 101 C1
Prince Consort Way
NE29 . . . . 42 A3
Prince Edward Ct NE34 . . . 60 A5
Prince Edward Gr NE34 . . 60 C6
Prince Edward Rd NE34 . . 60 A5
Prince Edward Rd E
NE34 . . . . 60 C6
Prince George Ave SR6 . . 75 D3
Prince Of Wales Cl NE34 . 59 E5
Prince Philip Cl NE15 . . . . 54 C5
Prince Rd NE28 . . . . 40 B3
Prince St Chopwell NE17 . . . 66 B1
Sunderland SR1 . . . . 103 A3
Prince's Gdns NE24 . . . . . . 17 C8
Prince's Meadow NE3 . . . . 38 A5
Princes Ave
Newcastle-upon-Tyne NE3 . . 38 B7
Sunderland SR6 . . . . 75 E5
Princes Cl NE3 . . . . 38 B8
Princes Gdns
Whitley Bay NE25 . . . . 31 E5
Sunderland SR6 . . . . 75 E5
Princes Pk Dunston NE11 . . 70 B6
Gateshead NE8 . . . . 70 C7
Princes Rd NE3 . . . . 28 B1
Princes St
Shiney Row DH4 . . . . 90 A5
Tynemouth NE30 . . . . 42 B7
Corbridge NE45 . . . . 47 A5
Princess Ct NE42 . . . . 50 D4
Princess Dr NE8 . . . . 100 A1
Princess Gdns DH5 . . . . . . 95 A5
Princess Louise Fst Sch
NE24 . . . . 17 D7
Princess Louise Rd NE24 . 17 E7
Princess Mary Ct NE2 . . . . 99 A4
Princess St
Gateshead NE10 . . . . 57 A1
Sunniside NE16 . . . . 69 B2
Sunderland SR2 . . . . 102 C1
Princess Way NE42 . . . . . . 50 C4
Princesway
Gateshead NE11 . . . . 70 C3
Gateshead NE11 . . . . 70 C5
Princesway Central NE11 . 70 C4
Princetown Terr SR3 . . . . . 85 E2
Princeway NE30 . . . . 42 D8
Prinn Pl NE16 . . . . 69 B2
Prior Terr Corbridge NE45 . . 46 F6
Hexham NE46 . . . . 45 A6
Prior's Ho NE30 . . . . 42 E7
Prior's Terr NE30 . . . . 42 D7
Priors Grange DH6 . . . . 96 B5
Priors Way NE28 . . . . 40 E2
Priors Wlk NE61 . . . . 8 E7
Priory Ave NE25 . . . . 31 F4
Priory Ct Tynemouth NE30 . . 42 E8
South Shields NE33 . . . . 42 D5
Gateshead NE8 . . . . 101 C3
Priory Gdns NE45 . . . . 46 F7
Priory Gn 20 NE6 . . . . 56 B6
Priory Gr SR4 . . . . 85 F5
Priory Grange NE24 . . . . . . 17 C8
Priory Mews 7 NE30 . . . . . . 42 D7
Priory Pl
Brunswick Village NE13 . . . . 28 A5
Stakeford NE62 . . . . 11 A8
Priory Prim Sch NE30 . . . . 42 D8
Priory Rd NE32 . . . . 58 C8
Priory Way NE5 . . . . 36 F4
Proctor Ct NE6 . . . . 57 A5
Proctor Sq SR3 . . . . 85 F2
Proctor St NE6 . . . . 57 A5
Promenade
Whitley Bay NE26 . . . . 32 B5
South Shields NE33 . . . . 42 F3
Newbiggin-by-the-Sea NE64 . . 7 E4
Sunderland SR2 . . . . 87 A3
Seaham SR7 . . . . 93 D1
Promontory Terr NE26 . . . . 32 C4
Promotion Cl 9 SR6 . . . . . . 75 E2
Prospect Ave
Seaton Delaval NE25 . . . . . . 23 C3
Wallsend NE28 . . . . 40 B3
Prospect Ave N NE28 . . . . . 40 B4
Prospect Cotts NE22 . . . . . . 11 C5
Prospect Cres DH5 . . . . 97 C8
Prospect Ct NE4 . . . . 98 A1
Prospect Gdns NE36 . . . . . 74 A7
Prospect Pl NE4 . . . . 98 A1
Prospect Row SR1 . . . . . . 103 C3
Prospect St
2 Chester le Street DH3 . . . 88 C4
Newbiggin-by-the-Sea NE64 . . 7 F5
Prospect Terr
1 Chester le Street DH3 . . . 88 C4
Ebchester DH8 . . . . 76 F4
Kibblesworth NE11 . . . . 81 C6
Burnopfield NE16 . . . . 79 A4
North Shields NE30 . . . . 42 C6
East Boldon NE36 . . . . 74 C7
Prudhoe NE42 . . . . 50 B2
Gateshead NE9 . . . . 71 D1
Providence Pl 18 NE10 . . . . 56 D1
Provident Terr NE28 . . . . . . 40 A2
Provost Gdns NE4 . . . . 54 D4
Prudhoe Castle* NE42 . . . 50 C3
Prudhoe Castle Fst Sch
NE42 . . . . 50 B2
Prudhoe Chare NE1 . . . . . . 99 A2
Prudhoe Com High Sch
NE42 . . . . 50 D1
Prudhoe Ct NE3 . . . . 37 E7
Prudhoe Gr NE32 . . . . 58 B3
Prudhoe Pl NE1 . . . . 99 A2
Prudhoe St
Newcastle-upon-Tyne NE1 . . 99 A2
North Shields NE29 . . . . 42 A5
8 Sunderland SR4 . . . . 85 F7
Prudhoe Sta NE42 . . . . 50 B4
Prudhoe Street Bacl 19
NE29 . . . . 42 A5
Prudhoe Terr
18 North Shields NE29 . . . . . 42 A5
Tynemouth NE30 . . . . 42 D8
Prudhoe West Fst Sch
NE42 . . . . 50 C2
Pudding Chare NE1 . . . . . . 99 A1
Pudding Mews NE46 . . . . . 45 B5
Puffin Cl NE24 . . . . 17 F3
Pullman Ct NE9 . . . . 70 E5
Purbeck Cl NE29 . . . . 31 F2
Purbeck Gdns NE23 . . . . . . 22 C7
Purbeck Rd NE12 . . . . 39 B6
Purley NE38 . . . . 84 A4
Purley Cl NE28 . . . . 40 F4
Purley Gdns NE3 . . . . 37 F4
Purley Rd SR3 . . . . 85 E2
Purley Sq SR3 . . . . 85 E2
Putney Sq SR4 . . . . 85 B4
Pykerley Mews NE25 . . . . . 31 E4
Pykerley Rd NE25 . . . . 31 E5

Q

Quadrant The
North Shields NE29 . . . . 41 E5
Sunderland SR1 . . . . 103 C3
Quality Row NE6 . . . . 56 A5
Quality Row Rd NE16 . . . . . 54 A1
Quantock Ave DH2 . . . . 88 A2
Quantock Cl
Longbenton NE12 . . . . 39 A6
Tynemouth NE29 . . . . 31 F2
Quarry Bank Ct NE4 . . . . . . 98 B1
Quarry Edge NE46 . . . . 45 C3
Quarry House Gdns DH5 . 94 C4
Quarry House La DH5 . . . . 94 D4
Quarry La
South Shields NE34 . . . . 60 B5
South Shields, Marsden NE34 . . . . 60 D6
Quarry Rd
Newcastle-upon-Tyne NE15 . 53 C6
Hebburn NE31 . . . . 57 E5
New Silksworth SR3 . . . . 92 B7
Quarry Row 19 NE10 . . . . . 56 D1
Quarry St SR3 . . . . 92 A7
Quarry View Inf & Jun Schs
SR4 . . . . 85 C6
Quarryfield Rd NE8 . . . . . . 101 C4
Quatre Bras NE46 . . . . 44 F5
Quay Rd NE24 . . . . 18 A7
Quay The DH5 . . . . 95 A3
Quay View NE28 . . . . 41 A2
Quayside
Newcastle-upon-Tyne NE1 . 101 B4
Newcastle-upon-Tyne, St Lawrence NE1,NE6 . . . . 56 A5
Blyth NE24 . . . . 17 F8
Quayside Ct 7 Blyth NE24 . 17 F8
North Shields NE30 . . . . 42 B5
Quayside Ho SR1 . . . . 103 B3
Queen Alexandra Rd
Tynemouth NE29 . . . . 42 A7
Sunderland SR2 . . . . 86 D3
Queen Alexandra Rd W
NE29 . . . . 41 E7
Queen Ann Ct 21 NE6 . . . . 56 C7
Queen Elizabeth Ave
NE9 . . . . 71 B6
Queen Elizabeth Dr DH5 . 97 D8
Queen Elizabeth High Sch
NE46 . . . . 44 E4
Queen Elizabeth Hospl
NE9 . . . . 71 B6
Queen Elizabeth II Ctry Pk*
NE63 . . . . 6 F6
Queen St Birtley DH3 . . . . . 82 B4
Hetton le Hole DH5 . . . . 95 A5
Newcastle-upon-Tyne NE1 . 101 B4
North Shields NE30 . . . . 42 B6
South Shields NE33 . . . . 42 C3
Lynmouth NE61 . . . . 2 A2
Morpeth NE61 . . . . 9 A8
Ashington NE63 . . . . 6 E4
Newbiggin-by-the-Sea NE64 . . 7 E5
Gateshead NE8 . . . . 70 C8
Sunderland SR1 . . . . 103 A3
Sunderland, Bishopwearmouth SR1 . . . . 102 C3
Sunderland, Grangetown SR2 . . . . 92 F8
Queen St E SR1 . . . . 103 B3
Queen Victoria Rd NE1,
NE2 . . . . 99 A3
Queen Victoria St NE10 . . . 57 A1
Queen's Cres
Wallsend NE28 . . . . 40 B3
Hebburn NE31 . . . . 57 D4
Sunderland SR4 . . . . 102 A1
Queen's Dr NE26 . . . . 32 A5
Queen's Gdns Blyth NE24 . . 17 C8
Morpeth NE61 . . . . 8 E7
Queen's Pk DH3 . . . . 88 D2
Queen's Rd
Newcastle-upon-Tyne NE2 . . 38 F1
Bedlington NE22 . . . . 11 D2

Queen's Rd *continued*
Whitley Bay NE26 31 F6
Sunderland SR5 75 B1
Queen's Terr NE2 38 F1
Queens Ave SR6 75 E5
Queens Ct Walbottle NE15 36 A1
Newcastle-upon-Tyne, Brunton Park NE3 28 C2
Newcastle-upon-Tyne NE4 98 B2
Gateshead NE8 100 C1
Queens Dr Sunniside NE16 69 B2
Whickham NE16 69 C5
Queens Gdns
Longbenton NE12 39 D6
Annitsford NE23 22 B1
Queens La NE1 101 A4
Queens Pl NE64 7 E5
Queens Rd Walbottle NE15 36 A1
Annitsford NE23 22 B1
Seaton Sluice NE26 24 D6
Newcastle-upon-Tyne NE5 37 A3
Queens Terr NE28 40 C3
Queens Way NE46 44 E5
Queensberry St SR4 102 B3
Queensbridge NE12 38 F7
Queensbury Dr NE15 36 B2
Queensland Ave NE34 58 F4
Queensmere DH3 88 C7
Queensway
Houghton-le-Spring DH5 94 F8
Ponteland NE20 25 D2
Newcastle-upon-Tyne, Brunton Park NE3 28 B1
Tynemouth NE30 42 D8
3 Washington NE38 83 E4
Newcastle-upon-Tyne, Fenham NE4 54 D8
Morpeth NE61 8 D7
Queensway N NE11 70 C5
Queensway S NE11 70 D4
Quentin Ave NE3 37 D5
Quigley Terr DH3 82 B6

R

Rabbit Banks Rd NE8 101 A3
Raby Cl Fence Houses DH4 90 A1
Bedlington NE22 10 D1
Raby Cres 7 NE6 56 C6
Raby Cross 10 NE6 56 C5
Raby Dr SR3 91 C7
Raby Gdns
Burnopfield NE16 78 E6
Jarrow NE32 58 B4
Raby Rd NE38 83 A5
Raby St
16 Newcastle-upon-Tyne, Byker NE6 56 B6
Newcastle-upon-Tyne, St Lawrence NE6 56 C5
Gateshead NE8 70 F8
Sunderland SR4 102 B2
Raby Way NE6 56 C5
Rabygate 6 NE6 56 C6
Rachel Cl SR2 92 C7
Rackly Way SR6 75 F8
Radcliffe Cotts 5 NE15 35 D2
Radcliffe Pl 3 NE5 37 D2
Radcliffe Rd
Hexham NE46 45 C4
Sunderland SR5 74 E2
Radcliffe St DH3 82 C3
Radlett Rd SR5 74 D2
Radnor Gdns NE28 41 A3
Radnor St NE1 99 B2
Radstock Pl NE12 39 C7
Rae Ave NE28 40 B4
Raeburn Ave NE38 83 E4
Raeburn Gdns NE9 71 B7
Raeburn Rd
Whiteleas NE34 59 D2
Sunderland SR5 74 C3
Raglan NE38 83 A5
Raglan Ave SR2 86 E3
Raglan Pl NE16 79 B6
Raglan Row DH4 90 C5
Raglan St NE32 58 C7
Railton Gdns NE9 71 B6
Railway Arches NE1 99 B1
Railway Cotts Birtley DH3 82 B4
Penshaw DH4 90 A8
Bebside NE24 16 E8
Cleadon NE36 59 D1
Wylam NE41 50 F5
Railway Mus NE41 51 B6
Railway Row SR1 102 B3
Railway St Newbottle DH4 90 D2
Hetton le Hole DH5 95 A4
Dunston NE11 54 F2
Dunston NE11 100 A1
10 North Shields NE29 42 A5
Hebburn NE31 57 F7
Jarrow NE32 58 A7
Newcastle-upon-Tyne NE4 100 B3
Sunderland SR1 103 C2
Railway Terr
New Herrington DH4 90 D6
Penshaw DH4 90 A8
Blyth NE24 17 D7
Blyth, South Newsham NE24 17 C2
Wallsend NE28 40 D1
North Shields NE29 42 A5
Washington NE38 83 F4

Railway Terr *continued*
Newcastle-upon-Tyne NE4 100 B3
2 Sunderland SR4 85 A6
Railway Terr N DH4 90 D7
Raine Gr SR1 103 B2
Rainford Ave SR2 86 E3
Rainhill Cl NE37 72 F1
Rainhill Rd NE37 72 F1
Rainton Bridge Ind Est DH4 94 C7
Rainton Cl NE10 72 C6
Rainton Gr DH5 94 E6
Rainton Meadows (Nature Reserve)* DH4 94 B6
Rainton St Penshaw DH4 90 B8
Sunderland SR4 102 A2
Rainton View DH4 94 A2
Rake La NE29 31 E1
Raleigh Cl NE33 59 B8
Raleigh Rd SR5 74 E2
Raleigh Sq SR5 74 D2
Ralph Ave SR2 92 E8
Ralph St NE31 57 F7
Ramilies SR2 92 D6
Ramillies Rd SR5 74 C3
Ramillies Sq SR5 74 C3
Ramparts The NE15 53 F8
Ramsay Rd NE17 66 B2
Ramsay Sq SR5 74 E3
Ramsay St Blaydon NE21 53 B1
High Spen NE39 67 A5
Ramsey St DH3 88 C2
Ramsgate Rd SR5 74 E3
Ramshaw Cl NE7 39 E3
Randolph St NE32 58 C7
Rangoon Rd SR5 74 C3
Ranmere Rd NE15 54 A5
Ranmore Cl NE23 22 B7
Rannoch Ave DH2 88 B1
Rannoch Cl NE10 72 C8
Rannoch Rd SR5 74 C3
Ranson Cres NE34 58 F5
Ranson St SR4,SR2 86 B4
Raphael Ave NE34 59 C2
Rathmore Gdns NE30 42 A7
Ratho Ct NE10 71 E6
Ravel Ct NE32 58 C6
Ravenburn Gdns NE15 53 F6
Ravenburn Wlk 6 NE15 35 D2
Ravenna Rd SR5 74 B3
Ravens Hill Dr NE63 6 A2
Ravensbourne Ave NE36 74 D8
Ravenscar Cl NE16 68 F5
Ravenscourt Pl NE8 101 A1
Ravenscourt Rd SR5 74 C3
Ravensdale Cres NE9 71 A6
Ravensdale Gr NE24 17 A7
Ravenshill Rd NE5 36 E1
Ravenside Rd NE4 54 E8
Ravenside Terr NE17 66 A1
Ravenstone NE37 83 B7
Ravenswood Cl NE12 39 E8
Ravenswood Gdns NE9 70 F3
Ravenswood Prim Sch NE6 39 C1
Ravenswood Rd
Newcastle-upon-Tyne NE6 39 C1
Sunderland SR5 74 B3
Ravenswood Sq SR5 74 B3
Ravensworth Birtley DH3 82 D5
Ryhope SR2 92 D6
Ravensworth Ave
Fence Houses DH4 90 A1
Gateshead NE9 71 C2
Ravensworth Cl NE28 40 F2
Ravensworth Cres NE16 79 D8
Ravensworth Ct
South Hetton DH6 97 F7
Dunston NE11 100 A1
Bedlington NE22 11 D3
Newcastle-upon-Tyne NE3 37 D7
Ravensworth Gdns NE61 1 D4
Ravensworth Rd
Birtley DH3 82 B5
Fence Houses DH4 89 F1
Dunston NE11 100 A1
Ravensworth St
Bedlington NE22 11 D3
Wallsend NE28 40 F2
Sunderland SR4 102 B3
Ravensworth Terr
Dunston NE11 70 A8
Bedlington NE22 11 D3
Jarrow NE32 58 B3
South Shields NE33 59 C8
Newcastle-upon-Tyne NE4 98 B1
Ravensworth Terrace Prim Sch DH3 82 C4
Ravine Terr SR6 75 F3
Rawdon Ct NE28 57 B8
Rawdon Rd SR5 74 E3
Rawling Rd NE8 70 D8
Rawlston Way NE5 37 C3
Rawmarsh Rd SR5 74 C3
Raydale SR5 74 E3
Raydale Ave NE37 83 B8
Raylees Gdns NE11 70 A7
Rayleigh Dr NE13 28 B7
Rayleigh Gr NE8 70 D8
Raynes Cl NE61 8 D7
Raynham Cl NE23 21 F3
Raynham Ct NE33 42 C2
Rea Pl NE3 38 A5
Readhead Ave NE33 42 E1
Readhead Bldgs 2 NE33 42 C2
Readhead Dr NE6 56 F4
Readhead Rd NE34 59 F8

Reading Rd
South Shields NE33 59 D7
Sunderland SR5 74 D3
Reading Sq SR5 74 D3
Reasby Gdns NE40 52 B5
Reasby Villas NE40 52 B5
Reavley Ave NE22 11 E3
Reay Cres NE35 74 B8
Reay Ct 4 DH2 88 C2
Reay Gdns NE5 37 A3
Reay Pl NE34 59 B5
Reay St NE10 57 B2
Rectory Ave NE3 38 E4
Rectory Bank NE36 74 A7
Rectory Dene NE61 8 F7
Rectory Dr NE3 38 E4
Rectory Gn NE36 73 F7
Rectory Gr NE3 38 D5
Rectory La
Whickham NE16 69 B7
Blaydon NE21 68 B8
Rectory Pk NE61 8 F7
Rectory Pl NE8 101 A1
Rectory Rd
Hetton le Hole DH5 95 A3
Gateshead, Carr Hill NE10 71 C7
Newcastle-upon-Tyne NE3 38 D4
Gateshead, Shipcote NE8, NE9 70 E8
Rectory Rd E NE10 71 D7
Rectory Terr NE3 38 E4
Red Admiral Ct NE11 70 B7
Red Barnes NE1 99 C1
Red Berry Way NE34 59 B4
Red Bglws NE9 71 E1
Red Hall Dr NE7 39 D3
Red House Dr NE25 31 C6
Red House Farm NE22 15 D8
Red House Rd NE31 58 A6
Red Lion La NE37 72 C2
Red Rose Prim Sch DH3 88 D1
Red Rose Terr DH3 88 D2
Red Row Dr NE22 11 C3
Red Wlk NE7 39 A1
Redburn Cl DH4 94 C8
Redburn Rd NE5 36 F4
Redby Cl 1 SR6 75 D2
Redby Prim Sch SR6 75 D2
Redcar Rd Wallsend NE28 41 A3
Newcastle-upon-Tyne NE6 39 D1
Sunderland SR5 74 E2
Redcar Sq SR5 74 E2
Redcliffe Way NE5 37 B3
Redcroft Gn NE5 37 B3
Redditch Sq SR5 74 D3
Rede Ave Hebburn NE31 57 E6
Hexham NE46 45 C4
Rede Ct NE61 1 E5
Rede St Gateshead NE11 70 C5
Jarrow NE32 58 A5
Redemarsh NE10 71 F6
Redesdale Ave
Blaydon NE21 67 F8
Newcastle-upon-Tyne NE3 38 A6
Redesdale Cheese Farm* NE19 123 A8
Redesdale Cl
Longbenton NE12 39 C8
Newcastle-upon-Tyne NE15 53 E7
Redesdale Fst Sch NE28 39 F4
Redesdale Gdns NE11 69 F7
Redesdale Gr NE29 41 D6
Redesdale Pl NE24 17 B7
Redesdale Rd
Chester le Street DH2 88 A1
North Shields NE29 41 D6
Sunderland SR5 74 C3
Redewater Gdns NE16 69 A6
Redewater Rd NE4 54 E8
Redewood Cl NE5 37 A1
Redford Pl NE23 29 C5
Redheugh Bridge Rd NE1,NE4 100 C3
Redheugh Ct NE8 70 B8
Redheugh Rd NE25 31 B5
Redhill SR6 75 E8
Redhill Dr NE16 68 E4
Redhill Rd SR5 74 D3
Redhill Wlk NE23 22 B7
Redhills Way DH5 95 A2
Redland Ave NE3 37 E6
Redlands DH4 90 A7
Redmayne Ct 1 NE10 71 D8
Redmires Cl DH2 81 E1
Redmond Rd SR5 74 E3
Redmond Sq SR5 74 E3
Rednam Pl NE5 37 B2
Redruth Gdns NE9 70 F2
Redruth Sq SR5 74 D3
Redshank Cl NE38 82 F2
Redshank Dr NE24 17 E4
Redstart Ct NE39 67 D2
Redwell Ct
South Shields NE34 60 C7
Prudhoe NE42 50 D2
Redwell La NE34 60 D7
Redwell Rd NE42 50 E2
Redwing Cl NE38 82 F3
Redwing Ct NE6 56 E7
Redwood Cl
Hetton le Hole DH5 94 F4
Killingworth NE12 29 C4
Redwood Gdns NE11 70 B5
Redwood Gr SR3 92 B7
Reed Ave NE12 29 C4
Reed St North Shields NE30 42 B6
South Shields NE33 59 C8
Reedham Ct NE5 37 B4

Reedling Ct SR5 74 C4
Reedside NE40 52 D5
Reedsmouth Pl NE5 54 B8
Reedswood Cres NE23 22 E5
Reestones Pl NE3 37 D5
Reeth Rd SR5 74 D2
Reeth Sq SR5 74 D2
Reeth Way NE15 35 C1
Regal Rd SR4 102 A3
Regency Ct NE2 99 C4
Regency Dr
Whickham NE16 68 F6
New Silksworth SR3 92 B8
Regency Gdns NE29 41 E7
Regency Way NE20 25 A5
Regent Ave NE3 38 B5
Regent Centre Sta NE3 38 C6
Regent Ct
Longbenton NE12 29 B2
Blyth NE24 17 D7
Hebburn NE31 57 D5
South Shields NE33 42 C1
Gateshead NE8 101 C2
Regent Ctr The NE3 38 C6
Regent Dr NE16 68 F4
Regent Farm Ct NE3 38 C5
Regent Farm Fst Sch NE3 38 A6
Regent Farm Rd NE3 38 B6
Regent Rd Wallsend NE28 40 A3
Newcastle-upon-Tyne NE3 38 C5
Jarrow NE32 58 C6
Ryhope SR2 93 A5
Regent Rd N NE3 38 C5
Regent St
Hetton le Hole DH5 95 A5
Blyth NE24 17 E8
Regent Terr
North Shields NE29 41 E6
Gateshead NE8 101 B2
Sunderland SR2 86 F2
Regents Ct NE28 39 E4
Regents Dr Prudhoe NE42 50 E4
Tynemouth NE30 32 C1
Regents Pk NE28 39 E3
Regina Sq SR5 74 D3
Reginald St
West Boldon NE35 73 F8
Gateshead NE8 56 B1
4 Sunderland SR4 85 F7
Reid Ave NE28 40 B3
Reid Park Cl NE2 38 F2
Reid Park Ct NE2 38 F2
Reid Park Rd NE2 38 F2
Reid St NE61 9 A8
Reid's La NE23 22 E1
Reigate Sq NE23 22 B7
Reiverdale Rd NE63 6 D4
Rekendyke Ind Est NE33 42 B1
Rekendyke La NE33 42 B1
Relton Ave NE6 56 D4
Relton Cl DH4 94 A7
Relton Ct NE25 31 E5
Relton PL NE25 31 E5
Relton Terr
Chester le Street DH3 88 C2
Whitley Bay NE25 31 E5
Rembrandt Ave NE34 59 C2
Remington Ave NE30 32 C1
Remscheid Way NE63 6 C1
Remus Ave NE15 34 D2
Remus Cl NE13 28 B5
Rendel St NE11 54 F1
Rendle Rd NE6 57 B4
Renforth St NE11 69 F8
Renfrew Cl NE29 41 C8
Renfrew Gn NE5 37 B3
Renfrew Pl DH3 82 D2
Renfrew Rd SR5 74 D3
Rennie Rd SR5 74 B3
Rennie Sq SR5 74 B3
Rennington NE10 72 A5
Rennington Cl
Tynemouth NE30 32 C1
Morpeth NE61 9 B5
Rennington Pl NE5 37 D2
Renoir Gdns NE34 59 D2
Renwick Ave NE3 37 E6
Renwick Ct NE8 70 C8
Renwick Rd NE24 17 D7
Renwick St NE6 56 D6
Renwick Wlk NE61 8 E8
Rescue Station Cotts DH5 94 F6
Resida Cl NE15 53 C8
Retford Rd SR5 74 D3
Retford Sq SR5 74 D3
Retreat The
Newburn NE15 52 F7
Sunderland SR2 102 B2
Revell Terr NE5 37 E1
Revelstoke Rd SR5 74 C3
Revesby St NE33 59 C6
Reynolds Ave
Killingworth NE12 29 B2
Whiteleas NE34 59 D3
Washington NE38 83 E4
Reyrolle Ct NE31 57 D5
Rheims Ct SR4 85 D7
Rheydt Ave NE28 39 F2
Rhoda Terr SR2 86 F1
Rhodes St NE6 57 A5
Rhodesia Rd SR5 74 D3
Rhondda Rd SR5 74 B3
Rhuddlan Ct NE5 37 B4
Rhyl Par NE31 58 A2
Rhyl Sq SR5 74 E3
Ribble Rd SR5 74 C2

Ribble Wlk NE32 58 C
Ribbledale Gdns NE7 39 E
Ribblesdale Penshaw DH4 90 E
Wallsend NE28 39 F
Ribblesdale Ave NE24 17 A
Richard Ave SR4 86 A
Richard Avenue Prim Sch SR4 86 A
Richard Browell Rd NE15 35 E
Richard St
Hetton le Hole DH5 95 A
Blyth NE24 17 E
Richardson Ave 2 NE34 58 F
Richardson Dees Fst Sch NE28 40 D
Richardson Rd NE1,NE2 98 C
Richardson St
Wallsend NE28 40 C
3 Newcastle-upon-Tyne NE6 56 C
Ashington NE63 6 E
Richardson Terr
Chopwell NE17 66 E
5 Washington NE37 83 D
6 Ryhope SR2 93 A
Richardson's Bldgs NE62 10 E
Richmond SR2 92 D
Richmond Ave
Gateshead NE10 57 C
Whickham NE16 54 E
Washington NE38 83 D
Richmond Cl NE22 10 E
Richmond Ct Jarrow NE32 58 A
Gateshead NE8 101 C
1 Gateshead, Low Fell NE9 70 F
Richmond Dr DH4 89 D
Richmond Gdns NE28 40 A
Richmond Gr NE29 41 E
Richmond Lodge NE3 38 D
Richmond Mews NE3 38 E
Richmond Pk NE28 39 E
Richmond Rd NE34 59 C
Richmond St SR5 102 C
Richmond Terr
Haswell DH6 97 F
13 Gateshead, Felling NE10 71 D
Walbottle NE15 35 F
Whitley Bay NE26 31 F
Gateshead NE8 101 E
Richmond Way
Ponteland NE20 25 A
Cramlington NE23 22 A
Rickaby St SR1 103 C
Rickgarth NE10 71 F
Rickleton Ave DH3 88 C
Rickleton Prim Sch NE38 88 F
Rickleton Way NE38 83 A
Riddell Ave NE15 54 C
Riddell Ct 7 DH2 88 C
Riddings Rd SR5 74 C
Riddings Sq SR5 74 D
Ridge Ct NE13 28 E
Ridge Terr NE22 10 E
Ridge The NE40 52 C
Ridge Villas NE22 10 E
Ridge Way NE25 23 E
Ridge Way The NE3 37 F
Ridgely Cl NE20 26 A
Ridgely Dr NE20 26 A
Ridgeway Birtley DH3 82 C
Gateshead NE10 72 B
Newcastle-upon-Tyne NE4 54 E
Stakeford NE62 11 A
Ashington NE63 7 A
Ryhope SR2 92 C
Ridgeway Cres SR3 86 B
Ridgeway Cty Jun Mix & Inf Sch NE34 59 F
Ridgeway The NE34 59 F
Ridgewood Cres NE3 38 F
Ridgewood Gdns NE3 38 E
Ridgewood Villas NE3 38 E
Riding Barns Way NE16 69 A
Riding Cl NE40 51 E
Riding Dene NE43 49 F
Riding Grange NE44 62 E
Riding La DH9,NE11 81 B
Riding Lea NE21 53 A
Riding Mill Sta NE44 62 F
Riding Terr NE43 49 F
Riding The NE3 37 E
Ridings Ct NE40 51 E
Ridings The NE25 31 C
Ridley Ave
Chester le Street DH2 88 B
Blyth NE24 17 F
Wallsend NE28 41 B
Sunderland SR2 92 F
Ridley Cl
Newcastle-upon-Tyne NE3 37 F
Hexham NE46 44 F
Morpeth NE61 8 E
Ridley Gdns NE16 54 A
Ridley Gr NE34 60 A
Ridley Mill Cotts NE43 64 B
Ridley Mill Rd NE43 64 B
Ridley Pl NE1,NE99 99 A
Ridley St Cramlington NE23 22 C
Blyth NE24 17 F
Gateshead NE8 70 E
Sunderland SR5 75 B
Ridley Terr
Gateshead NE10 71 E
Cambois NE24 12 D
Sunderland SR2 103 C
Ridsdale NE42 50 B
Ridsdale Ave NE5 36 E

Ridsdale Cl
Seaton Delaval NE25 .....23 C3
Wallsend NE28 .....40 C4
Ridsdale Ct NE8 .....101 A1
Ridsdale Sq NE63 .....6 C3
Rievaulx NE38 .....83 C4
Riga Sq SR5 .....74 C3
Riggs The
Houghton-le-Spring DH5 .....94 F8
Corbridge NE45 .....46 F7
Rignall NE38 .....84 A5
Riley St NE32 .....58 A7
Riley Street Ind Est NE32 .58 A7
Ringlet Cl NE11 .....70 B7
Ringmore Ct SR2 .....86 C2
Ringway Stakeford NE62 .....6 A1
Sunderland SR5 .....85 A8
Ringwood Dr NE23 .....22 B7
Ringwood Gn NE12 .....39 C7
Ringwood Rd SR5 .....74 D3
Ringwood Sq SR5 .....74 D3
Rink St NE24 .....17 F8
Ripley Ave NE29 .....41 E4
Ripley Cl NE22 .....10 D2
Ripley Ct NE9 .....71 B1
Ripley Dr NE23 .....22 A3
Ripley Terr NE6 .....56 E6
Ripon Cl NE23 .....21 F3
Ripon Gdns
Newcastle-upon-Tyne NE2 ..56 A8
Wallsend NE28 .....40 E3
Ripon Sq NE32 .....73 B8
Ripon St
Chester le Street DH3 .....88 C1
Gateshead NE8 .....101 B1
Sunderland SR6 .....75 E1
Rise The Ponteland NE20 .....25 B2
Ryton NE21 .....53 A4
Seaton Sluice NE26 .....24 E4
Newcastle-upon-Tyne NE3 ..37 E4
Gateshead NE8 .....56 B1
Rishton Sq SR5 .....74 C3
Rising Sun Cotts NE28 .....40 B5
Rising Sun Ctry Pk* NE28 .....40 B6
Ritson Cl NE29 .....41 E7
Ritson St SR6 .....75 E4
River Bank NE62 .....11 C8
River Bank E NE62 .....11 C8
River Dr NE33 .....42 C4
River La NE40 .....52 C6
River Terr 5 DH3 .....88 D4
River View
Blackhall Mill NE17 .....77 B6
Blaydon NE21 .....53 B2
Bebside NE22 .....11 D1
North Shields NE30 .....42 C6
Ryton NE40 .....52 E5
Ovingham NE42 .....50 A4
Prudhoe NE42 .....50 C2
Lynmouth NE61 .....2 A3
River View Cl NE22 .....11 D1
Riverbank Rd SR5 .....74 D2
Riverdale SR5 .....85 B8
Rivermead NE38 .....83 E1
Rivermede NE20 .....25 F7
Riversdale NE17 .....77 B6
Riversdale Ave NE62 .....11 A8
Riversdale Ct
Newcastle-upon-Tyne NE15 .53 C6
Stakeford NE62 .....11 A7
Riversdale Ho NE62 .....11 A7
Riversdale Terr SR2 .....102 B1
Riversdale Way NE15 .....53 C6
Riverside NE20 .....25 E6
Riverside Ave NE62 .....10 D7
Riverside Bsns Pk NE28 ..41 A1
Riverside Ct
Dunston NE11 .....100 A1
South Shields NE33 .....42 B2
Riverside Lo NE15 .....52 E7
Riverside Pk SR4 .....85 B7
Riverside Rd SR5 .....74 E2
Riverside The NE31 .....57 C7
Riverside Way NE11,NE16 .54 C3
Riverview Lodge NE4 .....54 D4
Roachburn Rd NE5 .....36 E2
Robert Owen Gdns NE10 .71 C7
Robert St Blyth NE24 .....17 E7
South Shields NE33 .....42 D1
New Silksworth SR3 .....92 B7
Sunderland SR4 .....102 A3
Robert Terr NE39 .....66 F4
Robert Terr Cotts NE39 ..66 F4
Robert Westall Way
NE29 .....42 A3
Robert Wheatman Ct
SR2 .....86 E2
Roberts St NE15 .....54 A5
Roberts Terr NE32 .....58 B5
Robertson Rd SR5 .....74 B2
Robertson Sq SR5 .....74 B3
Robin Ct DH5 .....94 C3
Robin Gr SR5 .....74 C1
Robin La
East Rainton DH4,DH5 .....94 C2
West Rainton DH4,DH5 .....94 C2
Robinson Gdns
Wallsend NE28 .....41 A3
2 Whitburn SR6 .....60 F1
Robinson Sq NE64 .....7 E5
Robinson St
8 South Shields NE33 .....42 D2
4 Newcastle-upon-Tyne
NE6 .....56 C6
Robinson Terr
Burnopfield NE16 .....79 A4
Washington NE38 .....83 F4
Robinson Terr *continued*
Sunderland SR2 .....103 C1
Robinswood 8 NE9 .....70 F5
Robsheugh Pl NE5 .....54 C8
Robson Dr NE46 .....44 F3
Robson Pl 10 SR2 .....93 A6
Robson St
Newcastle-upon-Tyne NE6 .56 B6
7 Gateshead NE9 .....70 F5
Robson Terr Tantobie DH9 .78 F1
High Spen NE39 .....67 B3
Rochdale Rd SR5 .....74 D3
Rochdale St
Hetton le Hole DH5 .....95 A2
Wallsend NE28 .....40 B1
Rochdale Way SR5 .....74 D3
Roche Ct NE38 .....83 C4
Rochester Cl NE63 .....7 A2
Rochester Gdns NE11 .....70 A8
Rochester Sq NE32 .....58 B1
Rochester St NE6 .....57 A4
Rochester Terr NE10 .....71 E8
Rochford Gr NE23 .....22 A3
Rochford Rd SR5 .....74 C3
Rock Gr 4 NE9 .....70 F5
Rock Lodge Gdns SR6 .....75 F3
Rock Lodge Rd SR6 .....75 F3
Rock Terr
Newcastle-upon-Tyne NE2 ..99 C2
9 Washington NE37 .....83 E8
Rockcliffe
Whitley Bay NE26 .....32 C5
South Shields NE33 .....42 F1
Rockcliffe Ave NE26 .....32 C4
Rockcliffe Fst Sch NE26 .32 C4
Rockcliffe Gdns
Newcastle-upon-Tyne NE15 .53 F7
Whitley Bay NE26 .....32 C4
Rockcliffe St NE26 .....32 C4
Rockcliffe Way NE9 .....71 D1
Rocket Way NE12 .....39 F8
Rockhope NE38 .....88 F8
Rockingham Rd SR5 .....74 C3
Rockingham Sq SR5 .....74 C3
Rockmore Rd NE21 .....53 C1
Rockville SR6 .....75 E4
Rockwood Gdns NE40 .....51 E1
Rockwood Hill Est NE40 ..66 E8
Rockwood Hill Rd NE40 ..51 F1
Rockwood Terr NE40 .....51 F1
Rodin Ave NE34 .....59 D2
Rodney Cl
Tynemouth NE30 .....42 D7
Ryhope SR2 .....92 C6
Rodney Ct NE26 .....31 D7
Rodney St NE6 .....56 B5
Rodney Way NE26 .....31 D7
Rodsley Ave NE8,NE9 .....70 F8
Roeburn Way NE3 .....37 F3
Roedean Rd SR5 .....74 E3
Roehedge NE10 .....72 B6
Rogan Ave 8 NE37 .....83 A6
Roger St NE6 .....56 B6
Rogerson Terr NE5 .....36 E3
Rogues La NE39 .....67 A5
Rokeby Ave NE15 .....53 D6
Rokeby Dr NE3 .....37 F4
Rokeby St
Newcastle-upon-Tyne NE15 .53 D6
Sunderland SR4 .....102 B2
Rokeby Terr NE6 .....39 C1
Rokeby View NE9 .....71 A1
Roker Ave
Whitley Bay NE25 .....31 F3
Sunderland SR6 .....75 E1
Roker Baths Rd SR6 .....75 E2
Roker Park Cl 10 SR6 .....75 E2
Roker Park Rd SR6 .....75 E3
Roker Park Terr SR6 .....75 F2
Roker Terr SR6 .....75 F3
Rokerby Ave NE16 .....69 C6
Roland Burn Way NE39 .....67 E2
Roland Rd NE28 .....40 E2
Roland St NE38 .....83 E4
Rollesby Ct NE5 .....37 B4
Rolling Mill Rd NE32 .....58 A8
Romaldskirk Cl SR4 .....85 B5
Roman Ave
Chester le Street DH3 .....88 D3
Newcastle-upon-Tyne NE6 .56 E6
Roman Rd Hedworth NE10 .72 E8
South Shields NE33 .....42 D4
Roman Rd N NE33 .....42 C4
Roman Road Prim Sch
NE10 .....72 A5
Roman Way NE45 .....46 F6
Roman Way The NE5 .....53 D8
Romford Cl NE23 .....22 A3
Romford Pl NE9 .....71 A8
Romford St 4 SR4 .....85 F6
Romilly St NE33 .....42 D2
Romley Gr NE10 .....72 D7
Romney Ave
Whiteleas NE34 .....59 D3
Washington NE38 .....83 E4
Sunderland SR2 .....86 E3
Romney Cl
Shiney Row DH4 .....90 C5
Whitley Bay NE26 .....32 C4
Romney Gdns NE9 .....71 B7
Romsey Cl NE23 .....22 B7
Romsey Dr NE35 .....73 E8
Romsey Gr NE15 .....53 C8
Ronald Dr NE15 .....54 A6
Ronald Gdns NE31 .....57 D4
Ronald Sq SR6 .....75 D3
Ronaldsay Cl 4 SR2 .....92 E8
Ronan Mews DH4 .....94 A2
Ronsdorf Ct NE32 .....58 B6
Rookery Cl NE24 .....17 B7
Rookery La NE16 .....68 E4
Rookery The NE16 .....78 F6
Rooksleigh 6 NE21 .....53 B1
Rookswood NE61 .....9 A6
Rookswood Gdns NE39 .....67 E3
Rookwood Dr NE13 .....28 C8
Rookwood Rd NE5 .....54 A8
Ropery La Bournmoor DH3 .88 F3
Chester le Street DH3 .....88 D2
Wallsend NE28 .....40 F2
Hebburn NE31 .....57 D6
Ropery Rd Gateshead NE8 .70 B8
Sunderland SR4 .....102 B4
Ropery The NE6 .....56 D4
Rosa St NE33 .....42 D2
Rosalind Ave NE22 .....11 B1
Rosalind St Ashington NE63 .6 E4
Ashington, Hirst NE63 .....6 E3
Rosamond Pl NE24 .....17 F7
Rose Ave
Fence Houses DH4 .....89 F1
Whickham NE16 .....69 B7
Cramlington NE23 .....21 F8
Rose Cotts NE16 .....78 E5
Rose Cres Bournmoor DH4 .89 D3
Whitburn SR6 .....60 F2
Rose Ct NE31 .....57 D5
Rose Gdns
Kibblesworth NE11 .....81 C6
Wallsend NE28 .....40 B4
Rose St
7 Houghton-le-Spring DH4 .94 D8
Hebburn NE31 .....57 D5
Gateshead NE8 .....100 C2
Sunderland SR4 .....102 B3
Rose St E DH4 .....90 B8
Rose St W DH4 .....90 B8
Rose Terr Greenside NE40 ..52 C2
Newcastle-upon-Tyne NE5 ..37 E1
Rose Villa La NE16 .....69 B7
Rosebank Cl SR2 .....92 E8
Rosebank Hall NE28 .....40 F2
Roseberry Grange NE12 ..30 A1
Roseberry Pl NE2 .....99 C4
Roseberry Terr 1 NE35 .....58 E1
Rosebery Ave Blyth NE24 ..17 D7
Tynemouth NE29 .....42 A8
South Shields NE33 .....42 E1
Gateshead NE8 .....71 A8
Rosebery Cres NE2 .....56 A8
Rosebery Pl NE2 .....56 A8
Rosebery St 4 SR5 .....75 D1
Rosedale Bedlington NE22 ..10 E1
Wallsend NE28 .....39 F4
Rosedale Ave SR6 .....75 E6
Rosedale Cres DH4 .....90 C2
Rosedale Ct NE5 .....36 D2
Rosedale Rd NE40 .....51 F3
Rosedale St
Hetton le Hole DH5 .....94 E1
Sunderland SR1 .....102 B2
Rosedale Terr
Newcastle-upon-Tyne NE2 ..99 C3
North Shields NE30 .....42 B7
Sunderland SR6 .....75 E4
Roseden Ct NE12 .....39 C7
Rosedene Villas NE23 .....22 D6
Rosefinch Lodge NE9 .....70 F5
Rosegill NE37 .....83 B6
Rosehill NE28 .....40 E2
Rosehill Rd NE28 .....40 F2
Rosehill Way NE5 .....37 C1
Roselea NE32 .....58 C1
Roselea Ave SR2 .....92 F7
Rosemary Gdns NE9 .....71 D2
Rosemary Rd SR5 .....74 D3
Rosemary Terr NE24 .....17 F6
Rosemount
Newcastle-upon-Tyne NE5 ..36 F2
Morpeth NE61 .....9 A7
Sunderland SR4 .....85 A5
Rosemount Ave NE10 .....72 B7
Rosemount Cl NE37 .....72 C2
Rosemount Ct NE36 .....74 B7
Rosemount Way
Whitley Bay NE25 .....31 C5
Newcastle-upon-Tyne NE7 ..39 C5
Roseneath Ct NE63 .....6 D3
Roseville St SR4 .....102 B1
Rosewell Pl NE16 .....69 A4
Rosewood NE12 .....29 F3
Rosewood Ave NE3 .....38 E6
Rosewood Cres
Seaton Sluice NE26 .....24 D4
Newcastle-upon-Tyne NE6 ..39 F1
Rosewood Gdns
Chester le Street DH2 .....88 B5
Newcastle-upon-Tyne NE3 ..37 F4
Gateshead NE9 .....71 B5
Rosewood Sq SR4 .....85 A2
Rosewood Terr
Birtley DH3 .....82 B5
Wallsend NE28 .....41 A2
Roseworth Ave NE3 .....38 D3
Roseworth Cl NE3 .....38 D4
Roseworth Cres NE3 .....38 D3
Roseworth Terr
Whickham NE16 .....69 B7
Newcastle-upon-Tyne NE3 ..38 C4
Roslin Pk NE22 .....11 C1
Roslin Way NE23 .....22 A3
Ross DH2 .....82 A1
Ross Ave NE11 .....54 F1
Ross Castle (N.T.)*
NE66 .....112 B8
Ross Gr NE23 .....21 F7
Ross Lea DH4 .....90 A5
Ross St SR5 .....75 C1
Ross Way
Whitley Bay NE26 .....31 E7
Newcastle-upon-Tyne NE3 ..37 F8
Rosse Cl NE37 .....83 B8
Rossendale Pl NE12 .....38 F6
Rosslyn Ave
Newcastle-upon-Tyne NE3 ..37 E5
Gateshead NE9 .....71 A6
Ryhope SR2 .....92 F7
Rosslyn Mews SR4 .....102 A2
Rosslyn Pl DH3 .....82 D2
Rosslyn St SR4 .....102 A2
Rosslyn Terr SR4 .....102 A2
Rosyth Rd SR5 .....74 E3
Rosyth Sq SR5 .....74 E3
Rotary Parkway NE63 .....6 B4
Rotary Way Blyth NE24 .....17 F5
North Shields NE29 .....41 E3
Rothay Pl NE5 .....37 C2
Rothbury SR2 .....92 D6
Rothbury Ave
Gateshead NE10 .....57 A1
Blyth NE24 .....17 B6
Newcastle-upon-Tyne NE3 ..38 B6
Hebburn NE32 .....58 A4
Rothbury Cl
Chester le Street DH2 .....88 A1
Killingworth NE12 .....29 C4
Rothbury Gdns
Dunston NE11 .....70 A5
Wide Open NE13 .....28 C6
Wallsend NE28 .....40 F3
Rothbury Rd SR5 .....74 D3
Rothbury Terr
North Shields NE29 .....41 D4
Newcastle-upon-Tyne NE6 ..56 C8
Rotherfield Cl NE23 .....22 B7
Rotherfield Gdns NE9 .....71 A2
Rotherfield Rd SR5 .....74 C3
Rotherfield Sq SR5 .....74 C3
Rotherham Cl DH5 .....94 D6
Rotherham Rd SR5 .....74 C3
Rothesay DH2 .....81 F1
Rothesay Terr NE22 .....11 C2
Rothlea Gdns NE62 .....11 A8
Rothley NE38 .....83 F2
Rothley Ave
Newcastle-upon-Tyne NE5 ..54 C7
Ashington NE63 .....6 D2
Rothley Cl Ponteland NE20 .25 D7
Newcastle-upon-Tyne NE3 ..38 D5
Rothley Ct
Killingworth NE12 .....29 D3
Sunderland SR5 .....74 F4
Rothley Gdns NE30 .....32 B1
Rothley Gr NE25 .....23 C3
Rothley Terr DH8 .....77 B1
Rothley Way NE26 .....31 E7
Rothsay Terr NE64 .....7 D3
Rothwell Rd
Newcastle-upon-Tyne NE3 ..38 C5
Sunderland SR5 .....74 C2
Roundhill NE32 .....58 D1
Roundhill Ave NE5 .....37 C2
Roundstone Cl NE7 .....39 D4
Roundway The NE12 .....39 B7
Row's Terr NE3 .....38 E5
Rowan Ave NE38 .....83 C1
Rowan Cl Bedlington NE22 ..10 F2
Sunderland SR4 .....85 B5
Rowan Ct
Longbenton NE12 .....39 F8
Blyth NE24 .....17 D6
4 South Shields NE34 .....59 A4
Rowan Dr
Hetton le Hole DH5 .....94 F4
Ponteland NE20 .....25 E7
Newcastle-upon-Tyne NE3 ..37 F6
Rowan Gr
Cramlington NE23 .....22 D5
Prudhoe NE42 .....50 B2
Rowanberry Rd NE12 .....39 B6
Rowans The NE9 .....71 D2
Rowantree Rd NE28,NE6 ..40 A1
Rowanwood Gdns NE11 .....70 B5
Rowedge Wlk NE5 .....37 A2
Rowell Cl SR2 .....92 C6
Rowes Mews NE6 .....56 C4
Rowlands Gill Inf Sch
NE39 .....67 F3
Rowlands Gill Jun Sch
NE39 .....67 F3
Rowlandson Cres NE10 ..71 D8
Rowlandson Terr
12 Gateshead NE10 .....71 D8
8 Sunderland SR2 .....86 E4
Rowley St NE24 .....17 E7
Rowlington Terr NE63 .....6 D2
Rowntree Way NE29 .....42 A3
Rowsley Rd NE32 .....58 C5
Roxburgh Cl NE21 .....68 A8
Roxburgh House NE26 .....32 A5
Roxburgh Pl 2 NE6 .....56 B7
Roxburgh St SR6 .....75 D2
Roxburgh Terr NE26 .....32 A5
Roxby Gdns NE29 .....41 E5
Royal Arc NE1 .....99 B1
Royal Cres NE4 .....54 E8
Royal Gram Sch NE2 .....99 B3
Royal Ind Est NE32 .....57 F8
Royal Quays Outlet Shopping
NE28 .....41 E2
Royal Victoria Infmy NE2 .98 C3
Royalty The SR2 .....102 B2
Roydon Ave SR2 .....86 E3
Royle St SR2 .....86 F2
Royston Terr NE6 .....57 A4
Ruabon Cl NE23 .....22 A3
Rubens Ave NE34 .....59 D3
Ruby St DH4 .....90 D2
Rudby Cl NE3 .....38 D8
Rudchester Pl NE5 .....54 C8
Ruddock Sq 1 NE6 .....56 C4
Rudyard Ave SR2 .....86 E3
Rudyerd Ct NE29 .....42 B5
Rudyerd St 13 NE29 .....42 A5
Rugby Gdns
Wallsend NE28 .....40 E3
Gateshead NE9 .....71 C3
Ruislip Pl NE23 .....21 F3
Ruislip Rd SR4 .....85 A5
Runcorn SR2 .....92 C7
Runcorn Rd SR5 .....74 C3
Runhead Est NE40 .....52 D4
Runhead Gdns NE40 .....52 D5
Runhead Terr NE40 .....52 E5
Runnymede SR2 .....92 D7
Runnymede Gdns NE17 ..77 B7
Runnymede Rd
Whickham NE16 .....69 A6
Ponteland NE20 .....25 C5
Sunderland SR5 .....74 D3
Runnymede Way
Newcastle-upon-Tyne NE3 ..37 E4
Sunderland SR5 .....74 D3
Runswick Ave NE12 .....38 F6
Runswick Cl SR3 .....92 C7
Rupert Sq SR5 .....74 E3
Rupert St SR6 .....60 F1
Rupert Terr NE15 .....52 F8
Rushall Pl NE12 .....39 B6
Rushbury Ct NE27 .....30 C5
Rushford SR2 .....92 D6
Rushie Ave NE15 .....54 C5
Rushley Cres NE21 .....53 C3
Rushsyde Cl NE16 .....68 E5
Rushton Ave SR2 .....86 E3
Rushyrig NE37 .....83 A6
Ruskin Ave
Easington Lane DH5 .....97 D8
7 Dunston NE11 .....54 F1
Longbenton NE12 .....29 D1
Ashington NE63 .....6 F2
Ruskin Cres NE34 .....59 B3
Ruskin Ct NE42 .....50 B1
Ruskin Dr
West Boldon NE35 .....74 A8
Newcastle-upon-Tyne NE7 ..39 E3
Ruskin Rd Birtley DH3 .....82 C4
Gateshead N10,NE9 .....71 B7
Whickham NE16 .....69 A8
Russel Ct NE2 .....38 F2
Russell Ave NE34 .....60 A6
Russell Ct NE8 .....100 C1
Russell Sq NE13 .....28 B8
Russell St
8 North Shields NE29 .....42 A5
Jarrow NE32 .....58 C7
7 South Shields NE33 .....42 C3
Washington NE37 .....83 C8
Sunderland SR1 .....103 B3
Russell Terr Birtley DH3 ..82 B6
Newcastle-upon-Tyne NE1,
NE2 .....99 C2
Bedlington NE22 .....15 F8
Rustic Terr NE64 .....7 E5
Ruswarp Dr SR3 .....92 B6
Ruth Ave NE21 .....53 C2
Rutherford Ave SR7 .....92 F1
Rutherford Cl NE62 .....10 E7
Rutherford Pl NE61 .....8 E7
Rutherford Rd
Washington NE37 .....72 E2
Sunderland SR5 .....74 B3
Rutherford Sq SR5 .....74 B3
Rutherford St
Newcastle-upon-Tyne NE1 ..98 C1
Blyth NE24 .....17 D7
Wallsend NE28 .....41 B3
Rutherglen Rd SR5 .....74 E3
Rutherglen Sq SR5 .....74 E3
Rutland Ave
Newcastle-upon-Tyne NE6 ..57 A7
New Silksworth SR3 .....91 F7
Rutland Pl
North Shields NE29 .....41 F6
Washington NE37 .....72 D2
Rutland Rd Wallsend NE28 .40 A1
Hebburn NE31 .....57 F3
Rutland Sq DH3 .....82 B5
Rutland St
Hetton le Hole DH5 .....94 F4
Ashington NE63 .....6 C3
Sunderland SR4 .....85 F7
Rutland Terr DH6 .....97 E1
Ryal Cl Blyth NE24 .....17 C7
Seaton Delaval NE25 .....23 E3
Ryal Terr NE6 .....56 F5
Ryal Wlk NE3 .....37 D4
Ryall Ave NE13 .....28 A4
Rydal NE10 .....72 A8
Rydal Ave
Easington Lane DH5 .....97 C8
Tynemouth NE30 .....32 A2
Rydal Cl Killingworth NE12 ..29 F3
East Boldon NE36 .....74 C8
Rydal Cres NE21 .....68 B8
Rydal Gdns NE34 .....59 E6
Rydal Mount
Newbiggin-by-the-Sea NE64 ..7 C4

Rydal Mount *continued*
Sunderland, Castletown SR5 .....85 A8
Sunderland, Monkwearmouth SR5 .....75 C3
Rydal Rd
Chester le Street DH2 .....88 C1
Newcastle-upon-Tyne, Lemington NE15 .....53 D8
Newcastle-upon-Tyne, Gosforth NE3 .....38 D5
Rydal St NE8 .....101 B1
Rydal Terr NE13 .....28 B4
Ryde Pl NE23 .....22 B7
Ryde Terr NE11 .....100 A1
Rye Cl NE15 .....35 E1
Rye Hill
Newcastle-upon-Tyne NE4 .100 B4
Newcastle-upon-Tyne NE4 .100 C4
Rye Terr NE46 .....44 F5
Rye View SR2 .....92 F7
Ryedale Wallsend NE28 .....39 F5
Sunderland SR6 .....75 F7
Ryedale Cl NE63 .....6 B2
Ryedale Ct 7 NE34 .....59 A4
Ryehaugh NE20 .....25 F6
Ryehill View DH5 .....94 C5
Ryemount Rd SR2 .....92 D7
Ryhope Engine Mus* SR2 .....92 E5
Ryhope Gdns NE9 .....71 D4
Ryhope General Hospl SR2 .....92 F5
Ryhope Grange Ct SR2 .....86 F1
Ryhope Inf Sch SR2 .....92 F7
Ryhope Jun Sch SR2 .....92 F7
Ryhope Rd Ryhope SR2 .....93 A8
Sunderland SR2 .....86 E3
Ryhope St
Houghton-le-Spring DH5 .....94 F8
Ryhope SR2 .....92 E7
5 Sunderland SR2 .....86 F2
Ryhope St S SR2 .....92 F7
Ryhope Village C of E Prim Sch SR2 .....92 F6
Ryton Com Inf Sch NE40 .52 A5
Ryton Com Jun Sch NE40 .....52 A5
Ryton Comp Sch NE40 .....52 B5
Ryton Ct NE33 .....42 D1
Ryton Hall Dr NE40 .....52 C6
Ryton Ind Est NE21 .....52 F5
Ryton Sq SR2 .....86 E3
Ryton Terr
Shiremoor NE27 .....30 D1
Newcastle-upon-Tyne NE6 ..56 F4

S

Sackville Rd
Newcastle-upon-Tyne NE6 ..39 C1
Sunderland SR3 .....85 E3
Sacred Heart High Sch NE4 .....54 D7
Sacred Heart Lower Sch NE4 .....54 F6
Sacred Heart RC Mid Sch Sch NE4 .....54 E7
Sacred Heart RC Prim Sch NE4 .....54 D7
Sacriston Ave SR3 .....85 F3
Sacriston Gdns NE9 .....71 C2
Saddleback NE37 .....83 B7
Saffron Pl NE6 .....57 A5
Saga Ct NE6 .....39 F1
Sage Cl NE15 .....53 C8
St Acca's Ct NE46 .....44 F5
St Agnes RC Prim Sch NE40 .....51 E4
St Agnes' Gdns NE40 .....51 E4
St Agnes' Gdns N NE40 .....51 E4
St Agnes' Gdns W NE40 .....51 E4
St Agnes' Terr NE40 .....51 E4
St Aidan's Ave
Wallsend NE12 .....30 C1
Sunderland SR2 .....86 F2
St Aidan's Cl NE29 .....41 D8
St Aidan's Cres NE61 .....9 A6
St Aidan's Ct NE30 .....42 C7
St Aidan's RC Comp Sch SR2 .....86 C4
St Aidan's RC Fst Sch NE63 .....6 D1
St Aidan's Rd
Wallsend NE28 .....40 A1
South Shields NE33 .....42 D4
St Aidan's Sq NE12 .....30 C1
St Aidan's St NE8 .....101 A1
St Aidan's Terr DH4 .....90 E6
St Alban's Cl NE25 .....31 A5
St Alban's Cres
Gateshead NE10 .....71 C7
Newcastle-upon-Tyne NE6 ..39 D2
St Alban's Pl NE10 .....71 C7
St Alban's RC Prim Sch NE10 .....57 A1
St Alban's RC Sch NE6 .....56 F6
St Alban's St SR2 .....86 F3
St Alban's Terr NE8 .....101 C1
St Albans Cl NE63 .....7 A2
St Albans View NE27 .....30 F2
St Aldate's Ct SR4 .....85 A2
St Aloysius RC Jun Mix Sch NE31 .....57 E7
St Aloysius View NE31 .....57 D6
St Andrew's Ct NE7 .....39 C5
St Andrew's Dr NE9 .....70 E3
St Andrew's La NE42 .....49 D4
St Andrew's RC Fst Sch NE24 .....17 C7
St Andrew's Rd
Tanfield Lea DH9 .....79 F1
Hexham NE46 .....45 A4
St Andrew's St
Newcastle-upon-Tyne NE1 ..98 C1
Hebburn NE31 .....57 C7
St Andrew's Terr
Ashington NE63 .....6 E3
3 Sunderland SR6 .....75 E2
St Andrews DH4 .....94 B8
St Andrews Ave NE37 .....83 B8
St Andrews Cl NE25 .....31 D5
St Andrews Ct 4 NE29 .....41 F8
St Ann's Cl NE1 .....56 A5
St Ann's St NE1 .....99 C1
St Anne's Ct NE25 .....31 E3
St Anne's RC Prim Sch
Newcastle-upon-Tyne NE4 .100 C4
Gateshead NE9 .....71 B2
Sunderland SR4 .....85 B5
St Anselm Cres NE29 .....41 C7
St Anselm Rd NE29 .....41 C7
St Anthony's CE Prim Sch NE6 .....56 F3
St Anthony's Ct NE6 .....56 F6
St Anthony's Ho NE6 .....56 F3
St Anthony's RC Girls Sch SR2 .....102 C1
St Anthony's Rd NE6 .....56 E4
St Anthony's Wlk NE6 .....56 F3
St Asaph Cl NE12 .....39 D4
St Augustine's RC Prim Sch NE10 .....72 A6
St Austell Cl NE5 .....37 C4
St Austell Gdns NE9 .....70 F2
St Barnabas DH4 .....89 D3
St Barnabas Way SR2 .....103 C1
St Bartholomew's CE Prim Sch NE12 .....39 D6
St Bartholomews Cl
Cresswell NE61 .....2 A7
Ashington NE63 .....6 F5
St Bede's NE36 .....74 D7
St Bede's Cl DH5 .....95 A4
St Bede's Dr NE8 .....101 C2
St Bede's Ho NE9 .....71 A7
St Bede's Inf Sch NE32 .....58 C7
St Bede's Pk SR2 .....103 A1
St Bede's Prim Sch NE37 .72 D1
St Bede's RC Fst Sch NE22 .....15 E8
St Bede's RC Prim Sch
Newcastle-upon-Tyne NE15 .54 A6
Jarrow NE32 .....58 C7
South Shields NE33 .....42 D2
St Bede's Terr SR2 .....103 A1
St Bedes Pl NE24 .....17 B4
St Bedes Rd NE24 .....17 B4
St Bedes Wlk NE27 .....30 C1
St Benedict's RC Mid Sch NE63 .....6 F3
St Benet Biscop RC High Sch NE22 .....15 E8
St Benet's RC Prim Sch DH2 .....81 F1
St Benets RC Prim Sch SR6 .....75 D2
St Bernadette's RC Prim Sch NE28 .....40 B5
St Buryan Cres NE5 .....37 C4
St Catherine's Ct SR5 .....74 D1
St Catherine's RC Prim Sch NE2 .....56 A8
St Catherines Gr NE2 .....56 A7
St Cecilia's Cl SR2 .....86 F4
St Chad's Cres SR3 .....91 B7
St Chad's Rd SR3 .....91 B7
St Chad's Villas 6 NE36 .....74 D7
St Charles' RC Prim Sch NE3 .....38 B6
St Christopher Way NE29 .41 C2
St Christopher's Ho NE61 ..8 E8
St Christopher's Rd SR3 ..86 A2
St Christophers Cl NE63 .....6 F5
St Clements Ct
Newcastle-upon-Tyne NE3 ..37 F8
Ashington NE63 .....7 A2
St Columba's Ct SR5 .....75 C2
St Columba's RC Prim Sch NE28 .....40 A2
Saint Ct SR3 .....92 A5
St Cuthbert Ave DH3 .....88 D3
St Cuthbert's Ave NE34 .....60 A8
St Cuthbert's Cave (N.T.)* NE70 .....108 C5
St Cuthbert's Cl DH5 .....95 A4
St Cuthbert's Ct
Newcastle-upon-Tyne NE3 ..38 A5
Gateshead NE8 .....101 A2
St Cuthbert's Dr NE10 .....71 F7
St Cuthbert's Gn NE5 .....54 C7
St Cuthbert's High Sch NE15 .....54 B6
St Cuthbert's La NE46 .....45 A4
St Cuthbert's Pl NE8 .....101 A1
St Cuthbert's RC Prim Sch
North Shields NE29 .....42 A5
Newcastle-upon-Tyne NE5 ..37 D4
Sunderland SR4 .....85 D3
St Cuthbert's Rd
New Herrington DH4 .....90 F7
Newbottle DH4 .....90 D3
St Cuthbert's Rd *continued*
Sunniside NE16 .....80 B7
Wallsend, Holystone NE27 ..30 C1
Wallsend, Holy Cross NE28 ..40 E3
Newcastle-upon-Tyne, Benwell NE5 .....54 B7
Newcastle-upon-Tyne, Fenham NE5 .....54 C8
Gateshead NE8 .....101 A2
Gateshead, Windmill Hills NE8 .....101 B3
St Cuthbert's Terr
Hexham NE46 .....45 A4
Sunderland SR4 .....102 B3
St Cuthbert's Wlk DH3 .....88 C3
St Cuthberts CE Jun Sch NE8 .....100 C1
St Cuthberts Cl
Wallsend NE27 .....30 C1
Prudhoe NE42 .....50 C2
Hexham NE46 .....45 A4
St Cuthberts Ct NE24 .....17 F7
St Cuthberts Lower Sch NE15 .....54 C6
St Cuthberts Pk NE16 .....80 A8
St Cuthberts RC Prim Sch DH3 .....88 D2
St Cuthberts Way
Blaydon NE21 .....53 D3
Wallsend NE27 .....30 C1
St David's Cl NE26 .....31 F8
St David's Way
Whitley Bay NE26 .....31 F8
Hedworth NE32 .....58 C1
St Davids Cl NE63 .....6 F5
St Ebba's Way DH8 .....76 E3
St Edmund Campion RC Sch NE9 .....71 D4
St Edmund's Ct NE8 .....56 A1
St Edmund's Dr NE10 .....71 F7
St Edmund's Rd NE8 .....101 C1
St Etienne Ct 12 NE10 .....56 D1
St Gabriel's Ave
Newcastle-upon-Tyne NE6 ..39 B1
Sunderland SR4 .....85 F5
St George's Ave NE33, NE34 .....59 E8
St George's Cl NE2 .....38 E2
St George's Cres NE29 .....41 F5
St George's Est NE38 .....83 C1
St George's Hospl NE61 .....4 A2
St George's Pl NE15 .....53 E5
St George's RC Sch NE15 .53 D5
St George's Rd
Newcastle-upon-Tyne NE15 .53 E5
Tynemouth NE30 .....32 C3
Hexham NE46 .....45 A4
St George's Terr
Newcastle-upon-Tyne, Lemington NE15 .....53 E5
Newcastle-upon-Tyne, West Jesmond NE2 .....38 E2
East Boldon NE36 .....74 D7
Sunderland SR6 .....75 F2
St George's Way SR2 .....103 A1
St Georges Cres NE25 .....31 F4
St Georges Ct NE10 .....72 B7
St Godric's Dr DH4 .....94 A2
St Gregory's Ct NE34 .....59 F5
St Gregory's RC Jun Mix & Inf Sch NE34 .....60 A7
St Helen's Cres NE9 .....70 E5
St Helen's St NE45 .....46 F6
St Hilda Ind Est NE33 .....42 C2
St Hilda St NE33 .....42 C2
St Hilda's Ave NE28 .....40 E3
St Hilda's RC Prim Sch SR5 .....75 A2
St Hilda's Rd NE46 .....45 A4
St Ignatius Cl SR2 .....103 B1
St Ives Way NE5 .....37 C4
St James Bvld NE1,NE4 ..100 C4
St James Cl NE44 .....62 F7
St James Ct NE8 .....56 B1
St James Lodge 4 NE4 ..54 D5
St James RC Prim Sch NE31 .....57 F4
St James Rd NE8 .....56 A2
St James Sq NE8 .....56 A2
St James St NE3 .....38 E5
St James Sta NE1 .....98 C1
St James Terr
Riding Mill NE44 .....63 A7
4 Morpeth NE61 .....3 F1
St James' Cres NE15 .....54 D4
St James' Gdns 6 NE15 ..54 D5
St James' Mall NE31 .....57 D5
St James' Pk (Newcastle Utd F.C.) NE1 .....98 C2
St James' Rd NE15 .....54 D5
St James' St NE1 .....98 C2
St James' Terr NE29 .....41 D3
St John & St Patrick's Church Sch SR1 .....103 C3
St John Bosco RC Prim Sch SR5 .....74 A4
St John Boste RC Prim Sch NE38 .....83 A5
St John St NE1 .....99 A1
St John the Baptist's RC Prim Sch NE10 .....71 D8
St John Vianney RC Prim Sch NE5 .....36 D1
St John's Ave NE31 .....57 D5
St John's Cl NE26 .....31 F8
St John's Cres NE22 .....11 D3
St John's Ct
Backworth NE27 .....30 C5
St John's Ct *continued*
Newcastle-upon-Tyne NE4 ..54 E4
St John's Gn NE29 .....41 D3
St John's Mall NE31 .....57 D5
St John's Pl Birtley DH3 ..82 C4
Bedlington NE22 .....11 D3
Whitley Bay NE26 .....31 F8
St John's Rd
High Pittington DH6 .....96 B5
Bedlington NE22 .....11 D2
Newcastle-upon-Tyne NE4 ..54 E4
St John's St NE29 .....41 D3
St John's Terr
North Shields NE29 .....41 D3
Jarrow NE32 .....58 B7
East Boldon NE36 .....74 E7
3 Seaham SR7 .....92 E1
St John's W NE22 .....11 D3
St John's Wlk
North Shields NE29 .....41 D3
Hebburn NE31 .....57 E5
Newcastle-upon-Tyne NE4 ..54 E4
St Johns SR1 .....103 C4
St Johns Pl NE10 .....71 D8
St Johns Rd NE46 .....45 A3
St Johns Vale SR4 .....85 A4
St Joseph's Ct
7 Birtley DH3 .....82 C5
Hebburn NE31 .....57 D3
St Joseph's RC Comp Sch NE31 .....57 D2
St Joseph's RC Mid Sch NE46 .....44 F4
St Joseph's RC Prim Sch
Newcastle-upon-Tyne NE15 .54 D4
Blaydon NE21 .....53 B3
Hedworth NE32 .....58 B1
Washington NE38 .....83 D6
Gateshead NE8 .....101 C2
Sunderland SR4 .....102 A3
St Joseph's RC Sch NE39 .67 B2
St Joseph's Way NE32 .....58 C1
St Jude's Terr NE33 .....59 C8
St Julien Gdns
Wallsend NE28 .....41 B3
Newcastle-upon-Tyne NE7 ..39 D2
St Just Pl NE5 .....37 C4
St Keverne Sq NE5 .....37 C4
St Kitt's Cl NE26 .....31 F8
St Lawerence's RC Prim Sch NE6 .....56 C6
St Lawrence Cl DH6 .....96 C5
St Lawrence Rd
High Pittington DH6 .....96 B5
Newcastle-upon-Tyne NE6 ..56 C4
St Lawrence Sq NE6 .....56 B5
St Leonard St SR2 .....86 F4
St Leonard's La NE61 .....3 B2
St Leonard's RC Prim Sch SR3 .....92 B7
St Leonard's Wlk NE61 .....3 C2
St Lucia Cl
Whitley Bay NE26 .....31 E8
Sunderland SR2 .....103 B1
St Luke's Rd
North Shields NE29 .....41 D3
Sunderland SR4 .....85 D7
St Luke's Terr SR4 .....85 F7
St Lukes Cl NE63 .....7 A5
St Lukes Ct NE31 .....57 D4
St Lukes Rd NE46 .....45 A4
St Margaret's Ave SR5 .....74 A1
St Margaret's Dr DH9 .....79 D4
St Margaret's Rd NE15 .....54 A4
St Margargets Ave NE12 ..39 D6
St Mark's Cl 11 NE6 .....56 C7
St Mark's Cres SR4 .....102 B2
St Mark's Ct NE29 .....41 D2
St Mark's RC Prim Sch NE5 .....36 F4
St Mark's Rd SR4 .....102 B2
St Mark's Rd N SR4 .....102 A2
St Mark's St
13 Newcastle-upon-Tyne NE6 .....56 C7
Morpeth NE61 .....3 E1
Sunderland SR4 .....102 B2
St Mark's Terr SR4 .....102 B2
St Mark's Way NE33 .....42 C1
St Marks Ct NE27 .....30 E3
St Marks Rd NE46 .....45 A3
St Martin's Cl NE26 .....31 E7
St Martin's Ct NE26 .....31 E7
St Mary & St Thomas Aquinas RC Prim Sch NE21 .....53 A4
St Mary Magdalene Hospl NE2 .....98 B4
St Mary RC Prim Sch NE32 .....58 D3
St Mary's Ave
Whitley Bay NE26 .....31 F7
South Shields NE34 .....59 F6
St Mary's Chare NE46 .....45 B4
St Mary's Church (Mus)* NE63 .....7 C6
St Mary's Coll NE4 .....54 E7
St Mary's College Flats NE4 .....54 E7
St Mary's Ct
South Shields NE33 .....59 B7
Gateshead NE8 .....101 C2
St Mary's Dr
West Rainton DH4 .....94 A2
Blyth NE24 .....17 B6
St Mary's Field NE61 .....8 F7
St Mary's Gn 4 NE16 .....69 B7
St Mary's Infs Sch NE8 ..101 B3
St Mary's Lodge NE26 .....31 F5
St Mary's or Bait Island* NE26 .....24 G2
St Mary's Pl
Newcastle-upon-Tyne NE1 ..99 A2
Walbottle NE15 .....35 E2
St Mary's Pl E NE1 .....99 A2
St Mary's RC Cath NE1 ..100 C4
St Mary's RC Comp Sch NE7 .....39 A5
St Mary's RC Fst Sch NE46 .....45 A4
St Mary's RC Prim Sch
Tynemouth NE30 .....32 A2
Sunderland SR2 .....86 B4
St Mary's St NE1 .....99 C1
St Mary's Terr
South Shields NE33 .....59 B7
East Boldon NE36 .....74 E7
Ryton NE40 .....52 B5
St Mary's Training & Enterprise Ctr NE4 .....98 B1
St Mary's Way SR1 .....103 A3
St Mary's Wynd
Seaton Sluice NE26 .....24 E4
Hexham NE46 .....45 B4
St Marys CE Jun Mix & Inf Sch NE33 .....59 B7
St Marys Cl DH2 .....88 B1
St Marys Dr NE63 .....6 F5
St Marys RC Prim Sch NE16 .....69 C7
St Mathews La NE42 .....50 D2
St Matthew's RC Fst Sch NE42 .....50 C2
St Matthew's RC Prim Sch NE32 .....58 B2
St Matthew's Terr DH4 ..90 D4
St Matthews Rd NE46 .....44 F3
St Matthews View SR3 ..92 A7
St Michael's Ave
New Hartley NE25 .....23 D6
South Shields NE33 .....42 E1
St Michael's Ave N NE33 ..42 D1
St Michael's Mount 3 NE6 .....56 C5
St Michael's RC Jun Sch NE4 .....54 F4
St Michael's RC Prim Sch DH5 .....94 E7
St Michael's Rd NE6 .....56 B5
St Michael's Way NE11 ..54 C1
St Michaels DH4 .....94 B8
St Michaels RC Inf Sch NE4 .....100 A3
St Michaels Way SR1 ..102 C2
St Michaels Workshops 10 NE6 .....56 B5
St Nichola's Cath NE1 .....99 B1
St Nicholas Ave
Newcastle-upon-Tyne, Gosforth NE3 .....38 C4
Newcastle-upon-Tyne, South Gosforth NE3 .....38 D4
Sunderland SR3 .....86 B3
St Nicholas Cl NE63 .....6 F5
St Nicholas Hospl NE3 ..38 A5
St Nicholas Rd
West Boldon NE36 .....74 A7
Hexham NE46 .....45 A4
St Nicholas View NE36 ..74 A7
St Nicholas' Church Yd NE1 .....99 A1
St Nicholas' Sq NE1 .....99 A1
St Nicholas' St NE1 .....101 A4
St Omers Rd NE11 .....54 F2
St Oswald Ave's NE6 .....56 E6
St Oswald's Gn NE6 .....56 E7
St Oswald's RC Prim Sch
Newcastle-upon-Tyne NE3 ..38 D7
Whiteleas NE34 .....59 D3
Gateshead NE9 .....71 C3
St Oswald's Rd
Wallsend NE28 .....40 E4
Hebburn NE31 .....57 F7
3 Hexham NE46 .....45 A4
St Oswald's Terr 2 DH4 ..90 B6
St Oswalds C of E Prim Sch NE31 .....57 F7
St Oswin's Ave NE30 .....32 C3
St Oswin's Pl NE30 .....42 D7
St Oswin's St NE33 .....59 D7
St Patrick's Cl NE10 .....71 D8
St Patrick's RC Prim Sch SR2 .....92 F6
St Patrick's Wlk NE10 .....71 D8
St Paul's CE Prim Sch NE4 .....100 B4
St Paul's Gdns NE25 .....32 A4
St Paul's Pl NE4 .....98 A1
St Paul's RC Fst Sch NE23 .....22 B5
St Paul's Rd NE32 .....58 C7
St Paul's Terr 5 SR2 .....92 F6
St Pauls Cl NE63 .....6 F5
St Pauls Ct NE8 .....100 C1
St Pauls Dr DH4 .....89 E8
St Pauls Rd NE46 .....44 F4
St Peter's Ave NE34 .....59 E7
St Peter's Ct NE6 .....56 C5
St Peter's Quayside E NE6 .....56 D4
St Peter's Quayside W 9 NE6 .....56 C4
St Peter's RC Mid Sch NE23 .....22 B4
St Peter's RC Prim Sch NE9 .....71 A6

St Peter's Rd
Wallsend NE28 .... 40 D3
Newcastle-upon-Tyne NE6 .. 56 C5
St Peter's View SR6 .... 103 A4
St Peter's Wharf NE6 .... 56 C4
St Peters Spec Sch NE3 .. 38 F4
St Peters Sta SR5 .... 103 A4
St Peters' Way SR6 .... 103 B4
St Philip Neri RC Prim Sch NE11 .... 70 A8
St Philips Cl NE4 .... 98 B1
St Philips Way NE4 .... 98 B1
St Robert of Newminster RC Sch NE38 .... 83 D2
St Robert's of Newminster RC Fst Sch NE61 .... 8 E8
St Rollox St NE31 .... 57 D5
St Ronan's Dr NE26 .... 24 B7
St Ronan's Rd NE25 .... 31 F4
St Ronans View NE9 .... 71 A2
St Simon St NE34 .... 59 A4
St Stephen's Cl NE25 .... 23 B3
St Stephen's RC Prim Sch NE12 .... 39 B7
St Stephen's Way NE29 .. 41 D3
St Stevens Cl DH4 .... 89 E8
St Teresa's RC Sch NE6 .. 56 B8
St Thomas Cl NE42 .... 50 D2
St Thomas Mews NE42 .. 50 D2
St Thomas More RC High Sch NE29 .... 41 D7
St Thomas More RC Sch NE21 .... 53 B3
St Thomas St 6 NE9 .... 71 A5
St Thomas' Cres NE1 .... 99 A2
St Thomas' Sq NE1 .... 99 A2
St Thomas' St
Newcastle-upon-Tyne NE1 .. 99 A2
Sunderland SR1 .... 103 A3
St Thomas' Street Bsns Ctr NE1 .... 99 A2
St Thomas' Terr NE1 .... 99 A2
St Vincent Ct NE8 .... 56 A1
St Vincent St
South Shields NE33 .... 42 E1
Gateshead NE8 .... 56 A1
Sunderland SR2 .... 103 B1
St Vincent's Pl NE26 .... 31 F8
St Vincent's RC Sch NE6 .. 56 E4
St Vincent's Way 1 NE26 .. 31 F8
St Vincents Cl NE15 .... 53 E8
St Vincents Ho NE30 .... 42 D7
St Wilfred's RC Mid Sch NE24 .... 17 D7
St Wilfred's Rd NE45 .... 47 A6
St Wilfrid's Ct 6 NE46 .... 45 A4
St Wilfrid's Rd NE46 .... 45 A4
St Wilfrid's RC Prim Sch NE10 .... 56 B2
Saint Wilfrid's RC Comp Sch NE34 .... 59 D6
Saints Peter & Paul RC Prim Sch NE33 .... 59 B6
Saker Pl 1 NE28 .... 40 B1
Salcombe Ave NE32 .... 58 D6
Salcombe Gdns NE9 .... 70 F2
Salem Hill SR2 .... 103 B1
Salem Rd SR2 .... 103 B1
Salem St Jarrow NE32 .... 58 C7
South Shields NE33 .... 42 C3
Sunderland SR2 .... 103 B1
Salem St S SR2 .... 103 B1
Salem Terr SR2 .... 103 B1
Salisbury Ave
10 Chester le Street DH3 .. 88 C2
Tynemouth NE29 .... 42 A7
Salisbury Cl
Cramlington NE23 .... 21 E6
9 Ashington NE63 .... 6 F2
Salisbury Gdns NE2 .... 56 A8
Salisbury Ho NE6 .... 56 A6
Salisbury Pl NE33 .... 42 E3
Salisbury St
Gateshead NE10 .... 57 A1
Blyth NE24 .... 17 D8
South Shields NE33 .... 42 D2
Morpeth NE61 .... 9 B8
Sunderland SR1 .... 103 B2
Sunderland, South Hylton SR4 .... 85 A7
Salisbury Way NE32 .... 58 B1
Salkeld Gdns NE9 .... 71 A8
Salkeld Rd NE9 .... 71 A6
Sally Davison Ct 4 NE63 .. 6 F2
Sallyport Cres NE1 .... 99 B1
Sallyport Ho NE1 .... 99 B1
Salmon St NE33 .... 42 D4
Saltburn Cl DH4 .... 90 C1
Saltburn Gdns NE28 .... 41 B3
Saltburn Rd SR3 .... 85 E3
Saltburn Sq SR3 .... 85 E3
Salter La SR3 .... 91 B8
Salter's La
Houghton-le-Spring DH5 .... 91 E1
Seaton DH5,SR7 .... 95 F6
Haswell DH6 .... 97 E6
Hetton le Hole SR7 .... 95 F6
Salterfen La SR2 .... 93 A8
Salterfen Rd SR2 .... 93 A8
Salters Cl NE3 .... 38 E6
Salters Ct NE3 .... 38 E6
Salters' La NE3,NE12 .... 38 F7
Salters' Rd NE3 .... 38 B4
Saltford NE9 .... 71 A2
Saltmeadows Rd NE10, NE8 .... 56 B4
Saltwell Park Mansion Mus* NE9 .... 70 E6
Saltwell Pl NE8 .... 70 D8
Saltwell Rd NE8 .... 70 D7
Saltwell Rd S NE9 .... 70 E4
Saltwell St NE8 .... 70 D8
Saltwell View NE8 .... 70 E7
Sam's Ct NE23 .... 28 F8
Samson Cl NE12 .... 29 C2
Sancroft Dr DH5 .... 94 E7
Sand Point Rd SR6 .... 75 F1
Sandalwood NE34 .... 59 E3
Sandalwood Sq SR4 .... 85 B2
Sanderling Cl NE40 .... 52 D4
Sanderlings 3 NE28 .... 40 B1
Sanders Gdns 3 DH3 .... 82 C5
Sanders' Memorial Homes DH2 .... 88 C3
Sanderson Rd
Newcastle-upon-Tyne NE2 .. 38 E2
Whitley Bay NE26 .... 31 F5
Sanderson St NE4 .... 54 F3
Sandfield Rd
Cambois NE22 .... 12 B4
Tynemouth NE30 .... 32 B3
Sandford Ave NE23 .... 16 B1
Sandford Mews NE13 .... 28 A5
Sandgate NE1 .... 99 C1
Sandgrove SR6 .... 60 A1
Sandhill NE1 .... 101 B4
Sandhill View Comp Sch SR3 .... 85 D2
Sandholm Cl NE28 .... 40 F5
Sandhurst Ave NE30 .... 32 C2
Sandiacres NE32 .... 58 C1
Sandison Ct NE13 .... 27 F6
Sandmartin Cl NE63 .... 11 E8
Sandmere Pl NE15 .... 54 A5
Sandmere Rd SR2 .... 86 D1
Sandoe Gdns NE15 .... 54 B5
Sandon Cl NE27 .... 30 C5
Sandown NE25 .... 31 D5
Sandown Cl NE25 .... 23 D2
Sandown Ct NE28 .... 41 A4
Sandown Gdns
Wallsend NE28 .... 40 F4
Gateshead NE8 .... 70 D8
New Silksworth SR3 .... 91 F8
Sandpiper Cl Blyth NE24 .. 17 F4
Washington NE38 .... 82 F2
Ryton NE40 .... 52 D4
Sandpiper Ct NE30 .... 42 D8
Sandpiper Pl NE12 .... 39 A7
Sandpiper Way NE63 .... 6 D1
Sandray Cl DH3 .... 82 D1
Sandridge NE64 .... 7 F5
Sandringham Ave NE12 .. 39 D6
Sandringham Cl NE25 .... 31 B4
Sandringham Cres SR3 .. 91 C6
Sandringham Ct
3 Longbenton NE12 .... 39 A6
6 Gateshead NE10 .... 71 C8
Sandringham Dr
Whickham NE16 .... 69 A7
Blyth NE24 .... 17 D3
Whitley Bay NE25 .... 31 C4
Sandringham Gdns NE29 . 42 A7
Sandringham Mews 8 NE28 .... 40 F4
Sandringham Rd
Newcastle-upon-Tyne, South Gosforth NE3 .... 38 E4
Newcastle-upon-Tyne, West Denton NE5 .... 53 E8
Sunderland SR6 .... 75 D2
Sandringham Terr SR6 .. 75 E2
Sandringham Way NE20 .. 25 C4
Sands Ind Est The NE16 .. 54 A1
Sands Rd NE16 .... 54 A1
Sandsay Cl SR2 .... 92 D8
Sandstone Cl NE34 .... 58 F3
Sandwell Dr DH4 .... 89 F8
Sandwich Rd NE29 .... 31 F1
Sandwich St NE6 .... 56 F3
Sandy Bank NE44 .... 62 F7
Sandy Chare SR6 .... 75 E8
Sandy Cres NE6 .... 56 E4
Sandy La
Brunswick Village NE13 .... 27 E6
Wide Open NE3,NE12 .... 28 F4
Riding Mill NE44 .... 62 E8
Ashington NE63 .... 7 B2
Gateshead NE9 .... 71 D1
Sandy Lane Ind Area NE3 . 28 E4
Sandyford Ave NE42 .... 50 F3
Sandyford Pk NE2 .... 99 C4
Sandyford Rd NE2 .... 99 B3
Sandygate Mews NE16 .. 69 B1
Sandypath La NE16 .... 79 A7
Sandysykes NE42 .... 50 B2
Sans St SR1 .... 103 B3
Sans St S SR1 .... 103 B2
Sarabel Ave NE62 .... 10 E7
Sargent Ave NE34 .... 59 D2
Satley Gdns
Gateshead NE9 .... 71 C2
Sunderland SR3 .... 86 B2
Saunton Ct DH4 .... 90 C3
Saville Lodge 5 NE33 .. 42 D3
Saville Pl SR1 .... 103 B2
Saville Row NE1 .... 99 A2
Saville St
North Shields NE30 .... 42 B5
4 South Shields NE33 .... 42 D3
Saville St W NE29 .... 42 A5
Savory Rd NE28 .... 40 F3
Sawmill Cotts DH9 .... 78 E1
Saxilby Dr NE3 .... 38 D8
Saxon Cl SR6 .... 59 E1
Saxon Cres SR3 .... 85 F3
Saxon Dr NE30 .... 32 C1
Saxon Way NE32 .... 58 C7
Saxondale Rd NE3 .... 37 E5
Saxton Gr NE7 .... 39 A4
Scafell DH3 .... 82 D1
Scafell Ct 22 SR3 .... 91 F6
Scafell Dr NE5 .... 37 D3
Scafell Gdns NE11 .... 70 A6
Scalby Cl NE3 .... 38 D8
Scales Cres NE42 .... 50 F2
Scarborough Ct
Cramlington NE23 .... 22 B5
Newcastle-upon-Tyne NE6 .. 56 D6
Scarborough Par NE31 .. 58 A2
Scarborough Rd
Newcastle-upon-Tyne NE6 .. 56 D6
New Silksworth SR3 .... 91 F8
Sceptre Ct NE4 .... 100 A4
Sceptre Pl NE4 .... 98 A1
Sceptre St NE4 .... 98 A1
Schalksmuhle Rd NE22 .. 10 F1
Schimel St SR5 .... 75 B2
School App NE34 .... 60 A6
School Ave Dunston NE11 .. 69 F8
Guide Post NE62 .... 10 F7
School Cl NE9 .... 71 D6
School Houses NE39 .... 78 B8
School La Whickham NE16 . 69 C7
High Spen NE39 .... 67 A3
School Loaning NE34 .... 59 B5
School Rd
East Rainton DH5 .... 94 C4
Bedlington NE22 .... 11 D3
School Row NE43 .... 64 F3
School St Whickham NE16 . 69 A7
Hebburn NE31 .... 57 F7
School Terr DH4 .... 89 E1
School View DH5 .... 97 D8
Schoolhouse La NE16 .... 79 E7
Scorer St NE29 .... 41 F5
Scorer's La DH3 .... 89 B1
Scot Terr NE17 .... 66 B1
Scotby Gdns NE9 .... 71 B3
Scotland Ct NE21 .... 53 A1
Scotland Head NE21 .... 68 A8
Scotland St SR2 .... 93 A6
Scotswood Rd NE15,NE4 .. 54 B4
Scotswood View NE11 .... 54 C2
Scott Ave NE23 .... 21 F8
Scott Cl NE46 .... 44 F2
Scott St NE23 .... 16 B3
Scott's Ave 12 NE40 .... 51 F3
Scott's Ct NE10 .... 72 B6
Scott's Terr DH5 .... 95 A4
Scoular Dr NE63 .... 7 A3
Scrogg Rd NE6 .... 56 F6
Scruton Ave SR3 .... 85 F3
Sea Banks NE30 .... 42 E8
Sea Crest Rd NE64 .... 7 E6
Sea La SR6 .... 75 E4
Sea Rd South Shields NE33 .. 42 E4
Sunderland SR6 .... 75 E4
Sea View Lynmouth NE61 .. 2 B3
Ashington NE63 .... 12 A8
Ryhope SR2 .... 93 A6
Sea View Gdns SR6 .... 75 E3
Sea View La NE64 .... 7 E5
Sea View Pk
Cramlington NE23 .... 22 D6
Whitburn SR6 .... 75 D8
Sea View Rd SR2 .... 86 E3
Sea View Rd W SR2 .... 86 D2
Sea View St SR2 .... 86 F2
Sea View Villas NE23 .... 22 D6
Sea Way NE33 .... 42 E3
Seaburn Ave NE25 .... 23 D6
Seaburn Cl SR6 .... 75 E4
Seaburn Dene Prim Sch SR6 .... 75 D5
Seaburn Dr 1 DH4 .... 94 C8
Seaburn Gdns
Gateshead NE9 .... 71 D3
Sunderland SR6 .... 75 E4
Seaburn Gr NE26 .... 24 C6
Seaburn Hill SR6 .... 75 E4
Seaburn Sta SR5 .... 75 C4
Seaburn Terr SR6 .... 75 F4
Seaburn View NE25 .... 23 D6
Seacombe Ave NE30 .... 32 C3
Seacrest Appartments NE30 .... 32 C1
Seacrest Ave NE30 .... 32 C2
Seafield Rd NE24 .... 17 E5
Seafield Terr NE33 .... 42 E3
Seafield View NE30 .... 42 D8
Seafields SR6 .... 75 E5
Seaforth Rd SR3 .... 86 A3
Seaforth St NE24 .... 17 E8
Seaham Cl NE34 .... 60 B6
Seaham Gdns NE9 .... 71 C2
Seaham Grange Ind Est SR7 .... 92 E2
Seaham Rd
Houghton-le-Spring DH5 .... 95 A8
Ryhope SR2 .... 93 A6
Seaham Sch SR7 .... 93 A1
Seaham St SR3 .... 92 A7
Seascale Pl NE9 .... 71 B4
Seatoller Ct 3 SR3 .... 91 F6
Seaton Ave
Houghton-le-Spring DH5 .... 95 A7
Annitsford NE23 .... 22 B1
Blyth NE24 .... 17 C4
Newbiggin-by-the-Sea NE64 .. 7 D4
Seaton Burn Com Coll NE13 .... 28 C8
Seaton Cl NE10 .... 72 B6
Seaton Cres Holywell NE25 . 23 F2
Seaton Cres *continued*
Whitley Bay NE25 .... 31 E5
Seaham SR7 .... 92 E1
Seaton Croft NE23 .... 29 C8
Seaton Delaval Fst Sch NE25 .... 23 B4
Seaton Delaval Hall* NE26 .... 24 A6
Seaton Gdns NE9 .... 71 C3
Seaton La SR7 .... 92 E1
Seaton Pl
Brunswick Village NE13 .... 28 A6
Newcastle-upon-Tyne NE6 .. 56 E3
Seaton Rd Shiremoor NE27 . 31 A4
Sunderland SR3 .... 85 D3
Seaton Sluice Fst Sch NE26 .... 24 D5
Seaton Sluice Mid Sch NE26 .... 24 B7
Seaton Terr NE22 .... 11 B1
Seatonville Cres NE25 .... 31 E3
Seatonville Gr NE25 .... 31 E3
Seatonville Rd NE25 .... 31 E3
Second Ave
Chester le Street DH2 .... 88 B2
Chester le Street DH2 .... 88 B8
Dunston NE11 .... 70 B6
Blyth NE24 .... 17 D6
North Shields NE29 .... 41 B4
Newcastle-upon-Tyne NE6 .. 56 C7
Morpeth NE61 .... 9 B7
Ashington NE63 .... 6 D4
Second Row Ellington NE61 . 1 E4
Linton NE61 .... 1 A3
Second St NE8 .... 101 A1
Secretan Way NE33 .... 42 C2
Sedbergh Rd NE30 .... 32 B2
Sedgeletch Ind Est DH4 .. 90 A2
Sedgeletch Rd DH4 .... 90 A2
Sedgemoor NE12 .... 29 D4
Sedgemoor Ave NE15 .... 54 A4
Sedgewick Pl NE8 .... 101 B1
Sedley Rd NE28 .... 40 B1
Sedling Rd NE38 .... 83 B2
Sefton Ave NE6 .... 39 C1
Sefton Ct NE23 .... 16 C1
Sefton Sq SR3 .... 85 E3
Segedunum Way NE28 .. 40 B1
Seghill Fst Sch NE23 .... 22 F1
Seine Ct NE32 .... 58 C6
Selborne Gdns NE2 .... 56 A8
Selbourne Cl NE23 .... 21 E6
Selbourne St
2 South Shields NE33 .... 42 D2
Sunderland SR6 .... 75 E1
Selbourne Terr NE24 .... 12 D3
Selby Cl NE23 .... 16 B1
Selby Ct 2 NE32 .... 58 B7
Selby Gdns Wallsend NE28 .. 40 B3
Newcastle-upon-Tyne NE6 .. 56 F8
Selby Sq SR3 .... 85 E3
Selby's Grave NE21 .... 67 F8
Sele Ct 9 NE46 .... 45 A4
Sele Fst Sch The NE46 .. 45 A5
Selina Pl SR6 .... 75 E1
Selkirk Cres DH3 .... 82 C6
Selkirk Gr NE23 .... 16 C1
Selkirk Sq SR3 .... 85 D3
Selkirk St NE32 .... 58 E3
Selkirk Way NE29 .... 41 C8
Selsdon Ave SR4 .... 85 A2
Selsey Ct NE10 .... 71 E6
Selwood Ct NE34 .... 59 F5
Selwyn Ave NE25 .... 31 D3
Selwyn Cl NE5 .... 37 D4
Senet Enterprise Workshop NE63 .... 6 D2
Serin Ho NE5 .... 37 A3
Serlby Cl NE37 .... 72 C1
Seton Ave NE34 .... 58 F4
Seton Wlk NE34 .... 58 F4
Setting Stones NE38 .... 89 A8
Settlingstone Cl NE7 .... 39 E3
Sevenoaks Dr SR4 .... 85 A2
Seventh Ave
Chester le Street DH2 .... 88 B4
Gateshead NE11 .... 70 D4
Blyth NE24 .... 17 D6
Newcastle-upon-Tyne NE6 .. 56 C7
Morpeth NE61 .... 9 B7
Ashington NE63 .... 6 E2
Seventh Row NE63 .... 6 B4
Severn Ave NE31 .... 57 E3
Severn Ct 8 SR3 .... 91 F6
Severn Dr NE32 .... 58 C2
Severn Gdns NE8 .... 71 B8
Severn Hos NH37 .... 84 A8
Severn St NE17 .... 66 C1
Severs Terr NE5 .... 36 B6
Severus Rd NE4 .... 54 E7
Sewingshields Wall Turrets & Milecastle* NE47 .... 127 E5
Sextant Ho 6 NE24 .... 17 F8
Seymour Ct
Dunston NE11 .... 100 A1
Ashington NE63 .... 7 B3
Seymour Sq SR3 .... 85 E3
Seymour St
Dunston NE11 .... 100 A1
North Shields NE29 .... 42 A4
Seymour Terr
Hetton le Hole DH5 .... 95 B1
Ryton NE40 .... 52 A5
Shadfen Cres NE61 .... 4 E3
Shadfen Park Rd NE30 .. 32 A3
Shadon Way DH3 .... 82 E3
Shaftesbury Ave
Whitley Bay NE26 .... 31 F6
Shaftesbury Ave *continued*
Jarrow NE32 .... 58 E5
Ryhope SR2 .... 92 E7
Shaftesbury Cres
Tynemouth NE30 .... 32 A3
Sunderland SR3 .... 85 F3
Shaftesbury Gr NE6 .... 56 B7
Shaftesbury Wlk NE8 .. 101 A2
Shafto Ct NE15 .... 54 B5
Shafto St
Newcastle-upon-Tyne NE15 . 54 A5
Wallsend NE28 .... 40 E3
Shaftoe Cl NE40 .... 51 F3
Shaftoe Cres NE46 .... 45 A5
Shaftoe Ct
Killingworth NE12 .... 29 D3
Newcastle-upon-Tyne NE3 .. 38 A7
Shaftoe Leazes NE46 .... 44 F4
Shaftoe Rd SR3 .... 85 D2
Shaftoe Sq SR3 .... 85 D2
Shaftoe Way NE13 .... 27 B7
Shakespeare Ave NE31 .. 57 E6
Shakespeare St
Houghton-le-Spring DH5 .... 94 E7
Newcastle-upon-Tyne NE1 .. 99 A1
Wallsend NE28 .... 40 F3
Jarrow NE32 .... 58 B8
18 South Shields NE33 .... 42 D1
Sunderland SR5 .... 75 B2
Shakespeare Terr SR2 .. 102 C1
Shalcombe Cl SR3 .... 92 A6
Shallcross SR2 .... 86 B4
Shallon Ct NE63 .... 6 C2
Shalstone NE37 .... 72 F1
Shamrock Cl NE15 .... 53 C8
Shandon Way NE3 .... 37 E5
Shanklea Fst Sch NE23 .. 22 B7
Shanklin Pl NE23 .... 21 E6
Shannon Cl SR5 .... 74 A1
Shannon Ct NE3 .... 37 C7
Shap Cl NE38 .... 83 D3
Shap Ct 2 SR3 .... 91 F6
Shap La NE5 .... 37 A1
Shap Rd NE30 .... 32 A2
Sharnford Cl NE27 .... 30 D5
Sharon Cl NE12 .... 29 B2
Sharpendon St NE31 .... 57 E7
Sharpley Dr SR7 .... 92 E1
Shaw Ave NE34 .... 59 B4
Shaw Gdns NE10 .... 72 B8
Shaw La DH8,NE17 .... 76 F4
Shawbrow Cl NE7 .... 39 E3
Shawdon Cl NE5 .... 37 B4
Shaws La Hexham NE46 .. 44 D4
Hexham NE46 .... 44 D5
Shaws Pk NE46 .... 44 E6
Shearlegs Rd NE8 .... 56 A3
Shearwater SR6 .... 60 F3
Shearwater Ave NE12 .... 39 A7
Shearwater Cl NE5 .... 37 B4
Shearwater Way NE24 .. 17 F4
Sheelin Ave DH2 .... 88 C1
Sheen Cl DH4 .... 94 A2
Sheen Ct NE3 .... 37 B5
Sheep Hill NE16 .... 79 B6
Sheepfolds N SR5 .... 103 A4
Sheepfolds Rd SR5 .... 103 A4
Sheepfolds S SR5 .... 103 A4
Sheepwash Ave NE62 .... 10 E7
Sheepwash Bank NE62 .. 10 E7
Sheepwash Rd NE61 .... 5 E3
Sheldon Ct NE12 .... 29 C1
Sheldon Gr
Cramlington NE23 .... 16 B1
Newcastle-upon-Tyne NE3 .. 38 A3
Sheldon Rd NE34 .... 42 F1
Sheldon St NE32 .... 58 B7
Shelford Gdns NE15 .... 53 E7
Shellbark DH4 .... 89 F6
Shelley Ave
Easington Lane DH5 .... 97 D8
South Shields NE34 .... 60 B5
West Boldon NE35 .... 74 A8
Springwell NE9 .... 71 F1
Shelley Cres NE24 .... 17 C5
Shelley Dr NE8 .... 56 A2
Shelley Rd NE15 .... 53 A7
Shepherd St SR4 .... 102 A3
Shepherd Way NE38 .... 83 F2
Shepherd's Quay NE29 .. 42 B4
Shepherds Way NE36 .... 74 A7
Sheppard Terr 1 SR5 .... 74 B1
Sheppey Ct SR3 .... 92 A6
Shepton Cotts NE16 .... 69 C3
Sheraton NE10 .... 72 A5
Sheraton St NE2 .... 98 B4
Sherborne Ave NE29 .... 41 D8
Sherburn Gn NE39 .... 67 F3
Sherburn Gr DH4 .... 90 C1
Sherburn Grange N NE32 . 58 A5
Sherburn Grange S NE32 . 58 A5
Sherburn Hill Prim Sch DH6 .... 96 D1
Sherburn Park Dr NE39 .. 67 F3
Sherburn Terr
Hamsterley NE17 .... 76 F5
Gateshead NE9 .... 71 C2
Sherburn Village Prim Sch DH6 .... 96 A2
Sherburn Way NE10 .... 72 C7
Sherfield Dr NE7 .... 39 D2
Sheridan Gn NE38 .... 83 A1
Sheridan Rd NE34 .... 59 A3
Sheridan St 5 SR4 .... 85 F7
Sheriff's Highway NE9 .. 71 A6

Sheriff's Moor Ave DH5 97 C8
Sheriffs Cl NE10 71 B8
Sheringham Ave NE29 41 D7
Sheringham Cl SR3 92 A4
Sheringham Dr NE23 21 E6
Sheringham Gdns NE15 35 B2
Sherringham Ave NE3 37 E4
Sherwood NE27 31 B2
Sherwood Cl
Tynemouth NE27 31 B2
Washington NE38 83 D5
Sherwood Ct 5 SR3 92 A6
Sherwood Pl NE3 28 C2
Sherwood View NE28 40 A4
Shetland Ct 1 SR3 92 A6
Shibdon Bank NE21 53 D2
Shibdon Bsns Pk NE21 53 E3
Shibdon Cres NE21 53 D2
Shibdon Ct NE21 53 C3
Shibdon Park View NE21 53 D2
Shibdon Pond Nature Reserve* NE21 53 E2
Shibdon Rd Blaydon NE21 53 D3
Blaydon NE21 53 E2
Shibdon Way NE21 53 F2
Shiel Gdns NE23 21 E6
Shield Ave NE16 54 B1
Shield Ct
Newcastle-upon-Tyne NE2 99 C3
Hexham NE46 45 B3
Shield Gr NE3 38 D6
Shield Rd SR6 75 C5
Shield St NE2 99 C2
Shieldclose 2 NE37 83 A6
Shieldfield Gn NE2 99 C2
Shieldfield Ho NE2 99 C2
Shieldfield La NE2 99 C2
Shields Rd
Chester le Street DH3 88 D5
Gateshead NE10 71 F8
Nedderton NE22 15 C5
Whitley Bay NE25 31 F3
Cleadon NE34 60 A3
Cleadon NE34,SR6 60 A2
Newcastle-upon-Tyne NE6 56 C7
Morpeth NE61 9 B7
Sunderland SR5,SR6 75 B5
Shields Rd W 5 NE6 56 A6
Shillaw Pl NE23 29 B5
Shilmore Rd NE3 37 F5
Shilton Cl NE34 60 B5
Shincliffe Ave SR5 74 C2
Shincliffe Gdns NE9 71 D3
Shiney Row Prim Sch DH4 90 B5
Shipcote La NE8 70 F8
Shipcote Terr NE8 70 F8
Shipley Art Gallery* NE8 70 F8
Shipley Ave
Newcastle-upon-Tyne NE4 54 E6
Sunderland SR6 75 E4
Shipley Ct NE8 101 C1
Shipley Pl 18 NE6 56 B6
Shipley Rd NE30 42 C7
Shipley Rise 8 NE6 56 C6
Shipley St NE15 53 C6
Shipley Wlk 23 NE6 56 B6
Shipton Cl NE35 58 E1
Shire Farm Gr NE63 6 A2
Shiremoor Mid Sch NE27 30 F4
Shiremoor Prim Sch NE27 30 E3
Shiremoor Sta NE27 30 F4
Shirlaw Cl
Newcastle-upon-Tyne NE5 36 F4
Newcastle-upon-Tyne NE5 37 A4
Shirley Gdns SR3 86 B3
Shirwood Ave NE16 69 A5
Shop Row DH4 90 C5
Shop Spouts NE21 53 C3
Shopping Ctr The 4 NE5 36 C2
Shore St SR6 75 D1
Shoreham Ct NE3 37 C7
Shoreham Sq SR3 85 E3
Shorestone Ave NE30 32 B3
Short Row NE5 36 B6
Shortridge St 1 NE33 42 D3
Shortridge Terr NE2 38 F1
Shot Factory La NE4 100 C3
Shotley Ave SR5 75 B3
Shotley Ct NE63 6 B2
Shotley Gdns NE9 71 A7
Shotton Ave NE24 17 E6
Shotton La
Cramlington NE23 15 C2
Shotton NE61,NE13 20 F8
Shotton St NE23 16 B3
Shotton Way NE10 72 E6
Shrewsbury Cl NE12 39 D4
Shrewsbury Cres SR3 85 F3
Shrewsbury Dr NE27 30 C5
Shrewsbury St NE11 69 F8
Shrewsbury Terr NE33 59 C7
Shrigley Gdns NE3 37 F5
Shunner Cl NE37 83 A6
Sibthorpe St NE29 42 B5
Side NE1 101 B4
Side Cliff Rd SR6 75 E3
Sidlaw Ave
Chester le Street DH2 88 A2
Tynemouth NE29 31 F1
Sidlaw Ct NE63 6 E1
Sidmouth Cl DH4 90 C4
Sidmouth Rd
North Shields NE29 41 C5
Gateshead NE9 70 F3
Sidney Gr
Newcastle-upon-Tyne NE4 98 A2
Gateshead NE8 101 A1
Sidney St Blyth NE24 17 D7
North Shields NE29 42 A5
West Boldon NE35 73 F8
Siemens Way NE28 41 A7
Silkey's La NE29 41 F5
Silkstun Ct 8 SR3 92 A7
Silksworth Cl SR3 91 F8
Silksworth Gdns NE9 71 C2
Silksworth Hall Dr SR3 91 F6
Silksworth La
New Silksworth SR3 91 F7
Sunderland SR3 86 A2
Silksworth Rd
New Silksworth SR3 92 A7
Sunderland SR3 91 C6
Silksworth Row SR1 102 C3
Silksworth Terr SR3 92 A7
Silkwood Cl NE23 16 B1
Silkworth La 1 SR3 92 A8
Silkworth Way SR3 91 E6
Silloth Ave NE5 54 A8
Silloth Dr NE37 72 C2
Silloth Pl NE30 32 B2
Silloth Rd SR3 85 D2
Silvas Ct NE61 4 A1
Silver Ct 3 NE9 71 A8
Silver Fox Way
Earsdon NE27 31 A1
Wallsend NE27 40 F8
Silver Lonnen NE5 54 B8
Silver St Tynemouth NE30 42 D7
Sunderland SR1 103 C3
Silverbirch Ind Est NE12 29 B4
Silverdale SR3 92 A4
Silverdale Ave NE10 72 D8
Silverdale Dr NE21 68 A8
Silverdale Rd NE23 16 B1
Silverdale Terr NE8 70 F8
Silverdale Way
Whickham NE16 68 F4
Brockley Whins NE34 58 F3
Silverhill Dr NE5 54 B7
Silverhill Sch The NE5 54 C7
Silverlink N The
Shiremoor NE27 30 E1
Wallsend NE27 40 F8
Silverlink The NE28 41 A6
Silvermere Dr NE40 52 D4
Silverstone NE12 29 E3
Silverstone Rd NE37 83 E8
Silvertop Gdns NE40 52 A1
Silvertop Terr NE40 66 F8
Silverwood Gdns NE11 70 B5
Simon Pl NE13 28 A5
Simonburn NE38 82 F4
Simonburn Ave
North Shields NE29 41 C6
Newcastle-upon-Tyne NE4 54 E8
Simonburn La 3 NE63 6 F2
Simonside
Seaton Sluice NE26 24 D4
Prudhoe NE42 50 B1
Simonside Ave
Wallsend NE28 40 F4
Stakeford NE62 11 B8
Simonside Cl
Seaton Sluice NE26 24 D4
Morpeth NE61 8 D7
Simonside Fst Sch NE5 36 F5
Simonside Hall NE34 58 F5
Simonside Ind Est NE32 58 E5
Simonside Jun Mix & Inf Sch NE32 58 D4
Simonside Pl NE9 71 D3
Simonside Rd
Blaydon NE21 53 C1
Sunderland SR3 85 D3
Simonside Terr
Newcastle-upon-Tyne NE6 56 C8
Newbiggin-by-the-Sea NE64 7 E4
Simonside View
Ponteland NE20 25 D7
Jarrow NE32 58 C4
Simonside Way NE12 29 F4
Simpson Cl NE35 73 E8
Simpson Ct NE63 7 A3
Simpson St Blyth NE24 17 E8
North Shields NE29 41 E5
Tynemouth NE30 32 C4
Sunderland SR4 102 B4
Simpson Terr
Newcastle-upon-Tyne, Shieldfield NE1,NE2 99 B2
Newcastle-upon-Tyne, Lemington NE15 36 B1
Simpsons Memorial Homes NE40 52 A4
Sinclair Dr DH3 88 D8
Sinclair Gdns NE25 23 D3
Sinderby Cl NE3 38 D8
Sir Charles Parsons Sch NE6 56 F7
Sir GB Hunter Memorial Hospl NE28 40 C2
Sir Godfrey Thomson Ct NE10 71 C8
Sixth Ave
Chester le Street DH2 88 B3
Gateshead NE11 70 C4
Blyth NE24 17 D6
Newcastle-upon-Tyne NE6 56 C7
Morpeth NE61 9 B7
Sixth Ave *continued*
Ashington NE63 6 E2
Skaylock Dr NE38 83 A3
Skegness Par NE31 58 A2
Skelder Ave NE12 39 B6
Skelton Ct NE3 37 E8
Ski View SR3 91 F8
Skiddaw Dr SR6 75 C5
Skiddaw Pl NE9 71 B4
Skinnerburn Rd NE1, NE4 100 C3
Skipper Cl NE11 70 B7
Skipsea View SR2 92 D7
Skipton Cl
Bedlington NE22 10 D2
Cramlington NE23 16 C1
Skipton Gn NE9 71 B2
Skirlaw Cl NE38 83 D4
Skye Ct 2 SR3 92 A6
Skye Gr NE32 58 E2
Slake Rd NE32 58 D8
Slaley NE38 83 E1
Slaley Cl NE10 72 C7
Slaley Ct Bedlington NE22 11 A1
4 Silksworth SR3 92 A6
Slatyford La NE5 54 A8
Sled La NE40, NE41 51 D3
Sleekburn Ave NE22 11 E3
Slingley Cl 4 SR7 92 E1
Slingsby Gdns NE7 39 D3
Slipway The NE10 57 A2
Sloane Ct NE2 99 B3
Sloping Hall SR6 60 A1
Smailes La NE39 67 C2
Smallholdings NE64 7 C6
Smeaton Ct 5 NE28 41 A1
Smeaton St 2 NE28 41 A1
Smith Gr SR2 92 E6
Smith St
South Shields NE33 59 B8
Ryhope SR2 92 F6
Smith St S SR2 92 F6
Smith Terr NE8 100 B1
Smith's Terr DH5 95 B1
Smithburn Rd NE10 71 E7
Smithy* TD12 107 B7
Smithy La NE11,NE9 70 F1
Smithy Sq NE23 22 B6
Smithy St 2 NE33 42 C3
Smithyford NE9 71 A1
Smyrna Pl SR1 103 B2
Snipes Dene NE39 67 E3
Snowdon Gdns NE11 70 A6
Snowdon Gr NE36 74 B7
Snowdon Terr NE39 66 F5
Snowdrop Cl NE21 53 A2
Soane Gdns NE34 59 D3
Softley Pl NE15 53 F7
Solar Ho SR1 102 C4
Solingen Est NE24 17 F5
Solway Ave NE30 32 B2
Solway Rd NE31 57 F4
Solway Sq SR3 85 E3
Solway St NE6 56 C4
Somerford NE9 71 F2
Somersby Dr NE3 37 E5
Somerset Cotts 4 SR3 92 A8
Somerset Gdns NE28 40 A3
Somerset Gr NE29 41 D8
Somerset Pl NE4 98 A1
Somerset Rd
Hebburn NE31 57 F3
Sunderland SR3 85 D3
Somerset Sq SR3 85 D3
Somerset St SR3 92 A8
Somerton Ct NE3 37 C6
Sophy St SR5 75 B2
Sorley St SR4 102 A2
Sorrel Cl NE63 6 C2
Sorrel Gdns NE34 59 E3
Sorrell Cl NE4 54 D7
Soulby Ct NE3 37 D8
Sourmilk Hill La NE9 71 A6
Souter Lighthouse* SR6 60 F5
Souter Rd NE3 38 A5
Souter View SR6 60 F2
South App DH2 88 C2
South Ave Whickham NE16 69 B5
South Shields NE34 59 F5
Washington NE37 83 C8
Ryton NE40 52 C5
South Beach Fst Sch NE24 17 E4
South Bend NE3 28 B1
South Bents Ave SR6 75 F6
South Benwell Prim Sch NE4 54 E4
South Benwell Rd NE15 54 C4
South Burn Terr DH4 90 C6
South Burns DH3 88 C4
South Cl
Easington Lane DH5 97 D8
South Shields NE34 59 F5
Ryton NE40 52 C4
South Cliff SR6 75 F2
South Cres
Great Lumley DH4 89 F1
West Boldon NE35 73 F8
Washington NE38 89 B8
South Croft NE12 39 E7
South Cross St NE3 38 C5
South Dene NE34 59 B6
South Dr Shot NE13 20 E6
Woolsington NE13 37 A8
Hebburn NE31 57 D4
Cleadon SR6 59 F1
South Durham Ct SR1 103 B2
South Eldon St NE33 59 B8
South End SR6 74 E8
South Farm NE22 15 A8
South Frederick St NE33 59 B7
South Front NE2 99 B4
South Gosforth Fst Sch NE2 38 E4
South Gosforth Sta NE3 38 E4
South Gr NE40 52 D4
South Grange Pk SR7 92 F2
South Hetton Ind Est DH6 97 F7
South Hetton Prim Sch DH6 97 F7
South Hetton Rd DH5, DH6 97 D8
South Hill Cres SR2 102 B1
South Hill Rd NE8 101 A1
South Hylton Prim Sch SR4 85 A6
South Hylton Sta SR4 85 B6
South La NE36 74 C7
South Lea NE21 53 C1
South Leigh DH9 79 D1
South Magdalene DH8 77 B1
South Market St DH5 95 B4
South Nelson Ind Est NE23 21 E8
South Nelson Rd NE23 21 E8
South Newsham Rd NE24 17 D3
South Par Gateshead NE10 57 B2
Whitley Bay NE26 32 B5
Stocksfield NE43 64 A7
Choppington NE62 10 E6
South Preston Gr 1 NE29 42 A5
South Preston Terr 2 NE29 42 A5
South Rd Chopwell NE17 66 C1
Prudhoe NE42 50 D2
South Ridge
Newcastle-upon-Tyne NE3 38 B8
Ashington NE63 7 B2
South Riggs NE22 15 F8
South Row NE8 56 A4
South Sherburn NE39 67 E1
South Shields Sta NE33 42 C3
South Shore Rd
Gateshead, East Gateshead NE8 56 B3
Gateshead, Saltmeadows NE8 56 A4
South Side NE61 2 B7
South St
Chester le Street DH2 88 B4
9 Fence Houses DH4 94 A8
Newbottle DH4 90 D3
West Rainton DH4 94 A2
East Rainton DH5 94 C4
Sherburn DH6 96 A1
Newcastle-upon-Tyne NE1 101 A4
Shiremoor NE27 30 F4
Newcastle-upon-Tyne, Coxlodge NE3 38 A5
Hebburn NE31 57 F7
High Spen NE39 66 F4
Gateshead NE8 101 C1
Sunderland SR1 103 A3
South Street Prim Sch NE8 101 C1
South Terr Chopwell NE17 77 B8
Wallsend NE28 40 E2
Morpeth NE61 3 F1
Sunderland SR5 75 B1
South Tynedale Railway* CA9 132 F1
South Tyneside Coll
Hebburn NE31 57 C2
South Shields NE33 59 E8
South Tyneside Coll Seamanship & Survival Ctr NE33 42 C4
South Tyneside General Hospl NE34 59 D5
South View Birtley DH3 82 D4
Shiney Row DH4 90 B6
Easington Lane DH5 97 D8
Sherburn Hill DH6 96 D1
Tantobie DH9 79 B2
Hazlerigg NE13 28 A4
Chopwell NE17 77 A8
East Sleekburn NE22 11 F3
Annitsford NE23 22 B1
Blyth NE24 17 C4
Cambois NE24 12 C6
Jarrow NE32 58 A6
Washington NE38 83 E1
High Spen NE39 66 F3
Crawcrook NE40 51 F4
Crawcrook NE40 51 F7
Prudhoe NE42 50 B2
Mickley Square NE43 49 E1
Newcastle-upon-Tyne NE5 53 E8
Pegswood NE61 4 F3
Guide Post NE62 10 E7
Ashington NE63 6 C4
Longbenton NE7 39 C5
Sunderland, South Hylton SR4 85 B5
Sunderland, Monkwearmouth SR6 75 D3
South View E NE39 67 C2
South View Gdns NE46 44 F4
South View Pl NE23 22 B6
South View Rd SR4 85 B5
South View Terr
Fence Houses DH4 94 B8
Whickham NE16 69 B6
South View Terr *continued*
Whickham, Swalwell NE16 69 B8
South View W
Rowlands Gill NE39 67 C2
Newcastle-upon-Tyne NE6 56 A6
South Wellfield Fst Sch NE25 31 B4
South Woodbine St 1 NE33 42 D2
Southburn Cl DH4 94 C8
Southcliff NE26 32 C4
Southcote NE16 69 A5
Southcroft NE38 83 D1
Southdowns DH2 88 C2
Southend Ave NE24 17 C6
Southend Par NE31 58 A2
Southend Rd
Gateshead NE9 71 B5
Sunderland SR3 85 E2
Southend Terr NE9 71 B6
Southern Cl NE63 7 B3
Southern Rd NE6 56 F4
Southern Way NE40 52 C4
Southey St NE33 59 D8
Southfield Gdns NE16 69 C6
Southfield Gn NE16 69 C6
Southfield La DH9,NE17 77 F3
Southfield Rd
Longbenton NE12 39 D6
Whickham NE16 69 C6
2 South Shields NE34 60 A8
Southfield Terr
Whickham NE16 69 C6
Newcastle-upon-Tyne NE6 57 A4
Southfields NE23 29 A8
Southfields Ho 1 NE6 56 B6
Southfork NE15 53 C8
Southgarth East 2 NE33 59 E8
Southgate NE12 29 D3
Southgate Wood NE61 9 A5
Southhill Rd NE34 60 A6
Southlands
Tynemouth NE30 32 B1
Hedworth NE32 58 D1
Hexham NE46 44 D4
Newcastle-upon-Tyne NE7 39 A2
Gateshead NE9 71 C2
Southlands Cty Mid Sch NE23 22 B3
Southlands Sch (Specl) NE30 32 A1
Southmayne Rd SR4 85 D4
Southmead Ave NE5 37 C1
Southmoor Rd NE6 56 F7
Southmoor Sch SR2 86 E3
Southport Par NE31 58 A3
Southridge Fst Sch NE25 31 D6
Southward NE26 24 D5
Southward Cl NE26 24 D5
Southward Way NE25 23 E1
Southway
Newcastle-upon-Tyne NE15 53 E7
Gateshead NE9 71 B6
Southwick Ind Est SR5 74 F2
Southwick Prim Sch SR5 75 A2
Southwick Rd SR5 75 C1
Southwold Gdns SR3 91 F8
Southwold Pl NE23 21 E6
Southwood Cres NE39 67 F2
Southwood Gdns NE3 37 F4
Sovereign Ct
Newcastle-upon-Tyne, Jesmond NE2 99 C4
Newcastle-upon-Tyne NE4 100 A4
Sovereign House 16 NE30 42 D7
Sovereign Pl NE4 100 A4
Spa Well Cl NE21 68 B8
Spa Well Dr SR5 74 C2
Spa Well Turn NE21 68 E7
Spalding Cl NE7 39 C4
Sparkwell Cl DH4 90 C4
Spartylea NE38 83 F1
Speculation Pl NE37 83 D8
Speedwell NE9 71 C5
Speedwell Ct NE63 6 B1
Spelter Works Rd SR2 86 F3
Spelvit La NE61 8 F7
Spen Burn NE39 67 A4
Spen La High Spen NE39 67 B3
Greenside NE39,NE40 66 F7
Spen Rd NE39 66 F5
Spence Terr 1 NE29 41 F5
Spencer Ct NE24 12 B1
Spencer Dr NE61 4 E3
Spencer Gr NE16 69 A8
Spencer Rd NE24 12 B1
Spencer St
20 North Shields NE29 42 A5
Hebburn NE31 57 F7
Newcastle-upon-Tyne NE6 56 C8
Spencer Terr NE15 36 B1
Spencers Bank 3 NE16 54 A1
Spenfield Rd NE5 37 D3
Spenser St NE32 58 B8
Spenser Wlk NE34 59 A3
Spetchells NE42 50 D3
Spinney Terr NE6 56 F6
Spinney The
Killingworth NE12 29 E2
Annitsford NE23 22 C1
Washington NE38 83 D2
Morpeth NE61 9 A6
Newcastle-upon-Tyne NE7 39 B2
Spinneyside Gdns NE11 69 F7
Spire Rd NE37 83 F7
Spires La NE6 56 C6
Spital Cres NE64 7 D3

Spital La NE46 44 F7
Spital Rd NE64 7 C3
Spital Terr NE3 38 D5
Spital Villas NE15 33 A3
Spittal Terr NE46 45 A5
Split Crow Rd NE10,NE8 71 B8
Spohr Terr NE33 42 D2
Spoor St NE11 100 A1
Spoors Cotts NE16 69 A6
Spout La Washington NE37 83 D7
Washington, Concord NE37 83 D8
Washington, Washington Village NE38 83 D6
Spoutwell La NE45 47 A5
Spring Garden Cl SR1 103 B3
Spring Garden La NE4 98 B2
Spring Gardens Prim Sch NE29 41 F6
Spring Gdns NE29 41 F5
Spring St NE4 98 B2
Spring Terr NE29 42 A6
Spring Ville NE22 11 F4
Springbank Rd
Newcastle-upon-Tyne NE2 56 A7
Sunderland SR3 85 D3
Springbank Sq SR3 85 D3
Springfeld NE10 71 F4
Springfell DH3 82 D3
Springfield
[5] North Shields NE29 42 A6
Ovington NE42 49 D4
Springfield Ave NE9 71 C1
Springfield Cl NE42 49 D4
Springfield Comp Sch NE32 58 B5
Springfield Gdns
Chester le Street DH3 88 C5
Wallsend NE28 39 F3
Springfield Gr NE25 31 E3
Springfield Pl NE9 71 A6
Springfield Rd
Newbottle DH4 90 D3
Blaydon NE21 53 C1
Hexham NE46 45 C4
Newcastle-upon-Tyne NE5 37 D2
Springfield Terr [1] NE10 71 C7
Springhill Gdns NE15 54 D6
Springhill Wlk NE61 8 E7
Springhouse Cl DH8 76 E2
Springhouse La DH8 76 E2
Springs The DH3 82 E3
Springsyde Cl NE16 68 E5
Springwell Ave
Jarrow NE32 58 C6
Newcastle-upon-Tyne NE6 56 E4
Gateshead NE9 71 C3
Springwell Cl NE21 53 D1
Springwell Dene Sch SR3 85 E3
Springwell Dr NE61 1 E4
Springwell Rd
Jarrow NE32 58 B5
Gateshead NE9 71 D3
Springwell NE9 71 F1
Sunderland SR3,SR4 85 D3
Springwell Terr
Hetton le Hole DH5 95 A2
Gateshead NE9 71 E3
Springwell NE9 71 F1
Springwell Village Prim Sch NE9 71 F1
Springwood NE31 57 C7
Square Houses NE10 71 C7
Square The
[3] Whickham NE16 69 B7
Ponteland NE20 26 C5
Riding Mill NE44 63 A8
Guide Post NE62 10 F7
Squires Gdns NE10 71 D7
Stadium Ind Pk NE10 56 B3
Stadium of Light (Sunderland FC) SR5 102 C4
Stadium Rd NE10 56 B3
Stadium Sta SR5,SR6 75 D1
Stadium Villas NE28 40 C2
Stadium Way SR5 102 C4
Stafford Gr Ryhope SR2 92 E6
Sunderland SR5 75 B2
Stafford St
Hetton le Hole DH5 94 F4
Sunderland SR1 103 C4
Stafford Villas NE9 71 F1
Staffords La [3] SR6 75 F8
Stagshaw NE12 29 C5
Stagshaw Rd NE45 46 F6
Staindrop NE10 72 A5
Staines Rd NE6 56 D4
Stainton Dr NE10 71 D8
Stainton Gdns NE9 71 C2
Stainton Gr SR6 75 C5
Staith La NE21 53 A4
Staithes Ave NE12 39 C6
Staithes La NE61 4 A1
Staithes Rd NE38 84 A3
Staithes St NE6 57 B6
Staiths Rd NE11 100 A2
Stakeford Cres NE62 11 B8
Stakeford Fst Sch NE62 11 C8
Stakeford La NE62 11 A7
Stakeford Rd NE22 11 C3
Stakeford Terr NE62 11 A7
Stalks Rd NE13 28 B6
Stamford NE12 29 D4
Stamford Ave
Seaton Delaval NE25 23 E1
Sunderland SR3 85 F3
Stamfordham Ave NE29 41 D5
Stamfordham Cl NE28 40 A2
Stamfordham Mews [7] NE5 37 D1
Stamfordham Rd
Ponteland NE15,NE5 35 D7
Newcastle-upon-Tyne NE5 36 C4
Woolsington NE5 36 C4
Stampley Cl NE21 68 A8
Stamps La SR1 103 C3
Stancley Rd NE42 50 E2
Standfield Gdns NE10 72 C8
Stanelaw Way DH9 79 F1
Staneway NE10 71 E5
Stanfield Bsns Ctr SR2 103 C1
Stanfield Ct NE7 39 E3
Stang Wlk NE12 39 C7
Stanhope NE38 83 A5
Stanhope Cl DH4 94 D7
Stanhope Cty Inf Sch NE33 59 C6
Stanhope Cty Jun Mix Sch NE33 59 C7
Stanhope Par [7] NE33 59 D8
Stanhope Rd Jarrow NE32 58 D5
South Shields NE33,NE34 59 C7
Sunderland SR6 75 E4
Stanhope St
South Shields NE33 42 C3
Newcastle-upon-Tyne NE4 98 B2
Greenside NE40 51 F1
Stanhope Way NE4 98 B2
Stanley Cres
[8] Whitley Bay NE26 32 B4
Prudhoe NE42 50 E3
Stanley Gdns Seghill NE23 22 F1
Gateshead NE9 71 C2
Stanley Gr
Bedlington NE22 11 B1
Newcastle-upon-Tyne NE7 39 B3
Stanley St
Houghton-le-Spring DH5 90 E1
Blyth NE24 17 F7
Wallsend NE28 40 F3
North Shields NE29 42 A5
Jarrow NE32 58 C7
South Shields NE34 59 B5
Newcastle-upon-Tyne NE4 54 F4
[2] Sunderland SR5 74 B1
Stanley St W NE29 42 A5
Stanley Terr
Chester le Street DH3 88 D2
[4] Penshaw DH4 90 B6
Stanmore Rd NE6 39 C1
Stannerford Rd NE40 51 F6
Stannington Ave NE6 56 B7
Stannington Fst Sch NE61 14 B4
Stannington Gdns SR2 86 C2
Stannington Gr
[5] Newcastle-upon-Tyne NE6 56 B7
Sunderland SR2 86 D2
Stannington Pl
Ponteland NE20 25 E8
[1] Newcastle-upon-Tyne NE6 56 B7
Stannington Rd NE29 41 D5
Stannington St NE24 17 F7
Stannington Station Rd NE61 14 D8
Stansfield St SR6 75 E1
Stanstead Cl SR5 85 A8
Stanton Ave Blyth NE24 17 B5
South Shields NE34 59 E7
Stanton Cl NE10 72 D7
Stanton Dr NE61 4 E3
Stanton Gr NE30 32 A1
Stanton Rd
Shiremoor NE27 30 E3
Tynemouth NE30 32 A1
Stanton St NE4 98 A2
Stanway Dr NE7 39 A3
Stanwick St NE30 42 D8
Stanwix [1] NE28 40 F4
Stapeley Ct [5] NE3 37 D5
Stapeley View NE3 37 D5
Staple Rd NE32 58 C6
Stapleford Cl NE5 37 B1
Stapylton Dr SR2 86 B4
Star of the Sea RC Prim Sch NE25 31 E2
Starbeck Ave NE2 99 C3
Starbeck Mews NE2 99 C3
Stardale Ave NE24 17 A6
Stargate Gdns NE9 71 C2
Stargate La NE40 52 E4
Starlight Cres NE25 23 C3
Starling Wlk NE16 69 C2
Station App
Gateshead NE11,NE9 70 D3
Longbenton NE12 39 D6
[1] South Shields NE33 42 C3
Cleadon NE36 74 E8
Station Ave DH5 95 A3
Station Ave N DH4 90 A1
Station Ave S DH4 90 A1
Station Bank Ryton NE40 52 C6
Mickley Square NE43 49 E2
Station Cl NE44 62 F8
Station Cotts
Ponteland NE20 25 E6
Seghill NE23 23 A1
Burnopfield NE39 78 C6
Morpeth NE61 9 A7
Station Field Rd DH9 79 F1
Station First Sch The NE22 11 D3
Station Ind Est NE42 50 B3
Station La DH2,DH3 82 B4
Station Mews [10] NE30 42 D7
Station Rd
Chester le Street DH3 88 C3
Houghton-le-Spring DH4 90 D1
Penshaw DH4 89 E8
Shiney Row DH4 90 A6
Washington, Fatfield DH4, NE38 83 E1
Hetton le Hole DH5 95 A2
High Pittington DH6 96 A6
Gateshead, Bill Quay NE10 57 B2
Killingworth NE12 29 B3
Longbenton NE12 39 D7
Newcastle-upon-Tyne, Kenton Bankfoot NE13 37 B6
Heddon-on-the-Wall NE15 35 A1
Newburn NE15 52 F7
Bedlington NE22 11 C2
Cramlington NE23 22 B7
Dudley NE23 28 F8
Seghill NE23 23 A1
Whitley Bay NE26 32 B4
Backworth NE27 30 D3
Wallsend NE28 40 B2
Wallsend, Willington Quay NE28 41 A1
North Shields NE29 41 D3
Newcastle-upon-Tyne, South Gosforth NE3 38 E5
Tynemouth NE30 32 C3
Hebburn NE31 57 D6
South Shields NE33 42 C2
Boldon Colliery NE35 58 E2
East Boldon NE36 74 D7
Washington, Columbia NE38 83 E4
Washington, Swan NE38 84 A4
Rowlands Gill NE39 67 F1
Crawcrook NE41 51 C5
Wylam NE41 51 B5
Prudhoe NE42 50 C3
Corbridge NE45 46 F4
Hexham NE46 45 C5
Newcastle-upon-Tyne, Wincomblee NE6 57 A5
Ashington NE63 6 B4
Gateshead, Low Fell NE9 70 E5
Ryhope SR2 93 A6
Sunderland SR5,SR6 75 D4
Station Rd N
Hetton le Hole DH5 95 A3
Longbenton NE12 39 D8
Station St Haswell DH6 97 F3
Bedlington NE22 11 D3
Blyth NE24 17 E8
Jarrow NE32 58 B7
Sunderland SR1 103 A3
Station Terr
Fence Houses DH4 89 F1
Tynemouth NE30 42 D7
East Boldon NE36 74 E7
[10] Washington NE37 83 E8
Station View DH5 95 A3
Staveley Rd SR6 75 C5
Stavordale Terr NE9 71 A7
Staward Ave NE25 23 D2
Staward Terr NE6 56 F4
Staynebrigg NE10 72 A6
Stead La NE22 11 C1
Stead Lane Fst Sch NE22 11 C1
Stead St NE28 41 A3
Steadings The
Seaton Sluice NE26 24 E4
Ashington NE63 6 A2
Steadlands Sq NE22 11 C1
Steads The NE61 9 A6
Stedham Cl NE37 72 E2
Steenbergs [8] NE1 56 A6
Steep Hill SR3 91 C7
Stella Bank NE21 52 F5
Stella Hall Dr NE21 53 A4
Stella Rd Blaydon NE21 53 B4
Ryton NE21 53 B4
Stephen Ct NE32 58 C6
Stephen St
East Hartford NE23 16 B3
Blyth NE24 17 E8
Newcastle-upon-Tyne NE6 56 A6
Stephenson Bldg NE2 99 C2
Stephenson Cl DH5 95 B4
Stephenson Ct
North Shields NE30 42 B5
Wylam NE41 51 C6
Stephenson Ind Est
Killingworth NE12 29 C2
Washington NE37 72 E2
Stephenson Meml Prim Sch NE28 41 A2
Stephenson Railway Mus* NE29 41 A7
Stephenson Rd
Washington NE37 72 E2
Newcastle-upon-Tyne NE7 39 B1
Stephenson St
Wallsend NE28 41 B1
North Shields NE30 42 B5
[1] Tynemouth NE30 42 D7
Gateshead NE8 70 D8
Stephenson Terr
Gateshead NE10 71 D8
Newcastle-upon-Tyne NE15 36 B1
Throckley NE15 35 D2
Wylam NE41 51 B6
Stephenson Way
Blaydon NE21 68 B8
Bedlington NE22 11 A4
Stephenson's La NE1 101 A4
Stepney Bank NE1 56 A6
Stepney La NE1 99 C1
Stepney Rd [1] NE1,NE2 56 A6
Sterling Cotts NE10 71 C7
Sterling St SR4 102 A2
Stevenson St DH4 94 D8
Steward Cres NE34 60 B6
Stewart Ave SR2 92 E6
Stewart Dr NE36 74 B7
Stewart St
New Silksworth SR3 92 A7
Sunderland SR4 102 B1
Stewartsfield NE39 67 D1
Stileford NE10 72 A7
Stillington Cl SR2 92 F5
Stirling Ave Jarrow NE32 58 E4
Rowlands Gill NE39 67 E1
Stirling Cl NE38 84 A4
Stirling Ct NE11 70 E2
Stirling Dr
Bedlington NE22 11 C2
Tynemouth NE29 41 C8
Stirling La NE39 67 F1
Stobart St SR5 102 C4
Stobhill Villas NE61 9 A7
Stockfold NE38 83 E2
Stockholm Cl NE29 41 B5
Stockley Ave SR5 74 C2
Stockley Rd NE38 83 F6
Stocksfield Ave NE5 54 C7
Stocksfield Avenue Prim Sch NE5 54 B7
Stocksfield Gdns NE9 71 B2
Stocksfield Hall NE43 64 A8
Stocksfield Sta NE43 64 A7
Stockton Rd
North Shields NE29 41 F3
Sunderland SR2 103 A1
Ryhope SR2,SR7 92 F2
Stockton Terr [8] SR2 86 F2
Stockwell Gn NE6 56 F8
Stoddart Ho NE2 99 C2
Stoddart St
Newcastle-upon-Tyne NE1, NE2 99 C2
South Shields NE34 59 C6
Stoker Ave NE34 58 F4
Stoker Terr NE39 67 A3
Stokesley Gr NE7 39 A3
Stokoe Dr NE63 7 A3
Stone Cellar Rd NE37 72 C2
Stone St NE10 71 C6
Stonechat Cl [3] NE38 82 F3
Stonechat Mount NE21 53 A4
Stonechat Pl NE12 39 A7
Stonecroft NE15 33 D1
Stonecroft Gdns NE7 39 D3
Stonecrop NE9 71 C5
Stonecross NE63 6 C2
Stonefold Cl NE5 37 B3
Stonehaugh Way NE20 25 B2
Stonelaw Mid Sch NE23 22 A4
Stoneleigh NE61 9 E4
Stoneleigh Ave NE12 39 A7
Stoneleigh Cl DH4 90 C2
Stoneleigh Pl [1] NE12 39 A6
Stonesdale DH4 89 E8
Stonethwaite NE29 41 E3
Stoney La Springwell NE9 71 F1
Sunderland SR5 75 A1
Stoneycroft NE37 83 C7
Stoneycroft East NE12 29 E2
Stoneycroft West NE12 29 E2
Stoneygate Gdns NE10 56 E1
Stoneygate La NE10 56 E1
Stoneyhurst Ave NE15 54 B5
Stoneyhurst Rd NE3 38 E4
Stoneyhurst Rd W NE3 38 D4
Stoneylea Cl NE40 51 E3
Stoneylea Rd NE5 53 F8
Stoneywaites NE40 66 E8
Stonybank Way NE43 64 E8
Stonyflat Bank NE42 50 E2
Store Bldgs NE35 73 E8
Store Farm Rd NE64 7 C5
Store St
Newcastle-upon-Tyne NE15 53 C6
Blaydon NE21 53 B1
Store Terr DH5 95 B1
Storey Cres NE64 7 C5
Storey La NE21 53 A4
Storey St NE23 22 C5
Stormont Gn NE3 37 F3
Stormont St NE29 42 A5
Stothard St NE32 58 C7
Stotts Rd NE6 57 A8
Stow The NE12 39 A5
Stowe Gdns NE61 4 E4
Stowell Sq NE1 98 C1
Stowell St NE1 98 C1
Stowell Terr NE10 71 E8
Straker Dr NE46 44 E3
Straker St NE32 58 D6
Straker Terr NE34 59 C5
Strand The SR3 91 E8
Strangford Ave [2] DH2 88 B1
Stranton Terr SR6 75 D2
Stratfield St SR4 85 F7
Stratford Ave SR2 86 E3
Stratford Cl
Killingworth NE12 29 E3
Cramlington NE23 21 E7
Stratford Gdns NE9 70 F6
Stratford Gr NE6 56 A7
Stratford Gr W NE6 56 A7
Stratford Grove Terr NE6 56 A7
Stratford Rd NE6 56 A7
Stratford Villas NE6 56 A7
Strathearn Way NE3 37 F7
Strathmore Ave NE39 67 E1
Strathmore Cres
Byermoor NE16 79 D8
Newcastle-upon-Tyne NE4 54 E6
Strathmore Rd
Gateshead N10,NE9 71 B7
Newcastle-upon-Tyne NE3 38 C7
Rowlands Gill NE39 67 E1
Sunderland SR3 85 E2
Strathmore Sq SR3 85 E2
Stratton Cl SR2 93 A8
Stratus Ct [12] SR3 92 A6
Strawberry Ave NE23 29 C5
Strawberry Cotts NE62 11 B8
Strawberry Gdns NE28 40 A4
Strawberry La NE1 98 C1
Strawberry Pl NE1 98 C2
Strawberry Terr NE13 27 F4
Street Gate Pk NE16 69 D3
Stretford Ct NE9 71 A1
Stretton Cl DH4 94 A7
Stretton Way NE27 30 C5
Stridingedge NE37 83 B6
Stronsay Cl [2] SR2 92 E8
Strothers Rd NE39 66 F5
Strothers Terr NE39 66 E4
Struan Terr NE36 74 E7
Struddars Farm Ct NE21 53 F2
Stuart Ct NE3 37 C6
Stuart Gdns NE15 35 D2
Stuart Terr NE10 56 D1
Stubbs Ave NE16 69 A8
Studdon Wlk NE3 37 D5
Studland Cl NE29 31 F1
Studley Gdns
Whitley Bay NE25 32 A4
[2] Gateshead NE9 70 F5
Studley Terr NE4 98 A3
Studley Villas NE12 39 E7
Sturdee Gdns NE2 38 E3
Styan Ave NE26 32 B5
Styford Gdns NE15 53 E7
Success Rd DH4 90 B4
Sudbury Way NE23 21 E6
Suddick St [2] SR5 75 B1
Suez St NE30 42 B6
Suffolk Cl NE63 6 A4
Suffolk Gdns
Wallsend NE28 40 E4
South Shields NE34 60 C7
Suffolk Pl Birtley DH3 82 D1
Gateshead NE8 56 A4
Suffolk Rd NE31 57 F3
Suffolk St
Hetton le Hole DH5 94 F4
Jarrow NE32 58 B6
Sunderland SR2 103 B1
Sugley Dr NE15 53 D6
Sugley St NE15 53 D6
Sugley Villas NE15 53 D6
Sulgrave Ind Est NE37 72 E1
Sulgrave Rd NE37 72 F1
Sullivan Wlk NE31 57 E5
Summer St NE10 56 D1
Summerfield NE17 77 A5
Summerfield Rd NE9 70 F7
Summerhill Blaydon NE21 53 B3
Hedworth NE32 58 D1
Newcastle-upon-Tyne NE4 100 A4
Sunderland SR2 102 B2
Sunderland, Middle Herrington SR3 91 B7
Summerhill Ave NE3 28 D1
Summerhill Gr NE4 98 B1
Summerhill Rd NE34 60 A7
Summerhill St NE4 98 B1
Summerhill Terr NE1 100 C4
Summerhouse Farm DH5 94 D5
Summerhouse La
Ashington, North Seaton NE63 7 B3
Ashington, Woodbridge NE63 7 B4
Summerson St DH5 95 B4
Summerson Way NE22 11 D2
Sun St NE16 69 B2
Sun View Terr SR6 59 E1
Sunbury Ave NE2 38 E2
Sunderland Ent Pk SR5 85 B8
Sunderland Eye Infmy SR2 86 D3
Sunderland High Sch SR2 103 A1
Sunderland High Sch Jun Sch SR2 86 D4
Sunderland Highway NE37,NE38 83 C6
Sunderland Mus & Art Gall* SR1 103 A2
Sunderland Rd
Newbottle DH4 90 E4
Gateshead, Felling NE10 71 E8
Gateshead, Heworth NE10 71 F8
Gateshead, Wardley NE10 72 C7
South Shields NE33 59 E8
South Shields, Harton NE34 59 F6
East Boldon NE36,SR5 74 E6
Sunderland SR5 75 A2
Cleadon SR6 75 B7
Sunderland Ret Pk SR6 75 D1
Sunderland Royal Hospl SR4 102 A2
Sunderland Ski Ctr* SR3 85 F1

Sunderland St
2 Houghton-le-Spring, New Town DH4 ...94 E8
Houghton-le-Spring DH5 ...90 E1
Newcastle-upon-Tyne NE1 .100 C4
Sunderland SR1 ...103 B3
Sunderland Sta SR1 ...103 A2
Sunderland Tech Pk SR1 ...102 C2
Sundew Rd NE9 ...71 C4
Sundridge Dr NE10 ...72 C7
Sunhill NE16 ...69 B2
Sunholme Dr NE28 ...40 A5
Sunlea Ave NE30 ...32 C2
Sunnidale NE16 ...68 E5
Sunnilaws NE34 ...60 A3
Sunningdale
Whitley Bay NE25 ...31 D5
South Shields NE33 ...42 E1
Sunningdale Ave
Wallsend NE28 ...40 C2
Newcastle-upon-Tyne NE6 ..57 A6
Sunningdale Cl NE10 ...71 D7
Sunningdale Dr NE37 ...72 C2
Sunningdale Rd SR3 ...85 E3
Sunningdale Sch SR3 ...85 E2
Sunnirise NE34 ...60 A4
Sunniside
North Shields NE29 ...41 E5
Sunderland SR4 ...85 A6
Sunniside Ct NE16 ...69 B3
Sunniside Dr NE34 ...60 A4
Sunniside Gdns
Newcastle-upon-Tyne NE15 .54 B6
Gateshead NE9 ...71 C2
Sunniside La NE34,SR6 ...60 B2
Sunniside Rd NE16 ...69 B3
Sunniside Sta* NE16 ...69 B1
Sunniside Terr SR6 ...60 A2
Sunny Brae NE40 ...66 F8
Sunnybank Ave NE15 ...54 D5
Sunnybrow SR3 ...91 F8
Sunnycrest Ave NE6 ...56 F6
Sunnygill Terr NE40 ...51 F2
Sunnyside NE23 ...22 A6
Sunnyway NE5 ...37 C2
Sunrise Ent Pk SR5 ...85 A8
Sunrise La 1 DH4 ...90 D1
Surrey Ave SR3 ...92 A6
Surrey Cl NE63 ...6 A4
Surrey Pl Penshaw DH4 ...90 C6
Newcastle-upon-Tyne NE4 ..98 A1
Surrey Rd
North Shields NE29 ...41 D6
Hebburn NE31 ...57 F3
Surrey St Penshaw DH4 ...90 C6
Hetton le Hole DH5 ...94 F4
Jarrow NE32 ...58 A6
Surrey Terr DH3 ...82 C1
Sussex Gdns NE28 ...40 E3
Sussex Pl NE37 ...72 D1
Sussex St 2 Blyth NE24 ...17 F8
Jarrow NE32 ...58 A6
3 New Silksworth SR3 ...92 A8
Sutherland Ave
Newcastle-upon-Tyne NE4 ..54 E7
Newbiggin-by-the-Sea NE64 ..7 D4
Sutherland Ct NE34 ...59 D2
Sutherland Grange DH4 ..90 D6
Sutherland St
Gateshead NE8 ...101 C1
Sunderland SR6 ...75 D2
Seaham SR7 ...93 B1
Sutton Cl DH4 ...90 A6
Sutton Ct NE28 ...39 F5
Sutton St NE6 ...56 E7
Sutton Way NE34 ...60 B5
Swainby Cl NE3 ...38 D8
Swaledale Wallsend NE28 ..39 F5
Sunderland SR6 ...75 F7
Swaledale Ave NE24 ...17 A7
Swaledale Cl DH5 ...94 F1
Swaledale Cres DH4 ...90 A8
Swaledale Ct NE24 ...17 A7
Swaledale Gdns
Newcastle-upon-Tyne NE7 ..39 B3
Sunderland SR4 ...85 F5
Swallow Cl NE63 ...11 E8
Swallow Ct NE12 ...29 C4
Swallow Tail Ct NE34 ...59 B5
Swallow Tail Dr NE11 ...70 B7
Swallows The NE28 ...40 E7
Swalwell Bank NE16 ...69 A8
Swalwell Cl NE42 ...50 C2
Swalwell Cty Prim Sch NE16 ...69 B8
Swan Ave NE28 ...40 D3
Swan Ct NE11 ...100 A1
Swan Dr NE11 ...100 A1
Swan Ind Est NE38 ...83 F4
Swan Ind Est (South) NE38 ...83 F3
Swan Rd Washington NE38 .83 F4
Newcastle-upon-Tyne NE6 ..57 B4
Swan St Gateshead NE8 ..101 C3
Sunderland SR5 ...75 C1
Swansfield NE61 ...8 E7
Swanton Cl NE5 ...37 B4
Swanway NE9 ...71 B7
Swards Rd NE10 ...71 E7
Swarland Ave NE7 ...39 B5
Swarland Rd NE25 ...23 D2
Swarth Cl NE37 ...83 A6
Sweetbriar Cl NE61 ...3 E2
Sweetbriar Way NE24 ...17 C4
Sweethope Ave
Blyth NE24 ...17 D8
Ashington NE63 ...6 F2
Sweethope Dene NE61 ...9 A6
Swiftdale Cl NE22 ...10 F1
Swiftden Dr SR4 ...85 A4
Swinbourne Gdns NE26 ...31 F6
Swinbourne Terr NE32 ...58 B3
Swinburn Rd NE25 ...23 D2
Swinburne Pl Birtley DH3 ..82 C3
Newcastle-upon-Tyne NE4 ..98 C1
Gateshead NE8 ...101 C3
Swinburne St
Jarrow NE32 ...58 E6
Gateshead NE8 ...101 B3
Swindale Cotts NE41 ...51 B6
Swindale Dr NE12 ...29 C3
Swindon Rd SR3 ...85 D3
Swindon Sq SR3 ...85 E3
Swindon St NE31 ...57 D6
Swindon Terr NE6 ...39 B1
Swinhoe Gdns NE13 ...28 B6
Swinhope NE38 ...89 A8
Swinley Gdns NE15 ...53 F6
Swinton Cl NE61 ...9 B6
Swire NE1 ...99 C1
Swirral Edge NE37 ...83 C7
Swyntoft NE10 ...72 B7
Sycamore DH2 ...88 A5
Sycamore Ave
Dinnington NE13 ...27 C7
Ponteland NE20 ...25 D4
Blyth NE24 ...12 D1
Whitley Bay NE25 ...31 F4
South Shields NE34 ...59 F4
Washington NE38 ...83 B1
Guide Post NE62 ...10 E7
Sycamore Cl NE2 ...38 F2
Sycamore Dr SR5 ...75 B3
Sycamore Gr
Gateshead NE10 ...71 E8
Prudhoe NE42 ...50 A2
Springwell NE9 ...71 F1
Sycamore Pl NE12 ...29 C4
Sycamore Rd
Blaydon NE21 ...53 C2
Whitburn SR6 ...60 F1
Sycamore St
Throckley NE15 ...35 D3
Wallsend NE28 ...40 C1
Ashington NE63 ...6 D3
Sycamore Terr DH6 ...97 F3
Sycamores The
Burnopfield NE16 ...79 C5
Newcastle-upon-Tyne NE4 .100 A3
Guide Post NE62 ...10 E7
Sunderland SR2 ...86 E3
Sydenham Terr
14 South Shields NE33 ...42 D3
Sunderland SR4 ...102 A1
Sydney Ct NE8 ...101 B3
Sydney Gdns NE34 ...58 F3
Sydney Gr NE28 ...40 A5
Sydney St DH4 ...89 E2
Syke Rd NE16 ...78 F5
Sylvan Cl NE61 ...8 D7
Sylverton Gdns NE33 ...42 F1
Symington Gdns SR3 ...91 F8
Symon Terr NE17 ...77 B8
Synclen Ave NE45 ...47 A6
Synclen Rd NE45 ...47 A6
Synclen Terr NE45 ...47 A6
Syon St NE30 ...42 D8
Syron NE16 ...68 F7
Syston Cl DH4 ...94 A7

T

Taberna Cl NE15 ...34 E2
Tadcaster Rd SR3 ...85 C1
Tadema Rd NE33 ...42 F2
Talbot Cl NE38 ...83 D4
Talbot Cotts DH3 ...82 C4
Talbot Gn NE5 ...53 F8
Talbot House Specl Sch NE15 ...35 F2
Talbot Rd
South Shields NE34 ...59 C6
Sunderland SR6 ...75 E3
Talgarth NE38 ...84 B5
Talisman View 6 NE9 ...71 A2
Talley Ct NE38 ...83 C5
Tamar Cl NE29 ...41 D8
Tamar Ct 6 SR3 ...91 F6
Tamar St DH5 ...97 C8
Tamarisk Way NE9 ...71 C5
Tamerton Dr DH3 ...82 D2
Tamerton St SR4 ...85 F6
Tamworth Rd NE4 ...98 A2
Tamworth Sq SR3 ...85 C1
Tanbark DH4 ...89 F6
Tanfield Gdns NE34 ...60 B6
Tanfield Lea Ind Est DH9 .79 D2
Tanfield Lea Jun & Inf Sch DH9 ...79 C1
Tanfield Lea South Ind Est DH9 ...79 F1
Tanfield Pl NE9 ...71 C2
Tanfield Rd
Newcastle-upon-Tyne NE15 .54 A6
Gateshead NE9 ...71 C2
Sunderland SR3 ...85 D1
Tanfield Rly* NE16 ...80 B7
Tanfield St SR4 ...85 E7
Tangmere Cl NE23 ...22 C7
Tankerville Pl 3 NE2 ...38 E1
Tankerville Terr NE2 ...38 E1
Tanners Row NE46 ...45 A5
Tanners' Bank NE30 ...42 C6
Tantallon DH3 ...82 D2
Tantallon Ct DH4 ...89 D1
Tantobie Rd NE15 ...54 A6
Tarlton Cres NE10 ...71 C8
Tarn Dr SR2 ...86 F1
Tarragon Way NE34 ...59 E3
Tarrington Cl NE28 ...40 F5
Tarset Dr NE42 ...50 D2
Tarset Pl NE3 ...38 A6
Tarset Rd NE25 ...31 B5
Tarset St NE1 ...56 A5
Tasman Rd SR3 ...91 C8
Tasmania Rd NE34 ...58 F3
Tate St 8 NE24 ...17 F8
Tatham St SR1 ...103 B2
Tatham Street Back SR1 ...103 B2
Tattershall SR2 ...86 B4
Taunton Ave
Tynemouth NE29 ...31 D1
Jarrow NE32 ...58 E5
Taunton Cl NE28 ...40 F5
Taunton Pl NE23 ...22 B8
Taunton Rd SR3 ...85 D2
Taunton Sq SR3 ...85 D2
Tavistock Ct DH4 ...90 C3
Tavistock Pl Jarrow NE32 ..58 D5
Sunderland SR1 ...103 A2
Tavistock Rd NE2 ...38 E2
Tavistock Sq SR3 ...92 A8
Tavistock Wlk NE23 ...22 B8
Tay Rd SR3,SR4 ...85 C2
Tay St Easington Lane DH5 ..97 D8
Chopwell NE17 ...66 C1
Taylor Ave
Wide Open NE13 ...28 C6
Rowlands Gill NE39 ...67 F1
Ashington NE63 ...7 B3
Taylor Gdns
Gateshead NE10 ...57 B2
Seaton Sluice NE26 ...24 D6
9 Sunderland SR2 ...86 E4
Taylor St Blyth NE24 ...17 A8
South Shields NE33 ...59 B8
Taylor Terr 8 NE27 ...30 E1
Taylor's Bldgs NE22 ...11 D2
Taynton Gr NE23 ...22 F2
Teal Ave NE24 ...17 F4
Teal Cl
7 Washington NE38 ...82 F3
Longbenton NE7 ...39 C5
Team St NE8 ...100 B1
Team Valley Bsns Ctr NE11 ...70 D6
Team Valley Trad Est NE11 ...70 D4
Teasdale St SR2 ...103 C1
Tebay Dr NE5 ...53 F8
Tedco Bsns Wks 1 NE33 .42 C2
Teddington Cl NE3 ...37 B7
Teddington Rd SR3 ...85 C2
Teddington Sq SR3 ...85 C2
Tedham Rd NE15 ...53 C7
Tees Ct South Shields NE34 .59 C6
18 Silksworth SR3 ...91 F6
Tees Rd NE31 ...57 E3
Tees St
Easington Lane DH5 ...97 D8
Chopwell NE17 ...66 C1
Tees Terr 9 NE37 ...83 D8
Teesdale Ave DH4 ...90 A8
Teesdale Gdns NE7 ...39 B3
Teesdale Gr NE12 ...39 D8
Teesdale Pl 3 NE24 ...16 F8
Teindland Cl NE4 ...54 E4
Tel-el-Kebir Rd SR2 ...86 E4
Telford Cl NE27 ...30 C5
Telford Ct
North Shields NE28 ...41 C2
Morpeth, Loansdean NE61 ...8 F5
Morpeth, Stobhill NE61 ...8 F6
Telford Rd SR3 ...85 D2
Telford St
North Shields NE28 ...41 C2
Gateshead NE8 ...70 D7
Tempest St Ryton NE21 ...53 A4
10 New Silksworth SR3 ...92 A7
Temple Ave NE24 ...17 C8
Temple Gn
South Shields NE34 ...59 E5
Gateshead NE8 ...70 C8
Temple Park Cty Inf Sch NE34 ...59 D3
Temple Park Jun Mix Sch NE34 ...59 D4
Temple Park Rd NE34 ...59 D6
Temple St
Newcastle-upon-Tyne NE1 .100 C4
Gateshead NE10 ...56 D1
South Shields NE33 ...59 B7
Temple St W NE33 ...59 B7
Temple Town NE33 ...59 B8
Tenbury Cres
Longbenton NE12 ...39 C7
Tynemouth NE29 ...31 E1
Tenby Rd SR3 ...91 C8
Tenby Sq NE23 ...22 C8
Tennant St Hebburn NE31 ..57 D5
3 South Shields NE34 ...59 A4
Tennyson Ave
Hebburn NE31 ...57 F6
West Boldon NE35 ...74 B8
Tennyson Cres NE16 ...69 A8
Tennyson Ct
Prudhoe NE42 ...50 B1
Gateshead NE8 ...56 A2
Tennyson Gn NE3 ...37 F3
Tennyson St
11 South Shields NE33 ...42 D2
6 Sunderland SR5 ...75 A2
Tennyson Terr NE29 ...42 B4
Tenter Garth NE15 ...35 C2
Tenter Terr NE61 ...9 A8
Tenth Ave
Chester le Street DH2 ...88 B3
Gateshead NE11 ...70 D2
Blyth NE24 ...17 E6
Newcastle-upon-Tyne NE6 ..56 C8
Morpeth NE61 ...9 B6
Tenth Ave W NE11 ...70 D2
Tern Cl NE24 ...17 F4
Terrace Pl NE1 ...98 C2
Terrace The
Longbenton NE12 ...39 C6
6 Boldon Colliery NE35 ...58 E1
5 East Boldon NE36 ...74 D7
Ovingham NE42 ...50 A4
Terraces The NE38 ...83 E4
Terrier Cl NE22 ...11 C1
Tesla St DH4 ...90 D4
Tetford Pl NE12 ...39 C7
Teviot NE38 ...83 A1
Teviot St
Easington Lane DH5 ...97 C8
Gateshead NE8 ...71 A8
Teviot Way NE32 ...58 A5
Teviotdale Gdns NE7 ...39 B3
Tewkesbury NE12 ...29 D4
Tewkesbury Rd NE15 ...53 C7
Thackeray Rd SR3 ...85 D2
Thackeray St DH4 ...94 D8
Thames Ave NE32 ...58 C2
Thames Cres DH4 ...94 A8
Thames Gdns NE28 ...40 B1
Thames Rd Hebburn NE31 ..57 F3
Sunderland SR3 ...91 C8
Thames St
Easington Lane DH5 ...97 C8
Chopwell NE17 ...66 C1
Gateshead NE8 ...56 A1
Thanet Rd SR3 ...85 D1
Tharsis Rd NE31 ...57 D5
Thatcher Cl NE16 ...69 A5
Theatre Pl 21 NE29 ...42 A5
Thelma St SR4 ...102 B1
Theme Rd SR3 ...91 C8
Theresa Russell Ho NE6 ..56 C6
Theresa St NE21 ...53 C3
Thetford NE38 ...83 D4
Thieves Bank NE61 ...5 E1
Third Ave
Chester le Street DH2 ...88 B3
Chester le Street DH2 ...88 B7
Gateshead NE11 ...70 C6
Blyth NE24 ...17 D6
North Shields NE29 ...41 B5
Newcastle-upon-Tyne NE6 ..56 C7
Morpeth NE61 ...9 B7
Ashington NE63 ...6 E3
Third Row Ellington NE61 ...1 E4
Linton NE61 ...1 A3
Third St NE28 ...40 D1
Thirkeld Pl DH4 ...90 A7
Thirlington Cl NE5 ...37 B3
Thirlmere Birtley DH3 ...82 E2
Gateshead NE10 ...72 A8
Cleadon SR6 ...60 A1
Thirlmere Ave
Chester le Street DH2 ...88 B1
Easington Lane DH5 ...97 C8
Tynemouth NE30 ...32 A2
Thirlmere Cl NE12 ...29 F3
Thirlmere Cres
Penshaw DH4 ...90 B6
Blaydon NE21 ...68 B8
Thirlmere Ct NE31 ...57 F4
Thirlmere Terr NE64 ...7 E4
Thirlmere Way Blyth NE24 .12 A1
Newcastle-upon-Tyne NE5 ..37 B1
Thirlmoor NE37 ...83 A6
Thirlmoor Pl NE62 ...11 A8
Thirlwell Gr NE32 ...58 B3
Thirlwell Rd NE8 ...56 A3
Thirsk Rd SR3 ...85 D2
Thirston Dr NE23 ...22 C6
Thirston Pl NE29 ...41 D7
Thirston Way NE3 ...37 D5
Thistle Ave NE40 ...52 A4
Thistle Ct NE31 ...57 D5
Thistle Rd SR3 ...85 C1
Thistlecroft DH5 ...94 E7
Thistledon Ave NE16 ...68 F6
Thistley Cl NE6 ...56 E8
Thistley Gn NE10 ...57 B1
Thomas Bell Ho 8 NE34 ..59 A4
Thomas Dr NE31 ...57 D6
Thomas Hawksley Pk SR3 ...86 A3
Thomas Hepburn Com Sch NE10 ...71 E7
Thomas Horsley Ho NE15 .54 B5
Thomas St
9 Chester le Street DH3 ..88 C2
Hetton le Hole DH5 ...95 B5
Whickham NE16 ...69 A7
South Shields NE33 ...42 C3
8 Washington NE37 ...83 E8
Newcastle-upon-Tyne NE5 ..36 F2
Gateshead NE9 ...71 D1
Ryhope SR2 ...92 F6
Thomas St N SR6 ...103 A4
Thomas St S Ryhope SR2 ..92 F6
Sunderland SR5 ...75 A1
Thomas Taylor Cotts NE27 ...30 C5
Thomas Walling Prim Sch The NE5 ...37 C2
Thompson Ave NE12 ...29 C4
Thompson Cres 7 SR5 ...74 B1
Thompson Gdns NE28 ...40 B2
Thompson Pl NE10 ...71 D8
Thompson Rd SR5 ...75 B2
Thompson St
Bedlington NE22 ...11 D3
Blyth NE24 ...12 D1
Blyth NE24 ...12 E1
Thompson Terr 8 SR2 ...93 A6
Thompson's Bldgs DH4 ...90 C5
Thorburn St SR6 ...75 D4
Thoresby Ho NE6 ...56 E4
Thorn Cl NE13 ...28 A5
Thorn Tree Dr NE22 ...10 F2
Thornbank Cl SR3 ...92 A4
Thornbeck Coll SR2 ...102 C1
Thornborough Ho 17 NE6 ...56 C6
Thornbridge NE38 ...84 A5
Thornbury Ave NE23 ...23 A2
Thornbury Cl
Newcastle-upon-Tyne NE3 ..37 B5
Boldon Colliery NE35 ...58 E1
Thornbury Dr NE25 ...31 C6
Thornbury St SR4 ...102 A3
Thorncliffe Pl NE29 ...41 E5
Thorndale Pl NE24 ...17 A8
Thorndale Rd
Newcastle-upon-Tyne NE15 .53 F5
Sunderland SR3 ...85 D1
Thorne Ave NE10 ...72 B8
Thorne Brake NE10 ...72 A7
Thorne Rd SR3 ...85 C1
Thorne Sq SR3 ...85 C1
Thorne Terr NE6 ...56 E7
Thornehill Gdns NE62 ...11 A8
Thorney Close Prim Sch SR3 ...85 D1
Thorney Close Rd SR3 ...85 D1
Thorneyburn Ave NE25 ...31 B5
Thorneyburn Cl DH4 ...90 C2
Thorneyburn Way NE24 ...17 C7
Thorneyfield Dr NE12 ...29 B2
Thorneyford Pl NE20 ...25 E7
Thornfield Gr SR2 ...86 E2
Thornfield Pl NE39 ...67 E3
Thornfield Rd NE3 ...38 B4
Thorngill NE37 ...83 C6
Thornhaugh Ave NE16 ...68 F6
Thornhill Cl
Gateshead NE11 ...70 A8
Seaton Delaval NE25 ...23 D2
Thornhill Comp Sch SR2 ...102 C1
Thornhill Cres SR2 ...102 C2
Thornhill Gdns
Burnopfield NE16 ...78 F5
Sunderland SR2 ...102 C1
Thornhill Park Sch (Thornhill Unit) SR2 ...102 C1
Thornhill Pk SR2 ...102 C1
Thornhill Rd
Longbenton NE12 ...39 D6
Ponteland NE20 ...25 E7
Thornhill St DH4 ...94 D8
Thornhill Terr SR2 ...102 C1
Thornholme Ave NE34 ...60 B6
Thornholme Rd SR2 ...102 C1
Thornhope Cl NE38 ...83 F6
Thornlea NE61 ...9 E4
Thornlea Gdns NE9 ...70 F6
Thornleigh Gdns SR6 ...60 A3
Thornleigh Rd NE2 ...38 E1
Thornley Ave
Gateshead NE10 ...72 B6
Cramlington NE23 ...22 C6
Thornley Cl NE16 ...69 A4
Thornley La NE21,NE39 ...68 A6
Thornley Rd NE5 ...53 F8
Thornley Terr NE62 ...11 C6
Thornley View NE39 ...67 F2
Thornley Wood* NE21 ...68 B6
Thornton Cl Penshaw DH4 .90 B7
Morpeth NE61 ...9 B6
Thornton Cotts NE40 ...52 C6
Thornton Cres NE21 ...53 C3
Thornton Ct NE38 ...83 C5
Thornton St NE1 ...98 C1
Thornton Terr NE12 ...30 A1
Thorntree Ave NE13 ...21 B1
Thorntree Cl NE25 ...31 B4
Thorntree Ct NE12 ...39 F8
Thorntree Dr
Newcastle-upon-Tyne NE15 .54 A7
Whitley Bay NE25 ...31 C4
Thorntree Gdns NE63 ...7 A2
Thorntree Mews SR3 ...85 C2
Thorntree Way NE24 ...16 F7
Thorntree Wlk NE32 ...58 D2
Thornwood Gdns NE11 ...70 B6
Thornyford House NE4 ...98 B2
Thornygarth NE10 ...71 E7
Thoroton St NE24 ...17 E8
Thorp Ave NE61 ...4 A2
Thorp Cl NE24 ...17 B5
Thorp Cotts NE40 ...52 A5
Thorpe Cl NE4 ...98 A2
Thorpe Dr NE40 ...52 E5
Thorpe St NE4 ...98 A2
Thorpeness Rd SR3 ...85 C1
Threap Gdns NE28 ...40 E4
Three Mile Ct NE3 ...38 C8
Three Rivers Ct NE36 ...74 A7

Threlkeld Gr SR6 75 C5
Thrift St NE29 42 A4
Thristley Gdns SR2 86 C3
Throckley Fst Sch NE15 35 C2
Throckley Mid Sch NE15 35 C2
Throckley Way NE34 59 B5
Thropton Ave Blyth NE24 17 C5
Newcastle-upon-Tyne NE7 39 B5
Thropton Cl
Chester le Street DH2 88 A1
Gateshead NE10 72 C6
Thropton Cres NE3 38 B6
Thropton Ct NE24 17 C7
Thropton Pl NE29 41 D7
Thropton Terr NE7 39 B2
Thrunton Ct 5 DH5 94 F8
Thrush Gr 2 SR5 74 C1
Thurleston DH4 90 C4
Thurlow Way DH5 94 D6
Thursby DH3 82 E2
Thursby Ave NE30 32 B2
Thursby Gdns NE9 71 B3
Thurso Cl SR3 85 B1
Tiberius Cl 6 NE28 40 B1
Tidings The NE10 57 B2
Tilbeck Sq SR3 92 A5
Tilbury Cl DH4 90 C5
Tilbury Gdns SR3 91 C8
Tilbury Gr NE30 32 A2
Tilbury Rd SR3 91 C8
Tileshed La NE36 59 D1
Till Ave NE21 53 B2
Till Gr NE61 1 E5
Till St 7 NE6 56 C4
Tilley Cres NE42 50 D3
Tilley Rd NE38 82 F5
Tillmouth Ave NE25 23 E2
Tillmouth Gdns NE4 54 C6
Tillmouth Park Rd NE15 35 D1
Tilson Way NE3 37 F6
Timber Beach Rd SR5 74 D1
Times Sq NE1 100 C4
Timlin Gdns NE28 41 B3
Timothy Duff Ct NE30 42 E7
Tindal Cl NE4 98 B1
Tindal St NE4 98 B1
Tindale Ave NE23 22 C6
Tindale Dr NE16 69 A6
Tinkler Terr DH3 89 B1
Tinkler's Bank NE45 46 F3
Tintagel Cl
Cramlington NE23 22 B8
Sunderland SR3 85 B1
Tintern NE38 83 C3
Tintern Cl DH4 90 C2
Tintern Cres
Tynemouth NE29 41 D8
Newcastle-upon-Tyne NE6 56 B7
Tintern St SR4 102 B2
Tiree Ct SR3 92 A6
Tirril Pl NE5 37 A1
Titan Rd NE6 57 A5
Titchfield Rd NE38 83 C4
Titchfield Terr
Pegswood NE61 4 F4
Ashington NE63 6 D2
Tithe Barn* TD15 104 D7
Tithe Cotts NE20 25 E7
Titian Ave NE34 59 C2
Titlington Gr NE31 57 D3
Tiverton Ave
Tynemouth NE29 31 C1
1 Newcastle-upon-Tyne NE4 54 E5
Tiverton Cl Newbottle DH4 90 C4
Wallsend NE28 41 A5
Tiverton Gdns NE9 70 F3
Tiverton Pl NE23 22 B8
Tiverton Sq SR3 85 C1
Tivoli Bldgs DH4 90 C6
Toberty Gdns NE10 72 B8
Todd's Nook NE4 98 B1
Togstone Pl 4 NE5 37 C1
Toll Bar Rd SR2 92 E8
Toll Bridge Rd NE21 53 F3
Toll Sq NE30 42 C6
Tollerton Dr SR5 74 A1
Tollgate Fields DH4 94 A1
Tollgate Rd NE39 77 F5
Tolls Cl NE25 31 C6
Tomlea Ave NE22 11 D1
Tonbridge Ave NE29 41 E4
Toner Ave NE31 57 D4
Toner Avenue Cty Inf Sch NE31 57 D3
Toner Avenue Jun Sch NE31 57 D3
Topcliff SR6 103 B4
Topcliffe Gn NE9 71 B2
Toppings St NE35 58 E1
Tor Mere Cl NE37 83 A6
Torcross Way NE23 22 B8
Toronto Rd SR3 85 D2
Toronto Sq SR3 85 D2
Torquay Gdns NE9 70 F3
Torquay Par NE31 58 A3
Torquay Rd SR3 85 D2
Torrens Rd SR3 85 D2
Torrington Cl DH4 90 C4
Torver Cl NE13 28 B5
Torver Cres SR6 75 D5
Torver Pl NE9 71 B4
Torver Way NE30 31 F2
Tosson Cl NE22 11 B1
Tosson Pl
North Shields NE29 41 D5
Ashington NE63 6 E3
Tosson Terr NE6 39 C1
Totnes Cl SR3 85 B1
Totnes Dr NE23 22 B8
Toward Rd
Sunderland SR1, SR2 103 A2
Sunderland SR2 103 B1
Toward St 10 NE6 56 B6
Tower Ct
Easington Lane DH5 95 C1
Dunston NE11 100 A1
Tower Gdns NE40 52 C5
Tower Ho NE1 99 C1
Tower Knowe Visitor Centre* NE48 121 A5
Tower Pl 1 SR2 86 E4
Tower Rd NE37 83 E7
Tower St
Newcastle-upon-Tyne NE1 99 B1
Sunderland SR2 103 C1
Tower St W SR2 103 B1
Tower View NE15 54 C6
Towers Ave NE2 38 E3
Towers Cl NE22 16 A8
Towers Pl NE34 58 E5
Towers The SR4 85 B5
Town End Prim Sch SR5 73 F4
Town Farm Field NE45 46 F6
Town Sq 9 NE28 40 B2
Towne Gate The NE15 34 E2
Towneley Cotts NE40 52 A4
Towneley Terr NE39 66 E4
Townend Ct NE34 59 C5
Townfield Gdns NE15 52 F8
Townley Fields NE39 67 F2
Townley Rd NE39 67 D2
Townsend Cres NE61 8 D6
Townsend Rd SR3 85 D1
Townsend Sq SR3 91 C8
Townsville Ave NE25 31 D3
Towton NE12 29 D4
Toynbee NE38 84 A5
Tracey Ave NE36 74 B8
Trafalgar House 17 NE30 42 D7
Trafalgar Rd NE37 72 F1
Trafalgar Sq SR1 103 C3
Trafalgar St NE1 99 B1
Trafford NE9 71 A1
Trafford Rd SR5 75 A1
Trafford Wlk NE5 36 E3
Trajan Ave NE33 42 D4
Trajan St NE33 42 D4
Trajan Wlk NE15 34 D2
Transbritannia Ct NE21 53 E4
Tranwell Cl
Newcastle-upon-Tyne NE3 37 F8
Pegswood NE61 4 E3
Tranwell Dr NE25 23 E2
Travers St DH4 90 C6
Treby St SR4 102 A3
Tredegar Cl NE5 37 B4
Tree Ct 26 SR3 91 F6
Treecone Cl SR3 92 A5
Treherne Rd NE2 38 D3
Trent Ave NE31 57 E3
Trent Dr NE32 58 C2
Trent Gdns NE8 71 B8
Trent Rd SR3 85 C1
Trent St
Easington Lane DH5 97 C8
Chopwell NE17 66 C1
Trentham Ave NE7 39 B5
Trentham Gdns NE61 4 F4
Trenton Ave NE38 83 D6
Trevarren Dr SR2 92 F7
Trevelyan Ave
Bedlington NE22 11 B1
Blyth NE24 17 C6
Trevelyan Cl SR3 85 B1
Trevelyan Ct 2 NE12 39 A6
Trevelyan Dr NE5 37 A4
Trevethick St NE8 70 D8
Trevone Pl NE23 23 A2
Trevor Gr SR6 75 A8
Trevor Terr NE30 42 B7
Trewhitt Rd NE6 56 C8
Trewit Rd NE26 32 B5
Tribune Pl NE9 71 B6
Trident Rd SR3 92 A7
Trimdon Gr NE9 71 D3
Trimdon St SR4 102 B3
Trimdon St W SR4 102 B4
Trinity Bldgs NE30 42 C5
Trinity Cl 2 NE29 42 A4
Trinity Ct NE8 101 C3
Trinity Ctyd NE6 56 D4
Trinity Gr NE23 23 A2
Trinity Maritime Mus* NE1 101 B4
Trinity Pk DH4 90 B5
Trinity Pl NE29 42 A4
Trinity Sq SR1 103 B3
Trinity St
North Shields NE29 42 A4
Sunderland SR5 74 F2
Trinity Terr 3 NE29 42 A4
Trinity Wlk NE33 42 B1
Trojan Ave NE6 56 E7
Tromso Cl NE29 41 C5
Trool Ct SR3 92 A5
Troon Cl NE37 72 C2
Trotter Gr NE22 11 C1
Trotter Terr SR2 92 F6
Troutbeck Ave NE6 56 F5
Troutbeck Gdns NE9 71 A3
Troutbeck Rd SR6 75 C5
Troutbeck Way NE34 58 F3
Troutdale Pl NE12 38 F6
Troves Cl NE4 54 E4
Trowbridge Way NE3 37 F5
Truro Gr NE29 41 D8
Truro Rd SR3 85 D1
Truro Way NE32 58 C1
Tuart St DH3 88 C3
Tudor Ave NE29 41 E6
Tudor Ct NE20 25 C4
Tudor Dr DH9 79 D3
Tudor Gr SR3 85 F3
Tudor Rd
Chester le Street DH3 88 D5
South Shields NE33 42 C2
Tudor Way NE3 37 B6
Tudor Wlk NE3 37 C6
Tudor Wynd NE6 39 D2
Tulip Cl NE21 53 B2
Tulip St Prudhoe NE42 50 B2
Gateshead NE8 56 C1
Tummel Ct SR3 92 A6
Tumulus Ave NE6 57 A8
Tunbridge Rd SR3 85 D2
Tundry Way NE21 53 F4
Tuneside NE10 72 B7
Tunis Rd SR3 85 E2
Tunstall Ave
South Shields NE34 60 B6
Newcastle-upon-Tyne NE6 56 D6
Tunstall Bank SR2,SR3 92 D7
Tunstall Hill Cl SR2 86 C2
Tunstall Hope Rd SR3 92 C8
Tunstall Pk SR2 86 C4
Tunstall Rd SR2 102 C1
Tunstall Terr
New Silksworth SR2 92 B7
Ryhope SR2 92 D7
Sunderland SR2 102 C2
Tunstall Terr W SR2 102 C2
Tunstall Vale SR2 86 C4
Tunstall View SR3 92 B8
Tunstall Village Gn SR3 92 C7
Tunstall Village Rd SR3 92 B7
Tunstall Villas SR3 92 B7
Turbinia Gdns NE7 39 D2
Turfside NE10 72 A7
Turn The NE61 8 F5
Turnberry Ouston DH2 81 F2
Whitley Bay NE25 31 C5
South Shields NE33 42 E1
Turnberry Cl NE37 72 C2
Turnberry Ct NE10 72 B7
Turnberry Way
Cramlington NE23 22 C6
Newcastle-upon-Tyne NE3 38 E6
Turnbull Ho 5 SR5 75 B1
Turnbull St SR1 103 C4
Turner Ave NE34 59 D2
Turner Cl NE40 52 D4
Turner Cres NE3 38 A5
Turner St NE27 30 E1
Turners Way NE61 8 D7
Turnham Rd SR3 85 C1
Turnstile Mews 7 SR6 75 E2
Turnstone Dr NE38 82 F3
Turret Rd NE15 53 F7
Tuscan Rd SR3 91 C8
Tweed Ave NE61 1 E5
Tweed Bridge* TD12 106 D8
Tweed Dr NE61 9 E1
Tweed Gr NE15 53 C7
Tweed St
Easington Lane DH5 97 C8
Chopwell NE17 66 C1
Hebburn NE31 57 E5
Jarrow NE32 58 A5
Washington NE38 83 F4
Newcastle-upon-Tyne NE4 54 F5
Ashington NE63 6 E4
Tweedmouth Ct NE3 38 E4
Tweedy St NE24 17 A8
Tweedy Terr NE6 56 F5
Tweedy's Bldgs NE40 52 B5
Twelfth Ave
Chester le Street DH2 88 B4
Blyth NE24 17 D6
Twentieth Ave NE24 17 C5
Twentyfifth Ave NE24 17 D5
Twentysecond Ave NE24 17 C5
Twentysixth Ave NE24 17 C5
Twentythird Ave NE24 17 C5
Twickenham Ct NE23 22 F2
Twickenham Rd SR3 85 C2
Twizell Ave NE21 53 B2
Twizell Pl NE20 25 E7
Twizell St NE24 17 F6
Two Ball Lonnen NE4 54 D8
Twyford Cl NE23 22 B8
Tyldesley Sq SR3 85 C1
Tyndal Gdns 4 NE11 54 F1
Tyne App NE32 58 A8
Tyne Ct NE46 45 A6
Tyne Dock Sta NE33 59 B6
Tyne Gdns
Washington NE37 72 D1
Ryton NE40 52 E4
Ovingham NE42 50 B4
Tyne Green NE46 45 A6
Tyne Green Country Park NE46 45 B6
Tyne Green Rd
Hexham NE46 45 A6
Hexham NE46 45 B6
Tyne Ho 20 SR3 91 F6
Tyne Main Rd NE10 56 C3
Tyne Mills Ind Est NE46 45 C5
Tyne Point Ind Est NE32 58 E5
Tyne Rd E NE8 100 C2
Tyne Riverside Ctry Pk* NE15 52 D8
Tyne Riverside Ctry Pk* NE42 50 B3
Tyne St
Easington Lane DH5 97 C8
Newcastle-upon-Tyne NE1 56 A5
Gateshead, Bill Quay NE10 57 A2
Gateshead, Felling Shore NE10 56 E2
Gateshead, Pelaw NE10 56 F2
Chopwell NE17 66 B1
Blaydon NE21 53 B1
North Shields NE30 42 B5
Jarrow NE32 58 B8
Ashington NE63 6 E4
Tyne Terr NE34 59 C5
Tyne Tunnel (Tynemouth) Trad Est NE29 41 B5
Tyne Valley Gdns NE40 52 A5
Tyne View
Newcastle-upon-Tyne NE15 53 D6
Blaydon NE21 53 C1
Hebburn NE31 57 C7
Crawcrook NE40 51 F7
Wylam NE41 51 B6
Tyne View Ave NE16 69 C8
Tyne View Com Prim Schs NE8 100 C2
Tyne View Gdns NE10 56 F1
Tyne View Pl NE8 100 C1
Tyne View Terr
North Shields NE28 41 C1
Wallsend NE28 41 C1
Prudhoe NE42 50 D3
Stocksfield NE43 64 D7
Tyne Wlk NE15 35 D1
Tynebank NE21 53 B2
Tynedale Ave
Whitley Bay NE26 31 F6
Wallsend NE28 40 B4
Tynedale Cl NE41 51 B6
Tynedale Cres DH4 90 B7
Tynedale Ct NE28 41 A4
Tynedale Dr NE24 17 A7
Tynedale Gdns NE43 64 D5
Tynedale Ho NE15 54 B5
Tynedale Mid Sch NE24 17 A7
Tynedale Rd
South Shields NE34 59 F8
Sunderland SR3 85 C1
Tynedale St DH5 94 E1
Tynedale Terr
Longbenton NE12 39 D6
Hexham NE46 44 F4
Tynegate Office Precinct NE8 101 C2
Tynemouth Castle* NE30 42 E7
Tynemouth Cl 3 NE6 56 B6
Tynemouth Coll NE29 41 F6
Tynemouth Ct 7 NE6 56 C7
Tynemouth Gr 9 NE6 56 C7
Tynemouth Pl 6 NE30 42 D7
Tynemouth Priory* NE30 42 E7
Tynemouth Rd
Wallsend NE28 41 A3
North Shields NE30 42 C6
Jarrow NE32 58 B2
Newcastle-upon-Tyne NE6 56 C7
Tynemouth Sealife Ctr* NE30 32 D1
Tynemouth Sq SR3 85 D1
Tynemouth Sta NE30 42 D7
Tynemouth Terr NE30 42 D7
Tynemouth Watch House (Mus)* NE30 42 E7
Tynemouth Way 8 NE6 56 C7
Tyneside Rd NE4 100 B3
Tyneside Ret Pk NE28 41 A6
Tynevale Ave NE21 53 C1
Tynevale Terr
Newcastle-upon-Tyne NE15 53 C6
Gateshead NE8 100 C1
Tyneview Pk NE12 39 D5
Tyneview Prim Sch NE6 57 A5
Tyneview Terr NE46 45 C3
Tyzack Cres SR6 75 D2

U

Uldale Ct NE3 37 E7
Ullswater Ave
Easington Lane DH5 97 C8
Hedworth NE32 58 D3
Ullswater Cl NE24 16 E8
Ullswater Cres NE21 68 B8
Ullswater Dr NE12 29 F3
Ullswater Gdns NE34 59 D6
Ullswater Gr SR5 75 C4
Ullswater Rd
Chester le Street DH2 88 B1
Newbiggin-by-the-Sea NE64 7 C3
Ullswater Terr DH6 97 E8
Ullswater Way NE5 54 B8
Ulverston Gdns NE9 71 B4
Ulverstone Terr NE6 56 E7
Umfraville Dene NE42 50 D3
Underhill Dr NE62 10 E6
Underhill Rd SR6 59 F1
Underhill Terr NE9 72 A1
Underwood NE10 72 A6
Underwood Gr NE23 16 A1
Union Alley NE33 42 C3
Union Hall Rd NE15 53 D7
Union La SR1 103 B3
Union Quay NE30 42 C5
Union Rd
North Shields NE30 42 C6
Newcastle-upon-Tyne NE6 56 C6
Union St
Hetton le Hole DH5 95 A4
Newcastle-upon-Tyne NE2 99 C2
Blyth NE24 17 F7
Wallsend NE28 57 B8
North Shields NE30 42 B5
Jarrow NE32 58 B8
South Shields NE33 59 B6
Sunderland SR1 103 A3
Sunderland, South Hylton SR4 85 A6
Union Stairs NE30 42 B5
Unity Terr Tantobie DH9 79 B2
Cambois NE24 12 D4
Univ of Newcastle-upon-Tyne NE1 99 A3
Univ of Northumbria at Newcastle
Newcastle-upon-Tyne NE1 99 B2
Newcastle-upon-Tyne NE7 39 C4
Univ of Sunderland SR1 102 C2
Univ of Sunderland Ashburne Ho (School of Arts, Design & Media) SR2 86 D4
Univ of Sunderland Bede Tower SR2 103 A1
Univ of Sunderland Benedict Bldg SR2 103 A1
Univ of Sunderland Langham Tower SR2 103 A1
Univ of Sunderland Liby
Sunderland SR1 102 C2
Sunderland SR2 103 A1
Univ of Sunderland St Peter's Campus SR6 103 B4
University Sta SR1 102 C2
Uplands NE25 31 D5
Uplands The Birtley DH3 82 D5
Newcastle-upon-Tyne NE3 37 F4
Uplands Way NE9 71 F2
Upper Camden St 10 NE30 42 A6
Upper Crone St NE27 30 F4
Upper Elsdon St 6 NE29 42 A4
Upper Fenwick Gr NE61 4 A2
Upper Norfolk St NE30 42 B6
Upper Pearson St NE30 42 B6
Upper Precinct The NE21 53 D3
Upper Queen St NE30 42 B6
Upton St NE8 100 C1
Urban Gdns NE37 83 D7
Urfa Terr 4 NE33 42 D4
Urswick Ct NE3 37 B5
Urwin St DH5 95 B3
Ushaw Rd NE31 57 F6
Usher St 3 SR5 75 B1
Usk Ave NE32 58 C3
Usworth Colliery Prim Sch NE37 72 E1
Usworth Cotts SR5 73 D3
Usworth Grange Prim Sch NE37 72 F1
Usworth Sch NE37 72 D2
Usworth Station Rd
4 Washington, Concord NE37 83 E8
Washington, Sulgrave NE37 83 F8
Uxbridge Terr 3 NE10 56 D1

V

Vale Ho NE2 56 A8
Vale St Easington Lane DH5 97 B8
Sunderland SR4 102 B1
Vale St E SR4 102 B1
Vale Wlk NE2 56 A8
Valebrook NE46 44 F4
Valebrooke SR2 102 C1
Valebrooke Ave SR2 102 C1
Valebrooke Gdns SR2 102 C1
Valehead NE25 31 D5
Valentia Ave NE6 56 E7
Valeria Cl NE28 40 E6
Valerian Ave NE15 34 F2
Valerian Ct NE63 6 B1
Valeshead Ho NE28 40 B2
Valeside NE15 35 C2
Valley Cres NE21 53 A2
Valley Ct SR2 103 B1
Valley Dene NE17 77 B7
Valley Dr Dunston NE11 69 F7
Whickham NE16 69 A8
Gateshead NE9 70 F7
Valley Forge NE38 83 D6
Valley Gardens Mid Sch NE25 31 D6
Valley Gdns
Whitley Bay NE25 31 D5
Wallsend NE28 40 D3
Gateshead NE9 71 A7
Valley Gn NE40 51 F2
Valley La NE34 60 C6
Valley Rd NE25 23 F2
Valley Road Inf Sch SR2 86 F4
Valley Road Jun Sch SR2 86 F4
Valley Shopping Village NE11 70 D4
Valley View Birtley DH3 82 B6
Hetton le Hole DH5 94 D1

Valley View *continued*
Newcastle-upon-Tyne, Lemington NE15 53 C7
Burnopfield NE16 78 F7
Newcastle-upon-Tyne, Jesmond NE2 38 F1
Jarrow NE32 58 B4
Washington NE38 83 E1
Rowlands Gill NE39 67 D2
Prudhoe NE42 50 E1
Hexham NE46 45 C4
Valley View Prim Sch NE32 58 B4
Vallum Ct NE4 98 B1
Vallum Pl NE9 71 B6
Vallum Rd Throckley NE15 35 E2
Newcastle-upon-Tyne NE6 56 E6
Vallum Way NE4 98 B1
Vanborough Ct NE25 23 D2
Vanburgh Gdns NE61 8 D7
Vance Bsns Pk NE11 70 B7
Vance Ct NE21 53 E4
Vancouver Dr NE7 39 D2
Vane St SR3 92 A7
Vane Terr SR2 103 C1
Vanguard Ct SR3 91 F6
Vardy Terr DH4 90 E6
Vauxhall Rd NE6 57 A8
Vedra St 1 SR5 75 B1
Velville Ct NE3 37 B6
Ventnor Ave NE4 54 F5
Ventnor Cres NE9 70 E5
Ventnor Gdns
Whitley Bay NE26 32 A6
Gateshead NE9 70 E6
Vera St NE40 66 F8
Verdun Ave NE31 57 E6
Vermont NE37 83 D8
Verne Rd NE29 41 D6
Vernon Cl NE33 59 B8
Vernon Dr NE25 31 E4
Vernon Pl NE64 7 E5
Vernon St NE37 83 D8
Veryan Gdns SR3 86 B3
Vespasian Ave NE33 42 D4
Viador DH3 88 C4
Viaduct St NE28 40 E2
Vicarage Cl SR3 91 F7
Vicarage La SR4 85 A6
Vicarage Rd SR3 92 A7
Vicarage St NE29 42 A4
Vicarage Terr NE22 16 A8
Vicars Way NE12 38 F6
Vicars' La NE7 39 A5
Vicarsholme Cl SR3 91 E5
Victor Ct SR6 75 E1
Victor St
5 Chester le Street DH3 88 C3
Sunderland SR6 75 E1
Victoria Ave
Gateshead NE10 71 C7
Longbenton NE12 39 D7
Whitley Bay NE26 32 B5
Wallsend NE28 40 B2
Sunderland, Grangetown SR2 86 E2
Sunderland, South Hylton SR4 85 B6
Victoria Ave W SR2 86 E2
Victoria Bldgs SR1 102 C2
Victoria Cres
8 North Shields NE29 41 F5
Tynemouth NE30 32 C3
Victoria Ct
Killingworth NE12 29 C1
Tynemouth NE30 32 C3
Hebburn NE31 57 D5
Gateshead NE8 100 C1
Victoria House NE8 100 C1
Victoria Ind Est NE31 57 C3
Victoria Mews
Newcastle-upon-Tyne NE2 56 A8
Blyth NE24 17 D7
Whitley Bay NE26 32 B5
Victoria Pl
Whitley Bay NE25 31 E4
7 Washington NE37 83 D8
Sunderland SR1 103 B2
Victoria Rd
South Shields NE33 42 C1
Washington NE37 83 D8
Gateshead NE8 70 C8
Victoria Rd E NE31 57 F6
Victoria Rd W NE31 57 D4
Victoria Sq
4 Gateshead NE10 71 D8
Newcastle-upon-Tyne NE2 99 B3
Victoria St
Hetton le Hole DH5 95 A4
Dunston NE11 100 A1
North Shields NE29 42 A4
Hebburn NE31 57 C6
Newcastle-upon-Tyne NE4 100 B4
Crawcrook NE40 51 F4
Victoria Terr
Penshaw DH4 90 C8
5 Gateshead, Felling NE10 71 D8
3 Throckley NE15 35 D2
Hamsterley NE17 77 B6
Bedlington NE22 11 C1
Whitley Bay NE26 32 B5
Jarrow NE32 58 A6
East Boldon NE36 74 C7
Rowlands Gill NE39 67 C1
Prudhoe NE42 50 D2
Victoria Terr *continued*
Newbiggin-by-the-Sea NE64 7 E4
Gateshead, Wrekenton NE9 71 C3
Springwell NE9 71 F1
Victoris Villas NE22 11 B1
Victory Cotts NE23 22 A1
Victory House 15 NE30 42 D7
Victory St SR4 85 E7
Victory St E DH5 95 B4
Victory St W DH5 95 B4
Victory Way SR3 91 C5
Viewforth Dr SR5 75 C3
Viewforth Gn 1 NE5 37 C1
Viewforth Rd SR2 92 F5
Viewforth Terr SR5 75 C3
Viewlands NE63 6 D4
Vigo La Birtley DH3 88 D8
Washington NE38 83 A1
Washington NE38 83 B1
Vigodale DH3 82 E1
Viking Precinct 8 NE32 58 B7
Villa Cl SR4 85 F6
Villa Pl NE8 101 B1
Villa View NE9 71 A6
Village Ct NE26 31 F5
Village Ctr
Washington, Albany NE37 83 B7
Washington, Donwell NE37 72 B1
Washington, Biddick NE38 83 D4
Washington, Glebe NE38 83 D5
Washington, Harraton NE38 88 F8
Washington, Lambton NE38 83 B3
Village E NE40 52 C6
Village Farm NE15 36 A1
Village Hts NE8 101 B2
Village La NE38 83 D6
Village Pl NE6 56 D5
Village Rd NE23 22 C6
Village The SR2 93 A6
Villas The Wide Open NE13 28 C5
Stannington NE61 13 C7
7 Sunderland SR5 74 C1
Villette Brook St 5 SR2 86 E4
Villette Path SR2 86 E4
Villette Rd SR2 86 E4
Villiers Pl 3 DH3 88 C4
Villiers St SR1 103 B3
Villiers St S SR1 103 B2
Vimy Ave NE31 57 E6
Vindolanda 2 NE28 40 F4
Vindomora Road DH8, NE17 76 E4
Vindomora Roman Fort* DH8 76 E4
Vindomora Villas DH8 76 E4
Vine Cl NE8 100 C1
Vine Ct NE46 45 B3
Vine La NE1 99 A2
Vine Pl
6 Houghton-le-Spring DH4 94 E8
Sunderland SR1 102 C2
Vine St Wallsend NE28 40 C1
South Shields NE33 59 C6
Vine Terr NE46 45 B4
Viola Cres DH2 81 F2
Viola St NE37 83 D8
Viola Terr NE16 69 B7
Violet Cl NE4 54 D4
Violet St
Houghton-le-Spring DH4 94 D8
Sunderland SR4 102 B3
Sunderland, South Hylton SR4 85 A6
Violet Terr DH4 89 D3
Violet Wlk NE4 54 D4
Viscount Rd 4 SR3 92 A7
Vivian Cres 1 DH2 88 C2
Vivian Sq SR6 75 D3
Voltage Terr DH4 90 D4
Vulcan Pl Bedlington NE22 16 A8
Sunderland SR6 75 D1
Vulcan Terr NE12 29 E1

W

Wade Ave NE15 33 A7
Wadham Terr NE34 59 B5
Wadsley Sq SR2 86 E3
Waggonway The NE42 50 D3
Wagon Way NE28 40 D1
Wagonway Rd NE31 57 E7
Wagtail Cl NE21 68 C8
Wakefield Ave NE34 60 B5
Walbottle Campus Tech Coll NE15 35 F2
Walbottle Rd
Wallbottle NE15 35 F1
Newburn NE15 52 F8
Walbottle St Cuthbert's RC Prim Sch NE15 35 F2
Walbottle Village Fst Sch NE15 35 F1
Walden Cl DH2 81 D2
Waldo St NE29 42 B5
Waldridge Cl NE37 83 A6
Waldridge Gdns NE9 71 D4
Waldridge La DH2 88 A2
Waldridge Rd DH2,DH3 88 B2
Waldron Sq SR2 86 E3
Walker Gate NE6 56 E8
Walker Gate Hospl NE6 39 E1
Walker Gate Ind Est NE6 57 B6
Walker Gate Sta NE6 56 E8
Walker Gr NE6 56 F8
Walker Park Cl NE6 57 A4
Walker Pl NE30 42 C6
Walker Rd NE6 56 E3
Walker Riverside Ind Pk NE6 57 B4
Walker Riverside Pk* NE6 56 F3
Walker Sch NE6 56 F6
Walker Terr NE8 101 B2
Walker View NE10 71 D8
Walkerburn NE23 22 B3
Walkerdene House NE6 57 B8
Walkergate Inf Sch NE6 56 E8
Walkergate Jun Sch NE6 56 E8
Wall Cl NE3 38 A5
Wall St NE3 38 A5
Wall Terr NE6 56 E7
Wallace Ave NE16 69 C8
Wallace Gdns NE9 71 E3
Wallace St
Houghton-le-Spring DH4 94 D8
Dunston NE11 100 A1
Newcastle-upon-Tyne NE2 98 B4
Sunderland SR5 75 C1
Wallace Terr NE40 52 C6
Waller St DH5 94 E7
Wallinfen NE10 71 F5
Wallingford Ave SR2 86 E2
Wallington (N.T.)* NE61 123 F4
Wallington Ave
Brunswick Village NE13 28 A6
Tynemouth NE30 32 A1
Wallington Cl NE22 11 C2
Wallington Ct
Killingworth NE12 29 C3
Seaton Delaval NE25 23 D3
Newcastle-upon-Tyne NE3 37 D7
Wallington Dr NE15 53 E8
Wallington Gr 9 NE33 42 D3
Wallington Rd NE63 6 F2
Wallis St Penshaw DH4 90 B8
12 South Shields NE33 42 C3
Wallridge Dr NE25 23 E1
Wallsend C of E Prim Sch NE28 40 E2
Wallsend Central Mid Sch NE28 40 D2
Wallsend Jubilee Fst Sch NE28 40 A4
Wallsend Rd
North Shields NE28,NE29 41 C3
North Shields, Percy Main NE29 41 D4
Wallsend Sports Ctr NE28 39 F2
Wallsend Sta NE28 40 C1
Walmer Terr NE9 71 D1
Walnut Gdns NE8 70 C8
Walnut Pl NE3 37 F3
Walpole Ct 1 SR4 85 F6
Walpole St
South Shields NE33 42 C1
Newcastle-upon-Tyne NE6 56 E8
Walsh Ave NE31 57 E7
Walsham Cl NE24 17 B5
Walsingham NE38 83 C4
Walter St
Brunswick Village NE13 28 A6
Jarrow NE32 58 B7
Walter Terr
Hetton le Hole DH5 95 B1
Newcastle-upon-Tyne NE4 98 A2
Walter Thomas St 3 SR5 74 F2
Waltham NE38 83 D4
Waltham Cl NE28 39 F4
Waltham Pl 4 NE5 37 B2
Walton Ave Blyth NE24 17 C8
Tynemouth NE29 41 F7
Walton Dr NE62 10 F8
Walton La SR1 103 B3
Walton Pk NE29 41 F8
Walton Rd
Washington NE38 84 B5
Newcastle-upon-Tyne NE5 37 A1
Walwick Ave NE29 41 D6
Walwick Rd NE25 31 B5
Walworth Ave NE34 60 C6
Walworth Gr NE32 58 B3
Wandsworth Rd NE6 56 B7
Wanless La NE46 45 B4
Wanley St NE24 17 E8
Wanlock Cl NE23 22 C3
Wanny Rd NE22 11 B1
Wansbeck NE38 83 A1
Wansbeck Ave Blyth NE24 17 E5
Tynemouth NE30 32 C2
Stakeford NE62 11 A8
Wansbeck Bsns Pk NE63 6 B5
Wansbeck Cl
Sunniside NE16 69 A3
Ellington NE61 1 E5
Wansbeck Cres NE61 4 E3
Wansbeck Ct 19 SR3 91 F6
Wansbeck General Hospl NE63 6 F4
Wansbeck Gr NE25 23 D6
Wansbeck Mews NE63 6 B4
Wansbeck Rd
Dudley NE23 28 F8
Jarrow NE32 58 B5
Ashington NE63 6 B2
Wansbeck Rd N NE3 38 A6
Wansbeck Rd S NE3 38 A6
Wansbeck Riverside Pk* NE62,NE63 5 F1
Wansbeck Road Sta NE3 38 A6
Wansbeck Sq NE63 6 C4
Wansbeck St
Chopwell NE17 66 C1
Morpeth NE61 9 A8
Wansbeck St *continued*
Ashington NE63 12 A8
Wansbeck Terr NE62 11 D7
Wansbeck View NE62 11 B8
Wansdyke NE61 3 D1
Wansfell Ave NE5 37 D3
Wansford Ave NE5 37 B1
Wansford Way
Whickham NE16 68 F5
Whickham NE16 69 A4
Wantage Ave NE29 41 D4
Wantage St NE33 59 D7
Wapping 1 NE24 17 F8
Wapping St NE33 42 B4
War Memorial Hospl NE46 45 B4
Warbeck Cl NE3 37 B6
Warburton Cres NE9 71 A8
Warcop Ct NE3 37 E7
Ward Ct SR2 103 B1
Warden Gr DH5 94 F7
Warden Law La SR3 91 F6
Wardenlaw NE10 71 F5
Wardill Gdns NE9 71 B7
Wardle Ave NE33 42 E1
Wardle Dr NE23 29 B8
Wardle Gdns NE10 71 E7
Wardle St NE3 38 E5
Wardle Terr NE40 51 F4
Wardley Ct NE10 72 D8
Wardley Cty Prim Sch NE10 72 B8
Wardley Dr NE10 72 D7
Wardley La NE10,NE31 57 C1
Wardroper House NE6 57 A4
Warenford Cl NE23 22 C4
Warenford Pl NE5 54 C7
Warenmill Cl NE15 53 B7
Warennes St 3 SR4 85 E7
Warenton Pl NE29 31 B1
Waring Ave NE26 24 B7
Wark Ave Shiremoor NE27 30 F4
North Shields NE29 41 C6
Wark Cres NE32 58 B2
Wark Ct NE3 38 E4
Wark St DH3 88 C1
Warkdale Ave NE24 17 A6
Warkworth Ave
Blyth NE24 17 E5
Whitley Bay NE26 32 A5
Wallsend NE28 40 C4
South Shields NE34 60 B7
Warkworth Castle* NE65 119 D6
Warkworth Cl NE38 83 B4
Warkworth Cres
Newburn NE15 52 F7
Newcastle-upon-Tyne NE3 38 B6
Ashington NE63 6 C3
Warkworth Dr
Chester le Street DH2 88 A1
Wide Open NE13 28 C6
Ellington NE61 1 E5
Pegswood NE61 4 F3
Warkworth Gdns NE10 71 C8
Warkworth Hermitage* NE65 119 D7
Warkworth La NE61 1 C6
Warkworth St
Newcastle-upon-Tyne, Lemington NE15 53 C6
2 Newcastle-upon-Tyne, Byker NE6 56 C6
Warkworth Terr
Tynemouth NE30 42 D8
Jarrow NE32 58 B3
Warnham Ave SR2 86 E2
Warnhead Rd NE22 11 B1
Warren Ave NE6 57 A8
Warren Cl DH4 90 C4
Warren Ct NE63 6 C2
Warren Sq SR1 103 C4
Warrenmor NE10 72 A7
Warrens Wlk NE21 53 A1
Warrington Rd
Newcastle-upon-Tyne, Fawdon NE3 37 E6
Newcastle-upon-Tyne, Elswick NE4 100 A4
Warton Terr NE6 56 C8
Warwick Ave NE16 69 B5
Warwick Cl
Whickham NE16 69 A5
Seghill NE23 22 E1
Warwick Ct NE3 37 D7
Warwick Dr
Houghton-le-Spring DH5 94 E7
Whickham NE16 69 B5
Washington NE37 72 D2
Sunderland SR3 91 C7
Warwick Gr NE22 10 D1
Warwick Hall Wlk NE7 39 D3
Warwick Rd
Wallsend NE28 40 B1
Hebburn NE31 57 F3
South Shields NE34 59 D7
Newcastle-upon-Tyne NE5 53 E8
Warwick St Blyth NE24 17 C4
Newcastle-upon-Tyne NE6 56 A7
Gateshead NE8 101 C2
Sunderland SR5 75 D1
Warwick Terr SR3 92 A8
Warwick Terr W SR3 92 A8
Wasdale Cl NE23 22 C3
Wasdale Ct SR6 75 C5
Wasdale Rd NE5 54 B8
Washington Arts Ctr NE38 83 D2
Washington Birtley Service Area DH3,NE38 82 E3
Washington F Pit Mus* NE37 83 C7
Washington Gdns NE9 71 C3
Washington Highway
Penshaw DH4,NE38 89 E8
Washington NE37,NE38 83 B4
Washington Hospl The NE38 88 E8
Washington Old Hall* NE38 83 E6
Washington Rd SR5 74 B2
Washington Sch NE37 83 D7
Washington St SR4 85 F6
Washington Terr NE30 42 C7
Washington Village Prim Sch NE38 83 E6
Washington Wildfowl & Wetlands Ctr* NE38 84 C5
Washingwell Com Prim Sch NE16 69 C6
Washingwell La NE16 69 D6
Washingwell Pk NE16 69 C6
Waskdale Cres NE21 68 B8
Waskerley Cl NE16 69 B3
Waskerley Gdns NE9 71 D3
Waskerley Rd NE38 83 F5
Watch House Cl NE29 42 A3
Watcombe Cl NE37 72 F2
Water Row NE15 52 E7
Water St NE4 100 B3
Waterbeach Pl NE5 37 B2
Waterbeck Cl NE23 22 C3
Waterbury Cl SR5 74 F3
Waterbury Rd NE3 28 B1
Waterfield Rd NE22 12 B4
Waterford Cl
East Rainton DH5 94 D4
Seaton Sluice NE26 24 D6
Waterford Cres 5 NE26 32 B4
Waterford Gn NE63 11 D8
Waterford Pk NE13 27 F6
Watergate NE1 101 B4
Waterloo Ct 5 NE37 83 E8
Waterloo Pl
North Shields NE29 42 A6
Sunderland SR1 103 A2
Waterloo Rd Blyth NE24 17 E7
Earsdon NE25 31 A5
Washington NE37 72 F3
Washington, Sulgrave NE37 72 E1
Waterloo Sq 10 NE33 42 C3
Waterloo St
Newcastle-upon-Tyne NE1 100 C4
Blaydon NE21 53 A1
Waterloo Vale 8 NE33 42 C3
Waterloo Wlk NE37 83 E8
Waterlow Cl SR5 74 F4
Watermill NE40 52 C5
Watermill La NE10 71 E8
Waterside Dr NE11 54 E2
Waterside Pk NE31 57 C6
Waterville Pl 16 NE29 42 A5
Waterville Prim Sch NE29 41 F4
Waterville Rd NE29 41 E4
Waterville Terr 9 NE29 42 A5
Waterworks Rd SR1 102 C2
Watford Cl SR5 74 F4
Watling Pl NE9 71 B6
Watling St
South Shields NE34 59 B5
Corbridge NE45 46 F5
Watson Ave Dudley NE23 29 A8
South Shields NE34 60 B5
Watson Gdns NE28 41 A3
Watson Pl NE34 60 B5
Watson St
Burnopfield NE16 79 B6
Jarrow NE32 58 C8
High Spen NE39 67 A5
Gateshead NE8 100 C1
Watson Terr
West Boldon NE35 73 F7
12 Morpeth NE61 9 A8
Watt St NE8 70 D7
Watt's La NE64 7 E5
Watt's Rd NE26 32 A6
Watts Moses Ho SR1 103 C3
Wavendon Cres SR4 85 E4
Waverdale Ave NE6 57 A7
Waverdale Way NE33 59 B7
Waverley Ave
Bedlington NE22 11 C2
Whitley Bay NE25 31 F4
Waverley Bldgs NE64 7 E5
Waverley Cl NE21 67 F8
Waverley Cres NE15 53 D7
Waverley Ct NE22 11 C2
Waverley Dr NE22 11 C2
Waverley Fst Sch NE15 53 E6
Waverley Lodge NE2 99 C3
Waverley Rd
Newcastle-upon-Tyne NE4 100 B4
Gateshead NE9 71 B1
Waverley Terr Dipton DH9 78 E1
Sunderland SR4 85 E7
Waverly Dr NE22 11 D2
Waverton Cl NE23 22 B3
Wawn St NE33 59 D8
Wayfarer Rd SR5 75 A1
Wayland Sq SR2 86 E1
Wayman St SR5 75 C1
Wayside
Newcastle-upon-Tyne NE15 54 B5
South Shields NE34 60 B6
Sunderland SR2 86 B4

Wealcroft NE10 71 F5
Wealcroft Ct NE10 71 F5
Wealleans Cl NE63 7 B3
Wear Ct NE34 59 C5
Wear Lodge DH3 88 C7
Wear Rd NE31 57 E3
Wear St
Chester le Street DH3 88 D2
Fence Houses DH4 94 A7
Hetton le Hole DH5 95 A3
Chopwell NE17 66 B1
Jarrow NE32 58 B7
Sunderland SR1 103 C2
Sunderland, South Hylton SR4 85 A7
Sunderland, Low Southwick SR5 75 A1
Wear Terr NE38 83 E4
Wear View SR4 85 B7
Weardale Ave
Longbenton NE12 39 D8
Blyth NE24 17 A8
Wallsend NE28 40 B4
Washington NE37 83 C8
Newcastle-upon-Tyne NE6 57 A6
Sunderland SR6 75 E7
Weardale Cres DH4 90 B7
Weardale St DH5 94 E1
Weardale Terr DH3 88 D2
Wearfield SR5 74 F1
Wearmouth Ave SR5 75 D2
Wearmouth Dr SR5 75 D2
Wearmouth St SR6 75 D1
Weathercock La NE9 70 F5
Weatherside NE21 53 B1
Webb Gdns NE10 72 A8
Wedder Law NE23 22 B3
Wedderburn Sq NE63 6 C3
Wedgewood Cotts NE15 53 D6
Wedmore Rd NE5 36 D3
Weetman St NE33 42 B1
Weetslade Cres NE23 29 A7
Weetslade Rd NE23 29 A7
Weetslade Terr NE23 29 C5
Weetwood Rd NE23 22 C4
Weidner Rd NE15,NE4 54 D6
Welbeck Com Fst Sch NE63 7 A2
Welbeck Gn NE6 56 E5
Welbeck Prim Sch NE6 56 D5
Welbeck Rd
Newcastle-upon-Tyne NE6 56 E5
Guide Post NE62 10 E7
Welbeck Terr NE61 4 F4
Welbottle Hall Gdns NE15 36 A1
Welburn Cl NE42 50 C5
Welbury Way NE23 22 B3
Weldon Ave SR2 86 E2
Weldon Cres NE7 39 B2
Weldon Pl NE29 41 D8
Weldon Rd
Longbenton NE12 39 B6
East Cramlington NE23 22 E5
Weldon Terr DH3 88 D2
Weldon Way NE3 38 B6
Welfare Cres
Ashington NE63 6 F3
Newbiggin-by-the-Sea NE64 7 C4
Welfare Rd DH5 95 A4
Welford Ave NE3 38 A5
Well Bank NE45 46 F5
Well Bank Rd NE37 72 B1
Well Close Wlk NE16 69 A6
Well Dean NE42 50 D3
Well La Tynemouth NE27 31 B2
Tynemouth NE27 31 C2
Well Rd NE43 64 B5
Well Ridge Cl NE25 31 C6
Well Ridge Pk NE25 31 C7
Well St SR4 85 F7
Well Way NE61 3 F1
Wellands Cl SR6 60 E1
Wellands Ct SR6 60 E1
Wellands Dr SR6 60 E1
Wellands La SR6 60 E1
Wellbank Sch NE37 72 B1
Wellbeck Terr NE63 6 D2
Wellburn Rd NE37 72 B1
Wellesley St NE32 58 B5
Wellesley Terr NE4 98 A1
Wellfield Cl NE15 35 C1
Wellfield Ct NE40 51 E3
Wellfield La NE5 37 B2
Wellfield Mews SR2 92 E5
Wellfield Mid Sch NE25 31 B4
Wellfield Rd
Rowlands Gill NE39 67 C2
Newcastle-upon-Tyne NE4 54 D5
Newcastle-upon-Tyne NE4 54 E5
Wellfield Terr
3 Gateshead NE10 71 C7
Ryhope SR2 92 E5
Wellgarth Rd NE37 72 B1
Wellhead Dean Rd NE62 5 F2
Wellhead Terr NE63 6 A4
Wellhope NE38 88 F8
Wellington Ave NE25 31 A5
Wellington Ct
2 Gateshead NE10 71 C8
6 Washington NE37 83 E8
Wellington Dr NE33 42 C4
Wellington La SR4 102 B4
Wellington Rd
Dunston NE11 54 E1
Dunston NE11 54 F1
Stakeford NE62 11 A7
Wellington Row DH4 90 C5
Wellington St
High Pittington DH6 96 B5
Gateshead, Felling NE10 71 C8
Newcastle-upon-Tyne, Lemington NE15 53 D6
Blyth NE24 17 F7
11 North Shields NE29 42 A5
Hebburn NE31 57 D5
Newcastle-upon-Tyne NE4 98 C1
Gateshead NE8 101 B3
Wellington St E 10 NE24 17 F8
Wellington St W 12 NE29 42 A5
Wellington Wlk 2 NE37 83 F8
Wellmere Rd SR2 86 F1
Wells Cl NE12 39 D4
Wells Gdns NE9 70 F2
Wells Gr NE34 60 A7
Wells St NE35 58 E1
Wellshede NE10 72 B7
Wellway NE32 58 B2
Wellway Ct 11 NE61 3 F1
Wellwood Gdns NE61 4 A1
Welton Cl NE43 64 D6
Welworth Way SR1 102 C3
Welwyn Ave NE22 11 D3
Welwyn Cl Wallsend NE28 39 F4
Sunderland SR5 85 A8
Wembley Ave NE25 31 E4
Wembley Cl SR5 74 F3
Wembley Gdns NE24 12 B6
Wembley Rd SR5 74 F3
Wembley Terr NE24 12 C6
Wendover Cl SR5 74 E4
Wendover Way SR5 74 E4
Wenham Sq SR2 86 B4
Wenlock NE38 83 C4
Wenlock Dr NE29 41 F8
Wenlock Pl 6 NE34 59 A4
Wenlock Rd NE34 59 A5
Wensley Cl Urpeth DH2 81 E1
Newcastle-upon-Tyne NE5 37 C4
Wensley Ho 2 SR3 91 F5
Wensleydale NE28 39 F5
Wensleydale Ave
Penshaw DH4 90 A7
Washington NE37 83 C8
Wensleydale Dr NE12 39 D8
Wensleydale Mid Sch NE24 17 F6
Wensleydale Terr NE24 17 F6
Wentworth NE33 42 E1
Wentworth Cl NE10 71 D7
Wentworth Ct NE20 25 C4
Wentworth Dr NE37 72 C2
Wentworth Gdns NE25 31 C4
Wentworth Grange NE3 38 D4
Wentworth Grth NE46 45 B5
Wentworth Pl
Newcastle-upon-Tyne NE4 100 B4
Hexham NE46 45 B5
Wentworth Terr SR4 102 B3
Werhale Gn NE10 71 D8
Wesley Ct
1 Gateshead, Felling NE10 71 C8
Blaydon NE21 53 D3
Wesley Dr NE12 30 B1
Wesley Gr NE40 51 E3
Wesley Mount NE40 51 E3
Wesley St
Newcastle-upon-Tyne NE2 99 C2
Prudhoe NE42 50 D2
Gateshead, Low Fell NE9 70 F5
Wesley Terr
Chester le Street DH3 88 C3
Sherburn Hill DH6 96 C1
Dipton DH9 78 D1
Prudhoe NE42 50 D2
Wesley Way
Longbenton NE12 30 B1
Throckley NE15 35 D2
Wessex Cl SR5 74 F4
Wessington Terr NE37 83 D7
Wessington Way
Sunderland, Castletown SR5 85 B8
Sunderland, Low Southwick SR5 74 E1
West Acres
Dinnington NE13 27 B8
Blaydon NE21 53 D2
West Ave Longbenton NE12 29 F1
Longbenton NE12 39 D6
Whitley Bay NE25 31 E5
North Shields NE29 41 D5
Newcastle-upon-Tyne, Gosforth NE3 38 C4
South Shields NE34 59 E6
Washington NE38 83 B1
Rowlands Gill NE39 67 D1
Newcastle-upon-Tyne, Westerhope NE5 36 F2
Guide Post NE62 10 D7
Whitburn SR6 60 E1
West Bailey NE12 29 B3
West Boldon Jun Sch NE36 74 A7
West Bridge St
Penshaw DH4 89 E8
Cambois NE24 12 D3
West Chirton (Middle) Ind Est NE29 41 B7
West Chirton (south) Ind Est NE29 41 C5
West Chirton North Ind Est NE29 41 B7
West Clifton NE12 29 C4
West Copperas NE15 53 F7
West Cres
Gateshead NE10 72 C8
West Cres *continued*
Chopwell NE17 77 B7
West Ct Blyth NE24 17 C6
Newcastle-upon-Tyne NE3 38 A5
West Dene Dr NE30 42 A7
West Denton Cl NE15 53 D8
West Denton Fst Sch NE5 36 D1
West Denton High Sch NE5 36 E2
West Denton Rd NE15 53 D8
West Denton Ret Pk NE5 37 A2
West Denton Way NE5 36 E1
West Dr Blyth NE24 17 C4
Cleadon SR6 74 E8
West End
Seaton Sluice NE26 24 D4
Wallsend NE28 40 A1
West Farm
Medomsley DH8 77 C2
Ponteland NE20 26 C6
Burdon SR3 92 B3
West Farm Ave NE12 39 A6
West Farm Ct NE23 22 B7
West Farm La DH8 77 C2
West Farm Rd
Wallsend NE28 40 F3
Newcastle-upon-Tyne NE6 56 E7
Cleadon SR6 75 B8
West Farm Wynd NE12 38 F6
West Ford Rd NE62 11 B8
West Gate Com Coll NE4 54 D6
West George Potts St 17 NE33 42 D1
West Gr SR4 85 B5
West Grange SR5 75 C3
West Greens 6 NE61 9 A8
West Hextol NE46 44 F4
West Hextol Cl NE46 44 F4
West High Horse Cl NE39 68 A4
West Hill Morpeth NE61 8 E7
Sunderland SR4 85 E4
West Holborn NE33 42 B1
West Jesmond Ave NE2 38 E2
West Jesmond Prim Sch NE2 38 E1
West Jesmond Sta NE2 38 E2
West La
Chester le Street DH3 88 C2
Killingworth NE12 29 D2
Byermoor NE16 68 C1
Medomsley NE17 77 B4
Blaydon NE21 68 A8
West Law Rd DH8 76 D1
West Lawn SR2 86 C4
West Lawrence St SR1 103 B2
West Lea
New Herrington DH4 90 D6
Blaydon NE21 68 C8
West Market St NE61 2 B3
West Mdws NE5 36 D4
West Meadows Dr SR6 75 A8
West Meadows Rd SR6 75 B8
West Moffett St 6 NE33 42 D1
West Monkseaton Sta NE25 31 D4
West Moor Ct NE12 29 B1
West Moor Dr SR6 75 A7
West Moor Terr 1 SR4 85 E7
West Mount
Killingworth NE12 29 C3
Sunderland SR4 85 E5
West Par Hebburn NE31 57 D5
Newcastle-upon-Tyne NE4 100 B4
West Park Gdns NE21 53 C1
West Park Rd
South Shields NE33 59 C7
Gateshead NE8,NE9 70 E7
Cleadon SR6 60 A1
West Park View NE23 28 F8
West Pastures
Hedworth NE36 73 C5
Ashington NE63 6 B2
West Percy Rd NE29 41 F5
West Percy St NE29 42 A5
West Pk Morpeth NE61 8 E7
Sunderland SR3 91 B6
West Quay Rd SR5 74 F1
West Rd Tantobie DH9 79 A1
Newcastle-upon-Tyne NE15, NE5 54 B7
Ponteland NE20 25 E6
Bedlington NE22 11 D2
Prudhoe NE42 50 B2
West Rig The NE3 37 E4
West Riggs NE22 15 F8
West Row DH3 82 E3
West Salisbury St 4 NE24 17 D8
West Sleekburn Mid Sch NE62 11 F6
West Spencer Terr NE15 36 B1
West St 4 Birtley DH3 82 C4
Whickham NE16 69 A7
Shiremoor NE27 30 D1
Wallsend NE28 40 A2
Hebburn NE31 57 F7
High Spen NE39 66 F4
Gateshead NE8 101 B3
Sunderland SR1 102 C3
New Silksworth SR3 92 A8
West Stainton St 5 NE33 42 D1
West Stevenson St 7 NE33 42 D1
West Sunniside SR1 103 A3
West Terr
Seaton Sluice NE26 24 D6
Stakeford NE62 11 C7
West Thorn Wlk NE16 69 A6
West Thorp NE5 36 F5
West Vallum NE15 53 F7
West View
Chester le Street DH3 88 C4
Bournmoor DH4 89 E3
Newbottle DH4 90 D2
Penshaw DH4 90 B8
Shiney Row DH4 90 B4
Haswell DH6 97 D1
Sherburn Hill DH6 96 C1
Kibblesworth NE11 81 D6
5 Longbenton NE12 39 D8
Wide Open NE13 28 B7
Newcastle-upon-Tyne, Lemington NE15 53 C6
Burnopfield NE16 79 A6
Blaydon NE21 53 C3
Bedlington NE22 11 C3
Annitsford NE23 29 A8
Seghill NE23 22 F1
Cambois NE24 12 C6
Earsdon NE25 31 A5
Newcastle-upon-Tyne, Elswick NE4 54 F4
Crawcrook NE40 51 E6
Wylam NE41 51 B6
Morpeth NE61 3 C5
Pegswood NE61 4 E3
Ashington NE63 6 D3
Gateshead NE9 71 C4
Ryhope SR2 92 E6
3 Sunderland, Castletown SR5 74 B1
Sunderland, Roker SR6 75 D3
West View Terr NE46 45 C4
West Walker Prim Sch NE6 57 A4
West Walls NE1 98 C1
West Walpole St NE33 42 B1
West Way Dunston NE11 70 A7
South Shields NE33,NE34 59 C7
West Wear St SR1 103 A3
West Wylam Dr NE42 50 E3
West Wynd NE12 29 D3
Westacre Gdns NE5 54 C7
Westacres Ave NE16 69 B5
Westacres Cres NE15 54 C6
Westbourne Ave
Newcastle-upon-Tyne, Gosforth NE3 38 C7
Newcastle-upon-Tyne, Walker NE6 56 F7
Stakeford NE62 6 A1
Gateshead NE8 70 E8
Westbourne Dr DH4 90 B5
Westbourne Gdns NE6 57 A6
Westbourne Gr NE46 44 F5
Westbourne Rd SR1 102 B2
Westbourne Terr
2 Shiney Row DH4 90 A6
Seaton Delaval NE25 23 E3
Westburn Gdns NE28 39 F4
Westburn Mews NE40 51 E3
Westburn Terr SR6 75 E2
Westbury Ave NE6 57 A8
Westbury Rd NE29 41 F8
Westbury St SR4 102 B3
Westcliffe Rd SR6 75 F4
Westcliffe Way NE34 58 F3
Westcott Ave NE33 42 E1
Westcott Rd NE34 59 C6
Westcott Terr DH4 90 C8
Westcroft Whiteleas NE33 59 E1
Whitburn SR6 60 E1
Westcroft Rd NE12 39 E8
Wester Ct 1 SR3 91 F5
Westerdale Penshaw DH4 89 E8
Wallsend NE28 39 F4
Westerdale Pl NE6 57 B6
Westerham Cl SR5 74 F3
Westerhope Fst Sch NE5 36 E3
Westerhope Gdns 11 NE5 37 D1
Westerhope Ind Unit NE5 36 F3
Westerhope Rd NE38 83 F5
Westerkirk NE23 22 C3
Western App
South Shields, High Shields NE33 42 C1
South Shields, Tyne Dock NE34 59 A6
Western App Ind Est NE33 42 C2
Western Ave
Gateshead NE11 70 C4
Seaton Delaval NE25 23 C3
Newcastle-upon-Tyne, Elswick NE4 54 E5
Prudhoe NE42 50 B2
Newcastle-upon-Tyne, West Denton NE5 36 D1
Western Ct 5 NE26 31 F8
Western Dr NE4 54 F5
Western Fst Sch NE28 40 A2
Western Highway NE38 83 B2
Western Hill Ryhope SR2 92 E7
Sunderland SR2 102 B2
Western Mid Sch NE28 40 A2
Western Rd
Wallsend NE28 40 F2
Jarrow NE32 58 A7
Western Terr Dudley NE23 28 F8
West Boldon NE36 74 B7
Western Terr *continued*
Washington NE37 83 D7
Western View NE9 71 C1
Western Way
Ponteland NE20 25 A2
Blaydon NE21 53 E2
Whitley Bay NE26 31 F8
Ryton NE40 52 C4
Westernmoor NE37 82 F6
Westfield Gateshead NE10 71 E6
Dudley NE23 28 F8
Newcastle-upon-Tyne NE3 38 B2
Hedworth NE32 58 C1
Morpeth NE61 8 E7
Westfield Ave
Brunswick Village NE13 28 A6
Whitley Bay NE25 31 D4
Newcastle-upon-Tyne NE3 38 C3
Crawcrook NE40 51 F3
Westfield Cl NE46 44 F5
Westfield Cres
Crawcrook NE40 51 F3
Newbiggin-by-the-Sea NE64 7 D4
Westfield Ct
Wallsend NE28 57 B8
Sunderland SR4 85 E4
Westfield Dr NE3 38 C3
Westfield Gr
Newcastle-upon-Tyne NE3 38 B3
Sunderland SR4 85 E4
Westfield La NE40 52 B6
Westfield Lodge NE9 70 E4
Westfield Pk
Wallsend NE28 40 A2
Newcastle-upon-Tyne NE3 38 C3
Westfield Rd
Newcastle-upon-Tyne NE15 54 C5
Gateshead NE8 70 E8
Westfield Sch NE3 38 B3
Westfield Terr
Hexham NE46 44 F5
Gateshead NE8 70 E8
Springwell NE9 71 E1
Westgarth NE5 36 F4
Westgarth Terr 7 NE37 83 E8
Westgate NE61 8 D7
Westgate Ave SR3 92 A8
Westgate Cl NE25 31 C6
Westgate Ct NE4 98 B1
Westgate Gr SR3 92 A8
Westgate Hill Sch NE4 98 A1
Westgate Hill Terr NE4 98 C1
Westgate Rd NE1,NE4 98 B1
Westgreen NE62 10 F5
Westheath Ave SR2 86 E1
Westhills DH9 79 A2
Westholme Gdns NE15 54 D6
Westholme Terr 1 SR2 86 F2
Westhope Cl NE34 60 A7
Westhope Rd NE34 60 A7
Westlands
Seaton Sluice NE26 24 C6
Tynemouth NE30 32 B1
Hedworth NE32 58 D1
Newcastle-upon-Tyne, West Denton NE5 36 C1
Newcastle-upon-Tyne, High Heaton NE7 39 A2
Sunderland SR4 85 F5
Westlea NE22 15 D8
Westleigh Rd DH4 90 C3
Westley Ave NE26 24 F1
Westley Cl NE26 24 F1
Westline Ind Est DH2 82 B2
Westloch Rd NE23 22 B3
Westmacott St NE15 52 E8
Westminster Ave NE29 41 B8
Westminster Cl NE26 32 C4
Westminster Cres NE31 57 E2
Westminster Dr NE11 69 F6
Westminster St
Gateshead NE8 70 D8
4 Sunderland SR2 86 F2
Westminster Way NE12 39 D4
Westmoor Dr NE12 29 B1
Westmoor Fst Sch NE12 29 C1
Westmoor Mid Sch NE12 29 B1
Westmoor Rd SR4 85 D7
Westmoreland St NE28 40 C2
Westmorland Ave
Bedlington NE22 10 E1
2 Wallsend NE28 41 B1
Washington NE37 72 D1
Newbiggin-by-the-Sea NE64 7 D4
Westmorland Ct NE31 57 D5
Westmorland Gdns NE9 70 F5
Westmorland La NE1 100 C4
Westmorland Rd
Newcastle-upon-Tyne, Elswick NE1,NE4 100 A4
Shiremoor NE29 41 B7
South Shields NE34 60 C7
Newcastle-upon-Tyne NE4 100 C4
Westmorland Way NE23 22 A6
Westmorland Wlk NE4 54 F3
Westoe Ave NE33 42 E1
Westoe Colliery Dr NE33 42 E2
Westoe Cty Inf Sch NE33 42 D1
Westoe Dr NE33 42 E1
Westoe Hall 1 NE33 59 E8
Westoe Rd NE33 42 D1
Weston Ave NE16 68 F5
Westover Gdns NE9 70 F7
Westport Cl SR5 74 F4
Westray DH2 88 B1

Westray Cl 3 SR2 92 E8
Westsyde NE20 25 B3
Westward Ct NE5 36 E3
Westward Gn NE25 31 C4
Westward Pl NE38 83 B1
Westway Throckley NE15 35 E3
Blaydon NE21 53 B2
Westway Ind Est NE15 35 D3
Westwell Ct NE7 38 F4
Westwood Ave NE6 39 B1
Westwood Cl NE16 79 B7
Westwood Gdns
Newcastle-upon-Tyne NE3 37 E4
Stakeford NE62 5 F1
Gateshead NE9 71 D3
Westwood La NE17 77 B5
Westwood Rd NE3 28 C1
Westwood St SR4 85 F6
Westwood View
Chester le Street DH3 88 C1
Crawcrook NE40 51 F3
Wetheral Gdns NE9 71 A3
Wetheral Terr NE6 56 F4
Wetherby Cl NE63 6 C2
Wetherby Gr NE8 70 D7
Wetherby Rd SR2 87 A1
Wettondale Ave NE24 17 A7
Weybourne Sq SR2 86 E2
Weyhill Ave NE29 41 D4
Weymouth Dr DH4 89 F5
Weymouth Gdns NE9 71 A2
Whaggs La NE16 69 B6
Whalebone La NE61 8 F8
Whalton Ave NE3 38 A6
Whalton Cl Sherburn DH6 96 A1
Gateshead NE10 72 C7
Morpeth NE61 9 B5
Whalton Ct
Newcastle-upon-Tyne NE3 38 A6
South Shields NE34 59 E6
Wharfdale Pl NE6 57 B7
Wharfedale Penshaw DH4 90 A8
Wallsend NE28 39 F5
Wharfedale Ave NE37 83 C8
Wharfedale Dr NE33 59 C7
Wharfedale Gdns NE24 17 A8
Wharfedale Gn NE9 71 B1
Wharmlands Gr NE15 53 F7
Wharmlands Rd NE15 53 F7
Wharncliffe St SR1 102 B2
Wharrier St NE6 56 F4
Wharrier Street Prim Sch
NE6 56 F4
Wharton Cl DH5 94 D4
Wharton St Blyth NE24 17 C5
South Shields NE33 42 D2
Wheatall Dr SR6 60 F2
Wheatear Cl 1 NE38 82 F3
Wheatfield Cl NE42 50 B5
Wheatfield Gr NE12 39 C7
Wheatfield Rd NE5 36 F3
Wheatfields NE25 23 B4
Wheatley Gdns NE36 74 A7
Wheatridge NE25 23 B4
Wheatsheaf Ct SR6 75 F1
Wheler St 3 DH4 90 D1
Whernside Cl 4 NE37 83 A6
Whernside Ct 24 SR3 91 F6
Whernside Pl NE23 22 B3
Whernside Wlk NE40 52 D4
Whetstone Bridge Rd
NE46 44 F4
Whetstone Gn NE46 44 F4
Whickham Ave 6 NE11 69 F8
Whickham Bank 5 NE16 69 A7
Whickham Cl DH4 94 C8
Whickham Gdns 14 NE6 56 C5
Whickham Highway
NE11,NE16 69 E7
Whickham Ind Est NE16 68 F8
Whickham Lodge NE16 69 C7
Whickham Lodge Rise
NE16 69 C7
Whickham Parochial CE Prim
Sch NE16 68 F5
Whickham Pk NE16 69 C7
Whickham Rd NE31 57 E6
Whickham Sch NE16 69 A6
Whickham St SR6 75 E1
Whickham St E SR6 75 E1
Whickham View
Newcastle-upon-Tyne NE15 54 A6
Gateshead NE9 71 A4
Whickhope NE38 83 E2
Whinbank NE20 25 D2
Whinbrooke NE10 72 A6
Whinbush Pl NE15 54 A5
Whinfell NE37 83 B7
Whinfell Cl NE23 22 C3
Whinfell Ct 4 SR3 91 F6
Whinfell Rd NE20 25 D3
Whinfield Terr NE39 67 D2
Whinfield Way NE39 67 C1
Whinham Way NE61 9 B5
Whinlatter Gdns NE9 71 A4
Whinlaw NE9 71 C4
Whinmoor Pl NE5 37 E1
Whinney Cl NE21 68 A8
Whinneyfield Rd NE6 56 F7
Whinny La Ebchester DH8 76 E1
Morpeth NE61 3 A8
Whinshaw NE10 71 F7
Whinstone Mews NE12 39 D6
Whinway NE37 83 B7
Whistler Gdns NE34 59 D3
Whitbay Cres NE12 39 C6
Whitbeck Ct NE5 37 A1
Whitbeck Rd NE5 54 A8
Whitbourne Cl NE37 72 E2
Whitburn Bents Rd SR6 75 F7
Whitburn Comp Sch SR6 75 F8
Whitburn Gdns NE9 71 D3
Whitburn Hall SR6 75 F8
Whitburn Jun Mix Sch
SR6 75 E8
Whitburn Pl NE23 22 B3
Whitburn Rd Cleadon SR6 74 F8
Sunderland SR6 75 F4
Whitburn Rd E SR6 60 B1
Whitburn St SR6 103 A4
Whitburn Terr
East Boldon NE36 74 D7
Sunderland SR6 75 D4
Whitby Ave Hexham NE46 44 F5
Sunderland SR6 75 F6
Whitby Cl NE8 101 C1
Whitby Dr NE38 83 D3
Whitby Gdns NE28 40 E4
Whitby St NE30 42 B6
Whitchester House NE4 98 B2
Whitchurch Cl
Boldon Colliery NE35 58 E1
Sunderland SR5 74 F4
Whitchurch Rd SR5 74 F4
White Cross NE46 45 A4
White Gates Dr DH5 95 B2
White Hill Rd DH5 97 C8
White Horse View NE34 60 C6
White House Pl SR2 103 C2
White House Rd SR2 103 B2
White House Way NE10 71 E5
White Mere Com Prim Sch
NE10 72 C7
White Mere Gdns NE10 72 C8
White Oaks NE10 71 E5
White Rocks Gr SR6 60 F3
White Rose Way NE10 72 E5
White St NE6 57 B6
White-le-Head Gdns
DH9 79 A1
Whiteacres NE61 9 A7
Whitebark SR3 91 E4
Whitebeam Pl NE4 100 B3
Whitebridge Cl NE3 38 D7
Whitebridge Ct NE3 38 C7
Whitebridge Parkway
NE3 38 D8
Whitebridge Pk NE3 38 D8
Whitebridge Wlk NE3 38 D8
Whiteburn NE42 50 B1
Whitecliff Cl NE29 41 F8
Whitecroft Rd NE12 29 B2
Whitedale Ave NE24 17 A6
Whitefield Cres
Penshaw DH4 90 A7
Pegswood NE61 4 E3
Whitefield Gdns NE40 66 F8
Whitefield Gr NE10 71 D8
Whitefield Terr NE6 39 D1
Whiteford Pl NE23 23 A2
Whitefriars Way NE12 39 A6
Whitegate Cl NE11 54 F2
Whitehall Rd
Walbottle NE15 35 F2
Gateshead NE8 101 B1
Gateshead, Shipcote NE8 70 D8
Whitehall St NE33 59 C6
Whitehall Terr 7 SR4 85 F6
Whitehead St
South Shields NE33 59 B7
South Shields, West Harton
NE33 59 B6
Whitehill NE10 71 F5
Whitehill Dr NE10 71 D5
Whitehill Hall Gdns DH2 88 A4
Whitehill Rd NE23 16 A1
Whitehorn Cres NE5 37 E2
Whitehouse Cres NE9 71 E4
Whitehouse La
Tynemouth NE29 41 D8
Gateshead NE9 71 E4
Whitehouse Prim Sch
NE29 41 E8
Whitehouse Rd
Newcastle-upon-Tyne, Delaval
NE15 54 C4
Newcastle-upon-Tyne, Old Benwell
NE15 54 B4
Whiteladies Cl NE38 83 D6
Whitelaw Pl NE23 22 C4
Whiteleas Cty Jun Sch
NE34 59 C2
Whiteleas Way
Whiteleas NE34 59 C3
Whiteleas NE34 59 D2
Whitelees Ct NE3 37 E7
Whiteley Cl NE40 52 A1
Whiteley Rd NE21 53 E4
Whitemere Cl SR2 86 E1
Whites Gdns NE31 57 D6
Whiteside NE44 62 F7
Whitethroat Cl 6 NE38 82 F3
Whitewell Cl NE40 52 C5
Whitewell La NE40 52 C5
Whitewell Rd NE21 53 C2
Whitfield Dr NE12 39 C6
Whitfield Rd
6 Longbenton NE12 39 D8
Newcastle-upon-Tyne NE15 53 F5
Seaton Delaval NE25 23 D3
Whitfield Villas NE33 59 B6
Whitgrave Rd NE5 37 D3
Whitgray Ho NE6 56 E4
Whithorn Ct NE24 17 C7
Whitley Bay High Sch
NE26 31 E6
Whitley Bay Sta NE25 32 B4
Whitley Ct NE9 71 D3
Whitley Lodge Fst Sch
NE26 31 E8
Whitley Memorial CE Fst Sch
NE22 16 A8
Whitley Pl NE25 23 E2
Whitley Rd
Longbenton NE12 40 A8
Earsdon NE25 31 A5
Whitley Bay NE26 32 B4
Whitley Terr
Bedlington NE22 11 D3
Seaton Delaval NE25 23 E2
Whitmore Rd NE21 53 C3
Whitrig Cty Mid Sch
NE25 23 C4
Whitsun Ave NE22 11 A1
Whitsun Gdns NE22 11 A1
Whitsun Gr NE22 11 A1
Whittingham Cl
Tynemouth NE30 32 C2
Ashington NE63 6 A2
Whittingham Ct NE8 101 A1
Whittingham Rd
Tynemouth NE30 32 C1
Newcastle-upon-Tyne NE5 37 A4
Whittington Gr NE5 54 C8
Whittleburn NE10 71 F5
Whitton Ave NE24 17 B5
Whitton Gdns NE29 41 D7
Whitton Pl
Seaton Delaval NE25 23 D3
Newcastle-upon-Tyne NE7 39 B4
Whitton Way NE3 38 B6
Whittonstall NE38 83 F1
Whittonstall Rd NE17 66 A1
Whittonstall Terr NE17 66 A1
Whittonstone House NE4 98 B2
Whitwell Terr NE40 52 C6
Whitworth Cl
Newcastle-upon-Tyne NE6 57 A5
Gateshead NE8 70 D7
Whitworth Pl NE6 57 A5
Whitworth Rd NE37 82 F7
Whorlton Grange Cotts
NE5 36 E4
Whorlton Pl 1 NE5 36 E3
Whorlton Terr NE5 36 B4
Whorral Bank NE61 4 B2
Whyndyke NE10 71 F5
Whytlaw Cty Fst Sch
NE23 22 A5
Whytrigg Cl NE25 23 B3
Wickham Ind Est NE16 54 A1
Wicklow Ct NE62 11 D8
Widdrington Ave NE34 60 B8
Widdrington Gdns NE13 28 C6
Widdrington Rd NE21 53 C2
Widdrington Terr
Ryton NE21 53 A4
4 North Shields NE29 42 A5
Widnes Pl NE12 39 C7
Wigeon Cl NE38 83 A2
Wigham Terr NE16 79 A4
Wigmore Ave NE6 56 E4
Wilber Ct 9 SR4 85 F7
Wilber St SR4 85 F6
Wilberforce St
Wallsend NE28 57 B8
Jarrow NE32 58 C7
Wilberforce Wlk NE8 100 C2
Wilbury Pl NE5 37 C2
Wild Cattle Park*
NE66 112 B8
Wildbriar NE38 83 E2
Wilden Ct SR3 86 B2
Wilden Rd NE38 84 A3
Wildshaw Cl NE23 22 C3
Wilfred St
Chester le Street DH3 88 C2
West Boldon NE35 73 F8
Newcastle-upon-Tyne NE6 56 A6
Sunderland SR4 85 E7
Wilfrid St DH3 82 C3
Wilkes Cl NE5 36 F2
Wilkinson Ave NE31 57 D3
Wilkinson Ct 4 NE32 58 B7
Wilkinson Terr SR2 92 E6
Wilkwood Cl NE23 22 C4
Willerby Dr NE3 38 D8
William Allan Homes
NE22 15 D8
William Armstrong Dr
NE4 54 F3
William Cl NE12 40 A8
William Doxford Ctr SR3 91 F6
William IV Yd NE8 101 B4
William Morris Ave NE39 67 B2
William Roberts Ct NE12 29 D1
William St
Chester le Street DH3 88 C3
Gateshead NE10 56 D1
9 Whickham NE16 69 A7
Chopwell NE17 66 B1
Blyth NE24 17 E6
North Shields NE29 42 A5
Newcastle-upon-Tyne NE3 38 E5
Hebburn NE31 57 D7
6 South Shields NE33 42 C3
Pegswood NE61 4 F3
Sunderland SR1 103 A3
8 Sunderland, South Hylton
SR4 85 A6
William St W
14 North Shields NE29 42 A5
Hebburn NE31 57 D6
William Terr NE31 57 D7
Williams Pk NE12 39 C6
Williams Terr SR2 92 E6
Williamson Terr SR6 103 A4
Willington Comm High Sch
NE28 40 F4
Willington Terr NE28 40 E3
Willis St DH5 95 A5
Willmore St SR4 102 A2
Willoughby Dr NE26 31 E7
Willoughby Rd NE29 41 E6
Willoughby Way NE26 31 E7
Willow Ave Dunston NE11 69 F8
Blyth NE24 12 D1
Newcastle-upon-Tyne NE4 54 D8
Willow Bank Rd SR2 86 C3
Willow Cl Whickham NE16 69 B6
Morpeth NE61 9 B8
Willow Cres
Easington Lane DH5 95 D1
Blyth NE24 17 C4
Willow Ct Ryton NE40 52 D6
Stakeford NE62 11 B7
Willow Dyke NE45 47 A6
Willow Gdns NE12 29 C4
Willow Gr Gateshead NE10 71 E8
Wallsend NE28 40 D1
South Shields NE34 59 F5
Willow Grange NE32 58 A7
Willow Pl NE20 25 E4
Willow Rd
Houghton-le-Spring DH4 94 C8
Blaydon NE21 53 D2
Willow View NE16 79 A6
Willow Way NE20 25 E3
Willow's Cl NE38 83 F4
Willowbank Gdns NE2 38 E4
Willowdene NE12 29 E1
Willowfield Ave NE3 37 F6
Willowford Bridge
Abutment* CA6 126 B3
Willows Cl NE13 28 A5
Willows The
Throckley NE15 35 D1
Hebburn NE31 57 E4
Hedworth NE32 58 C1
Washington NE38 84 A4
Newcastle-upon-Tyne NE4 100 A3
Morpeth NE61 9 A8
Willowvale DH2 88 A5
Wills Mews NE7 39 E2
Wills Oval NE7 39 E2
Wilmington Cl NE3 37 B6
Wilson Ave Birtley DH3 82 C5
Cambois NE22 12 B3
Wilson Dr NE36 74 B8
Wilson Gdns NE3 38 B3
Wilson St Dunston NE11 69 F8
Wallsend NE28 40 B2
South Shields NE33 42 C2
Sunderland SR4 85 F6
Wilson St N SR5 102 C4
Wilson Terr
1 Longbenton NE12 39 D8
New Silksworth SR3 92 A8
Wilson's La NE9 70 F5
Wilsway NE15 35 C2
Wilton Ave NE6 56 E4
Wilton Cl
Cramlington NE23 22 C3
Whitley Bay NE25 31 C5
Wilton Cotts 5 NE35 58 E1
Wilton Dr NE25 31 B5
Wilton Gdns N NE35 58 E1
Wilton Gdns S NE35 58 E1
Wilton Manse NE25 31 B4
Wilton Sq SR2 86 E1
Wilton Terr DH8 76 E4
Wiltshire Cl SR5 74 E4
Wiltshire Dr NE28 39 F4
Wiltshire Gdns NE28 40 A3
Wiltshire Pl NE37 72 D2
Wiltshire Rd SR5 74 E3
Wimbledon Cl SR5 74 F3
Wimborne Cl NE35 73 E8
Wimbourne Ave SR4 85 E4
Wimbourne Gn NE5 36 F3
Wimpole Cl NE37 72 E2
Wimslow Cl NE28 39 F3
Winalot Ave SR2 86 E2
Wincanton Pl NE29 41 E4
Winchcombe Pl NE7 39 A3
Winchester Ave NE24 17 E7
Winchester Cl 8 NE63 6 F2
Winchester Ct NE32 58 B1
Winchester St 7 NE33 42 D3
Winchester Terr NE4 98 B1
Winchester Way NE22 10 F2
Winchester Wlk NE13 28 B6
Wincomblee Rd NE6 57 B4
Windburgh Dr NE23 22 B3
Windermere Birtley DH3 82 D2
Cleadon SR6 60 A1
Windermere Ave
Chester le Street DH2 88 C1
Easington Lane DH5 97 C8
Gateshead NE10 71 F8
Windermere Cl NE23 22 B3
Windermere Cres
Penshaw DH4 90 C6
Blaydon NE21 68 B8
Hebburn NE31 57 F4
Hedworth NE32 58 D3
South Shields NE34 59 E6
Windermere Dr NE12 29 C3
Windermere Gdns NE16 69 C7
Windermere Rd
Newcastle-upon-Tyne NE5 54 B8
Newbiggin-by-the-Sea NE64 7 C3
Windermere St
Gateshead NE8 101 B1
Sunderland SR2 86 F2
Windermere St W NE8 101 B1
Windermere Terr NE29 41 F6
Windhill Rd NE6 56 F3
Winding The NE13 27 B7
Windlass Ct NE34 59 C5
Windlass La NE37 83 C7
Windmill Ct NE2 98 C4
Windmill Gr NE24 17 A8
Windmill Hill
South Shields NE33 42 B1
Hexham NE46 45 A5
Ellington NE61 1 E5
Windmill Hill Cl NE61 1 E6
Windmill Hills Prim Sch
NE8 101 B2
Windmill Hts NE61 1 E6
Windmill Ind Est NE23 15 C2
Windmill Sq SR5 75 C4
Windmill Way
Hebburn NE31 57 E8
Morpeth NE61 9 B8
Windshields Wlk NE15 35 C1
Windsor Ave
Whitley Bay NE26 32 C4
Newcastle-upon-Tyne NE3 38 E4
Gateshead NE8 70 E8
Windsor Cl
Whickham NE16 69 A4
Wallsend NE28 41 A4
Windsor Cotts NE28 41 A4
Windsor Cres
Houghton-le-Spring DH5 94 F8
Whitley Bay NE26 32 C4
Hebburn NE31 57 F6
Ovingham NE42 50 B5
Newcastle-upon-Tyne NE5 37 A3
Windsor Ct
7 Gateshead NE10 71 C8
Bedlington NE22 15 F8
Cramlington NE23 16 A1
Newcastle-upon-Tyne,
Kingston Park NE3 37 E7
Newcastle-upon-Tyne,
South Gosforth NE3 38 E5
Corbridge NE45 47 A6
Windsor Dr
Houghton-le-Spring DH5 94 E6
South Hetton DH6 97 F8
Blyth NE24 17 D3
Wallsend NE28 41 A4
New Silksworth SR3 92 A7
Cleadon SR6 59 F1
Windsor Fst Sch NE64 7 D3
Windsor Gdns
Gateshead NE10 71 C8
Bedlington NE22 15 F8
Whitley Bay NE26 31 F6
Tynemouth NE29 42 A7
South Shields NE34 59 E7
Windsor Gdns W NE26 31 F6
Windsor Pk NE28 39 F3
Windsor Pl
Newcastle-upon-Tyne NE2 99 B3
Ponteland NE20 25 B4
Longbenton NE27 30 C1
Windsor Rd Birtley DH3 82 B6
Whitley Bay NE25 31 E5
Newbiggin-by-the-Sea NE64 7 D4
Springwell NE9 71 F1
Windsor St 2 NE28 40 B2
Windsor Terr Haswell DH6 97 F2
Newcastle-upon-Tyne NE2 99 B3
Whitley Bay NE26 32 C4
Newcastle-upon-Tyne,
South Gosforth NE3 38 E4
Crawcrook NE40 52 A4
Corbridge NE45 47 A6
Hexham NE46 44 F5
Choppington NE62 10 F4
Newbiggin-by-the-Sea NE64 7 D4
3 Sunderland, Grangetown
SR2 86 F2
Sunderland, East Herrington
SR3 91 C6
Windsor Villas NE62 11 A7
Windsor Way NE3 37 D7
Windsor Wlk
Newcastle-upon-Tyne NE3 37 D7
Ashington NE63 7 A2
Windt St NE13 28 A5
Windy Gyle NE63 6 E4
Windy Nook Prim Sch
NE10 71 D6
Windy Nook Rd N10,NE9 71 B6
Windy Ridge NE10 71 C7
Windy Ridge Villas NE10 71 C7
Wingate Cl
Houghton-le-Spring DH4 94 D8
Newcastle-upon-Tyne NE15 53 E6
Wingate Gdns NE9 71 D3
Wingrove NE39 67 D1
Wingrove Ave
Newcastle-upon-Tyne NE4 54 F6
Sunderland SR6 75 E3
Wingrove Gdns NE4 54 F7
Wingrove Ho NE33 59 C6
Wingrove Prim Sch NE4 54 F6
Wingrove Rd NE4 54 F7
Wingrove Terr NE9 71 F1
Winifred Gdns NE28 40 C1
Winifred St SR6 75 E3

Winifred Terr SR1 ....103 B2
Winlaton Care Village
NE21 ....67 F6
Winlaton West Lane Com Prim Sch NE21 ....68 A8
Winsford Ave NE29 ....31 F1
Winshields NE23 ....22 C4
Winshields Milecastle*
NE47 ....127 C3
Winship Cl NE34 ....59 C3
Winship St NE24 ....17 C4
Winship Terr 14 NE6 ......56 C6
Winskell Rd NE34 ....59 A4
Winslade Cl SR3 ....92 B8
Winslow Cl
Boldon Colliery NE35 ....58 F2
Newcastle-upon-Tyne NE6 ..57 A6
Sunderland SR5 ....74 F4
Winslow Gdns NE9 ....70 E5
Winslow Pl NE6 ....57 A6
Winster NE38 ....83 A1
Winster Pl NE23 ....22 B3
Winston Cres SR4 ....85 E4
Winston Ct NE9 ....71 F1
Winston Gn DH4 ....89 F8
Winston Way NE43 ....64 C3
Winton Cl NE23 ....23 A2
Winton Way NE3 ....37 F5
Wirralshir NE10 ....72 A6
Wiseton Ct NE7 ....38 F5
Wishart Ho NE4 ....54 E4
Wishart Terr NE39 ....66 F4
Wishaw Cl NE23 ....22 C4
Wishaw Rise NE15 ....53 E7
Witham Gn NE32 ....58 C2
Witham Rd NE31 ....57 F3
Witherington Cl NE7 .....39 E3
Withernsea Gr SR2 ......92 D7
Witherwack Prim Sch
SR5 ....74 F4
Witney Cl SR5 ....74 F4
Witney Way NE36 ....73 E7
Witton Ave NE34 ....60 A6
Witton Ct
Newcastle-upon-Tyne NE3 ..37 E6
Washington NE38 ....83 B4
Sunderland SR3 ....86 B2
Witton Gdns Jarrow NE32 .58 B3
Gateshead NE9 ....71 D2
Witton Gr DH4 ....94 C7
Witton Rd Shiremoor NE27 .30 F3
Hebburn NE31 ....57 F8
Witty Ave NE31 ....57 F5
Woburn NE38 ....83 D4
Woburn Cl
Cramlington NE23 ....16 A1
Wallsend NE28 ....39 F3
Woburn Dr
Bedlington NE22 ....11 C2
Silksworth SR3 ....92 A6
Woburn Way NE5 ....37 A2
Wolmer Rd NE24 ....17 F5
Wolseley Cl NE8 ....100 C1
Wolseley Gdns NE2 ......56 A8
Wolseley Terr SR4 ......102 A1
Wolsey Ct NE34 ....59 C6
Wolsingham Ct NE23 .....21 F7
Wolsingham Gdns NE9 ...71 D3
Wolsingham Rd NE3 .....38 B4
Wolsingham St NE4 .....100 A3
Wolsley Rd NE24 ....17 E7
Wolveleigh Terr NE3 .....38 D5
Wolviston Gdns NE9 .....71 D3
Wood Fields NE20 ....25 F6
Wood Gr NE15 ....53 E7
Wood La NE22 ....11 B1
Wood Lea DH5 ....95 A7
Wood St Dunston NE11 ....69 F8
Burnopfield NE16 ....79 A6
Sunderland SR4 ....102 A3
Wood Terr
Gateshead NE10 ....57 B2
Jarrow NE32 ....58 A4
South Shields NE33 ....59 D8
4 Washington NE37 ......83 D8
High Spen NE39 ....67 A2
Woodbine Ave
Wallsend NE28 ....40 B2
Newcastle-upon-Tyne NE3 ..38 C4
Woodbine Cl NE4 ....54 F4
Woodbine Cotts NE40 ....52 B5
Woodbine Pl NE8 ....101 B1
Woodbine Rd NE3 ....38 C5
Woodbine St
2 South Shields NE33 .....42 D3
Gateshead NE8 ....101 B1
Sunderland SR1 ....103 C2
Woodbine Terr
Birtley DH3 ....82 D4
Gateshead, Bill Quay NE10 ..57 B2
Gateshead, Felling NE10 ...71 B8
Blyth NE24 ....17 F6
Corbridge NE45 ....47 A6
Hexham NE46 ....44 F5
Gateshead, Bensham NE8 .101 B1
Sunderland SR4 ....85 F8
Woodbine Villas NE8 ....101 B1
Woodbrook Ave NE5 .....54 A8
Woodburn NE10 ....71 E5
Woodburn Ave NE4 ......54 E8
Woodburn Cl NE21 ....68 A8
Woodburn Dr
Burnside DH4 ....90 C1
Whitley Bay NE26 ....31 E7
Woodburn Gdns NE11 ....70 A6
Woodburn Sq NE26 ......31 D7
Woodburn St NE15 ....53 C7
Woodburn Terr NE42 .....50 B2
Woodburn Way NE26 .....31 E7
Woodchurch Cl NE12 .....39 D4
Woodcroft Cl NE23 ....22 B1
Woodcroft Rd NE41 ......51 A6
Woodend NE20 ....25 D2
Woodend Way NE3 ....37 D8
Woodford NE9 ....70 F1
Woodford Cl SR5 ....74 F4
Woodgate Gdns NE10 ....57 B1
Woodgate La NE10 ....57 B2
Woodhall Cl DH2 ....81 E2
Woodhall Ct NE25 ....23 C3
Woodhall Spa DH4 ....90 A4
Woodhead Rd
Prudhoe NE42 ....50 F3
Newcastle-upon-Tyne NE6 ..56 F8
Woodhill Dr NE61 ....8 E8
Woodhill Rd NE23 ....22 C4
Woodhorn Colliery Mus*
NE63 ....6 F5
Woodhorn Cotts NE63 .....6 F5
Woodhorn Cres NE64 ......7 D5
Woodhorn Dr NE62 ....10 F8
Woodhorn Gdns NE13 ....28 B6
Woodhorn La NE64 ....7 E5
Woodhorn Rd
Ashington NE63 ....6 E4
Newbiggin-by-the-Sea NE64 ..7 D5
Woodhorn Villas NE63 .....6 F5
Woodhouses La
Whickham, Fellside NE16 ..68 E6
Whickham, Swalwell NE16 ..69 A8
Woodhurst Gr SR4 ....85 A2
Woodkirk Cl NE23 ....23 A2
Woodland Cres NE15 .....54 C4
Woodland Dr SR4 ....85 E4
Woodland Grange DH4 ...89 F1
Woodland Mews NE2 .....38 F2
Woodland Rise SR3 ......91 E6
Woodland Terr
Penshaw DH4 ....90 A8
5 South Shields NE33 .....42 D4
Washington NE37 ....83 E8
Woodland View DH4 .....94 A1
Woodlands
Chester le Street DH3 ......88 C4
Great Lumley DH4 ....89 F1
Throckley NE15 ....35 C2
Ponteland NE20 ....25 D3
Tynemouth NE29 ....42 A7
Newcastle-upon-Tyne NE3 ..38 C3
Washington NE38 ....88 E8
Hexham NE46 ....45 D4
Seaham SR7 ....93 A1
Woodlands Cl
Earsdon NE25 ....31 A5
High Spen NE39 ....67 A3
Woodlands Ct
Kibblesworth NE11 ....81 D6
Throckley NE15 ....35 C2
Woodlands Dr SR6 ....75 A8
Woodlands Grange NE12 .29 E1
Woodlands Ho NE24 ......17 B8
Woodlands Park Dr
NE21 ....53 D2
Woodlands Park Villas
NE13 ....28 C4
Woodlands Pk NE13 ......28 C5
Woodlands Rd
Newcastle-upon-Tyne NE15 .53 D7
Rowlands Gill NE39 ....67 D2
Ashington NE63 ....7 A2
Cleadon SR6 ....75 A8
Woodlands Terr
Gateshead NE10 ....71 C8
Longbenton NE12 ....29 E1
Woodlands The NE11 .....81 D6
Woodlands View SR6 .....75 A8
Woodlawn Sch NE25 .....31 D3
Woodlea Killingworth NE12 .29 D1
Newbiggin-by-the-Sea NE64 ..7 E5
Woodlea Cl DH5 ....95 A4
Woodlea Cres NE46 ......45 C4
Woodlea Ct NE29 ....41 E3
Woodlea Gdns NE3 ....38 E6
Woodlea Rd NE39 ....67 B2
Woodlea Sq NE29 ....41 E3
Woodleigh Rd NE25 ......31 E4
Woodleigh View NE5 .....37 E3
Woodman Cl NE61 ....8 E7
Woodman St NE28 ....41 B3
Woodmans Way NE16 ....68 F4
Woodpack Ave NE16 .....68 F6
Woods Gn NE10 ....57 C1
Woods Terr NE8 ....101 C1
Woodside Ponteland NE20 .25 C2
Bedlington NE22 ....11 C1
Blyth NE24 ....17 F6
Prudhoe NE42 ....50 F2
Hexham NE46 ....45 D4
Morpeth NE61 ....8 D7
Sunderland SR2 ....102 C1
Sunderland, East Herrington
SR3 ....91 C6
Woodside Ave
Walbottle NE15 ....35 E2
Seaton Delaval NE25 ......23 D2
Corbridge NE45 ....47 B6
Newcastle-upon-Tyne NE6 ..57 B7
Woodside Cl NE40 ....52 C5
Woodside Cres NE12 .....39 E8
Woodside Ct NE12 ....39 D8
Woodside Gdns NE11 .....69 F7
Woodside Gr
Tantobie DH9 ....79 C3
Sunderland SR3 ....91 C6
Woodside La
Greenside NE40 ....52 B3
Woodside La *continued*
Ryton NE40 ....52 B4
Woodside Rd NE40 ....52 B5
Woodside Terr
Chopwell NE17 ....77 B8
Sunderland SR3 ....91 C6
Woodside Villas NE46 ....45 D4
Woodside Way
South Shields NE33 ....59 B7
Ryton NE40 ....52 C5
Woodside Wlk NE39 ......67 C1
Woodstock Ave SR2 ......86 E2
Woodstock Rd
Newcastle-upon-Tyne NE15 .54 A5
Gateshead NE9 ....71 B2
Woodstone Terr DH4 .....89 D1
Woodthorne Rd NE2 .....38 E3
Woodvale NE20 ....25 C2
Woodvale Dr NE31 ....57 C4
Woodvale Gdns
Newcastle-upon-Tyne NE15 .53 E7
Wylam NE41 ....51 B6
Gateshead NE9 ....71 C6
Woodvale Rd
Killingworth NE12 ....29 C4
Blaydon NE21 ....53 D2
Woodville Cres SR4 ......85 E4
Woodville Ct SR4 ....85 E4
Woodville Rd NE15 ....53 D8
Woodwynd NE10 ....71 F6
Wooler Ave NE29 ....41 D4
Wooler Cres NE8 ....70 C8
Wooler Gn NE15 ....53 B7
Wooler Sq
Wide Open NE13 ....28 C7
Sunderland SR2 ....86 E3
Wooler Wlk NE32 ....58 A4
Woolerton Dr
Gateshead N10,NE9 ....71 C6
Newcastle-upon-Tyne NE15 .53 E7
Gateshead NE9 ....71 B6
Wooley St NE28 ....40 B1
Woolmer Ct NE7 ....39 E3
Woolsington Ct NE22 .....10 F1
Woolsington Gdns NE13 ..36 F8
Woolsington Pk S NE13 ...36 F8
Woolsington Rd NE29 ....41 C7
Woolwich Cl SR5 ....74 F4
Woolwich Rd SR5 ....74 F4
Wooperton Gdns NE5 ....54 C7
Worcester Gn NE8 ......101 B2
Worcester St SR2 ....102 C1
Worcester Terr SR2 .....102 C2
Worcester Way NE13 .....28 C5
Wordsworth Ave
Easington Lane DH5 ....97 D8
Whickham NE16 ....69 B8
Blyth NE24 ....17 C6
Hebburn NE31 ....57 E6
Wordsworth Ave E DH5 ...94 E7
Wordsworth Ave W DH5 ..94 E7
Wordsworth Cres NE9 ....71 F1
Wordsworth St NE8 ......56 A2
Worley Ave NE9 ....70 F4
Worley Cl NE4 ....98 B1
Worley Mews NE9 ....70 F4
Worley St NE4 ....98 B1
Worley Terr DH9 ....79 A1
Worm Hill Terr NE38 ......83 E1
Worsdell St NE24 ....12 E1
Worsley Cl NE28 ....39 F4
Worswick St NE1 ....99 B1
Worthing Cl NE28 ....39 F3
Worthington Ct NE2 ......99 C4
Wouldhave Ct NE33 ......42 E3
Wouldhave St NE33 ......42 E3
Wraith Terr SR2 ....92 E6
Wraysbury Ct NE3 ....37 D7
Wreay Wlk NE23 ....22 C3
Wreigh St NE31 ....57 D6
Wreken Gdns NE10 ....72 C8
Wrekenton Row NE9 .....71 C2
Wren Cl NE38 ....83 A3
Wren Gr 1 SR5 ....74 C1
Wretham Pl NE2 ....99 C2
Wright Dr NE23 ....29 A7
Wright St NE24 ....17 D8
Wright Terr DH4 ....90 A5
Wrightson St NE23 ....16 B3
Wroxham Ct
Newcastle-upon-Tyne NE5 ..37 B4
Sunderland SR2 ....86 E2
Wroxton NE38 ....83 C3
Wuppertal Ct NE32 ....58 B6
Wych Elm Cl NE61 ....1 D4
Wych Elm Cres NE7 ......39 C3
Wychcroft Way NE5 ......37 C2
Wycliffe Ave NE3 ....37 F3
Wycliffe Rd SR4 ....85 F4
Wydon Pk NE46 ....45 A3
Wye Ave NE32 ....58 C3
Wye Rd NE31 ....57 E3
Wylam Ave NE25 ....23 F2
Wylam Cl NE34 ....59 E5
Wylam Fst Sch NE41 .....51 B6
Wylam Gdns NE28 ....40 F4
Wylam Gr SR1 ....103 B2
Wylam Rd NE29 ....41 F3
Wylam St NE32 ....58 B7
Wylam Sta NE41 ....51 C5
Wylam View NE21 ....53 B2
Wylam Wood Rd NE41 ....51 B5
Wyles Hill NE41 ....51 B6
Wynbury Rd NE9 ....71 A5
Wyncote Ct NE7 ....39 B2
Wynd The
Killingworth NE12 ....29 F1
Throckley NE15 ....35 D1
Wynd The *continued*
Newcastle-upon-Tyne NE3 ..38 A4
Tynemouth NE30 ....42 A8
Wynde The
Ponteland NE20 ....25 D4
South Shields NE34 ....59 D5
Wyndfall Way NE3 ....38 A3
Wyndham Ave NE3 ....37 F3
Wyndham Prim Sch NE3 .38 A3
Wyndham Way NE29 ......41 B8
Wynding The
Bedlington NE22 ....10 E1
Annitsford NE23 ....22 B1
Wyndley Cl NE16 ....68 F5
Wyndley House NE3 ......37 F3
Wyndley Pl NE3 ....37 F3
Wyndrow Pl NE3 ....37 F3
Wyndsail Pl NE3 ....38 A3
Wyndtop Pl NE3 ....38 A3
Wyndways Dr DH9 ....78 E1
Wynn Gdns NE10 ....56 F1
Wynyard DH2 ....88 A3
Wynyard Dr NE22 ....11 C3
Wynyard Gdns NE9 ....71 C2
Wynyard Sq SR2 ....86 E2
Wynyard St
Fence Houses DH4 ....94 A8
Dunston NE11 ....69 F8
New Silksworth SR3 ....92 A7
Wythburn Pl NE9 ....71 B4
Wyvern Sq SR2 ....86 E2

Y

Yardley Gr NE23 ....22 A8
Yarmouth Dr NE23 ....22 A8
Yatesbury Ave NE5 ....37 B3
Yeadon Ct NE3 ....37 C7
Yeavering Bell (Camp)*
NE71 ....107 B2
Yeavering Cl NE3 ....38 B4
Yellow Leas Farm NE36 ..74 C7
Yelverton Cres NE6 ....56 F3
Yelverton Ct NE23 ....22 A8
Yemeni Sch The NE33 ....42 B1
Yeoman St NE29 ....42 B5
Yeovil Cl NE23 ....22 A8
Yetholm Ave DH2 ....88 B2
Yetholm Pl NE5 ....37 A4
Yetholm Rd NE8 ....100 B1
Yetlington Dr NE3 ....38 A4
Yew Tree Dr NE22 ....10 F2
Yewburn Way NE12 ......39 C6
Yewcroft Ave NE15 ....54 A6
Yewdale Gdns NE9 ....71 A4
Yewtree Ave SR5 ....74 F2
Yewtree Gdns NE6 ....40 A1
Yewtrees NE10 ....71 E5
Yewvale Rd NE5 ....37 D1
York Ave NE32 ....58 B3
York Cl NE23 ....22 A8
York Cres DH5 ....94 F4
York Ct DH3 ....88 D2
York Dr NE28 ....40 B1
York Gr NE22 ....10 D2
York Ho SR5 ....74 A4
York Rd Birtley DH3 ....82 C1
Whitley Bay NE26 ....32 B5
York St Hetton le Hole DH5 .94 E1
Gateshead NE10 ....57 A1
Jarrow NE32 ....58 A6
Newcastle-upon-Tyne NE4 ..98 B1
Sunderland SR1 ....103 A3
New Silksworth SR3 ....92 A8
York Terr
Chester le Street DH3 ......88 D2
Gateshead NE10 ....71 D8
7 North Shields NE29 .....42 A5
York Way NE34 ....60 A6
Yorkdale Pl NE6 ....57 A6
Yorkwood NE31 ....57 C7
Young Rd NE12 ....29 F1

Z

Zetland Dr NE25 ....31 F2
Zetland Sq SR6 ....75 E1
Zetland St SR6 ....75 E1
Zion St SR1 ....103 B3
Zion Terr Blaydon NE21 ....53 B2
Sunderland SR5 ....75 C3

Street Atlases from Philip's

Philip's publish an extensive range of regional and local street atlases which are ideal for motoring, business and leisure use. They are widely used by the emergency services and local authorities throughout Britain.

Key features include:

◆ Superb county-wide mapping at an extra-large scale of 3½ inches to 1 mile, or 2½ inches to 1 mile in pocket edition

◆ Complete urban and rural coverage, detailing every named street in town and country

◆ Each atlas available in three handy formats – hardback, spiral, pocket paperback

'The mapping is very clear... great in scope and value'

★★★★ BEST BUY AUTO EXPRESS

1 Bedfordshire
2 Berkshire
3 Birmingham and West Midlands
4 Bristol and Bath
5 Buckinghamshire
6 Cambridgeshire
7 Cardiff, Swansea and The Valleys
8 Cheshire
9 County Durham and Teesside
10 Derbyshire
11 Edinburgh and East Central Scotland
12 North Essex
13 South Essex
14 Glasgow and West Central Scotland
15 North Hampshire
16 South Hampshire
17 Hertfordshire
18 East Kent
19 West Kent
20 Lancashire
21 Leicestershire and Rutland
22 London
23 Greater Manchester
24 Merseyside
25 Northamptonshire
26 Nottinghamshire
27 Oxfordshire
28 Staffordshire
29 Surrey
30 East Sussex
31 West Sussex
32 Tyne and Wear and Northumberland
33 Warwickshire
34 East Yorkshire and Northern Lincolnshire
35 South Yorkshire
36 West Yorkshire

How to order

The Philip's range of street atlases is available from good retailers or directly from the publisher by phoning 01933 443863